Principles of
Educational and
Psychological Testing

Principles of Educational and Psychological Testing

third edition

Frederick G. Brown
Iowa State University

Holt, Rinehart and Winston

New York   Chicago   San Francisco   Philadelphia
Montreal   Toronto   London   Sydney   Tokyo
Mexico City   Rio de Janeiro   Madrid

Library of Congress Cataloging in Publication Data

Brown, Frederick Gramm.
  Principles of educational and psychological testing.

  Bibliography: p.
  Includes index.
  1. Educational tests and measurements. 2. Psychological tests. I. Title.
LB3051.B7636   1983   371.2′6   82-15642

ISBN 0-03-060103-7

Address correspondence to
383 Madison Avenue
New York, N.Y. 10017

CBS College Publishing
Holt, Rinehart and Winston
The Dryden Press
Saunders College Publishing

Preface

WHEN preparing the third edition of this book I asked myself several questions: What were my goals for the previous editions? How well were they accomplished? Have some of these goals changed or additional ones been added? In what ways could the book be improved, both in its presentation of current knowledge of educational and psychological testing and as a teaching tool?

As with the previous editions, my primary goal is to provide readers with the necessary background so that they can make informed and critical evaluations of tests (and other assessment methods) when the need arises. Because each testing situation is unique, one cannot say that a particular test is good or bad. Rather, test users must combine their knowledge of the principles of psychological measurement (which are presented in this book) with their knowledge of the test takers, the testing situation, and the proposed use of the test to make a reasoned evaluation of the usefulness of the test in a particular situation. Stated differently, my goal is for readers to learn what questions to ask when evaluating a test or a particular use of a test.

I believe that this goal can best be accomplished by stressing the logic of psychological measurement. By logic I mean the underlying principles that explain why psychological measurement proceeds as it does. Thus we must consider such questions as: Why do we measure psychological characteristics? What types of characteristics can be measured? Why should tests be reliable, valid, and standardized? What assumptions are made when measuring achievement, abilities, and personality characteristics? What do these assumptions imply regarding the nature of the measurement process and the interpretation and use of test scores? Consideration of these "why" questions leads to the "how" questions, those dealing with the methods for constructing and evaluating tests.

I also emphasize the applied aspects of testing, stressing how tests can be used to make educational and vocational decisions and to promote the development of individuals. Although this emphasis, in part, reflects my training as an applied psychologist, what is more important is that applied aspects are stressed because most readers will be test takers and test users rather than test developers or researchers. But test users, as well as test developers and researchers, must understand the nature of the measurement process and the reasoning and assumptions underlying it. As anyone who has followed the controversies over educational and psychological testing—both in the popular press and in professional journals—can attest, there is widespread misunderstanding and ignorance of the nature and purposes of psychological measurement. Only by knowing how tests are developed, and why they are developed as they are, will you be able to make informed judgments about the reasonableness of the various arguments and points of view about the uses (and misuses) of educational and psychological tests.

Readers and instructors may ask how this book differs from others covering similar material. To me, the most distinctive feature is the emphasis on the logic of measurement—the emphasis on the basic principles and assumptions of psychological measurement. As a consequence, I have not attempted to survey or provide an extensive catalog of available instruments; instead, specific tests are introduced only to illustrate a particular principle, concept, or method. Another distinctive feature is the sequential development of topics from the nature of measurement, to consistency, to validity, to interpreting scores. This approach is used to emphasize that unless tests are carefully constructed, measure consistently, and are valid, interpretation of scores will be questionable. Only after the basic principles have been presented are particular types of tests described. Thus we are able to show how the basic principles of measurement are applied to the construction, interpretation, evaluation, and use of various types of tests and assessment methods. Third, I have emphasized certain topics that receive minor consideration in other books; for example, the decision-making approach to validity, base rates, incremental validity, and homogeneity.

A number of techniques have been incorporated to make the book an effective learning tool. All statistics used are described, both in the chapter on statistics (Chapter 3) and as they are applied to specific problems. Examples of statistical analyses are described in the text and illustrated. Statistical concepts are presented both verbally and by formulas. Each chapter has a summary reviewing the major points of the chapter and includes an annotated list of further readings for readers who want to pursue a topic in more depth. Numerous examples of test items, uses of tests, and types of analyses are described, as are guidelines for writing items and interpreting scores. A glossary of important terms is included at the end of the book and these terms are highlighted (by italics) in the text. Instructors may find the *Instructor's Manual* a useful source of test items, problems, and suggestions for class activities.

There are a number of changes from the previous editions. All chapters have been extensively rewritten, both to clarify the presentation and to include discussion of new and revised tests, new methods, and current issues. The two chapters on consistency have been combined into one chapter in order to integrate the material and give a more proper emphasis to this topic. On the other hand, the discussion of typical performance measures has been expanded to three chapters. The chapter on uses of tests has been deleted and the material integrated into other chapters. Information on published tests has been updated and topics of current concern have been discussed more extensively, including content-referenced (criterion-referenced) tests, test bias, competency tests, latent trait approaches, and coaching. And a glossary has been added.

Two comments on stylistic matters. Literature references have been cited in the text only when a point is controversial, to give credit to persons who have developed a new technique or method, and to help readers locate sources that treat a topic in more depth. (The suggested readings at the end of each chapter also serve this third purpose.) And I have tried to balance male and female referents in examples.

Preparation of this edition was greatly helped by the thoughtful, detailed comments of Dr. John T. Cowles, Dr. Dale B. Harris, and Professor Peter Prunkl, who reviewed the manuscript in depth. I express my appreciation for their contributions.

Ames, Iowa
October 1982   **F. G. Brown**

Contents

Principles of
Educational and
Psychological Testing

· part one ·
measurement in psychology and education

MEASUREMENT pervades all aspects of our lives. Your birth certificate lists the date and time of your birth, and your birth length and weight—all measured characteristics. Every day you encounter measurements: when you receive a score on a test, when you price articles in a store, when you select clothes, and when you determine the distance you will travel on your vacation, to name but a few examples. Magazines and newspapers are filled with measurements—inflation and crime rates, athletic statistics, the cost of living index, and election returns. Science, of course, depends heavily on measurements. Perhaps the most famous equation of all time, Einstein's $E = mc^2$, shows the relationship among three measured quantities.

Educators, psychologists, and other behavioral scientists also make extensive use of measurements. Their focus, however, is not on economic or physical variables. Instead they measure abilities, achievements, aptitudes, interests, attitudes, values, and personality characteristics. These measurements are used for purposes such as planning and evaluating instruction, selecting workers and assigning them to jobs which match their abilities and interests, placing students in courses, counseling and guidance, and studying differences between groups and the nature and extent of individual differences. Underlying these uses of measurement is the belief that accurate information about characteristics of individuals is necessary for effective planning, decision making, and evaluation.

This book is concerned with the measurement of individual characteristics and focuses on one particular method, the psychological test. This first part is an introduction to and an overview of the book. Chapter 1 describes the nature of psychological measurement, contrasts psychological and physical measurement, and defines what is meant by a test. Chapter 2 describes the essential characteristics of a good test and the steps in constructing good tests. Inasmuch as measurement is a quantitative endeavor and relies on statistical analyses, Chapter 3 reviews the descriptive statistics needed to understand the quantitative concepts used in testing. The topics introduced in these three chapters provide the foundation for the material discussed in the remainder of the book.

Chapter 1 • The Nature of Psychological Measurement

THAT people differ in numerous ways is apparent even to the most casual observer. Some people are short, others tall; some have blue eyes, others brown; some can run 100 yards in less than 10 seconds, others take 15 seconds or longer. People differ not only in physical appearance and skills, but in their abilities and personality characteristics as well. Some people find math easy, whereas others are unable to do simple calculations; some people are extroverted and outgoing, whereas others are quiet and retiring; some people emerge as leaders, whereas others are content to follow.

Because of these wide variations, the study of individual differences has been a continuing focus of interest in psychology. Part of this interest reflects our natural curiosity about other people—about what they are like and how they behave. Thus, in psychology as in everyday conversation, most terms used to describe people refer to characteristics that vary widely between people, such as intelligence, aggressiveness, mathematical ability, flexibility, and creativity, to name but a few. These differences also have practical consequences, perhaps the most obvious being that different skills and abilities are required in various occupations.

Psychologists interested in individual differences are concerned with a number of questions: In what ways do people differ? How large are these differences? How can these differences be most accurately measured? What are the practical implications of these differences? These are the types of questions addressed in this book. Although the focus will be on the identification and measurement of individual differences, the ultimate goal will be to apply this knowledge to help individuals live more satisfying and productive lives.

why measure psychological characteristics?

The goal when measuring psychological attributes—be they abilities, skills, interests, attitudes, or personality characteristics—is to obtain an accurate description of an individual or group of individuals. For some people the primary goal is to understand more about the nature and range of individual differences, as when a psychologist studies the range of intellectual abilities in a particular population. For others the goal is to understand and predict behavior more effectively. For example, a teacher might measure students' mathematical skills in order to determine what abilities are needed to solve problems and what teaching method will be most appropriate for each student. Others will be interested in making practi-

3

cal decisions, such as which applicants to hire for a position. In each situation, accurate information about abilities or personality characteristics is needed.

As you can see, there are various reasons for measuring the characteristics of individuals. To give a flavor of some of the common uses of psychological measurement, I will briefly describe several applications of psychological measurement. In these examples the characteristics of interest are measured by tests; keep in mind, however, that tests are only one of several possible methods for measuring psychological characteristics.

Descriptive Uses

In some situations tests are used to provide descriptions of an individual. For example, tests are frequently administered during counseling to provide clients with descriptions of their abilities, interests, or personality characteristics. Or an elementary school teacher may be interested in the abilities, knowledge, and study habits of his students. In other situations we may want to describe a particular population; for example, the academic ability of students attending Androscoggin College. (In turn, we might use these data to compare an individual student's ability either with that of other students attending Androscoggin or to compare the students at Androscoggin with students at other colleges.)

When using tests descriptively, we generally are interested in using the information at more than one time and for various purposes. Thus descriptive information is of most value when there is continuing contact between the test user and test taker over an extended period of time. For example, a classroom teacher can use students' scores on ability and achievement tests in a variety of interactions with students throughout the school year, not just at one particular time. Or a counselor may use test scores to help a client select courses, plan a program of study, improve study methods, or make a career choice. In other words, use of the test data is not restricted to one particular decision. Thus, descriptive uses generally involve measurement of broad abilities and characteristics, often ones that are relatively stable over time.

Decision-Making Uses

In contrast to the broad-based assessments just described, tests are also used as an aid in making specific, practical decisions. These decisions may involve individuals, such as who should be hired for a particular job or admitted to medical school, or groups, such as which of two methods of teaching physics results in higher achievement. In either case a decision must be made and the test scores are used as one basis for making the decision. Thus, in contrast to descriptive uses, the test content will usually be narrower and more focused on the specific situation.

The following paragraphs describe some common decision-making uses of tests.

Selection. Selection decisions are common in both academic and business settings. In selection there are more applicants than can be accepted or hired and the decision is which one (or ones) to accept. To illustrate, if a medical school has places for only 100 students in its first-year class and 800 students apply, the admissions committee must decide which applicants to admit and which to reject. The role of a test in this situation is to help identify the most promising applicants—that is, those with the highest probability of success.

Placement. In placement, or classification, there are several individuals and several alternative courses of action; for example, there may be several academic tracks, training programs, or jobs, and each person is to be assigned to one alternative. The goal is to match individuals and alternatives in an optimal manner. Examples include using tests to assign recruits to occupational specialties in the armed services or college freshmen to various levels within a sequence of French courses.

Ranking. An illustration of the use of tests for ranking is grading. In most courses, grades must be assigned. Frequently all, or a large part, of the grade is determined by performance on examinations. The scores on the various tests and assignments are then combined, students are ranked in order of their achievement, and grades assigned on the basis of these ranks. In this situation, the decision involves which grade to assign to each level of performance.

Proficiency. Tests can also be used to establish proficiency. A familiar example is the examination required to obtain a driver's license. This examination usually consists of both a written test (on traffic laws and regulations) and a behind-the-wheel driving test. You must perform at a certain minimal level in order to obtain a license.

Other examples of proficiency tests include licensure exams in professions such as law and medicine, Red Cross swimming and lifesaving tests, and minimum competency tests for high school graduation. "Test-out" examinations in schools can also be considered as proficiency exams in that students who demonstrate the desired level of proficiency either receive credit for the course and/or are exempt from taking it.

The distinguishing feature of proficiency testing is that a minimal level of performance is specified in advance; the decision involves determining whether performance meets this standard. Usually there are only two possible outcomes: pass or fail.

Diagnosis. Diagnosis involves comparing an individual's performance in several areas in order to determine relative strengths and weaknesses. Generally, diagnostic procedures are instituted when an individual is having difficulty in some area. Once the areas of disability are identified, a program of remediation can be undertaken. Thus a diagnostic reading test might provide scores in phonetics, word meaning (vocabulary), sentence meaning, paragraph meaning, and reading rate. Here the goal would be to identify the student's particular weaknesses and strengths. Once the specific area of disability is identified, a program of remedial help can be arranged.

Evaluation.   The previous examples all concerned decisions about individuals. But test scores can also be used to evaluate educational programs, treatments (such as alternative types of therapies), or procedures. Consider the example introduced at the beginning of this section, evaluating the effectiveness of two different methods of teaching physics. We could design an experiment where some students take a physics course taught by one method and others are taught by a second method. At the end of the term, both groups would be given the same final examination. By comparing the scores of the two groups of students on this exam, we could determine which course produced higher achievement.

To review, consider the decision made in each situation. In selection, the decision is whether to select or reject each applicant; in placement, which alternative course of action to instigate; in ranking, which grade or category to assign; in proficiency, whether or not the person attained the minimal level of performance; in diagnosis, which treatment to use; in evaluation, which method is more effective. Since no test (or other assessment method) is 100 percent accurate, the primary question is not whether the test provides accurate or inaccurate information but whether it increases the number the correct decisions made.

Note also that we referred to tests as decision-making "aids" because a test is usually only one of several elements in the decision-making process. Rarely are decisions made solely on the basis of test scores. Rather, all available relevant information should be used when making a decision. As stated in the *Standards for Educational and Psychological Tests:*

> For most purposes, . . . a single assessment or assessment procedure rarely provides all relevant facets of a description. . . . Decisions about individuals should ordinarily be based on assessment of more than one dimension; when feasible, all major dimensions related to the outcome of the decision should be assessed. . . (*Standards*, 1974, pp. 61–62)[1]

Because human behavior is complex, many factors enter into a decision; test scores are only one. Thus, when tests are used as decision-making aids, accurate test data alone will not guarantee accurate decision making; other factors and variables that contribute to the decision will also affect the quality of the decision.

Defining Constructs

In addition to descriptive and decision-making uses, tests can also aid in the development of educational and psychological theories. Theories in education and psychology, like those in other disciplines, involve both constructs and laws (Kerlinger, 1973). One way of operationally defining constructs is by tests. Suppose, for example, we are interested in anxiety. One way to measure anxiety would be to ask people to rate their degree of anxiety in various situations. The score on this test (the sum of these ratings) would be the operational definition of anxiety.

To validate a theory we conduct experiments. One possibility would be to

---

[1] Literature references can be found in the bibliography at the end of the book. For brevity, the *Standards for Educational and Psychological Tests* will be referred to as the *Standards*.

study the effects of anxiety on problem solving. We might hypothesize that the more anxious a person is, the poorer his or her performance on problem-solving tasks will be. To test this hypothesis we could administer an anxiety test to a group of subjects, administer the problem-solving tasks, and then see whether the predicted relation held. If it did, we would have more confidence in our theory. By conducting other studies we could increase our knowledge of the construct of anxiety and whether our test was a good measure of anxiety.[2]

The previous example illustrates the use of psychological measurement in *hypothesis testing*. That is, the anxiety measure was used to test a hypothesis about the relationship between anxiety and problem solving. In this example the anxiety measure was the independent variable, since we tested the effect of anxiety on problem solving. We could, by designing a different study, have used the anxiety measure as a dependent variable. For example, we could study whether anxiety test scores increase under stressful conditions.

Suggesting Hypotheses

Tests can also be used for *hypothesis building*. This use is illustrated by surveys and the use of tests in counseling. Suppose that a survey shows that persons living in a certain part of the United States score lower on achievement tests than persons of comparable age and education in other states. Why? Several hypotheses could be developed. One is that the people living in that area are less intelligent. Another is that the results reflect differences in the quality of education. A third hypothesis might attribute the effects to socioeconomic and cultural differences. These hypotheses could then be checked by further studies.

Counselors and therapists often use test results to build hypotheses about their clients. Suppose tests show that Clarence, whose father is an engineer, has excellent scholastic aptitude, is interested in literary and artistic activities, is submissive, and has conflicts with authority figures and a problem with family relationships. He is now enrolled in engineering and is failing. From the test data the counselor might hypothesize that Clarence is in engineering because of parental pressure. Unable to confront his parents directly with his dislike for engineering, he has chosen the indirect method of failing his courses. This hypothesis could then be checked through further interviews.

how are psychological characteristics measured?

A second question is: How can psychological characteristics be measured? For most characteristics, a wide variety of methods are available. Suppose, for example, we are interested in the mathematical ability of high school students. Several indices of ability come readily to mind: grades in math courses, scores on math tests, teachers' ratings, self-ratings, and performance in courses or situations requiring use of mathematics. (You can probably think of others.) Or, if we are interested in anxiety, we could have observers rate each person's level of anxiety, have people rate their own anxiety level or answer test items asking about their

---

[2] For further discussion see the section on construct validity in Chapter 7.

anxiety in various situations, or use a physiological measure such as GSR or blood pressure. The point should be clear: Most psychological characteristics can be measured by a variety of methods.

In this book we will focus on tests. One reason is that tests use standard procedures,[3] thus are less susceptible to bias and the influence of irrelevant factors. Also, methods are available for determining how well a test measures the characteristic(s) it is designed to measure. And, third, tests have been shown to be more valid and useful than other assessment methods in a variety of situations. Even though we will focus on tests, *the principles and guidelines discussed for constructing and evaluating tests apply to any procedure used for assessing psychological characteristics* whether or not it is called a test.

Definition of a Test

The term "test" is one of those common words that everyone feels he or she understands and therefore seldom takes time to define precisely. We shall define a *test* as *a systematic procedure for measuring a sample of behavior*. This definition can best be understood by considering the implications of the various components of the definition.

The phrase "systematic procedure" indicates that a test is constructed, administered, and scored according to prescribed rules. Test items are systematically chosen to fit the test specifications, the same or equivalent items are administered to all persons, and the directions and time limits are the same for all persons taking the test. The use of predetermined rules for evaluating (scoring) responses ensures agreement between different persons who might score the test.

Using standard procedures serves to minimize the possible influence of irrelevant personal and situational variables on test scores. For example, instructions about how to respond when uncertain decrease individual differences in guessing behaviors. Another reason for standard procedures is to enable scores of different persons to be compared directly. If two individuals responded to different items, or had different amounts of time to complete the same items, we could not compare their scores.

A second crucial term is behavior. In the strictest sense, a test measures only the responses a person makes to the test items. Thus we do not measure a person directly; rather, we infer his characteristics (traits) from his responses to test items. If the behaviors exhibited on the test adequately mirror the construct being measured, the test will provide useful information. If the test does not adequately reflect the underlying characteristic, inferences made from test scores will be in error.

Third, a test contains only a sample of all possible items. No test includes every possible item that might be developed to measure the behavior or characteristic. One could think of exceptions, such as an addition test covering every possible combination of two one-digit numbers, but these exceptions are rare and generally trivial. Thus any particular test is better thought of as a sample of possible items.

[3] Standardization of testing procedures is discussed in greater detail in Chapter 2. This term, and other important terms, are also defined in the Glossary at the end of the book.

Because a test contains only a sample of all possible items, two problems arise. First, we must be assured that the items included on the test are a representative sample of all possible items. The second problem involves the question of whether a person would obtain the same score if he or she responded to a different sample of items drawn from the same domain. In other words, would an individual obtain the same score on an equivalent form of the test? The former is a validity problem, the latter a problem of reliability.

Finally, a test is a measuring instrument. Since any measurement process results in the assignment of a numerical value to performance, test scores will be expressed in quantitative terms. Because the concept of measurement underlies many of the topics in this book, it will be discussed in detail later in this chapter.

Before leaving our definition of a test, however, it should be noted that nothing in the definition requires that one particular format (for example, paper and pencil) be used, that test takers make specific preparations for the test, or that they even be aware they are being tested. Although test takers generally are aware they are being evaluated and often prepare for a test, these are not necessary conditions.

An Example

To illustrate the various aspects of the definition of a test, consider a typical, comprehensive final examination in a college course. This exam uses systematic procedures in that items are chosen to fit certain specifications (that is, to cover the material taught in the course), the same items are administered to all students, and the directions, time limits, testing conditions, and scoring procedures are the same for all students. It is a measurement as scores are expressed numerically, usually as the total number of points earned over all items. It is a sample because not all possible questions are included, only a sample of the possible questions. And, finally, it measures behavior, the students' responses to the items. Of course, the instructor uses this sample of behavior as a basis for making inferences about students' command of all the material in the course.

what is measured?

We have said that tests measure characteristics of individuals. The use of the term "characteristics" was deliberate, to indicate both that we can measure only observable behaviors and that we measure only some facet of an individual's personality. We have talked about characteristics such as intelligence, anxiety, extroversion, and mathematical ability. These are relatively broad terms, summarizing a variety of behaviors and reactions made in a variety of situations. And these characteristics are not measured directly. Consider, for example, the basis for making statements about a person's mathematical ability. We might administer a test containing a variety of mathematical problems; persons answering many of the items correctly would be said to have high mathematical ability. But this would be a summary statement based on their responses to a number of items. What was measured directly was a set of responses to individual problems. Then, looking at a person's performance on these items, we made a statement about his or her mathematical ability. Thus, the concept of "mathematical ability" is an abstraction based on a number of observable responses.

The number of specific responses we could observe is, for all practical purposes, infinite. One investigator, for example, has identified over 40,000 terms that have been used to describe people. Thus, we need a method of identifying categories of behaviors or reactions that can be measured and studied. One approach is trait theory (see, e.g., Allport, 1966; Anastasi, 1970; Ferguson, 1954; Hogan, DeSoto, & Solano, 1977; Mischel, 1968).

Trait Theory

A trait can be defined as a cluster of interrelated, or intercorrelated, behaviors. That is, a trait is a term that describes a group of behaviors that tend to occur together. The typical procedure for identifying traits is to have a group of people respond to a large number of items, then statistically analyze the data to find which items cluster together. For example, we might administer a questionnaire covering a large number of vocational and avocational activities and ask people to respond by indicating whether they like or dislike each activity. Suppose that people who say they like to repair their own car also say that they like to work with power tools, would like to have a home workshop, enjoy working with their hands, like to know how machines work, and like to read *Popular Mechanics*. We have now identified a trait that we might label "mechanical interest." Similar procedures could be used to identify other cognitive and personality traits.

To be useful as descriptive constructs, traits must be relatively stable over time and in different situations. If a person's behavior is not consistent, then predictions of behavior and reactions from situation to situation and from time to time will be inaccurate and of little use. Although most ability and cognitive traits are quite stable, personality characteristics tend to fluctuate more widely.

To summarize, traits are categories for the orderly description of behavior (Anastasi, 1970). They are a way of classifying and talking about behavior, a classification based on clusters of interrelated behaviors or reactions. They are abstractions, a convenient fiction that helps us conceptualize and understand human behavior.

Alternative Approaches

Although the trait approach has proved useful in many areas of psychological research, it has some limitations. For example, it has been more useful in describing cognitive characteristics than personality characteristics (Mischel, 1968). What, then, are the possible alternatives?

One possibility is to use *typologies*, to consider people as falling in independent classes. Typologies would classify some people as introverted and others extroverted, some people as smart and others dumb, or some as having a criminal personality. The basic assumption is that people fall into distinct, qualitatively different, and independent groups. We talk this way in everyday conversation even though this view is not supported by the empirical data. Although we may refer to some people as smart and others dumb, in actuality the distribution of intelligence is continuous. Thus, to talk about distinct classes of people is an oversimplification.

At the other extreme, we could study only *specific behaviors* and not postulate anything like traits. One problem with this approach is, of course, that the number of specific behaviors is virtually limitless. In addition, certain behaviors tend to occur together. Although we can call these classes something other than traits, we still need to develop an economical classification scheme in order to generalize our statements about behavior and develop psychological theories.

measurement

A psychological test is a measuring instrument. But what is meant by measurement? Measurement is the description of data in terms of numbers (Guilford, 1954). More precisely, measurement has been defined as the assignment of numerals to objects or events according to rules (Stevens, 1951). In the context of testing, this definition could be restated: *Measurement is the assignment of numerals to behavior according to rules.* Therefore, measurement of any characteristic involves the utilization of certain procedures (operations) and specified rules to assign numerical values to a person's performance. Implicit in the definition is the idea that these numerical values will be expressed on a well-defined scale. In other words, we have a continuum measuring some dimension, and our goal is to place each person at the proper place on this continuum.

Measurement Scales

To understand the preciseness of psychological measurement, we must consider the nature of the scale used. Depending on the mathematical and logical assumptions made, several types of scales are possible. These scale levels are hierarchical in that the higher-level scales meet all the assumptions of the lower-order scales plus additional ones characteristic of their particular level. From lower to higher order, from simpler to more complex, the scales are called nominal, ordinal, interval, and ratio.

Nominal Scales. Measurement on a nominal scale is simply assigning persons to qualitatively different categories. For example, people can be classified as male or female. If desired, numerals can be assigned to each group. Thus, males might be coded 1 and females 2. These numerals are used for identification only, to denote membership in a certain class; they do not imply magnitude. We can, however, count the number of people in each group; for example, we might have 20 males (group 1) and 30 females (group 2).

Ordinal Scales. Ordinal scales rank people on some dimension. For example, when we rank schoolchildren in order according to their height, from tallest to shortest, we cannot say how much taller one child is than another; we can only compare their relative heights. Thus, on an ordinal scale we have classification (two children can be the same height) and ranking (some children are taller than others), but can say nothing about the size of the scale units (how much taller one child is than another).

In many situations ranking is sufficient. If we want to select the 25 best math students from a class of 100, we have only to give a math test and identify the 25 highest scorers. We do not need to know how much higher they scored than the rest of the class; we only need to know that they obtained the highest scores. In general, when we are interested in selecting only a top (or bottom) group of people, ranking will suffice.

Interval scales. On an interval scale, a difference of a certain magnitude means the same thing at all points along the scale. In other words, the score units can be shown to be equivalent at all points on the scale.[4] Thus, an interval scale involves classification, ranking and equal-sized units. Consequently, the crucial operation in the development of an interval scale is to establish that we do have equal-sized units. We must be able to show that a given interval on the scale, say a 5-point difference, is equivalent at any place on the scale.

Suppose that we administer a science test consisting of 50 items of varying difficulty and that the scores are the number of items answered correctly. Can we say that a 5-point difference at one part on the scale is equivalent to a 5-point difference on any other part of the scale? For example, is the difference between scores of 10 and 15 equivalent to the difference between scores of 40 and 45? From one point of view, yes, because each is a 5-point difference. From another point of view, the difference between 40 and 45 is greater than the difference between 10 and 15 because to increase one's score from 40 to 45 requires answering five relatively difficult questions while an increase from 10 to 15 requires answering five additional easy items. On an interval scale, these differences would be equivalent.

Ratio Scales. The fourth level of measurement is the ratio scale. In addition to equal intervals, ratio scales also have a meaningful zero point. Since a meaningful absolute zero point is virtually impossible to define for most psychological characteristics (consider, for example, how to define "zero intelligence") and since interval scales are sufficient for most purposes, we shall not be overly concerned with attempting to develop tests that measure on ratio scales.[5]

What Level Is Psychological Measurement? There is general agreement that tests measure at least on an ordinal scale—that is, can rank people. Whether they measure on an interval scale has been a subject of much debate (see, e.g., Anderson, 1961; Gaito, 1980; Gardner, 1975; Nunnally, 1978; Stevens, 1951; Wolins, 1978). We will take a pragmatic view and argue: (1) Although test construction procedures do not guarantee interval scales, they at least approximate them; and (2) treating test scores as if they were on interval scales produces useful and

---

[4] Strictly speaking, the requirement is for equal-sized intervals between scale points.

[5] Some recent approaches to test construction claim to attain a type of absolute scaling (see, e.g., Lord, 1980).

interpretable results. In short, we will assume an interval scale and proceed as if we had one.

Characteristics of Psychological Measurement

Three characteristics of psychological measurement put some limitations on the interpretation and use of psychological tests. First, *psychological measurement is descriptive.* A test score indicates the level of performance on a particular set of tasks under a specific set of conditions. The score only describes the performance; it does not interpret or evaluate it. Thus, an IQ score of 115 describes a person's performance on a particular test administration; to interpret the score requires further information, such as the performance of other people and knowledge of the test taker's background.

As a corollary, a score describes the person's performance at a particular time; it does not tell why the person performed that way. True, by looking at performance on individual items or considering other information we can make some hypotheses about why the person scored as he or she did, but the test score does not provide this information directly. Thus, if students from a school with a high socioeconomic status score higher on a reading test than children from a ghetto school, the test scores describe the difference in performance but do not tell the reasons for the difference.

Even though scores are descriptive and nonevaluative, value judgments do enter into the testing process—for example, when deciding what to test and how scores are to be used.

Second, *psychological measurement is relative.* Scores usually are interpreted by comparisons with other people. One reason is that there are few, if any, absolute and nonarbitrary standards of performance in the areas that we test. Even measurements that we often consider absolute—such as an A grade in a course or running a 4-minute mile—take on meaning only when compared with the performance of other people. Another reason is that differences between people usually are more interesting and useful than absolute measures. For example, in most athletic contests awards are based on relative performance (who finishes first) rather than the absolute level or performance; most grades are based on relative achievement, and employers hire the best-qualified applicant rather than taking anyone who meets their minimum standards.

Third, *psychological measurement is indirect.* In the discussion of traits we showed how characteristics are inferred from specific behaviors rather than being measured directly. Thus we are always confronted with the question of whether the test is measuring the characteristic it is designed to measure.

Psychological and Physical Measurement

Another way to understand the nature of psychological measurement is to contrast it with physical measurement.[6] An obvious difference is that in psychological measurement there are more variables to control. For example, when measuring

[6] For interesting discussions of the nature of physical measurement see Astin (1968), Faller (1967), Hall (1978), or Hunter (1980).

reading speed we have to be concerned with the nature of the items (their wording, length, vocabulary level), the testing conditions (directions, time limits, physical environment), and the state of the test taker (motivation, illness). None of these variables affect physical measurements to any significant degree.

A second difference is that psychological measurement is less precise than physical measurement. When a teacher grades an essay question, he or she assigns a limited range of scores, say 1–10 or A–F; even then, differences between successive points may not be clear-cut. On the other hand, given appropriate instruments you could measure the length of an object to 0.0001 inch, or even more precisely.

Third, in psychological measurement, knowing that you are being evaluated may affect the results of the measurement. Many people become very anxious when being observed or evaluated. Other people, knowing they are being evaluated, try extraordinarily hard to do well. In either case the outcome of the measurement may be affected.

In addition, experiences during the test may affect performance. Several very hard items at the beginning of a test may result in a loss of confidence, and consequent poor performance. Or, conversely, if a person who is unsure of herself finds that she can easily do the first several items, her confidence may increase and result in better performance on the rest of the test. Changes can also be more permanent. Counselors sometimes report that clients who take interest inventories note that just thinking about the items causes them to reconsider their vocational plans. These examples have no parallel in physical measurement.

Measurement, Evaluation, and Assessment

A common confusion in psychological testing is the failure to make a clear distinction between measurement and evaluation. Measurement answers the question: how much? That is, measurement provides a description of a person's performance; it says nothing about the worth or value of the performance. However, when we interpret a person's performance, we usually place some value or worth on it. At this point we are going beyond description. We are attempting to answer the question: how good? This is evaluation.

Perhaps an example can illustrate the difference between measurement and evaluation. Suppose that I give a 50-item test to my class. John Jacobs asks me how he did, and I reply that he obtained a score of 36. His test score is a measurement, a description of his level of performance. He then asks me what grade he received, and I reply that a 36 is a B. Now I have made an evaluation because I have made a judgment of how good his performance was. In other words, the objective description of his performance (his test score) is a measurement; my subjective judgment of its quality (the grade) is an evaluation.

Another frequently used term is assessment. *Assessment* refers to the global process of synthesizing information about individuals so as to describe and understand them better. Implicit in this definition is the idea that a variety of sources of information, both formal and informal, may be used to arrive at a description. Thus, although tests and other measurement procedures may be used in assessment, the assessment process is not restricted to formal measurement procedures and may encompass other methods of obtaining information about an individual.

attitudes toward testing

People hold various views regarding the efficacy of psychological tests (Brim et al., 1969; Goslin, 1967). On the one hand, a large number of people overestimate the accuracy of tests. They tend to see test scores as providing almost perfect indications of a person's abilities and personality characteristics. These people think that if a test shows Johnny's IQ to be 120, then he is more intelligent, and should do better in school, than Sam, whose IQ is only 117. Or if Chuck's score on a mechanical comprehension test is relatively low, these people would discourage him from becoming a mechanic, neglecting the fact that he rebuilt the engine on his car. This view of tests provides an easy way to make decisions; there is no need to weigh a variety of factors, just do what the test scores indicate.

Another large group of persons feel that psychological tests are essentially useless. These people argue that relying on tests will, in many cases, result in making wrong decisions; thus tests should not be used. This argument is buttressed with examples: the girl who was told that she lacked the ability to complete college, but who later became a successful physician; the company president who "failed" the employment test of his own company; the sullen "genius" who obtained a low score on the intelligence test because he rebelled against being asked to submit to the test.

Other people object to testing on equalitarian grounds, feeling that using tests to differentiate between people is inconsistent with the principles of a democratic society. An obvious example of this occurs whenever test results are used in making comparisons between racial or ethnic groups. Others feel that personality tests invade an individual's privacy when they probe areas such as religion, sex, and politics. Yet others feel that the human personality is so complex that no objective, scientific method can adequately capture its richness and diversity.

These are important issues that must be attended to by test constructors and users. But since they can be debated only if one has an understanding of the testing process, we will postpone our discussion of them until after we have presented the basic principles of psychological measurement.

summary

There are a number of reasons for measuring psychological characteristics. Among the most important are to describe the abilities and/or personality characteristics of individuals, to aid in making practical decisions, to help define psychological constructs, and to suggest hypotheses for further investigation.

One common technique for measuring psychological characteristics is to use tests. A test can be defined as a systematic procedure for measuring a sample of behavior. Thus comparable items are administered to all test takers, testing conditions are similar for all people, and responses are evaluated using the same rules.

Because there are an almost infinite number of abilities, skills, and behaviors that could be measured, a method is needed to categorize these diverse behaviors. The most common approach is trait theory. A trait can be defined as a cluster of interrelated behaviors. Traits are but labels referring to orderly classifications of related behaviors; they are hypothetical constructs, not real entities.

As tests are measuring instruments, they report performance in quantitative terms. That is, to measure an individual's standing on some dimension of interest, we must establish certain rules and measurement procedures that result in performance being expressed on some well-defined scale. Although psychological measurement is similar to physical measurement, it differs in that more variables may affect the measurement, including knowledge that one is being assessed and reactions to the testing situation. Consequently, psychological measurement is usually less precise than physical measurement. It is also important to remember that psychological measurement is descriptive, indirect, and generally relative rather than absolute.

Whenever we attempt to measure psychological characteristics, our goal should be to measure as accurately as possible. When evaluating measurement methods, including tests, the question is not whether the method is good or bad in some absolute sense; rather, it is whether the measurement procedure results in more accurate and usable results than would be obtained with other available methods. Finally, although we will discuss tests, keep in mind that the same principles and standards apply to all types of methods used to assess psychological abilities and characteristics.

Suggestions for Further Reading

Allen, M. J., & Yen, W. M. *Introduction to measurement theory.* Monterey, Calif.: Brooks/Cole, 1979. Chapter 8 describes the various levels of measurement scales and methods for obtaining them.

Anastasi, A. On the formation of psychological traits. *American Psychologist,* 1970, *25,* 899–910. A description of the major approaches to studying the nature and development of psychological traits; a basic article on trait theory.

Dawes, R. M. Suppose we measured height with rating scales instead of rulers? *Applied Psychological Measurement,* 1977, *1,* 267–273. A clever study showing that similar results can be obtained from different measuring techniques.

DuBois, P. H. *A history of psychological testing.* Boston: Allyn and Bacon, 1970. An overview of the history of testing from ancient times to the 1970s.

Gardner, P. L. Scales and statistics. *Review of Educational Research,* 1975, *45,* 43–57. A review of various views on the distinctions, and interrelations, between measurement and statistics; for readers with good statistical backgrounds.

Ghiselli, E. E., Campbell, J. P., & Zedeck, S. *Measurement theory for the behavioral sciences.* San Francisco: Freeman, 1981. Chapter 2 describes the types of variables and scales used in psychology and how these variables are measured.

Hunter, J. S. The national system of scientific measurement. *Science,* 1980, *210,* 869–874. A description of the requirements for an adequate measuring system in the physical sciences.

Jones, L. V. The nature of measurement. In R. L. Thorndike (Ed.), *Educational measurement,* 2d ed. Washington, D.C.: American Council on Education, 1971. A concise, but thorough and readable introduction to the nature and problems of psychological measurement.

Kelly, E. L. *Assessment of human characteristics.* Belmont, Calif.: Brooks/Cole, 1967. Chapters 1–3 are a good introduction to the nature and goals of personality assessment.

Kerlinger, F. N. *Foundations of behavioral research,* 2d ed. New York: Holt, Rinehart and Winston, 1973. Chapter 3 describes the nature and functions of constructs and variables in psychological theory and research; Chapter 25 is a brief, clear introduction to educational and psychological measurement.

Tyler, L. E., & Walsh, W. B. *Tests and measurements,* 3d ed. Englewood Cliffs, N.J.: Prentice-Hall, 1979. A short book covering the nature of psychological measurement and the types and uses of psychological tests.

Chapter 2 • Test Development: An Overview

THE procedures used to construct tests are designed to ensure that the test attains its desired goals and purposes. This aim is accomplished through application of the measurement principles discussed in Chapter 1. Although the process will vary, depending upon the type of test, a general sequence of steps can be identified. These include defining the purpose of the test and the construct to be measured, developing a set of operational procedures for obtaining the measurement, and specifying a scale for expressing performance.

This chapter presents an overview of the test development process, describing the characteristics of a good test and showing, in broad outline, the steps in the process. The individual steps will then be considered in more detail in this and following chapters. Throughout the discussion, keep in mind that the process of test development is both a science and an art, uses both statistical and logical reasoning, and balances practical with theoretical considerations. The goal is to develop an instrument that is both technically sound and practical.

characteristics of a good measuring instrument

Before discussing the steps in the test development process, we will look briefly at the characteristics desired in any test or other assessment device—characteristics that should be built into the test during the test construction process and scrutinized when evaluating a test. They are important regardless of what the test measures and what is the purpose of the measurement. Unless the test has these properties, there is no assurance that the test measures what it purports to measure, that it measures accurately, or that it will be a practical and useful instrument.

Specification of Purpose

Any test should have a clearly defined purpose. More specifically, the test developer should describe what construct the test is designed to measure, how the results of testing will be used, and who will take the test. The answers to these questions give direction to the test construction process and provide a framework for evaluating the completed instrument.

Suppose a test is designed to measure the reading comprehension of elementary school children. This definition both guides the test constructor and sets some constraints. For example, specifying that the test is to measure reading comprehension suggests appropriate types of items, such as having test takers read selections and answer questions about their meaning. Knowing that the test is designed for elementary school children sets some limits on item content, the complexity of the reading material, and the difficulty of the items. In addition, the possible uses for the test suggest further guidelines. For example, different types of items might be used if the test is to provide an overall index of students' reading comprehension than if it is to be used as a diagnostic instrument to identify specific reading problems.

Because of the importance of specifying the test purpose, we will discuss this topic in more detail later in this chapter.

Standard Conditions

In testing, our goal is to obtain as accurate an estimate of the test taker's performance as possible. Accurate estimation in psychological testing, as in other scientific procedures, depends upon control of errors—that is, minimizing the influence of factors irrelevant to the purposes of the testing. This is accomplished by making the test situation as similar as possible for all individuals.

The process of developing these controls is called *standardization*. Standardization means various things to different authors. All agree that standardization implies that the same (or equivalent) items are presented to each test taker and that there are specific rules for administering and scoring the test. Other authors would add the requirement that performance norms be available. The definition of standardization adopted in this book will include only the requirements of common item content and standard administration and scoring procedures. In other words, standardization will refer to the procedures for obtaining scores, not the provision of data necessary to interpret scores.[1]

Standard conditions refer to three aspects of the testing process: content, administration, and scoring. Unless the same or comparable items are administered to all test takers, their scores cannot be directly compared, as they will be based on different samples of items. Although this requirement may seem obvious, it is not always met. Perhaps the most common example is when students are allowed to select from among various essay questions on classroom examinations. Only when the various items require comparable amounts of knowledge and preparation, and are of equal difficulty, can scores on the various questions be directly compared.

Even when the same items are administered to all test takers, they must also be administered under the same conditions. All students should have the same amount of time to work on the test, should receive the same directions, and be tested under similar conditions. To use an obvious example, on a classroom test it would be unfair to allow some students to refer to the text while others had to rely on their memory or to give some students 20 minutes and others 45 minutes to complete the test.

Since a test may be administered to different persons, at various times and places, and possibly even by different examiners, testing conditions will differ.

---

[1] The term "standardized test" is also applied to tests developed by commercial test publishers that meet all the conditions outlined above and also provide normative data to aid interpretation of scores.

However, much extraneous variability can be eliminated by carefully following the prescribed directions for administering the test.

The third element is scoring. Ideally, scoring procedures should guarantee high agreement between different scorers. This can be best accomplished by determining scoring rules and procedures in advance, then following them conscientiously.

To summarize, testing can be said to be standardized if the same (or comparable) items are administered to all test takers, under similar testing conditions, with responses scored using specified procedures. The reasons for using standardized testing conditions are to minimize the effects of irrelevant variables and to allow for accurate interpretations of scores. Unless each person is tested under the same conditions, different factors may influence the scores; thus scores cannot be unambiguously interpreted, either by comparison to each other or to some performance standard.

Consistency

Unless a test measures consistently, little faith can be placed in the accuracy of the test scores. That is, an individual should obtain approximately the same scores on another administration of a test. Without consistency, testing would be analogous to measuring with a rubber ruler. Different results would be obtained on each occasion (measurement), depending on how much the ruler was stretched. Thus we would not know whether the score obtained from a particular administration of the test was an accurate index of the test taker's performance.

Methods for determining the consistency (or reliability) of a test will be discussed in Chapter 5. At this point we will only say that obtaining a reliable measure involves control of variables that might produce instability in scores from time to time or from occasion to occasion. One way to do this is to use standard testing conditions. Other ways are to write unambiguous items (so that test takers know what is expected of them) and to increase the test length by adding more items. Use of clear items and standardized testing conditions both reduce irrelevant influences; using more items increases reliability because chance factors, such as guessing, tend to cancel each other out, thus producing a more accurate estimate.

Validity

The most important characteristic of a test is validity. *Validity* refers to the extent to which a test measures what it is designed to measure, and nothing else. Without evidence of the validity of a test, we do not know what characteristic the test actually measures, and in turn, cannot interpret scores.

How to determine the validity of a test depends on the nature of the construct measured and the purpose of the testing. The methods of determining validity fall into three broad classes. *Content validity* involves establishing that the test items representatively sample a particular content domain. *Criterion-related validity* involves establishing an empirical relationship between test scores and some external measure, the criterion. *Construct validity* involves collecting evidence that better defines the nature of the construct measured by the test. These types of validity will be described in Chapters 6 and 7.

The test construction process, particularly the method of selecting items, is an important determiner of the test's validity. For example, when developing a test to predict success on some job, we would select only those items whose scores correlate with a measure of job success. Because a test may be valid in one situation but less valid in another, presumably comparable situation, validity data must be collected in various situations and for various groups. The test constructor's obligation is to provide sufficient validity data to inform test users what characteristic the test measures.

Scores

All of the characteristics discussed thus far have one goal—to insure that the test scores provide useful information. Unless a test is reliable and valid, there is no assurance that scores will provide information that can be used in making practical decisions or theoretical statements. In turn, reliable and valid scores are obtained by careful test construction strategies, including use of standardized conditions.

In Chapters 8 and 9 we will distinguish between three broad classes of scores. *Norm-referenced scores* are interpreted by comparing a person's score to scores of other people. For example, when a teacher says that a student scored higher on an exam than 85 percent of the students in the class, she has made a norm-referenced interpretation. *Content-referenced scores* are interpreted by comparison to a predetermined performance standard. Thus, saying that a teenager drives well enough to obtain a driver's license is a content-referenced interpretation, as her driving skills have exceeded the minimum level needed to obtain a license. *Outcome-referenced scores* are interpreted in terms of performance on some other measure. For example, if a counselor tells a client that students who obtain a particular score on a college admissions test usually obtain a B average at State College, he is making an outcome-referenced interpretation.

Practicality and Efficiency

The final consideration is practicality. The simpler the procedures for administering, responding to, and scoring the test, the more likely we are to obtain accurate and useful results. If directions are unclear, they may be misunderstood; if procedures are unduly complex, they may not be followed; if scoring is difficult, errors will be made.

But other considerations are also important. One is time: not only the time needed to administer the test but also the time needed to score the test and interpret the results. Another is cost. Tests vary widely in their costs, both direct (the cost of the test and scoring materials) and indirect (costs associated with administering, scoring, and interpreting the test). We must also consider the qualifications needed to administer, score, and interpret the test. Some tests, such as multiple-choice achievement tests, can be administered, scored, and interpreted by most users with little training. Others, such as individual intelligence tests, require highly trained administrators and can be interpreted only by persons having strong backgrounds in psychology or education.

The practical constraints will vary in each situation. However, the goal should be to use the simplest procedures possible within the limits imposed by the nature of the test and the situation. Regardless of the situation, practical considerations always should be of less importance than the quality of the test. To use a poorer test just because it is cheaper or more efficient is a false economy because the results will probably be less useful and will result in less accurate decisions.

the test purpose

The first step in constructing any test is to define clearly what the test will measure and how it will be used. Specifically, the following three questions must be addressed: What construct or characteristic will the test measure? What are the expected uses of the test? Who will take the test? Answers to these questions will direct the test construction process by suggesting answers to such questions as what content the test will cover, what types of items will be used, how long the test will be, and how scores will be expressed.

The need for carefully considering the purpose and potential uses of a test cannot be overstressed. Unless we know what we want to measure, and how the test will be used, we will have no guidelines to follow in developing the test. Or, as someone once said, "If you don't know where you are going, you may end up somewhere else."

An example of a succinct definition of the purpose of a test is provided in a pamphlet sent to students planning to take the College Entrance Examination Board's Scholastic Aptitude Test (SAT):

> The SAT is a multiple-choice test made up of separately timed verbal and mathematical sections. Verbal questions measure your ability to understand what you read and the extent of your vocabulary. Mathematical questions measure your ability to solve problems involving arithmetic reasoning, algebra, and geometry. These abilities have been shown to be related to successful academic performance in college. The SAT does not measure other kinds of abilities which may be associated with success in college, such as special talents or motivation.
>
> Your high school record is probably the best evidence of your preparation for college. Because applicants have taken different courses and come from high schools with different grading practices, college admissions officers need a common measure of ability, such as the SAT. However, scores on the SAT are just part of the information used in making an admissions decision. (CEEB, 1978, p. 3)

Note that this description not only gives the purpose and intended uses of the test, it also indicates what types of items will be used and what content will be covered.

The manual for a published test should indicate the purpose of the test. The *Standards* (1974) make this clear in two standards:

> B2. The test manual should state explicitly the purposes and applications for which the test is recommended. (p. 14)
> B3. The test manual should describe clearly the psychological, educational, and other reasoning underlying the test and the nature of the characteristic it is intended to measure. (p. 15)

Thus, whether a new test is being developed or an existing test is being considered for use, we must first look at the purpose of the test.

It should also be noted that a test may measure more than one characteristic or have several intended uses. For example, interest inventories may measure interest in a number of occupations, college majors, and/or broad occupational fields. And, though designed primarily for vocational and educational counseling, they also have been used in selection and placement. Thus it is important to consider all the characteristics a test may measure and all its potential uses.

Types of Test Purposes

The purposes and functions of tests can be viewed in a number of ways. Chapter 1 presented one classification. In this section we will look at three other ways of classifying test purposes, ones that have important implications for the test construction process, as well as for evaluating and interpreting tests.

Maximal and Typical Performance Tests. On *maximal performance tests* test takers attempt to make the highest possible score; the goal is to measure the upper limits of their abilities. This set is engendered by the test directions and the test taker's knowledge of the test purpose. For example, the directions for classroom examinations imply that you should try to make a high score and your knowledge of the use of the scores (for grading) encourages you to do your best. Thus, such tests are maximal performance measures. In addition to achievement tests, aptitude and ability tests are also maximal performance measures.

In contrast, *typical performance measures* assess a person's habitual reactions and behaviors. Here the interest is not in a person's best possible performance, rather in her typical reactions or behavior. Thus, if on an interest inventory you are asked about your liking of various courses, the question of concern is your usual reaction to these courses. Again, this set is produced by the test directions. As might be expected, most personality, interest, and attitude tests are typical performance measures.

Because maximal and typical performance measures differ in both content and directions, different test construction strategies are needed. In particular, the task must be structured so as to obtain the desired response, either the test taker's best possible performance or typical reactions.

Tests That Represent and Tests That Predict. Another classification scheme distinguishes between tests that represent and tests that predict. This distinction refers to whether the test items and the relevant nontest behavior are similar or different. If the test and nontest behavior are essentially similar, the test is said to represent the relevant behavior; if they are different, the test is said to be a predictor. A classroom test would be an example of a test that represents, as the items measure the skills and knowledge taught in the class; a college admission test would be an example of a test that predicts, as scores are used to predict a qualitatively different variable, success in college.

Goodenough (1949) made a further distinction within the class of tests that represent. She distinguished between tests as samples and tests as signs. The primary basis of her distinction is the clarity with which one can define the behavioral domain being sampled. In her classification, a test is a sample when the items are drawn from a clearly defined universe; a test is a sign when the universe is open-ended and not completely defined. The implication of the term "sign" is that the test points to, or signals, the nature of the universe being sampled. Thus tests that are samples can be viewed as describing the domain, tests that are signs as explaining the domain.

In general, the sampling concept is most appropriate with achievement tests, in which the content and skills to be measured are usually clearly specified. When measuring constructs used in psychological theories, such as creativity or intelligence, the domain is usually incompletely defined. Here conceptualizing tests as signs seems more appropriate.

Sometimes a test serves more than one of these functions. Consider a test covering high school mathematics. The same test might serve as a sample of material taught in high school mathematics courses, as a sign of mathematical aptitude or ability, or as a predictor of success in college mathematics courses. However, the test construction process would vary depending on the test's primary purpose. If the test is to be used primarily as a sample, items will be selected so as to sample the mathematics taught in high school. If the test will serve primarily as a sign, items will be selected to represent the various components of mathematical ability. If the test is to serve primarily as a predictor, items will be selected on the basis of their ability to predict performance in math courses. Thus, even though a test may serve several purposes, one purpose will probably be stressed in the test construction process.

Norm-Referenced and Content-Referenced Tests. The distinction between norm-referenced and content-referenced tests is in how scores are interpreted. On norm-referenced tests, an individual's scores are interpreted by comparing them to those of other people in some specified comparison group. If a teacher tells you that your exam score was higher than those of 75 percent of the students in the class, she has made a norm-referenced interpretation because she has compared your performance with that of other class members. Content-referenced scores[2], in contrast, interpret performance with reference to a standard of content mastery, one that is independent of the performance of other people. Thus, if the teacher said that you answered 75 percent of the items correctly, she would be making a content-referenced interpretation.

The distinction between norm-referenced and content-referenced tests influences the test construction process at two places: selection of items and development of scales for expressing scores. In selecting items for content-referenced tests, more explicit definitions of the content domain are generally used, often ones based on instructional objectives. With reference to scores, norm-referenced tests require use of scales that allow for comparisons between individuals, whereas content-referenced scores require scales that express performance in terms of content mastery.

---

[2] What we refer to as content-referenced scores are frequently called criterion-referenced scores (Glaser, 1963; Millman, 1974; Popham & Husek, 1969). We will follow the usage of the *Standards* and refer to them as content-referenced scores.

Test Takers

The other major consideration is the composition and characteristics of the groups for which the test is intended. Here the test constructor must take into account such variables as the test takers' ages, intellectual levels, education, socioeconomic and cultural backgrounds, and reading levels. Which variables will be relevant in any specific circumstance will, of course, depend upon the type and purposes of the test. For example, since the SAT is designed for applicants to American colleges and universities, the large majority of persons taking the test will be high school juniors and seniors, who are 16 to 18 years old and have been exposed to a common core of educational experiences. Therefore, the items in the SAT are designed to be of appropriate difficulty and coverage for this particular group.

An Ethical Consideration

When considering a test's potential uses, the test developer must address another important question: Should the test be used in its intended manner? As Messick states:

> [T]wo questions [should] be explicitly addressed whenever a test is proposed for a specific purpose: First, is the test any good as a measure of the characteristic it is [intended] to assess? Second, should the test be used for the proposed purpose in the proposed way? (Messick, 1980b, p. 1012)

In other words, one must always consider how a test will be used and the consequences of its various uses.

Consider an illustration that has been the basis of several court cases. Intelligence tests frequently are used as one basis for assigning students to special educational classes. In some localities, a larger proportion of minority group children than white children are assigned to special educational classes. Although part of the controversy centers on the adequacy of tests as measures of intelligence, another facet relates to whether tests should be used to support a practice that, in the view of some people, results in discriminatory classification of children. Thus, even a well-constructed test may be used for purposes that some people find objectionable.

constructing a test: the basic steps

The first step in test construction is to specify the purpose of the testing and the nature of the construct to be measured. The next step is to translate these specifications into an operational measurement procedure—that is, to construct the test. This process requires development of certain procedures that accomplish the desired purposes through application of the principles of measurement. As standardized measuring conditions have certain advantages (which have been discussed previously), we will describe the steps in developing such measures, focusing on three aspects of the process: specifying content, administrative conditions, and scoring. In this section we will discuss the various steps in general terms; in the next section we will illustrate these steps as applied to the construction of three types of tests.

Test Content and Formats

The content domain will vary with the nature of the construct to be measured and the purpose of the testing. For example, when developing a test to serve as a sample, such as a classroom achievement test, the first step is to delineate the content domain to be covered by the test. A test might cover the sonnets of Shakespeare, the laws of permutations, the social and economic factors in the rise of the Nazi party, or the principles of achievement test construction. The content may be further specified by reference to particular materials; for example, in a classroom exam, content might be defined by reading assignments and the material covered in lectures. In addition to specifying the content, the test constructor may also specify the skills to be tested (for example, knowledge, applications, analysis, evaluation).

If the test is being developed to measure a particular psychological trait or characteristic, the test constructor's job is somewhat different. First he must define, as explicitly as possible, the trait being measured. Then he must indicate the behaviors through which the trait will be manifested. That is, he will describe the observable behaviors, skills, or abilities that are indicators of the trait being measured.

When a test is being developed to serve as a predictor, the first step is to make a systematic analysis of the performance we are attempting to predict. In other words, a job analysis is conducted. The results of this analysis should identify those traits and behaviors that are necessary for satisfactory performance.

Test Plans. The vehicle used to specify content is the test plan. A *test plan* is an outline specifying the coverage of the test. One type of plan is a table showing the topics to be covered, the cognitive skills[3] to be measured, and the relative emphasis given to each content/skill category. An example of a simple test plan, for a unit on descriptive statistics, is shown in Figure 2.1.

Figure 2.1. Example of a Test Plan

Test on Descriptive Statistics

	Concepts	Computation	Interpretation
Distributions	10%	10%	5%
Central tendency	10%	10%	5%
Variability	15%	5%	5%
Correlation	15%	0%	10%

[3] Cognitive skills refer to the type of processing or thinking required to respond to an item. One well-known classification (Bloom et al., 1956) distinguishes between six levels of cognitive skills: knowledge, comprehension, application, analysis, synthesis, and evaluation.

An alternative approach, often used on content-referenced tests, is to start with a list of behavioral objectives. *Behavioral objectives* are statements of educational outcomes that specify what the test taker will know or do, under what conditions, and to what level of proficiency. For example:

- The student can factor four of five quadratic equations within 10 minutes.

- The student can make seven out of ten free throws.

- The student can list four economic outcomes of World War II.

- The student can correctly balance five out of six chemical equations involving the reaction of an acid with a base.

Given the list of objectives, test items are written to measure attainment of each objective. More than one item may be needed for an objective; for example, the first objective would require five equations (items) and the last one would require six.

A test plan serves two purposes. In the item-writing stage, it indicates how many and what sort of items need to be written. Later, we can compare the actual distribution of items on the final test form to the proportions suggested in the test plan, and thereby determine whether the test items do, in fact, adequately sample the domain.

Test Formats. Other decisions involve the test format. That is, how will the items be presented and how will the test taker respond. Some common variations in formats include:

Verbal or written presentation. Items can be presented in writing or orally. Although test items most often are printed in individual test booklets, they can be written on the board or presented by slides or an overhead projector. Oral presentation can be made by the test administrator or by tape recordings.

Written, oral, or psychomotor responses. Test takers can respond in writing, orally, or, in the case of performance tests, by manipulating some object or apparatus or by performing some physical or psychomotor act.

Alternative-choice or free response items. On alternative-choice items, test takers select from among given alternatives, such as on multiple-choice, true-false, and matching items. On free response items, test takers supply the answer in their own words, as on short answer and essay items.

Group or individual administration. Group tests can be administered to more than one person at a time, thus usually involve written responses. Individual tests can be administered to only one person at a time; thus most oral and performance tests are individual tests.

Speed or power tests. On a speed test, items are quite simple, the time limit is stringent, and scores measure differences in response rates. On power tests, items are of varying difficulty, test takers have time to complete all items, and the score reflects the level of difficulty of items the test taker can answer correctly.

Any test will combine several of these dimensions; that is, the typical classroom test involves written questions and responses, is a power test, and uses group administration. In addition, it may include several different item types, both alternative-choice (such as multiple-choice, true-false) and free response (such as short answer and essay).

As, in most instances, any item can be presented in several formats, one problem is to select the "best" format. Two considerations aid in deciding between possible formats: the characteristics of the group to be tested and practical factors. The role of the composition of the group tested can be illustrated by the practice of administering tests orally to young children and persons with limited reading skills and using tests with minimal verbal content with persons having language deficits. Practical considerations are exemplified by the use of multiple-choice items in college admissions tests, where, because of the volume of tests administered, the only feasible method of scoring is to use high-speed electronic scoring machines.

Item Writing. Having made these preliminary decisions, the test developer is now ready to start writing items.[4] Again, he has several options as to how to proceed. Consider the sources that might be used in developing individual items. For a classroom exam the teacher can use textbooks, reading assignments, lectures, and class discussions as sources of items. In contrast, on achievement tests developed for use in a variety of schools, item writers consider not just one text, but several widely used texts; not the opinions of only one teacher, but those of a variety of teachers and curriculum experts. Personality inventory items are usually suggested by personality theories, by terms and phrases used to describe personality, by statements found in clinic records, by statements people use to describe themselves, and even by items on other personality inventories.

The process of developing good items is one of writing, editing, tryout, and revision. These steps are then repeated until a satisfactory item is developed. Consider, as an example, tests developed by test publishers. Groups of specialists, working from the test plan, write items to cover the designated content-skill areas. To start, several times as many items are written as will be needed, since many items will be eliminated by succeeding analyses. The first drafts of items are then reviewed and edited, both by the original item writers and by other persons. Editing involves correcting ambiguous wording, strengthening weak alternatives, and eliminating duplicate and otherwise unusable items.

Item Tryout and Analysis. On some tests, such as classroom achievement tests, pretesting of items is seldom possible before the test is administered in its final form. On standardized tests, items that have survived the initial screening are combined into one or more *pretests* and administered to a sample of people similar to those who will take the completed test. For example, on achievement tests, pretests would be administered to a sample of students of the same grade

---

[4] Although some test items are not, strictly speaking, written (for example, performance test items), we will use the term "item writing" to refer to the construction of all types of test items, since the same general guidelines and procedures are used.

level and educational background as students who will take the completed test. The goal of pretesting is to obtain information on how test takers respond to the items. This analysis will include both qualitative comments by test takers, such as perceived ambiguities in items, and quantitative analyses.

The quantititative analysis of test items, called *item analysis,*[5] typically investigates three characteristics of each item. One is the difficulty of the item, defined as the percentage of test takers who answer the item correctly. The second is the discrimination power, the extent to which the item differentiates between people having greater or lesser degrees of knowledge or ability, or, in the case of personality measures, persons having varying degrees of the trait. The third analysis is of distracters. Here the interest is in identifying weak alternatives, ones that do not attract many responses. Those items that have statistical weaknesses are revised or eliminated and the better items retained.[6] Sometimes additional items may need to be written and the procedure repeated with a revised form of the pretest. Pretesting continues until there is a large enough pool of satisfactory items to form a test.

Assembling the Test.   The next step is to prepare the final form, or forms, of the test. The results of the item analyses are used to select those items that provide the best discrimination, are of appropriate difficulty, and have no weak alternatives or ambiguities. This selection requires balancing and compromising in that it may be necessary to include less discriminating items in order to ensure the desired content balance. If equivalent forms of the test are built, the test constructor has the further task of equating the forms in terms of content, difficulty, and discrimination power, and along other relevant dimensions.

After any final editorial changes have been made, the test is printed. Now, for the first time, the test exists as a distinct entity. At this point we have a collection of good items but not necessarily a good test. Whether the test will be good or mediocre depends on further analyses.

Test Administration

How a person performs on a test is not simply a function of the content of the test; performance also can be affected by the testing conditions (see, e.g., Anastasi, 1976, Chapter 2; Hattie, 1977; Jensen, 1974, 1980; Rumenik, Capasso, & Hendrick, 1977; Sattler, 1970). Of particular importance are directions, time limits, and the physical and psychological climate during testing.

Directions.   Two sets of directions are required: one for the test taker and the other for the test administrator. The former should explain, as clearly and simply as possible, how and where the test taker should respond. These directions should be printed at the beginning of the test, preferably on a separate page. If

---

[5] For a further discussion of item analysis see Chapter 10.

[6] Examples of weaknesses in items shown by statistical analyses include identifying alternatives that are seldom or never chosen and incorrect responses that are selected more often than the keyed correct response.

the test has several sections or includes several types of items, additional directions should be presented at the beginning of each new section. On some tests, simple, even one-sentence, directions may suffice; for example, the directions for a multiple-choice classroom test might be:

> For each item, select the correct alternative and mark its letter in the appropriate place on the answer sheet.

On standardized tests, directions generally will be more complex (see Figure 2.2).

Directions to the test taker should indicate the nature of the desired response, how and where to make the response (for example, in the test booklet or on a separate answer sheet), and the time limits, if any. There may also be directions about filling in identifying information on the answer sheet. Some tests also include directions about how to respond when uncertain—that is, whether to guess. Usually it is desirable to include sample items. This is essential if the test format may be unfamiliar to test takers.

On published tests, directions for the test administrator are usually printed in a separate manual. These directions should include the specific directions the test administrator should give to the test takers. They should also explain the rationale for the testing procedures and include details about such things as the arrangement of the testing room, distributing and collecting test materials, timing, and how to handle problems and questions arising during the testing session. If you are to obtain a standardized measure, *directions should be followed exactly as printed in the manual.*

Figure 2.2. Example of Test Directions

I. VOCABULARY

Each test word, in capital letters, is followed by five possible answers. The correct answer is the word which *means most nearly the same* as the test word. Make a *heavy* line with your pencil between the pair of dotted lines at the right which are lettered the same as the correct answer. **EXAMPLE:**

FREQUENT: A) always B) often
          C) never D) very E) soon

    A B C D E

Mark an answer for every word. If you don't know the meaning of a word, make the best choice you can.

You will have *three minutes* to work on this test.

DO NOT TURN THE PAGE UNTIL YOU ARE TOLD TO DO SO.

Source: E.E. Cureton et al., *The Multi-Aptitude Test.* New York: The Psychological Corporation, 1955.

Time Limits. Another salient factor is *time limits.* Although time limits some-times are dictated by practical constraints, such as the length of class periods, preferably they should be determined by psychometric considerations and the purpose of the test. For example, when speed of responding is an important aspect of performance, such as on a typing test or a test of facility in performing simple computations, rather stringent time limits should be used, to differentiate between people who work rapidly and those who are slower. On the other hand, when measuring the depth of a student's knowledge, time limits should be liberal, if they are used at all. Many standardized achievement and ability tests use a com-promise procedure. Items are arranged in order of increasing difficulty and time limits set so that about 90 percent of the test takers can complete all the items in the time allowed. Thus, although most people will have time to attempt all items they can answer correctly, the practical advantages of having a set time limit are retained.

Time limits for maximal performance tests can be set using any of several procedures. One is to set the time limit arbitrarily by estimating how long test takers will need to complete the test. A somewhat better procedure is to admin-ister the test to a sample of people, see how long they take, and then set the time limits so that the desired proportion of people (say 90 percent) can finish. An even better procedure is to consider not only the proportion of people who finish in a given time limit, but also the effects of various time limits on reliability and validity (see Nunnally, 1978, for procedures). Thus, for example, if a 30-minute time limit results in as valid and reliable measurement as a 45-minute time limit for a test, the shorter, more efficient time limit can be used with no loss of accu-racy.

Most typical performance measures are administered without time limits, as response rate is of little interest. However, directions often suggest that test takers respond rapidly, giving their first reactions rather than puzzling over items.

Testing Conditions. A third consideration is the testing conditions. Require-ments regarding the physical conditions should be obvious. For example, the testing room should be well-lighted, ventilated, and free from noise and distrac-tions; each test taker should have sufficient room for the testing materials and be comfortable; if materials other than a test booklet are used (for example, specimens for a geology or biology test), all test takers should have access to these materials; if the test requires use of apparatus, it should be in working order.

The psychological climate should also be optimal. Although it is probably im-possible to eliminate all test anxiety and evaluation apprehension, several things can be done to alleviate anxiety. One is to be certain that test takers know why the test is being given and how the results will be used. Another is to make sure the test takers know well in advance what will be covered on the exam. (This does not mean that they should be told the content of specific items, only that they know what topics will be covered.) They should also be told what types of items will be included and how they will be scored. In short, giving test takers information about the nature and purpose of the test will often ease the tension.

The test administrator can also contribute to good testing conditions. Although it is necessary to follow directions precisely, the examiner should be willing to answer questions, attempt to put test takers at ease, improve any undesirable physical conditions, and have a friendly approach to the test takers. All these behaviors help make testing less stressful and consequently increase the probability of obtaining useful results.

Scoring

When scoring a test, the goal is to obtain agreement between various possible scorers. Thus procedures must be developed that specify how items are to be scored, ones that increase agreement among scorers. The reason is obvious: When there is disagreement between scorers, differences in scores will reflect differences between scorers as well as differences between test takers on the characteristic measured.

Objective Scoring. Scoring procedures are considered *objective* if there is close agreement between two or more trained scorers when they follow the prescribed scoring procedures. In other words, if two persons scored the same test independently, they would obtain the same score for each test taker. Ideally there would be perfect agreement between any two scorers; in practice, especially with free response items, agreement may be less than complete. The goal, however, should always be to obtain as much agreement as possible.

Although a myriad of scoring techniques are available, from hand scoring to high-speed electronic scoring machines, the requirements for objective scoring can be reduced to three basic steps. The first is immediate and unambiguous recording of responses. When the test taker responds by marking an answer sheet, or by writing a letter, a number, a word, a phrase, a sentence, or a paragraph or more, we can use this record. If answers are given orally, responses should be recorded immediately and completely. If the test taker manipulates some apparatus or performs some physical act, the results should be recorded, again immediately and completely. These permanent records avoid possible distortions due to faulty memory and provide the basis for classifying responses.

The second requirement is a list of acceptable responses or correct responses, a *scoring key*. For alternative-choice items, the key will indicate the letter (or number) of the correct or scored responses; for short-answer items, it would be a list of correct responses and acceptable variations; for an essay item, it might be an outline of the major points to be covered in the response. If various responses receive different weights, these weights should be indicated on the key.

The third requirement is to specify a procedure for comparing responses to the key; that is, a procedure for classifying responses. On alternative-choice items, the procedure usually is straightforward and obvious. When judgment is involved in scoring responses, as on short-answer and essay items, detailed directions for assigning scores need to be developed. An example of how this can be done is provided by in the manual for the Wechsler Adult Intelligence Scale (see Figure 2.3). Note that the manual provides rules for scoring and examples of acceptable responses. The scorer compares responses to the examples, then assigns the

Figure 2.3 Example of a Scoring Manual

SCORING CRITERIA AND SAMPLE ANSWERS: VOCABULARY.   In general, any recognized meaning of the word is acceptable, disregarding elegance of expression. However, *poverty of content* is penalized to some extent; indication of only a vague knowledge of what the word means does not earn full credit. Responses are scored 2, 1, or 0. The following are general principles for scoring responses to the Vocabulary items.

---

2 Points

---

1. A good synonym.
2. A major use.
3. One or more definitive or primary features.
4. General classification to which word belongs.
5. Several correct descriptive features which are not precisely definitive but which cumulatively indicate understanding of the word.
6. For verbs, definitive example of action or causal relation.

---

1 Point

---

1. A response that is not incorrect but which shows poverty of content.
2. A vague or inexact synonym.
3. A minor use, not elaborated.
4. Attributes which are correct but not definitive or not distinguishing features.
5. An example using the word itself, not elaborated.
6. Correct definition of a related form of the word, e.g., "haste" instead of "hasten".

---

0 Points

---

1. Obviously wrong answers.
2. Verbalisms, e.g., "Repair a car," when no real understanding is shown after inquiry.
3. Responses which show great poverty of content or are very vague even after questioning.

SAMPLE ANSWERS: VOCABULARY

---

1. Chair

---

2 points—a piece of furniture to sit in; to conduct a meeting; to sit in . . . to sit on . . . sit on while eating
1 point—furniture made of wood
0 points—sitting down . . . soft object . . . be at a meeting

---

2. January

---

2 points—first month of the year; a month . . . first month . . . cold winter month
1 point—after December . . . starts year . . . New Year's is January 1
0 points—a Roman God

---

3. Construct

---

2 points—to build or devise something; something built systematically; to build . . . erect something . . . put together using a plan
1 point—construct a building . . . make . . . process of building
0 points—divide . . . tighten, draw together . . . helpful

To preserve the security of the test actual WAIS items were not used. The hypothetical items used are similar to the WAIS vocabulary items and the format of the scoring manual similar to the WAIS manual.

score of the most nearly comparable sample response. Although this procedure does not ensure perfect agreement between scorers, differences in scores assigned are generally minor. Thus, scoring can be said to be objective.

Analyses of Total Scores

The procedures we have discussed are designed to ensure that the test provides a standardized measure. But this does not complete our task. Several types of analyses must be performed on the completed test.

Regardless of the type of test, we must determine the reliability and validity of our measure. That is, we need evidence that the test measures consistently and that it measures what it is designed to measure. Furthermore, these analyses should be done for each group and use of the test. Procedures for doing these analyses will be described in Chapter 4–7.

We also will want to obtain information about the distribution of scores for various groups of test takers. Although information of this type is useful when interpreting scores on any test, it is essential for norm-referenced tests, where scores are interpreted by comparison to the performance of other people. Thus the test should be administered to various groups, and the mean, the standard deviation, and the shape of the distribution should be determined. These procedures will be discussed in Chapters 3, 8, and 9.

examples of test development

As a review and to provide integration, we will briefly describe the steps in the construction of three types of tests: one where the test samples a content domain, one where the test defines a construct, and one where the test is a predictor. These examples are used only as illustrations, not as an exhaustive list of possible test development strategies.

The major steps in the test construction process are shown in Figure 2.4. Not all steps can be included for all tests; for example, pretesting of items is not always possible. Note also that, at this point, we will not describe how to determine the test's reliability, validity, and norms. This does not mean that these steps are not essential; they are an integral part of the test development process. Because of their importance they will be discussed more fully in later chapters.

A Test as a Sample

To illustrate the construction of a test used as a sample, consider a familiar example: a classrooom final exam—specifically, a comprehensive final examination in a general psychology course at the college level.

The instructor's first step is to define the purpose. In this case it is obvious, to measure students' knowledge of the material covered in the course. Development of a test plan is straightforward. The instructor lists the various topics covered (probably the text chapter titles), the skills to be measured (for example, knowledge, comprehension, and application), and their relative emphases. Items are drawn both from the text and lectures and will be of various types (multiple-choice, short answer, and essay). The instructor may use items from the instructor's manual supplied by the text publisher and/or write his own items. All items, however, cover important concepts or principles covered in the course.

Figure 2.4. Steps in Test Construction.

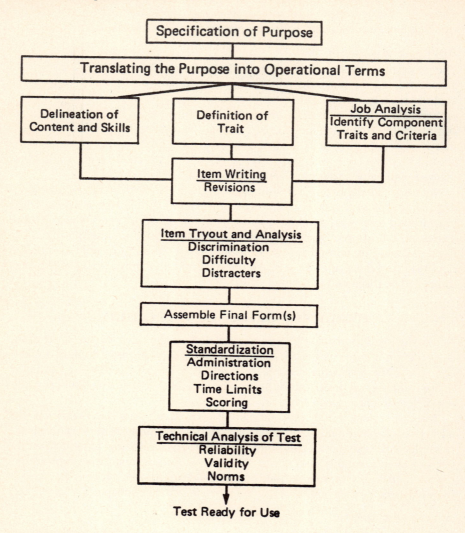

To ensure a balanced test, he writes many more items than he plans to use. Since items cannot be pretested, he will have to rely on his own judgment in selecting items. Thus, after writing the original items, he will edit and revise them, and then select enough of them to attain the desired length and content coverage. These items constitute the final form of the exam. Writing the necessary directions, duplicating the test, and preparing the answer key complete his task.

A Test to Define a Construct

As a second example, consider a psychologist who wants to develop a test that can be used to study the creative ability of high school students. In essence, the test will be an operational definition of the construct called creative ability or creativity.

Her first step is to define what she means by creativity. Surveying the various definitions proposed in the literature on creativity, she adopts as a working definition "the ability to supply original responses." The next task is to operationalize this definition, to develop tasks that measure this ability. She decides to use two tasks: suggesting possible uses for familiar objects and completing drawings involving geometric figures. In the first task, students are asked to list all possible uses for common objects such as a paper clip, a credit card, and a brick. In the second task students are presented with drawings of a circle, a triangle, a square, and other geometric forms and asked to make a drawing incorporating these figures. She constructs 20 items of each type and groups them into two subtests, object uses and drawings.

To pretest the items, she administers the two subtests to samples of high school students. In this situation, pretesting serves two purposes. One is to develop scoring criteria. As her index of creativity is originality, she tabulates the responses to each item to see which responses are common and which are uncommon, hence original. For example, if many students say a brick can be used as a doorstop, this would not be a creative response; however, if only a few say a brick can be used as a hammer, this could be a creative response. The second use of the pretest data is to identify items that, for various reasons, do not work; for example, ones that get few or a narrow range of responses. These items would be revised or eliminated.

The data from the pretesting would be used to develop tentative scoring criteria. She would then score each person's test, using the tentative scoring procedures, and look at the distribution of scores to see whether they gave a wide enough range. She would also look at the interrelations between the items on each subtest and the correlation between scores on the two subtests to determine whether she was measuring two separate abilities or only one. She would then revise the items, modify the administrative procedures (if necessary), and prepare revised forms of the test. These revised forms would then be administered to another sample and similar analyses conducted. This process of revisions and analyses would continue until she had a test that attained the quality needed for use in studies of creativity.

A Test as a Predictor

As a third example, consider a test used to predict the performance of mechanical draftsmen—that is, a test used to select mechanical draftsmen for a particular company.

The first step is to analyze the job, to determine what skills and abilities are needed to perform the job. Observing employed workers, we find that two main skills are required: translating rough sketches and objects into finished drawings and drawing diagrams to different scales. In terms of abilities, we hypothesize that a successful worker needs three abilities: spatial visualization (being able to visualize three-dimensional objects in two dimensions), mathematical skill (especially being able to transform scales), and drawing skills. We would then construct a pool of items to measure each of these abilities, again using separate subtests for each skill. And, since workers do not have unlimited time to complete their work, these tests would be administered with a time limit.

Pretesting would be used primarily to identify items that predict job performance. One approach would be to give the pretests to mechanical draftsmen and people working in other jobs. We would then compute the percent of each group who could answer each item correctly, keeping only those items that differentiated between the two groups. As an alternative, we might compare the responses of draftsmen rated above and below average. In either case, we would keep the items that provided the best differentiation. At this point, or after further pretesting, the best items would be combined into the final form of the test and directions and time limits established. The final form of test could then be administered to future applicants for the position.

summary

The process of test construction involves application of the principles of measurement to build an instrument that measures the desired characteristic and can be used for its intended purposes. Although the specific procedures and steps will vary depending on the nature and purpose of the test, three general steps must be followed: specifying the purpose, coverage, and intended uses of the test; developing operational procedures for building the test; and specifying a scale for reporting performance.

Certain characteristics are desired in any test. These include a clearly specified purpose and content domain, standard conditions for administration and scoring, consistent measurement, valid measurement, interpretable scores, and practicality.

Any test should be constructed for a clearly specified purpose or set of purposes. The first step is to clearly define the construct to be measured, the population to which the test will be administered, and the intended uses of the test. Although tests can be classified in various ways, three broad classifications help clarify thinking about test construction and evaluation. Some tests are maximal performance tests, in that they measure test takers' best possible performance; others are typical performance tests and measure usual or habitual behaviors. Some tests are designed to represent a particular content domain; others are designed to predict external behaviors. Some tests are norm-referenced, in that performance is interpreted by comparison to other people; others are content-referenced and compare performance to a predetermined proficiency standard.

To interpret either norm-referenced or content referenced scores accurately, testing conditions must be standardized. Standardization involves three components: content, administration, and scoring. With respect to content, the important condition is that the same or comparable items are administered to all test takers. This pool of items is obtained by specifying the domain to be measured, writing a test plan and a pool of potential items, carefully editing items, and, whenever possible, pretesting items before use. Standardized test administration procedures ensure that all examinees take the test under similar conditions. Here we are concerned with such factors as directions, time limits, the physical setting, and the psychological climate. Scoring should be objective; that is, procedures should be developed so that trained scorers will agree on the scores assigned to various responses.

Test construction is both a science and an art and must balance practical with psychometric considerations. In all cases, however, the goal is to obtain a valid measure of the characteristic of interest.

Suggestions for Further Reading

Educational Testing Service. *ETS builds a test*. Princeton, N.J.: Educational Testing Service, 1965. A pamphlet describing the process a test publisher follows when constructing a standardized test.

Glaser, R. The future of testing: A research agenda for cognitive psychology and psychometrics. *American Psychologist,* 1981, *36*, 923–936. Glaser argues that knowledge of cognitive processes is essential for understanding abilities and thus has implications for the test construction process.

Green, B.F. A primer of testing. *American Psychologist,* 1981, *36*, 1001–1011. A brief, interesting introduction to the major concepts and procedures in psychological measurement.

Hively, W., Maxwell, G., Rabehl, G., Sension, D., & Lundin, S. *Domain-referenced curriculum evaluation : A technical handbook and a case study from the MINNEMAST Project.* Los Angeles: Center for the Study of Evaluation, University of California at Los Angeles, 1973. Describes the domain-referenced approach to constructing tests to measure educational outcomes as applied to mathematics and science courses.

Krathwohl, D. R., & Payne, D. A. Defining and assessing educational objectives. In R. L. Thorndike (Ed.), *Educational measurement,* 2d ed. Washington, D.C.: American Council on Education, 1971. Describes the construction, evaluation, and use of instructional objectives.

Messick, S. Test validity and the ethics of assessment. *American Psychologist,* 1980, *35*, 1012–1027. Argues that psychologists must be concerned both with the scientific questions about a test as a measuring device and with ethical questions concerning how a test is used.

Popham, W. J., & Lindheim, E. The practical side of criterion-referenced test development. *NCME Measurement in Education,* 1980, *10(4)*. A brief description of the process of constructing criterion-referenced tests using an amplified objectives approach.

Serling, A. M. The measurement of public literacy. *College Board Review,* Winter 1979–80, *114*, 26–29. A discussion of the issues and problems involved in the measurement of literacy, including problems in defining what is meant by literacy.

Shoemaker, D. M. Toward a framework for achievement testing. *Review of Educational Research,* 1975, *45*, 127–147. Argues that the implementation of an item domain provides the answer to many problems in the measurement of achievement.

Tinkleman, S. N. Planning the objective test. In R. L. Thorndike (Ed.), *Educational measurement,* 2d ed. Washington, D.C.: American Council on Education, 1971. Descriptions of the various practical problems in constructing a test, such as developing a test plan, selecting item formats, and determining the appropriate number and difficulty of items.

Traub, R. E., & Fisher, C. W. On the equivalence of constructed-response and multiple-choice tests. *Applied Psychological Measurement,* 1977, *1*, 355–369. An empirical study of the comparability of short-answer items, multiple-choice items, and multiple-choice items with more than one correct response.

Chapter 3 • Some Basic Statistics

IN order to perform surgery, a physician must understand human anatomy. To build a bridge, an engineer must know some basic principles of physics. Similarly, in order to understand many of the concepts in educational and psychological testing, it is necessary to know some basic descriptive statistics.

Descriptive statistics summarize and describe a set of data in quantitative terms. This chapter will explain and illustrate several types of descriptive statistics. Specifically, we will consider methods for:

Presenting and describing test scores in tabular and graphic form;
obtaining an average value for a set of test scores;
describing the variability in a set of test scores;
transforming scores from one scale to another scale; and
describing the degree of relationship between two sets of scores.

All statistics used in this book will be variations on the methods described in this chapter.

There are several advantages to using descriptive statistics to describe data, such as test scores. One is economy. Descriptive statistics allow us to summarize a large amount of data by one or a small number of values; for example, most test score distributions can be described by two statistics, the average score and a measure of variability. Using descriptive statistics also facilitates communication between test users, since a common set of statistics can be used to describe distributions and relationships. Moreover, these descriptive statistics form the basis of more complex statistical analyses of test scores.

raw scores

Scores obtained directly from test performance are called *raw scores.* On maximal performance tests, the most commonly used raw score is the number of items answered correctly. However, other measures can be used, such as the number of errors, the sum of points over various items, the time taken to complete the test, a rating, or a letter grade. On objectively scored typical performance tests the raw score is obtained in a slightly different manner. Here items are generally keyed to represent the dominant response of some specified group, and the score is the number of items answered in the keyed direction. On other typical performance measures, raw scores may be ratings, frequencies of certain responses or classes of behavior, or response latencies.

Raw scores are frequently transformed to another scale before they are analyzed or interpreted. For example, the number of items answered correctly (a raw score) can be transformed to a percent correct score by dividing the number correct by the maximal possible score, then multiplying by 100 percent. We will discuss transformed scores later in this chapter and in Chapters 8 and 9.

Composite Scores

Most tests are composed of a number of separate items, with the raw score being obtained by summing the scores on the various items. Such a score is referred to as a *composite score* because it is formed by combining several individual scores.

Several types of composite scores are used on tests. One possibility is to obtain a *total score* by including scores of all items in one composite. Another possibility is to combine scores on only a particular subset of items, to obtain *subtest scores*. When several subtest scores are obtained on a test, they may or may not be combined into one total score. Finally, we may form a composite of scores on several different tests.

There are several possible ways of forming composites. Consider the case of combining items.[1] Most frequently, test scores are unweighted composites of individual item scores. In the simplest case each item would have unit weight with the total (composite) score being the number of items answered correctly. For example, if a 50-item multiple-choice test were administered, and each item scored 1 for correct answers and 0 for incorrect answers, each person's total score would be the number of items answered correctly.

A slightly more complicated case would occur if we had several items, each carrying more than unit weight, but with each item having the same value. For example, a teacher might give a test consisting of five essay questions with each item being worth ten points. In this situation, a student could obtain a score of 0–10 on each item, with the total score being the sum of scores on the five questions.

It is also possible to weight individual items differentially. For example, a test might consist of 20 one-point multiple-choice items, two short essays worth five points each, and one longer essay worth 15 points. Even though the individual items carry different weights, the composite score would still be the sum of points over all items.

describing score distributions

Usually we are concerned with the scores of a group of persons. Sometimes we want to describe the performance of a particular group. At other times we may want to compare the performance of two or more groups. Or we may want to compare the performance of several individuals with that of some relevant group in order to interpret their scores. In all these situations, methods are needed to summarize the performance of a group of individuals.

---

[1] We shall discuss methods of forming composite (test) scores from item scores. The same methods, however, apply to all types of composites; for example, combining subtest scores or scores of several separate tests.

The first part of this section describes some simple tabular and graphical methods for displaying a set of scores. Although these methods show the pattern of performance quite clearly, it is useful to summarize the performance of the group with two numbers—one to describe the average level of performance and another to describe how widely the individual scores are scattered around this average value. Statistics describing the average level of performance are called measures of *central tendency;* statistics describing the scatter or dispersion are called measures of *variability.* We shall describe the common indices of central tendency and variability, using one set of data as an illustration.

Frequency Distributions

Suppose that we administered a nine-item quiz to a class of 30 students, and their scores were as follows:

4 8 3 0 8 2 4 5 5 6 7 4 3 5 2 3 6 7 1 5 6 7 6 4 5 9 4 5 1 6

This arrangement tells us little except that there were 30 scores and that the range of scores was from 0 to 9 points. However, we could obtain a clearer picture if the scores were presented in a table showing how many people obtained each score. Such a table is called a *frequency distribution.* To illustrate, using the scores in our example:

Raw Score (X)	0	1	2	3	4	5	6	7	8	9	Σ
Frequency (f)	1	2	2	3	5	6	5	3	2	1	30

In the table X = the raw score, f = the frequency of each score, and Σ means "the sum of." Note also that Σf = the total number of scores (n).

Graphical Presentations. Frequency distributions can be presented graphically by plotting the number of people who obtain each score. Traditionally, scores are placed on the horizontal axis, with lower scores to the left and higher scores to the right. Frequencies are placed on the vertical axis, with frequencies increasing as we go up the axis.

Scores usually are plotted as frequency polygons or histograms. When making a *frequency polygon* we place a dot corresponding to the frequency of each score, then connect these dots by lines. In constructing a *histogram* we use a stairlike approach with the height of each stairstep corresponding to the frequency of the score. These methods are shown in Figure 3.1, using the data from our previous example.

Four types of test score distributions are commonly encountered (see Figure 3.2). When scores cluster at the high end and trail off toward the lower end we obtain a *negatively skewed distribution.* Conversely, when scores cluster at the low end and are less frequent at the higher end we have a *positively skewed distribution.* If there are two high points (two scores that occur more frequently than other scores), the distribution is *bimodal.*

The distribution we will refer to most often is the *normal distribution,* which is a symmetric, bell-shaped curve. Although the normal curve is a mathematical

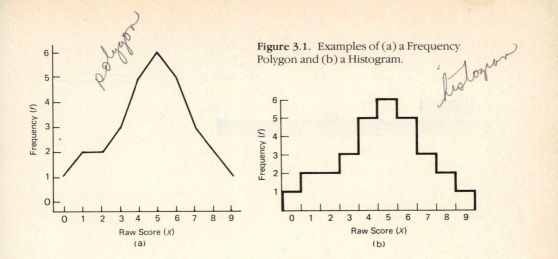

polygon *histogram*

Figure 3.1. Examples of (a) a Frequency Polygon and (b) a Histogram.

Figure 3.2. Examples of Score Distributions.

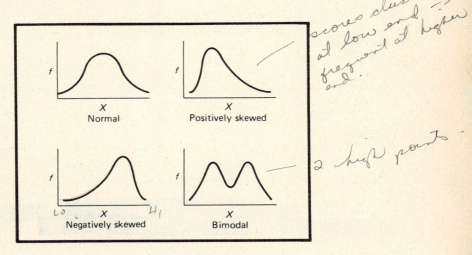

scores cluster at low end — less frequent at higher end.

2 high points —

abstraction, distributions of test scores frequently approach a normal distribution. Thus it serves as a useful model when describing test score distributions and interpreting scores.

Measures of Central Tendency

It is often useful to have one number which describes the average score of a group. For example, we might want to know the average score on a quiz (as in our example), the average grade-point of freshmen at a particular college, the average income of workers in a certain occupation, or the average height of members of a basketball team.

Three measures of central tendency are commonly used—the mean, the median, and the mode. Which one will be most appropriate and useful depends on the nature of the score distribution and how the data will be used.

The Mean. The most useful measure of central tendency is the *mean* $(\overline{X})$, which is nothing more than the arithmetic average:

$$\overline{X} = \frac{\Sigma X}{n} \tag{3.1}$$

To compute the mean, we sum all the scores (ΣX) and divide by the number of scores (n). In our example:

$$\Sigma X = 4 + 8 + 3 + \cdots + 1 + 6 = 141$$

and

$$\overline{X} = \frac{\Sigma X}{n} = \frac{141}{30} = 4.70$$

The mean could also have been computed from the frequency distribution using the formula:

$$\overline{X} = \frac{\Sigma f_i X_i}{n} \tag{3.1a}$$

where f_i = the number of scores in a particular class (X_i). That is, multiply each score by its frequency, sum the products, and divide by n. In our example:

$$\Sigma f_i X_i = (1)(0) + (2)(1) + (2)(2) + \cdots + (1)(9) = 141$$

and

$$\overline{X} = \frac{141}{30} = 4.70$$

which is the same value that was obtained using Equation (3.1).

The Median. The *median* is the score that divides the distribution into halves; the score above and below which 50 percent of the scores fall. To compute the median, arrange the scores in order of magnitude and find the score that divides the distribution in half. In our example, since there are 30 scores, this point will be between the 15th and 16th score. Referring to the frequency distribution, we see that the 15th and 16th scores are both 5; thus the median would be 5.

The median will be the appropriate measure of central tendency when the raw scores are expressed as ranks, when the distribution is markedly skewed, or when a few extreme scores might distort the mean. If the distribution is symmetrical and contains few extreme scores, the mean and the median will be (approximately) the same.

The Mode. The *mode* is the score with the highest frequency. In our example the mode is 5, since this score occurs more frequently ($f = 6$) than any other single score. The mode is used when scores are so highly skewed that one value predominates or when we have nominal data. For example, to describe the average age of children in a particular grade we would use the mode because almost all children would be of the same age.

Measures of Variability

Measures of central tendency provide valuable information about score distributions; however, they are not sufficient by themselves. For example, two score distributions may have the same mean, but in one distribution the scores may be closely bunched whereas in the other the scores vary more widely (see Figure 3.3a). These two distributions are obviously different. Conversely, two distributions may have similar variability but different means (see Figure 3.3b). Thus, to describe a distribution we need a measure of variability as well as a measure of central tendency.

At first glance it might seem that the range of scores would be an appropriate index of variability, the range being the difference between the highest and lowest score. However, the range is not the best measure of variability. One reason is that it depends solely on the two extreme scores. That is, one extremely high or low score would produce a high range even if the other scores were closely bunched. A second, more important, reason is that it is useful to have a measure of variability that indicates dispersion around some central point, such as the mean.

We will discuss two measures of variability, the variance and the standard deviation. Although these two measures are related, they are used for different purposes. The standard deviation is the measure of choice when we want to describe a particular score distribution while the variance will be used in most statistical analyses and for making certain theoretical statements.

The Variance. The *variance* (s^2) is a measure of the total amount of variability in a set of test scores and is defined as:

$$s_x^2 = \frac{\sum x^2}{n} \qquad (3.2)$$

Figure 3.3. Examples Showing Need for Measure of Dispersion as well as of Central Tendency.

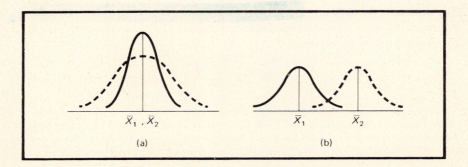

$$\overline{X}_1, \overline{X}_2$$

(a)

$$\overline{X}_1 \qquad \overline{X}_2$$

(b)

where the x is a *deviation score* $(X - \overline{X})$. As can be seen, the variance is the average squared deviation from the mean.[2]

When computing the variance, especially with a large number of scores, formula (3.2) is not used because computing the deviation scores would be too tedious. Rather we would use an equivalent raw score formula:

Variance $\longrightarrow$
$$s_x^2 = \frac{1}{n}\left[\sum X^2 - \frac{(\sum X)^2}{n}\right] \qquad (3.3)$$

This formula contains two expressions that we have not previously used, $\sum X^2$ and $(\sum X)^2$. The first of these, $\sum X^2$, the sum of squares, can be obtained from the raw scores:

$$\sum X^2 = (4)^2 + (8)^2 + (3)^2 + \cdots + (6)^2 = 803$$

or from the frequency distribution:

$$\sum X^2 = \sum f_i X_i^2 = (1)(0^2) + (2)(1^2) + (2)(2^2) + \cdots + (1)(9^2) = 803$$

The other, $(\sum X)^2$, is obtained by squaring the sum of scores. As we previously found, $\sum X = 141$:

$$(\sum X)^2 = (141)^2 = 19{,}881$$

These two expressions are frequently confused. When computing $\sum X^2$, you first square each individual score, then sum the squares; when computing $(\sum X)^2$, in contrast, you first sum the scores, then square this sum.

Given these two values, we can now compute the variance:

$$s_x^2 = \frac{1}{30}\left[803 - \frac{(141)^2}{30}\right] = 4.68$$

Note that the variance is expressed in raw score units squared.

Because variances are additive, the proportion of variability in a set of test scores attributable to each of several variables (or their interactions) can be determined. Thus statements about the relative influence of each variable can be made. This property makes the variance a useful statistic for conceptualizing certain properties of tests (such as reliability and validity) and for determining the effects of varying conditions on test performance. Thus, many statistical analyses use the variance.

The Standard Deviation. When describing a particular set of test scores, the standard deviation is used rather than the variance. The *standard deviation (s)* is the square root of the variance:

$$s_x = \sqrt{\frac{\sum x^2}{n}} \qquad (3.4)$$

---

[2] When computing the variance we use n in the denominator as we are describing the variance of a particular sample of scores. We would use $(n - 1)$ if we wanted to estimate the variance of the population from which the sample was drawn. Similar reasoning applies to the computation of the standard deviation.

where all terms have been previously defined. Note that the standard deviation is expressed in raw score units.

As with the variance, an equivalent raw score formula is usually used in any computations:

$$s = \frac{1}{n}\sqrt{n\Sigma X^2 - (\Sigma X)^2} \qquad \text{standard deviation} \qquad (3.5) \checkmark$$

Applying this formula to our example, where $\Sigma X = 141$, $\Sigma X^2 = 803$, and $n = 30$:

$$s_x = \frac{1}{30}\sqrt{(30)(803) - (141)^2} = 2.16$$

The standard deviation is an index of how widely the scores are dispersed around the mean; the larger the standard deviation, the more widely scattered the scores.

Interpreting a Standard Deviation. A working knowledge of the meaning of the standard deviation can best be obtained by reference to the normal curve. While the normal curve is a mathematical abstraction, not an empirical concept, it can be used as a working model for interpreting standard deviations. In a normal distribution, a specified proportion of scores fall within each standard deviation range (see Figure 3.4). Thus, if we know the mean and standard deviation of a score distribution, we can determine what proportion of the scores fall within certain score limits. Conversely, we can determine the scores needed to encompass any proportion of the scores.

Applying these relationships to our example, the following relations would be expected to hold: 68 percent of the scores will fall between 2.5 and 6.9; that is,

Figure 3.4. Percent of Scores Falling in Various Areas of the Normal Curve.

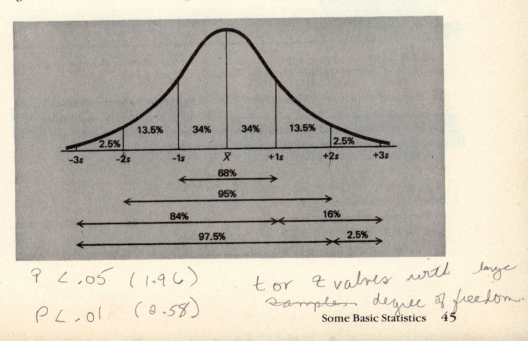

$P < .05 \ (1.96)$

$P < .01 \ (2.58)$

t or z values with large samples degree of freedom.

$$\overline{X} \pm 1s = 4.7 \pm 2.2$$

and 95 percent of the scores will fall between 0.3 and 9.1; that is,

$$\overline{X} \pm 2s = 4.7 \pm 2(2.2)$$

Comparing the obtained frequencies to these expected frequencies will indicate whether the empirical distribution approaches a normal distribution.

Consider another example. Suppose that a college reports that the mean ACT Composite score of their entering freshmen is 22 and the standard deviation is 4 points. If the score distribution is normal, we can imply that approximately 68 percent of the freshmen had ACT scores between 18 and 26 (mean ± 1 standard deviation), 95 percent had scores between 14 and 30 (mean ± 2 standard deviations), 16 percent of the students scored 26 or higher, and so on.

transformed scores

Sometimes raw scores are transformed to a different scale. This may be done for various reasons: to eliminate negative or fractional scores, to facilitate further analyses, to aid in interpretation of scores, or because of some undesirable property of the original score scale (e.g., scores may be highly skewed). Scores expressed on scales other than raw scores are called *derived scores* or *transformed scores*.

How to Transform Scores

There are various ways to transform scores, some simple and others quite complex. We will illustrate only *linear transformations*. If we make a linear transformation and then plot the derived scores against the original scores, the plot of the two sets of scores will fall on a straight line. Thus, a linear transformation changes the scale units without changing the relative position of each score or the relationships between scores.

One possible transformation would be to add a constant to each score. This is usually done to eliminate negative values. Suppose, for example, a test was scored by counting one point for each correct answer and subtracting a point for each incorrect answer. In this situation some scores might be negative. To eliminate these negative values, we could add a constant to each person's score. Thus, if the lowest score was −5, by adding 5 to each score the lowest score would become 0 and every other score would increase 5 points. Note that this transformation will change the mean (by the amount of the constant added, in this case 5) but will not change the standard deviation or the relative positions of the scores.

Another possibility is to multiply (or divide) each score by a constant. Suppose that we gave a 50-point test but wanted to express scores on a 100-point scale. One way to do this would be to multiply each score by two. This procedure will change both the mean and the standard deviation.[3] Another example of this type

---

[3] Multiplying scores by a constant (C) changes the mean and standard deviation by a factor C and the variance by C^2. That is, the mean of the transformed scale will be $C\overline{X}$, the standard deviation Cs_x, and the variance $C^2 s_x^2$.

of transformation is changing feet to inches by multiplying by 12.

We could, of course, apply both procedures simultaneously:

$$X' = a + bX \qquad (3.6)$$

where X' is the transformed score and a and b are constants. That is, we multiply each score by b, and add a points to each score. This transformation will change both the mean and the standard deviation but not the relative position of individuals. Because this is a linear transformation, a plot of X versus X' will be a straight line.

Standard Scores

In testing, the most common and useful transformation is to convert raw scores to standard scores. A *standard score* (z) expresses performance in terms of the deviation from the mean in standard deviation units:

$$z = \frac{X - \overline{X}}{s_x} = \frac{x}{s_x} \qquad (3.7)$$

The distribution of standard scores will have a mean of 0 and a standard deviation of 1 because subtracting the mean from each score makes the average score equal to zero and dividing by the standard deviation results in a scale with standard deviation units.

Consider two illustrations from our previous example. If a student had a raw score of 8, the standard score would be:

$$z = \frac{(X - \overline{X})}{s_x} = \frac{8 - 4.7}{2.2} = \frac{3.3}{2.2} = +1.50 \qquad \text{above the mean}$$

If a student had a raw score of 2:

$$z = \frac{(2 - 4.7)}{2.2} = \frac{-2.7}{2.2} = -1.23 \qquad \text{below the mean}$$

In other words, a score of 8 is 1.50 standard deviations above the mean and a score of 2 is 1.23 standard deviations below the mean.

One advantage of standard scores lies in their relationship to the normal distribution. Previously we described how a standard deviation could be interpreted in relation to the hypothetical normal distribution. Comparing that discussion to Equation (3.7), you can see that it makes no difference whether we express scores in terms of standard scores or standard deviations from the mean; that is, a z score of $+1.0$ is one standard deviation above the mean, a z score of -2.0 is two standard deviations below the mean, and so on. Thus the relations shown in Figure 3.4 hold for standard (z) scores, as well as for standard deviations.

Appendix A shows the relationships between the areas of the cumulative normal distribution and z scores, in units of .05 standard score points. You should become familiar with this table and learn how to use it. As an illustration, consider our two examples. The first student (raw score $= 8$) had a z score of $+1.50$.

Looking at Appendix A we find that this score is higher than 93.3 percent of the scores (column C) and lower than 6.7 percent of the scores (column D). The second example (raw score = 2) is slightly more complex, as the z score (-1.23) is negative and falls between two tabled points. If we use the closest tabled value ($z = 1.25$), we find that this score is higher than 10.6 percent of the scores (column D is used because with negative z scores the smaller proportion will be below the score) and 89.4 percent of the other scores are higher (column C). If we interpolate, the values will be 10.9 and 89.1 percent respectively.

correlation

Often we have scores on several variables and want to know the relationship between these scores.[4] For example, we might be interested in the relationship between scores on two exams in a course, between students' English and math grades, between scores on a college admissions test and grades in college, between scores on a mechanical aptitude test and performance as an auto mechanic, or between scores on two different measures of creativity.

This is the problem of correlation (literally co-relation). What we need is an index that describes the degree of relationship between the two sets of scores. This relationship is described by the *correlation coefficient*. There are a number of possible correlation coefficients that can be used. Which one is appropriate depends on the nature of the data and the form of the relationship between the two variables. Since we shall generally be concerned with relatively continuous distributions of scores and linear relationships, we shall use the *Pearson product-moment correlation coefficient (r).*

The Correlation Coefficient

A correlation coefficient is an index of the degree of relationship between two sets of scores obtained from the same group of people. Conceptually it can be defined as:

$$r_{xy} = \frac{\Sigma z_x z_y}{n} \tag{3.8}$$

where the subscript "xy" indicates that we are correlating variable X with variable Y and $n =$ the number of individuals (that is, the number of pairs of scores).

The value of the correlation coefficient can range from -1.00 through 0.00 to $+1.00$, with any intermediate value being possible. If we think of the correlation coefficient as indicating how accurately scores on one variable can be predicted from scores on the other (which is one way to view a correlation coefficient), then the closer the value of the coefficient is to 1.00, the more accurate the prediction.

---

[4] When there are more than two variables, we compute the correlation between each pair of variables. For example, if we had three variables (A, B, C), we could compute the correlation beween A and B, between A and C, and between B and C.

Conversely, when $r = 0.00$ there is no systematic relation, and predictions will be no better than chance. Thus the absolute value of the coefficient indicates the degree of relationship, the predictive accuracy.

The sign of the coefficient indicates the direction of the relationship. If high scores on one variable go with high scores on the other, and low with low, the correlation will be positive. Conversely, if high scores on one variable are associated with low scores on the other, the coefficient will be negative. However, as the absolute value of the coefficient indicates the degree of relationship, correlations of $+0.68$ and -0.68 indicate an equivalent degree of predictability.

An Example.   Suppose that the teacher in our previous example gave another 9-point quiz a week later and the results were as follows:

$$\times \quad s = \frac{1}{n} \sqrt{n \Sigma x^2 - (\Sigma x)^2}$$

$$= \frac{1}{10} \sqrt{10 \, (} \quad ?$$

X	Y		
9	9		
8	8 7	$\overline{X} = 4.70$	$s_x = 2.16$
7	9 8 7	$\overline{Y} = 5.33$	$s_y = 2.07$
6	8 7 6 6 5		
5	7 6 6 6 5 5	$\Sigma XY = 874$	
4	6 5 4 4 4	$n = 30$	
3	4 3 3		
2	4 2		
1	3 1		
0	2		

This table lists the scores on the second test (Y) of people who obtained each score on the first test (X). For example, of the two people who scored 8 on the first test, one scored 8 and the other 7 on the second test.

Our question is: What is the correlation between scores on the two quizzes?

Scatterplots.   Before computing the correlation coefficient, we will plot the scores graphically, listing scores on the first quiz (X) on the horizontal axis and scores on the second quiz (Y) on the vertical axis. We then plot each individual, that is, each pair of scores. The resulting figure (Figure 3.5) is called a *scatterplot*.

Looking at the scatterplot tells us several things about the relationship between the test scores. First, as high scores on X go with high scores on Y and low scores on X are associated with low scores on Y, the correlation will be positive. Second, the relation is generally linear; that is, it can be best described by a straight line. Third, the various points (corresponding to the pairs of scores) cluster closely around the best-fitting straight line. In short, we will expect to find a high positive correlation.

Computation of the Correlation Coefficient.   To use formula (3.8) to compute r would be inefficient. Rather we can use one of two alternative raw-score formulas:

Figure 3.5 Scatterplot: Data from Text Example.

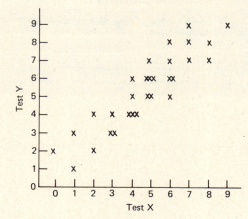

$$r = \frac{n\Sigma\, XY - (\Sigma\, X)(\Sigma Y)}{\sqrt{n\Sigma\, X^2 - (\Sigma\, X)^2}\,\sqrt{n\Sigma Y^2 - (\Sigma Y)^2}} \qquad (3.9a)$$

or

$$r = \frac{\Sigma\, XY/n - (\overline{X})(\overline{Y})}{s_X\, s_Y} \qquad (3.9b)$$

All of the terms in these two formulas have been defined previously, except $\Sigma\, XY$ which is the *sum of cross-products*. This is obtained by multiplying the corresponding X and Y scores for each individual:

$$\Sigma\, XY = (9)(9) + (8)(8) + (8)(7) + (7)(9) + \cdots + (0)(2) = 874$$

or by multiplying each X score by the sum of its corresponding Y values:

$$\Sigma\, XY = (9)(9) + (8)(15) + (7)(24) + \cdots + (0)(2) = 874$$

This term indicates how the pairs of scores covary; that is, how scores on X and Y are related.

To calculate the correlation coefficient we will use formula (3.9b):

$$r_{xy} = \frac{(874/30) - (4.70)(5.33)}{(2.16)(2.07)} = +0.91$$

Similar results, within rounding errors, would be obtained by using formula (3.9a).[5] The value of the correlation coefficient, +0.91, describes the degree of relationship between the scores on the two tests.

---

[5] Formula (3.9a) is slightly more accurate than Formula (3.9b) because fewer rounding errors are involved in the computation.

Interpretation of a Correlation Coefficient

There are a number of ways to interpret a correlation coefficient. We have already mentioned two: as the strength of relationship between two variables and in terms of the accuracy of predicting one variable from another. Applied to our example, where the correlation was +0.91, we can say that there was a high positive correlation between scores on the two tests and, consequently, that scores on the second test can be predicted with a high degree of accuracy from scores on the first test.

Another method of interpreting a correlation coefficient is in terms of the proportion of variance shared by the two measures. The square of the correlation coefficient is an index of the proportion of variance in one variable shared in common with, or attributable to variations in, the other variable.[6] Again referring to our example, $r^2 = (.91^2) = .8281$, which means that 83 percent of the variability in the two measures is shared in common. Another way of saying this is that 83 percent of the differences (variance) in scores on one variable are predictable from scores on the other. This type of interpretation is useful when making theoretical statements about relationships.

One other aspect of the correlation is often overlooked. A correlation indicates the relation between the relative rankings of scores in the two distributions. In order to predict exact scores, we have to make appropriate scale corrections. To illustrate, if every person's score on Y was exactly two points higher than his or her score on X, the correlation would be +1.00; however, this does not mean that each person obtained the same score on Y as on X.

Correlation and Causation. It cannot be overemphasized that r indicates only the degree of relationship between two variables; it does *not* indicate causation. If variables X and Y are highly correlated, there are at least three possible explanations: (1) X causes Y, and thus changes in X result in changes in Y; (2) Y causes X, and thus the changes in X reflect changes in Y; or (3) X and Y are both influenced by some other variable. In other words, a correlation coefficient is never a sufficient basis for inferring causation.

To illustrate, suppose a study finds a high positive correlation between intelligence and reading ability. Several interpretations are possible. One is that good reading ability increases intelligence. Conversely, it may be that more intelligent people learn to read better. Or, as a third possibility, it may be that both intelligence and reading ability are determined by some third factor, such as the quality of education obtained or the emphasis on intellectual activities in the home environment.

---

[6] The variance in Y ($s_Y{}^2$) can be divided into two independent components: that predictable from X ($s_{\hat{Y}}^2$) and that not predictable from X ($s_{Y \cdot X}^2$). It can be shown (e.g., A. L. Edwards, 1976) that $r_{XY}^2 = s_{\hat{Y}}^2 / s_Y{}^2$; that is, r^2 is the proportion of predictable variance. Since the relation holds in both directions (predicting X from Y as well as Y from X), r^2 also indicates the proportion of shared variance. The value of r^2 is sometimes called the *coefficient of determination* and $1 - r^2$ the *coefficient of nondetermination*.

summary

In this chapter we discussed the descriptive statistics needed for understanding the concepts and applications of psychological testing. Descriptive statistics summarize and describe a set of test scores or data in quantitative terms. We described methods for presenting test scores in tabular and graphical form, obtaining an average score (a measure of central tendency), describing the variability of a score distribution, transforming scores to another scale, and describing the relationship between two sets of scores.

Scores obtained directly from a test are called raw scores and usually are composites formed by combining scores on various items. They may be used as such or transformed to other scales. Transformations involve multiplying (or dividing) scores by a constant and/or adding (or subtracting) a constant. The most common transformation is to standard scores (z scores), which are deviation scores (the raw score minus the mean) divided by the standard deviation. Standard scores express performance in terms of distance from the mean in standard deviation units.

To describe a set of test scores requires both a measure of central tendency and a measure of variability. The most common measure of central tendency is the mean, which is the arithmetic average. Other measures of central tendency are the median (the score that divides the distribution into halves), and the mode (the most frequently occurring score).

Measures of variability include the standard deviation and the variance. Both are indices of the dispersion of scores around the mean; the higher the standard deviation (or variance) the greater the scatter of scores around the mean. The standard deviation is used when describing a specific distribution. When a distribution is normal, 68 percent of the scores fall within plus-or-minus one standard deviation of the mean and 95 percent of the scores fall within two standard deviations of the mean. The variance is used primarily in conceptual and theoretical derivations, particularly for estimating the magnitude of the effects of various variables on test scores.

A correlation coefficient describes the degree of relationship between scores on two tests (or variables) administered to the same group. Although there are various correlation coefficients, we will generally use Pearson's product-moment correlation coefficient (r), which assumes a linear relation between the two variables. The correlation coefficient is an index of how accurately scores on one variable can be predicted from scores on the other. Its value can range from $+1.00$ to -1.00 with the magnitude of the correlation indicating the degree of relationship and the sign indicating the direction of scaling of the two variables. The square of the correlation coefficient indicates the proportion of variance the two variables share in common and the proportion of variance in one variable that is predictable from scores on the other variable.

Suggestions for Further Reading

Allen, M. J., & Yen, W. M. *Introduction to measurement theory.* Monterey, Calif.: Brooks/Cole, 1979. Chapter 2 describes the basic statistical concepts used in testing in somewhat more detail than the present chapter.

Blommers, P. J., & Forsyth, R. A. *Elementary statistical methods in psychology and education,* 2d ed. Boston: Houghton Mifflin, 1977. An introductory statistics text; see particularly chapters on frequency distributions (Chapter 3), central tendency (Chapter 6), variability (Chapter 7), and correlation (Chapter 17).

Edwards, A. L. *The measurement of personality traits by scales and inventories.* New York: Holt, Rinehart and Winston, 1970. Chapter 1 reviews basic statistics in the context of constructing scales for personality inventories.

Edwards, A. L. *An introduction to linear regression and correlation.* San Francisco: Freeman, 1976. A relatively brief book providing an introduction to correlation and regression but also considering advanced topics and applications.

Ghiselli, E. E., Campbell, J. P., & Zedeck, S. *Measurement theory for the behavioral sciences.* San Francisco: Freeman, 1981. Chapter 4 discusses transformations of raw scores to other scales; Chapter 5 describes the concept and methods of correlation.

Hays, W. L. *Statistics,* 3d ed. New York: Holt, Rinehart and Winston, 1981. A relatively advanced text, with readable chapters on frequency distributions (Chapter 2), central tendency and variability (Chapter 9), and correlation (Chapter 13).

Hopkins, K. D., & Glass, G. V. *Basic statistics for the behavioral sciences.* Englewood Cliffs, N.J.: Prentice-Hall, 1978. Another good introductory text with chapters on frequency distributions (Chapter 3), central tendency (Chapter 4), variability (Chapter 5), standard scores (Chapter 6), and correlation (Chapters 7–9).

Wainer, H., & Thissen, D. Graphical data analysis. *Annual Review of Psychology,* 1981, *32,* 191–241. Reviews, describes, and discusses a variety of methods for presenting and analyzing data graphically.

Young, R. K., & Veldman, D. J. *Introductory statistics for the behavioral sciences,* 4th ed. New York: Holt, Rinehart and Winston, 1981. Another good introductory text with chapters on central tendency (Chapter 4), variability (Chapter 5), standard scores (Chapter 6), and correlation (Chapter 9).

· part two ·
consistency
and validity

IF you were asked to determine whether someone was a good driver, you could use various methods. For example, you could observe him driving, you could look at his accident and arrest records, you could ask the person's friends to rate his driving skills, or you could ask him to take the behind-the-wheel portion of the driver's license examination. The results you would obtain could vary in at least two ways. Some methods would produce more consistent results than others; that is, some methods would give similar results each time you measured driving skill, whereas others would be more variable. The methods would also differ in how well they measure driving skill; some would clearly indicate the person's driving skill, whereas others would give only a rough estimate of his skill.

When constructing and evaluating tests we are interested in the same two characteristics. That is, a good test measures consistently and clearly describes the characteristic being measured. In psychological testing, the former property is called consistency or reliability, the latter validity.

Consistency is concerned with the replicability of measurements. A reliable test gives scores that are consistent from time to time, occasion to occasion, or situation to situation. Attaining reliable measurements depends on controlling factors that cause scores to vary from occasion to occasion. If a test does not measure consistently, scores cannot be related to scores on other measures, thus limiting the usefulness of the test.

Validity is concerned with determining how well the test measures what it is designed to measure. Validation studies are directed toward such questions as: What trait or characteristic does the test measure? How well does it measure this characteristic? What outcomes or behaviors can be predicted from the test scores? Attaining a valid test depends on controlling the influence of variables that affect test scores but are irrelevant to the purpose of the measurement. Validity is the most important property of a test. If we do not know what the test measures, we cannot interpret its scores.

Chapter 4 presents an overview of the concepts of reliability and validity, emphasizing the types of errors that can influence test scores. Chapter 5 describes various methods for determining reliability. Chapter 6 focuses on criterion-related validity (the extent to which test scores can predict other behaviors and outcomes). Chapter 7 discusses content validity (how well the test items sample the domain of interest) and construct validity (how well the test measures the trait of interest). Besides providing a basis for evaluating tests, the material in Chapters 5 through 7 suggests how tests can be constructed to maximize their reliability and validity.

Chapter 4 • Consistency, Validity, and Measurement Errors

[handwritten: goal of testing = provide accurate scores]

[handwritten: Good test ① consis ② valid]

HAVING defined what a test is and described how tests are constructed, we now turn to the question of what is a "good" test. From the psychometric viewpoint, a test is a good measuring instrument if it measures consistently and is valid. By *consistency* (or *reliability*), we mean that test takers would obtain (approximately) the same score if they took an alternative form of the test, or took the same test at a different time or under different conditions. By *validity* we mean that a test measures what it is designed to measure and not other, extraneous variables.

The importance of consistency and validity can be shown by several examples. Suppose a teacher administers two, presumably comparable forms of a final examination. Here two questions are paramount: Would students obtain the same score regardless of which form they took? Does the test measure students' command of the course material? The first is a reliability question, the second a question of validity. When several judges rate a gymnastics competition, we are interested in the agreement between the judges' ratings (their reliability) and whether their ratings do, in fact, identify the better performers (their validity). Or, when a doctor takes patients' blood pressure we are interested in the reliability of this measurement (Would the blood pressure be the same if measured under different conditions?) and its validity (Does abnormal blood pressure indicate certain physical problems?).

This chapter will present an overview of the theory underlying the concepts of consistency and validity. The next three chapters will discuss these concepts more extensively. The concepts discussed in these chapters will be clearer if you keep two important points in mind. First, consistency and validity are properties of a test, not of individual scores. We cannot talk about the reliability and validity of an individual's score, only of a set of test scores. Second, there are a variety of methods for estimating reliability and validity. Which method will be most appropriate depends on the nature of the test and how it is used. In addition, different estimates of reliability and validity will be obtained when testing different groups and in different situations. Thus, it makes no sense to talk about *the* reliability or *the* validity of a test; rather we must discuss reliability and validity for a particular use of a test.

sources of variance in test scores

Any particular measurement or observation is only one of various possible measurements of a characteristic. That is, each measurement is obtained under a unique set of conditions. For example, a classroom examination measures knowledge of a limited amount of information, as measured by certain types of items, at one time, in a particular situation. Or a golfer's score for an 18-hole round reflects her performance on one day, on a particular course, under certain weather conditions. In each case the score obtained is a description of the person's performance in that specific situation. However, it is not a complete description of the person's ability; it is only a measure obtained under one set of conditions.

The fact that any test is only one of various possible measurements has many important implications for test use. At this point we will be concerned with only one; many factors influence the score obtained from any measurement. When discussing these factors, it will be helpful to think in terms of differences between people (that is, variances) rather than individual scores. Thus, in the first example we would consider the differences between the scores of students who took the exam.

Although there are various ways to classify the sources of influences on scores, we will use three broad categories. First, some differences reflect differences in the ability or characteristics being measured. Thus, in our first example, one reason why students obtain different scores is that they vary in their knowledge of the material tested.

A second source of variance has to do with differences between individuals on characteristics that are irrelevant to the purposes of the testing but have systematic effects on scores. Usually these are stable, long-term differences. For example, if the test items were long and complexly worded, differences in reading ability would probably influence the scores. Or, if the test contained essay items, differences in writing skill might affect scores. Both of these variables are irrelevant because the purpose of the test is to measure knowledge of the material, not reading or writing skills.

The third source of variance has to do with more temporary, chance influences. For example, an item may be particularly easy for a student who glanced at that part of his notes just before the exam. Or a student may misread an item, mismark the answer sheet, or suffer a memory block. This category includes all factors that cause a person's score to differ from the score she would obtain if she took a different sample of items, or took the test at another time or under different circumstances.

As the second and third categories result in less accurate measurement, they can be considered as sources of *error* in test scores. Because the idea of error underlies the concepts of reliability and validity, we will first consider the various sources of error in test scores and then discuss reliability and validity.

Two Types of Errors

The goal in testing is to obtain scores that reflect, as accurately as possible, the ability or characteristic being measured. Thus, the effects of variables that reduce the accuracy of the measurement must be controlled or minimized. As indicated above, we must be concerned with both systematic and random errors.

Systematic errors are produced by variables that have consistent effects but are irrelevant to the purpose of the measurement. The effects are consistent because they reflect broad, relatively permanent characteristics that differentiate between people—characteristics that influence various measurements. Two were cited in our example, reading ability and writing skill. Other examples include quantitative ability, reaction speed, test-taking skills, and, on personality tests, the willingness to say undesirable things about oneself. Because these are quite stable characteristics, they will have similar effects on several measures of a given trait. Thus they will have little effect on reliability but will effect validity. That is, the validity of a test will be reduced if it measures irrelevant factors in addition to what it is designed to measure.

The other type of error, *random errors*, includes influences due to any variables that produce differences in scores on various measures of the same trait. These are called random errors, or *errors of measurement*, since they reflect influences that are so specific to particular items or testing conditions, or occur in such a haphazard manner, as to produce no identifiable systematic effects. Random errors can be produced by such factors as the content of individual items, errors in directions or timing, mistakes in marking answer sheets, guessing, illness, and momentary lapses in attention. The concept of reliability is concerned with the degree of influence of such measurement errors. But, since the validity of a measure is limited by its reliability, measurement errors also influence validity.

Although we can distinguish between the types of errors conceptually, in practice a variable may produce either systematic or random errors, depending on the situation. For example, people differ widely in vocabulary level. Thus differences in vocabulary may produce systematic effects on scores on various types of verbal tests. However, at the individual item level, the effects may be more or less random. This would occur if some test takers answered an item incorrectly because they did not know the meaning of a particular word used in an item but would answer an alternative form of the item correctly if that word was not used. Or, when the same test is administered more than once (say, as a pretest and posttest in a course), motivation will have systematic effects if students have the same motivation on both tests but will operate as a random effect if some students' motivation varies widely between the two tests.

Although the particular sources of error will vary with the group being tested, the type of test, and the testing conditions, certain common sources have been identified (Thorndike, 1951). Some errors result from the test itself, primarily variations resulting from the particular sampling of items included on a specific form of the test. A second class of error variables relates to the conditions of the particular test administration, such as the physical situation, directions, distracting factors, and errors in timing. A third class of error variables involves changes within the test taker. These may be long-term effects resulting from education, maturation, and changes in environment, or they may be relatively short-term fluctuations in mood, health, or attention.

Sources of Error within the Test

The entire test construction process is designed to minimize errors attributable to the test per se. However, any aspect of a test that causes a test taker to respond to an item on bases other than knowledge of the "correct" or appropriate response may introduce error. Thus ambiguity in the wording of an item, or in specifying the procedures for responding, may produce unstable responses. Difficult items that require the test taker to guess may introduce errors. Restrictive time limits, which encourage hasty reading and responding, frequently produce unstable performance.

The major source of inconsistency within the test, however, has to do with the sampling of items that comprise the test. This effect is clearest when we have several equivalent forms of the test. In order to be equivalent, test forms must be matched, item by item, on content and difficulty, and the distributions of test scores must be similar. These requirements are straightforward, but in practice such equivalence is difficult to attain, coming only as a result of exceedingly careful item construction and analysis. If several forms of the test do not yield equivalent scores, error has been introduced into the measurement, since the test taker would obtain different scores depending upon the particular sample of items (that is, form of the test) administered.

Errors due to item sampling can also occur within a single form of a test. Such errors are of particular importance when the test is designed to measure a single trait or characteristic. If the test is to measure a single trait, every item on the test should measure that trait, and nothing else. However, for various reasons most items are not pure measures of a single trait. Even if they were, different test takers might not react similarly to any given item (for example, any particular math problem will be easy for some persons, difficult for others). Thus, the choice of the particular items included on a test becomes a potential source of error.

Sources of Error in the Test Administration

As psychological tests have become more common and administrative procedures more standardized, errors attributable to test administration conditions have decreased. However, because misunderstanding of directions, mismarking of answer sheets, mistakes in timing, and unforeseen interruptions and other distractions do occur, it is essential that the test administrator be alert to conditions that might result in inaccurate scores. These errors are most likely to occur in tests with complex procedures or directions, in situations in which the test administrator has considerable leeway in setting the testing conditions (such as individually administered tests), and when tests are administered to young children or other persons who are unfamiliar with testing procedures.

Some examples of disruptions of administrative procedures that the author has experienced include having his watch stop during a timed section of the test; having the air conditioning fail and thus produce almost intolerable ventilation; having a custodian use the testing room as a passageway when emptying trash cans; having the microphone used for giving directions go "dead"; finding test booklets and answer sheets misprinted; having to deal with persons caught cheating; and having a student suffer a seizure. In each instance the test administrator must handle the immediate situation so as to produce minimal inconvenience and distraction to the other persons, estimate whether the disturbance was serious enough to result in inaccurate scores, and, when necessary, make plans for retesting.

On individually administered tests, the examiner becomes a potential source of variance. For example, we might ask whether children from minority groups would obtain higher scores on intelligence tests administered by persons of their own race than on tests administered by white examiners? This is a very controversial question. Reviews of studies on examiner effects (Hattie, 1977; Jensen, 1974, 1980; Rumenik, Capasso, & Hendrick, 1977; Sattler, 1970) indicate that effects due to examiners are generally small when tests are administered according to standard procedures, but may be significant in individual cases.

Error may also be introduced in the scoring of the test. As mentioned in Chapter 2, scoring errors can be minimized by the use of objective scoring methods, such as the utilization of electronic scoring machines to score multiple-choice exams. Under these conditions scoring errors should be negligible. On essay tests and other free response tests, scorers may disagree, thus producing large error effects. On these tests, an index of interscorer agreement (reliability) is essential.

Of the three sources of error, those concerned with the test administration are probably easiest to control or minimize. This is because experience with testing has resulted in the development of detailed instructions for administering (and scoring) tests. These instructions minimize errors by outlining specific procedures for the test administrator to follow, thereby reducing irrelevant variability. Thus, unless there is some compelling reason for altering procedures, the test administrator should always follow the instructions exactly as printed in the manual.

Sources of Error Associated with the Test Taker

The sources of variation that are most difficult to control are those associated with the test taker. Even when a well-constructed test is administered under standard conditions, there will be errors attributable to the test takers. Some of these result from pervasive and long-term changes in the individual; others reflect transient factors associated with a particular test administration. In this section we will consider some of the most important personal variables; other factors will be introduced in later chapters, when we discuss specific types of tests and test uses.

Motivation. Measurement errors will be introduced if a particular person, or subgroup of people, has a different motivation than do the majority of the test takers. Whenever this occurs, there is the question of whether the test results are comparable with those of other people or whether similar results would be obtained under different testing conditions. For example, most people view an achievement test as a situation calling for maximal performance, since our society stresses doing one's best. However, in certain segments of the population this achievement drive does not operate as it does in middle- and upper-class children. Thus, even though a test is designed as a measure of maximal performance, some children may have little motivation to do well, and may even respond randomly. An analogous situation occurs when a personality inventory is given as part of a selection process. Although the employer may be interested in the applicant's typical performance, the applicant may feel that it would be to his advantage to make a good impression. Thus, for the applicant, the testing situation becomes a maximal performance situation (showing his best possible profile) rather than presenting a picture of his typical behavior.

These examples show that atypical motivational patterns may manifest themselves in several ways. If a systematic bias is introduced, one that operates in a constant manner on repeated testings, scores might be less valid but not necessarily less consistent. If a test taker's motivation produces haphazard and erratic responding (as in the first example) there will be both a systematic effect (underestimation of the person's ability) and a variable error; only the latter would decrease reliability.

Experience with Tests. In order for the scores of different individuals to be compared, the test takers' experiences prior to testing must be similar, at least within broad limits. These experiences are of two types: ones that provide the opportunity to learn the skill or behavior measured and ones that familiarize the test taker with the testing procedures. Although the former is important when interpreting scores, at this point we will focus on the latter consideration: familiarity with testing procedures.

Any time a new item format[1] or procedure for responding (for example, a different type of answer sheet) is introduced, there is the possibility of misunderstanding, and consequently of introducing error into the measurement. Thus practice problems and illustrations should be included whenever a new, or uncommon, test format or response mode is used. In most circumstances this small amount of practice will be sufficient to ensure that the item format does not produce extraneous variability. For persons with very limited exposure to testing, more extensive practice may be needed. In any case, the test administrator should always ascertain that everyone understands the test procedures before the test is administered.

A reverse phenomenon also occurs. Some persons have developed their test-taking skills into a fine art. These people are experts in understanding the subtler aspects of testing—for example, in detecting nuances that indicate correct answers and in knowing how to make the optimal use of their time. Through application of these skills, they frequently receive higher scores than persons with equal ability but less well-developed test-taking skills (see, e.g., Millman, Bishop, & Ebel, 1965; Rowley, 1974; Sarnacki, 1979).

To aid the development of test-taking skills, some test publishers (e.g., Bennett & Doppelt, 1967) have developed materials designed to provide practice with various types of test items and materials. Other publishers distribute practice tests so that potential test takers can become familiar with the test content and procedures.[2] The goal in each case is to reduce errors due to unfamiliarity with the

---

[1] New, as used here, means new to the test taker.

[2] For example, students taking college and professional school admission tests generally receive a practice test, including correct answers, as part of their registration materials.

testing procedures so that the scores will better reflect test takers' knowledge and abilities.

One other factor can also influence scores. Whenever a person takes the same test more than once, alternative forms of a test, or similar tests, there may be a *practice effect*. That is, test takers may learn some things about the nature and content of the items and test-taking skills from the first administration that increase their scores on the second administration. Thus, students applying to selective colleges or professional schools often take entrance examinations more than once, hoping to obtain a higher score the second time, thus improving their chances for admission. How large the practice effect will be depends on the specific test. Because practice effects do occur, test users must be alert to them when interpreting scores on retests.

Coaching. A closely related concern is with the effects of coaching. As with experience with tests, coaching can be directed toward the test content or procedures. That is, coaching can be directed toward improving one's abilities or test-taking skills.

The crucial question regarding coaching is whether it increases the person's skill or knowledge or just increases his test score. Coaching that produces long-term increases in knowledge is desirable. On the other hand, coaching directed toward specific items and that results in only temporary increases in scores without longer-range effects only results in inaccurate measurement.[3]

Test Anxiety. Some people get very tense, nervous, and upset at the prospect of taking a test. Since excess anxiety can have a detrimental effect on performance and often produces erratic responding (Sarason, 1980; Tryon, 1980; Wine, 1971), test anxiety can be a source of error. Often this anxiety results from the test taker being unfamiliar with testing procedures or being unsure of his or her ability. Minor cases of test anxiety can often be alleviated by giving a clear explanation of the purposes of the testing, ensuring that the person is familiar with the testing procedures, and providing practice items. In more severe cases, special testing procedures or counseling (for example, use of systematic desensitization procedures) may be needed.

Temporary States. We all have bad days. Tests taken when we are ill or fatigued may yield different results than tests taken when we are healthy and alert. Or, on a long test, the test taker may suffer momentary lapses of attention, thus decreasing performance. Although evidence tends to indicate that when motivation remains high, fatigue and illness do not influence test performance significantly, the tester should be alert to the potential effect of these variables. If there is any indication that performance may have been affected by physiological or psychological disturbances, the safest procedure is to readminister the test under more favorable conditions.

Long-Term Changes. Every test reflects the test taker's experiences prior to the test. When measuring broadly defined characteristics, changes due to education

---

[3] Research on the effects of coaching is discussed in Chapter 13.

and developmental processes can result in either true changes in ability (if they are relevant to the domain tested) or produce systematic errors. Thus they have little effect on reliability, especially when the several measures are administered within a short time span.

There is one situation in which these factors are of more concern: when some educational or training program intervenes between repeated testings on the same measure. When all test takers receive the same amount of training, various people will learn different amounts and their scores will be affected differentially. Thus retest scores will reflect true differences in ability. However, if test takers receive differing amounts of education, the effect becomes more complex. If more education results in more learning (which, presumably, it will), differences in posttest scores will reflect both differences in ability and differences in the amount of intervening training. Unless our purpose is to measure the effects of different amounts of education, interpretation of results will be confounded. In both cases, differential learning will lower the correlation between pretest and posttest scores.

Reducing Error Variance

We have seen that various factors can influence test scores besides the characteristic we want to measure. As all these factors reduce accuracy, and consequently the usefulness of the test, the question becomes: How can errors be reduced? (We say reduced, because it is never possible to eliminate all error-producing factors completely.) While, in one sense, this entire book is an attempt to answer this question, we will conclude this section by noting some obvious methods for minimizing errors.

Random errors can be reduced by using clear and unambiguous tasks (items), standarized testing conditions, and a sufficient number of items. Clear items and standardized conditions reduce errors by controlling the effects of variables that might produce errors. Using more items reduces errors because the various errors tend to cancel each other out. (See, e.g., Nunnally, 1978, for a statistical proof.) For example, since over a large number of items lucky guesses will be counterbalanced by unlucky ones, the number of answers guessed correctly will be approximately the same for all test takers.

Systematic errors can be reduced by carefully constructing test items so that they reflect only the desired trait and by using testing conditions that do not introduce extraneous variability. To use an obvious example, to measure knowledge of American history, items should cover only material from an American history course and be worded so that all students understand them, and time limits should be set so that all students have ample time to display their knowledge.

We now turn to consideration of the two basic psychometric characteristics of a good measuring instrument: reliability and validity.

consistency

The problem of consistency of measurement has been likened to the money problem: it is only the lack of it that causes any trouble (Kerlinger, 1973). If we can be assured that a test measures consistently, we have no cause for concern. But since human behavior, including test-taking behavior, tends to fluctuate from time to time and situation to situation, we have to be concerned with consistency in test scores. Furthermore, any test contains only a sample of all possible items and is administered at a particular time. Thus, the sampling of items and the circumstances of the test administration, as well as the characteristics of the test taker, may introduce error into the measurement.

The need for consistency of measurement may be so obvious that you have not thought about it, at least in the terms that we are concerned with in psychological testing. Most physical characteristics (such as length, weight, speed, volume) can be measured with high precision (little variation) from occasion to occasion. However, such precision does not occur in psychological measurement because test scores are more readily influenced by extraneous conditions. For example, you probably have had the experience of getting a higher than expected mark on an exam because it just happened to stress the areas you had studied most thoroughly. Or you may have obtained a lower than expected mark because there was a heavy emphasis on material that you had skimmed over. Or, another time, you may have felt that your performance was adversely affected because you were not feeling well on the day of the test. Or you may, in your haste, have mismarked an answer sheet, thus obtaining a lower score. In each of these cases you may have felt that the test was not a measure of your true ability. In these circumstances, you implied that if the test content were changed, or the test was administered under different circumstances, your score would have been a more accurate reflection of your ability. It is such concerns that have caused psychologists to study the consistency of their measurements.

The generic term given to the problem of consistency of measurement is *reliability*. When studying reliability we are basically interested in two sets of questions. The first set involves the degree of consistency of test scores: What is the relationship between scores obtained under varying testing conditions? How much will a person's score change on retesting? How close is an individual's obtained score to his or her "true score"? Does the test measure consistently enough that it can be applied in practical situations? The second set of questions revolves around the causes of discrepancies between test scores: What factors produce inconsistent scores? What is the relative magnitude of their effects? How do they operate? Traditionally, the study of reliability has placed more emphasis on the first set of questions, concentrating on the development of methods for making more precise estimates of the degree of consistency of measurement.

The Basic Equation

The fundamental concepts of reliability theory can best be presented by introducing the idea of a "true score." A *true score* can be defined as the score that a person would obtain if the test measured without error. Since this definition is rather circular, many people prefer an alternative definition: The true score is the score an individual would obtain if he took all the items in the domain. Or, a true score is the person's average score on a large number (theoretically, infinite) of equivalent forms of a test.

no correlation between T + E scores for an ind.

Each of these definitions states, in essence, that the score a person obtains on a test is a function of both his true score and the error involved in the measurement. Expressed as an equation:

ind ⟶
$$X = T + E \tag{4.1}$$

where X is the obtained, or observed, score; T, the hypothetical true score; and E, the measurement error.

The measurement error term (E) represents the contribution of any variables that produce inconsistencies in measurement. This error component can be either positive or negative. If it is positive, the person's true score will be overestimated by his obtained score; if negative, his true score will be underestimated. Two assumptions are made about error. First, if averaged over many administrations of the test, or over a group of people, the average error will be zero. Second, true scores and measurement error are independent (uncorrelated). These assumptions are merely saying that error effects are random.

averaged error = 0

T & E not correlated

Equation (4.1) shows the relation between observed scores, true scores, and measurement error for a particular individual. But because reliability is a property of a test, not of an individual score, we need an analogous equation for a group of persons. We can write this equation:

group ⟶
$$s_X^2 = s_T^2 + s_E^2 \tag{4.2}$$

- does not define reliability
- only relationship

or the variance of observed scores (s_X^2) equals the variance of the true scores (s_T^2) plus error variance (s_E^2).

Reliability Defined

Equation (4.2) shows the relationship between obtained scores, true scores, and error, but does not define reliability. *Reliability can be defined as the ratio of true variance in a set of test scores to the total, or obtained, variance:*

proportion of true + error variance

$$r_{XX} = \frac{s_T^2}{s_X^2} \tag{4.3}$$

where r_{XX} is the reliability of the test, s_T^2 the variance of true scores, and s_X^2 the variance of the obtained scores.

If you understood the definitions and equations, you are probably now saying, "Fine; but since you do not know a person's true score, how can you determine reliability?" We cannot do so from Equation (4.3). But by substituting Equation (4.2) in Equation (4.3) and performing some algebra, we obtain:

$$r_{XX} = 1 - \frac{s_E^2}{s_X^2} \tag{4.4}$$

That is, reliability can be defined in terms of error variance and observed score variance. Because error can be defined as the difference between scores on two administrations of a test, we can compute error variance. And, because we can compute the variance of observed scores, we can compute the reliability of our measure.

reliability limits validity

Types of Reliability Estimates

Depending on which error sources are of greatest concern, we can calculate one of several types of reliability estimates. Some are derived from comparing performance on two administrations of the same measure. Thus, if we are interested in the stability of performance over time, we would administer a test, readminister the same test to the same people at a later date, then correlate the scores. This is called the *coefficient of stability* or *test-retest reliability*. If we have two forms of a test, we could administer both forms to the same sample of people, then correlate the scores. This is called the *coefficient of equivalence, parallel forms reliability*, or *alternative forms reliability*. We could, of course, combine these two procedures by administering one form of a test, then administering the alternative form at a later date. This is the *coefficient of equivalence and stability*.

When we have only one form of a test, we have two options. One is to divide the test into two parts and compare scores on the two parts. This is, not surprisingly, called *split-half reliability*. The other option is to investigate the consistency of performance over the various items comprising the test. This analysis determines whether all items on the test measure the same trait or characteristic. Such indices are called *internal consistency* or *homogeneity coefficients*.

All of these consistency estimates provide evidence on the quality of the test. Test users, however, are concerned with another question: How much will an individual's score be expected to change on retesting with the same or an alternative form of a test? A statistic, the *standard error of measurement*, provides this information.

The methods for determining reliability, and their interpretation, will be discussed in Chapter 5.

validity

Like consistency, validity is a generic term given to a class of related concepts and procedures. When investigating the validity of a measure, we are interested in such questions as: What trait is measured by the test? How well? Are the test items a representative sample of some defined domain? What behaviors can be predicted by the test scores? How accurately? Does the test supply information that can be used in making more accurate decisions? In short, the major validity questions are: (1) What does the test measure?, and (2) How well does it measure what it is designed to measure?

Although we talk about the validity of a test, or of test scores, strictly speaking we validate inferences made from the scores. That is, when discussing the validity of a test as a measure of a particular trait, we really are talking about the validity of the inference that the test measures the trait. Or, when determining how well a test predicts some external behavior, we are really validating our predictions.

Validity Defined

Whereas reliability was defined in terms of the proportion of true and error variance, conceptually *validity* (r^2_{XY}) *can be defined as the proportion of observed variance that is relevant to the purposes of the testing.* As implied by the definition, what is relevant depends on the purpose of the testing. When a test serves as a representation, relevant variance will be that variance attributable to the ability, trait, or construct the test is designed to measure. When a test serves as a predictor, relevant variance will be that shared by the test (the predictor) and the criterion—or, in other words, the proportion of criterion variance predictable from the test scores.

The definition of validity can also be expressed by equations. Equation (4.2) stated that the total variance in a set of test scores equals true variance plus measurement error variance:

$$s_X{}^2 = s_T{}^2 + s_E{}^2$$

Defining validity as the proportion of relevant variance implies that true variance can be divided into two components:

$$s_T{}^2 = s_V{}^2 + s_I{}^2 \tag{4.5}$$

where $s_V{}^2$ is the relevant (valid) variance and $s_I{}^2$ is irrelevant but reliable variance.[4] Substituting (4.5) into (4.2):

$$s_X{}^2 = s_V{}^2 + s_I{}^2 + s_E{}^2 \tag{4.6}$$

In other words, the total variance in a set of test scores is composed of three components: valid variance, stable but irrelevant variance, and error variance. Furthermore:

$$r^2{}_{XY} = \frac{s_V{}^2}{s_X{}^2} \tag{4.7}$$

as validity (r^2_{XY}) was defined as the proportion of relevant variance.[5]

As mentioned previously, what is relevant will depend on the purpose of testing. For example, suppose a statistics instructor is interested in students' ability to use correct statistical methods and gives a test consisting of a series of problems. Here relevant variance would reflect knowledge of statistical methods, irrelevant variance might be introduced by differences in computational skills or speed of responding, and error variance could be introduced by chance events such as misreading or miscopying a number used in a solution. The problem in validation studies is to identify and separate these various sources of variance.

Types of Validity

Although there are numerous types of validity, all fall into three main classes: criterion-related validity, content validity, and construct validity (see *Standards*,

---

[4] Irrelevant variance generally results from the effects of several variables. For example, on an essay exam, irrelevant variance may be due to differences in writing skill, speed of responding, grading biases, and other factors besides knowledge of the material tested. To simplify the equations, we have lumped all these variables together as irrelevant sources of variance.

[5] Note that in this conceptual definition, validity is represented by a *squared* correlation coefficient (r^2_{XY}). This is necessary when using a proportion of variance interpretation of correlation (see Chapter 3). A validity coefficient, however, is the simple, unsquared correlation between a predictor and a criterion measure (r_{XY}). This difference will be discussed further in Chapter 6.

1974). These three types will be briefly introduced here; they will be discussed in more detail in Chapters 6 and 7.

Criterion-related Validity   One frequent use of psychological tests is to predict an individual's future performance on some external variable (the criterion). For example, we might want to predict the grade averages of prospective college students or the job performance of workers. The basic question in these situations is: How well do scores on the test predict performance on the criterion? An index of this predictive accuracy is a measure of the validity of the test.

Note that the most important aspect of the situation is the criterion, hence the label criterion-related validity. What is of ultimate interest is the individual's performance on the criterion variable; the test score is important only in that it predicts the criterion. Thus the major concern in constructing the test will be to select items that predict the criterion. Here the test operates as a predictor, rather than as a representation or sample.

[margin notes: concurrent & predictive / predict a criterion / validity of test]

Content Validity   In other situations, the test user wants to know: How would the individual perform in the universe of situations of which the test is but a sample? For example, the typical classroom exam samples an individual's knowledge in a variety of areas; scores on this sample of items are then used to make inferences about the student's knowledge of the total domain covered by the exam. Since the test represents a well-defined domain, the test content will closely parallel the tasks constituting the domain under study, and performance on individual items—both the accuracy of the response and the process used to answer the item—will be of primary interest.

Because this type of test requires making inferences from a sample to a domain, evaluation of the content validity of a test will be in terms of the adequacy of the item sampling. Since no quantitative index of sampling adequacy is available, evaluation will necessarily be a rational, judgmental process.

[margin notes: for achievement tests. / item samp / how rep? / evaluation]

Construct validity   A third use of psychological tests is in the study of psychological traits and their manifestations. Here the basic question is: What trait does the test measure? Knowing what trait, or traits, a test measures allows the test to be used for studies of individual differences and for the development of psychological theories. The focus of construct validity, therefore, is on the relationship between the test and the trait.

Construct validation proceeds by an accumulation of evidence as to what trait the test does, in fact, measure. Evidence may be accumulated in various manners and from various sources, including studies of content and criterion-related validity. As evidence accumulates, the trait-test relationship is clarified and the trait definition becomes sharper. As with content validity there is no single quantitative index of the construct validity of a test.

In the discussion that follows we shall treat each class separately, although, as we shall see, they are interrelated. Moreover, evidence on all three types of validity will generally be appropriate in evaluating any test.

[margin notes: trait, charact. / ind diff / develop of theories.]

the relationship between reliability and validity

Validity refers to the relationship between test scores and some other variable, either a hypothetical trait or construct or some overt behavior. This relationship enables us to make sense of test scores, by indicating what the test measures. Yet, at least theoretically, it would be possible to develop a perfectly reliable test whose scores did not correlate with any other variable. Such a test would be of no use, since scores would relate to nothing but scores on another administration or form of the test. The test would measure reliably but have no validity. Conversely, if a test is unreliable, its potential validity will be limited. If we cannot measure something consistently, we cannot consistently relate it to the other measures or variables. Thus, reliability is a necessary, but not a sufficient condition for validity. In other words, just because a test is reliable does not mean it will be valid; however, if it is unreliable, its validity will be limited.

Figure 4.1 is a schematic representation of the relationship between reliability and validity. Consider each rectangle to represent the observed variance (s_x^2) of scores on a test. Both tests (a) and (b) are reliable measures, but (a) is also quite valid, since relevant variance is large, whereas (b) is a less valid measure. Tests (c) and (d) are less reliable, but again have different degrees of validity. Note, too, that even though the reliability of measure (c) is lower than that of measure (b), the validity of (c) is higher. These diagrams show that although reliability limits validity, there is not a linear relationship between reliability and validity.

Figure 4.1. Relationship between Reliability and Validity.

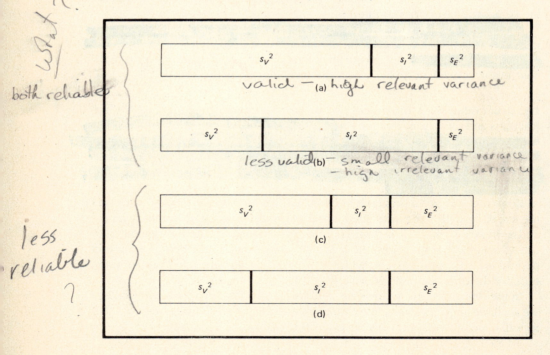

The relationship between reliability can also be shown in a number of other ways. One, which has been emphasized in this chapter, is in terms of type of errors. Reliability is concerned with estimating the effects of random measurement errors; validity is concerned with systematic errors. Another is by considering the similarity of the two measures. In analyses of reliability we study the relationship between items in a measure or between two forms or administrations of the same measure; in validity, scores on one measure are related to some other qualitatively different measure or to a hypothetical construct.

The relationship can also be shown by a statistic called the *correction for attenuation:*

correction for unreliability

$$\hat{r}_{XY} = \frac{r_{XY}}{\sqrt{r_{XX}} \sqrt{r_{YY}}} \qquad (4.8)$$

where r_{XY} is the observed relationship between two variables, r_{XX} and r_{YY} are their reliabilities, and $\hat{r}_{XY}$ is the correlation corrected for unreliability. This formula allows us to estimate what the relationship between two variables would be if the variables were measured more (or less) reliably.

The effect of reliability on validity can be shown more clearly if we manipulate this formula. Assume that the criterion measure can be measured with perfect reliability ($r_{YY} = 1.00$), which would be the case when measuring some theoretical construct (Y). Then, by doing some algebra we find that:

$$r_{XY} = \hat{r}_{XY} \sqrt{r_{XX}} \qquad (4.9)$$

Since r_{XY} is a validity coefficient, this equation shows that the observed validity of a measure will always be limited by its reliability. Furthermore, if the error-free correlation between the measures was perfect ($\hat{r}_{XY} = 1.00$), the observed validity of a measure would equal the square root of its reliability.

Finally, a practical problem should be mentioned. Often, test users must choose between measuring a narrower trait with high precision (reliability) and measuring a broader trait with less reliability. This is an aspect of the bandwidth-fidelity dilemma (Cronbach, 1970, 1971; Cronbach & Gleser, 1965). If a test user chooses to measure one, or a small number of characteristics with high reliability, she may lose much generality, and hence validity. On the other hand, given the same amount of time for testing, she might choose to measure more diverse characteristics, yet measure each one less reliably. Which approach should she choose? Cronbach concludes, "When several questions are of about equal importance, it is more profitable to use a brief test giving a rough answer to each than to use a precise test answering only one or two questions." (Cronbach, 1970, p. 180) In other words, be more concerned with validity than reliability.

summary

From a psychometric point of view, a test should be both reliable and valid. By reliable we mean that test takers would obtain (approximately) the same scores if they took alternative forms of a test or took the same test at a different time or under different conditions. Validity means that the test measures the trait or construct it is designed to measure and not extraneous factors. Both are properties of the test scores, not of individual scores.

Observed scores on any test reflect three major sources of variation: the characteristic the test is designed to measure, stable but irrelevant influences (systematic errors), and unsystematic influences (random errors or measurement errors). Systematic errors are of primary concern when determining validity; measurement errors when determining reliability.

Errors come from three sources. Some are associated with the test itself; these are primarily differences between items or samples of items. Others are associated with the test administration; these reflect variations in such factors as directions, timing, and scoring. Still others are associated with the test takers; these include differences in motivation, test-taking skills and experiences, coaching, temporary states, and long-term changes in individuals. Random errors can be minimized by writing clear items, using standard testing conditions, and using a sufficient number of items. Systematic errors are controlled by carefully constructing the test so as to measure only the desired characteristic.

Any observed score is a function of both the person's true score and measurement error. Consistency, or reliability, is defined as the ratio of true score variance to observed score variance or, alternatively, as one minus the proportion of error variance in observed scores. Reliability estimates indicate the extent to which scores will be expected to vary over items (internal consistency), test forms (equivalence), or time (stability).

Validity is concerned with what trait or characteristic the test measures, how well it measures this trait, and what behaviors and outcomes can be predicted by the test scores. Content validity focuses on the adequacy of sampling of items from a defined domain. Construct validity is concerned with how well the test measures a particular trait or construct. Criterion-related validity is concerned with how accurately test scores predict other behaviors.

A test's potential validity is limited to the extent that the test fails to measure consistently. Conversely, even a highly reliable test may not measure the characteristic it is designed to measure. Hence, reliability is a necessary, but not a sufficient, condition for valid measurement.

Suggestions for Further Reading

Clemans, W. V. Test administration. In R. L. Thorndike (Ed.), *Educational measurement,* 2d ed. Washington, D.C.: American Council on Education, 1971. A discussion of the concerns in test administration from the viewpoint of the test author, examiner, and test taker; the emphasis is on control of the variables that may influence test scores.

Ebel, R. L. Must all tests be valid? *American Psychologist,* 1961, *16,* 640–647. Ebel points out some limitations of the concept of validity and argues that some tests can provide useful information without support from traditional validity evidence.

Guion, R. M. Open a new window: Validities and values in psychological measurement. *American Psychologist,* 1974, *29,* 287–296. The author argues that psychologists should take a broader view of the types of evidence used to determine the quality and usefulness of a test, for example, job relatedness.

Jensen, A. R. The effect of race of examiner on the mental test scores of white and black pupils. *Journal of Educational Measurement,* 1974, *11,* 1–14. An empirical study showing that the race of the examiner has negligible effects on test performance.

Marso, R. N. Test item arrangement, testing time, and performance. *Journal of Educational Measurement,* 1970, *7,* 113–118. Two studies showing that the order of item presentation has little effect on performance on a classroom achievement test.

Messick, S. The effectiveness of coaching for the SAT. *New Directions for Testing and Measurement,* 1981, *11,* 21–53. A review of the research and discussion of issues regarding effects of formal coaching on performance on college admissions tests.

Messick, S., & Jungeblut, A. Time and method in coaching for the SAT. *Psychological Bulletin,* 1981, *89,* 191–216. A more technical discussion of the coaching problem, with emphasis on the relationship between the type and length of coaching and score changes.

Rowley, G. L. Which examinees are most favored by the use of multiple-choice tests? *Journal of Educational Measurement,* 1974, *11,* 15–23. An empirical study showing that students who are testwise and willing to take risks may be favored by the use of multiple-choice items.

Tryon, G. S. The measurement and treatment of test anxiety. *Review of Educational Research,* 1980, *50,* 343–372. A review of the validity of various measures of test anxiety and of the effectiveness of methods for treating test anxiety.

Wine, J. Test anxiety and direction of attention. *Psychological Bulletin,* 1971, *76,* 92–104. A review of literature on test anxiety concluding that test-anxious people split their attention between the task and their own feelings.

Wing, H. Practice effects with traditional mental test items. *Applied Psychological Measurement,* 1980, *4,* 141–155. An extensive study showing that practice effects occur on various types of aptitude tests but have the largest effect on tests requiring the use of specific types of rules.

Chapter 5 • Consistency

CHAPTER 4 introduced the basic notions of the theory of measurement error and reliability. We indicated that all tests measure imperfectly, with random measurement errors causing scores to vary from time to time and occasion to occasion. Thus one problem is to estimate the degree of inconsistency introduced into measurements by these random errors. The concept of reliability, defined as the ratio of true variance to observed variance in a set of test scores, provides this information.

The discussion in Chapter 4 was at a conceptual level. This chapter will discuss consistency in more practical terms, describing the computation and interpretation of various reliability estimates. We will first describe methods for determining consistency over time and test forms and then discuss measures based on the relationship between items on a test. Next we will discuss the interpretation of measures of consistency, including variables that influence the magnitude of reliability estimates, error in individual scores, and what is considered an acceptable level of reliability. We will conclude by describing some problems and situations involving use of reliability data.

One frequently misunderstood point should be kept in mind when reading this chapter. As the term is used in psychological measurement, reliability refers to the consistency of measurement of a single measure or alternative forms of a measure. When we investigate the relationship between scores on two different tests, even ones designed to measure the same characteristic, we are not determining reliability. Only if the two test forms are specifically constructed to measure the same domain, using the same guidelines for selecting items, can they be considered alternative forms. Thus, the correlation between Forms A and B of the E-Z Reading Test would be an estimate of reliability; however, the correlation between scores on the E-Z Reading Test and on the C-U Reading Test would not be a reliability measure.

types of reliability estimates

As indicated in Chapter 4, any particular measurement, test, or observation is only one of various possible measurements of the characteristic of interest. The dimensions along which the measurement can vary are almost limitless: content, item format, time, testing situations, test administrators, and scorers, to name but a few. Traditionally, however, estimates of reliability have been concerned with consistency over only two of these dimensions: samples of items (test forms) and time. One reason is that the effects of many other variables can be minimized by using standardized testing conditions. But, more important, these two dimensions reflect practical concerns in testing. When there is more than one form of a measure, we want to be assured that test takers will obtain (approximately) the same score regardless of which form they take.[1] And, when test scores are used to predict future behavior, we must be assured that scores will be stable over time.

Reliability Coefficients

At first glance it might seem that an appropriate quantitative index of consistency would be the percent of scores that were the same on two administrations of a test. That is, we could administer the same test twice, or administer alternative forms of a test, and determine what percent of the scores did not change. In some cases this index is appropriate; usually, however, it is not. The reason being that when a test has a wide range of scores, exact matches will be rare and the degree of consistency may be underestimated.

Another possibility would be to use some function of the difference in scores, such as the mean or standard deviation of the distribution of discrepancy scores (differences in individual's scores on two administrations). Indices of this nature are frequently used in the physical sciences and engineering. And, as we shall see later, they are also used in psychological measurement. However, most common indices of reliability are expressed as correlation coefficients.

A *reliability coefficient* is nothing more than the correlation between scores from two administrations of a test to the same sample of people. The correlation coefficient is used because it can be shown (see, e.g., Nunnally, 1978; Stanley, 1971) that a reliability coefficient derived in this manner is equivalent to reliability as defined earlier:

$$r_{XX} = \frac{s_T^2}{s_X^2} \tag{5.1}$$

where r_{XX} is the reliability coefficient (the subscripts indicate that the correlation is between two forms or administrations of the same test). Thus, if the reliability of a test is .90, we can say that 90 percent of the variance in observed scores represents variance in true scores and 10 percent is measurement error variance. Three points about reliability coefficients should be noted. First, the particular value obtained for any reliability coefficient will depend upon the group being tested and the sources of error that influence the scores. Thus, there is no such thing as *the* reliability of a test. Rather, there will be many reliability coefficients for any test—as many as there are different conditions for estimating the reliability.

Note, too, that a reliability coefficient is a measure of the amount of inconsistency; it does not indicate the causes of this lack of consistency. It tells how much the scores may be expected to vary, not why they vary. Thus, if we have reliability

[1] Ideally, measures would be perfectly reliable and test takers would get the same score on each administration. In practice, perfect reliability is never attained and scores will vary somewhat. Thus, whenever we say test takers will obtain the same score, read it to mean *approximately* the same scores.

coefficients for two tests, obtained under similar conditions, we can tell which of the two tests measures more consistently. But without further analyses we cannot know why one test measures more accurately than the other.

Third, as a correlation coefficient indicates the agreement in relative rankings on the two measures, systematic changes (either increases or decreases) in scores will not be detected. Suppose, for example, a reading test was administered to third grade students in October and again six months later. If each student's reading score increased by about the same amount, the relative rankings would not change much and the reliability coefficient would be high, even though students obtained different scores on the two tests. On the other hand, if changes in reading skill varied widely among students, the reliability coefficient would be lower, since the relative position of many students would change.

The Coefficient of Stability

There are several situations in which the stability of test scores over time is of interest. One is when measuring characteristics presumed to be relatively stable over time, such as many abilities and personality characteristics. In this case, if the data indicate that test scores are not stable, we would need either to develop a more stable measure or to revise our thinking about the stability of the trait. Another is when using the test to make decisions involving long-range plans. For example, when using vocational interest inventories in career planning with college students, the implicit assumption is that interests are stable over time. If they were not, and interests changed radically, the test would be of little use in making long-range plans inasmuch as interests at, say, age 35 would be different from the student's interests when in college. Finally, even when we are not interested in stability over long periods, a test may be readministered to estimate the amount of error due to a particular test administration or to measure short-term stability.

The paradigm for the coefficient of stability is quite simple. The test is administered, a period of time elapses, and the same test is readministered. We then compute the correlation between scores on the test and the retest (see Table 5.1, steps 1 and 2, for an example):

$$\text{TEST} \xrightarrow{\text{(time)}} \text{RETEST}$$

Because the procedure consists of a test and a retest, the coefficient of stability is also referred to as *test-retest reliability*.

The time interval between testings can vary from several minutes to several years. Thus, different values of the reliability coefficient will be obtained depending on the time between testings. If we were to plot the relationship between the magnitude of the reliability coefficient and the time between test administrations, we would usually find that reliability decreases over time. Of course, it is not time per se that causes the changes in scores; rather, it is the experiences of the individual between testings.

Because a coefficient of stability involves two administrations of the test, any variable that influences performance on one administration but not the other will

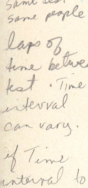

Test problem!

Same test same people lapse of time between test. Time interval can vary.

if Time interval to great, reliability ↓.

Item content doesn't influence reliability because same items are used for each test.

reduce the correlation. Examples include errors in timing or interruptions during one testing session. Thus, any errors associated with a specific administration of the test will affect the test-retest reliability. So, also, will day-to-day fluctuations in mood, health, and motivation. If the time between testings is relatively long, differential training or learning may become a factor. Item sampling does not affect the coefficient of stability since the same test form (i.e., the same collection of items) is used on both administrations.

There are two situations where a coefficient of stability should not be used. One is when test takers might remember items from the first administration and thus make the same responses on the second administration. In this situation the coefficient will be spuriously inflated. The other situation is when education, training, or other relevant experiences intervene between the two administrations of the test. In this case, interpretation of the coefficient will be ambiguous because changes in scores will reflect true gains in knowledge or changes in behavior, as well as measurement errors.

The Coefficient of Equivalence

Because any test contains only a sample of all possible items, a number of parallel forms of the test can be constructed. Parallel forms cover the same content, use the same types of items, and are of equal difficulty. Such parallel forms are needed whenever retesting with the same test is not feasible or desirable. For example, many math and science problems that are useful because they present a new situation, upon repetition present only a routine calculation exercise.

When we have equivalent forms, the reliability question becomes: How consistent are scores on the two forms of the test? To determine the equivalent forms reliability we would administer one form (Form A) of the test and then, with a minimum time lag,[2] administer a second form (Form B). Correlating the scores on the two forms gives a coefficient of equivalence (see Table 5.1, steps 1 and 3, for an example). Diagrammatically the procedure would be:

$$\text{FORM A} \xrightarrow{\text{(minimal time)}} \text{FORM B}$$

In practice, to counterbalance any effects due to order of administration, half the group would be administered Form A followed by Form B and the other half Form B followed by Form A. Because the procedure involves use of equivalent, or parallel, forms of the test, this method is also called *parallel forms reliability* or *alternate forms reliability*.

In this method, inconsistencies in scores can be attributed primarily to differences in item sampling (that is, test forms). Since the two forms of the test are given close together in time, long-term fluctuations are eliminated; however, short-term fluctuations in the test taker's mood or differences in administration of the two forms are not entirely controlled. Thus, a pure measure of equivalence

[2] Theoretically, the two forms would be administered simultaneously. Since this is not possible, the two forms generally are administered within a few days of each other.

test - retest reliability

Table 5.1
Calculation of the Coefficients of Stability, Equivalence, and Stability and Equivalence

(1) Assume that two (equivalent) forms of a 16-item test were administered to a group of 20 persons on a total of three occasions—Form A on March 1, Form B also on March 1, and Form A again on May 1. These administrations will be referred to as A_1, B_1, and A_2, respectively. Scores were as follows:

	A	B	C	D	E	F	G	H	I	J	K	L	M	N	O	P	Q	R	S	T
A_1	15	14	13	12	12	11	11	10	10	10	10	10	9	9	9	8	8	7	6	5
B_1	16	14	14	12	13	10	11	11	10	10	9	10	8	9	9	8	7	7	6	6
A_2	15	14	16	15	13	12	11	13	12	12	10	11	11	11	10	9	10	7	8	8

cross product =

The summary statistics were as follows:

use bias estimate   *standard deviation*

Test	ΣX	ΣX^2	$\overline{X}$	s	\multicolumn{3}{c}{Cross-products (ΣXY)}
					A_1	B_1	A_2
A_1	199	2101	9.95	2.46	—	2118	2375
B_1	200	2144	10.00	2.68		—	2397
A_2	228	2714	11.40	2.40			—

(2) *Coefficient of stability.* The coefficient of stability is the correlation between scores on two administrations of the same form of the test, separated by a time period—in this example the correlation between A_1 and A_2:

$$r_{xx} = r_{(A1)(A2)} = \frac{\Sigma(X_{A1})(X_{A2})/N - (\overline{X}_{A1})(\overline{X}_{A2})}{(s_{A1})(s_{A2})}$$

standard deviation

Substituting in the data from the example and solving:

$$r_{(A1)(A2)} = \frac{2375/20 - (9.95)(11.40)}{(2.46)(2.40)} = .90$$

true variance + error *10% is error*

(3) *Coefficient of equivalence.* The coefficient of equivalence is the correlation between scores on parallel forms of the test, administered with a minimal time lag between testing—in the example, the correlation between A_1 and B_1:

$$r_{(A1)(A2)} = \frac{\Sigma(X_{A1})(X_{B1})/N - (\overline{X}_{A1})(\overline{X}_{B1})}{(s_{A1})(s_{B1})}$$

Substituting in the data and solving,

$$r_{(A1)(B1)} = \frac{2118/20 - (9.95)(10.00)}{(2.46)(2.68)} = .97$$

should have high reliability

(4) *Coefficient of equivalence and stability.* This coefficient is the correlation between two parallel forms of the test administered at different times—in the example, the correlation between B_1 and A_2:

$$r_{(B1)(A2)} = \frac{\Sigma(X_{B1})(X_{A2})/N - (\overline{X}_{B1})(\overline{X}_{A2})}{(s_{B1})(s_{A2})}$$

Substituting in the data and solving,

$$r_{(B1)(A2)} = \frac{2397/20 - (10.00)(11.40)}{(2.68)(2.40)} = .91$$

coefficient of stability formula →   *// form*

(5) *Interpretation of the coefficients.* The very high value ($r = .97$) obtained for the coefficient of equivalence, plus the similarities in means and standard deviations, indicate that forms A and B are, in fact, parallel forms. As both stability indices were also high ($r \sim .90$), the trait tested evidently is quite stable, at least over a period of two months. Note also that there is some practice effect operating (i.e., the mean on A_2 is higher than the mean on A_1).

---

is not obtained. However, the major source of variance will be the difference between items on the two forms of the test.

If the coefficient of equivalence is high, rankings of test takers will be similar on the two test forms. If, in addition, the two forms have comparable means and standard deviations (which they should have, to be considered parallel forms), scores on the two forms will be approximately the same for most test takers. However, as with test-retest reliability, systematic increases or decreases in scores will not be reflected in the parallel forms coefficient. Thus, a high coefficient of equivalence does not necessarily guarantee equivalent scores on the two test forms.

Stability and Equivalence.   If alternative forms of a test are available, it is possible to determine reliability by a combination of the two preceding methods. The procedure would be to administer one test form (Form A), allow a period of time to pass, then administer the other form (Form B):

$$\text{FORM A} \xrightarrow{\text{(time)}} \text{FORM B}$$

The coefficient of stability and equivalence will be the correlation between the two sets of scores. As with equivalent forms reliability, the experimental design would involve some people taking Form A first, others taking Form B first. (See Table 5.1, steps 1 and 4.)

Since all the factors that produce inconsistencies in scores in the test-retest paradigm plus all the factors that produce inconsistencies in the parallel forms design can operate in this design, we would expect the greatest inconsistency in scores (that is, the lowest reliability coefficients) using this method of estimating reliability. Thus the coefficient of stability and equivalence will generally give the lowest estimate of reliability.

Split-Half Reliability

In some situations it is not possible to use either equivalent forms or stability indices of reliability. For example, a teacher typically will not administer alternative forms of a classroom test nor will the same exam be repeated at a later date. Nevertheless, some estimate of reliability may be needed. Fortunately, several methods are available for estimating reliability in these situations. One common method involves splitting the test into two equivalent halves—hence the designation split-half reliability.

Unless there is some systematic bias (such as alternating types of items or the response to one item being dependent on the response to a previous item), this split can usually be accomplished by using the odd-numbered items as one form and the even-numbered items as the other. In other words, we would obtain separate scores for the odd- and even-numbered items. The correlation between these two scores gives an estimate of reliability.

One problem with this procedure is that each score is based on only half the items in the original test. Since reliability varies with test length (see below), the reliability estimated from the correlation between odd and even items will be lower than the reliability expected from a test of the original length. To estimate the reliability of a test of the original length we can use the *Spearman-Brown* formula:

$$r_{xx} = \frac{2 r_{hh}}{1 + r_{hh}} \tag{5.2}$$

where r_{hh} is the split-half reliability coefficient and r_{xx} is the estimate of the reliability of the test of the original length. The equation estimates the reliability of a test of the original length from the split-half reliability.

The Spearman-Brown formula assumes that the variability of the two halves of the test are equal. An alternative formula (Guttman, 1945) does not make this assumption:

$$r_{xx} = 2 \left[1 - \frac{s_a^2 + s_b^2}{s_x^2} \right] \tag{5.3}$$

where s_a and s_b are the standard deviations of the two subtest scores and s_x is the standard deviation of the total score. Other formulas are presented by Thorndike (1951) and Stanley (1971).

The split-half reliability coefficient can be considered as a special case of the coefficient of equivalence or as a type of internal consistency. Because it is based on the correlation between two samples of items, differences in item sampling can affect the size of the correlation. So, too, can differences in the distributions of scores on the two halves of the test. Because all items are administered at one time, only short-term fluctuations in personal variables will influence the coefficient.

An illustration of the computation of a split-half reliability coefficient is presented in Table 5.2.

internal consistency

Another approach to consistency focuses on the interrelations between the various items comprising a test. Here the basic question is: Do all items on the test measure the same trait or characteristic? Although measures of internal consistency are related to other measures of reliability, particularly the coefficient of equivalence, we will consider them separately because they answer a somewhat different question. In our discussion, we will use the terms internal consistency and homogeneity interchangeably.

Table 5.2
Calculation of Split-Half Reliability

(1) Form B of the test described in Table 5.1 was split into two halves—odd-and even-numbered items—and each half scored separately. Scores were as follows:

	A	B	C	D	E	F	G	H	I	J	K	L	M	N	O	P	Q	R	S	T
										Subject										
Odds	8	8	7	6	6	5	6	5	5	5	4	6	4	4	5	4	3	4	3	3
Evens	8	6	7	6	7	5	5	6	5	5	5	4	4	5	4	4	4	3	3	3
Total	16	14	14	12	13	10	11	11	10	10	9	10	8	9	9	8	7	7	6	6

The summary data were:

	ΣX	ΣX^2	$\overline{X}$	s	
Odds	101	553	5.05	1.47	$\Sigma X_o X_e = 532$
Evens	99	527	4.95	1.36	
Total	200	2144	10.00	2.68	

(2) The split-half reliability is computed by correlating scores on the odd-numbered items (o) with scores on the even-numbered items (e):

$$r_{xx} = r_{oe} = \frac{\Sigma X_o X_e / N - (\overline{X}_o)(\overline{X}_e)}{(s_o)(s_e)}$$

Substituting in the data and solving:

$$r_{oe} = \frac{532/20 - (5.05)(4.95)}{(1.47)(1.36)} = .80$$

The value, $r = .80$, is the *uncorrected* split-half reliability coefficient.

(3) As each half of the test contained only eight items, and the full test contained 16, we can use the Spearman-Brown formula to estimate the reliability of a 16-item test:

$$r_{xx} = \frac{2\,r_{oe}}{1 + r_{oe}} = \frac{2(.80)}{1 + .80} = .89$$

The value, $r_{xx} = .89$, is the *corrected* split-half reliability coefficient.

(4) We could also estimate the split-half reliability using the alternative formula:

$$r_{xx} = 2\left[1 - \frac{s_a^2 + s_b^2}{s_x^2}\right] = 2\left[1 - \frac{s_o^2 + s_e^2}{s_x^2}\right]$$

$$= 2\left[1 - \frac{(1.47)^2 + (1.36)^2}{(2.68)^2}\right] = .88$$

Note that the two formulas produce essentially the same value for r_{xx} (.88 and .89) and that these values approximate the value found for the coefficient of equivalence.

Homogeneity Defined

Analyses of internal consistency seek to determine the degree to which the test items are interrelated. If the scores on the various items comprising a test inter-correlate positively, the test is homogeneous (DuBois, 1970b; Loevinger, 1947). As a corollary, given a homogeneous test, knowing how a person performs on one item allows us to predict how he or she will perform on other items. Note that the emphasis is on performance (scores), not on the content or format of the items. If item scores are intercorrelated positively, the test is homogeneous, regardless of the item content.

Some authors make a further distinction between homogeneity and unidimensionality (Bejar, 1980; DuBois, 1970b; Loevinger, 1947; Terwilliger & Lele, 1979). A test is said to be unidimensional if it measures only one trait. If a test is homogeneous, we might presume that all items measured a common characteristic. However, all items could measure the same combination of characteristics and thus be highly intercorrelated. Thus, a homogenous test may or may not be unidimensional. Conversely, a heterogeneous test may contain clusters of homogeneous items.

The need for homogeneous measures is most apparent when considering how psychological constructs are defined. In psychological research, constructs are frequently defined by, or inferred from, scores on psychological tests. Only when the tests used to define these theoretical constructs are homogeneous do we have "pure" measures of the constructs. Defining theoretical constructs and making inferences from test scores would be simpler if each test measured only one construct.

Domain Sampling Theory

The concept of homogeneity can best be understood through an approach to testing called the *domain sampling theory* (Nunnally, 1978). This approach assumes that associated with every trait is a hypothetical domain of items that measure that particular construct. To develop a test, we would randomly sample items from this domain. By repeated sampling of items from the domain, we can develop any number of parallel tests that measure the construct of concern. Since any test is a random sample of items from the domain, an individual's score on the test (item sample) will be an estimate of his true score (X_T) and the reliability of a test will be the average correlation between that test (a particular item sample) and all other parallel tests of the same length drawn from the same domain.

A particularly useful derivation relates the internal consistency of a test to the intercorrelations among the items:

$$r_{kk} = \frac{k\bar{r}_{ij}}{1 + (k - 1)\bar{r}_{ij}} \tag{5.4}$$

where k is the number of items comprising the test and $\bar{r}_{ij}$ is the average correlation between items in the domain. Equation (5.4) states that reliability can be expressed in terms of the average interitem correlation. As should be obvious from this formula, a test will be more homogeneous when the average interitem correlation is high—that is, when the items tend to measure the same trait.

To summarize briefly, domain sampling theory postulates that for each trait there is a domain of items, all of which measure the trait. A test is defined as a random sample of k items from this domain. Parallel forms of a test can be constructed by drawing other random samples of k items from the domain. Using the average intercorrelations between the items in the domain, formulas can be derived for determining the reliability of a test from the item intercorrelations. In all cases, the higher the average interitem correlations, the higher the internal consistency (homogeneity) of the measure.

Measures of Internal Consistency

Measures of internal consistency indicate the degree to which the items comprising a test are intercorrelated. Thus they are designed to answer the question: Do all items measure the same characteristic? These indices place primary emphasis on the internal structure of the test, specifically the relationships between items. This is in contrast to the other reliability indices discussed previously, which were based on the correlation between forms or administrations of a test.

As internal consistency estimates are obtained from one administration of a test, errors associated with a particular test administration are not detected and long-term changes in test takers are not a factor. Because the indices are derived from item intercorrelations, the primary source of error lies in the items comprising the test. More specifically, the major source of error in internal consistency estimates is differences between the items in their ability to measure the trait tested.

A number of indices of internal consistency have been developed. We will present three: Cronbach's coefficient alpha, Kuder-Richardson formula 20, and a procedure developed by Hoyt that uses analysis of variance.

Coefficient Alpha.   One widely used measure of internal consistency, which can be derived from the previous equation, is Cronbach's coefficient alpha (Cronbach, 1951):

$$r_{kk} = \frac{k}{k-1}\left[1 - \frac{\Sigma s_i^2}{s_x^2}\right] \tag{5.5}$$

where k is the number of items on the test, Σs_i^2 is the sum of the variances of the item scores, and s_x^2 is the variance of the test scores (that is, the scores on all k items). Coefficient alpha can be interpreted as the expected correlation between a test and another test of the same length drawn from the same domain or as the average expected correlation between all k-item tests constructed from this domain.

Kuder-Richardson Formulas.   Kuder-Richardson formula 20 (Kuder & Richardson, 1937; Richardson & Kuder, 1939) can be considered as a special case of coefficient alpha when the items are scored dichotomously (that is, either correct or incorrect). Although Kuder and Richardson developed several formulas,[3] the most useful one is formula 20 (K-R 20):

$$r_{kk} = \frac{k}{k-1}\left[\frac{s_x^2 - \Sigma p_i q_i}{s_x^2}\right] \tag{5.6}$$

where

$$
\begin{aligned}
k &= \text{the number of items on the test}\\
s_x^2 &= \text{the variance of (total) scores on the test}\\
p_i &= \text{the proportion of people passing an item}\\
q_i = 1 - p_i &= \text{the proportion failing an item}
\end{aligned}
$$

[3] Formulas (5.5) and (5.6) are algebraically equivalent except for the item variance term. When computing coefficient alpha we use Σs_i^2 for item variances; in K-R 20 the analogous term is $\Sigma p_i q_i$.

An example of the calculation of K-R 20 is given in Table 5.3.

Table 5.3
Computation of a Coefficient of Internal Consistency

Suppose 22 students took a 16-item true-false test and you want to determine the internal consistency of the test. Since the items are scored dichotomously, you can use either coefficient alpha or Kuder-Richardson formula 20; we shall use K-R 20.

1. The first step is to compute the descriptive statistics for the total test score. These were: mean = 11.27, standard deviation = 2.30, and variance = 5.289 (original data and work not shown).
2. The other value needed is the sum of the item variances. This can be obtained by:
   (a) finding the number of students who correctly answered each item;
   (b) dividing this value by the number of test takers (22) to obtain the proportion (p) answering each item correctly;
   (c) multiplying p by $(1 - p = q)$ to obtain the item variance; and
   (d) summing the item variances over all 16 items.

This procedure is shown in the table below.

[handwritten: P = # People who got answer correct / TOTAL POEPLE (N)]

[handwritten: .95 × .05 = .04Y.   pq]

Item	Number Correct	p		pq
1	21	.95	.5	.048
2	11	.50	–5	.250
3	18	.82		.148
4	16	.73		.197
5	17	.77		.177
6	21	.95		.048
7	21	.95		.048
8	17	.77		.177
9	19	.86		.120
10	12	.55		.248
11	13	.59		.242
12	13	.59		.242
13	2	.09		.082
14	16	.73		.197
15	19	.86		.120
16	12	.55		.248
				$2.592 = \Sigma pq$

[handwritten: the grand chain]

[handwritten: sum of item variance + score variance are different!]

3. To compute K-R 20 use Equation (5.6):

$$r_{kk} = \frac{k}{k-1}\left[\frac{s_x^2 - \Sigma pq}{s_x^2}\right] = \frac{16}{15}\left[\frac{5.289 - 2.592}{5.289}\right] = 0.54$$

[handwritten: low reliability – easy items p value = above]

4. The obtained value (.54) is relatively low. One reason is that the test contained a number of easy items (items 1, 6, 7, 9, 15) and one very hard item (item 13). As can be seen, very easy and very hard items have low variances and thus decrease internal consistency.

[handwritten: intpret ?]

Reliability by Analysis of Variance. Internal consistency can also be determined by another statistical technique, analysis of variance (Hoyt, 1941). In this approach, the total variance in a set of test scores is apportioned to three sources—differences between people, differences between items, and differences due to the interaction between people and items. True score variance is estimated from the differences between people (mean square for persons) and measurement error variance from the person by item interaction. In analysis-of-variance terms, reliability is:

$$r_{XX} = \frac{MS_{\text{persons}} - MS_{\text{persons} \times \text{items}}}{MS_{\text{persons}}} \qquad (5.7)$$

useful for calcul rate of reliability

where MS_{persons} is the mean square (variance) associated with differences between people and $MS_{\text{persons} \times \text{items}}$ is the mean square associated with the persons-by-items interaction. This reliability estimate is interpreted as any other internal consistency measure. The reader desiring further information and examples is referred to Hoyt's article or to Kerlinger (1973).

To illustrate how this approach can be used to study interrater (or scorer) reliability, one needs only to substitute raters for items. Then the data would consist of the scores the various raters assigned to different persons on the component rated. The error would reflect differences between raters in scores assigned, with high agreement shown by a low rater by person interaction.

interpretation of reliability coefficients

Having discussed the methods of estimating reliability, we now turn to three interrelated questions: What factors affect the size of reliability coefficients? How is a reliability coefficient interpreted? What is an acceptable level of reliability?

Factors Influencing Reliability Coefficients

When discussing the various types of reliability coefficients, we mentioned some sources of error that influenced each estimate. In addition, four other factors must be considered when interpreting any reliability coefficient: the length, difficulty, and speededness of the test, and the heterogeneity of the group tested.

Test Length. Longer tests are generally more reliable than shorter tests. Therefore, increasing the number of items on a test generally increases reliability. This occurs because, as the number of items increases, random measurement errors tend to cancel each other out. Consequently, observed scores are a better approximation to true scores and the test is more reliable. Of course, this holds only when the additional items are as reliable as the original ones; adding poor-quality items will increase error and reduce reliability.

test length

Spearman Brown

The relationship between test length and reliability can be shown by the *Spearman-Brown formula*:

$$r_{kk} = \frac{k r_{XX}}{1 + (k - 1) r_{XX}} \qquad (5.8)$$

length of test reliability

where k is the ratio of the increased length to the original length, r_{XX} is the reli-

long test more reliable

ability of the original test, and r_{kk} is the estimated reliability of a test k times as long. This formula allows us to estimate the reliability of any longer, or shorter, test. Moreover, by solving for k we can determine how much a test would have to be lengthened to reach a desired level of reliability.

To illustrate, suppose that we have a ten-item test whose reliability is .50 and we want to estimate what the reliability would be if the test were increased to 30 items. Here $k = 3 = 30/10$. Applying the Spearman-Brown formula, the reliability of a 30-item test would be:

$$r = \frac{3(.50)}{1 + (3 - 1)(.50)} = \frac{1.50}{2.00} = .75$$ *reliability of 30 items*

If we wanted to know how long the test would have to be to obtain a reliability of .90, we would solve for k as follows:

$$.90 = \frac{k(.50)}{1 + (k - 1)(.50)}$$

from which we find that $k = 9$. Thus we would need a 90-item test; that is, we would have to add 80 items to our original ten.

Range of Scores.   Like all correlation coefficients, reliability coefficients are influenced by the variance of the test score distribution, which, in turn, depends on the nature of the group tested. In general, as groups become more homogeneous, variability decreases and the correlation coefficient decreases. Conversely, as groups become more heterogenous, variability is greater and the correlation coefficient increases. A wider range of scores can also be obtained by adding more items to the test, thus producing a wider range of scores.

To illustrate how variability is important, assume you measure the spelling ability of fourth grade students using a test designed for use in several grades, say fourth through sixth. Assume, also, that reliability data are available only for a combined sample of students in the fourth, fifth, and sixth grades. As this sample will be more heterogeneous than a sample composed solely of fourth graders, the variance for the combined sample will also be larger. Consequently, reliability will be higher in the combined sample than in the fourth grade sample; and reliability coefficients based on the combined sample will overestimate the consistency of measurement in the more restricted fourth grade sample.[4]

Similar concerns arise whenever a test is used in a group that differs in variability from the sample used to compute the reliability data. Usually the group tested will be more homogeneous than the standardization sample. For example, a reading test standardized on a national sample may be administered in a particular school or class. As the variability of the school or class scores will be less than those of the standardization sample, the coefficients reported in the test manual will overestimate the reliability of the test for the particular class. In such situa-

[4] Another way of viewing this situation is to consider the difference in rankings produced by a change of x points. When the range of scores is narrow (low variance), the change in position will be relatively large; when the range of scores is wide, the change will be relatively small.

tions, a better indication of the reliability can be obtained either by calculating the reliability for that particular group (the preferable approach) or by applying a formula correcting the coefficient for restriction in range (see, e.g., Ghiselli et al., 1981).

Test Difficulty. There is no simple relationship between the difficulty of the test and its reliability. Nor is there a simple relation between the level of performance of a group and reliability. However, whenever the range of scores is reduced, reliability will be also reduced. Thus, if the test is too difficult or too easy for a group, the range of scores will be narrowed and reliability reduced. This implies that to maximize reliability, the level of difficulty of a test should be such as to produce the widest possible distribution of scores.[5]

A specific problem occurs when the test is so difficult that test takers respond to many items randomly—for example, by guessing. When a person responds randomly we cannot place any confidence in his scores. If only a few people respond randomly, reliability will be only slightly affected. However, if many people guess or otherwise respond randomly, the reliability coefficient will approach zero.

Speededness. On speeded tests, internal consistency estimates are not appropriate.[6] So, too, are split-half estimates, unless the test is administered in two separately timed sections. To show why this is so, assume that you give a 100-item test of simple arithmetic facts to fourth graders. The problems are ones that, with sufficient time, the students would get correct. However, by setting a restrictive time limit, such that not everyone can finish, we produce a speeded test. Under these circumstances, a child who completes 90 items will probably get 90 correct, 45 even and 45 odd; a child who finishes 80 items will get 80 correct, 40 even and 40 odd; and so forth. Thus each child will get the same score (with the exception of a few errors) on both halves. In this situation the split-half coefficient will be spuriously inflated.

How, then, can the reliability of speeded tests be estimated? One possibility is to use test-retest and/or equivalent forms methods. Or you could use a split-half method but administer the test in two separately timed sections. In some situations, the effects of speed can be estimated (Nunnally, 1978, Chapter 16). The important point to remember is that reliability estimates obtained from one administration of a speeded test will generally be overestimates and should be taken with a grain of salt.

Ways of Interpreting Reliability Coefficients

We now turn to the question of how to interpret reliability coefficients. That is, what do the data tell about consistency of measurement? When we interpret reli-

[5] It can be shown that the largest variance will be obtained when the probability of obtaining a correct response is .50; that is, when half the test takers answer an item correctly. If guessing is considered, the optimal level will be higher; how much higher depends on the number of alternatives. A range of item difficulties of .50 to .75 will generally produce an acceptable distribution of total scores.

[6] This is because the items near the end of the test will not be answered by many test takers; thus the variance of these items will be low, as will the correlation between these items and other items.

ability coefficients, three considerations must be kept in mind. First, the reliability of a test as estimated by one technique, in one situation, with one sample will not be the same as an estimate obtained with a different technique, in a different situation, or with a different sample. Thus, we shall always be interpreting a specific reliability coefficient, not making statements about *the* reliability of the test. Second, a reliability coefficient is only an estimate of the magnitude of inconsistency in test scores; it does not indicate, except indirectly, the causes of the inconsistency. Third, high reliability is not an end in itself but rather a step on a way to a goal. That is, unless test scores are consistent, they cannot be related to other variables with any degree of confidence. Thus reliability places limits on validity, and the crucial question becomes whether a test's reliability is high enough to allow satisfactory validity.

Reliability as the Proportion of True Variance.   Earlier we defined reliability as the proportion of true score variance in observed scores. It can also be shown that reliability is equal to the squared correlation between true and observed scores:

$$r_{XX} = r_{XT}^2 \tag{5.9}$$

where r_{XT} is the correlation between true and obtained scores. Thus, a reliability coefficient can be interpreted in terms of the proportion of variance in the obtained scores that represents variation in true scores. For example, if $r_{XX} = .90$, we can say that 90 percent of the variability in obtained scores is due to differences in true scores and only 10 percent is due to errors of measurement. At the extremes, if $r_{XX} = 1.00$, there is no measurement error, all variability being true score variance; if $r_{XX} = .00$, all score differences reflect errors of measurement.

Reliability as the Correlation between Measures.   Many reliability coefficients are nothing more than the correlation between two measures. Stability estimates are correlations between two administrations of the same test, separated in time; equivalence estimates are correlations between forms of a test; split-half estimates are correlations between two halves of a test. In addition, coefficient alpha and K-R 20 can be interpreted as the average correlation between parallel forms of a test derived from the same domain. Thus all these estimates indicate the expected correlation between scores on one administration of a test and scores that would be obtained if the test were administered again or another form of the test were administered.

Reliability as Error in Individual Scores.   When interpreting scores we are often interested in the amount of error in individual scores. We can ask this question in either of two ways: How close is the person's observed score to her true score? Or, how much would her score be expected to change on retesting? We will discuss a statistic that provides this information, the standard error of measurement, later in this chapter.

Another way of approaching this issue is to consider how much a person's relative rank would change on retesting. If a test measured without error (that is, if r_{XX} were 1.00), then every person would keep the same relative position (rank) on retesting. If r_{XX} is less than 1.00, then there will be changes in rankings between tests. Thorndike and Hagen (1977) have provided charts that show how relative ranks will change as reliability changes. To give but one example, suppose that two individuals' scores place them at the 75th and 50th percentile on a test (that is, they scored higher than 75 percent and 50 percent of the group, respectively). When the test's reliability is .60, there is about one chance in three that these two individuals would reverse positions on a retest; however, when $r_{XX} = .95$, there is only one chance in 50 that they will change positions. In other words, the higher the reliability, the less change in relative position.

[margin handwriting: ↑ reliability the less change in relative position]

What Is an Acceptable Level of Reliability? Ideally, tests would be perfectly reliable; in practice, this standard is never attained. The question then becomes: What is an acceptable level of reliability? Although the answer will vary with the nature of the test, how it is used, and what type of reliability estimate is calculated, some guidelines can be provided.

One possible guideline is the level of reliability attained by the better available tests. Many maximal performance tests have equivalent forms and internal consistency reliabilities of .90 or higher. For example, the corrected split-half reliabilities for the Full Scale IQ on the Wechsler Intelligence Scale for Children are .95 or .96 for various age groups; the K-R 20s for the Composite score on the SRA Assessment Survey range from .96 to .98 for various age levels. Similar tests should be expected to attain this level of reliability. Reliabilities of typical performance measures are generally slightly lower, but values of .85–.90 and even higher are common. Thus, from a pragmatic point of view, the reliability of any test should be as high as that of the better tests in the same area. The danger of this approach is, of course, that attainment of the present norm becomes an acceptable goal rather than being viewed as a minimum standard.

These guidelines are appropriate when individual scores will be interpreted. When making comparisons between groups, a lower degree of reliability can be tolerated. However, even in this case, we should use the most reliable measures available.

Variability of Individual Scores

A reliability coefficient provides evidence essential to evaluate a test. It does not give a direct indication of the amount of error in individual test scores. In many practical situations, however, we are interested in the degree to which an individual's score may be expected to vary on retesting. Suppose, for example, that a school psychologist administers the Wechsler Intelligence Scale for Children (WISC) to a child who obtains an IQ of 116. He knows that the child would probably not obtain exactly the same score on retesting, and wonders how much variation can be expected if the child were retested. This is the question we now address.

The Standard Error of Measurement. Our problem, in technical terms, is to estimate the person's true score and the magnitude of the error component. As described earlier in Equation (4.1), measurement theory postulates that any obtained score is a function of the true score plus some error:

$$X = T + E$$

Because of measurement errors, we know that on some occasions the obtained score will be higher than the true score, sometimes the true score will exceed the obtained score, and occasionally the two scores will be equal. In other words, the obtained score may overestimate, underestimate, or equal the true score.

Hypothetically we could test a person an infinite number of times, and compute the mean and standard deviation of the distribution of his (obtained) scores. In this hypothetical distribution the mean would be the individual's true score and the standard deviation would be an index of the magnitude of the errors of measurement. This procedure is obviously unfeasible. However, if we know the reliability of a test, we can estimate the amount of error using a statistic called the *standard error of measurement*:

Standard Error of Meas $\rightarrow$
$$s_m = s_x \sqrt{1 - r_{xx}} \tag{5.10}$$

where s_m is the standard error of measurement, s_x is the standard deviation of the distribution of obtained scores, and r_{xx} is the reliability coefficient for the test. Thus, knowing the standard deviation of the obtained scores and the reliability of the test, we can estimate the magnitude of error in individual scores. Table 5.4 shows an example of the computation of the standard error of measurement.

Interpretation of the Standard Error of Measurement. The standard error of measurement is the standard deviation of the distribution of errors of measurement. It is also the standard deviation of the distribution of observed scores around an individual's true score. Thus the probability is .68 that a given observed score will fall within plus or minus one standard error of measurement of the true score and .95 that an observed score will fall within $\pm 1.96 s_m$ of the true score.

Test users generally approach the problem from another direction because they know only observed scores. At times we want to estimate the limits within which an individual's true score falls. Thus, in our example (see Table 5.4), since the standard error of measurement is 0.78 point, 95 percent of the time a person's true score will fall within 1.53 points of his or her obtained score.[7]

More frequently, test users have another question: How much will an individual's score vary on retesting? This estimate is made by setting confidence limits around a person's observed score, using the standard error of measurement to set these limits. To illustrate, suppose a child obtains an IQ of 80 on the Wechsler Intelligence Scale for Children (WISC). As the standard error of measurement for WISC IQs is about 3 IQ points, the probability is .68 that the child's IQ would vary by no more than ± 3 points on retesting (that is, $\pm 1 s_m$) and .95 that it will not vary

---

[7] Although this procedure is technically incorrect (see, e.g., Dudek, 1979), it can be shown that it will not introduce any large amounts of error when the reliability coefficient is high and we are not considering extreme scores (McHugh, 1957). Also, if there are any practice effects associated with retesting, they must be taken into account.

Table 5.4

Computation and Interpretation of the Standard Error of Measurement

(1) For illustrative purposes we shall use data from the reliability example presented in Table 5.1. We shall use scores on the first administration of Form A and use the coefficient of stability as our reliability estimate. The mean ($\bar{X}_{A1}$), standard deviation (s_{A1}), and reliability coefficient (r_{A1A2}) were

$$\bar{X} = 9.95 \qquad s_X = 2.46 \qquad r_{XX} = .90$$

(2) To compute the standard error of measurement (s_m) for this example use Equation (5.10):

$$s_m = s_X \sqrt{1 - r_{XX}}$$

$S_m = 10 \sqrt{1-}$

Substituting the appropriate values into the equation and solving for s_m:

$$s_m = 2.46 \sqrt{1 - .90} = .78$$

(3) Suppose that an individual scored 12 on Form A of the test and we want to know the 95 percent confidence limits for his true score. The limits are

$$X \pm 1.96 s_m$$

and, substituting in the values from the example,

$$12 \pm (1.96)(.78) = 12 \pm 1.53 = 10.47 - 13.53$$

We can say that the true score for an individual with $X = 12$ is between 10.5 and 13.5 points—or, rounded off, between 10 and 14.

---

by more than ± 6 points ($\pm 1.96 s_m$). (Note that this range is the same as that for true scores.) Thus, the standard error of measurement can be used either to estimate the expected change in scores on retesting or the range in which a person's true score falls.

Two further points should be considered when interpreting a standard error of measurement. First, since there are many possible estimates of the reliability of the test, there will also be many possible estimates of s_m. This problem can be alleviated by using the reliability estimate most appropriate for the particular situation of interest. For example, if we are interested in the stability of an individual's score over a six-month period, we would use as the reliability estimate a coefficient of stability computed with a six-month interval between testings. Second, this estimate assumes that s_m is the same at all score levels—that is, that s_m is the same for high scores as for low scores. This is not the case; the standard error of measurement as computed above is an index of the *average* error of measurement throughout the entire score range. If more precise estimates are needed, more complicated procedures are needed (see e.g., Lord, 1957, or Magnusson, 1967).

Test Scores as Best Estimates

The standard error of measurement has a very important function: It forces us to think of test scores as ranges or bands of scores and not as exact points. The obtained score on the test (X) will be the best available estimate of the person's true score (X_T); but, because of measurement error, it is not an exact indicator. How precise an estimate of the true score any given obtained score will be is indicated by the magnitude of s_m and, indirectly, by the reliability of the test. Since

r_{xx} never is 1.00, *test scores must be thought of as ranges, or bands, not as precise points*. The larger the s_m (or the lower the reliability), the more imprecise is our measurement and the wider this range. If we constantly think of scores as ranges, rather than points, we will avoid the habit of overinterpreting small differences between scores.

some special situations

Our discussion has focused on methods for determining the reliability of individual measures. Before we leave the topic of consistency, however, several other practical problems relating to the consistency of measurement need to be considered. These include the problem of determining consistency between scorers or raters; situations where there is more than one score, including ones where scores from several measures are combined and ones where the difference between scores on several measures is of interest; and methods for estimating the reliability of content-referenced tests. Finally, we will look briefly at alternative approaches to consistency.

Scorer and Rater Reliability

Whenever more than one person scores a test, or more than one rater judges a performance, the question of interscorer (or interrater) reliability arises. That is, do the scorers assign the same score to each individual's performance? If they do, there is no problem. However, if the scores vary, error has been introduced into the measurement. In addition, there would also be the question of which score to use. This latter question, however, is usually sidestepped by using the average score or rating assigned.

A variety of methods can be used to obtain a measure of interscorer agreement (Mitchell, 1979). The simplest and most common method is to calculate the percentage of scores (either total scores and/or scores on individual items) that agree.[8] While this method is straightforward and easy to apply it presents two problems. First, will only exact matches be counted as agreements or will scores varying within some range also be counted as agreements? If the latter approach is adopted, scores would be counted as being in agreement if they varied by no more than, say, one point. The second problem is that cases in which the scores assigned vary widely are treated no differently than mild disagreements. Yet they would seem to represent differing degrees of accuracy.

One way to avoid this problem is to use the average disagreement as the index of interscorer agreement. That is, each scorer would score all papers, the difference in scores assigned to each test taker would be obtained, and the mean of these discrepancy scores would be calculated. This value would be the index of interscorer reliability. This approach would be preferred to the first method (percent of agreement) when the range of potential scores is wide, since in this situation exact matches would be uncommon, and consequently the percent agreement index might give a misleading picture of the actual agreement between scorers.

[8] Although we shall discuss interscorer agreement, similar points and methods apply to estimating interrater agreement.

A third possibility is to use the correlation between scorers as the index of reliability. That is, we could calculate the correlation between the scores assigned by two scorers. This approach essentially considers scorers as equivalent forms of a test. Although the correlation indicates whether scorers ranked persons in the same order, it does not indicate whether they assigned the same mean and range of scores. To obtain this information we would have to look at the means, standard deviations, and distributions of scores assigned by each scorer.

The previous discussion assumed that there were only two scorers. However, there are two other possibilities: There could be only one scorer or more than two scorers. When there is only one scorer, we could obtain estimates of scorer reliability using the methods designed for a single administration of the test. For example, we could use a modified version of the split-half technique and compare scores assigned on two comparable halves of the test. When there are more than two scorers, we can apply the techniques used with two scorers to each pair of scorers, then determine the average degree of agreement—for example, the average percent agreement or the average correlation. We could also use Hoyt's method in this situation.

As when determining the reliability of test scores, high scorer agreement can best be obtained by using standardized testing procedures and objective scoring methods. In the case of ratings, the trait or behavior rated should be clearly defined and the rules for assigning scores clearly specified.

Subtest and Composite Scores

Although many tests yield only one score, others provide scores on several subtests. These subtest scores may be combined into a total score or inferences drawn from individual subtest scores. If reliability data are available for each subtest, there is no cause for concern. Too frequently, however, reliability data are available for the composite score but not for subtest scores. Because reliability is dependent on test length, subtest scores will almost certainly be less reliable than the composite score. Thus the test user must always check to see whether reliability estimates are reported for each subtest. If no estimate is reported, she cannot be sure that the subtest possesses acceptable reliability.

The reliability of composite scores generally presents less of a problem. Usually the test manual will give reliability data for any composite scores used. If not, and the reliabilities of the subtests are known, the reliability of the composite scores can easily be computed (see, e.g., Nunnally, 1978, and Stanley, 1971, for formulas). Since composite scores will be based on more observations than the subtest scores, they usually will be more reliable than the subtest scores. One exception is measures of internal consistency. Even if each of several subtests has a high degree of internal consistency, if these subtests are combined, the total (composite) test will be heterogeneous because it will measure several distinct abilities or traits. Thus its internal consistency will be lower than that of the individual subtests.[9]

[9] As internal consistency formulas also consider the number of items in addition to interitem correlations, in practice a relatively high coefficient of internal consistency often is obtained for total scores on long, heterogeneous tests.

Difference and Change Scores

In many circumstances we want to compare an individual's performance on two tests or subtests. For example, an elementary school teacher may want to know whether a student scored higher on the arithmetic or language sections of an achievement battery. Or a counselor may want to compare a student's quantitative and verbal abilities.

Since any score is somewhat unreliable, differences between scores will also be unreliable. The reliability of the difference between two test scores can be estimated by the following formula:

$$r_{j-k} = \frac{r_{jj} + r_{kk} - 2r_{jk}}{2(1 - r_{jk})} \tag{5.11}$$

where r_{j-k} is the reliability of the difference scores $(X_j - X_k)$; r_{jj} and r_{kk} are the reliabilities of tests j and k, respectively; and r_{jk} is the correlation of tests j and k.

Since the reliability of a difference score will be lower than the average subtest reliability, the standard error of measurement will be larger. Also, the range of difference scores generally will be less than the range of scores on either test. Consequently, an apparently large difference in scores may be attributable only to measurement error. Thus, extreme caution must always be used when interpreting differences between scores.

A special case of difference scores that is often encountered in psychology and education is *change scores.* For example, we might measure changes in skills or attitudes as the result of a training program, changes in students' abilities and achievement from year to year, or changes in personality or behavior as the result of psychotherapy. In each case, an appropriate experimental design would be to administer equivalent forms of a test as a pretest and a posttest. The difference (posttest-pretest) would be a change score.

The problems associated with change scores are beyond the scope of this book (see, e.g., Cronbach & Furby, 1970, or Harris, 1963, for a discussion of the issues involved). The major problem is that if the experiences between the tests (e.g., the training program or therapy) have been effective, change scores will reflect both real changes in individuals and the unreliability of the measure. Furthermore, the more effective the treatment, the greater the changes in the scores will be and the less the consistency between pretest and posttest scores. One way to untangle these effects is to establish the equivalence of the pretest and posttest on an independent sample in which the subjects do not receive any intervening treatment. The data obtained will help estimate the amount of difference in scores attributable to measurement errors in the test, as distinct from changes produced by the treatment.

Content-Referenced Tests

The methods of estimating reliability we have discussed were developed for norm-referenced tests, tests constructed to have a relatively wide range of individual differences. However, a recent trend in educational measurement has been the development of content-referenced and mastery tests. These tests, you will recall, specify a particular level of performance as the passing (mastery) level and classify persons into only two groups: masters (those who exceed the mastery level) and nonmasters (those whose scores fall below the passing level).

Since these tests de-emphasize individual differences, and scores are classified into only two groups, the variability of scores is restricted. Thus the traditional methods of determining reliability, which assume high between-individual variance, are not appropriate. This is particularly true when a large proportion of the test takers attain the mastery level, which is the goal in educational programs based on the mastery system.

A number of possible indices for determining the reliability of content-referenced tests have been proposed (see, e.g., Berk, 1980a; Brennan, 1980; Hambleton & Novick, 1973; Huynh, 1976; Livingston, 1972; Millman, 1974). Some are based on agreement in classification. That is, if students took two equivalent forms of a content-referenced test designed to measure mastery of a certain area, would their classification (pass or fail) be the same on both tests? In other words, would the mastery-nonmastery decision be consistent across test forms? Other indices are based on deviations from the passing score or the consistency in estimating domain scores across parallel tests. Sometimes, traditional indices, such as K-R 20, are reported.

The problem is further complicated by the fact that the reliability estimate may vary depending on where the mastery score is set. That is, more reliable scores might be obtained using one passing score rather than another. Although certain methods have potential advantages (Berk, 1980a), the question of what is an appropriate index of reliability for content-referenced tests is an unresolved issue. However, it is an object of intense current study.

Generalizability Theory

An alternative approach to the consistency of measurement, *generalizability theory,* has been proposed by Cronbach and his colleagues (Cronbach, Rajaratnam, & Gleser, 1963; Gleser, Cronbach, & Rajaratnam, 1965; Cronbach et al., 1972). This approach considers any observation (such as a test score) as being but one sample from a universe of possible observations. The conditions under which an observation is obtained can vary along many dimensions; for example, any test is administered at only one of many possible times, is composed of a particular sample of items, is administered by one of many possible administrators, and so forth. The major measurement problems are to determine, first, what effects these various sources of variation have on the specific observation, and second, how accurately the universe score (true score) can be estimated from the observation (obtained score). Because the basic concern is with making inferences about a universe from an observation, the primary problem of consistency is the generalizability of the meaning of an observation.

In their papers, the authors derive formulas and consider experimental designs for various types of studies, both of generalizability (reliability or consistency) and of decision making (validity). Their designs have the important advantages of estimating the magnitude of the various error effects as well as providing generalizability indices. One index, the ratio of the expected universe score variance to the expected observed score variance, is directly related to reliability as it is traditionally defined (r_{xx}). Their approach also emphasizes the fact that there is no one reliability for a test; that is, reliability is situation-specific. It also provides a unifying framework by viewing the varying approaches to reliability as aspects of the problem of generalizability across observations.

summary

To be useful as a measuring instrument a test must measure consistently from time to time, from situation to situation, or across items. The technical term used to describe consistency of measurement is reliability. Reliability can be defined as the ratio of true score variance to observed score variance in a set of test scores or, alternatively, as one minus the proportion of measurement error variance in observed scores. Error is defined as inconsistency in scores from time to time, or across items or clusters of items (alternative test forms).

There are a variety of methods for estimating the reliability of a measure. Which coefficient will be appropriate depends on the purpose of the testing and the sources of error that are of greatest concern. The coefficient of equivalence (also called parallel forms or alternative forms reliability) is the correlation between two forms of a test. The coefficient of stability (test-retest reliability) is the correlation between two administrations of the same measure. The coefficient of equivalence and stability is the correlation between two forms of a test administered at separate points in time. When there is only one form of a test and only one administration, the split-half reliability coefficient is used.

Measures of internal consistency (homogeneity) are based on the intercorrelations between items comprising a test. The usual indices are coefficient alpha and Kuder-Richardson formula 20. These coefficients indicate whether all items on a test measure the same trait or characteristic.

A number of factors can influence the magnitude of an obtained reliability coefficient. Longer tests are generally more reliable than shorter tests; the more heterogeneous the sample tested, the higher the reliability coefficient; reliability will be reduced if a test is too easy or too difficult; and reliability estimates based on one administration of a test are inappropriate for speeded tests. We also noted that change and difference scores tend to be quite unreliable, that methods for determining the reliability of test scores can also be applied to the measurement of interscorer and interrater agreement, and that there is no agreement on methods for estimating the reliability of content-referenced tests.

Reliability coefficients can be interpreted in various ways. One is in terms of the proportions of true and error variance. For example, if the reliability of a test was .85, then 85 percent of the differences in observed scores would represent true score differences and 15 percent would represent errors of measurement. Another is in terms of the correlation between two measures. For example, the coefficient of equivalence is the correlation between two parallel forms of a test, and coefficient alpha is the expected correlation between a test and any other test of the same length drawn from the same domain. A third method, the standard error of measurement, indicates the amount of error in individual scores. It can be used to estimate the range in which a person's true score will fall or the expected change in scores on retesting.

To obtain optimal levels of reliability, the test items should be clear and unambiguous, the test should be administered under standardized conditions, and enough items should be used to ensure consistent results.

Suggestions for Further Reading

Allen, M. J., & Yen, W. M. *Introduction to measurement theory.* Monterey, Calif.: Brooks/Cole, 1979. Chapter 3 presents the statistical basis of classical test theory; Chapter 4 describes the various methods of determining reliability.

Cronbach, L. J. *Essentials of psychological testing,* 3d ed. New York: Harper & Row, 1970. Chapter 6 is a somewhat rambling discussion but contains many valuable insights into reliability; for example, it stresses balancing the need to obtain accurate information on one trait with the need to obtain a broad range of information about an individual.

Dudek, F. J. The continuing misinterpretation of the standard error of measurement. *Psychological*

Bulletin, 1979, *86,* 335–337. Differentiates between procedures for setting confidence limits around true scores and around obtained scores.

Ghiselli, E. E., Campbell, J. P., & Zedeck, S. *Measurement theory for the behavioral sciences.* San Francisco: Freeman, 1981. Chapters 8 and 9 present a more complex and comprehensive, though still readable, discussion of the topics presented in this chapter.

Goldberg, L. R. The reliability of reliability: The generality and correlates of intra-individual consistency in responses to structured personality inventories. *Applied Psychological Measurement,* 1978, *2,* 269–291. A study of the various types of reliability evidence derived from widely used personality inventories; focuses on factors responsible for inconsistencies between and within individual scales.

Kerlinger, F. N. *Foundations of behavioral research,* 2d ed. New York: Holt, Rinehart and Winston, 1973. Chapter 26 is an excellent, brief introduction to the topic of reliability.

Mitchell, S. K. Interobserver agreement, reliability, and generalizability of data collected in observational studies. *Psychological Bulletin,* 1979, *86,* 376–390. A description and evaluation of methods used to determine the reliability of observational data.

Standards for educational and psychological tests. Washington, D.C.: American Psychological Association, 1974. Section F (pp. 48–55) gives standards and guidelines for information about reliability to be included in test manuals; all test users should be familiar with this source.

Stanley, J. C. Reliability. In R. L. Thorndike (Ed.), *Educational measurement,* 2d ed. Washington, D.C.: American Council on Education, 1971. A detailed, technical discussion of reliability theory and the methods for obtaining reliability evidence.

Thorndike, R. L. Reliability. In E. F. Lindquist (Ed.), *Educational measurement.* Washington, D.C.: American Council on Education, 1951. A relatively nontechnical discussion of reliability with emphasis on the variety of factors that can influence test reliability.

Chapter 6 • Criterion-Related Validity

VALIDATING a test involves determining what domain or characteristic the test measures and/or what outcomes it predicts. If we do not know what a test measures, we cannot interpret individual scores or use the test as a measure of a theoretical construct. Thus validity is the most important property of a test.

Although there are numerous types of validity, all can be categorized into three classes. Content validity studies determine whether the test items representatively sample the domain of interest; thus they are appropriate when a test serves as sample. Construct validity studies provide evidence as to the nature of the trait or characteristics measured; thus they are appropriate when defining constructs or when a test is used as a sign. Criterion-related validity studies investigate how well test scores correlate with some external behavior; thus they are appropriate when using a test as a predictor. In this chapter we shall discuss criterion-related validity; content and construct validity will be covered in the next chapter.

the validation process

One use of tests is to predict future behavior. For example, scholastic aptitude tests are used to predict success in college and professional schools, aptitude and ability tests are used to predict job performance, and personality inventories have been used to predict who will have automobile accidents. In each of these situations the function of the test is to predict an individual's performance in some qualitatively different situation. The performance being predicted is called the criterion, hence the designation criterion-related validity.

Although we sometimes make a prediction to test a theoretical hypothesis, more often we are using the test to help make some practical decision. In our previous examples the decisions would be which students to admit, whom to hire, and what insurance premium rate to assess. In each situation, the more accurately we can predict the outcome (criterion), the more useful the test will be.

There are three audiences for criterion-related validity data, each of which has a somewhat different interest. The test developer is interested in the data because they provide evidence about the quality of the test and its potential uses. The test user is interested in the data because it indicates how useful the test will be in making practical decisions. Test takers also have an interest in the process because the test results will be the basis of decisions affecting their lives. Note, too, that test takers and test users generally are interested in the validity of the test in a specific situation, whereas the test developer is interested in the test's validity in a variety of situations.

The Paradigm

The general paradigm for investigating criterion-related validity involves establishing the relationship between scores on the test and the criterion:

$$\text{TEST} \longrightarrow \text{CRITERION}$$

Because the test predicts the criterion, criterion-related validity is sometimes referred to as predictive validity. And, since determining criterion-related validity always involves collection of empirical data on the relationship between test scores and the criterion measure, some writers refer to it as empirical validity.

The designation criterion-related validity emphasizes the fact that the fundamental concern is with criterion performance. We are interested in the test scores because they predict some important external behavior. Thus the content of the test is of secondary importance, and the test items need bear no obvious relation to the criterion. What is vital is that the test scores can, in fact, predict criterion performance.

A distinction can be made between two types of criterion-related validity: predictive validity and concurrent validity. *Predictive validity* refers to situations in which the criterion data are collected at some future time. Thus, when college admissions tests administered in high school are used to predict college grades, or an employment test is used to predict job tenure, we are interested in predictive validity.

In *concurrent validity* studies, however, the test scores and criterion data are collected at the same point in time. Here the purpose is to determine whether test scores can be substituted for actually collecting the criterion data. For example, can scores on a personality inventory, administered by a clerk, be used in place of an examination by a psychiatrist to determine the degree of psychopathology? Obviously such a substitution would be valuable only if (1) there was a high degree of relationship between the test scores and the criterion measure (in our example, between a diagnosis made from the test and a psychiatrist's diagnosis) and if (2) use of the test is more efficient, or less expensive, than actually collecting the criterion data. Hence, concurrent validity is different from predictive validity in that it involves a substitution of the test for the criterion rather than a prediction of a criterion from the test.

Criterion-Related Validity and Decision Making

Implicit in the concept of criterion-related validity is the idea that tests are used as part of a decision-making process. When a scholastic aptitude test is used to predict college grades, the decision is whether to admit the prospective student; when a test is administered to a job applicant, the decision is whether he or she should be hired. In each situation there is a decision to be made, one that will be influenced by the individual's test score. The test will be valid to the degree that it improves the effectiveness of the decision making.

There are several aspects of the decision-making situation that merit specific attention. First, a decision must be made regarding the treatment of individuals. If every individual received the same treatment (for example, if all students were allowed to enter college or all applicants were hired), there would be no need for testing. Only when a decision must be made can a test provide any useful information.

Second, the relative influence of test scores, as opposed to other sources of information used in determining the course of action, may vary widely between situations. In some situations, decisions may be made solely on the basis of test scores; in others, test scores may be one of several variables used; in yet others, test scores may be used only when a decision cannot be reached using other data. In every case, however, the relative weight given to test scores (and other sources of information) should be determined empirically. This weight should be based on the proportional contribution test scores make to decision-making accuracy. The point of view taken in this book is that *the proper measure of a test's criterion-related validity is its contribution to predictive or decision-making accuracy*.

Third, in each situation there is some outcome (the criterion), specified or implicit, that is regarded as the "desirable" outcome. The goal of the decision-making process is to select or assign individuals so as to maximize performance on this criterion. Because the validity of a test is judged by its relationship to the criterion, if the criterion measure does not adequately reflect the desired outcome, the decision-making process will be less effective. However, this decreased effectiveness will be attributable to deficiencies in the criteria, not in the test. For example, consider the use of grades as a criterion of success in college. If a test predicted grades accurately, it would increase the proportion of students admitted who would obtain high grades. The test would not select students with other desired characteristics, unless these characteristics were correlated with grade-getting ability.

Fourth, strictly speaking we validate inferences made from test scores, not the test scores per se; that is, test scores are used to make an inference about performance on the criterion measure. For example, we might infer that people who score high on a mechanical aptitude test will perform well in an auto mechanics course. The validation study checks on the accuracy of these inferences.

Fifth, validity data obtained on one sample usually will be used to make predictions about people who are not members of that particular sample. For example, after we have validated a selection test on one pool of job applicants, the information will be used when selecting among future applicants. Thus, the data will be most useful when the validation sample is similar to future groups who will take the test.

Finally, validity is always determined for a group of test takers. Thus, logically, statements about the validity of a test always refer to a set of scores, not to individual scores. Although inferences can be made about individuals, based on their test scores, errors in individual predictions may be quite large. However, inferences regarding the effectiveness of a test as applied to groups of individuals often can be made with reasonable accuracy. For example, whereas a test may not be able to predict with much accuracy whether Jane will be a better worker than

Janis, if applied to large numbers of job applicants it may result in a significant increase in the number of good workers hired.

Criteria

If a test is designed to predict performance in an area, some standard or measure of performance must be identified; this is the criterion. For instance, what is the criterion of success as a college student? The most common approach is to use grade point average; but grades are only one, and not necessarily the best, criterion of academic success. Other criteria are also possible, such as amount learned (which is not necessarily the same as the amount known at the end of a given course), ability to apply what one has learned, ability to evaluate knowledge critically, ability to learn by oneself, or development of positive attitudes toward education and learning.

Thus talking about *the* criterion is an oversimplification, as several writers have pointed out (see, e.g., Dunnette, 1963; Ghiselli, 1956; Weitz, 1961). In most situations multiple criteria are desirable. Choosing one criterion is simpler, but it neglects much valuable information. How to combine several criteria, however, is a knotty problem. If the various criteria are highly related, using a combination of criteria will not improve decision making greatly since all criteria are measuring essentially the same behavior. Conversely, if the various criteria are not inter-related, combining them may produce a hodgepodge since they measure different things.

Ghiselli (1956) has also pointed out two other problems besides the problem of combining criteria. One revolves around the fact that criteria may change over time. What is a good measure of success at the present time may not be a good measure at some future time. For example, to succeed as a physician a person must be able to master formal course work; later her success is judged by her effectiveness in treating patients. The other problem relates to individual differences. Two persons may perform the same job in quite different ways, yet be rated as equally successful. For example, one football receiver may get free by utilizing his speed, another by deceptive moves. Or one student may get high grades because he grasps material easily, whereas another succeeds only through long hours of studying.

A major problem in test validation is failing to appreciate the fact that there is no such thing as *the* criterion. This implies that the validation process should relate test scores to a variety of criteria in a variety of situations. The caveat to the test user, therefore, is to consider carefully the criterion measures used in validating a test and to be aware of the limitations that use of these particular criteria impose on the interpretation of the test scores.

Types of Criterion Measures. In discussing criteria we must distinguish between a criterion and a criterion measure (Astin, 1964). A criterion is the global concept of successful performance, what Astin calls the *conceptual criterion*. But, as in all measurement, this conceptual concept must be identified by an operational measure. Thus, the conceptual criterion might be success in college, the criterion measure grade point average; the conceptual criterion success as a salesman, the criterion measure dollar volume of sales. In short, even an ideal conceptual criterion will be useless unless an adequate measure of the criterion behavior is available.

A wide variety of variables can be used as criterion measures. The most obvious are direct measures of output, performance, or persistence. In industrial and business settings, volume of sales, production, salary, advancement, number of customers serviced, or tenure on the job may be used. In academic settings, the criterion measure might be grades, level of education attained, or graduation from a program. In other situations, the criterion measure may be performance on a test. Examples include course examinations, tests given at the end of training programs, and tests to certify competency in certain professions (for example, CPA exams and tests in medical specialties). Where objective measures of output or performance are unavailable or inappropriate, ratings by supervisors or peers are often used as criterion measures. In other situations the criterion measure might be membership in a defined group. For example, intelligence tests frequently use an age differentiation criterion; that is, items are considered valid if the proportion of children passing the item increases with age. Interest inventories are considered valid if they differentiate between persons in various occupations; personality tests if they differentiate between people with various syndromes; aptitude tests if they differentiate between successful and unsuccessful workers.

Characteristics of a Good Criterion Measure. Although criterion measures can be of many types, certain characteristics are desired in any criterion measure. The most important characteristic of a criterion measure is its *relevance*. A criterion measure must actually reflect the important facets of the conceptual criterion. Thus grade point average will be a relevant measure of college success only if the characteristics considered indications of college success are reflected in the student's grade point average. Or, output will be a relevant criterion measure of job performance only if it directly reflects the individual's skill rather than some characteristic of the work situation.

A criterion measure also should be *reliable*. The reason is obvious; if criterion performance varies from time to time or situation to situation, it cannot consistently relate to other measures, including predictors. Criterion reliability can often be increased by obtaining a larger sample of behavior and/or sampling over several occasions.

A third requirement is *freedom from bias*. This problem is particularly crucial when the criterion measure is a rating. If a rater assigns a criterion score on bases other than actual performance, such as his general opinion of the worker, the criterion score will be biased. (See Chapter 17 for a further discussion of ratings.)

A common source of bias is criterion contamination. *Criterion contamination* refers to the situation in which a person's criterion score is influenced by a rater's knowledge of his predictor score. Suppose that we want to determine whether an intelligence test predicts English grades. If the teacher assigning the grades knows the students' IQs, her evaluation of students may be influenced by this knowledge. For example, a student may receive a lower grade because the teacher thinks, on the basis of his IQ, that he should have done better and thus should be reprimanded by a lower grade. Criterion contamination can be avoided by not allowing the person making the criterion rating to see the predictor scores. Predictor scores can be collected and filed, criterion ratings collected, then related to the criterion. This procedure would ensure independence of predictor and criterion scores.

Finally, other things being equal, the best criterion measure is the one that has the most *practical advantages*—that is, one that is the simplest to use, and is readily available and inexpensive. It should be emphasized, however, that this is generally the least important consideration; relevance, reliability, and freedom from bias are more crucial determiners of the adequacy of a criterion measure.

Indices of Criterion-Related Validity

There are various possible indices and methods for assessing criterion-related validity. All provide a quantitative index of the degree of relationship between test and criterion scores.

Our discussion will focus on two types of indices, validity coefficients and indices of selection efficiency. *Validity coefficients,* which are the most common indices of criterion-related validity, are nothing more than the correlation between test and criterion scores. Indices of *selection efficiency* or *decision-making accuracy,* as the label implies, indicate how many correct decisions will be made using the test as a predictor. We shall also consider two other indices that may be used in certain situations: group separation indices and utility measures.

When first presenting the various techniques we shall use a selection situation with one predictor and one criterion measure as an illustration. Although this is a somewhat simplified and perhaps unrealistic situation, it should help to clarify the basic logic of the various procedures.[1]

validity coefficients

The most frequently used method for establishing criterion-related validity is to correlate test scores (X) with criterion scores (Y). In a concurrent validity study the process involves four steps: selecting an appropriate group to study, administering the predictor test, collecting the criterion data, and correlating the test and criterion scores. The resultant correlation, the validity coefficient (r_{xy}), is an index of how accurately criterion performance can be predicted from test scores.

Predictive validity studies involve a similar process except that a period of time intervenes between collecting the test and criterion scores. In addition, some relevant treatment usually occurs during this time period. For example, when we predict success in a training program, the treatment is the training program; when we predict outcomes of therapy, the treatment is the therapeutic process. Again, the validity index is the correlation between test and criterion scores.

Since a validity coefficient is a correlation coefficient, any factor or variable that influences a correlation coefficient can also affect the magnitude of a validity coef-

---

[1] Multiple prediction will be discussed later in the chapter.

ficient. Two are particularly relevant. One is the form of relationship between predictor and criterion scores. Since Pearson's *r* assumes a linear relationship, if the predictor and criterion scores are not linearly related the validity coefficient will underestimate the degree of relationship. In this case, nonlinear correlational methods will better estimate the degree of relationship.

Second, the magnitude of a correlation depends on the range of individual differences—that is, the variance of the predictor and criterion scores. Any factor that restricts the range of predictor or criterion scores will limit the size of the validity coefficient. One situation where this becomes important is when conducting validity studies on preselected groups. Suppose that scores on the Graduate Record Examination (GRE) are used as one basis for selecting students for graduate work in psychology. If we correlate GRE scores with graduate grades, the validity will be lower than in an unselected sample because the range of GRE scores has been restricted. Restriction of range also becomes important when not all people complete a treatment. For example, if we predict job success using only workers who have been employed for at least a year, many of the workers who could not perform the job adequately would have already left or been fired. Again our validity coefficient would be limited by this restriction in range—in this case restriction of criterion scores.

An Example

Suppose that a high school mathematics teacher finds that some of his students have trouble in first-year algebra. He would like to identify these students so that they could take a different math course. He decides to run a study to see whether he can differentiate between students who experience varying degrees of success in algebra. Because he thinks that sudents who have trouble in algebra lack the ability to reason mathematically, he develops a short (eight-item) test of mathematical reasoning, which he administers to all students the first day of class. He does not score the tests, but files them away for further use. At the end of the term, after grades have been assigned, he scores the tests. He decides to compute a validity coefficient to see whether the test is a valid predictor.

The relation between test scores and algebra grades is shown in Table 6.1 (step 1). Scores on the math reasoning test serve as the predictor; the criterion is algebra grades. For his analysis, he assigns a numerical value to each grade (from 4 for an A to 0 for an F). He then computes the necessary summary statistics (step 2) and the validity coefficient (step 3). He finds a value of .60 for his validity coefficient. Since the correlation is positive and moderately high, his belief that mathematical reasoning ability may be an important determiner of grades in algebra is confirmed.

Interpretation of Validity Coefficients

There are several ways of interpreting validity coefficients. As a validity coefficient is an index of the degree of relationship between predictor and criterion scores, the higher the correlation the more accurately scores on the criterion can be predicted from test scores. Thus, for example, if in a given situation the validity

Table 6.1
Calculation of a Validity Coefficient

(1) A high school math teacher wants to determine whether scores on a short mathematical reasoning test predict grades in algebra (see text). The distribution of scores is:

		1	2	3	4	5	6	7	8
Algebra	A					2	8	7	7
Grade	B			1	3	14	20	8	2
(Y)	C	4	8	26	42	29	9	2	
	D	8	11	8	6	3			
	F	8	1	1	1	1			

Mathematical Reasoning Test (X)

(2) Coding grades on a five-point scale ($A = 4, B = 3$, etc.), the summary statistics for these data are:

$$\overline{X} = 4.30 \quad s_X = 1.79 \quad \overline{Y} = 2.15 \quad s_Y = 1.22 \quad \Sigma XY = 2534 \quad n = 240$$

(3) The validity coefficient will be the correlation between the scores on the mathematics reasoning test and the algebra grades. Using Equation (3.9b):

$$r_{XY} = \frac{\Sigma XY/n - (\overline{X})(\overline{Y})}{s_X s_Y} = \frac{2534/240 - (4.30)(2.15)}{(1.79)(1.22)} = 0.60$$

(4) The value $r_{XY} = .60$ is the validity coefficient. One interpretation is that 36 percent (that is, $r^2 = 60^2 = .36$) of the differences in algebra grades are predictable from scores on the math reasoning test.

---

coefficient was .40 for Test A and .50 for Test B, we would use Test B because it predicts the criterion more accurately.

Validity coefficients can also be interpreted in terms of percent of variance in the criterion accounted for by differences in predictor scores. The percent of variance accounted for is obtained by squaring the correlation coefficient. Thus, if $r_{XY} = .60$, as in our example, we can say that 36 percent of the variance (that is, $.60^2 = .36 = 36$ percent) is shared by the two measures, or that 36 percent of the variance in criterion scores is attributable to variations in predictor scores. (Note that r_{XY} must be .71 if half of the variance in the criterion is to be accounted for by predictor scores.) The squared correlation coefficient (r^2) is called the *coefficient of determination*.

A more concrete interpretation of the meaning of a validity coefficient has been provided by Brogden (1946, 1949). Suppose we have 40 positions, 100 workers, and predictor and criterion scores on all 100 workers. We could calculate the average criterion scores of three different groups of 40 workers: the 40 best workers (the 40 with the highest criterion scores), the 40 having the highest test scores (the 40 with the highest predicted criterion scores), and 40 workers selected at random. Ideally, of course, we would select the first group, those with the highest criterion scores. At the time of hiring, however, we do not know the criterion scores, only the test scores. The question then becomes: What does the validity coefficient tell us about the criterion performance of those workers selected by the test?

Brogden showed that the productivity of this group (as compared to the ideal group) is proportional to the validity coefficient. That is, if we consider the means of the three groups:

$$r_{xy} = \frac{\text{(Test-selected)} - \text{(Random)}}{\text{(Criterion-selected)} - \text{(Random)}}$$

200 − 100

To be even more concrete, suppose that the criterion-selected group produces an average of 200 widgets an hour and the randomly selected group produces an average of 100 widgets an hour. If the validity coefficient was .50, the test-selected group would be expected to produce an average of 150 widgets per hour.[2]

A fourth method involves prediction errors. Before discussing prediction errors, we must first consider how to predict criterion scores.

Predicted Criterion Scores and Prediction Errors

One advantage of the correlational approach is that knowing an individual's test score and the validity coefficient, a prediction of his or her expected criterion score can be made. The procedure is based on the fact that the relationship summarized by a validity coefficient can also be described by a straight line, called a *regression line,* that best fits the data points. Such a line can be described by a *regression equation* of the form:

non standards scores require a

$$Y' = a + b_{YX}X \quad \text{actual score}$$

(6.1)

where Y' is the predicted criterion score; a is an intercept constant, to correct for differences in the means; b_{YX} is the slope, or regression constant, which indicates the rate of change in Y as a function of changes in X; and X is the score on the predictor. An example is given in Table 6.2.

if standard scores, forget a.

What is predicted (Y') is the average criterion score made by persons with the same predictor score (X). The actual criterion scores of people with the same predictor score will vary; some people will obtain criterion scores higher than the average, and some lower. The discrepancy between actual and predicted criterion scores will be prediction error. Unless $r_{XY} = 1.00$, there will be some error in each prediction.

The magnitude of the prediction errors is indicated by the *standard error of estimate* (s_{est}):

refers to validity

$$s_{est} = s_y\sqrt{1 - r_{XY}^2}$$

(6.4)

The standard error of estimate is the standard deviation of the distribution of prediction errors. If we have both predicted (Y') and actual (Y) criterion scores, we can obtain a measure of prediction error from the difference between these scores $(E = Y - Y')$. If we then plot the distribution of these error scores for all individuals in the group, the standard deviation of the resulting distribution will be the standard error of estimate.

The standard error of estimate can be interpreted like any other standard deviation. The probability is .68 that the actual criterion score will fall within $\pm 1s_{est}$

[2] When $r_{xy} = .50$, the equation would be $.50 = (X - 100)/(200 - 100)$ and X would be 150, the average number of widgets produced per hour by the test-selected group.

of the predicted criterion score and .95 that the actual criterion score will fall within $\pm 1.96s_{est}$ of the predicted criterion score. An example is presented in step 4 of Table 6.2.

Advantages and Limitations

The correlational approach to validity has several advantages. The validity coefficient summarizes the relationship between the predictor and criterion over the entire range of scores. An expected criterion score for each individual can be computed using the regression equation. Validity coefficients are also widely used, thus providing comparability between studies. Moreover, most of the analyses involving multiple scores are based on the correlational model.

Validity coefficients also have some limitations. If the predictor-criterion relationship is not linear, the degree of relationship will be underestimated unless special correlational methods are used. A more important limitation is that validity coefficients do not directly provide the type of information many test users want. In practical situations, test users may want to know how many correct decisions will be made or how much criterion performance will be improved by using the test. Validity coefficients do not provide this information (Brogden's procedure is an exception). Furthermore, as we shall see later, the meaning of a validity coefficient will vary with the proportion of people selected and the proportion judged successful. Thus, in many situations, other indices will provide more useful information.

decision-making accuracy

In many situations, tests are used as aids in making practical decisions. In selection, the decision is which applicants to select and which to reject. In placement, the decision is which alternative treatment or program to assign to each individual. In diagnosis, the decision is which diagnostic category to assign. In each of these situations, the goal is to maximize the number of correct decisions and minimize the number of incorrect decisions. Thus an obvious index of the effectiveness of the decision-making process is the proportion of correct decisions made. When decisions are made on the basis of test scores, the most valid test will be the one that results in the highest proportion of correct decisions.

In this section we shall discuss validity indices based on the proportion of correct decisions made. We shall again use the selection situation as an example, although the procedures can be generalized to other types of problems, such as placement. We shall discuss two indices: the *total hit ratio*, which considers all decisions, and the *positive hit ratio*, which considers only selected applicants. Both are indices of decision-making accuracy or, when applied to the selection situation, indices of selection efficiency.

Indices of Decision-Making Accuracy

To derive an index of decision-making accuracy we must classify test scores into two or more independent categories, similarly classify the criterion data, and then compare the two sets of data. The division of criterion scores will be in terms of

Table 6.2
Predicted Criterion Scores and Prediction Errors

(1) To derive a regression equation, we first must determine the values of the two constants. Using raw scores, these formulas are:

[handwritten: st. Dev. of y]

$$b_{YX} = \frac{r_{XY}s_Y}{s_X},$$ (6.2)

[handwritten: st. Dev. of x.]

and

$$a = \bar{Y} - b_{YX}\bar{X}$$ (6.3)

[handwritten: constant that correct scales.]

(2) We shall use as an example the data from Table 6.1:

$$\bar{X} = 4.30 \quad s_X = 1.79 \quad \bar{Y} = 2.15 \quad s_Y = 1.22 \quad r_{XY} = 0.60$$

Substituting these values in the equations and solving, we obtain:

[handwritten: slope or regression constant] $b_{YX} = .60(1.22/1.79) = 0.41$

$$a = 2.15 - (4.30)(.41) = 0.39$$

(3) Substituting these values into the regression equation, we find that:

$$Y' = 0.39 + 0.41X$$

This equation can be used to obtain a predicted criterion score (Y') for any predictor score. For example, suppose that a student scores 6 on the math reasoning test. His expected algebra grade would be:

$$Y' = 0.39 + 0.41(6) = 2.85$$ *[handwritten: predicted criterion score for that subject with score of 6.]*

or, most probably, a B grade.

(4) For prediction errors we apply Equation (6.4) for the standard error of estimate, and obtain:

$$s_{est} = s_Y\sqrt{1 - r_{XY}^2} = 1.22\sqrt{1 - .60^2} = 0.98$$

That is, the standard error of estimate is 0.98 points. We know that a person scoring 6 on the test has a predicted algebra grade of 2.85 (see step 3 above). The 95 percent confidence limits around this predicted score are as follows:

$$Y' \pm 1.96s_{est} = 2.85 \pm 1.96(.98) = 0.91 - 4.79$$

Thus, although our best estimate of his grade is 2.85 (a B), because our prediction is not perfect, the 95 percent confidence limits will extend over a broad range—from 0.91 to 4.79 or from an A to a D.* In fact, about all that we can say, using these confidence limits, is that it is very improbable that he will fail the course.

---

*In this example, as sometimes happens in practice, the theoretical confidence limits exceed the range of possible scores.

performance—for example, success or failure, acceptable or unacceptable. The division of test scores will be in terms of score levels. Actually, our classification of test scores is in terms of predicted outcomes—for example, predict success versus predict failure—or in terms of the decision to be made—hire or not hire, admit or reject. Thus we will be comparing a predicted outcome to the actual outcome.

In the simplest case, where both predictor and criterion data are dichotomized, there will be four groups: persons predicted to be successful who were successful, persons predicted to be successful who were unsuccessful, persons predicted to be unsuccessful who were successful, and persons predicted to be unsuccessful who were unsuccessful. In diagrammatic form:

Test Prediction	Criterion Performance Failure ($-$)	Success ($+$)
Success ($+$)	(A) MISS	(B) HIT
Failure ($-$)	(C) HIT	(D) MISS

We shall call correct decisions (predictions) hits and incorrect ones misses.

One obvious index would be the proportion of all decisions that were correct. We shall call this the *total hit ratio* (P_{CT} or proportion correct-total). This index is the ratio of correct decisions (hits) to total decisions:

$$P_{CT} = \frac{\text{Hits}}{\text{Hits} + \text{Misses}} = \frac{B + C}{A + B + C + D} \qquad (6.5)$$

where A, B, C, and D are the number of people in the cells of the decision table.

Two aspects of this index deserve special note. First, the index takes into account all decisions made. Second, both correct and incorrect decisions are weighted equally. Note, however, that differential weighting of categories could be handled by assigning different values (weights) to correct and incorrect decisions.

In some situations another index of accuracy may be more appropriate. For example, an employer typically is concerned only with the success or failure of applicants he hires and not with the fate of persons he does not hire. A college admissions officer, too, is more concerned with the potential success of students who are admitted than of those students not admitted. In these situations, a more appropriate index of decision-making effectiveness will be the *positive hit ratio* (P_{CP} or proportion correct-positive); the proportion of those selected who will be successful:

$$P_{CP} = \frac{B}{A + B} = \frac{\text{Number successful}}{\text{Number selected}} \qquad (6.6)$$

This is the appropriate validity index when the goal of the selection procedure is to maximize the proportion of people selected who will be successful. Although it is recognized that incorrect decisions will be made by not accepting some people who would have been successful, this category of decisions is considered less important and given no weight in the computation of this index.

An Example

As an example, consider the problem used to illustrate validity coefficients. The problem, you will remember, was to predict performance in algebra from scores on a math reasoning test. If we consider a grade of A, B, or C in the algebra course to represent successful performance, and grades of D and F to represent unsuccessful performance, the data would be:

Predictor (Test) Score	Criterion Performance (Algebra Grade)		
	Successful	Unsuccessful	Total
8	9	0	9
7	17	0	17
6	37	0	37
5	45	4	49
4	45	7	52
3	27	9	36
2	8	12	20
1	4	16	20
Total	192	48	240

The table shows, for example, that of the 49 students who obtained a score of 5 on the test, 45 were successful (obtained a grade of A, B, or C) and 4 were unsuccessful (obtained a D or F grade).

Suppose we use a score of 5 as the *cutting score*; that is , we allow only those students scoring 5 or higher on the test to take algebra. This is the same as predicting that students with scores of 5 or above will be successful in algebra and those with scores below 5 will be unsuccessful. Using this cutting score, the decision will be as follows:

Test Prediction	Criterion Performance	
	Successful	Unsuccessful
Successful	108	4
Unsuccessful	84	44

We can now compute the two indices of decision-making accuracy. The total hit ratio will be:

$$P_{CT} = \frac{108 + 44}{240} = \frac{152}{240} = .63$$

In other words, 63% of the decisions would be correct. The positive hit ratio would be:

$$P_{CP} = \frac{108}{112} = .96$$

or, 96 percent of those accepted (those with scores of 5 or above) will be successful.

Although we have computed the two indices, we have left an important question unanswered: Does the use of the test increase decision-making accuracy? In order to answer this question we must consider another statistic, the base rate.

Base Rates

We have previously stated that the most valid test was the one whose use resulted in the most correct decisions. However, a test that makes a large number of correct decisions, or has a high validity coefficient, still may not be a useful instrument. To understand why this is so requires consideration of another parameter, base rates. The *base rate* may be defined as the rate of occurrence of a phenomenon in an unselected population. In the selection situation, the base rate would be the proportion of people in an unselected group who would be successful. ✓ Actually, all groups probably are selected in some way, formally or informally, or by self-selection. Thus, in validity studies, the base rates more appropriately refer to the rate of occurrence of the phenomenon in the group selected by present procedures.

To be of use a test must improve on the base rates; that is, more correct decisions must be made using the test than on the basis of the base rate alone. To illustrate, in our example 192 of the 240 students successfully completed algebra (received a grade of A, B, or C). Thus .80 (that is, 192/240) is the base rate for successful performance in this situation. Note, however, when using a cutting score of 5, only 63 percent of the decisions were correct. Thus, using this cutting score would result in poorer decision making than going with the base rate and admitting everyone. However, it is possible that use of another cutting score would result in an improvement in decision making accuracy. We shall consider that possibility in the next section.

base gives something to compare values to

Determining the Optimal Cutting Score

The optimal cutting score is the score that, when used as the minimal acceptable predictor score, results in the highest proportion of correct decisions. To determine this score we prepare a selection efficiency table (Table 6.3). The first four columns in this table list the various combinations of predicted and actual criterion scores for each test score level. For example, for a cutting score of 5, the table shows that 108 students had test scores of 5 or higher and were successful in algebra (had A, B, or C grades), 4 had scores of 5 or higher but were unsuccessful (obtained D or F grades), 84 had scores of 4 or lower but were successful, and 44 had scores of 4 or lower and were unsuccessful.

The next two columns are used to calculate the total hit ratio. The first gives the number of correct decisions. Thus, for a score of 5, there were 152 correct decisions (the 108 students predicted to succeed who did plus the 44 predicted to be unsuccessful who were unsuccessful). Dividing 152 by the total number of students (240) gives .63, the total hit ratio. When we do this for every possible cutting score, we find that the proportion of correct decisions ranges from .24 to .87 and that the optimal cutting score is 3. Using this cutting score would produce a 7 percent improvement over the use of the base rate.

When there is a positive correlation between predictor and criterion scores, the cutting score that maximizes total correct decisions will be in the middle of the distribution, not at the extremes. If the cutting score is set too high, a number of people who would be successful will be rejected; if it is set too low, a number

Table 6.3
Determining the Optimal Cutting Score

The table below can be used to determine the optimal cutting score. It also indicates the number of correct decisions made and the selection ratio at each cutting score. See text for explanation.

Cutting Score	Predict ABC		Predict DF		TOTAL HITS		POSITIVE HITS			
	ABC*	DF	ABC	DF	No.	P_{CT}	No. Sel.	No. Suc.	P_{CP}	SR
8	9	0	183	48	57	.24	9	9	1.00	.04
7	26	0	166	48	74	.31	26	26	1.00	.11
6	63	0	129	48	111	.46	63	63	1.00	.26
5	108	4	84	44	152	.63	112	108	.96	.47
4	153	11	39	37	190	.79	164	153	.93	.68
3	180	20	12	28	208	.87	200	180	.90	.83
2	188	32	4	16	204	.85	220	188	.85	.92
1	192	48	0	0	192	.80	240	192	.80	1.00

*Actual criterion performance
No. Sel. = Number selected
No. Suc. = Number successful (grades of A, B, or C)
SR = Selection ratio

of people who would be unsuccessful will be selected. In the middle ranges, these two types of errors are counterbalanced. Exactly where the optimal cutting score will fall depends on the distribution of test and criterion scores and the correlation between the two sets of scores.

The next three columns are used to calculate the positive hit ratio. The first column indicates the number of people who would be selected using a particular cutting score. Thus, when the cutting score is 5, we would select 112 students, since there are 112 students with scores of 5 or above. The next column indicates the number of these students who were rated as successful. The positive hit ratio is determined by dividing the second column by the first. In our example, the positive hit ratio for a score of 5 is .96 (that is, 108/112). In other words, 96 percent of the students scoring 5 or above on the test would be expected to receive A, B, or C grades in algebra.

When the goal is to maximize positive hits, only one type of decision error is of concern: people predicted to be successful who will not be successful. By setting a high cutting score, we would minimize this type of error. However, we would admit only a small proportion of the students. Thus another statistic becomes important, the selection ratio. The *selection ratio* (shown in the last column) is the proportion of persons who would be selected using each cutting score.[3] If we used a cutting score of 5, we would only admit 47 percent (152/240) of the applicants to the class.

As in any validation study of a decision-making process, statistics computed on one sample would be applied on future samples. In our example, data obtained from one year's class would be used to decide which students to admit to algebra in future years. Note, too, in our example, that all decisions were weighted

[3] In other words, the selection ratio is the proportion of applicants selected—that is, the number selected divided by the total number of applicants.

equally. If desired, the various outcomes could be weighted differentially. For example, if it was considered a more serious error to reject a student who might succeed than to admit a student who later failed, the various errors could be weighted to reflect this emphasis.

Advantages and Limitations

The main advantage of the decision-making accuracy (selection efficiency) approach is that it closely parallels the "real-life" situation. Although a validity coefficient provides an index of the relationship between predictor and criterion scores throughout the entire score range, the decision-making accuracy approach is concerned with effectiveness at a specific decision point. Thus the model is a closer representation of "reality" than the correlational model. Other advantages include its computational simplicity and the ease of understanding.

A frequent criticism of this approach is that, due to the errors of measurement, it is unfair to people whose scores fall just below the cutting line. However, perhaps unfortunately, in any practical situation a select-reject line must be drawn at some point. A more telling criticism is that using groups (for example, accept-reject) rather than a continuum of scores reduces precision. The reply to this criticism would be that the precision of the regression approach is a false precison, because the critical question is accuracy at the decision point, not throughout the score range.

other validation methods

In addition to validity coefficients and indices of decision-making accuracy, several other validity indices are sometimes used. We shall consider but two. To compare two or more existent groups, we can use an index of group differentiation. And, when we are interested in the costs and benefits of testing, in either financial or other terms, we may use an index of utility.[4]

Group Differentiation

Sometimes a test is validated by comparing the scores of two or more independent groups whose performance would be expected to differ—for example, by comparing the intelligence test scores of children of different ages; by comparing achievement test scores of people who have and have not completed a particular course, set of courses, or training program; or by comparing scores of people in various occupations on an interest inventory. In each case, significant differences in the predicted direction would provide support for the test's validity.

All of these examples contrast naturally occurring groups. We could also determine whether people attaining different criterion score levels obtain different test scores. For example, in our previous illustration we divided the students into two groups on the basis of their criterion performance: those who received an A, B, or C in algebra were classified as successful; those who received a D or F were

---

[4] Other indices are needed for different types of problems, such as placement and diagnosis. For discussions of these measures see, for example, Cronbach (1970, Chapter 12; 1971), Dunnette (1966), Hills (1971), Horst (1954, 1955), or Magnusson (1967, Chapter 12).

Table 6.4
Validity by Group Separation

(1) Using data from the previous example (Table 6.1), we shall define two subgroups: successful (those who obtained an A, B, or C in algebra) and unsuccessful (those who obtained a D or F). The relevant summary statistics are:

Successful	$\overline{X}_s = 4.79$	$s_s{}^2 = 2.43$	$n_s = 192$
Unsuccessful	$\overline{X}_u = 2.40$	$s_u{}^2 = 1.70$	$n_u = 48$

These values refer to the test scores of the two groups.

(2) To find whether there is a statistically significant difference in the test scores of the two groups we shall use the t statistic. This procedure compares the difference in means to a measure of sampling error (see, e.g., Hays, 1981). Applied to our example:

$$t = \frac{\overline{X}_s - \overline{X}_u}{\sqrt{(s_s{}^2/n_s) + (s_u{}^2/n_u)}} = \frac{4.79 - 2.40}{\sqrt{(2.43/192) + (1.70/48)}} = 9.19$$

The table of significant t values indicates that this large a difference would occur by chance less than one time in a thousand ($p < .001$). Thus we can say that the test scores of successful and unsuccessful students were different; that is, the math reasoning test does predict success in algebra.

---

classified as unsuccessful. We could compare the scores of these two groups to determine whether there is a statistically significant difference in their test scores. In other words, do successful students obtain significantly higher test scores than unsuccessful students? This procedure is illustrated in Table 6.4. As can be seen, the two groups do have significantly different test scores.

A problem with using group separation to indicate validity is that the statistical significance of the difference between group means is a function of the size of the groups. As group size increases, smaller differences in average scores become statistically significant. With large groups, as are often used in testing, small differences between average scores often will be statistically significant, but the test may be of little practical value in discriminating between groups. To avoid this shortcoming, we could determine the amount of overlap between the two distributions. Two possible indices are the percentage of scores in one group that exceed the mean score of the other group and the percentage of area common to the two distributions (Tilton, 1937).

Utility

Utility is concerned with the analysis of the costs and benefits of various courses of action. Therefore, to use utility as an index of the validity of the test involves determination of the benefits attained and costs incurred by using the test.

To illustrate, consider a selection situation in which there is no concern with persons who are not hired. In this situation three classes of costs and benefits can be estimated: the benefit to the company of hiring a worker who is successful, the cost to the company of hiring a worker who later proves unsuccessful, and the cost of the selection program. The calculation of each of these values is a complex cost-accounting procedure. For example, the benefits derived from hiring a successful worker will be a function of his productivity minus the costs of his salary, fringe benefits, equipment needed to perform his job, training costs, and other overhead costs. (A more thorough analysis might include such factors as expected job tenure, his influence on the productivity of other workers, and social costs and benefits associated with the employment of the worker.) Costs of hiring an unsuccessful worker would include such things as training costs and the expense of hiring a new worker to replace the unsuccessful one.

Let us assume, however, that the benefits of hiring a successful worker and the costs of hiring a worker who later proves to be unsuccessful can be established. Then utility could be calculated, using a formula of the form:

$$\text{Utility} = B(N_s) - C(N_u) - S \tag{6.7}$$

where B is the average benefit accrued by a successful worker; C the cost associated with hiring a worker who proves to be unsuccessful; N_s and N_u are the numbers of successful and unsuccessful workers hired, respectively; and S is the cost of the selection program. Although Equation (6.7) is highly simplified (cf. Cronbach & Gleser, 1957, 1965), it does show that for any selection program to have utility the gains obtained through testing must exceed the costs of the testing program.

In situations in which costs and benefits can readily be translated in exact values, such as dollars, a utility analysis will have the advantage of translating validity into units that are meaningful to the decision maker. However, in many situations exact values cannot be assigned to the various outcomes. For example, in most educational situations outcome values cannot be precisely determined. Although attempts have been made to apply the model in educational situations (for example, to determine the economic value of higher education), these applications do not include the intangible values of an education (such as a more satisfying life) and frequently must assign somewhat arbitrary values to certain costs and benefits.[5]

multiple predictors

When describing the methods of criterion-related validation we used illustrations involving only a single predictor. Often, however, we have scores on more than one variable available. For example, college admissions officers consider students' high school grades, scores on ability and achievement tests, letters of recommendation, special accomplishments, and other data when deciding which applicants to admit. Or employers may look at previous work history, interview ratings, recommendations, and even test scores when deciding which applicants to hire.

For the test user the important question is how to combine scores on these variables so as to obtain the most accurate prediction. In terms of validation the question is how to determine the validity of the composite. (We may, of course, also be interested in the validity of each score that makes up the composite.)

[5] For example, Page (1972) has described a method for determining the benefits of various educational outcomes.

There are a number of ways of combining scores to make predictions. Perhaps the most common is to make an intuitive prediction based on clinical judgment. Because this method is less accurate than actuarial methods (see, e.g., Meehl, 1954), statistical methods of combining scores are to be preferred. Here, again, there are a variety of possible methods. We will describe only two common methods—the multiple cutoff method and multiple regression.

Multiple Cutoff

The multiple cutoff method involves determining the minimally acceptable score on each variable. Using a procedure analogous to that used with a single predictor, it is possible to develop cutting scores on two (or more) predictors operating jointly. If an individual's scores are above the cutting score on *both* variables, he is accepted; if his score on *either* variable falls below the cutting score, he is rejected. This paradigm can be generalized to any number of predictors. Regardless of the number of predictors, if a person's score falls below the cutting line on *any* variable, he is rejected; if he is to be accepted his scores must exceed the cutting score on *all* variables.

Several points about the multiple cutoff model should be noted. First, the model is noncompensatory. That is, poor performance (score) on one variable cannot be compensated for by superior performance on another variable. If a person obtained exceedingly high scores on all tests except one, but fell below the cutting score on that one, he would be eliminated. Therefore, this model is appropriate only when there is evidence that the variables are, in fact, noncompensatory. If the predictors are compensatory, and the multiple cutoff model is used, classification errors will be made.

Second, the model is most appropriate when there are definite cutting lines that differentiate persons having the necessary abilities from those who lack the relevant skills. In these circumstances the cutting line represents this minimal ability level. If there are no definite ability thresholds, the cutting scores can be set to maximize certain outcomes. In this latter situation, the several variables must be manipulated simultaneously to obtain the desired cutting scores; in the former case, cutting scores can be determined for each variable independently.

Third, the decision will be either to accept or reject. Each individual is placed in one of two categories: those meeting the minimum requirements and those not meeting the minimum standards. Thus we obtain a pool of acceptable candidates, with no ranking of people within the pool. If we want to distinguish between minimally acceptable applicants (for example, rank them), we must use some other procedure.

Fourth, the validity of a multiple cutoff procedure can be evaluated by determining the number of correct decisions made. As with the single-predictor case, the criterion may be either total correct decisions or positive hits. The number of correct decisions must also be compared to the base rates, and to the number obtained by other techniques, to determine whether multiple cutoff is the optimal strategy.

Successive Hurdles. In practice predictor data are often collected sequentially. Rather than have all applicants take all predictors, only applicants who pass one go on to the next step in the sequence, the others being eliminated. Since the successful applicant must surmount a series of hurdles, the method is referred to as *successive hurdles*.

If a sequential selection procedure is to have the maximum validity, the most valid predictor should be used first, followed by the next most valid predictor, and so on. Although the last step would utilize the least valid predictor, the pool of surviving applicants is the best possible pool, given the validity of the predictors. Thus the validity of the selection procedure will be only slightly affected by the use of a poorer predictor at this point.

In practice, the order of presentation of the predictors is usually determined by practical and economic considerations, rather than their validity. Because it is more economical to send one recruiter to a university to interview 50 students than to send 50 students to the company plant for interviews, the on-campus interview will usually be conducted before the plant interview, regardless of the validity of the two interviews. Similarly, relatively simple and inexpensive selection methods, such as application blanks and tests, are often administered early in an employment procedure. The more costly and time-consuming, though not necessarily more valid, selection methods occur later in the sequence and are applied only to those that have survived the first hurdles. In this way the total cost of the selection process is minimized.

Advantages and Limitations. The multiple cutoff method is applicable whenever minimum cutting scores can be established on certain crucial variables. Because the model is noncompensatory, high performance on one variable cannot compensate for deficiencies in other areas. The model is appropriate for sequential selection strategies and when the variables combine in a nonlinear manner. The model is also compatible with a decision-making approach to validity. In addition, its computation ease and ready interpretability are desirable features.

The model also has several disadvantages. By the use of classes rather than continuous measurement, some precision is sacrificed. Unless there are definable minimal standards (cutting scores), people who would have succeeded through utilization of a compensatory skill or ability will be eliminated. Also, the technique provides a pool of acceptable candidates, not a rank ordering, and thus does not provide the information necessary for selecting from the pool those persons with the greatest probability of success.

Multiple Regression

The multiple cutoff method assumed no compensation between predictors; however, in most situations involving psychological variables some degree of compensation does occur. One student may study long hours to compensate for his lesser ability or weaker background in a course, while another student, possessing a more retentive memory, studies hardly at all; or two workers may attain the same production level, one by working rapidly and producing a large number of both acceptable and defective units and the other by working slowly but rarely spoiling a unit. In both of these situations a high degree of one skill or ability compensates for a relative weakness in another relevant area.

In situations in which compensation between abilities is the rule, multiple regression is the most frequently used model for combining scores. Multiple regression is similar to the regression procedure described previously, except that more than one predictor is used.

The basic logic of multiple regression can best be illustrated by the *multiple regression equation*:

$$Y' = a + b_1 X_1 + b_2 X_2 + b_3 X_3 + \cdots + b_k X_k \tag{6.8}$$

where Y' is the predicted criterion score, X_1 to X_k are the scores on the k predictor variables, b_1 to b_k are the weights assigned to each predictor, and a is an intercept constant needed to correct for differences in the predictor and criterion means. Equation (6.8) is written using raw scores; a comparable formula could be written using standard scores.

Although it is possible, and some people would even argue desirable, to weight the various predictors equally (Wainer, 1976), usually the weights assigned to each variable are determined empirically with each predictor receiving a weight proportional to its contribution to predictive accuracy.

To illustrate the compensatory nature of the model, consider a case with two predictors. In this situation the regression equation will be of the form:

$$Y' = a + b_1 X_1 + b_2 X_2 \tag{6.9}$$

Since a, b_1, and b_2 are constants, the only values that can vary are the test scores, X_1 and X_2. Various combinations of scores on X_1 and X_2 can produce the same predicted criterion score (Y'). Suppose that the actual equation was:

$$Y' = 10 + 2X_1 + 3X_2$$

In this case the same Y' might be obtained by scoring high on Test I (such as 35) and low on Test II (such as 5), scoring low on Test I (5) but high on Test II (25), or scoring in the middle ranges on both tests (20 and 15, respectively).

The Analysis.   Since the computational procedures of multiple regression analysis are quite complex, they will not be discussed in detail here; instead, only a general description of the procedure will be given. The reader who is interested in the details of the analysis can consult any of a number of texts; for example, A. L. Edwards (1976, 1979); Ghiselli, Campbell, & Zedeck (1981); Kerlinger & Pedhazur (1973); or Nunnally (1978).

The input data for the analysis are the means and standard deviations of the predictors and the criterion, and a correlation matrix showing the correlations between all pairs of variables. The analysis consists of solving a series of simultaneous equations, a task usually done by computer. This analysis weights the predictors so as to obtain the weighted combination of test scores that predicts the criterion with the least error. The output has two components of prime interest: (1) a regression equation indicating the weights assigned to the various predictors; and (2) a *multiple correlation coefficient, R,* which indicates the correlation between the predictors (considered as a composite) and the criterion measure.

In this model the validity of the composite prediction is indicated by the magnitude of the multiple correlation coefficient (R), which is the correlation between the predictors considered jointly (that is, as a composite) and the criterion. As with r, the square of the multiple correlation coefficient (R^2) gives the proportion of variance in the criterion scores associated with, or predictable from, variance in the predictors. Also, we can compute a standard error of estimate for a multiple correlation using the same formula as before, only substituting R for r in the formula. Thus we have a method for determining the magnitude of prediction errors.

In some cases we are interested in the validity of the individual predictors as well as the validity of the predictors considered as a set (the multiple correlation). Although we could look at the correlation between each variable and the criterion, we are generally interested in a somewhat different question: Does inclusion of a variable increase predictive accuracy over and above the level attained when it is not included in the multiple correlation? This increase in accuracy, called *incremental validity* (Sechrest, 1963), is evaluated by the increase in R or R^2 produced by including the variable in the prediction equation. In practice, variables correlated with the criterion may not be included in the prediction (regression) equation if they are highly correlated with variables previously included—that is, if they measure some characteristics already tapped by another variable. These variables would be eliminated from the equation since they add no new information. Because predictors often intercorrelate positively, the asymptote of predictive accuracy is usually reached with a small number of variables—rarely more than four or five.

An Example.   An example of a multiple regression/correlation problem is shown in Table 6.5. The problem is predicting college grades from high school performance and test scores. The analysis was done by a *stepwise* procedure. In this procedure the best predictor is included first; then we add the predictor that in combination with the best predictor increases R the greatest amount. The next predictor included is the one that in combination with the first two adds the greatest amount to R; and so on. We terminate the analysis when additional variables no longer significantly increase the multiple correlation coefficient. The computational steps are not shown in the table—only the summary data for each step.

The data in Table 6.5 illustrate several of the points made earlier. The first variable used (HSR) was the one with the highest correlation with the criterion ($-.544$). Other variables were added if they had high correlations with the criterion and low correlations with the predictors previously added. Using two variables (HSR, MATH) resulted in almost as accurate prediction as using four variables (.574 versus .578). That is, the additional variables did not contribute much additional information.

Advantages and Limitations.   The multiple correlation coefficient is the maximum correlation between the predictors, considered as a composite, and the criterion. The procedure allows a predicted criterion score to be derived for each individual by substituting individual test scores in the regression equation. Thus individuals can be ranked according to their predicted criterion performance. Another advantage is that, because of the compensatory nature of the model,

Table 6.5
An Example of Multiple Regression

PROBLEM.   Scores on seven predictors—two scholastic aptitude tests (ACT, MSAT), a test of reading speed (RS) and comprehension (RC), an English test (ENGL), and a math test (MATH)—plus the student's rank in his high school class (HSR) were used to predict grade point average (GPA) during the freshman year. The sample consisted of 660 freshmen in the college of engineering at a midwestern university.

ANALYSIS.   Analysis was done using a stepwise multiple regression procedure (see text).

THE INPUT DATA.   The input data consisted of the means and standard deviations on all variables, plus the matrix of intercorrelations among the variables:

Variable	$\bar{X}$	s	GPA	HSR	ACT	MSAT	RS	RC	ENGL
GPA	2.317	.625							
HSR	21.4	17.0	−.544						
ACT	26.1	3.3	.444	−.621					
MSAT	52.2	12.4	.384	−.553	.760				
RS	40.4	9.2	.237	−.313	.497	.456			
RC	28.5	9.3	.327	−.431	.675	.661	.844		
ENGL	186.3	28.5	.390	−.589	.705	.741	.468	.594	
MATH	40.5	10.9	.471	−.592	.681	.598	.374	.481	.591

Note that HSR is scaled so that a score of 1 is the highest possible score, and 100 the lowest; thus HSR correlated negatively with other variables. GPA is on a scale where A = 4, B = 3, and so on.

STEP 1. The first step selected the single best predictor, HSR:

$$R_{\text{GPA,HSR}} = .544$$

The regression equation, using only HSR, is:

$$\text{GPA}' = 2.75 - 0.02(\text{HSR})$$

where GPA' is the predicted GPA. Note also, that the important fact is the magnitude of the correlation between HSR and GPA, not the sign of the correlation.

STEP 2. The second step selected the variable, MATH, that in combination with HSR gave the highest value of R:

$$R_{\text{GPA,HSR + MATH}} = .574$$

and the regression equation is:

$$\text{GPA}' = 2.10 - 0.01(\text{HSR}) + 0.01(\text{MATH})$$

STEP 3. The next step selected the variable, ACT, that in combination with HSR and Math gave the highest R; that is:

$$R_{\text{GPA,HSR + MATH + ACT}} = .577$$

and the regression equation is:

$$\text{GPA}' = 1.80 - 0.01(\text{HSR}) + 0.01(\text{MATH}) + 0.01(\text{ACT})$$

(Since none of the remaining variables increased R more than .01, they were not added to the regression equation.)

SUMMARY. The results can be summarized by showing R, R^2, and the increase in R produced by each additional variable.

Table 6.5 (continued)
An Example of Multiple Regression

Variables	R	R^2	Increase in R
HSR	.544	.296	.544
MATH, HSR	.574	.330	.030
ACT, MATH, HSR	.577	.333	.003
All variables	.578	.334	.001

The analysis showed that the asymptote of predictive accuracy was reached using three of the seven variables, and that using only two variables resulted in essentially as accurate prediction as using three predictors.

various combinations of ability patterns are equally acceptable. An index of predictive accuracy (R or R^2) is provided, along with an estimate of prediction error (the standard error of estimate). Finally, the selection of the variables to be included in the regression equation, from among all possible predictors, is objective.

The disadvantages are several. Having a predicted criterion score may give an aura of exact predictability when, in actuality, the predicted criterion score is really a best estimate—the mean of the distribution of criterion scores for all individuals having the same predictor scores. However, the standard error of estimate can be computed for R in a manner analogous to that for r. Also, the model is inappropriate when compensation among abilities cannot be assumed and when the predictor-criterion relation is not linear.

interpreting criterion-related validity data

We now turn to a discussion of several factors to be considered when interpreting and using the results of validation studies: variables that influence the magnitude of a validity index, the generalizability of validity data, and possible biases in predictions. We shall conclude with the question: What is an acceptable level of criterion-related validity?

Factors Influencing Criterion-Related Validity Indices   R B C S S

Any variables that affect the predictor (test) scores, the criterion measure, or the situation in which the validity data are collected may influence a validity index. Thus they must be considered when interpreting validity data. In this section we will discuss some of the more important influences, paying particular attention to those not discussed in detail earlier in the chapter.

The Sample.   Validity data should be collected on groups and in situations similar to those in which the test will be applied. Thus, for example, validation studies of college admissions tests should use applicants for college, industrial selection and placement tests should be validated using job applicants, and personality measures designed to predict therapeutic outcomes should use clients undergoing therapy. Needless to say, any validation sample should be representative of the target population and large enough to allow for stable and statistically significant data.

Even when these general requirements are met, there still remain several alternative sampling strategies (Cronbach, 1971). One approach is to include all members of the relevant group, or at least a random sample, in the validity study. Thus in an industrial selection situation the selection test would be administered to all applicants; all (or a random sample) would be hired, irrespective of their test scores, and allowed to work for a set period of time; criterion data would be collected; and the validity of the test would be determined. Although in many ways this is the ideal procedure, since data are collected along the entire range of predictor and criterion scores, it is often unfeasible. Because employers want immediate results from the selection procedure, and costs or facilities do not allow all applicants to be hired, some applicants are rejected. Inasmuch as the eliminated persons generally have lower ability, the range of individual differences is restricted by eliminating the lower end of the predictor scale.

A second design utilizes only "screened applicants"; that is, those people who have survived some initial culling. This initial selection may be made on the basis of the predictor variable (the test being validated) or another variable. In the latter case, if the variable used for screening is positively correlated with the test being validated, as is generally the case, individual differences on the predictor test will be reduced; if the two variables are independent, there will be no effect. Screening using the scores on the predictor test will, of course, reduce the range of scores. In either case, the most likely outcome is that the range of individual differences will be restricted, thereby reducing validity (see Dawes, 1975).

When viewed within the framework of decision-making effectiveness, this second design is appropriate when our concern is with positive hits; the first design is appropriate when the concern is with total hits. Although this second design does not allow us to calculate the predictor-criterion relationship throughout the entire score range, it closely reflects the practical situation.

A third sampling procedure is sometimes used. In this approach, presently employed workers are divided into groups on the basis of their criterion performance (for example, successful and unsuccessful workers). Tests are then administered to see what variables differentiate the groups. This design has several major shortcomings. First, only persons who have survived all screening procedures and persisted until the criterion data were collected will be included—certainly an unrepresentative group. Second, the skills or characteristics that differentiate the two groups may have developed on the job and not have been present when the groups were hired. Third, the skills needed to perform the job may be common to everyone on the job but seldom found in other groups. The design does not allow these variables to be detected. Thus, the approach should be used only in preliminary investigations and, even then, results must be interpreted with extreme caution. Either of the first two sampling methods is preferable. Needless to say, regardless of which design is chosen, the actual sampling of subjects must be random or representative so as not to introduce any further biases.

Restriction of Range. As noted in the discussion of studies using screened applicants, if the variance of the predictor and/or criterion scores is restricted, the magnitude of the validity index will be reduced. Restriction of range on predictor scores is most likely to occur when the group is preselected, either using the predictor variable or a variable that is correlated with the predictor variable. Criterion score variance can be restricted by preselection or when established groups are used as the validation sample. Restriction is most likely to occur in the latter case when the least successful people have already been culled out.[6] The effects of restriction of range can be minimized by using unselected validation samples (ones that do not have a restricted range of scores) or by applying statistical formulas to correct for restriction in range.

The Criterion. In any validation study we predict a particular criterion measure or a limited range of criteria. Thus, as mentioned earlier, the nature of the specific criterion measure must be considered when interpreting validation data. Even when criteria appear to be similar or related, a test may predict one criteria more accurately than another. To use a previous example, a test may predict grade averages but not graduation from a program. Thus the test should be validated against all criteria of interest.

Base Rates. When discussing indices of decision-making accuracy, we stated that a test was valid only if the number of correct decisions improved on the base rates. Analogously, when using validity coefficients, predictive accuracy should be higher using the predictor being validated than when using other predictors and, when considering utility, the measure being validated should have greater utility than other possible methods. In short, a valid test is one that improves on current procedures.

The importance of base rates is particularly apparent when the phenomenon being predicted occurs either very frequently or very infrequently. In these circumstances, any prediction made on bases other than the base rates is likely to result in more errors than predicting the most likely outcome. Suppose, for example, that you want to identify people who will attempt to commit suicide. If only 5 persons in 1000 attempt suicide, and if you predict that no one will attempt suicide (even knowing that some people will) your accuracy rate will be .995, or 5 errors per 1000. Hence it is highly unlikely that a test will be useful in identifying potential suicides. Conversely, when selecting persons for a job that is so simple that 95 percent of the applicants can perform it adequately, the optimal selection strategy is to go with the base rates, to hire people as they apply. The reason, of

---

[6] If the less successful people have either quit or been terminated, the range of possible criterion scores will be reduced. It may also be reduced if criterion scores are adjusted to take into account preselection; for example, the range of grades awarded in advanced college and professional school courses is usually less than those awarded in freshman courses.

course, is that no test can identify successful persons with greater than .95 accuracy, the accuracy obtained using the base rates. (For a further discussion, see Meehl & Rosen, 1955.)

Selection Ratios. A final consideration is the *selection ratio*, the proportion of persons selected out of the number of applicants. If a predictor is positively related to the criterion, by being more and more selective we can increase the probability that any person selected will be successful. That is, we can select only from ranges of the population that have high probabilities of success; we can take the cream of the crop.

The effect of the selection ratio on the proportion of total correct decisions is shown in Figure 6.1, which is adapted from Taylor and Russell (1939). This figure shows the effect of different selection ratios on the proportion of correct decisions in a situation where the base rate is .60 (that is, 60 percent of the workers are rated as successful). Four different levels of validity are plotted: .20, .40, .60, and .80. Several important relations can be seen in this figure. First, for any given validity coefficient, the proportion of correct decisions decreases as the selection ratio increases. Second, for any given selection ratio, the proportion of correct decisions increases as the validity coefficient increases. Third, the same propor-

Figure 6.1 Effect of Selection Ratio on Correct Decisions

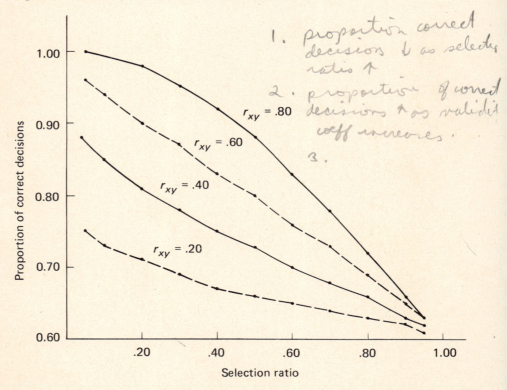

tion of correct decisions can be obtained using various combinations of selection ratios and validity coefficients. For example, 75 percent correct decisions will be made when the validity coefficient is .40 and the selection ratio is .40, when the validity coefficient is .60 and the selection ratio is .65, and when the validity coefficient is .80 and the selection ratio is .75. The major point is clear: Even a relatively invalid test can be quite useful if the pool of applicants is large enough that we can use a low selection ratio; that is, hire only the most qualified persons.

Note, too, that when a cutting score is utilized, fewer applicants will be selected than under the current selection procedures. What if the number selected is insufficient to fill all open positions? Here you have two options. One is to recruit a larger pool of applicants. For example, if there were 200 applicants for 150 positions and use of the cutting score resulted in only 100 being selected (i.e., if the selection ratio was .50), 50 positions would remain unfilled. By increasing the applicant pool to 300, however, you could retain the same cutting score and selection ratio yet obtain 150 qualified applicants. The other alternative is to lower the cutting score. This alternative would increase the selection ratio, resulting in more applicants being hired, but would do so at the cost of making more incorrect decisions. You might, however, be able to reduce the number of unsuccessful workers by instituting a training program that would equip these potentially unsuccessful workers with the skills needed to perform the job satisfactorily.

Generalizability of Validity Data

It should now be apparent that *validity data are situation-specific.* That is, the results of any validity study are dependent upon the characteristics of the specific situation in which the data were collected. This statement has two important implications. First, a test will have not one, but many validities. Second, even though validity has been established in one situation, it cannot be assumed that the test will be equally valid in another, presumably comparable, situation. Thus, in any situation, adoption of a test must always be tentative until its validity has been established empirically. The need to evaluate a test independently for each specific use cannot be overstressed. In this author's opinion, using a test without evaluating its effectiveness is both poor practice and borders on the unethical.

When considering the results of a particular validation study, two questions should be asked. First, would the results be the same if the study were replicated on another sample drawn from the same population? This is the problem of *cross-validation.* Second, over what range of situations and samples will the results hold? The first part is a question of generalizability (Brennan & Kane, 1979; Cronbach, Gleser, Nanda, & Rajaratnam, 1972; Cronbach, Rajaratnam, & Gleser, 1963) and the second part a question of *population validity* (Breland, 1979). Together they constitute the question of *validity generalization.*

Cross-Validation. Cross-validation refers to the process of determining a relationship from two or more samples independently drawn from the same population. In validity studies this would involve establishing the predictor-criterion relationship on two separate samples drawn from the same population. Although computation of a validity index in two samples will not detect systematic effects, it will detect variable errors; that is, it will establish the reliability of the validity data. Thus the magnitude of chance errors, those associated with one sample, can be estimated and the data corrected accordingly.

Cross-validation, in the single predictor situation, would proceed as follows. Test scores and criterion data would be collected on one sample, r_{XY} computed, and a regression equation derived. A second sample would then be independently drawn from the same population. For each person in this second (cross-validation) group, the regression equation derived from the first sample would be used to calculate a predicted criterion score. Actual criterion scores would then be collected and the correlation between predicted and actual criterion scores calculated. This correlation should not differ markedly from the validity coefficient established on data from the first sample. If it does, we know that the first correlation was a poor estimate of the relationship. The coefficient calculated on the cross-validation sample will generally be slightly lower than the original correlation since chance factors that tend to maximize the original correlation will not operate in the cross-validation sample. Thus the cross-validated correlation is a better estimate of the true degree of relationship.

Validity Generalization. Cross-validation involves only generalization over various samples drawn from the same population. However, we can consider generalization over at least five dimensions: predictors, criteria, situations, samples or populations of subjects, and methods of establishing validity.

Rather than review each of these dimensions, we will only draw several conclusions about the need for validity generalization studies. First, because validity is influenced by many variables, systematic collection of validity data is essential. Most validity studies are conducted to justify use of a particular test (for example, the data provided in a test manual) or represent the hit-or-miss, shotgun approach of many investigators, each pursuing his or her own particular interests. Although attempts have been made to summarize available validity data for particular occupations, or tests, more studies that deliberately and systematically vary the relevant parameters to establish the limits of the validity of commonly used tests are needed.

Second, more adequate methods of summarizing validity data are needed. Although one single summary index of validity may not be possible, the variables influencing a particular test and the effects of manipulating each one could be specified. Perhaps some of the recently proposed methods for combining data from several studies can be adapted to this problem.[7]

Third, there is close relation between the data and concepts of validity and reliability. Many of the variables influencing validity generalization are similar to those that influence consistency. In both types of analysis we are interested in generalizability over certain salient dimensions and variables, the difference being in the number and nature of the dimensions over which generalizations are made. Thus, Cronbach and his colleagues (Cronbach, Gleser, Nanda, & Rajaratnam, 1972) have subsumed both reliability and validity under a common theory, generalizability theory.

[7] See, for example Glass (1976, 1977), Light and Smith (1971), Pillemer and Light (1980), Rosenthal (1978), and Smith and Glass (1977).

Bias in Predictions

reread

Sometimes a population consists of several distinct subpopulations; for example, a group may include both males and females or members of one or more minority groups. An important question in these situations is whether the test is equally valid for all groups. If not, the possibility of test bias must be entertained.

The term *test bias* is one that has different meanings for different authors (see, e.g., Arvey, 1979; Cleary et al., 1975; Cole, 1973, 1981; Darlington, 1971; Flaugher, 1978; Hunter & Schmidt, 1976; Hunter, Schmidt, & Hunter, 1979; Novick & Ellis, 1977; Petersen & Novick, 1976; Reschley, 1979; Thorndike, 1971b). Since our concern at this point is with predictive validity, the primary question is whether the test has comparable predictive or decision-making accuracy for various subgroups. You should be aware, however, that there are other types of test bias. For example, in addition to bias in predictions, Reschley (1979) has indicated that bias can occur in the test content, in the test administration, and in how the test results are used.

To put our discussion in more concrete terms, consider determining a test's validity for two subgroups from a broader population. We can compute the validity coefficient for each group separately and also for the combined group. One possible result would be that the validity coefficient is of similar magnitude in both groups. In this case we would probably use validity data from the combined group. Another possibility is that the validity coefficient differs in the two groups. In this case, using the same prediction equation for everyone (either one based on data from the combined group or from the larger group) will result in larger prediction errors for the atypical subgroup. If, in addition, the data are such that we systematically underpredict the criterion performance of one group, we will have biased predictions. One possible solution is to use different predictors for each group, preferably ones that result in comparable levels of predictive accuracy.

bias if validity coef. diff for 2 groups drawn from same pop.

Even if the validity coefficients are similar for the two groups, there is still a possibility of bias. To see why this can occur, consider the distribution of scores for the two groups on the predictor and criterion. If, for example, the two groups have comparable mean criterion scores but differ in predictor scores, and if we select applicants on the basis of predictor scores, members of the group scoring lower on the predictor test will have less chance of being selected, even though they perform as well on the criterion. (This situation is shown in Figure 6.2a.) Conversely, if the two groups have similar predictor scores but differ on the criterion performance, we will systematically overpredict the performance for members of the group having lower criterion scores and systematically underpredict the performance of members of the group having higher criterion scores (see Figure 6.2b). In short, when looking for possible prediction bias we have to examine the distribution of scores on both the predictor and the criterion as well as the magnitude of the validity coefficient. Differences in any of these parameters may indicate bias.[8]

bias if validity co. similar for 2 groups

When studying bias, we must take several other factors into account. One is the

[8] Bias due to differences in criterion performance level are called intercept bias; those due to differences in validity coefficients are called slope bias.

Figure 6.2 Examples of Prediction Bias.

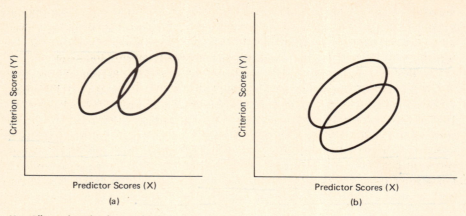

Note: Ellipses show distribution of scores for two groups.

nature of the sample. In many situations there are few members of any minority group available for study. Thus data from these groups will not be as reliable as data from the larger, majority group. Furthermore, the sample of minority group members may be unrepresentative of all the broader population for that group. Then, too, when criterion data are based on ratings or factors other than performance records, the criterion measure itself may be biased. Finally, since there are various statistical definitions of bias, what is considered as evidence of bias using one method may not appear as bias using another method.

What Is an Acceptable Level of Validity?

We have avoided an explicit discussion of the question that plagued the discussion on reliability—the question of how high is high, or, in more technical terms, what is an acceptable level of validity? Because of the situation-specific nature of validity, the variety of validity coefficients, and the multitude of factors that influence a validity coefficient, it is impossible to give one definite answer. At best one can set certain minimal requirements: (1) The cross-validated relationship between predictor and criterion scores must be statistically significant—that is, be more than a chance relationship. (2) Using the test must result in more correct decisions being made than would be made by resorting to base rates alone. (3) The test must possess some utility; it must result in some gain to the user. (4) The effectiveness of the test must be greater than other available decision-making tools; that is, the test should provide some unique information. If these requirements are not met (at least the ones that can be evaluated in the particular situation), use of the test is not justified.

Finally, although test results are ultimately used to make decisions about individuals, the validity of a test is established by determining its effectiveness for a group of persons. Because there is no logical link that allows group results to be applied unerringly to any individual member of the group, the effectiveness of a test must be evaluated in terms of decisions made regarding the group collectively. Although the decision made about John Jones is of utmost importance, with imperfect tests errors will be made in individual cases. Our goal is to minimize errors in individual cases. Yet, until the day arrives, if it ever does, when tests predict with perfect accuracy, some errors will be made in individual cases. When evaluating tests the appropriate question is not "Will errors be made in individual cases?"—a question that obviously can only be answered "Yes." Rather the crucial question is: "Will fewer errors be made in individual cases using the test or by using some other technique?"

summary

Criterion-related validity studies investigate the empirical relationship between scores on a test (the predictor) and some other behavior or outcome (the criterion). In predictive validity studies, criterion scores are collected later in time than test scores and the focus is on how accurately criterion scores can be predicted by test scores. In concurrent validity studies, both test and criterion scores are collected at the same point in time. Here the interest is in whether one method can be substituted for another. Both investigate the accuracy of the inferences about criterion performance made from test scores. Thus criterion-related validity is evaluated in terms of the test's contribution to increased predictive or decision-making accuracy.

Although criterion-related validity studies are used to determine the range of behaviors and outcomes a test can predict, a more common use is in practical, decision-making situations, such as selection and placement. In these situations the focus is on the criterion behavior; the test is of interest only because it predicts the criterion. Thus the most essential aspect of a criterion measure is its relevance: Does it adequately reflect the behavior we want to predict? Other desired properties of criterion measures are reliability, freedom from bias and contamination, and practicality.

The most commonly used measure of criterion-related validity is a validity coefficient, which is the correlation between predictor and criterion scores. A validity coefficient is an index of how well criterion scores can be predicted from test scores. The squared validity coefficient indicates the proportion of shared variance or the proportion of variance in criterion scores predictable from test scores. It can also be interpreted as the gain in average criterion performance attained by using the test as a predictor. Validity coefficients enable us to predict criterion scores (through use of regression equations) and to estimate the magnitude of prediction errors (by use of the standard error of estimate).

Another approach is to use indices of decision-making accuracy or selection efficiency. These indices tell how many correct decisions will result from use of the test. Two indices are the total hit ratio (the proportion of correct decisions made, considering all possible decisions) and the positive hit ratio (the proportion of selected persons who will be judged successful). When such indices are used, validity will vary with the cutting score—the optimal cutting score being the one that best balances the various types of errors and consequently results in the highest proportion of correct decisions. A valid predictor is one that improves on the base rates; that is, it results in more correct decisions than would be made without using the test as a predictor.

Two other methods of validation are also used. Group differentiation involves determining whether persons having different levels of criterion performance obtain different average test scores. Indices of utility determine whether use of the test results in greater benefits than costs.

When more than one predictor is available we are interested in the validity of the composite as well as of individual predictors. The multiple cutoff procedure is noncompensatory and identifies a pool of minimally acceptable persons (ones who surpass the minimal cutting line on each predictor). The multiple regression procedure is compensatory and weights each predictor in relation to its contribution to predictive accuracy.

The magnitude of a validity index depends on several factors, the most important of which are the nature of the validation sample, the range of predictor and criterion scores, the nature of the criterion measure, the base rates, and the selection ratio. When validity indices are obtained by studying a sample of a population, they should be cross-validated using another sample from the same population. To determine the range of situations in which the test is valid, validity generalization studies can be performed. We must also be concerned with possible bias in predictions.

Although no one minimal value establishes that a test is valid, certain guidelines should be met: The cross-validated index of criterion-related validity should be statistically significant; use of the test should result in more correct decisions than use of the base rates; the test should have utility; and the test should be more valid than other available predictors.

It is also important to remember that criterion-related validity studies indicate the validity of a test for a particular use in a particular situation. A test that is valid in one situation or for one use may not be valid in other, even similar, situations or for other uses. Thus tests should be validated for each use and situation.

Suggestions for Further Reading

Anastasi, A. *Psychological testing,* 4th ed. New York: Macmillan, 1976. Chapters 6 and 7 are a good introduction to validity, covering material similar to this chapter; Chapter 6 describes the basic concepts of validity and Chapter 7 focuses on methods for determining validity.

Breland, H. M. *Population validity and college entrance measures.* Research Monograph No. 8. New York: The College Board, 1979. A review of studies on the predictive validity of the SAT with particular emphasis on validity for different populations.

Cronbach, L. J. Test validation. In R. L. Thorndike (Ed.), *Educational measurement,* 2d ed. Washington, D.C.: American Council on Education 1971. An excellent, comprehensive discussion of validity and validation strategies; probably the best single reference on this topic.

Fincher, C. Personnel testing and public policy. *American Psychologist,* 1973, *28,* 489–497. Discusses implications of legal rulings and governmental regulations for the validation of psychological tests.

Fincher, C. Is the SAT worth its salt? *Review of Educational Research,* 1974, *44,* 293–305. An analysis of the validity and usefulness of the SAT in a statewide system of higher education over a 13-year period.

Ghiselli, E. E., Campbell, J. P., & Zedeck, S. *Measurement theory for the behavioral sciences.* San Francisco: Freeman, 1981. Chapter 10 describes the types of validity, methodological and statistical problems in validation, and alternative indices of validity.

Hartnett, R. T., & Willingham, W. W. The criterion problem: What measure of success in graduate education? *Applied Psychological Measurement,* 1980, *4,* 281–291. A nontechnical analysis of the strengths and weaknesses of various possible criteria for evaluating the performance of graduate students.

Kerlinger, F. N. *Foundations of behavioral research,* 2d ed. New York: Holt, Rinehart and Winston, 1973. Chapter 27 is an excellent, brief discussion of validity.

Meehl, P. E., & Rosen, A. Antecedent probability and the efficiency of psychometric signs, patterns, or cutting scores. *Psychological Bulletin,* 1955, *52,* 194–216. A classic article, the one that first suggested using measures of selection efficiency and improvement over the base rates in validation studies.

Principles for the validation and use of personnel selection procedures. Washington, D.C.: American Psychological Association, Division of Industrial/Organizational Psychology, 1975. A brief pamphlet explaining how the *Standards* apply to the validation and use of tests and other instruments in personnel selection.

Standards for educational and psychological tests. Washington, D.C.: American Psychological Association, 1974. Section E (pp. 25–48) describes standards and guidelines regarding information on validity and validation studies.

Chapter 7 • Content and Construct Validity

In Chapter 2 a distinction was made between tests that represent and tests that predict. Our discussion of criterion-related validity focused on the use of tests as predictors. In this chapter we shall focus on tests that represent. Thus, rather than being concerned with how well test scores predict an external criterion, we shall be concerned with how well the test measures the domain or trait of interest.

Tests that represent, you will recall, can be further subdivided into tests that serve as samples and those that serve as signs. A test is a sample when the items are drawn from a clearly specified content or behavioral domain. A test serves as a sign when the domain is open-ended; here the test helps point out the nature of the domain being sampled. This distinction, between samples and signs, has a parallel in the types of validity—content validity being the analog of tests as samples, construct validity of tests as signs. Thus, content validity focuses on the process of evaluating how adequately a set of items (the test) samples the relevant domain. Construct validity, in contrast, focuses on the definition of the trait measured by the test and on the ability of the test to provide information concerning the nature of the trait.

content validity

Evidence of content validity is needed whenever performance on a sample of items (the test) is used to make inferences about the broader domain of which the test items are a sample. Most frequently these situations involve achievement testing. For example, classroom teachers are constantly confronted with the problem of assessing their students' knowledge and/or skills. Usually they are interested in a relatively well-defined content area. If time permitted, they might administer an extensive examination, covering all important aspects of the subject matter. Obviously such a procedure, desirable as it may be, is unfeasible. Thus some substitute procedure must be devised, one that provides a valid estimate of each student's knowledge in a reasonable amount of time. Frequently the solution is to administer an achievement test.

In these situations the variable of interest is students' knowledge of the subject matter domain. The test serves as a sample, or representation, of the content domain. Scores on the test are not ends in themselves; rather, they are used to make inferences about performance in the wider domain. Because he cannot ask every possible question, the teacher selects a sample of the possible items to serve as the test. On the basis of the student's performance on this sample of items, the teacher makes inferences about the student's knowledge of (all) the material in the unit. To the extent that the items are a good sample of the total pool of potential items, the inferences will be valid; to the extent that any bias is introduced into the item selection, the inferences will be invalid.

The Content Domain

When evaluating content validity, the basic question is: Do the items comprising the test constitute a representative sample of the content domain of interest? Or, as stated in the *Standards:*

> To demonstrate the content validity of a set of test scores, one must show that the behaviors demonstrated in testing constitute a representative sample of behaviors to be exhibited in a desired performance domain. (*Standards,* 1974, p. 28)

Thus, content validation is the process of determining the adequacy of sampling items from the domain of potential items. As we will show, determination of content validity is usually a judgmental process that provides no quantitative index or measure of validity.

Describing the Domain. Content validity, as its name indicates, focuses on the content of the test items. That is, we are concerned with the knowledge, skills, or behaviors measured by the test items. However, we may also be concerned with the cognitive processes used to answer the items. Thus, for example, on achievement tests we could look at both the subject matter covered (e.g., permutations and combinations, the novels of Charles Dickens, measures of central tendency) and the cognitive processes (e.g., comprehension, analysis, synthesis) used to answer the items.

As the focus is on the content domain, the first step in content validation is to specify the domain of interest in a clear manner. As we saw in Chapter 2, this is usually done in one of two ways: by a content/skills test plan or by a list of behavioral objectives. To clearly specify the domain, the boundaries of the domain must be delineated. Although some authorities would insist that content validity requires an explicitly defined, finite universe of items (see Bornmuth, 1970; Hively et al., 1968), most people interpret this requirement to mean that the test constructor must, as clearly as possible, specify what materials and skills the test is designed to cover. On achievement tests the content usually is specified by topical areas (for example, the theory of reliability, alcoholism in women), by the assignments covered, or by specification of behavioral objectives for a unit.

Some people would suggest using even more detailed specifications. For example, Popham and Lindheim (1980), in discussing the construction of content-referenced tests, suggest that after identifying the attribute to be measured, a detailed list of test specifications be written. These specifications would include a general description of the nature of the task, a list of stimulus attributes (which specifies the nature of the items), a list of response attributes (which specifies the nature of permissible responses), and sample test items. This procedure describes both the content domain and the nature of the test items used to measure the domain.

Another point of debate is the relative emphasis to be placed on the cognitive process dimension when specifying the domain. Some experts feel that since different persons may answer the same item using different processes (for example, the item "multiply 11 by 12" might involve computation by one child and recall of a learned fact by another), inclusion of process factors introduces unnecessary ambiguity. Other experts, however, feel that failure to consider process dimensions is both sterile and a poor educational practice. They would argue that the types of achievement tests that are so widely criticized (for example, tests composed solely of items testing factual recall) would never be developed if the test constructor considered process variables (see, e.g., Bloom et al., 1971).

Representative Sampling. The definition of content validity stated that the test items must be a representative sample of the domain of possible content or behaviors. Note that the definition specifies *representative sampling,* not random sampling. Representative sampling means selecting items in proportion to their emphasis or importance. For example, in a typical instructional unit, some of the material repeats what has been learned previously, some is trivial or included as filler, and some is otherwise inappropriate for test items. These materials will not be included on the test. The test will include only material that, in the judgment of the test constructor, represents important content and/or skills. The test items, therefore, need not be representative of the total content of the course or unit, but only of the material judged to be relevant and important.

When constructing a test, after defining the domain the next step is to write a pool of potential items. Several items are written for each content/skill category or objective. Then items are sampled from each subcategory until the desired proportional emphasis is attained. In practice, this sampling often is not random. One reason is that the items selected generally have to meet certain statistical requirements; for example, they should be of appropriate difficulty. Another reason is that a balance of content may be desired. And, third, items sometimes are chosen to serve a specific function—for example, to be easy "warm-up" items or to test the limits of the best students' knowledge.

Content Bias. When constructing test items or evaluating content validity, the possibility of content bias should be considered. In the most general sense, content bias can occur whenever test takers do not have equal opportunity to learn the material or behaviors covered by the test. However, whether a test is, in fact, biased varies with the use of the test. For example, if a classroom test included material only some students had an opportunity to learn, it would unfairly discriminate against students who did not have the opportunity to learn this material.[1] On the other hand, if a job requires workers to read instructions written in English, a selection test might include items requiring applicants to read instruc-

---

[1] We shall use the term "discriminate" synonymously with differentiate. Thus most tests discriminate; for example, achievement tests are designed to discriminate between persons with varying degrees of knowledge of the subject tested. Unfair discrimination, or bias, occurs when discrimination results from factors irrelevant to the primary purpose of testing—because of the test taker's race or sex, for example.

tions written in English. This test would be a fair measure of applicants' ability to perform the job requirements, thus would not be biased, even if applicants unfamiliar with English would obtain lower scores.

The practical issue is how to detect and eliminate possible content bias. Whenever members of various subgroups perform differently on an item or test, the possibility of content bias should be investigated. One method is to have members of each affected group inspect the items and judge which ones may be biased; these items can be revised or replaced. A better approach is to use item analysis data to identify biased items (see Chapter 10). These methods are better because the determination of bias is based on empirical data, not just subjective opinions.

Other Domains.   Although content validity is usually associated with achievement tests, its use is not restricted to such tests. For example, a mechanical aptitude test might sample the various skills and abilities that constitute mechanical ability; a test of ethnocentrism might sample reactions to various types of people; a vocational interest test might sample reactions to various courses, jobs, and activities; or a proficiency test used for hiring, placement, or promotion might sample the tasks a worker would have to perform on the job. In short, content validity can be investigated whenever the boundaries of the domain being measured can be adequately specified and the test is designed to sample this domain.

Methods for Determining Content Validity

The usual process of content validation involves having expert judges systematically compare the test items to the postulated content domain.[2] If the test items appear to these judges to represent the domain adequately, the test has content validity. This process is logical and rational, involving a judgment of the correspondence between the test items and the underlying domain.

To determine the content validity of a test requires, first, a well-specified content domain—both a broad definition and detailed subcategories. Next, which items are designed to measure each subcategory should be identified. Expert judges can then evaluate the test. At one level, judges can evaluate the adequacy of the definition of the domain. This, however, is usually taken as a "given." At another level, judges can evaluate whether the various classes or categories of items adequately represent the domain. Finally, they can judge whether individual items do, in fact, reflect the aspect of the domain they are supposed to measure. Based on these considerations, judges make an overall evaluation of the content validity of the measure.

There are certain, rather obvious, weaknesses with this procedure. First, there is no quantitative index of content validity. Second, any lack of clarity in defining the domain or in the classification of individual items will make the judgments more difficult. Third, since various judges may use different standards and criteria, they may not agree as to the content validity of a test.

---

[2] Who is an expert judge depends on the type of test and its intended uses. For example, expert judges of the content validity of an achievement test would be people who teach the courses in the subject area the test covers.

In an attempt to standardize these procedures, Guion (1977) proposed five conditions to be met if a test can be said to have content validity: (1) the content domain must be described in terms of behaviors that have generally accepted meanings; (2) the domain must be described unambiguously; (3) the domain must be relevant to the intended use of the test; (4) qualified judges must agree that the domain has been adequately sampled; and (5) responses must be reliably observed and evaluated. Unless these five conditions are met, we do not have adequate evidence of content validity.

Specificity of Content Validity.   In one sense, content validity is a general property of a test rather than being situation-specific. If the test constructor clearly defines the content domain and selects items to represent this domain, he either does or does not succeed (more precisely, succeeds to a certain degree) in attaining his goal. Although we may disagree with his definition of the domain, we must evaluate the test in terms of how well the test attains the specified goal, by how well the test represents the domain as the test constructor defined it.

In another sense, however, content validity is situation-specific. A test user will always apply a test in a specific situation to measure certain behaviors that he considers important. If the domain as defined by the user and as defined by the test constructor are congruent, there is no problem. If, however, the user defines the domain differently than did the test constructor, a conflict arises. Now the test is not a good representation of the domain as the user defines it, and thus will be less valid for his purposes. In this sense, content validity is situation-specific.

To illustrate, suppose that a standardized test is constructed to measure achievement in mathematics as traditionally taught in the upper elementary grades. Assume also that the test has well-constructed items that measure important concepts—in short, assume that the test has content validity as a measure of mathematics as traditionally taught in the upper elementary grades. If this test is used in a school system that teaches math in the traditional manner, it should be a valid measure of achievement. True, there may be some differences in emphasis and coverage due to the particular text used and teacher preferences, but, by and large, these will be minor differences. On the other hand, if the test is used in a school system which teaches the "new" math, some items will cover concepts that are not taught or emphasized and some of the concepts stressed in the new math will not be covered on the test. In this situation, the disparity in definitions of the content domain would be so great as to render the test inappropriate—in essence, to reduce its validity.

Other Measures of Content Validity.   Most evidence of content validity is of the judgmental nature just described. However, other methods have been suggested. For example, Cronbach (1971) proposed that content validity could be evaluated quantitatively by comparing scores on two forms of a test, independently constructed from the same domain. By "independently constructed" he means that two separate test construction teams, each working from the same definition of the content domain and following agreed-upon guidelines (such as the number and form of items), would construct a test. A high correlation between scores on the two forms would be presumptive evidence of content validity.

A second method uses a pretest-posttest design. That is, we could administer a pretest to persons having no background in the area covered by the test, expose the group to a course or training program covering the relevant material, then administer a posttest. If scores increased significantly, we would have evidence that the test did cover the relevant domain (that is, the material taught in the course). This approach is particularly appropriate with achievement tests.

A third possibility is to correlate scores on a test with scores on other tests presumably measuring the same domain. This method has limited use because even though the tests may cover similar material, the definitions of the domains may vary. Then, too, a relatively high correlation may be obtained whenever two tests measure related abilities or content areas, even if the domains are clearly different.

Finally, it should be possible to develop standard rating scales judges could use when evaluating content validity. Scales could be developed for the overall validity of the test and/or for certain dimensions, such as content coverage, stress on important points, and appropriateness of item format to content. The ratings of various judges could then be compared statistically with agreement between the various judges' ratings being an estimate of interrater reliability. If the level of interrater reliability were sufficiently high, the mean rating could be used as an index of content validity.

Face Validity. Content validity is frequently confused with face validity. A test has face validity when the items seem to measure what the test is supposed to measure. That is, when a test taker looks at the items, they appear relevant to the purpose of the testing. Thus a test containing items that ask the individual's reactions to such activities as basketball, geometry, selling as a career, and working with people would have face validity as an interest inventory but not as an intelligence test. In short, face validity is determined by a somewhat superficial examination of the test by the test taker, and considers only obvious relevance. Content validity, in contrast, is established by a thorough and systematic evaluation of the test by a qualified judge, and considers both subtle and obvious aspects of relevance.

Face validity may be an important consideration if the apparent relevance of the items influences the motivation of the test takers. In some situations, particularly in employment testing, if a test lacks face validity, test takers may not be motivated to do well, feeling that the test is irrelevant to the decision being made. In other situations, such as when measuring personality characteristics, a high degree of face validity may be undesirable because it may threaten test takers and/or encourage them to dissimulate (bias their responses). Thus face validity, though not guaranteeing accurate measurement, may have an important influence on motivation and therefore on validity.

Advantages and Limitations

Content validity, as a concept and as a method, has both its strong points and limitations. The emphasis on evaluating the correspondence between the test items and the domain sampled both ensures care in item selection and requires careful specification of the domain to be sampled. Thus considerations of content validity are an essential aspect of the construction of any test. Content validity is clearly the most appropriate method for evaluating the validity of achievement tests (unless, of course, the achievement test is used primarily as a predictor). It is also an appropriate method for validating most proficiency tests. Moreover, content validity, as a concept, reminds us that our major concern is not with the test itself but with the inferences we draw about students' performance in the broader domain from which the items were sampled.

The major limitation of content validity is, of course, the lack of quantitative indices that summarize the degree of validity. Lack of available quantitative indices hinders communication of information about the content validity of a test. As a first step we should attempt to develop clearly specified methods, techniques, and procedures for determining content validity and scales, or a set of standards that can be used to summarize and communicate the degree of content validity. Such procedures and scales are, in principle, attainable; however, as yet, they are not used.

construct validity

As stated in the *Standards* (1974), "... construct validity is implied when one evaluates a test or other set of operations in light of the specified construct" (p. 29). Thus, construct validity is important whenever a test is designed to measure some attribute or quality (construct) that people are presumed to possess. Construct validity studies attempt to answer the questions: What psychological construct is measured by a test? How well does the test measure this construct? Thus the focus is on the construct, the characteristic being measured.

Frequently in psychology, constructs are not definable solely in operational terms. That is, the definition of a construct may include statements that, though anchored in observable data, contain elements that go beyond observable behaviors. Such definitions are often broader and more meaningful than definitions involving a mere rephrasing of empirical relationships. Thus construct validity is evaluated by an accumulation of evidence, and no single quantitative index of construct validity is possible. To determine the construct validity of a test, one must examine the entire body of evidence surrounding the test: what sort of items are included on the test, the stability of the test scores under varying conditions, the homogeneity of the test, its correlation with other tests or variables, the effects of experimental manipulations on test performance, and any other data that cast light on the meaning of test scores. By evaluating, sifting, and refining the evidence about the test, a clearer definition of the construct measured by the test emerges.

The process of construct validation can also be conceptualized as an attempt to answer the question: What proportion of the variance in test scores is attributable to the variable the test measures? That is, to what extent does performance on the test reflect the construct the test is designed to measure?

The Logic of Construct Validation

In many ways the logic of construct validity, as well as its methods, are essentially those of the scientific method. Construct validation can be viewed as building a miniature theory about a test. This theory building involves three steps. First, on the basis of his currently held theory about the test, the investigator derives certain hypotheses about the expected behavior of persons obtaining different scores on the test. He then gathers data that will confirm or disconfirm these hypotheses. On the basis of the accumulated data he decides whether the theory does, in fact, adequately explain the data. If it does not, he must revise his theory and repeat the process until a more adequate explanation is available. Since no one set of data ever provides a complete and unambiguous explanation, the process is one of continual reformulation and refinement.

Clarification of the meaning of any concept in a theory occurs by including more lawful relationships or by making the existing laws more specific and definite. Many methods can be used to study these relationships, and several operations, even qualitatively different ones, can be used to measure a concept. Note, too, that when we validate a test used to measure a theoretical construct, we will simultaneously be validating the test and the theory.[3] However, we shall focus on what such studies tell about the validity of the test as a measure of the construct.[4]

Construct Validity Studies. The validation procedure implied by this view involves deducing testable hypotheses from the theory, then collecting data to test these hypotheses. Suppose that the results of an empirical study give us reason to believe that our hypotheses have been substantiated. What do the results mean? Certainly they do not "validate" or "prove" the entire theory, since we were dealing with only one portion of the theory. Instead, we retain our belief that the test measures the construct and can have more faith in our adoption of the concept.

What of negative results, of the data failing to confirm our hypothesis or prediction? Here there are at least three possible interpretations. The test may not measure the construct. Or the theoretical framework may have been in error, thus allowing for an incorrect inference to be made. Or, perhaps, the design of the experiment did not permit an appropriate test of the hypothesis. Unfortunately, it is not always clear which of these three possibilities is operating in a specific instance. The third interpretation, faulty experimental design, is usually easiest to detect; the other two are more likely to be confounded. Therefore, failure to confirm a prediction indicates that some revision is needed in the theoretical network and/or the experimental procedure, but the exact locus of the failure is not always clearly identified. This ambiguous interpretation of negative results is an obvious drawback of the construct validation procedure.

Tests as Signs. The picture we have presented, that of a formalized theory involving well-defined constructs and a set of specified laws, is overly idealistic. Many psychological constructs and laws are vaguely and incompletely defined,

---

[3] Some writers (e.g., Birnbaum, 1974; Campbell, 1960) make a distinction between validating a theory and validating a construct. Their view is that psychological theories are not well enough developed to allow validation, but individual constructs are often defined clearly enough to allow their validation.

[4] A test may, of course, measure more than one construct. We shall talk about a test measuring a single construct because there are advantages to using tests that measure but one construct (homogeneous tests) and because the awkward wording "construct or constructs" is thereby avoided.

and systematic theories are relatively rare. Construct validation aids progress toward this ideal, however, because in addition to clarifying existing constructs and laws, validation studies may also point out relationships that heretofore have gone undetected. When this occurs, the test is serving as a sign; that is, it provides information that clarifies the nature of the behavioral domain of interest.

Methods of Construct Validation

Construct validity can be investigated by a variety of methods. We shall consider six types of evidence: analyses of the internal structure of the test, correlations with other measures, criterion-related studies, studies involving experimental manipulation of variables, generalizability studies, and the multitrait-multimethod matrix approach. Although this categorization is somewhat arbitrary, and the methods are not completely independent, it does illustrate the most frequent approaches to construct validation.

Internal Structure. One source of evidence of construct validity is studies of the internal structure of the test: analyses of the test content, the processes used when responding to items, and the relationships between items and/or subtests. For example, if a test is designed to measure a single construct, indices of internal consistency (homogeneity), such as coefficient alpha or the K-R 20 reliability coefficient, will provide relevant data. If a test is composed of several scales or subtests, intercorrelations among the subtests will indicate whether the subtests all are measuring the same construct or measuring several distinct constructs.

Information on content validity also falls in this category. Specification of the domain sampled by the test items helps define the nature of the construct measured. Thus, for example, if "verbal ability" is defined as the ability to define words, reason using verbal analogies, and use words appropriately in context, a test of verbal ability should sample this domain.

Sometimes we are interested in the cognitive processes a test taker uses when responding to items as well as the responses per se. In these situations, process analyses can be used to identify the skills, abilities, or response tendencies test takers use when responding. This information may be obtained by observing test takers respond to the items, statistically analyzing responses, or asking people why they responded as they did. For example, we might be interested in whether a person solved certain mathematics problems using a formula or empirically.

Internal analyses help circumscribe the domain measured by the test and thereby help define the construct. However, they provide no evidence about the relationship of test scores with other variables.

Correlations with Other Measures. Another source of information is the correlations between the test being validated and other measures. In general, these methods are designed to indicate whether various tests measure the same construct and/or what features the tests do, and do not, share in common.

The simplest procedure, called *congruent validity,* is to correlate scores on a new test with scores on an established test measuring the same construct. For example, new intelligence tests are usually compared to well-validated individual measures such as the Stanford-Binet or one of the Wechsler Intelligence Scales. If the correlation is high, the two tests measure the same construct, and scores on the newer test can be interpreted as scores on the older test. We can also infer that scores on the new test will relate to other variables in somewhat the same manner as scores on the established test. These statements hold only when the two tests are highly correlated. The lower the intercorrelation between the two tests, the less faith we can have in generalizing from one test to the other.

In a more general sense, whenever we investigate the correlations between two or more tests presumed to measure the same construct, or the correlations between two or more methods of measuring the same construct, we are investigating *convergent validity.* Here we are trying to establish whether several approaches give the same information. But there is also an opposite side of this coin: We also need to establish that measures of different traits are not highly intercorrelated. This is called *discriminant validity* (Campbell, 1960; Campbell & Fiske, 1959). For example, several tests of creativity should intercorrelate positively (have convergent validity) but measures of creativity should be relatively independent of measures of different traits, such as intelligence (have discriminant validity). If measures of presumably dissimilar traits are highly correlated, we are actually measuring the same construct with both tests, but have given them different names. Although convergent validity evidence is often available for a test, evidence of discriminant validity is less common.

Another method used to study the relations among a set of tests or measures is factor analysis. *Factor analysis* is a statistical method for determining how many factors (constructs) are needed to account for the interrelations among a set of test scores. A factor analysis provides three types of information: (1) how many factors are needed to account for the intercorrelations among the tests, (2) what factors determine performance on each test, and (3) what proportion of the variance in the test scores is accounted for by these factors. In terms of construct validation, factor analysis indicates what factor (construct) a particular test measures and what other tests measure the same construct.

Criterion-Related Validity Studies. The nature and types of criteria predicted by the test scores also give an indication of what construct the test measures. Thus criterion-related validity coefficients can provide relevant data for construct validation. For example, a scholastic aptitude test should, of course, predict grades in academic subjects; a test of finger dexterity should predict success in an occupation, such as watch repairing, where fine movements are essential; a test of sociopathic tendencies should predict delinquency. Confirmation or disconfirmation of these predictions would strengthen or weaken, respectively, our confidence in the test as a measure of the purported trait.

Another type of criterion-related validity data is provided by studies of group separation or differentiation. For example, scores on occupational scales of interest inventories should differentiate between people in a particular occupation and people in general. Scores on intelligence tests should differentiate between children of various ages. Or a test of creativity should differentiate between artists who are acknowledged to be highly creative and ones whose work is judged to be stereotyped and mundane.[5] In each case, if the results of the study confirm our predictions, we have more confidence that the test measures the postulated construct.

Conversely, groups can be constructed on the basis of their test scores (for example, those scoring in the upper and lower portions of the score distributions) and the distinguishing characteristics of the groups identified. These characteristics serve to define the construct. For example, Barron (1963) showed that graduate students who scored high on an Ego Strength scale were rated as being alert, adventuresome, determined, independent, (having) initiative, outspoken, persistent, reliable, resourceful, and responsible; low scorers were rated as being dependent, effeminate, mannerly, and mild. These descriptions give the flavor of the construct being measured by the test, thus defining its nature.

Experimental Manipulation.   Useful information can also be obtained by manipulating some variable and observing its effects on test scores or the relation between test scores and some criterion. For example, suppose that we define "test anxiety" as the fear of failure on examinations when results have significance for a person's self-concept. From this definition we could hypothesize that performance on an examination would be negatively related to test anxiety (that is, high anxiety produces poor performance) if the exam were structured as being important to the person (for example, used to make some decision about his educational future), but that test-taking anxiety and examination scores would be unrelated if the test were structured so as to produce no threat to the individual (for example, if the test were presented as part of a standardization project and the student responded anonymously). If such an experiment were conducted and scores on the anxiety test did have the predicted relationships with examination scores, we would have evidence that the test did, in fact, measure test anxiety.

The category of experimental manipulation also includes evidence on variations resulting from naturally occurring events. For example, if the definition of a trait (construct) implies that the trait is resistant to environmental effects and is stable over time, the coefficient of stability should be high. Note that here reliability data are used as validity evidence—another illustration of the close relationship between the two concepts. Or if intelligence is defined so as to imply that it will increase with age, then a test presuming to measure intelligence must show increasing scores with age.

Generalizability Studies.   For most constructs we are interested in the range of situations and conditions in which the test provides useful and valid information. These conditions are essentially the same ones discussed under validity generalization in Chapter 6. Thus, for example, we might study the validity of a test under different administrative conditions (for example, various time limits or direc-

---

[5] Usually this type of validity is built into the test during the test construction process. For example, items included on occupational scales of interest inventories are chosen because they differentiate between people in an occupation and people in general, and items on intelligence tests are selected only if performance increases with age.

tions), when administered to different populations or age groups, using different response modes, or when the test is used for different purposes. To cite several examples, a test might be a good measure of the intelligence of children but not of adults, a problem-solving test might identify high-ability students but not differentiate between average and low-ability students, a college admissions test might predict grades in certain types of colleges but not in others, or a math ability test might be more valid when given with a restrictive time limit than with a more generous time limit. Thus, studies that investigate the distribution of scores and the validity of a test under varying conditions, or when administered to different groups, help establish the limits of its validity as well as clarify the nature of the construct measured.

The Multitrait-Multimethod Matrix. Any test measures a given trait by a given method; that is, any single measurement confounds trait and method effects. Thus, if we want to separate the effects of the trait we are measuring from the method of measurement, we must measure several traits by several methods. One possible method of analysis is the *multitrait-multimethod matrix* (Campbell & Fiske, 1959).

To illustrate the problem, consider scores on a personality inventory measuring several traits. The scores obtained may be attributable to the particular characteristics measured (the traits), or to the method of measurement (an inventory, rather than some other method), or to some combination of trait and method. If we studied different traits, or the same trait using a different method, we might obtain different results. Therefore, if we want to separate the relative contributions of trait and method components, we must study more than one trait and more than one method simultaneously. In essence, we are studying convergent and discriminant validity: convergent validity by looking at the correlations between the same traits measured by different methods; discriminant validity by looking at the correlations between different traits measured by the same method.

An example of a multitrait-multimethod matrix is shown in Table 7.1. This table shows the (hypothetical) correlations obtained when three traits (A, B, C) were measured by three different methods (1, 2, 3). The three traits might, for example, be dominance, social sensitivity, and self-assurance as measured by three methods: self-reports, projective techniques, and peer ratings. Or they might be measures of verbal comprehension, numerical reasoning, and general information as measured by a paper-and-pencil test, an individually administered test, and teacher's ratings. Any number and type of traits and methods can be utilized, with the number of traits not necessarily being equal to the number of methods. The three traits and methods used in the example were arbitrary choices.

The correlations in Table 7.1 can be divided into four categories. The correlations in the major diagonal are the reliabilities (measuring the same trait by the same method). The triangles outlined by dashed lines show the correlations between separate traits measured by different methods. The values within the triangles outlined by solid lines are the correlations across traits using a single

Table 7.1
An Example of a Multitrait-Multimethod Matrix

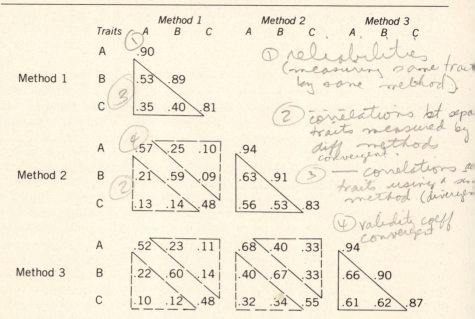

method (measures of method variance). Finally, the values in the diagonals between the dashed triangles are validity coefficients. Validity, in this approach, means convergent validity, since the values show the correlations between the same trait measured by different methods.

Several lines of evidence from the matrix are relevant to validity. First, different measures of the same trait should be positively correlated. Second, correlations between different methods of measuring a single trait (validity diagonals) should be higher than correlations between different traits measured by the same method (values in solid triangles). This means that trait differences should be greater than method differences. Third, validity coefficients should be higher than correlations involving both different traits and different methods (dashed triangles).

Two aspects of the multitrait-multimethod matrix approach deserve further mention. First, note that reliability is defined as the agreement between two measurements of the same trait using the same method, whereas validity is defined as the agreement between two measurements of the same trait using different methods. Thus the fundamental distinction between reliability and validity is in the similarity of the measurement methods. Second, this matrix provides evidence of possible method bias—for example, by showing the relationship between various traits measured using the same method. This evidence is not obtained in the usual validity study because each trait is measured by only one method, thus making it impossible to separate the effects of the trait, the measurement method, and their interaction. Only when multiple methods are utilized can we be sure that our results are attributable to trait differences rather than being artifacts of the measurement method.

Two Examples of Construct Validation

Since construct validation is a rather complex and abstract process, more concrete examples may help clarify its nature. We shall discuss two examples. The first, Barron's development of an Ego Strength (ES) scale (Barron, 1963) was chosen because a variety of types of evidence was used; it represents a blending of theory and empiricism, and it illustrates how a test can serve as a sign to point out the nature of the behavioral domain. The second example, a test-taking anxiety scale, is hypothetical but parallels the work in Sarason (1980).

Ego Strength.　Barron's original goal was to build a scale to predict which neurotics would respond favorably to psychotherapy. He administered the Minnesota Multiphasic Personality Inventory (MMPI), a test consisting of about 550 personality items, to a group of patients prior to therapy. After therapy the group was divided into two groups: those rated improved and those rated as unimproved. With improvement as the criterion, an item analysis was conducted, and 68 items that discriminated between the two groups were selected for the ES scale. Odd-even reliability and a coefficient of stability were calculated and found to be of an acceptable level. Barron then did a content analysis by classifying the scale items into rational groups and attempting to summarize the content of the scale. On the basis of this analysis, and such other data as a study of adjectives rated descriptive of persons obtaining high and low scores on the scale, Barron postulated that the test measured something broader than response to psychotherapy; he called this trait "Ego Strength," and proposed a tentative description of the construct.

Barron next predicted that scores on the ES scale would be related in certain ways to other variables. He tested these relationships in various groups, and in most instances his predictions were confirmed. For example, he hypothesized that ES and measures of intellectual ability would be moderately positively correlated, and found such relationships. He also correlated ES with characteristics exhibited in social interactions—self-confidence, drive, submissiveness—and found the correlations with variables such as tolerance, ethnocentrism, and measures of psychopathology. These relationships were viewed as supporting his interpretation of the ES scale. Barron also cross-validated the ES scale with three separate groups of psychotherapy patients.

At this point Barron defined "Ego Strength" as a construct expressed in characteristics such as physiological stability and good health, a strong sense of reality, feelings of personal adequacy and vitality, permissive morality, lack of ethnic prejudice, emotional outgoingness and spontaneity, and intelligence.

From this definition certain implications and hypotheses were drawn, then tested in further studies using various groups of normal subjects. ES scores were related to a variety of variables including intellectual performance, spatial orientation, ability to play charades, performance in the Asch experiment, and courage under fire in the Korean War. A cluster analysis to determine the item groupings was also conducted.

Although far from exhausting the possible relationships and studies, and being collected in a somewhat unsystematic manner, these data all served to clarify the meaning of the construct "Ego Strength." In addition, they provided the basis for a set of laws relating Ego Strength to other concepts. Thus they are a good beginning for the continual process of validating the ES scale as a measure of the construct "Ego Strength."

Test-Taking Anxiety.   Suppose that you were interested in measuring test-taking anxiety (TTA). You tentatively define this construct as the tendency to become apprehensive and display physiological symptoms of anxiety in evaluative situations. You devise a self-report inventory containing items such as:

> I feel tense during exams.
> My mind often goes blank during exams.
> I have obtained a low grade on an exam because of tenseness.
> I take exams in stride.

Students respond by indicating whether or not the statements describe their behavior. The total score on the test is used as the measure of test-taking anxiety.

What sorts of evidence could you provide to support the construct validity of your test? If you considered TTA to be a homogeneous dimension, you could compute coefficient alpha. As another type of internal analysis, you might ask students to cite particular experiences that they thought of when answering particular items. These experiences could be sorted into categories and otherwise analyzed to determine whether they fit your definition of TTA.

You might also correlate scores on your test with other measures of test-taking anxiety. Or you might correlate scores with physiological measures of anxiety. For example, you might obtain blood pressure measures, galvanic skin responses, or Strahan's sweat-bottle method (Strahan et al., 1974) to obtain a physiological measure of anxiety just before or when students were taking an examination. You could also correlate TTA scores with course or examination grades. Here you would look both at the simple correlation of grades with TTA scores and also check to see whether TTA was related to grades when ability was controlled.

One example of an experimental manipulation study was discussed previously. Another possibility would be to teach a group of students relaxation methods and/or test-taking skills. In this situation we could use a pretest-posttest design, with the hypothesis being that TTA scores should be lower after the training sessions than before.

We might also do a series of generalizability studies. For example, the results of each of the studies described above could be analyzed separately for males and females to see whether the effects were similar for both sexes. Or we could look at the correlation between TTA scores and performance in situations other than classroom examinations (e.g., job performance) to determine whether TTA operates only in formal classroom settings or generalizes to a broader range of evaluative situations.

You can probably think of other types of studies that can be done. The main point, however, is that establishment of construct validity is a gradual process based on the accumulation of various types of evidence, each of which serves to clarify the nature of the construct and indicate how well the test measures the construct.

Advantages and Limitations

Reactions to the concept of construct validity have ranged over the entire spectrum. Some writers (e.g., Loevinger, 1957; Messick, 1981b) believe that the construct validity is the essence of validity and that all other concepts of validity can be subsumed under construct validity. At the other extreme are writers (e.g., Bechtoldt, 1959; Ebel, 1961) who attack the notion of construct validity, primarily on the grounds that it violates the canons of operationalism. Other psychologists approve of the idea but suggest some modifications. For example, Campbell (1960) suggested that there are really two varieties of construct validity, *trait validity* and *nomological validity,* with the former focusing on the trait (construct) and the latter being concerned with the test as representing a term in a formal theoretical network.

Probably the greatest contribution the concept of construct validity has made is to focus attention on psychological tests as instruments of psychological theory. Thus tests are viewed in broader perspective than solely as tools to aid in practical decision making. Even when no formal theory is involved, construct validity forces the investigator to precisely define the trait being measured and to specify the relationships expected between test scores and other variables. It has also placed an emphasis on collecting a variety of data to support one's claims, rather than relying on only one technique or measure.

Construct validity also has several disadvantages. Many persons have tried to pawn off sloppy evidence as indications of construct validity; this, however, is more a fault of the investigator than of the concept. Also, the necessary operational steps and procedures are not unambiguous. For example, negative evidence has several possible interpretations, and no clear indication is presented of which way to proceed after obtaining negative evidence. Third, there is no single summary index to describe the degree of validity. Although the proportion of variance attributable to the trait being measured would appear to be a simple quantitative index of construct validity, this value may vary between situations. Fourth, unless all parties agree upon the definition of the construct, the results of various studies will not be comparable. In psychology, where terms frequently are only vaguely defined, it is not unusual for the same term to be applied to different concepts, and the same construct to be given different names by different authors. Unless there is agreement on definitions of basic terms, the investigators will just talk past each other.

a review and integration

Before leaving the discussion of validity, we shall provide a brief review and emphasize several points that were implied throughout the discussion.

Validity studies address two broad questions: What does the test measure? And, what outcomes can be predicted from test scores? More specifically, we described three types of validity (see Table 7.2). Criterion-related validity is concerned with the relationship between test scores and an external criterion. Content validity is concerned with the sampling of items from a defined domain. Construct validity focuses on the trait or construct measured by the test. Which type(s) of validity evidence will be most appropriate will depend on the particular use of the test. However, all serve to clarify what the test measures, and how well, and thus provide a basis for accurate interpretation of test scores.

A first point needing emphasis is that validity evidence will always be situation-specific; thus any test will have many different validities. The first part of this statement reminds us that validity is always established for a particular use of a test in a particular situation. For example, a selection test that is valid when used in one company may be less valid when used in another company, even when the jobs are similar. Or a test that predicts production on a job may not predict tenure. Thus, when evaluating validity data we must always consider the particular situation and how the test was used.

Table 7.2
Summary of Differences between Content, Criterion-Related, and Construct Validity

Content validity

> Question asked: How would the individual perform in the universe of situations of which the test items are a sample?
> Evaluation: By estimating the adequacy of sampling.
> Orientation: Toward the task or behavior, the test process.
> Example: A classroom exam sampling the content of a given unit of the course.

Criterion-related validity

> Question asked: How well do scores on the test predict status or performance on some independent measure?
> Evaluation: By comparing scores on the test with scores on the independent (qualitatively different) measure.
> Orientation: Toward the criterion, the predicted variable.
> Examples: Using a scholastic aptitude test to predict college grade average; using a mechanical aptitude test to predict success as an automobile mechanic; using a personality inventory to predict which automobile drivers will have accidents.

Construct validity

> Question asked: What trait does the test measure?
> Evaluation: By accumulation of evidence as to what the test does and does not measure.
> Orientation: Toward the trait being measured by the test.
> Examples: Developing a test to define a trait such as intelligence or creativity.

The second part of the statement reminds us that not only must we consider a test's validity for different uses, we must also consider the various types of validity evidence. Just because a test has content validity as a measure of knowledge of English grammar does not mean that it will necessarily predict success in composition courses. Although some tests may be valid in a wider variety of situations, or for more different uses, it makes no sense to talk about the validity of a test without the appropriate qualifications.

Second, although validity is usually discussed in connection with the final form of a test, the basic philosophy of validity plays an integral role in the test construction process. The pool of potential test items is composed of items that measure some important construct, sample some relevant content or behavioral domain, and/or are presumed to be predictive of the relevant criteria. Items are selected from this pool of potential items on the basis of their content or criterion-related validity. Items not meeting certain requirements dictated by the nature of the trait measured (for example, those that reduce homogeneity) are eliminated. Thus the concepts and procedures of validity are an essential element in the test construction process.

Finally, once again the relationship between consistency and validity should be emphasized. Unreliable measurement, of either the test or the criterion, limits validity. Then, too, certain types of consistency data often provide relevant information in construct validation studies. Finally, both reliability and validity are concerned with the generalizability of test data, the difference being in the dimensions over which we wish to make generalizations.

summary

In this chapter we discussed two types of validity—content validity and construct validity—that are used when a test is designed to represent a particular behavioral domain or theoretical construct.

Content validity studies evaluate whether the test items representatively sample a particular domain of knowledge, skill, or behavior. If a test has content validity, scores on the test can be used to make inferences about performance in the broader domain of which the test items are a sample. Thus the primary focus is on the domain being measured. Although content validity is particularly appropriate when evaluating achievement tests, it can be applied to other types of tests as well.

In most situations, content validity is established by having expert judges review the test items to determine whether they sample the domain of interest. Thus there is no quantitative index of content validity. Other methods of content validation include constructing two independent measures of the same domain, then correlating scores on the two tests; correlating scores on the test with other tests presumed to measure the same domain; and investigating changes in scores produced by relevant training or education.

Construct validity studies seek to determine and clarify the nature of the trait or construct measured by a test. It is most appropriate when the construct being measured cannot be defined solely in operational terms. Thus construct validity is most appropriate for ability, aptitude, and personality tests; that is, when the test serves as a sign.

Construct validity is established by collecting a variety of evidence about a test. Each study serves to define more clearly the nature of the construct by establishing its relation with other measures, behaviors, and outcomes. A number of methods for collecting evidence of construct validity were discussed. Analyses of the internal structure of a test help define the domain measured, as do internal consistency reliability coefficients, process analyses, and content validity studies. A second class involves correlations with other measures, such as studies of congruent validity, convergent and discriminant validity, and factor analyses. A third class, criterion-related validity studies, indicates what outcomes can be predicted by the test scores. A fourth class, experimental manipulation studies, investigates changes in test scores as a result of various experimental treatments or naturally occurring events. The fifth class, generalizability studies, seeks to establish the range of situations or conditions in which the test is valid. The sixth method, the multitrait-multimethod matrix, is useful for separating trait and method variance and for establishing the convergent and discriminant validity of a measure.

The chapter concluded with a brief review of some important points about validity. We emphasized that the validity of a test will vary depending on the situation, how the test is used, and the method of determining validity. Thus the validity of a test will always be specific to a particular situation and use, and any test will have many validities. In addition, we pointed out that not only is validity evaluated after a test is constructed, but certain types of validity are built into the test during the test construction process. Finally, we emphasized that collection of validity evidence is a continuing process, not something that is done once then forgotten.

Suggestions for Further Reading

Campbell, D. T., & Fiske, D. W. Convergent and discriminant validity by the multitrait-multimethod matrix. *Psychological Bulletin,* 1959, *56,* 81–105. The article that originally introduced the concepts of convergent and discriminant validity, stressed the need to consider method variance, and described the multitrait-multimethod approach.

Cronbach, L. J., & Meehl, P. E. Construct validity and psychological tests. *Psychological Bulletin,* 1955, *52,* 281–302. The classic paper describing the concept of construct validity and its philosophical rationale.

Ebel, R. L. And still the dryads linger. *American Psychologist,* 1974, *29,* 485–492. Discusses the problems and misconceptions in measuring broad psychological constructs such as intelligence, creativity, and motivation.

Guion, R. Content validity—The source of my discontent. *Applied Psychological Measurement,* 1977, *1,* 1–10. Discusses the problems involved in the concept of content validity and gives requirements for acceptable evidence of content validity.

Kerlinger, F. N. *Foundations of behavioral research,* 2d ed. New York: Holt, Rinehart and Winston, 1973. Chapter 27 includes an excellent, brief discussion of construct validity.

Messick, S. The standard problem: Meaning and values in measurement and evaluation. *American Psychologist,* 1975, *30,* 955–966. Argues that all psychological measures should be construct-referenced (that is, should clearly indicate what they measure) and that test users must consider their values and how the test will be used.

Nunnally, J. *Psychometric theory,* 2d ed. New York: McGraw-Hill, 1978. Chapter 3 is a theoretical discussion of validity with emphasis on construct validity.

Standards for educational and psychological tests. Washington, D.C.: American Psychological Association, 1974. Pages 28–33 and 45–48 describe standards and guidelines for evidence on construct validity.

Ward, W. C., Frederiksen, N., & Carlson, S. B. Construct validity of free-response and machine-scorable forms of a test. *Journal of Educational Measurement,* 1980, *17,* 11–29. An empirical study showing that different types of test items measuring the same content may measure different abilities and cognitive processes.

• part three •
interpreting
test scores

HOW did you do? This question is asked frequently—for example, of students who have just had a test returned, of athletes finishing competition, and of gamblers returning from Las Vegas. Perhaps the student obtained a score of 40, the athlete high-jumped 6 feet, and the gambler lost $500. These numbers only partially answer the question. The meaning of a test score of 40 depends on the grade assigned; whether high-jumping 6 feet is good depends on the age and sex of the athlete; whether losing $500 is important depends on the financial resources of the gambler. Determining the meaning of these quantitative values requires other information, often a comparison to some type of performance standard.

Testing also results in quantitative values—scores—that describe test takers' levels of performance. As with other types of measurements, test scores take on meaning only as they are interpreted and used. In this part of the book we will describe various types of test scores and how they are interpreted and used. We will focus on two areas. One is how to develop scoring scales that are both statistically sound and psychologically meaningful. This is the concern of the test developer. The other is the interpretation and use of test scores. This is the concern of the test user.

Chapter 8 describes norm-referenced scores, which compare an individual's performance to that of other people. Chapter 9 covers content-referenced scores, which express performance relative to a predetermined standard of content mastery, and outcome-referenced scores, which express performance in terms of predicted performance on some other criterion measure.

The placement of the chapters on scores at this point in the book was deliberate—to emphasize that unless a test is carefully constructed, and unless it is reliable and valid, we can have little faith in the score interpretations. Particularly, we wanted to stress that unless we have evidence of what a test measures or predicts (that is, validity evidence), score interpretation will be a fruitless exercise.

Chapter 8 • Norm-Referenced Scores

MOST readers of this book probably will never have to determine the reliability or validity of a test. However, you probably will have numerous opportunities to interpret test scores. These may include scores on tests you yourself take; ones you interpret in your role as a teacher, counselor, or employer; or when reading reports of studies using test data. To aid you in this task, this chapter and the next one will describe the construction and interpretation of the common varieties of test scores.

When interpreting test scores you must consider three questions: What is the person's present level of performance? What factors caused this person to perform at this level? And what are the implications for his or her future behavior? The first question reminds us that test scores provide a description of a person's present level of performance—no more and no less. The score tells how the person performed, not why. The second question reminds us that interpretation of scores often requires knowledge of the test taker's experiences prior to testing and of the nature of the test. For example, the same score on a reading test might mean quite different things if obtained by a child attending an academically oriented private school or by a child from an inner-city ghetto school. The third question reminds us to consider how the test scores will be used and what implications they will have for the test taker's life.

types of test scores

One stage in the test interpretation process is the development of scoring procedures and scales that are statistically sound and accurately reflect test takers' performance. This is the task of the test developer. The other is communication of accurate and useful information to test takers and others using the scores. This is the joint responsibility of the test developer and the test user. The test developer must develop scoring scales that users can understand and supply information to aid score interpretation (e.g., normative data); the test user must be able to communicate the meaning of the scores to various people who will use this information. In this section we shall address the first problem, development of scales for reporting test scores.

Raw Scores

After a test is administered, an individual's responses are compared to a *key* to obtain his or her score on the test. On achievement and ability tests, the keyed responses are the correct answers. On interest and personality inventories, the keyed responses are usually the predominant choices of a particular criterion group (e.g., psychologists, schizophrenics, submissive people). Other performance measures can also be used as scores—for example, the number of errors, the sum of points on various items or problems, the time taken to complete the test, or a rating. Any such score obtained directly from the test is called a *raw score*.

At the most microscopic level, raw scores are obtained for each individual item. However, scores on individual items are seldom interpreted as such. More often we interpret scores on groups of items such as a total score (the score over all items on a test). Sometimes we interpret scores on *subtests* or *scales*.[1] At other times we may interpret scores from several independent tests, either expressed as a composite (summing scores over various tests) or as differences or ratios.

Raw scores are seldom meaningful in and by themselves. Only when a test covers an explicitly defined domain, and when an absolute standard of performance is available, does a raw score have meaning. Otherwise, a raw score must be compared to the scores of comparable individuals or to some defined standard, or expressed in terms of some outcome or criterion. Each of these approaches requires transforming raw scores to a different scale. Since the new scale is derived from the raw scores by a statistical transformation, they are called *transformed* or *derived scores*.

Transformed Scores

1. norm reference — higher compare in d with group
2. content — (st of mastery).
3. outcome — predict future performance

There are a number of possible ways of classifying transformed scores (see, e.g., Angoff, 1971a; Carver, 1974; Glaser, 1963; Lyman, 1978, 1980; Mayo, 1980; or *Standards*, 1974). We shall use a classification scheme that focuses on the basis for interpreting scores. This classification includes three types of scores: norm-referenced scores, content-referenced scores, and outcome-referenced scores. Norm-referenced scores will be discussed in this chapter, the others in the next chapter.

With *norm-referenced scores* an individual's score is compared to those of other people in some relevant reference group, the norm group. Norm-referenced scores, either directly or indirectly, indicate the person's relative position or ranking within the norm group. Thus, to say a student scored higher than 75 percent of his classmates on a mechanical ability test is a norm-referenced interpretation.

With *content-referenced scores* an individual's performance is compared with a standard of mastery or proficiency. This standard is based on mastery of the skill or material covered by the test, not on the performance of other individuals. For example, to say that a person can drive well enough to obtain a license is a con-

---

[1] A *subtest* is a group of items administered as a separate part of a test; i.e., with separate directions and time limits. A *scale* is a group of items measuring a common characteristic but not administered as a separate section of a test; that is, items are interspersed throughout the test among items measuring other characteristics. Separate scores are obtained from each subtest or scale. Subtests are more common on maximal performance tests, whereas scales are more common on typical performance tests.

tent-referenced interpretation. Note that the decision to issue a license is based on a minimal level of driving proficiency, not on a comparison with other drivers.

Outcome-referenced scores interpret performance in terms of behavior on some other measure. In essence, the interpretation is a prediction of future performance. Thus, to say students with a certain score on a college admissions test are likely to obtain a B average at Old Siwash is an outcome-referenced interpretation. In order to use outcome-referenced scores we must have validity data; unless we know the relationship between the test scores and the predicted behaviors (the criterion), our interpretations will be of little value.

All three types of scores might be used on the same test. For example, suppose a mathematics achievement test is administered to high school seniors. If we had the necessary data, scores could be interpreted in terms of relative ranks compared with other high school seniors (norm-referenced interpretation), in comparison with minimal graduation requirements (content-referenced interpretation), and as predictions of probable grades in college-level mathematics courses (outcome-referenced interpretation). More commonly, any score is interpreted in only one of these ways.

normative data

In norm-referenced measurement, an individual's score is compared with the scores of other individuals in a relevant reference group, the *norm group*. The norm group is composed of people who share certain characteristics with the individual. For example, on a classroom examination the norm group will be other persons taking the same course; on an intelligence test, children of the same age; on college admissions tests, students planning to attend college. Thus developing norm-referenced scores involves identifying a relevant comparison group, obtaining the test scores of members of this group, and converting raw scores to a scale that expresses performance as a relative ranking within this norm group.

The use of norm-referenced scores emphasizes that psychological measurement is relative rather than absolute. As mentioned earlier, in educational and psychological measurement absolute scales or standards seldom are available. Also, in most situations, differences between indidividuals are more important, or at least more interesting, than similarities. Both of these factors argue for expressing performance in comparative terms—that is, on norm-referenced scales.

Norm Groups

The norm group provides a basis for comparison by showing the scores of a standard, defined reference group. Potentially, there are a number of possible norm groups for any test. Since a person's relative ranking may vary widely depending on the norm group used for comparison, the composition of the norm group is a crucial factor in the interpretation of norm-referenced scores. Thus, when developing norms, the first question is: What are the various possible norm groups?

From the test developer's viewpoint, this question becomes: In what populations will the test be used? The norm groups should be chosen to represent these populations. If the test is designed to assess high school seniors' aptitude for college work, the norm group should consist of high school seniors who plan to attend college. If the test is designed to measure the personality characteristics of adolescents, the norm group would consist of a cross section of adolescents. If the test is designed to measure the reading readiness of kindergarten students, the norm group should consist of kindergarten students who have not begun reading instruction. Since most tests are designed for use with various groups, more than one norm group generally will be needed.

The test user looks at norms from a different vantage point. His primary question is: Which of the available norm groups is most appropriate? Again, several norm groups may be relevant. For example, when counseling a high school student who plans to study engineering in college, a counselor might compare the student's scores on a college admission test with those of other high school students planning to attend college, with those of entering freshmen at the universities the student is thinking of attending, and with those of freshmen engineering students at the universities the student is thinking of attending.

Requirements for Norm Groups. The test developer or user must consider several factors when constructing or evaluating norm groups. The first requirement is that *the composition of the norm group be clearly defined*. Although the general specifications of the norm groups will be dictated by the purposes and uses of the test, within this range there is a variety of potential norm groups. Therefore a concise, yet clear, description of the nature and characteristics of each norm group is necessary. A statement that a norm group is composed of "5000 college freshmen" is insufficient. Even the following statement provides only a minimal description:

> The norm group consists of entering freshmen, male and female, enrolled in liberal arts curricula at land-grant universities.

Some questions we might ask are: What is an "entering freshman"? What curricula are subsumed under "liberal arts"? What are "land-grant universities"?

If a norm group is composed of people in a particular job or occupation, the title of the job should be given along with its code in the *Dictionary of Occupational Titles;* the job duties should be specified, and the type of business or industry, its geographic location, the years of experience of the workers, and other relevant information should be included. For achievement tests, the basic information should include the grade level of the students, the type of school, socioeconomic and other demographic data, and the students' experience in the subject matter area being tested.

In most instances a norm group consists of a sample drawn from the relevant population rather than the entire population. Thus a second requirement is that *the norm group must be a representative sample of the designated population*. For example, if a test is designed for use with junior high students, it should include proportionate numbers of students from each grade level, urban and rural areas, various races, both high and low socioeconomic areas, various areas of the country, and so forth. Failure to obtain a representative sample will bias the norm data and make interpretation of scores more difficult. Since norm data are easier to obtain from certain groups (for example, it is easier to collect a sample of college students than 18-year-olds who are working), the possibility of biased sampling is ever present.

Implicit in the previous paragraph is a third requirement: *The sampling procedure must be clearly described*. To return to our previous example, the description of the sampling, and thus of the norm group, might be:

> The norm group consisted of 5000 entering freshmen tested in the first week of classes in September 1975; 250 students (125 male and 125 female) were randomly selected from students enrolled in liberal arts curricula at each of 20 universities randomly selected from among all land-grant institutions.

As with the description of the population, the more precise and comprehensive the description the better.

A fourth requirement is that *the norm groups be based on a sample of adequate size*. What constitutes "adequate size" is hard to define precisely. However, since the amount of sampling error varies inversely with sample size, the larger the sample the better. Certainly it is not unreasonable to expect national norms on standardized tests to include several hundred cases in each sampling cell. However, the need for large samples, which provide more stable estimates, must be tempered by the requirement of representative sampling. That is, obtaining scores from a smaller, more representative sample is generally more desirable than a set of scores from a larger but vaguely defined group. (See Angoff, 1971a, for a discussion of the procedures of developing norm groups.)

A final consideration is the recency of the norms. With changes in education and job requirements, norms that were developed a number of years ago may no longer be appropriate. Thus *norms should be updated periodically* and old norms looked upon with appropriate skepticism.

Deriving Norm-Referenced Scores. While the process of deriving norm-referenced scores will vary with the nature of the test, the basic process is quite simple. The first step is to define the norm group. The second step is to select an appropriate sample. The test is then administered to members of this sample. After the test is scored, a distribution of raw scores is obtained.[2] These raw scores are then converted into the one or more types of derived scores. Finally, tables or charts are prepared to show the relationship between the raw scores and transformed scores for each norm group.

In many ways, the most critical and difficult step is obtaining an adequate sample. Here the goal is to obtain a sample that is representative of the population along various important dimensions. Consider, for example, developing national norms for a reading test designed for use in grades 4–8. Because reading skills increase with age, we would want separate norms for each grade level. Within each grade level, the norm group should reflect the parent population along certain dimensions—for example, geographic region of the country, sex, size of community, type of school, and perhaps others. To draw an adequate sample, we

---

[2] If a test yields more than one score, such as when subtests are used, separate distributions are made for each score. The remaining steps also apply to each score that will be interpreted.

would first have to classify each dimension into various groups (for example, several levels of community size, public versus private schools). We would then consult appropriate demographic data to find the proportion of students falling in each group. (For example, what percent of sixth-grade students reside in the New England states?) Given these data, we could build a sampling plan that would indicate the proportion of students in each category (e.g., males attending public schools in large midwestern cities). Next we would sample schools, classrooms, and/or individuals to attain the desired proportional representation. Although various sampling strategies could be used, the final sample should represent the composition of the population along all relevant dimensions.

The common types of transformed scores are described later in this chapter. For a discussion of other types of scores and norm groups, see Angoff (1971a), Lyman (1978), and Mayo (1980).

Subgroup Norms. Frequently various subgroups within a population obtain different average scores or have different distributions of scores. When this occurs, separate norms may be constructed for each subgroup. For example, men generally perform better than women on tests of mechanical aptitude; conversely, women score higher than men on clerical aptitude tests. Therefore, separate normative data for men and women are usually provided on these tests. Variables that frequently are related to test performance, and thus may constitute the basis of separate norm groups, include sex, age, education, socioeconomic status, intelligence, occupation, geographic region, race, and amount of special training.

Whether separate subgroup norms are necessary or desirable will depend on the use of the test. For example, as stated above, males and females generally obtain different average scores on mechanical aptitude tests. If we want to interpret scores by comparing a person's performance with that of other people having similar experiences, we would use separate norms for each sex; that is, males would be compared to the male norms and females to the female norms. However, if we were using the scores to make inferences about a person's probable success on a job requiring mechanical aptitude, we would be better advised to use a combined (male + female) norm group since we would want to compare the applicant's performance with that of all other applicants, regardless of their gender.

Local Norms

A test user may find than none of the available norm groups fits his or her purposes. Or the user may want to utilize a more limited norm group than those presented in the test manual, which are usually rather broad in scope. For instance, a classroom teacher may want to compare the performance of her students to other students in her class or in the local school system. In this situation, one solution is to construct *local norms*.

Developing local norms is simple and straightforward (Ricks, 1971). Since norm tables are basically frequency distributions, the procedure involves obtaining scores for all people in the local group (or a sample of this group), compiling a frequency distribution, and calculating derived scores.

The main advantage of local norms is, of course, that they allow for comparisons between a person and his immediate associates. Because each class, school, or company is in some ways unique, its members will differ from the members of the norm groups listed in the manual. For example, the students in any particular class or school will not have had the same educational experiences as students in the national norm group. The local students will probably also differ from the national norm group on factors related to school achievement, such as abilities or socioeconomic background. When such differences occur between local and national norm groups, a local norm group may represent a better standard of comparison. Of course, a test user can use both local and national norms, and thus extract the maximal amount of information from test scores.

The advantage of local norms—providing a more immediate comparison group—is also its major weakness. Although local norms provide information relevant to immediate local decisions, they do not allow the interpretations in a broader context. For example, data from local groups may be more valuable in helping a student decide whether to take Geometry A or Geometry B; they will be of limited use in counseling the student about a career in mathematics. In the latter case, broader norms will provide better information.

A Brief Summary

Our discussion of norms can best be summarized by paraphrasing several general principles formulated by Seashore and Ricks (1950). They suggest that one should use well-defined norm groups and avoid vaguely defined people-in-general norms; use separate subgroup norms whenever populations differ and combine groups only when the combination makes sense; report all useful norm data (that is, provide norms on various groups); develop and use local and special group norms; make all normative data available to other test users; and use the available normative data when interpreting scores.

types of norm-referenced scores

All norm-referenced scores compare an individual's score to those of other people in a designated norm group; they indicate the test taker's relative standing or ranking within the norm group. We shall discuss four classes of norm-referenced scores: percentile ranks, standard scores, developmental scales, and ratios. For each type of score we shall describe its rationale and computation, give an example, describe how the score is interpreted, and cite its advantages and limitations.

Percentile Ranks

Probably the most widely used method of expressing test scores is percentile ranks. *The percentile rank for a score is defined as the percentage of persons in the norm group who obtain lower scores.* Thus, a percentile rank of 78 indicates that 78 percent of the people in the norm group obtained lower scores; a percentile rank of 5 indicates that only 5 percent of the norm group obtained lower scores. In other words, a percentile rank indicates the person's relative ranking in percentage terms. The important point is that percentile ranks involve percentages of people. (This is in contrast to percentage scores, which express performance in terms of percent of content mastered; that is, a percentage score of 78 means that the student correctly answered 78 percent of the items.)

Computation of Percentile Ranks. A percentile rank indicates the proportion of people in a norm group who score lower than a particular score. However, three definitions of "score lower" can be used. Some people use the literal definition; that is, the proportion of scores that are lower than a particular score. Others interpret it to mean the proportion obtaining that score or a lower score. Still others interpret it to mean score at or below the midpoint of a given score interval. We will use this last approach.

An example of the computation of percentile ranks is given in Table 8.1; for other methods, see Ebel (1972) or Angoff (1971a). The first step is to prepare a frequency distribution. Next find the proportion of people who score below the score in question. This is called the *cumulative frequency* (*CF*) or, more precisely, the cumulative frequency to the lower limit of the score interval (see step 2 in Table 8.1). Next add one-half the number of scores in the interval to the cumulative frequency (step 3). This gives the cumulative frequency to the midpoint of the score interval (*CF*$_{mp}$). Next divide this value by the total number of scores to obtain the *cumulative proportion* (step 4). Finally, multiply the cumulative proportions by 100 to obtain the percentile ranks (step 5).

Percentile ranks can also be obtained graphically. In this method, we would first plot the cumulative frequency for each test score, then draw a smoothed curve between the points (see Figure 8.1). Percentile ranks could then be obtained by drawing a perpendicular from the test score to the curve, then drawing another perpendicular to the percentile rank axis. The point at which this line intersects the vertical axis is the percentile rank for that score. In our example, we have drawn such lines to show that an ACT score of 27 is equal to a percentile rank of 53, which is essentially the same value we found in Table 8.1.

Interpretation of Percentile Ranks. Interpretation of percentile ranks is straightforward. All you have to remember is that a percentile rank indicates the number of people out of 100 who scored lower than the score in question. To illustrate, in our example (Table 8.1), a raw score of 25 was equivalent to a percentile rank of 31. Thus a student who scored 25 on the ACT scored higher than 31 percent of her classmates and lower than the other 69 percent.

Percentile Points. When computing percentile ranks we determined the proportion of individuals who scored lower than a given test score. Sometimes, however, we want to know what test score divides a distribution into certain proportions; for example, we might want to find the test score corresponding to a percentile rank of 80. This can be done by finding the cumulative proportion associated with the percentile rank, then finding the point on the raw score scale corresponding to this cumulative proportion. The point on the score scale corresponding to the desired percentile rank is called a *percentile point,* or, more simply, a *percentile.*

Table 8.1
Computation of Percentile Ranks

The following steps illustrate the procedure for computing percentile ranks. The data used are the ACT Composite scores for a sample of 177 entering freshmen women in a midwestern liberal arts college.

1. Prepare a frequency distribution of the scores.
2. Find the cumulative frequency (CF) to the lower limit of each score. This is the sum of all scores below the score in question. For example, the CF for a score of 23 is: $1 + 3 + 12 = 16$, the number of students scoring 22 or lower.
3. Find the cumulative frequency to the midpoint of the score interval (CF_{mp}). This is obtained by adding one-half the number of scores in the interval to the CF. For example, for a score of 23:

$$CF_{mp} = 16 + (.5)(14) = 23.0$$

4. Find the cumulative proportion (CP) by dividing CF_{mp} by n, the total number of scores. For a score of 23:

$$CP = \frac{23.0}{177} = .130$$

5. To find the percentile rank (PR), multiply CP by 100. Again, with a score of 23:

$$PR = (.130)(100) = 13$$

A percentile rank of 13 means that 13 of every 100 students (13 percent) scored lower than 23 on the ACT and 87 of every 100 (87 percent) scored higher.

X	f	CF	CF_{mp}	CP	PR
32	4	173	175.0	.989	99
31	7	166	169.5	.958	96
30	17	149	157.5	.890	89
29	22	127	138.0	.780	78
28	18	109	118.0	.667	67
27	28	81	95.0	.537	54
26	15	66	73.5	.415	42
25	22	44	55.0	.311	31
24	14	30	37.0	.209	21
23	14	16	23.0	.130	13
22	12	4	10.0	.056	6
21	3	1	2.5	.014	1
20	1	0	0.5	.003	<1

To illustrate, let us find the raw score, that divides the top 20 percent of the distribution from the remaining 80 percent. From Table 8.1 we can see that a raw score of 30 has a CP of .890 and a raw score of 29 has a CP of .780; interpolating, we find that a raw score of 29.2 is equivalent to a percentile rank of 80. Similar procedures would be used to find what raw score was needed to obtain various percentiles' ranks—such as 90, 80, 70, and so on.

Percentile Bands. As all test scores contain some error of measurement, any obtained score should be viewed as only a best estimate. Thus, rather than reporting exact scores, performance could be reported as bands or ranges. These ranges generally will be some function of the standard error of measurement; for

Figure 8.1. Obtaining Percentile Ranks Graphically.

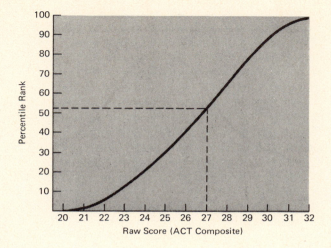

example, the obtained score plus or minus one standard error of measurement. Since the standard error of measurement can also be applied around percentile ranks, some test publishers report percentile ranks as ranges. To illustrate, in our example, the standard error of measurement would be approximately .5 raw score points. Thus, rather than reporting a percentile rank of 30 for a score of 24, we might report a range of 23–37.[3] Such ranges are called *percentile bands.*

Quartiles and Deciles. Percentiles divide the distribution into 100 parts. When broader divisions are sufficient, two other related scores are sometimes used. *Quartiles* are scores that divide the distribution into four equal parts. Thus, the first quartile is equivalent to a percentile of 25, the second quartile to a percentile of 50 (which is also the median), and the third quartile is equivalent to a percentile of 75. *Deciles* divide the distribution into ten parts. Thus, the first decile is equivalent to a percentile of 10, the second decile to a percentile of 20, and so on.

Advantages and Limitations. The major advantage of percentile ranks is that their meaning is clear to most test users. Knowing a person's relative ranking in a relevant comparison group is, to most persons, a simple, readily comprehensible, and meaningful index of performance. Also, for many purposes, ranking within a group is sufficient; thus more complex transformations are not needed.

Percentile ranks have two major limitations. First, being on an ordinal scale they cannot legitimately be added, subtracted, multiplied, or divided. This is not a serious limitation when interpreting scores, but it is a serious liability in statis-

---

[3] The standard error of measurement was computed by using .96 as the reliability of the ACT scores (ACT, 1972) and the standard deviation of 2.76 for our sample (see Table 8.2). We then computed percentile ranks for scores of 23.5 and 24.5 and used these percentile ranks as the limits of the percentile band.

Figure 8.2 Relationship between Distributions of Raw Scores and of Percentile Ranks.

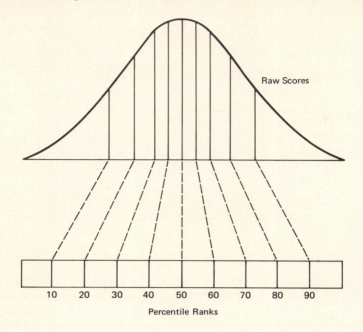

tical analyses. A second limitation is of more concern to the test user. Percentile ranks have a rectangular distribution, whereas test score distributions generally approximate the normal curve. As a consequence, small raw score differences near the center of the distribution result in large percentile differences. Conversely, large raw score differences at the extremes of the distribution produce only small percentile differences (see Figure 8.2). Unless these relations are kept in mind, percentile ranks can easily be misinterpreted; in particular, seemingly large differences in percentile ranks near the center of the distribution tend to be overinterpreted.

Standard Scores

While percentile ranks are easy to interpret, they are less useful when we want to analyze scores statistically or make certain types of comparisons between scores. This is because they provide only rank-order scores and because the relationship between percentile ranks and raw scores is not the same at all points on the scale. Standard scores avoid both of these problems.

A standard score (z) is the deviation of a raw score from the mean in standard deviation units:

$$z = \frac{X - \bar{X}}{s} \tag{8.1}$$

problem: (+) & *(-) values*

ind →

not a normal transformation – its linear

on st-scores: mean = 0 st. dev = 1

Since the scale unit is the standard deviation, such scores are referred to as standard scores.

Inasmuch as z scores are linear transformations of raw scores, the distribution of z scores will have the same shape as the distribution of raw scores. If the raw score distribution is normal, so will be the z-score distribution; if the raw score distribution is skewed, the z-score distribution will be similarly skewed. Since the mean of the raw scores is subtracted from each score, the mean of the z scores will be 0; moreover, since each *deviation score* $(x = X - \overline{X})$ is then divided by the standard deviation, the standard deviation of the z scores will be 1. The sign of the z score tells whether the raw score is above or below the mean; scores above the mean have positive z scores, whereas scores below the mean have negative z scores. The absolute value of the z score tells how many standard deviations the score is from the mean. Finally, in a normal distribution, the range of z scores will be approximately -3.0 to $+3.0$, a range of about six standard deviations.

Computation of Standard Scores. The computation of standard scores is illustrated in Table 8.2; the data are those used to illustrate the computation of percentile ranks. The first step is to compute the mean and standard deviation of the raw scores (step 1 in Table 8.2). To compute the z score for any raw score, first obtain the deviation score (x) by subtracting the mean from the raw score (step 2), then divide this deviation score by the standard deviation (step 3). The resultant z score expresses performance in terms of how many standard deviations the score is from the mean.

Transformed Standard Scores. Because z scores can have decimal and negative values, they usually are transformed to yet another scale by a transformation of the form:

$$Z = a + bz \tag{8.2}$$

where a and b are constants. In effect, multiplying z scores by the constant b converts scores to a scale having a standard deviation of b points; adding a to each score converts scores to a scale having a mean of a. Since the transformation is linear, the relationships between scores will be the same regardless of whether scores are expressed as Z scores, z scores, or raw scores.

Although any set of constants can be used, the recommended procedure is to convert scores to a scale having a mean of 50 and a standard deviation of 10 (see step 4 in Table 8.2). This can be accomplished by the following formula:

$$T = 50 + 10z \tag{8.3}$$

The resultant scale will have a range of approximately 20 to 80 in a normal distribution. All T scores are rounded to whole numbers.[4]

[4] T scores originally were defined in relation to a specific norm group (McCall, 1922). However, they are now generally used for all standard score scales using a mean of 50 and a standard deviation of 10.

Table 8.2
Computation of Standard Scores

The following steps illustrate the computation of standard scores. The data are those used in Table 8.1.

1. Compute the mean and standard deviation. For these data you will obtain $\overline{X} = 26.54$ and $s = 2.76$.

2. For each raw score, find the deviation score (x), which is the raw score minus the mean. For example, when $X = 25$:

$$x = 25 - 26.54 = -1.54$$

$$z = \frac{x - \overline{X}}{s_x}$$

↳ # of standard deviations

3. Find z for each score. Remember, $z = x/s$. For $X = 25$:

$$z = \frac{-1.54}{2.76} = -0.56$$

The z score expresses the raw score in terms of standard deviation units from the mean. Our example indicates that a raw score of 25 is 0.56 standard deviation below the mean.

4. To eliminate decimals and negative numbers, we transform z scores to another scale. The recommended transformation is to a scale with a mean of 50 and a standard deviation of 10. This can be accomplished using the formula $T = 50 + 10z$. Applied to our example, with $X = 25$:

$$T = 50 + 10(-0.56) = 50 - 5.6 = 44.4, \text{ or } 44$$

Our scores are now expressed on a standard score scale with mean of 50 and standard deviation of 10 points.

The computational routine is as follows:

Z score = how many standard deviation score is from mean

X	$(x - \bar{x})$ x	z	T
32	5.46	1.98	70
31	4.46	1.62	66
30	3.46	1.25	62
29	2.46	0.89	59
28	1.46	0.53	55
27	0.46	0.17	52
26	−0.54	−0.20	48
25	−1.54	−0.56	44
24	−2.54	−0.92	41
23	−3.54	−1.28	37
22	−4.54	−1.64	34
21	−5.54	−2.01	30
20	−6.54	−2.37	26

Normalized Standard Scores. The standard scores described (z, T) are linear transformations of raw scores. When using these scores, we assumed that the raw score distribution was approximately normal. What if the score distribution is not normal?

When raw scores are not normally distributed, we can make an *area transfor-*

not linear transformation most used in test batteries

164 Interpreting Test Scores

mation and force scores into a normal distribution. Scores derived in this manner are called *normalized standard scores;* the word "normalized" indicates that scores have been forced into a normal distribution. In order to normalize scores there must be some basis for assuming that scores on the characteristic being measured are, in fact, normally distributed. If scores cannot be assumed to be normally distributed, forcing them into a normal distribution only distorts the distribution. Therefore, normalized standard scores are computed only when an obtained distribution approaches normality but, because of sampling errors, is slightly different. This situation frequently occurs in standardization of tests on large, heterogeneous samples.

To calculate normalized standard scores requires finding the z scores that divide the distribution into the desired proportions. (We will label these scores z', to distinguish them from other z scores described above.) The procedure involves, first, finding the cumulative proportion associated with each raw score (as in step 4 of Table 8.1) and then, from Appendix A, finding the z' score corresponding to this division. For scores above the mean, refer to Column C; for scores below the mean, to Column D. Thus, as the *CP* for a score of 29 was .780, the corresponding z' score (after interpolating) would be 0.77; for a score of 23 the CP was .130, so the corresponding z' score (again after interpolating) would be -1.13, the negative sign indicating the score is below the mean.

As with z scores, normalized standard (z') scores are usually transformed to another scale to eliminate decimals and negative values. The procedure is the same as above. Although we can use any constants, again the recommended conversion is to a scale with a mean of 50 and a standard deviation of 10.

Other Standard Scores.   Many commercially published tests use standard scores for reporting performance, most often normalized standard scores. For example, the College Board's Scholastic Aptitude Test (SAT) and the Graduate Record Examination (GRE) report standard scores on a scale with a mean of 500 and a standard deviation of 100 points and scores on the American College Testing Program (ACT) Assessment have a mean of 20 and a standard deviation of 5 points for college-bound students.

The *intelligence quotients (IQs)* on the commonly used individual intelligence tests, the Stanford-Binet Intelligence Scale and the various Wechsler Intelligence Scales, are also standard scores. On the Stanford-Binet the mean IQ at each age level is 100 and the standard deviation is 16 points; on the Wechsler scales the mean is also 100 at each age level but the standard deviation is 15 IQ points.

Another well-known variety of standard scores is the *stanine,* stanine being an abbreviation for "standard nine." The stanine scale is a nine-step standard score scale with a mean of 5 and a standard deviation of 2, with the middle seven categories each being one-half standard deviation wide. Though stanines have the advantage of being one-digit scores, of necessity they sacrifice some precision.

The relationships between various score scales are shown in Figure 8.3. This figure shows the relationships for a normal distribution; when the distribution is not normal, the relations will not hold as precisely.

Figure 8.3. Relations between Common Score Scales.

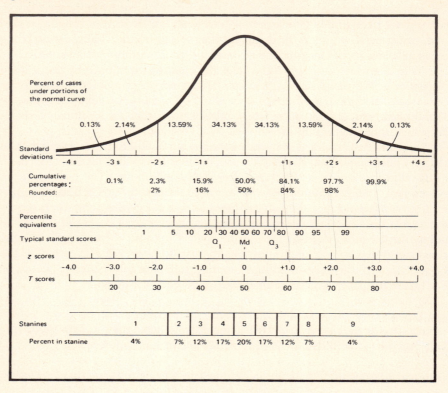

Interpretation of Standard Scores. All standard scores report performance in terms of standard deviations from the mean. Therefore a z of +1.0, a T of 60, and a transformed normalized standard score of 60 all indicate a raw score one standard deviation above the mean. Similarly, a z of −1.5 or a T of 35 indicates the raw score was 1.5 standard deviations below the mean. Thus one way to interpret standard scores is in terms of the number of standard deviation units a person's score is from the mean.

For a person unfamiliar with the concept of the standard deviation such an interpretation will, at best, be vague. However, when using normalized standard scores, or when the distribution of linearly transformed standard scores approaches normality, standard scores can be converted into percentile ranks with reference to the normal curve. Thus, a score of 60 is equivalent to a percentile rank of 84 and a standard score of 35 is equivalent to a percentile rank of 7. These relationships between standard scores and percentile ranks hold regardless of the nature and content of the test. Thus, normalized standard scores and T scores can be converted to and interpreted as percentiles. When interpreting tests to people unfamiliar with standard scores, you will probably want to use a percentile-based interpretation.

When interpreting standard scores, you must also consider several other factors. One, of course, is the nature of the transformation used. A standard score of 80 would mean quite different things if the transformed scale had a mean of 50 than if the mean was 100. It would also mean different things if the standard deviation were 10 or 15 points. Second, you must consider whether the scores are normalized or not. Generally, however, this will be of little concern since both scores will be similar unless the original distribution is far from normal. Third, you should consider the nature of the norm group used. For example, we said IQs are standard scores based on a particular age group. Thus, although an IQ of 100 would represent the same relative position among agemates for a six-year-old child and a nine-year-old child, the IQs would represent quite different levels of performance (raw scores). Finally, you must consider whether the center point of the score scale really corresponds to the mean of the distribution for any norm group. To illustrate, whereas the score of 500 on the Mathematics section of SAT represents the average score of the original norm group, the average for current college-bound students is significantly lower. Thus, a score of 500 is well above average for current students.

Using Standard Scores to Compare Performance on Several Tests.   One advantage of standard scores is that scores on several subtests or tests can be placed on the same scale. This is possible because converting raw scores to standard scores adjusts for any differences in means and standard deviations on the tests.

For example, suppose Dan takes both a Quantitative and a Verbal Ability test, each has 100 items, and he scores 70 on the Quantitative and 65 on the Verbal test. At first glance it might appear that he did better on the Quantitative test. Suppose, however, that the Quantitative test has a mean of 40 and a standard deviation of 20 and the Verbal test has a mean of 50 and a standard deviation of 10 points. Computing standard scores we find:

$$z_q = \frac{70 - 40}{20} = +1.50 \qquad z_v = \frac{65 - 50}{10} = +1.50$$

Thus, even though his raw scores differed, he performed at the same level on both tests.[5]

Advantages and Limitations.   Since standard score scales have equal-sized units, they are preferable to percentile ranks for most statistical operations and analyses, such as combining subtest scores into a composite score. In addition, they allow for conversion to other scales, such as percentile ranks, for interpretation. And, as we have just seen, they are useful when comparing scores on tests having different means and standard deviations.

Standard scores, being statistically more complex and less familiar than percentiles, are harder for the layman to understand. Also, standard score systems

---

[5] In our example, both tests contained the same number of items; however, the same procedure could be used with tests containing different numbers of items.

utilize different means and standard deviations, and scores are often referred to only as standard scores, with no distinction made between normalized and linearly transformed scores. Therefore, the test user must always ascertain the scale values used in the particular scale and whether the scores are normalized or a linear transformation of the raw scores. Finally, normalizing standard scores forces the scores into a normal distribution. This procedure is justified to smooth out sampling errors; otherwise it will only distort the shape of the distribution.

Developmental Scales

Many abilities, skills, and characteristics develop in a systematic manner over time. For example, a child's ability to read increases with age and with additional years of schooling. So, too, do most other intellectual abilities and skills. Because these abilities increase systematically, score scales can be developed that compare an individual's performance with that of the average person of various developmental levels. On these scales, an individual's score indicates the developmental level that his or her performance typifies. As might be expected, developmental scales generally report performance as an age or grade equivalent.

Age Scales.   When Alfred Binet built the first intelligence test, he measured mental growth by comparing a given child's performance with that of the average child of various age levels. He first identified intellectual tasks (items) that discriminated between children of various ages—that is, items on which performance varied systematically with age. Each item was then placed at the age level at which the majority of children could successfully complete it. By developing a number of appropriate items for each age level, Binet constructed a scale that assessed the level of mental development of children. The score a child received was the age level that his performance best typifies. Such a score is referred to as a *mental age.*

All age scales are developed using essentially the same reasoning and procedures. The task is to find items that typify the performance of children of different ages, typifying meaning that at least half of the children of that age can answer the question correctly.[6] For example, if the majority of eight-year-olds can answer the item "What is nine times nine?", but fewer than half of the seven-year-olds can, this item would be assigned to the eight-year level. By using a number of such items, an age score can be assigned each child. These scores are usually reported in years and months; a score of 10-5 indicating, for example, that the person performed at the same level as the *average* child ten years and five months old. Use of the word "average" is essential to correct interpretations because there could be a wide range of performance within each age level.

When skills vary systematically with age, age scores are straightforward and easy to interpret. However, when the rate of development varies from year to year, age scores are difficult to interpret due to differing amounts of growth be-

---

[6] The norm sample should, of course, be representative of the desired target population. In our example, we would want to have representative samples of seven- and eight-year-old children.

tween years. (That is, unit sizes are not equal.) For example, most intellectual abilities develop at a fairly constant rate throughout childhood but the rate of growth begins to decelerate during adolescence. Therefore, the amount of increase in, say, reading comprehension, will be less between the ages of 17 and 18 than between ages 7 and 8. Thus, a difference of one year in age scores will have different implications at various ages.

Grade Scales. An analogous type of score is the *grade-equivalent* or *grade placement score*. On grade scales, the procedures for selecting items and assigning scores are similar to those used on age scales except that grade levels are used instead of age levels. Thus, grade-equivalent scores compare a child's performance to students at various grade levels and the score represents the grade level her performance typifies. Thus, if Jenny's grade-equivalent score on an arithmetic test is 3.5, her performance is comparable to that of the *average* student in the fifth month of the third grade. (Again, note the emphasis on average.)

Although grade-equivalent scores would seem to be an appropriate method of describing the achievement of elementary and high school students, they have a number of properties that make them easy to misinterpret, and thus their usefulness is limited. For example, when norming the test, some students will score below the average for the lowest grade category and, conversely, some will score higher than the average of the highest grade. These scores are generally assigned by extrapolation, which requires making assumptions about the nature of growth in the subject; thus they may be somewhat inaccurate.

Another problem is that, by definition, half of the students will score below average for their grade. This is obvious but is often overlooked when interpreting scores. Thus, if a student in the second month of fourth grade obtains a reading placement score of 3.9, many people would conclude that his reading is not up to expectation and he should get some remedial help. In reality, his score probably is well within the average range for students at his grade level.

Other problems have to do with the nature of the typical curriculum. Some subjects are more sequential and cumulative than others, and learning depends more on specific school experiences. Mathematics falls into this category, in contrast to, say, reading and writing skills.[7] These differences affect the variability of scores since year-to-year changes would not be the same in all subject matter areas. Thus, for example, for a sixth-grader, a grade placement score of 7.8 might represent a greater degree of acceleration in mathematics than in English; that is, it would be less likely that she would obtain a grade-equivalent score of 7.8 in mathematics than in English.

A related way of viewing this problem is to consider what a grade-equivalent score tells about the skills a student has mastered. To illustrate, suppose that a junior high level mathematics test consisting of 75 items—50 arithmetic and 25 algebra items—is administered in the sixth month of the school year. Suppose

[7] Because the rate of development varies between content areas, separate grade-equivalent scores must be derived for each subject matter area (test).

also that the average score for eighth grade students is 40 and for ninth grade students 50, and that algebra is taught only in the ninth grade. Albert, an eighth grade student, takes this test and obtains a raw score of 50—the average score for ninth grade students. What does this score mean? Albert probably obtained his score by being extremely accurate on the arithmetic items, whereas the average ninth grade student obtained the same score by correctly answering some of the arithmetic and some of the algebra items. In other words, Albert and the average ninth grade student both obtained the same scores but correctly answered different items. Thus Albert's knowledge of mathematics is not necessarily equivalent to that of the average ninth grade student, because he has not studied algebra.

When deriving grade placement scores we assume that achievement increases systematically with grade level. Since scores are based on a comparison to the typical student at various grade levels, normative data must be based on a representative sample of students at each grade level. Besides being concerned with typical sampling problems (such as sampling different types of schools and geographic areas), when using grade placement scores test developers must decide what to do with students who are not in the grade typical for their age—that is, students who have either been accelerated or held back a grade. To control for such diversity some publishers use *modal age grade norms,* norms based only on students who are in the grade typical for their age level.

Because of the many problems in interpreting grade placement scores, many people, the author included, suggest avoiding their use. A better alternative in most situations is to use *percentile ranks within grades;* that is, to express students' achievement in terms of their relative ranking within a particular grade level. Thus, in our example, Albert's score might fall at the 95th percentile rank for eighth grade students.

Advantages and Limitations. The main advantages of developmental scales are that they report scores in readily understandable units—in terms of age or grade equivalents; they provide a direct comparison with the performance of one's peers; and they provide a basis for intraindividual comparisons and the study of growth over time. Their main disadvantages are that they are appropriate only when the characteristic measured changes systematically with age, thus being limited mainly to use with younger children; scale units at various ages or grade may not be equal; and extrapolations from one grade or age level to another are risky. In short, age and grade scales cannot be interpreted as unambiguously as superficial consideration might suggest.

Ratios and Quotients

There have been numerous attempts to develop scales that use the ratio of two scores. Probably the best known of these is the intelligence quotient (IQ). On Binet's original intelligence test, scores were expressed on an age scale. As his test was used, some psychometricians pointed out that a mental age of 10 could have differing meanings and implications if it was obtained by a child of 8, a child of 10, or one of 15. Consequently they suggested that the rate of mental development should be measured as well as the level of development (that is, the mental age). The intelligence quotient, defined as the ratio of the child's mental age to his chronological age, was proposed as an index of the rate of intellectual development:

$$IQ = \frac{\text{Mental age}}{\text{Chronological age}} \times 100 \qquad (8.4)$$

As can be seen from this formula, a child whose intellectual development is average for his age (that is, one whose mental age equals his chronological age) will obtain an IQ of 100, children whose mental development is more rapid than average will obtain scores over 100, and those whose development is slower than average will obtain IQs below 100. The more the rate of development deviates from the average, the farther the IQ will differ from 100.

An IQ computed in this manner is called a *ratio IQ*. This approach has several weaknesses, the main one being that the variability of IQs is not the same at each level (Terman & Merrill, 1937). Thus, ratio IQs are no longer used on the major intelligence tests. Rather, as we indicated earlier, the IQs reported are normalized standard scores. These are called *deviation IQs,* to indicate that IQs are based on deviations from the average score of children of a particular age.

The IQ measures the rate of general intellectual development. In educational testing, one frequently encounters measures that purportedly indicate the rate of educational development or achievement. These go by various names, such as *educational quotients* or *achievement quotients*. These indices are all ratios that use as their numerator some measure of achievement and as the denominator chronological age, a measure of intellectual ability, or grade placement. The purpose of such ratios is to compare a person's actual achievement to his expected achievement (as estimated from his age, grade, or intelligence). These quotients have two major drawbacks. First, the ratio of two scores will be less reliable than either individual measure. Thus the quotient will, typically, be a statistically unsound measure. Second, comparing a measure of achievement to one of intellectual ability assumes that achievement is determined solely by intellectual ability. This assumption is both constricting and inconsistent with empirical facts. In this author's opinion, achievement quotients based on the comparison of achievement test scores to measure intellectual development can best be ignored.

methods of presenting norm-referenced scores

Having described norm groups and various types of norm-referenced scores, we now turn to methods for summarizing and presenting normative data. We shall discuss two types of methods: tabular (conversion tables) and graphical (score profiles). The former are used as a basis for converting raw scores to derived scores and the latter as a basis for interpreting performance on a series of tests.

When considering these methods, several important points should be kept in mind. First, a description of the composition of the norm group(s) used should be included with the scores. Although a brief description may be provided with the table or profile, a more complete description should be presented in the test manual. Second, each type of score used should be described fully. This is essential when using standard scores or any type of scaled score that may not be familiar to test users. Again, this information should be included in the test manual.

Third, all data in a conversion table, or on a profile, should be derived from the same norm group.[8] This, of course, is no problem when only one score is reported. However, it becomes a consideration when conversion tables or profiles report performance on various subtests, scales, or tests. If all scores are not derived from the same norm group, scores will not be directly comparable, as performance may vary across norm groups. Fourth, without relevant validity data, norm-referenced scores will tell only the student's relative ranking within the group—and nothing more. This latter point cannot be overstressed. Too often the availability of normative data is taken as a license to interpret performance on the test as indicative of probable high performance on some criterion. *Without validity data, conversion tables only translate raw scores into another type of score.*

Conversion Tables

A *conversion table* shows raw scores and equivalent derived scores for a particular norm group. The essential elements in a conversion table are a list of raw scores and a corresponding list of derived scores. Having this information, a test user can convert raw scores into derived scores or find the raw score equivalents of various derived scores. Conversion tables, for each type of derived score and each norm group, should be presented in the test manual.

An example of a conversion table is shown in Table 8.3. This table shows the

Table 8.3
Example of a Conversion Table for ACT Composite Scores

Score	Percentile Rank	Standard Score
32	99	70
31	96	66
30	89	62
29	78	59
28	67	55
27	54	52
26	42	48
25	31	44
24	21	41
23	13	37
22	6	34
21	1	30
20	1	26

$n = 177$ freshman female liberal arts majors at a midwestern university.

[8] Furthermore, all tests should be administered under comparable conditions. For example, if some tests had been administered as an admissions requirement and others for advising, scores might not be comparable in the two groups.

Table 8.4
Example of a Conversion Table Showing Norms for Several Subtests

Score	English	Math	Social Studies	Natural Science	Composite
35		99			
34		95		99	
33		90	99	96	
32		84	97	91	99
31		76	93	83	97
30		66	86	75	92
29	99	56	79	65	84
28	97	46	72	55	74
27	93	36	62	45	62
26	87	28	54	34	50
25	79	22	45	25	39
24	69	18	35	19	29
23	59	14	27	15	21
22	48	11	21	11	14
21	37	8	16	8	9
20	28	6	12	6	6
19	20	4	8	5	4
18	14	3	6	3	2
17	9	2	5	2	2
16	5	1	3	2	1
15	3		3	1	
14	2		2		
13	1		1		

Table shows the percentile equivalents on the four subtests (plus composite) of the American College Testing Program (ACT). Sample was 2087 entering freshmen at a midwestern university.

percentile rank and standard score equivalents of the ACT Composite scores for a particular norm group.[9] (The data are those used in Tables 8.1 and 8.2). To read the table, consider the scores in a given row. For example, if Marcie's ACT score was 27, her percentile rank would be 54 and her T score 52. Thus, compared to other freshmen women at this college, Marcie's score was 0.2 standard deviation above the mean ($T = 52$) and was higher than 54 percent of the other students ($PR = 54$).

Another type of conversion table shows the derived score equivalents for several subtests or tests. For example, Table 8.4 shows the percentile ranks on the four subtests and for the Composite score on the ACT Assessment for a particular norm group. Again we can use the table either to convert ACT scores to percentile

[9] The ACT scores we have been using are not, strictly speaking, raw scores. Rather they are the scores reported to test takers, which are transformations of raw scores to a standard scale system using a national norm group. However, they can be used as raw scores in our examples since we are illustrating how to find derived scores for a particular norm group that is different from the group used to derive the original scores. The same procedures would be followed if we had started with raw scores.

Table 8.5
Example of a Conversion Table Showing the Performance of Several Norm Groups on the Same Test

Score	A	B	College C	D	E
36		99		99	
35	99	98		97	
34	96	94	99	92	99
33	94	88	98	86	97
32	90	81	96	77	94
31	82	74	95	67	90
30	72	66	92	57	84
29	62	58	87	45	75
28	55	52	82	35	65
27	50	44	76	26	59
26	43	36	67	17	52
25	35	29	59	11	44
24	28	24	53	8	36
23	20	18	45	5	29
22	14	13	38	3	24
21	11	11	30	2	19
20	8	7	24	1	14
19	6	4	17		10
18	4	3	13		7
17	3	2	9		4
16	1	1	5		2
15			3		1
14			2		
13			1		
n	177	486	340	528	307

Table presents percentile equivalents of ACT mathematics test scores for five colleges within the same university. (See text for explanation.)

ranks or to find the ACT score equivalent of a percentile rank. To illustrate the former case, a score of 25 would be equivalent to a percentile rank of 79 on English, 22 on Math, 45 on Social Studies, 25 on Natural Science, and 39 on the Composite. To illustrate the latter, to obtain a percentile rank of at least 90, a student would have to obtain a score of 27 on English, 33 on Math, 31 on Social Studies, 32 on Natural Science, and 30 on the Composite.

A third type of conversion table presents the data from one test for several different norm groups. An example is shown in Table 8.5, which shows the percentile equivalents of the ACT Mathematics score in several colleges. With this type of conversion table, a person's score can be compared to several norm groups simultaneously; in this case, compared to students at several colleges. This table also allows us to compare the performance of various norm groups. For example, a score of 28 would be percentile rank of 82 at College C and a percentile rank of 35 at College D; thus College D is a tougher norm group. This differ-

Figure 8.4 An Example of a Normal Percentile Chart: The Edwards Personal Preference Schedule.

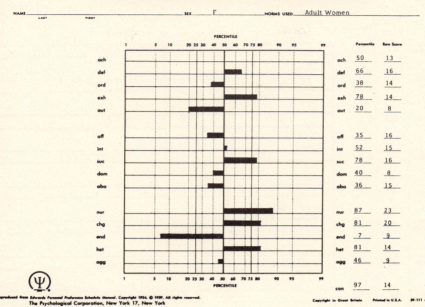

Edwards Personal Preference Schedule

NAME _____ SEX __F__ NORMS USED __Adult Women__
　　　　LAST　　　　FIRST

	Percentile	Raw Score
ach	50	13
def	66	16
ord	38	14
exh	78	14
aut	20	8
aff	35	16
int	52	15
suc	78	16
dom	40	8
aba	36	15
nur	87	23
chg	81	20
end	7	9
het	81	14
agg	46	9
con	97	14

ence reflects the differences in mathematics preparation and ability of students enrolling in the two colleges (thus illustrating the value of local norms).

Our illustrations have shown conversions to percentile ranks and, in one case, to standard scores. Similar procedures could be used to develop conversion tables for any type of norm-referenced score.

Profiles

Converting raw scores to derived scores is the first step in the test interpretation process. When one score is reported, this will usually be sufficient. However, when we have scores on several subtests or tests, it often is helpful to look at the pattern of scores. One way is to plot a profile of the test scores. A *test profile* is nothing more than a graph on which a series of test scores are plotted. The profile shows the configuration of an individual's scores on the various tests, thus indicating the relative positions of the scores.

When developing a profile, the guidelines discussed earlier should be followed. That is, the norm group and score scales should be clearly described and the same norm group used for all tests whose scores are reported. In addition, when using profiles, all scores should be plotted on the same scale; that is, all scores should be expressed either as percentiles or some other type of score.

Figure 8.5 An Example of a Profile Using a Band Approach: The Differential Aptitude Tests.

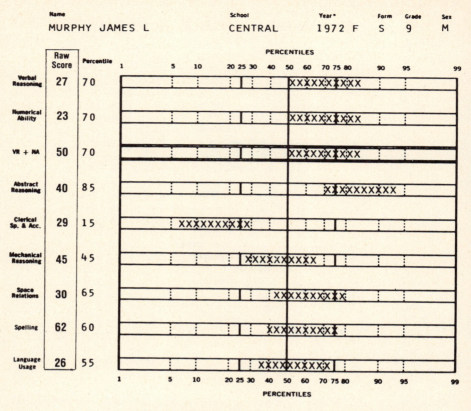

When interpreting profiles, as when interpreting any other scores, we must be aware of the possibility of overinterpreting small differences, especially for scores near the center of the distribution. One way to guard against this tendency is to use normal percentile charts. A *normal percentile chart* is a profile in which scores are reported as percentile ranks but the dimensions of the scale are drawn to correspond to a standard score scale (see Figure 8.4). In other words, a percentile rank scale is superimposed on the standard score scale. This compresses differences in percentile ranks near the center of the score distribution (to better reflect the raw score distribution) and stretches them out at the extremes. This approach thus incorporates the advantages of both percentile ranks and standard scores and minimizes the chances of overinterpreting small differences in scores.

Since every score contains some error of measurement, some profiles plot scores as bands or ranges, rather than exact points (see Figure 8.5). These bands usually are some function of the standard error of measurement. A particularly useful approach is to set these ranges so that when the bands overlap, the differences between scores are not statistically significant.

When interpreting test score profiles, the test user can look at various features. First, what is the general level of the scores? Are scores generally high, in the middle range, or low? Second, what is the scatter of scores? Are the scores all about the same level or does performance vary widely over the various tests? Third, what is the pattern of scores? That is, in what area or areas are scores high and low? This patterning gives an indication of the test taker's relative strengths and weaknesses.

Two Final Points

Before leaving our discussion of norm-referenced scores, two points should be emphasized. The first has been pointed out at various points: Norm-referenced scores indicate only relative ranking within a designated norm group. If we want to use the scores to make inferences about behavior in other situations, we must have relevant validity data. For example, just because a student has a high score on a college admission test, or a job applicant has a high score on a selection test, does not necessarily mean that the individual will perform at the same high level in college or on the job. To make such inferences we need validity evidence relating test scores to the criterion of interest.

The other point is: What can we do when there are no appropriate normative data? This situation may occur when testing members of minority groups or when other than standardized testing conditions are used (for example, when testing students with a visual handicap). If possible, we could construct special norms; however, this will often be unfeasible. In these cases we might use the test as an observation of the test taker's performance, to observe how the person approaches the task. Combining these observations with other data (e.g., interviews, reports of persons acquainted with the test taker, specially devised tests) may allow some inferences to be made. The important point is that the absence of normative data should not be used as an excuse for doing nothing or avoiding a decision. As stated in the *Standards,* "Efforts to help solve educational or psychological problems should not be abandoned simply because of the absence of an appropriate standardized instrument" (1974, p. 71).

summary

Raw scores are usually transformed to another scale to aid interpretation. When scores are compared with those of other test takers, scores are norm-referenced; when they are compared with a proficiency standard, they are content-referenced; when they are expressed in terms of predicted performance on another variable, they are outcome-referenced. This chapter considered norm-referenced scores, ones where performance is expressed as a relative ranking within a designated comparison group, the norm group.

What will be an appropriate norm group depends on the nature of the test and its intended use. In general, norm groups will be composed of people who share certain salient characteristics with the test taker. For example, the usual norm group for a classroom achievement test will be all members of the class; a norm group for a reading comprehension test generally will be other students in the same grade. Norm groups can be national in scope or represent the performance of a more limited group, such as local norms. When scores of various subgroups differ, subgroup norms may be constructed.

Normative data should be provided (in the test manual) for each score reported. In many cases, scores may be compared with several norm groups.

To obtain normative data we must first define the relevant population, then administer the test to that population or a representative sample of it, tally the scores, and convert them to the desired transformed scores.

Various types of norm-referenced scores are used. The most common is percentile ranks, which indicate the percentage of test takers who obtain a given score or a lower score. Another common variety is standard scores, which express performance in terms of standard deviation units from the mean. Standard scores may be either linear transformations of raw scores or area transformations (normalized standard scores). In most cases, standard scores are further transformed to another scale, such as a scale with a mean of 50 and a standard deviation of 10 points. Transformations to standard scores put all scores on the same scale; thus they are particularly useful for comparing performance of tests having different means and standard deviations.

When test performance varies systematically with age, developmental scales can be used. Age scores compare the test taker's performance with that of average children of various ages; grade-equivalent, or grade placement, scores compare test takers to the average child in various grade levels.

Normative data can be presented in conversion tables or as profiles. A conversion table gives the derived score equivalents of various raw scores. They may serve as a basis for converting scores or show performance on various tests or subtests and/or for various norm groups. Profiles are graphic representations of scores on various tests or subtests, all obtained from the same norm group and plotted on a common scale.

When interpreting normative data, you must consider various factors, the most important of which are the nature of the characteristics measured, the composition of the norm group(s), the type of scale used to report scores, and the amount of error in the scores. This information should be found in the test manual. Finally, it is important to remember that norm-referenced scores only indicate the test taker's position in a designated norm group. To make inferences about behavior in other situations requires relevant validity data.

Suggestions for Further Reading

Angoff, W. H. Scales, norms, and equivalent scores. In R. L. Thorndike (Ed.), *Educational measurement,* 2d ed. Washington, D.C.: American Council on Education, 1971. A thorough discussion of the various types of derived scores, methods for obtaining normative data, and equating test scores.

Angoff, W. H. Criterion-referencing, norm-referencing, and the SAT. *College Board Review,* 1974, *92,* 2–5, 21. Points out that norm-referenced and criterion-referenced scores are not incompatible, but rather are two separate ways of expressing test performance.

Baglin, R. F. Does "nationally" normed really mean nationally? *Journal of Educational Measurement,* 1981, *18,* 97–107. A survey showing how the willingness of schools to participate affects the representativeness of norms; includes suggestions for improving the norming process.

Carver, R. P. Two dimensions of tests: Psychometric and edumetric. *American Psychologist,* 1974, *29,* 512–518. Distinguishes between tests used to measure individual differences (psychometric uses) and tests used to measure learning outcomes (edumetric uses).

Ebel, R. L. The case for norm-referenced measurements. *Educational Researcher,* 1978, 7(11), 3–5. A defense of norm-referenced tests, emphasizing their advantages and differences from criterion-referenced tests.

Echternacht, G. Grade equivalent scores, and Plas, J. M. If not grade equivalent scores—then what? *NCME Measurement in Education,* 1977, 8(2). Two views on the usefulness of grade-equivalent scores with suggestions for possible alternatives.

Glaser, R. Instructional technology and the measurement of learning outcomes. *American Psychologist,* 1963, *18,* 519–521. The article that presented the original distinction between norm-referenced and criterion-referenced measurement.

Gold, A. M. The use of separate-sex norms on aptitude tests: Friend or foe? *Measurement and Evaluation in Guidance,* 1977, *10,* 162–171. Argues for use of combined sex norms on standardized ability tests on basis of social, legal, and psychometric grounds.

Jaeger, R. M. The national test-equating study in reading. *NCME Measurement in Education,* 1973, *4*(4). A description of a large-scale project designed to equate scores on various standardized reading tests.

Lyman, H. B. *Test scores and what they mean,* 3d ed. Englewood Cliffs, N.J.: Prentice-Hall, 1978. A short book describing the various types of test scores and their interpretation; a good reference for anyone who interprets test scores.

Mayo, S. T. (Ed.). Interpreting test performance. *New Directions for Testing and Measurement,* 1980, *6.* Four articles describing the interpretation of various types of test scores (norm-referenced, criterion-referenced, latent trait) and methods for improving score interpretation.

Standards for educational and psychological tests. Washington, D.C.: American Psychological Association, 1974. Section D (pp. 19–24) discusses standards for scores and norms; section J (pp. 68–73) describes standards for the interpretation of test scores.

Chapter 9 • Content- and Outcome-Referenced Scores

NORM-REFERENCED scores are interpreted by comparing an individual's performance to a relevant norm group. The interpretation is in terms of a relative ranking or position, such as saying a student's knowledge of American history is better than 73 percent of a national sample of ninth grade students. When comparisons are made between individuals, norm-referenced scores provide the necessary information.

Sometimes, however, other types of information may be needed. Consider a parent discussing a fifth grade student's achievement with a teacher. The teacher may tell the parent that Karen scored at the 90th percentile rank compared to the national norms on an arithmetic achievement test and that she is one of the best arithmetic students in the class. The parent replies, "Fine, but what sorts of arithmetic problems can she do? Can she multiply fractions? Can she manipulate decimals?" Norm-referenced scores do not provide this sort of information. To answer these, and similar questions, we need a method of interpreting performance that describes performance in terms of what test takers know and what skills they have mastered. Such scores are called *content-referenced scores.*

There is also another type of situation in which norm-referenced scores do not provide the necessary information. Suppose a high school senior is trying to decide which college to attend. She takes a college admissions test and scores higher than 85 percent of all college-bound students and higher than 80 percent of the entering freshmen at State College. Yet she still has another question: "What grade average might I expect to obtain if I go to State College?" To answer this question we need yet another type of score, one which we shall call an *outcome-referenced score.* Outcome-referenced scores express test results in terms of expected performance on some other variable.

The terminology used to describe these various classes of scores is, unfortunately, not standard. Although there is general agreement on the meaning of norm-referenced scores, the other two terms are not used by all authors. For example, many people refer to what we call content-referenced scores as *criterion-referenced scores* (Glaser, 1963; Glaser & Nitko, 1971; Popham & Husek, 1969); however, we shall refer to scores interpreted in terms of content mastery as content-referenced scores. In addition, what we call outcome-referenced scores are sometimes called criterion-referenced scores (*Standards,* 1974). To complicate matters further, some authors use the label criterion-referenced to refer both to what we call content-referenced and outcome-referenced scores. As in other labeling controversies, the important point is not the label, but understanding how each type of score is developed, interpreted, and used.

There is also some controversy over whether these terms apply to scores, to score interpretations, or to the measurement process—that is, whether we should properly refer to norm-referenced scores, norm-referenced score interpretations, or norm-referenced measurement. We will ignore the subtleties of such arguments and use the terms interchangeably.

In this chapter we shall describe the development and interpretation of content-referenced and outcome-referenced scores, discuss some problems that arise when interpreting scores, and provide some guidelines for interpreting scores.

content-referenced scores

Content-referenced scores compare an individual's performance to a standard of proficiency or mastery of the material covered by the test. Thus performance is expressed in terms of what the test taker knows or can do, not as a relative ranking. Although this approach is most obviously useful for achievement tests, it is not necessarily limited to them.

The concept of content-referenced testing was introduced by Glaser (1963), who described content-referenced tests as measuring the degree to which a desired criterion level of performance was obtained.[1] In a later article, he said that scores on these tests are "directly interpretable in terms of specified performance standards" (Glaser & Nitko, 1971, p. 653). In 1974, the *Standards* stated, "*Content-referenced* interpretations are those where the score is directly interpreted in terms of performance at each point on the achievement continuum being measured." (*Standards,* 1974, p. 19.) In the same year, Carver made a related distinction but referred to it as the *edumetric dimension* of tests, which he defined to mean "the extent to which it [the test] reflects . . . within-individual growth" (Carver, 1974, p. 512). In all of these articles, content-referenced measurement was contrasted with norm-referenced measurement, with the major distinction being that content-referenced scores are interpreted in terms of some standard of content mastery, not in comparison with the performance of other test takers.

Development of Content-Referenced Scores

Developing content-referenced scores involves two major steps: specifying the domain to be covered and generating a scale on which performance can be reported. Although both of these requirements are attainable in principle, when one turns to constructing such scales the problems involved are at best difficult and often insoluble.

Consider first the problem of specifying the domain. This would seem to be a rather straightforward task, in that all you have to do is circumscribe the content or skills you wish to measure. In certain cases, this is not difficult (see, e.g., Born-

[1] As noted previously, Glaser called these tests criterion-referenced.

muth, 1970; Hively, Patterson, & Page, 1968). For example, we can easily specify certain basic arithmetic operations (such as addition, subtraction, multiplication, division) and, without too much trouble, we can also delimit the range of problems to which these operations will be applied—say, whole numbers of no more than four digits. As we proceed to more abstract or less well-defined subject matter areas, the problem becomes more complex. Try to define the domain of algebraic problem solving, Civil War history, or reading comprehension. You will soon see that adequately describing the domain is no easy task.

A useful description of how to define a domain has been provided by Popham and Lindheim (1980). The first step is to define the knowledge or skill to be measured. This definition should have an appropriate scope and describe a behavior that is teachable. What they consider a definition of appropriate scope is shown by the following statement:

> The student will be presented with a factual selection such as a newspaper or magazine article or a passage from a consumer guide or general-interest book. After reading that selection, the student will determine which one of four choices contains the best statement of the central point of the selection. This statement will be entirely accurate as well as the most comprehensive of the choices given. (p. 5).

Note that this definition is broad enough to describe a useful skill yet clearly enough defined so that there is little ambiguity as to what is being measured.

Popham and Lindheim then amplify this definition by providing descriptions of the necessary stimulus attributes (the nature of the test items) and descriptions of the response attributes (the nature of the alternative responses). For example, under stimulus attributes they list the following requirements:

1. Items will be of the form, "Which one of the following is the best statement of the selection you just read?"
2. Selections will be 125–250 words long and each set of five items will consist of no more than 1000 words.
3. Two of the five selections will be more than one paragraph long.
4. Reading selections will be factual material from newspapers, magazines, general-interest books, and consumer guides.
5. Each reading selection will have one main idea.
6. Selections will be at a reading level ranging between the seventh and ninth grades.

Requirements for response alternatives include the following:

1. There will be four one-sentence alternatives for each question.
2. Incorrect alternatives should lack accuracy or appropriate scope, or both.
3. The three distractors will include at least one that lacks accuracy and another that lacks appropriate scope.
4. The correct answer will be a statement that is both accurate and of appropriate scope.

They also give examples of items meeting these criteria. Together these statements define the domain measured and the nature of the test.

The other task is to define the scoring scale. This involves identifying a continuum on which scores should be reported, such as the number of correct responses or the percent correct. When content-referenced tests are used to determine whether the test taker has reached a designated level of proficiency, a second decision must be made: Some point on the score scale must be set to differentiate between passing and failing. Where this score should be set is a complex and debatable question (see, e.g., Glass, 1978; Hambleton, 1978; Koffler, 1980; Linn, 1978; Meskauskas, 1976; Millman, 1973; Shepard, 1980a).

Types of Content-Referenced Scores

Let us assume that we have, at least to a minimally acceptable degree, specified the domain to be measured. We can then turn to the major focus of our discussion, the types of scales used to report performance. The essential element of any such scale is that it communicates the test taker's level of performance in terms of content mastery. We shall discuss several types of scores that purport to do this. Although we shall discuss total scores, the same points apply to subtest scores or scores on any cluster of items.

Percent Correct Scores. The simplest score to use would be the number of items answered correctly or, when items have other than unit weight, the total number of points earned. Since tests vary in length, such scores are usually transformed to percent correct scores:

$$\text{Percent correct} = \frac{\text{Number items correct}}{\text{Total number of items}} \times 100\% \qquad (9.1)$$

or, with multipoint items:

$$\text{Percent correct} = \frac{\text{Points earned}}{\text{Maximal number of points}} \times 100\% \qquad (9.1a)$$

The percent correct score indicates what percent of items the test taker answered correctly or, in the case of multipoint items, the percent of the maximum number of points earned.

Because of their computational simplicity and apparent meaningfulness, percent correct scores have a certain appeal. A little reflection, however, suggests that things are not so simple. For one thing, a percent score will not have meaning unless "percent of what?" can be defined. Strictly speaking, we are talking of percent of test items answered correctly; by implication, we are talking of the percent of the domain mastered. But unless the test items representatively sample the domain, and unless the domain is clearly described, we find ourselves taking a percent of some unknown area.

Another factor of concern is the difficulty of the items. A given score, say 75 percent, would mean different things on a difficult or an easy test. From one point of view this may not be a problem. This would be the case when we are willing to assume that some domains cover more difficult material than others. On the other hand, one could argue that even within the same domain it would be possible to construct items of varying levels of difficulty. In this case the meaning of a percent correct score would be unclear because the score would reflect the item difficulty as well as the test takers' knowledge. Of course, if the items are not representative of the domain, in either content and/or difficulty, the meaning of a percent correct score will be ambiguous.

Mastery Scores.   The emphasis on content-referenced scores has closely paralleled the development of certain individualized approaches to education, particularly mastery learning. The basic philosophy of mastery learning is that almost all students can learn if given sufficient time and adequate instruction (Block, 1971, 1974; Bloom, 1976; Carroll, 1963). Thus, testing under a mastery learning approach involves determining whether a student has mastered an area to a designated level of proficiency (Bloom, Hastings, & Madaus, 1971; Mayo, 1970). For this purpose, content-referenced scores are more appropriate.[2]

Instruction under a mastery learning system typically is divided into units. Students study each unit, then take a test to determine whether they have mastered the material in the unit. Each unit has designated objectives, and the test covers these objectives. For each test a predetermined level of proficiency is designated as the mastery level. If a student attains this level, he passes the unit and goes on to the next unit; if he does not attain this level, he does further work, then takes an alternative form of the test. This process continues until the student passes the unit test.

Usually the mastery level is set in the range of 80 to 85 percent correct responses. But how is this level set? Usually somewhat arbitrarily (Glass, 1978). The essential requirement is that the score be set at a level that guarantees that the student has command of the material in the unit and/or has sufficient background to learn the material in the next unit. Ideally, there would be empirical evidence to support the choice of the mastery score; in practice it is usually a judgmental matter. Note, too, that the score will be used to make a pass/fail, mastery/nonmastery decision. Thus, if the mastery level is 85 percent, a score of 98 percent will be treated the same as a score of 85 percent (both will result in pass decisions), and a score of 36 percent will be treated the same as a score of 84 percent (both will result in a fail decision).

Content Standard Scores.   Ebel (1962) proposed what he calls *content standard test scores*. The word "content" implies that the scores are based directly on the tasks that make up the test—that is, its content. By "standard" Ebel means both that scores must be expressed on a common scale (such as percent correct) and, more important, that the process of test construction, administration, and scoring are standardized. Ebel also stresses that content scores are not substitutes for normative scores, but rather that content and normative scores should be utilized in conjunction with each other.

---

[2] Nitko (1980b) has argued that mastery scores are different from content-referenced scores. However, since they are based on a standard of content proficiency, we shall consider them as a type of content-referenced score.

Obviously the crucial steps in constructing any content standard scale are to specify the content domain and the scale clearly. Given these specifications, one could interpret scores in content terms. Alternatively, the interpretation process could start with the total score on the test. By specifying the types of items answered correctly or incorrectly by the "typical" person attaining each score level, an individual's scores could be interpreted. This interpretation would indicate the skills or difficulty of problems solved by persons at this score level.

Rating Scales.   In some domains proficiency cannot be determined by having students answer test questions. One example is handwriting. Other examples are found in industrial education, physical education, art, and music. Still others are found in industry and skilled trades; for example, can a plumber fix a leaking faucet? In these areas the skills required (the domain) can be defined; the question is how to determine proficiency.

In most academic areas this problem is sidestepped by using grades as a method of evaluation. These grades may be based on comparative performance (thus be norm-referenced); be based on some, at least implicit standard of mastery; or be a combination of both approaches. An alternative approach would be to develop content-anchored rating scales. To illustrate, consider handwriting. One approach that has been used is to have judges rate the quality of samples of children's handwriting. Various levels of quality, from illegible to legible, are identified, and samples of handwriting typifying the various levels are included as standards for comparison. To rate the quality of a child's handwriting, the teacher would compare his handwriting to the standard samples. The child's score (rating) would be the level that best corresponds to the quality of his handwriting.

Latent Trait Scores

Scores obtained on any test will be a function of at least two variables: the ability[3] of the test takers and the difficulty of the items. If test takers having high ability take an easy test, scores will be high; if they take a more difficult test, their scores will be lower. Similarly, if low-ability students take a difficult test, scores will be low; if the test contains easier items, scores will be higher. In short, scores on any test will vary with the ability level of the test takers and the difficulty of the items. Furthermore, since these two sources of variance are confounded, unless we have an independent measure of one or the other, we do not know which is more responsible for determining the level of scores obtained.

In recent years a variety of methods have been proposed to solve this problem. These methods go under different names: latent trait approaches, item characteristic curve theory, or item response theory. Although these methods differ, they share several common attributes. All assume that a test is designed to measure some underlying hypothetical continuum of ability, the *latent trait*. All use as their basic data the responses of individual test takers to individual items. All scale

---

[3] As used in this context, ability refers to ability in the specific domain measured, not to a more general concept of ability.

items and ability using statistical models based on item characteristic curves, which are graphs showing the probability of attaining the correct response to an item at various ability levels. And all provide an ability estimate for each individual that will be constant regardless of the particular sample of items answered.

Since the methods used to calibrate responses are too complex to discuss in detail here (see, e.g., Hambleton, 1980; Hambleton & Cook, 1977; Hambleton et al., 1978; Lord, 1977, 1980; Wright & Stone, 1979), we shall only describe the general logic of the approach. The basic data, as mentioned above, are the responses of test takers to individual items. Then, assuming a particular form of the item characteristic curve, certain statistical operations are performed that allow items to be calibrated in terms of difficulty and persons in terms of ability. If only items that meet a specified statistical criterion are selected, a pool of items can be calibrated for difficulty. Because these item difficulties have known relations with ability levels, the same items do not have to be administered to all test takers. Rather, any individual can take any particular sample of items and, from performance on this sample of items, his or her ability level can be estimated.

Latent ability scores are reported on an arbitrary scale, but one with known statistical properties. These scores are then usually transformed to some other scale for reporting. These scores can also be interpreted as norm-referenced scores by comparing them to a particular norm group. The model can also be used on such problems as equating test forms, tailored testing, and studying item bias.

We have classified these scores as content-referenced scores since they provide a method of showing where the student's performance falls along an ability continuum. For example, after items have been calibrated for difficulty, say on a mathematics test, we could select items of varying levels of difficulty to make up a test. By finding what level of difficulty an item a student can correctly solve, we can place him on an ability continuum for mathematics. As his proficiency increases, we can test his skill with more difficult items. Because the items have all been calibrated on a common scale, scores on each test can be reported on the same scale, even though different items are used on each test. By observing performance on the various tests (item samples), we have a measure of the student's growth in proficiency in mathematics. Furthermore, we can directly compare the ability levels of various students, even though they take different samples of items (tests).

Advantages and Limitations

The major advantage of content-referenced scores is, of course, that they describe performance in terms of the level of content or skills the individual has mastered. That is, they indicate what a student knows and can do, rather than his or her relative ranking in a norm group. In most educational and training programs, this is the most useful type of evidence. For example, it is more useful for a teacher to know that Johnny can multiply whole numbers and decimals but cannot cope with fractions than for her to know that his multiplication skills are better than those of 60 percent of sixth graders. Only if she knows what skills he has and has not mastered can she adequately prescribe instruction.

When interpreting content-referenced scores you must also consider the fact that two test takers can obtain the same score by answering different items correctly. This point also applies to norm-referenced tests, but the implications are more crucial in content-referenced testing because content-referenced scores are used to make inferences about test takers' level of competency. If different test takers answer different items correctly, they may have different competencies; to interpret their scores similarly may result in incorrect inferences. This problem can be avoided by testing over narrow homogeneous domains, by setting the mastery score high enough to ensure that test takers have mastered all the skills in the domain, and/or by using a range of item difficulties so that knowing a person's score also gives a good indication of the level of difficulty or complexity of items he or she can answer correctly (Nitko, 1980b; Wright, 1977; Wright & Stone, 1979).

Another problem concerns how we define proficiency levels. Previously we mentioned that mastery scores are usually determined arbitrarily, although they could be developed empirically. If you asked a teacher how he determines an appropriate passing score, he would probably say: "By the level of performance I expect of a child in this grade." But how does he know what level to expect? The only way, other than using some ideal standard, is to consider what skills children in that grade typically master. This, of course, is a normative interpretation. Similar arguments can be advanced with all types of content-referenced scores. In other words, content-referenced scores generally have at least an implicit normative base.

This fact should not dissuade us from using content-referenced scores. Rather, it points out that content-referenced and non-referenced scores are but two ways of looking at an individual's performance. In some circumstances, one or the other approach may provide more information; in many situations, both content- and norm-referenced scores may provide valuable information. For example, we may want to know whether Mary has mastered the basic arithmetic operations (a content-referenced approach) and also how her arithmetic skills compare with those of other children in her grade (a norm-referenced interpretation). There is no reason why both types of scores cannot be used, even on the same test.

outcome-referenced scores

Norm-referenced scores express performance as a relative ranking within a norm group. Content-referenced scores express performance in terms of content mastery and/or in comparison with a performance standard. Neither provides a direct basis for making predictions about a person's performance in other situations. To make such predictions we also need validity data.

Frequently validity and normative data are combined to make predictions through an indirect process. Suppose we have scores on a test of Economic Drive for a number of applicants for a job as a life insurance salesman. Suppose also that we know that scores on the test are positively correlated with success as a life insurance salesman (defined as the amount of insurance sold). By combining these two sources of information we could infer that applicants scoring, say, 28 on the test will sell more insurance than applicants scoring, say, 20. Although this approach is often used, it would be preferable to have a method that allowed us to interpret test scores directly in terms of the amount of insurance sold. Outcome-referenced scores express performance in this manner. It should be apparent that this approach will be most useful when tests are used to make predictions about expected performance on some external criterion, such as when making selection and placement decisions.

To develop outcome-referenced scores we must have validity data relating test scores to the relevant criterion measure(s). We then must develop a method of converting test scores into predicted criterion (outcome) scores, a method that incorporates the validity data. We shall discuss two methods: expectancy tables and tables or graphs that show predicted performance levels.

Expectancy Tables

An *expectancy table* shows the probability that people with a given predictor score, or range of predictor scores, will obtain each of various possible criterion scores. An example of a simple expectancy table, using one predictor, is shown in Table 9.1. This table shows the probability of obtaining a particular grade point average (GPA) during the first term in college for students with various scores on a college admissions test (the ACT). Using the table, we can estimate each student's probable GPA if we know their test scores. For example, the table shows that 34 percent of the students who obtained an ACT score of 28 obtained a GPA of 3.0 or higher, 55 percent had GPAs between 2.0 and 2.9, and 11 percent had GPAs 1.9 or lower. Or, as applied to a student who scores 28 on the ACT, the chances are 34 out of 100 that her GPA will be 3.0 or higher, 55 out of 100 that it

Table 9.1

Example of an Expectancy Table, With One Predictor: Predicting College GPAs from ACT Composite Scores

Test Score	College Grade Point Average*		
	3.0–4.0	2.0–2.9	0.0–1.9
32 or higher	93	6	1
30–31	58	39	3
28–29	34	55	11
26–27	19	56	25
24–25	14	49	37
22–23	5	47	48
20–21	4	45	51
18–19	2	42	56
17 or lower	3	33	64

*GPA is expressed on scale where A = 4.0, B = 3.0, and so on.

will be between 2.0 and 3.0, and 11 in 100 that it will be 1.9 or lower. In addition, if we combine categories, it can be seen that the chances are 89 out of 100 (34 + 55) that the student will obtain a GPA of 2.0 or higher.

Expectancy tables can also be constructed using two predictors. An example is shown in Table 9.2, which presents the same data as in Table 9.1 with high school rank added as a second predictor. To interpret the table, find the cell at the intersection of the row corresponding to the ACT score and the column corresponding to the high school rank. To illustrate, suppose a student scores 28 on the ACT and ranked in the top 10 percent of her high school class. Looking at the appropriate cell in the table we find the figures 52-42-6. This means that 52 percent of the students with this combination of scores obtained a 3.0 average or higher; 42 percent obtained a GPA between a 2.0 and 2.9; 6 percent obtained GPAs of 1.9 or lower, and 94 percent (52 + 42) obtained a GPA of 2.0 or higher.

Constructing an Expectancy Table.   The process of constructing an expectancy table is straightforward. The basic data are the predictor and outcome scores. These scores are then grouped into classes or categories. Predictor scores are usually divided into classes of about equal size, each of which contains a sufficient number of cases to allow stable estimates. Outcome scores are usually grouped on some logical basis; in our example, we used major grade point divisions, such as 3.0 (a B average) and 2.0 (a C average). In most cases, at least one division point will be the minimally acceptable level of performance; in our example, a C (2.0) average.

The next step is to find the frequencies in each cell of the table; that is, the frequency of each combination of predictor and criterion scores. These frequencies are then converted into proportions, percentages, or, more commonly, the

Table 9.2
Example of an Expectancy Table With Two Predictors: Predicting College GPAs from High School Rank and ACT Composite Scores

Test Score	High School Class Rank						
	Top 10%	2nd 10%	3rd 10%	4th 10%	5th 10%	6th 10%	Low 40%
30 or higher	82-16-2*	26-67-7					
28–29	52-42-6	21-68-11	16-76-8	30-50-20	7-40-53		
26–27	37-56-7	18-63-19	9-56-35	5-61-34	17-35-48	0-36-64	
24–25	35-58-7	19-51-30	4-57-39	13-36-51	3-34-63	0-40-60	8- 8-84
22–23	17-78-5	7-56-37	4-57-39	3-38-59	3-37-60	0-32-68	6-19-75
20–21	22-56-22	4-63-33	5-45-50	3-40-57	5-47-48	0-36-64	0-45-55
18–19			0-31-69	0-38-62	6-39-55	8-33-59	0-33-67
17 or lower					0-20-80		4-22-74

*Figures within table show percent of people obtaining GPAs of 3.0–4.0, 2.0–2.9, and 0.0–1.9, respectively. (Blank cells have too few cases for a stable estimate of percentages.)

number of cases out of 100. This conversion is done separately for each level of predictor score because we want to find the probability of each outcome, given the predictor score. Table 9.3 illustrates this procedure for a problem involving one predictor; similar procedures would be used with more than one predictor.

Although we could construct an expectancy table whenever we have both predictor and outcome scores, it makes no sense to construct one unless there is a significant correlation between predictor and criterion scores. In these cases, predictions will differ for each score level. Conversely, if the predictor and criterion scores were independent, the same predictions would be made regardless of score level; thus use of an expectancy table would not increase the accuracy of the predictions.

It should also be noted that the procedure we used did not smooth out any irregularities in the distributions. There are procedures that smooth out minor irregularities, either by using a regression equation or by other methods (see, e.g., Kolen & Whitney, 1978; Perrin & Whitney, 1976).

Advantages and Limitations. The major advantage of expectancy tables is that, by incorporating validity data, they enable test scores to be interpreted in terms of expected outcomes. In many circumstances this type of interpretation is more useful than a relative ranking. For example, a prospective college student may be more interested in knowing his chances of attaining a B (or a C) average at a particular college than knowing how his rank compared with that of other prospective students. The fact that his test score places him at the 55th percentile does not tell him whether this indicates almost certain academic success, a 50-50 chance of success, or probable failure.

Expectancy tables also have several limitations. By grouping predictor and criterion scores, we sacrifice some precision. Unless the sample is large, some cells may contain few cases and thus provide relatively unstable estimates. Unless there are meaningful points for separating categories (such as the 2.0 GPA in our example), the classification scheme may be somewhat arbitrary. In addition, no index of the amount of prediction error is given. Finally, when there are more than two predictors, several tables or a three-dimensional table will be needed to present the data.

Expectancy tables also clearly illustrate a dilemma that plagues psychological testing: how to apply group data to an individual. The figures within the cells of an expectancy table show the probability of various levels of criterion performance given the predictor score. These data are derived from groups and directly interpretable only for groups. For example, if the probability of success on the job is .63 for applicants having a particular predictor score, then an employer can expect 63 percent of the applicants that he hires who have this particular predictor score will be successful. When considering a specific individual, however, difficulties are encountered. Any individual will either succeed or fail; that is, for an individual the probability is either 1.00 (succeed) or 0.00 (fail). To say that an individual has a 63 percent chance of success is logically meaningless. Thus, when

Table 9.3
Construction of an Expectancy Table

DATA. The data used are scores on the Graduate Record Examination (GRE) and graduate degree earned. GRE scores were the sum of scale scores on the Verbal and Quantitative sections of the test. Outcomes were classified into three categories: (1) earned a Ph.D. degree, (2) earned an M.S. degree, (3) did not obtain a graduate degree. Scores were collected for 129 students who entered a graduate program in Psychology over a five-year period. The data were:

GRE Score	Degree Earned Ph.D.	M.S.	No Degree	Sum	
1320–1600	13	5	4	22	
1240–1319	11	12	5	28	
1160–1239	10	17	9	36	
1080–1159	5	11	3	19	
1000–1079	4	14	6	24	n = 129

COMPUTATION. The first step is to compute the proportion of people in each predictor score range who obtain each outcome. This is done by dividing the number attaining each outcome by the total number in that score range. To illustrate, for the GRE score range 1320 or higher, the computations would be:

$$\text{Ph.D. degree:} \quad 13/22 = .591$$
$$\text{M.S. degree:} \quad 5/22 = .227$$
$$\text{No degree:} \quad 4/22 = .182$$

Similar procedures would be used for each predictor score range.

THE EXPECTANCY TABLE. An expectancy table shows the percentage, or number of people out of 100, who obtain each outcome, given the predictor score. Thus the proportions obtained above would be changed to 59 (out of 100), 23, and 18, respectively. Following similar procedures for each score range, the completed expectancy table would be:

GRE Score	Ph.D.	M.S.	No Degree
1320–1600	59	23	18
1240–1319	39	43	18
1160–1239	28	47	25
1080–1159	26	58	16
1000–1079	17	58	25

INTERPRETATION. Of the students who obtain a GRE score of 1200, 28 out of 100 (28 percent) will obtain a Ph.D. degree, 47 of 100 (47 percent) will obtain an M.S. degree, and 25 of 100 (25 percent) will receive no degree. In terms of an individual student, and using broader categories, we could say that a student with a GRE score of 1200 has about one chance in four of obtaining a Ph.D., one chance in two of obtaining an M.S., and one chance in four of receiving no degree.

interpreting data from expectancy tables to an individual, it must be stressed that the predictions are group averages. In other words, these data only give an estimate of the success of a group of people obtaining similar predictor scores.

Tabular and Graphic Presentations

Outcome-referenced scores also can be presented by a variety of tabular and graphic methods. The essential requirement is that the table or graph clearly show the relationship between predictor and criterion scores. We will illustrate several useful methods; for discussions of other methods that can be adapted to present outcome-referenced scores see, for example, Macdonald-Ross (1977), Tufte (1970, 1974), Tukey (1977), or Wainer & Thissen (1981).

Constructing Tables and Graphs. As with expectancy tables, the basic data are scores on the predictor and criterion variables. Given these data, we can proceed in one of two ways. One is to determine the average criterion score for each predictor score,[4] then present these average scores either tabularly or graphically. The second method utilizes regression equations. Previously we showed that the correlation between a predictor, or set of predictors, and a criterion can be used to construct a regression equation to predict criterion performance. Thus, in this approach, we would compute the correlation between the predictor(s) and criterion, develop a regression equation, then construct a table showing the predicted criterion score for each score level on the predictor test.

In either approach, the outcome data will be predicted criterion performance. More specifically, the tabled values will be the average criterion performance associated with each test score level. They will be averages because, unless the correlation is perfect, there will be a range of criterion scores associated with each test score. Thus the tabled value will be a best estimate, and should be interpreted as such.

Some Examples. To illustrate the types of tables that can be used, we shall use the same data as in the expectancy table examples. The simplest type of table would be similar to the conversion tables discussed in Chapter 8; that is, the table would show the predicted criterion score for each predictor score. An example is provided in Table 9.4, which shows the predicted GPAs for various ACT scores for 330 entering freshmen at a midwestern college. The table was developed by using a regression equation to obtain the predicted GPAs.[5] To interpret the table (and thus the scores) we have only to find the predicted GPA for a score. Thus, students scoring 30 on the ACT have a predicted GPA of 2.95, those scoring 24 a predicted GPA of 2.29, and on one.

The data in this table also can be presented in several other ways. In Figure 9.1 we have presented the same data as a *bar graph,* with the length of each line showing the predicted GPA. Figure 9.2 presents the same data as a *nomograph.* In this figure the solid line is the regression line for predicting GPAs from ACT scores. To find the predicted GPA for a score we would draw a perpendicular from the test score to the regression line, then draw another from the regression line perpendicular to the GPA (vertical) axis. The point where this perpendicular intersects the GPA axis is the predicted GPA. For example, the lines in Figure 9.1

---

[4] The same points and principles apply when predictor scores are grouped—that is, when each predictor category represents a range of predictor scores rather than a single score.

[5] The tables illustrated were all developed using regression equations. Tables developed using average outcome scores for each predictor score would be similar in appearance.

Table 9.4

Example of an Outcome-referenced Prediction Table: GPAs Predicted from ACT Scores

ACT Composite	Predicted GPA
32	3.17
31	3.06
30	2.95
29	2.84
28	2.73
27	2.62
26	2.51
25	2.40
24	2.29
23	2.18
22	2.07
21	1.96
20	1.85

The data are based on a sample of 330 entering freshmen at a midwestern college. The regression equation is:

$$\text{GPA}' = 0.11\,(\text{ACT}) - 0.35$$

GPAs are reported on a four-point scale (A = 4, B = 3, and so on). Note also that predicted GPAs cover a narrower range than actual GPAs; this is a statistical artifact that could be corrected for, if desired.

Figure 9.1 Bar Graph: GPAs Predicted from ACT Scores.

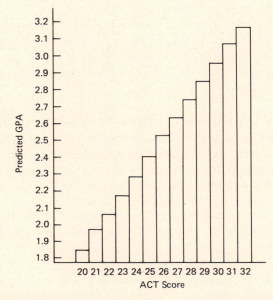

show students having ACT scores of 27 have a predicted GPA of slightly over 2.6, which is the same as the value reported in Table 9.4.

Figure 9.2 Nomograph for GPAs Predicted from ACT Scores.

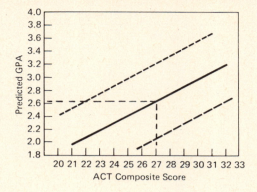

Figure 9.2 also shows another important point. Because all predictions will contain some error, confidence limits can be set around the predicted scores. These generally will be some function of the standard error of estimate; in this example, the (dashed) lines were drawn so that the band includes the predicted criterion score plus and minus one standard error of estimate.[6] To illustrate, students having an ACT score of 27 had a predicted GPA of 2.62. Using the confidence intervals, the probability is 68 out of 100 that their GPAs will fall in the range 2.02 to 3.12, or between a B and a C average.

Similar figures using two predictor variables could be built by using the predictor scores as the axes and showing the predicted criterion scores by lines within the graph (with separate lines for each level of predicted criterion scores). Data from expectancy tables can also be plotted graphically, for example, as a bar diagram with the lengths of the bars representing the probability of the various outcomes. Many other types of tables or graphs could be used; the ones presented illustrate only some common methods.

Advantages and Limitations of Outcome-Referenced Scores

Tabular and graphic presentations clearly show the relationship between predictor and criterion scores.[7] As the data presented are easy to understand, for many people tables and graphs are ideal ways to present outcome-referenced scores. And, as we have seen, indices of predictive error can be built into the graphs, thus alerting users to possible overinterpretation of scores.

There are also some problems with these methods. One is that they become cumbersome when more than one or two predictors are used, often requiring

---

[6] The standard error of estimate was .60 for this set of data.

[7] Note that the data used in developing any prediction table are based on a sample of people whose predictor and criterion scores were both available. The usefulness of these tables is that they can be used as a basis for interpreting scores of future test takers who are similar to the people in the sample used to develop the tables. This, of course, is also true of other types of scores.

use of several tables or graphs. The other problem is more technical, having to do with regression effects. Whenever regression equations are used, the range of predicted criterion scores will be narrower than the range of observed criterion scores. This is because the regression equation takes into account the imperfect correlation and regresses all predicted scores toward the mean. As a result, the equation underestimates criterion scores above the mean and overestimates scores below the mean. Note, for example, the range of predicted scores in Table 9.1 was 1.85 to 3.17, while the obtained GPAs ranged from below 1.00 to 4.00 (an A average). There are formulas to correct for this restriction in range, ones which make the range of predicted criterion scores more similar to the range of observed criterion scores (see, e.g., Ghiselli et al, 1981; Hopkins & Glass, 1978).

If criterion data are not available, or if the criterion data are not inherently meaningful or of interest, then outcome-referenced scores are inappropriate. The first case is obvious, but the second may not be. To illustrate, personality tests are sometimes validated using ratings or judgments as a criterion measure. For example, one might validate a test of aggressiveness using teachers' ratings of children's aggressiveness as a criterion. To express such data in outcome-referenced terms would only give us a prediction of teacher's ratings—hardly an item of interest.

Another important consideration is the strength of the relationship between test scores and the criterion measures. The higher the validity, the less error in our predictions; the lower the validity, the greater the error. Using average predicted criterion scores may mask this fact. The solution, of course, is to incorporate some index of error into our prediction and thus build it into the table. This margin would be based on the standard error of estimate. The result would be to report predicted (outcome) scores not as exact points, but as ranges.

interpretation of test scores

Two groups of people are interested in test score interpretations: test takers and test users. Although we shall focus on test interpretation from the point of view of the test user, the test taker should not be forgotten. In my opinion, test takers should always receive reports of their scores. This does not necessarily mean that they will always receive an exact score; however, they should always be told the implications of their scores and how their scores will be used.

The term "test user" refers to anyone who selects tests, interprets test scores, or makes decisions on the basis of test scores. The responsibilities of test users are clearly stated in the *Standards* (1974):

G1. A test user should have a general knowledge of measurement principles and of the limitations of test interpretations. (p. 58)

G2. A test user should know and understand the literature relevant to the tests he uses and the testing problems with which he deals. (p. 58)

J2. Test scores should ordinarily be reported only to people who are qualified to interpret them. If scores are reported, they should be accompanied by explanations sufficient for the recipient to interpret them correctly. (p.68)

In other words, test interpreters should know how tests are developed, what constitutes an adequate measure, and how scores are derived; know about the particular instrument they are using; and be able to interpret scores in a manner so that the meaning of scores is clear.

But accurate test interpretation also requires knowledge of the test taker's background and of the testing situation. Testing and test interpretation do not occur in a vacuum; test scores gain meaning only when related to other aspects of the test takers' lives. To illustrate, scores on maximal performance tests are frequently misinterpreted because test interpreters draw improper conclusions about the effects of prior experiences on test performance.

One point deserves particular emphasis since it often leads to improper interpretations. It is easy to think of factors, either in the test taker's background or in aspects of the testing situation, that may influence an individual's performance. Usually it is easier to identify factors that might interfere with performance, thus causing lower scores, than factors that will produce better performance. Combining this with our seemingly natural tendency to say good things about people and avoid the bad may result in a tendency to explain away poor performance—that is, to think of reasons why the person may have obtained a low score. In other words, we often overemphasize possible reasons for weak performance. This is not to imply that reasons for poor performance do not exist; they do. The point is that these reasons should be placed in proper perspective, so as not to present an excessively rosy picture to the test taker.

One way to avoid this problem is to separate the level of performance from the reasons for this performance, even though we know they are related. Consider an example. Many students from disadvantaged backgrounds, not having had the experiences of middle-class children, score low on achievement and ability tests. When interpreting their scores, we cannot neglect this fact. However, the student's level of performance may provide valuable information, regardless of why the score was obtained. For example, if a student's reading skills are poor he will probably experience difficulty in any class or situation that requires reading skills. This is the interpretation we make from his level of performance on the reading test. When considering how to improve the student's reading skills, however, knowledge of the relevant background factors becomes an important bit of information.

In the remainder of this chapter we shall discuss some other important considerations in test interpretation. First, we shall review the sources of error in test scores. Next, we shall discuss two common problems in test use and interpretation—equating scores on several tests and interpreting change and differences scores. Finally, we shall provide some guidelines for interpreting test scores to test takers and test users.

Sources of Error in Test Scores

Throughout this book we have emphasized that test scores are influenced by many factors besides the trait or construct being measured. As stated in the *Standards* (1974):

J1. A test score should be interpreted as an estimate of performance under a given set of circumstances. It should not be interpreted as some absolute characteristic of the examinee or as something permanent and generalizable to all other circumstances. (p. 68)

The score is an estimate because various sources of error can affect scores. These error effects arise from three sources: those due to unreliability, those due to invalidity, and those due to limited normative data. In this section we shall consider how these error sources may affect test interpretations.

Unreliability. In our discussion we assumed that a given raw score could be directly transformed into an equivalent derived score. That is, test scores were treated as precise indicators. However, we also pointed out that since, in practice, tests are never perfectly reliable, test scores should be treated as ranges or bands rather than as exact points. This means that one must always consider the standard error of measurement. Many test publishers have developed conversion tables or profiles that utilize a band approach to score interpretation. That is, derived scores are reported as ranges (bands) rather than as exact points. Even if the test publisher has not used this approach, the test interpreter should provide his own band interpretation to test scores. If exact scores are used, it should be with the understanding that such scores are not precise indicators but rather the best estimate that we have of the person's "true" score. In other words, a percentile rank of 55 should not be interpreted as the person's exact rank; rather it should be considered as the best available estimate of his rank (see Figure 8.5).

Invalidity. No test has perfect validity. Thus inferences from test scores will vary in accuracy, depending on the validity of the test. Obviously, the more valid the test, the more valid will be the score interpretations and the more valid will be the inferences made from the test scores. Although this point is generally recognized, it is not always followed in practice. Too often, tests are interpreted as if they were highly valid measures of the characteristic suggested by the test title although validity data are limited, fragmentary, or even nonexistent.

When using norm-referenced scores, the very fact that normative data are available often provides a subtle temptation to interpret test scores as if the test's validity had been clearly established. Thus, for example, if a test is labeled as a measure of mathematical aptitude, and if appropriate normative data are available, it is only too easy to interpret scores as if they predicted success in activities requiring mathematical ability. But, to repeat what now should be obvious: *Normative data are not sufficient for accurate test interpretation; one also needs validity data.*

Similar reasoning also applies to content-referenced and outcome-referenced scores. When interpreting content-referenced scores, we wish to generalize from test scores to performance in a broader domain—the content domain that the test samples. Such generalizations will be warranted only if the content validity of the test for that particular use has been established. When interpreting outcome-referenced scores we predict performance on some external variable from the test scores. Here the accuracy of such interpretations will depend on the magnitude of the relationship between the test scores and the outcome being predicted—that is, the validity of the test.

Limited Norms.   When using norm-referenced interpretations we assume that the available norm group(s) will provide an appropriate basis for comparisons. To the extent that an individual test taker differs from the members of the norm group, interpretations will be in error. If no norm group is clearly appropriate as a basis for interpreting scores, we sometimes can develop new normative data, such as local or subgroup norms. When this procedure is not feasible, the test interpreter has two options: either to disregard the test scores or use them as one source of evidence in deriving hypotheses about the individual's behavior. The latter approach will generally be preferred because, as was indicated earlier, the absence of appropriate normative data should not be used as an excuse for failing to make decisions or take appropriate action.

Equating Scores

Test users sometimes encounter a situation similar to the following:

> A high school student, Jimmy Jones, applies to Midwest State and Prestige U. As part of the application procedure to Prestige U he takes the XYZ College Aptitude Test. He also submits his scores on the XYZ Test to Midwest State. Unfortunately, Midwest State requires the ABC College Aptitude Test and asks Jimmy to submit scores on the ABC Test. Jimmy may well ask why scores on the XYZ Test cannot be substituted for scores on the ABC Test since both tests purportedly measure aptitude for college.

The basic problem in this situation is that of equating test scores; that is, of placing both scores on a common scale.

How can scores on tests be equated? One common procedure is called the *equipercentile method* (see Angoff, 1971a; Jaeger, 1973). In this technique both tests are administered to the same sample, and raw scores are translated into percentile ranks. Then, using the percentile ranks as pivot points, a table of equivalent raw scores can be prepared. That is, if a raw score of 55 on Test ABC is at the 90th percentile rank and a raw score of 36 on Test XYZ is also at the 90th percentile, scores of 55 on Test ABC and 36 on Test XYZ can be considered as equivalent scores.[8]

Several alternative approaches to equating also can be used (Angoff, 1968, 1971a; Jaeger, 1981; Kolen, 1981). When tests are used as predictors they can be equated in terms of (predicted) criterion scores; that is, rather than using equal percentile ranks as the pivot point, equal outcome scores could be used as the basis for equating. Another approach would be to anchor several tests to one

---

[8] These scores represent equivalent ranks; they would not represent equivalent knowledge unless the content of the two tests was similar (Wesman, 1958).

common test; that is, rather than equating each test with every other test, we could equate each test with one common, anchor test. And, as we saw earlier, test construction strategies based on item characteristic curves and latent traits, by calibrating individual items allow for interpretation of scores on a common scale, even when different examinees take different items.

Change and Difference Scores

Most of our discussion has been concerned with a single score. There are, however, at least two common situations in which we must consider more than one score. One is when we are concerned with repeated measurements over time (change scores). The other is when we want to compare scores on two or more tests, scales, or subtests.

When measuring change we obtain scores on the same measure at several points in time, then calculate some index of change. Perhaps the most common illustration is measuring academic growth over time. Suppose, for example, that a school administers a standardized reading comprehension test each October. If Mike's grade-equivalent score were 5.4 one year and 6.1 the next, we could say that he showed 7 months' growth. Since "normal" growth would be 10 months,[9] we might conclude that Mike showed less than normal growth in reading ability.

There are several problems with such an interpretation (even neglecting our concern with grade-equivalent scores per se). One is the large error of measurement due to the unreliability of difference scores. The other is that we do not usually know the distribution of growth scores. Although we can infer (from the score development procedure) that the average amount of growth will be 10 months, we do not know how many students improve by only 7 months. Such information would aid our interpretations.

The other common situation involves interpreting differences between several scores obtained at the same time. For example, a teacher might want to know whether Mary's verbal ability is better than her quantitative ability or whether Kirk's arithmetic computational skills are better than his problem-solving skills. Here again, we are confronted with the same problem—the unreliability of difference scores. Fortunately, it is possible to determine whether a given difference between pairs of scores is statistically significant. Some test publishers incorporate this information into their interpretive material, either (1) by reporting scores as bands, with nonoverlapping bands indicating significant differences, or (2) by stating that a difference of a certain number of points is statistically significant. Such practices should be encouraged. The important point is that unless we have evidence that the observed differences are true differences, we cannot imply that the person performed differently on the two tests or occasions. Because of the large error of measurement in difference scores, the difference needed for significance is usually larger than might be expected at first glance. Thus we

[9] Remember grade-equivalent scores are based on a ten-month school year.

should always be cautious when interpreting difference scores so as not to draw conclusions from chance differences.

Guidelines for Communicating Test Scores

Even if the tester has the necessary technical background to interpret a test score, there is no guarantee that this information will be effectively communicated to the test taker. Thus, in this section we shall suggest several guidelines to aid you in communicating scores in such a way that the client will understand their meaning. These suggestions will not make you an expert; it is hoped, however, that they will provide a starting point (for a detailed treatment see Goldman, 1971; Lyman, 1978; or Mayo, 1980).

1. *Use language the client understands.* Testing, like other specialized fields, has its own vocabulary. Just because you understand a term doesn't mean that the client will. For example, you know what standard deviations and standard scores are; however, it is unlikely that the client will. Thus, you will have to explain standard scores in nontechnical terms; generally, using an interpretation involving relative position (that is, percentile ranks) will suffice. If in doubt, ask the client whether he understands. Better yet, ask him to tell you what your interpretation meant.

2. *Be sure the client knows what the test measures or predicts.* This is the validity question. Here again, we do not need a detailed technical explanation, just the major implications. For example, you don't need to give a client a short course on the construction of interest inventories, but he should know that the occupational scales compare his interests to people in that occupation and high scores mean that the person will probably stay in an occupation if he enters it. Another aspect might be called the *labeling problem.* To tell the client that a certain scale measures, say, Dominance will probably not be sufficient. You may well have to explain what the test constructor means by Dominance. This is particularly important with emotionally laden personality dimensions, such as Heterosexuality or Masculinity-Femininity.

3. If the scores are norm-referenced, *be sure that the client knows what group he is being compared to.* For example, a student's ranking on a college aptitude test, such as the ACT or SAT, will vary widely depending on whether he is being compared to a cross section of high school seniors, students at a local community college, or students at a highly selective Ivy League college.

4. *Be sure the client recognizes that scores are only "best estimates."* Here we are referring both to unreliability and prediction errors (invalidity). The important point to be communicated is that the scores, or predictions, are "best estimates," and that there will always be some degree of error involved when considering an individual score. To do this without creating the impression that scores are so error-filled that they are worthless often involves treading a narrow path.

5. *Be sure the client knows how his scores will be used.* This is particularly important when tests are used in selection and placement. Our concern is with the role test scores will play in the decision-making process. Will the test scores

be an important factor or will they be used only in borderline cases? Are there minimal cutting scores on any variable? Often this information is not available, particularly in counseling situations. However, we often have some information that may be useful. For example, suppose a student is thinking of applying for graduate work in Psychology at Old Ivy, and we know that the average GRE-Verbal score of students in this program is 700. If John Smith scored only 500 on the GRE-V, we can probably safely imply that his chances of acceptance will be low, even if we do not know exactly how much weight is placed on GRE scores by the admissions committee.

6. *Consider what the impact of knowing his test scores will be on the client.* Take the example in the previous paragraph. Will John be discouraged because his scores were low? Or will it confirm what he already suspects about his abilities? Will it cause him to abandon some long-held plans? Or will it cause him to work harder to show that his score is not a true indication of his ability? In short, how will your interpretation affect the client?

Furthermore, how will you handle his reaction? Although we usually think of the possible upsetting reactions when scores are lower than the person expects, we must also be prepared for the opposite situation. If a student thinks he has only average ability, what will be the effect if he finds that his ability is quite high? How will he reconcile this with his previous self-image? These are the sorts of questions a test interpreter must be prepared to face.

7. Implicit in many of the previous guidelines is our final point: *Let the client be an active participant in the test interpretation process.* After all, the scores are his, not yours, and the decisions to be made will affect his life, not yours. Thus, at all stages of the process you should solicit his reactions, encourage him to ask questions, and help him reflect upon the implications of his scores. Although a test score is only one limited piece of information, finding out the score may set off a chain of events that drastically changes an individual's life. Thus, you must be assured that he thoroughly understands the meanings and implications of his scores. Unless the client is an active participant in the process, you may not be aware of how well he understands his scores.

summary

In this chapter we discussed content-referenced and outcome-referenced scores. Content-referenced scores, which are frequently called criterion-referenced scores, express test results in terms of performance levels in a specified content domain. They indicate what test takers know or can do, not how they compare to other persons, and are most frequently used on achievement tests.

To develop content-referenced scores involves two steps: describing the content domain and specifying the scale on which performance will be expressed. The domain indicates what skills, knowledge, or behaviors are tapped by the test items; the scale indicates the performance level.

Several types of content-referenced scores were described. The simplest is percent correct scores. Although these scores are easy to compute and use, their meaning varies with the difficulty of the test items and the definition of the domain. Mastery scores indicate whether performance meets a predetermined standard, usually 80 to 85 percent correct. With mastery scores there are only two interpretations: pass or fail (or mastery/nonmastery). If scores are above the mastery level, the test taker passes; otherwise he fails. Content standard test scores report performance in a clearly specified domain on a scale with a well-accepted meaning. Finally, when performance is not assessed by answering test questions, standardized rating scales can sometimes be used.

A related type of score is a latent trait score. These scores are developed by calibrating ability and item difficulties using a particular model for the item characteristic curve. They have the advantage of allowing scores of test takers who take different item samples to be reported on the same scale.

Outcome-referenced scores express test performance in terms of predicted performance on some other variable. Thus they incorporate validity data directly into the test interpretation process. The most common method of presenting outcome-referenced scores is by expectancy tables. An expectancy table shows the probability of various outcomes for each level of predictor score. We also illustrated several graphic and tabular methods for presenting outcome-referenced scores. The essential element in all methods was that scores show expected (predicted) performance on another variable.

We also discussed several problems in interpreting test scores. We pointed out that accurate interpretation of scores requires knowledge of the test takers' background and the testing conditions, as well as technical knowledge regarding the particular type of scores used. We also noted that the accuracy of scores—and thus of score interpretations—depends on the reliability and validity of the test and, when relevant, the appropriateness of the normative data. Several methods of equating scores, including the equipercentile and equal predicted outcomes methods, were discussed. We also pointed out that change and difference scores are generally quite unreliable and reflect both measurement errors and true changes, thus are frequently misinterpreted.

The chapter concluded with a presentation of some guidelines for interpreting scores. The main points in this discussion were that test takers and test users should always be informed of the implications and planned uses of the test scores and should be active participants in the test interpretation process.

Suggestions for Further Reading

Glass, G. V. Standards and criteria. *Journal of Educational Measurement,* 1978, *15*, 237–261. The major paper in an issue of JEM devoted to problems of standard setting; describes and critiques methods proposed for setting standards; responses to the paper by other authors follow this article.

Goldman, L. *Using tests in counseling,* 2d ed. New York: Appleton–Century–Crofts 1971. A comprehensive discussion of the use of tests in counseling, with particular emphasis on the interpretation of scores and communicating their meaning to test takers and clients.

Harris, C. W., Alkin, M. C., & Popham, W. J. *Problems in criterion-referenced measurement.* Los Angeles: Center for the Study of Evaluation, University of California at Los Angeles, 1974. A series of papers on criterion-referenced measurement; emphasis on test construction and psychometric problems.

Mehrens, W. A., & Ebel, R. L. Some comments on criterion-referenced and norm-referenced achievement tests. *NCME Measurement in Education,* 1979, *10*(1). A brief discussion of the construction and use of norm- and criterion-referenced achievement tests; concludes that each has appropriate uses and the major question is when to use each type of test.

Millman, J. Criterion-referenced measurement. In W. J. Popham (Ed.), *Evaluation in education.* Berkeley, Calif.: McCutchan, 1974. A clearly written introduction to the issues and problems in criterion-referenced measurement, illustrated with many examples.

Nitko, A. J. Criterion-referencing schemes. *New Directions for Testing and Measurement,* 1980, *6*, 35–71. A description and categorization of the various types of criterion-referenced scores; includes extensive bibliography on criterion-referenced measurement.

Popham, W. J. The case for criterion-referenced measurements. *Educational Researcher,* 1978, *7*(11), 6–10. A defense of criterion-referenced tests and a response to Ebel's arguments in favor of norm-referenced tests (see Suggestions for Further Reading in Chapter 8).

Popham, W. J. *Modern educational measurement.* Englewood Cliffs, N.J.: Prentice-Hall, 1981. A recent text stressing criterion-referenced measurement, written by the major proponent of this approach.

Popham, W. J., & Husek, T. R. Implications of criterion-referenced measurement. *Journal of Educational Measurement,* 1969, 6, 1–9. A discussion of the major differences between norm-referenced and criterion-referenced measurement and the implications for test construction, evaluation, and use.

Shepard, L. Standard setting issues and methods. *Applied Psychological Measurement,* 1980, 4, 447–467. A review of the various methods for setting standards for test performance and recommendations for which method to use for various purposes.

· part four ·
maximal
performance
tests

W E live in a competitive, achievement-oriented society. Most of us have come to accept the importance of "doing our best" in whatever we undertake. And, throughout our lives, we have been in competition with other people—for grades, for jobs, and in athletics. But we also compete with ourselves, as when we want to prove to ourselves that we can master the calculus or a foreign language, try to do our job better, or attempt to improve our golf or tennis game. In all of these situations we are trying to exhibit our best possible performance.

In education, the results of our efforts are frequently measured by tests. Our performance on the job or in athletics is measured more informally, but in ways that share many features with tests. For example, a golf score is a sample of the golfer's skill under a standard set of conditions—playing a particular course, under certain conditions, and following a defined set of rules.

Given the competitive nature of many of our activities, it is not surprising that many tests are designed to measure the test taker's best possible performance. These tests are called maximal performance tests and include measures of achievement, aptitudes, and abilities.

The next five chapters will discuss these tests. Chapter 10 is an overview of this unit. In it we differentiate between the types of maximal performance tests and consider two problems common to all maximal performance tests: how to identify good items and how to ensure that a test is unbiased. Chapter 11 describes the construction and uses of the most common type of test, the teacher-built classroom achievement test. Chapter 12 discusses the other type of achievement test, the standardized achievement test. Chapter 13 focuses on tests of general mental ability, such as intelligence, scholastic aptitude, and college admission tests. Chapter 14 describes ways of measuring a variety of other abilities, both cognitive and psychomotor. Throughout these chapters we have tried to illustrate how the basic principles of measurement (discussed in Chapters 1 through 9) apply to the construction, interpretation, evaluation, and use of each type of maximal performance test.

Chapter 10 • Measures of Maximal Performance

In Chapter 2 we made a distinction between tests of maximal performance and tests of typical performance. This distinction was based on the purpose of the measurement. On measures of maximal performance we are interested in obtaining an estimate of the person's best possible performance; on measures of typical performance we are interested in usual or habitual performance. The set to respond to a testing situation, as either maximal or typical performance, is usually engendered by the test directions. That is, on measures of maximal performance, test takers are instructed to "do their best," to "obtain the highest possible score." In contrast, on measures of typical performance test takers are directed to express their usual or habitual reactions.

As might be expected, items on maximal performance measures usually have definite correct answers. Thus this category encompasses tests that measure outcomes of educational or training programs (achievement tests), tests that measure a person's developed skills in an area (ability tests), and tests that indicate whether a person has the necessary skills and abilities to succeed in further work in an area (aptitude tests). Measures of typical performance are appropriate when we want to know how a person typically behaves or reacts, not whether he or she knows the appropriate reaction for a particular situation. Personality, interest, and attitude tests are examples of typical performance measures.

Chapters 10 through 14 focus on maximal performance measures; typical performance measures will be discussed in Chapters 15 through 17. When discussing the various types of tests in each category we shall consider the assumptions underlying each type of test, how the tests are constructed, their reliability and validity, how scores are interpreted, and appropriate uses of the tests. Examples of published tests will be used only to illustrate the various concepts and principles discussed; no attempt will be made to provide a comprehensive survey of the available tests in each category.

In this chapter we shall differentiate between the major categories of maximal performance tests—achievement, aptitude, and ability tests. We shall also consider two topics that apply to all types of maximal performance tests: item analysis and test bias. The item analysis section will describe statistical methods for identifying good and poor items; the test bias section will describe methods for detecting whether a test (or items) is unfair to certain groups of test takers. The remaining chapters in this section consider various types of maximal performance tests in greater detail.

aptitude, achievement, and ability

As we have noted, maximal performance tests can be classified into three broad categories: aptitude tests, ability tests, and achievement tests. Although these three categories are not mutually exclusive, and although a particular test may serve more than one of these functions, there are enough differences in emphasis to consider these types of tests separately. We shall start with the type of test you are probably most familiar with, achievement tests.

Achievement Tests

Undoubtedly you have taken many achievement tests during your educational career. For example, classroom examinations clearly are achievement tests. So are the test batteries that you took during your elementary and secondary school days that measured your mastery of arithmetic and mathematics, spelling, history, natural sciences, reading, and other basic skills. You probably also could specify the types of items included on such tests—for example, questions measuring knowledge of specific facts, principles, and concepts; problems involving the manipulation of numbers and formulas; questions requiring you to draw conclusions from information contained in a reading passage; items requiring application of your knowledge to new situations; and, at least on classroom exams, essay questions requiring you to evaluate or integrate material.

A question remains, however: How can achievement tests be differentiated from other types of tests? Probably your first response would be that achievement tests measure what a person has learned. This is obviously true, but a little reflection will show that all tests measure what an individual has learned. You might take another tack and say that achievement tests assess mastery of academic subjects. Yet the written test that you took to obtain a driver's license was an achievement test. Trying again, you might try to distinguish achievement tests by their uses. That is, if a test is designed to evaluate teaching or learning, it is an achievement test. However, there are instances where achievement tests are used primarily to predict future performance, since past performance is frequently the best predictor of future performance.

In this book a test will be classified as an achievement test if it measures learning that has occurred as a result of experiences in a relatively circumscribed learning situation, such as in a classroom or training program, and when the focus is on what *has been learned*.

Aptitude Tests

Most persons, if asked to give an example of a psychological test, would probably cite an intelligence or aptitude test. "IQ tests" and "tests that tell you what you can do" have become known as the psychologist's stock-in-trade. We will consider a test to be an aptitude measure if it measures the results of both general and incidental learning experiences and if the goal of testing is to predict what can be learned in the future.

Test designed to predict future learning
aptitude = ability to learn

This latter point, that aptitude tests predict future learning, is the hallmark of the definition of aptitude. Most definitions state that *aptitude* is *the ability to acquire certain behaviors or skills given appropriate opportunity*. Thus aptitudes indicate the probability that certain other behaviors will be acquired or learned. What is to be learned may vary from a complex intellectual skill, such as a foreign language or calculus, to simple motor or physical acts. Thus the definition of aptitude encompasses the ability to learn a variety of skills or behaviors, with the common thread being the ability to learn, not the type of skills learned.

Aptitude can also be defined in another manner. Advocates of mastery learning (e.g., Block, 1971, 1974; Bloom, 1971, 1974, 1976; Carroll, 1963) believe that most students can learn if given sufficient time. That is, differences in performance result not from differing abilities to learn but because students take different amounts of time to learn the material to a given level of proficiency. Thus, in their view, aptitude is more properly defined in terms of the amount of time necessary to learn the material.[1] Note that in this approach, although aptitudes would be measured by tests of skills or abilities, the appropriate measure of aptitude is the amount of time it takes a student to learn to a given criterion level.

Although the term *aptitude* has a long history in psychological testing, some people object to its use. The primary reason for their objection is that, to many people, the concept connotes highly stable, perhaps even innate, abilities. They would argue that because the skills constituting aptitudes are learned, they are not as immutable as many people think. They would prefer that the more neutral term, *ability,* be used for any developed skills and abilities, including those commonly called aptitudes.

Ability Tests

What, then, do we mean by ability? We shall define *ability* as *the power to perform a task*. Thus ability tests measure a person's level of skill in a particular area. In contrast to aptitudes, abilities refer to a current state rather than to a prediction of future performance. However, since current ability generally is the best predictor of future performance, ability tests can be used to predict future performance. In this sense they function as aptitude measures. And, by referring to current level of skill, ability tests are similar to achievement tests. However, they differ from achievement tests in two major ways: (1) The term *achievement* is usually used to refer to the outcome of relatively well-specified learning experiences, whereas ability refers to the results of more general or broad learning experiences; and (2) abilities refer to both verbal and performance skills, whereas achievement tests generally measure only verbal knowledge and skills.[2]

To summarize, achievement tests measure the results of relatively well-specified learning experiences and have a past or present reference; ability tests measure the results of broad learning experiences and have a present reference;

---

[1] This is a highly simplified view as learning also depends on such factors as the time available for learning, the quality of instruction, and the student's persistence (Block, 1971; Carroll, 1971).

[2] Ability tests, especially in the perceptual and psychomotor areas, can also measure skills not generally considered to be learned, such as dexterity, strength, and hand-eye coordination.

aptitude tests measure the results of broad learning experiences and have a future reference.

Developed Abilities

Although achievement, aptitude, and ability tests can be distinguished by their content and uses, they share an important feature: All measure developed abilities. That is, they reflect what a person has learned, both as a result of formal and informal learning experiences, prior to the time of testing. More generally, performance on any test reflects at least three broad classes of influences: the test takers' potentials for learning, their experiences prior to the test, and the testing conditions (including the nature of the test).

This point of view has several important implications for the interpretation and use of maximal performance tests. To the extent that people differ in their potential to learn, they may obtain different scores. (The degree to which people differ in learning potentials is, of course, a controversial issue. However, the evidence seems to indicate that there are individual differences in the ability to learn.) Second, and more important, people who have not had the opportunity to learn the material covered on a test cannot be expected to perform well on the test. This problem can be handled in two ways, either by ensuring that all test takers do have the opportunity to learn the material or skill tested or by taking differences in the opportunity to learn into account when interpreting scores. Third, a test will not accurately reflect a person's knowledge or skill unless the test items and testing conditions allow him to exhibit his knowledge. To use an obvious example, a Spanish-speaking student's skill in mathematics would not be accurately assessed if the test items were written in English.

The concept of developed abilities also implies that, when interpreting scores, we must consider where an individual falls on the continuum of learning a particular ability. Test takers having different prior learning experiences may be at different points on their individual learning curves for the skill tested. Thus, even if two people obtain the same score on a test, the implications may be quite different. One person may have had ample opportunity to learn and, consequently, her score may represent the limit of her ability on the task. The other, having had less opportunity to learn, may improve her score with further training. To know which interpretation applies requires more than a test score, it requires knowledge of the individual's previous learning experiences.

With these considerations in mind, we now turn to an overview of achievement and ability tests. In this chapter, we shall present some basic principles and concepts; specific types of tests and their uses will be discussed in more detail in following chapters.

achievement tests

Achievement tests, as we have indicated, are designed to measure the knowledge and skills developed in a relatively circumscribed content domain. This area may be as narrow as one day's class assignment (for example, computing the mean, the battle of Bull Run) or as broad as several years' study (such as high school mathematics or college French). Although we are measuring what a person knows or can do at a particular point in time, our reference is usually to the past; that is, we are interested in what has been learned as a result of a particular course or experience or a series of experiences. Because it generally is not feasible to measure every bit of knowledge and every possible skill, the test items usually are only a sample of all the possible items in the domain.

Assumptions Made When Measuring Achievement

When measuring achievement, we make three basic assumptions. The first is that the content and/or skill domain covered by the test can be specified in behavioral terms; that is, in a manner that is readily communicable to other persons. As a corollary, important goals must be differentiated from peripheral or incidental goals. Because of time limitations, only certain outcomes can be measured; these outcomes should be the most important ones.

A second assumption is that the test does, in fact, measure these important behaviors. This is an assumption of content validity. Consider an example used earlier, algebra word problems. To solve such problems requires several skills: being able to read the problem, to translate it into algebraic form, and to do the necessary arithmetic computations. If the test is designed to measure students' ability to solve algebraic word problems, we have no concerns. If, however, we are only interested in students' ability to manipulate algebraic formulas, the test will also measure a skill (reading ability) that is irrelevant to the purposes of the testing. In short, we must always be sure that our test measures only those outcomes that we want to measure, not irrelevant factors.

The third assumption is that the test takers have had the opportunity to learn the material covered by the test. This assumption is generally well met on classroom exams, since all students are in the same course and the instructor has specified what assignments will be covered on the exam. The problem of unequal educational experiences becomes an issue when dealing with standardized achievement tests. Because standardized tests are administered in a variety of schools, of necessity they cover material that is widely taught. To the extent that the subject matter taught in any particular school differs from that covered on the test, or the students in a particular school have not had equivalent experiences to those of the norm group, normative interpretations will be inappropriate.

Types of Achievement Tests

Achievement tests can be classified in various ways. One major distinction is between standardized and teacher-built classroom achievement tests. *Standardized* tests are constructed by test publishers and are designed for use in a wide variety of schools. Thus their coverage is necessarily broad and includes materials taught in many schools. Norms are generally national in scope. *Teacher-built tests*, in contrast, are constructed by the classroom teacher, or possibly by several teachers in the same school. The content area will be more circumscribed, being based on the curriculum of a particular course or school. And, because the test covers a narrower domain, materials will be covered in more detail. Scores will be interpreted with reference to the student's immediate competitors, his or her classmates.

Another obvious basis for classification is by content area. Some achievement tests measure knowledge of spelling, others arithmetic, others United States history, others chemistry, and so forth. The content area can be defined very broadly (for example, calculus, reading, American history) or narrowly (for example, economic causes of the Civil War, squaring a polynomial). Many academic achievement tests are batteries, measuring several major content areas rather than only one area. With these tests an appropriate basis of classification would be by grade level; that is, some batteries are designed for primary grades and others for upper elementary grades, junior high school, or high school.

Achievement tests can also be classified by their function. *Survey tests* are designed to provide an estimate of a student's overall level of knowledge in a given content area. Survey tests, therefore, generally sample a broad range of content and yield only one total score. The typical classroom final exam is an illustration of a survey test. A *diagnostic test,* in contrast, attempts to assess relative strengths and weaknesses in important component skills. Thus diagnostic tests are divided into subtests, and scores are provided for each important component. For example, a diagnostic reading test might include subtests covering word recognition, word comprehension, vocabulary, rate of reading, story comprehension, identification of sounds, and syllabication. By studying the pattern of scores, the psychologist can determine the areas in which the individual needs remedial work. A *readiness test* indicates whether the individual possesses the skills needed to learn the material at the next higher level. The most common examples of readiness measures are reading readiness tests, which are administered at the end of kindergarten or beginning of first grade, to determine whether a child has learned the skills necessary to start formal reading instruction. *Proficiency tests* are designed to measure whether a student has attained a designated level of competence in a particular area. "Test-out" examinations (that is, examinations for credit) in courses and driver's license examinations are examples of proficiency tests.

One final distinction, between norm-referenced and content-referenced achievement tests, is important enough to merit separate consideration.

Norm-Referenced and Content-Referenced Tests

Historically, most achievement tests have been norm-referenced, as the primary purpose of testing was considered to be to distinguish between students having varying degrees of knowledge. Thus items were selected by their ability to differentiate between students having varying levels of knowledge, and scores were interpreted as a relative ranking within a designated comparison group.

Beginning with Glaser's article in 1963 there has been an increasing emphasis on content-referenced achievement tests. (Remember, these tests are called criterion-referenced by many people.) On content-referenced tests, the primary concern is to determine an individual's level of mastery of the material tested. Thus, rather than selecting items primarily to differentiate between students, items are selected to cover important instructional outcomes. And, rather than expressing a person's score in comparison with scores of other students, scores are interpreted in relation to a content-defined standard. Sometimes this standard is a minimal level of competence; at other times it is a continuum. The important point, however, is that scores are interpreted in terms of content mastery.

The difference between these two types of tests is also reflected in their basic philosophy and intended uses. At the risk of oversimplification, advocates of norm-referenced testing believe that the most important use of testing is to differentiate between students in terms of knowledge and skills. Thus norm-referenced tests are used to make comparisons between individuals and groups and for selection and placement decisions. In contrast, advocates of content-referenced testing stress the use of testing to improve instruction and learning. They argue that to plan instruction for a student, you must know what a student knows and can do and what is yet to be learned. This information cannot be obtained from norm-referenced tests because they report only relative levels of achievement; they do not directly tell what each student can and cannot do. This requires a different type of testing, one in which test items are based on educational objectives and scores indicate whether these goals have been attained.

To some people (e.g., Angoff, 1974; Brown, 1981; Mehrens & Ebel, 1979) the distinction between norm-referenced and content-referenced tests is not as marked as the advocates of the two positions would suggest. They feel that both types of tests have their place in education but serve different purposes. It has even been suggested that both types of information could be obtained from the same test. That is, an overall score could be interpreted in a norm-referenced manner, and scores on items—or clusters of related items—could be interpreted in a content-referenced manner.

Validation of Achievement Tests

As achievement tests are designed to measure command of a specified content and/or skills domain, and as the test items are selected to represent this domain, in most situations the appropriate method of validation is content validation. That is, the most important question is whether the test items do, in fact, represent the content domain. As noted in Chapter 7, this will generally be a judgmental evaluation rather than a quantitative index.

It should be stressed that evaluation of content validity will always be in reference to a particular use of the test. When achievement tests are developed for use in one particular situation, as are most classroom examinations, this requirement presents no problem. It may, however, be a problem when using standardized achievement tests, because the content domain as defined by the test developers will not be precisely the same as the test user's definition. In these situations, each test user must compare the test items to his definition of the domain and judge whether the content validity is sufficient for his particular situation and use of the test.

In some situations, other types of validity evidence are appropriate. When achievement tests are used to make selection and placement decisions, evidence of criterion-related validity is needed. When other tests measuring the same domain are available, correlations between the tests (convergent or congruent validity) can be computed. When an achievement test is used to evaluate learning or instruction, increases in scores from a pretest to a posttest provide validity evidence.

aptitude and ability tests

The other two types of maximal performance tests, aptitude tests and ability tests, will be discussed in this section. As we noted, there are some unfortunate connotations attached to the term "aptitude"; thus we shall generally refer to both aptitude and ability tests as ability tests. However, whenever principles apply solely to aptitude tests, we shall make a distinction between the two types of tests.

Some Basic Assumptions

When measuring abilities we make the same three basic assumptions that we made when measuring achievement. That is, we assume that the characteristic measured can be defined, that the test measures the characteristic, and that all test takers have had the opportunity to develop the skill being measured by the test. However, when measuring abilities we often have less assurance that these assumptions are met. In the case of the first two assumptions, the main reason is that the construct being measured is frequently defined more generally than on achievement tests. Thus there is more room for disagreement regarding the definition and as to whether the test samples the domain. And, as ability tests generally measure the results of broader, less structured learning experiences, the requirement of equal opportunity to learn is harder to establish.

When measuring abilities, we usually adopt a trait view. That is, abilities are conceptualized as being organized and expressed through combinations of intercorrelated behaviors and responses. To say that someone has mathematical ability is, in essence, to say that she possesses a set of abilities and characteristics which are expressed through high performance on mathematics tests and problems. These skills and characteristics are the ability. Thus ability is a summarizing term, a theoretical construct rather than an entity. This approach is also normative in that a person's ability is compared to other people rather than to an absolute standard. To say that Jane has high mathematical ability means that she can learn mathematics faster, with less effort, or to a greater level of complexity than most of her peers. To say that Debbie lacks mathematical ability does not mean she knows no mathematics; it only means that she knows less or finds learning mathematics harder than most of her peers.

Aptitudes. When measuring aptitudes we usually make several other assumptions. One is that aptitudes are quite stable over time. If a trait (aptitude) is to predict future performance, it must be relatively stable over time. This emphasis on stability has led many people to conclude that aptitudes are inherited characteristics that are unchanging throughout life. (Note such common expressions as a "God-given talent" or a "natural athlete.") There is no doubt that some aptitudes do have genetic bases; there is also no doubt that aptitudes also reflect prior learning and environmental effects. Given the proper set of circumstances, aptitudes can be drastically influenced by environmental and situational characteristics (see, e.g., Anastasi, 1958; Bayley, 1968; Bloom, 1964, 1980; Brim & Kagan, 1980; Hunt, 1961; Vernon, 1971, 1972, 1979).

Our definition also stated that aptitudes assess the ability to learn, given the opportunity to learn. Hence, when we say that Johnny has an aptitude for art, we are actually predicting that Johnny will become a better than average artist *if* given proper training. There is no reason to believe that he will develop his artistic ability without the relevant training. Thus our prediction from an aptitude test is that a certain combination of abilities and skills (the aptitude) coupled with appropriate training will lead to a certain behavior.

Alternative Views. Although ability testing has a long history (DuBois, 1970a), in recent years there has been increasing dissatisfaction with the methods used to measure abilities. One point of view is that while ability tests may provide good indications of the results of learning, they tell little, if anything, about the learning processes that determine performance. Thus some people (e.g., Estes, 1974; Glaser, 1972, 1981; Sternberg, 1979, 1980) have suggested that ability testing should be more closely tied to cognitive psychology and learning theory. This view suggests that tests should be devised not to measure traits identified by the methods of differential psychology (such as factor analysis) but rather to measure processes that have been shown to be important in learning. Such tests, presumably, would provide more useful information for understanding the learning process and improving people's skills and abilities.

Another point of view (see, e.g., McClelland, 1973; Tyler, 1978) suggests that too much emphasis in ability testing has been placed on comparing individuals. They suggest that tests should identify the range and nature of a person's competencies, rather than stressing normative comparisons. For example, Tyler argues that we are constantly making choices—of what activities to pursue, of what skills to develop, of what educational opportunities to pursue. Because our time is finite, we cannot pursue all possible activities. Thus our weaker performance in some areas may, in many cases, result from a conscious decision not to develop our skills in this area, not from any inability to learn the skill. As, in most situations, there is more than one way to perform adequately (for example, most jobs can be satisfactorily performed in many different ways, by people with various skills), it is more important to know the person's range of competencies, not how well the person will perform on certain preselected skills.

Types of Ability Tests

Probably the most well-known types of intelligence tests are *general intelligence tests*—what the man in the street calls "IQ tests." These tests are designed to obtain a broad, overall measure of a person's intellectual functioning. The original, and still most important, general intelligence tests are the individually administered tests, such as the Stanford-Binet Intelligence Scale and the various Wechsler Intelligence Scales. These *individual intelligence tests* all report performance in terms of an overall, or full-scale, IQ (intelligence quotient) even though they may contain various types of items (for example, both verbal and performance tests).

Because individually administered intelligence tests require a trained administrator, and therefore are costly in terms of time and money, a number of *group intelligence tests* have been developed. In many ways, these tests are similar to the verbal portions of individually administered tests, but, of necessity, they are restricted to measuring skills that can be tested by a paper-and-pencil format. Thus they do not contain performance items. As might be expected, group tests are used in educational and industrial settings, where large numbers of people have to be tested. In contrast, individual tests are more appropriate when working intensively with single individuals—as in counseling, or with children needing special educational programs.

Closely related to general intelligence tests are *academic ability* or *scholastic aptitude tests*. These include the various college and professional school admission tests as well as more general academic ability measures. In contrast to group intelligence tests, academic ability tests focus directly on skills that are necessary for success in formal educational settings. Thus, for example, although both group intelligence tests and scholastic aptitude tests might contain vocabulary items, only a scholastic aptitude test would include reading comprehension items. Furthermore, group intelligence tests are constructed to sample the various skills that make up intellectual ability; items included on scholastic aptitude tests are ones that predict future academic success.

Some psychologists believe that intellectual ability can be subdivided into a small number of relatively broad abilities. This view has led to the construction of *multiple aptitude (multiaptitude) batteries*. These batteries are integrated series of tests, each measuring one of the major group factors. For example, the Differential Aptitude Test contains separate tests measuring Verbal Reasoning, Numerical Ability, Abstract Reasoning, Mechanical Reasoning, Space Relations, (Perceptual) Speed and Accuracy, and Language Usage.

There are also a number of tests that measure more specific abilities. We shall refer to these as tests of *special abilities*. Some of these test cognitive abilities such as critical thinking, creativity, or divergent thinking. Others measure musical and artistic abilities. Still others measure more vocationally oriented abilities, such as tests of perceptual speed and accuracy, spatial visualization, manual dexterity, and mechanical abilities. In contrast to most other types of ability tests, special ability tests frequently require a psychomotor performance and/or are not entirely verbal in either content or responses.

Validation of Ability Tests

The appropriate method of validating an ability test will depend on the use of the test. In most cases content validity is an important consideration. That is, the test items must cover the content and skills domain that constitutes the ability. An obvious example would be a test constructed to measure the abilities required on a particular job. Here the test items should sample the knowledge and skills workers use on the job. As might be expected, content validity is built into the test during the test construction process.

When ability tests are used for decision making, evidence of criterion-related validity is needed. For example, when an ability test is used to select workers, place workers on jobs, or place students in various sections of a course, evidence of criterion-related validity is needed to determine whether the test adequately performs its intended function.

Since ability tests can be used as both independent and dependent variables in psychological research and are used to define constructs in psychological and educational theories, evidence of construct validity is also frequently relevant when using ability tests. In these situations the test is used as an operational measure of the construct of interest. The important question here is: Is this test an acceptable measure of the construct? As noted in the discussion of construct validity (Chapter 7), this is not a question that can be answered by one study or one set of data.

When tests are used as measures of constructs, another problem must be considered—the difference between process and outcomes. As mentioned, most ability tests measure the outcomes of a learning process. When scores do not directly indicate what process was used in responding to the items, we must infer that a particular learning process occurred from the responses made. In some cases the line of inference is rather tight, as when different responses reflect alternative types of learning.[3] In many situations, however, the reasoning will be more indirect and speculative, depending on our general knowledge of the skill being measured. It is this problem that has caused writers to suggest that ability tests should be designed so that they will directly reflect the learning processes needed to provide correct responses to the items.

item analysis

A test is only as good as the items it contains. Thus, when constructing a test, we must be concerned with the quality of the items. When evaluating the quality of items, various criteria are used. For one, an item should measure the knowledge or skill it is designed to measure. Thus, for example, on achievement tests items are included only if they measure attainment of an important instructional objective. Besides the content of the item, we must also be concerned with the quality of expression: Items should be clearly written, grammatical, and at the appropriate reading level. But we are also concerned with the statistical characteristics of the item. In this section we shall concentrate on statistical indices of item quality.

The statistical analysis of test items is called, not surprisingly, *item analysis*. Although various types of analyses can be done, they usually serve one of two purposes. One, of course, is to identify good and poor items. This is obviously important in the test construction process. The other major use of item analyses is to identify knowledge and skills test takers have and have not mastered. For example, suppose an item on a classroom test is answered incorrectly by a majority of the students. This information tells the teacher something is wrong. Unfortunately, without further investigation, it does not tell her what went wrong. The item may have been misleading or poorly constructed, the material have been so difficult the students were not able to learn it, or the instruction may have been

---

[3] For example, incorrect responses on an English composition test may indicate what sorts of grammatical errors a student makes or observing the steps students use in solving mathematics problems can indicate whether they used a formula, an empirical process, or a trial-and-error procedure.

incomplete. Only further analyses will tell which is the most likely explanation. The information gathered from the item analysis, however, can be useful in planning further instruction and/or testing.

Item analysis data can also be used for other purposes. As we shall see later in this chapter, many approaches to identifying biased items rely on item analysis data.

With this general introduction, we shall now discuss item analysis in more detail, describing the procedures used, the indices computed, and how item analysis data can be used.

Procedures

The exact procedures used in an item analysis will depend on several factors: the type of items and test, the number of test takers, the computational facilities available, and the purpose of the analysis. However, most item analyses are concerned with three aspects of an item: first, the *difficulty* of the item, which is most simply defined as the proportion of people who answer an item correctly; second, the *discrimination* power of the item—that is, whether it differentiates between people with varying degrees of knowledge or ability; and third, the effect of the *distracters*—that is, whether they attract any responses and, if so, the pattern of the responses.

When analyzing difficulty and distracters we are interested in the performance of the total sample of test takers. When analyzing discrimination we compare people with varying degrees of ability.[4] If we have an external criterion, it can be used as a measure of ability. When no external criterion is available, the total score on the test is used as the measure of ability. That is, test takers who score high on the test are compared with those who score lower. In this type of analysis, we assume that the test as a whole is a reasonable measure of ability.

Since item statistics can be quite variable across samples of test takers, one essential requirement is to obtain a large number of tests for analysis. On standardized tests this is usually no problem; in fact, often only a sample of the tests is used in an item analysis. One common procedure is to select 370 tests randomly, and then use only the 100 highest and the 100 lowest scores in the analysis. On classroom tests we are not likely to have a large number of tests for analysis. In these situations, especially when there are less than 100 tests, a good procedure is to break the distribution at the median and compare the upper and lower halves. This procedure provides a more stringent test of the items because all scores are used, not just high and low scores.

Indices

As mentioned above, item analyses are concerned with three aspects of an item: its difficulty, its discrimination, and its distracters. Although many quantitative indices have been developed for each of these aspects, we shall describe only several of the simpler ones as these are the ones that you are most likely to use. Also empirical evidence suggests that comparable results generally will be ob-

---

[4] Some analyses of distracters also compare high and low groups.

tained from various indices (Englehart, 1965; Feldt & Hall, 1964; Oosterhof, 1976). In all our examples we shall use multiple-choice items; however, most of the procedures described can be adapted for use with other types of items. (For other discussions of item analysis see, e.g., Anastasi, 1982, and Henryssen, 1971.)

Difficulty. Item difficulty indices indicate the percent (or proportion) of test takers who answer an item correctly. One simple method is to count the number of test takers who answer each item correctly, then convert these into proportions or percentages. The difficulty index (p, for proportion correct) can be computed as follows:

$$p = \frac{\text{Number answering correctly}}{\text{Number of test takers}}$$ (10.1)

[handwritten annotation: q = those who didn't get item correct.]

When the tests have been divided into groups, the average difficulty can be used. For example, if the total group were divided into upper and lower halves, the formula would be:

$$p = \frac{p_h + p_l}{2}$$ (10.1a)

where p_h and p_l are the proportion of people in the high and low groups, respectively, who answered the item correctly.

Interpretation of item difficulty indices is not as straightforward as might appear on first blush because the difficulty of the item and (the degree of) students' learning are confounded. That is, an item may be easy because of something about the way the item was constructed (for example, the answer is obvious) or because students have learned the material thoroughly. Conversely, an item may be difficult because it is poorly constructed (for example, it is ambiguous), because the item covers intrinsically difficult material, or because students, for some reason, did not learn this material. Or the item may even be miskeyed. Thus, we always have to look at the wording of the items, and consider students' learning experiences and the structure of the subject matter when interpreting item difficulty indices.

Another important question is the optimal level of difficulty for an item. It can be shown that, if the goal of measurement is to maximize differences between students, items with difficulties of .5 are best.[5] Since there is little difference in discrimination power between items with difficulties of .5 and .7, a useful rule of thumb is to use items that 50 to 70 percent of the students can answer correctly.

There are also several situations where items of other levels of difficulty may be more appropriate. One would be when using "warm-up" items at the beginning of a test to build confidence or get students used to the testing situation. These items should be quite easy (yet cover important material). Another is on content-referenced tests, where students are expected to attain certain levels of performance. For example, if a mastery test had a passing level of 85 percent, we would not want an average item difficulty of 50 percent. Similar reasoning would

---

[5] When the item difficulty is .5, the item variance ($= pq$) is at a maximum.

hold whenever grades are awarded on a percentage basis, such as 90 percent for an A, 80 percent for a B, and so on. Third, if tests are designed to discriminate at a particular point, the average item difficulty should be close to that point. Thus, if we wanted to differentiate the top 20 percent of a group from the rest of the test takers, the best procedure would be to use items that only 20 percent of the test takers answer correctly; that is, items with an average difficulty of around 20 percent. Finally, when guessing may affect scores, use items that have difficulties slightly higher than 50 percent to take guessing into account.[6]

Discrimination. Item discrimination indices indicate whether an item differentiates between test takers having varying degrees of knowledge or ability. Ideally this differentiation would be made using an external criterion.[7] For example, items on a scholastic ability test should differentiate between students obtaining high and low grades. That is, students with higher grade averages should answer an item correctly more frequently than students with lower grade averages. Here one possible discrimination index would be the correlation between scores on the item and scores on the criterion (in this case, grades).

On most achievement tests, particularly teacher-built tests, such external criteria are not available. Thus the total score on the test is generally used as the criterion. This procedure assumes that the test as a whole is an adequate measure of the domain. Although this may seem like a tenuous assumption, empirical data support the use of this procedure (Ebel, 1968; Horn, 1966).

The problem, therefore, is to derive an index that measures this relationship. One procedure is to use the item-test correlation. That is, we can correlate scores on an individual item with (total) scores on the test. If students who score high on the test tend to answer the item correctly and those who score low answer incorrectly, the item-test correlation will be positive. If there is no relation between answering an item correctly and the test score, the discrimination index will be zero. In other words, discriminating items will correlate positively with the total score. A good rule of thumb would be to require r to be .20 or higher.

When the group is divided into two (or more) subgroups on the basis of total test scores, we can compare the percentage of students in each group answering an item correctly. Thus, when we have divided a class into halves, a possible discrimination index (D) would be:

$$D = p_h - p_l \qquad (10.2)$$

Here, again, we are looking for a high positive value. As a rule of thumb, we can say that any difference of 15 to 20 percent (.15–.20) or higher would indicate good discrimination.

Distracters. The third aspect of an item analysis concerns the pattern of responses to the various distracters. Obviously, one thing we are looking for is

[6] In these cases some students will attain the correct answer by guessing; item difficulties can be corrected to allow for this factor (Nunnally, 1978).

[7] Item discrimination indices computed using an external criterion measure are often referred to as *item validity indices* to differentiate them from indices using total test scores as a criterion measure.

alternatives that do not attract any responses. These alternatives contribute nothing to the test, except to increase reading time. Here a rule of thumb is that an alternative should be eliminated or revised unless one of every 50 students (2 percent) select it. Other analyses are more subtle but may provide useful information. For example, if an incorrect alternative is chosen by many students in the "high" group but few in the "low" group, it might suggest that this respose is, at least in some aspects, also correct.

Since the three parts of an item analysis are obviously interrelated, we should always look at the total picture when considering an item. To illustrate, if an item is very easy or very difficult, it cannot discriminate well. Or, if an item is very easy, few people will choose any of the distracters. Whether this means the item is weak depends on our criteria; as mentioned earlier, an easy item might be used as a warm-up item. Or a teacher might include an item because it covers important material that he thinks should be tested; whether this item discriminates will be of secondary importance. Or, to give a final example, consider what response pattern would suggest that students guessed at an item. If responses reflected pure guessing, the item difficulty would be at the chance level (for example, .25 in a four- choice item), the item would not discriminate, and approximately equal numbers of people would select each alternative.

We should also mention that the typical item analysis provides more than item data. For example, the item analysis program at the school where I teach also gives the class mean, standard deviation, and variance; provides a Kuder-Richardson reliability index; prints a distribution of scores that includes frequencies, percentile ranks, and standard scores; provides a list of students (by name or identification number) with their test scores; and prints another list indicating which items each student answered incorrectly.

An Example

An example of item analysis data for four test items is shown in Table 10.1. The items were constructed by members of an undergraduate educational psychology class and administered to other students in the class. Two different item analyses procedures are shown in the table. In part I, the analysis is based on all 177 students who took the test and shows the number of students who selected each alternative, the item difficulty index (p), and the item discrimination index (CORR, for item-total test correlation). In part II, the papers were divided into high and low groups by dividing tests at the median. Responses to each alternative are shown separately for the high and low groups. In this analysis, the item difficulty was computed using Equation (10.1a) and the discrimination using Equation (10.2).

Similar conclusions would be drawn from both analyses. Item 1 was moderately easy but did discriminate; item 2 was very easy and did not discriminate. In addition we can see that item 1 has one weak distracter (C) and one that could be improved (D). While none of the distracters on item 2 draw many responses, C and D are especially weak. Note, also, that the high-low analysis of item 1 (part II) provides an additional bit of information not obvious from the total group analysis (part I): 20 of the 25 people who selected alternative A were in the low group.

Thus we can infer that the major problem for test takers, and the reason why the item discriminated, was differentiating between alternatives A and B.

I will leave it to you to interpret the results for items 3 and 4.

Mastery Tests

On mastery tests item analyses are somewhat different.[8] Since we expect (hope?) that most students will have mastered the objectives, on items administered after instruction most students will obtain the correct answer and there will be little variance in responses. Thus the typical item analysis procedures will be inappropriate. Indices of item difficulty will still provide useful information, by indicating what skills students have and have not mastered. However, the usual item discrimination indices will not work. How, then, can we identify discriminating items? One possibility is to administer the same item both before instruction (as a pretest) and after instruction. Before students have studied the material, few students should obtain the correct answer; after instruction, most students should obtain the correct answer. Thus, a discriminating item will be one in which there is a large difference in the proportion of correct answers from pretest to posttest. This procedure has another advantage. If we select items which students cannot answer correctly before instruction but can after instruction, we have some assurance that the material was learned as a result of the instruction (unless, of course, students learned it elsewhere at the same time as the instruction).

A discrimination index could also be obtained by forming two groups of students, those who passed the test and those who did not. We could then compare the percentages of students in each group that answered each item correctly. The main problem with this approach is that the two groups may vary widely in size (since most students will pass the test), and thus the statistics may be much more accurate for the "pass" group than for the "not pass" group.

Uses of Item Analysis Data

We have already suggested several possible uses for item analysis data. Let us now review and summarize these uses.

One obvious use is to determine which items to include on a test. On standardized tests, this means trying out the items and using the item analysis data as a basis for selecting items for the final forms of a test. In general, we select items of appropriate difficulty that discriminate well. However, the procedure is not quite this simple. We also have to look at the intercorrelations between items (see, e.g., Nunnally, 1978) and, of course, we must be concerned with the content balance of the test.

Item analysis can also be used to improve items and item writing skills. If the test writer finds an item to be defective in some respect (for example, it is too easy or one distracter does not work), this is a signal for the item to be revised. This is one obvious reason for pretesting items. At a more general level, item writers, through experience, come to know what sorts of items work well and which items "bomb out." Thus by considering their past experiences (both mistakes and suc-

---

[8] Similar considerations apply to all content-referenced tests, not just mastery tests.

Table 10.1
An Example of an Item Analysis

ITEMS

1. Incorrect choices on multiple-choice tests are called:
   (A) alternatives (B) distracters (C) relatives (D) deceivers
2. Which of the following is NOT an alternative-choice item?
   (A) true-false (B) short-answer (C) matching (D) multiple-choice
3. Difficult test items can best be used to:
   (A) challenge students to do better.
   (B) separate the better and average students.
   (C) let poor students know where they need help.
   (D) reinforce the better students.
4. A psychologist who strongly favors true-false items is:
   (A) Ebel (B) Bloom (C) Tyler (D) Ausubel

I. ANALYSIS OF TOTAL GROUP

Item	Omit	A	B	C	D	p	CORR
1	2	25	141[a]	2	7	.81	.31
2	0	6	170[a]	1	0	.96	.14
3	0	21	130[a]	10	16	.73	.39
4	5	45[a]	41	39	47	.25	.03

II. ANALYSIS BY HIGH-LOW GROUPS

Item-Group[b]	Omit	A	B	C	D	%R	p	D
1-High	1	5	80[a]	0	2	91	.80	.22
-Low	1	20	61	2	5	69		
2-High	0	0	88[a]	0	0	100	.96	.08
-Low	0	6	82	1	0	92		
3-High	0	4	75[a]	4	5	85	.74	.23
-Low	0	17	55	6	11	62		
4-High	2	23[a]	19	20	24	26	.25	.02
-Low	3	22	22	19	23	24		

[a] Indicates correct answer.
[b] High group consists of the 88 highest scores; the low group, the 89 lowest scores.

cesses), they learn what characteristics (such as wording and types of problems) produce good items. Instructors can also develop a file of good items for use on future tests.

The results of an item analysis also provide useful information for improving instruction. The instructor can look at the items a student misses, identify weaknesses in knowledge, and suggest appropriate remedial instruction. One application of this procedure has been suggested by Dunstan (1973). His item analysis program provides each student with a list of the items that he or she missed and indicates where (in the reading assignments) the material was covered. Thus, each student is directed to the appropriate source for remedial help.

The teacher can look at the results of an item analysis for a class and identify what items, or types of items, many students missed and what ones they have mastered. She can then plan instruction accordingly—for example, by going over the material covered by items that many students answered incorrectly. By looking at the pattern of incorrect answers, she may also get some clues as to why students missed a particular item. Suppose, for example, that an item analysis of an arithmetic test shows that many of Ms. Piaget's fifth grade students had difficulty on items involving decimals. She could then spend more time teaching decimals. If, in addition, the item analysis showed that most wrong answers involved misplacing the decimal point, she could focus her instruction on this particular operation.

Fortunately, many test publishers will supply item analysis data, in addition to scores and normative data—for a small fee, of course. Given the potential value of such information for improving instruction and facilitating students' learning, expenditure of the necessary funds to obtain item analysis data would seem to be a worthwhile investment.

bias in maximal performance tests

The goal in developing any test is to obtain an accurate measurement of an individual's characteristics. But, in addition, the test procedures should be fair and unbiased. Although there is no agreed upon definition of test fairness or bias,[9] a common thread runs through the various definitions: *A test can be considered biaised if it differentiates between members of various groups* (for example, between men and women or between blacks and whites) *on bases other than the characteristic being measured.* That is, a test is biased if its content, procedures, or use result in a systematic advantage (or disadvantage) to members of certain groups over other groups and if the basis of this differentiation is irrelevant to the test purpose.

Note that this definition does not imply that a test is biased solely because members of various groups perform differently (have different mean scores or distributions). When two groups perform at different levels on a test, but the scores reflect differences in the ability being measured, the test would not be biased. Thus, if students who had not taken a statistics course scored lower on a statistics exam than students who had taken a statistics course, we would not say the test was a biased measure of knowledge of statistics. Although the test did differentiate between persons with varying degrees of knowledge of statistics, it would not be an unfair test.

On the other hand, whenever there are differences in the average performance of two groups, the possibility of bias should be investigated. Suppose, for example, that among students who had completed a statistics course, we found that men obtained higher scores than women. Suppose also that some of the items

[9] See, for example, Arvey, 1979; Bond, 1981; Cleary, Humphreys, Kendrick, & Wesman, 1975; Cole, 1973, 1981; Cronbach, 1976; Flaugher, 1974; 1978; Gardner, 1978; Hunter & Schmidt, 1976; Linn, 1973; McNemar, 1975; Novick & Ellis, 1977; Petersen & Novick, 1976; Schmidt & Hunter, 1974; Shepard, 1981; Thornike, 1971b; and *On bias in selection,* 1976. A good summary of the various approaches and definitions can be found in Jensen (1980).

used examples that would be more familiar to men than women. In this case the test would be biased because it differentiated between men and women on an irrelevant basis, not on the basis of their knowledge of statistics.

We shall discuss the problem of bias in maximal performance tests from two perspectives, first by considering attempts to build culture-fair tests and then by considering the various types of test bias.

Culture-Fair Tests

The problem of cultural influences on test performance has been studied for many years. Originally, investigators attempted to develop tests that would eliminate all effects of culture and, thus, presumably measure the individual's abilities more accurately. However, it soon became apparent that any attempt to develop completely *culture-free tests* was doomed to failure. Consequently, the emphasis in test construction has shifted to the development of *culture-fair tests*—tests that, though not eliminating cultural effects, attempt to control certain critical variables such as the role of language, the emphasis on speed of responding and competitive motivation, and the differing emphasis given to various skills in different cultures.

Test Construction Strategies.   One possible strategy is to develop, use, and validate the test in only one culture. Unless the test is applied to a different cultural group, no problems arise. If a test is needed to do a similar job in a different culture, a new test can be constructed within that culture. Such a strategy obviously sidesteps the basic issue.

A second possible approach is to develop a test in one culture, then to validate it in other cultures. For example, tests developed in one country have often been translated into foreign languages and used in other countries (see, e.g., Lonner, 1968). Another example is the use of tests in various subcultures within a single country. For example, tests standardized on predominantly white samples are often administered to black or Chicano students. The question then becomes: Are the tests valid in the particular subculture tested? The largest amount of evidence has been collected on scholastic aptitude and college admission tests administered to black students.[10] Here the data indicate that these tests are as good or better predictors for black students as for white students (see, e.g., Breland, 1979; Cleary, 1968; Jensen, 1980; Munday, 1965; Stanley & Porter, 1967; Thomas & Stanley, 1969). As a general rule, however, tests are usually more valid in the culture in which they were developed than in other cultures in which they happen to be applied.

A third strategy focuses on the item selection process. By first identifying skills and content common to many cultures, and including on the test only items that measure these universal elements, one could develop a culture-fair measure. The effectiveness of the test construction procedure is subsequently checked by validation studies in a variety of cultures. The fundamental step in this procedure is the identification of skills and relationships that are common to a number of cultures.

[10]   For a review of studies using employment tests see Hunter, Schmidt, & Hunter (1979).

Examples of Culture-Fair Tests. Items on culture-fair tests must either reflect cultural universals or involve purely abstract reasoning. An example of the former is the *Draw-a-Man Test,* which has frequently been used in cross-cultural studies. Since the task, drawing a figure of a man (or woman), involves content and skills that seem to be universal, the test would seem to be quite appropriate for cross-cultural studies. Yet data from cross-cultural studies show that scores on the test vary between cultural groups, with higher average scores occurring in cultures stressing skill in representational art.

Other tests that have been used in cross-cultural studies emphasize abstract reasoning. For example, *Raven's Progressive Matrices Test* consists of geometric matrices from which one section has been removed. The test taker must choose, from among six to eight alternatives, the element that completes the design. In each case, the relationship rather than the design is the important feature (see Figure 10.1)

Many psychologists now feel that even the quest for a culture-fair test is illusory. If we eliminated all culturally relevant material, we would be left with trivia. Furthermore, we would be unable to predict any socially meaningful criteria because criteria themselves are culturally laden. Thus we are caught on the horns of a dilemma. To complicate matters further, seemingly less culturally loaded materials, such as nonverbal items, have proved to be as culturally loaded as verbal items. Thus rather than attempting to develop additional or better culture-fair tests, research now concentrates on understanding the factors that produce different performance in various cultural groups.

Figure 10.1 Example of an Item Similar to Those Used on the Raven's Progressive Matrices Test.

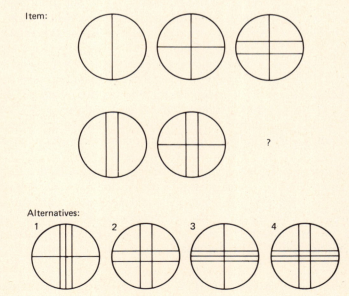

Types of Test Bias

Recent approaches to studying bias in maximal performance tests have focused on the components of the testing situation that produce bias and the ways in which bias can be identified and controlled. (See, Jensen, 1980, for a detailed discussion of these methods.) To organize our discussion we will use a classification of types of bias developed by Reschley (1978, 1979) who described four types of possible test bias: content bias, atmosphere bias, bias in use–prediction, and bias in use–social consequences.

Content Bias.   Content bias occurs when the content of test items gives a systematic advantage to a particular group of test takers. Usually the bias reflects differences in the opportunity to learn the material tested. Since interpretations of scores on maximal performance tests are based on the assumption that all test takers have had equal opportunity to learn the material, then the test may be unfair to the extent that members of any group have not had the opportunity to learn the material.

As mentioned previously, differential performance per se is not sufficient to establish bias; we must also consider the opportunity to learn. Unless all test takers have had the opportunity to learn the material tested, the test will be unfair to those who have not. On the other hand, if members of various groups have had the equal opportunities to learn, yet performance differed, we would not have persuasive evidence of content bias.

You should also note that a test that is content biased according to the above definition may be a valid and useful measure in a particular situation. Suppose a worker must be able to read an instruction manual written in English in order to perform a job satisfactorily. If a test of the ability to read and comprehend English were used as a job selection device, persons who did not read English would be at a disadvantage. Yet the test would be a valid selection device. This example illustrates how content bias is intertwined with test use. That is, what is defined as content bias may vary, or be of lesser importance, depending on the specific use of the test.

The practical problem is how to detect and control content bias. One method is to have representatives of the potentially affected group review items for possible bias during the test construction process. If they find certain items objectionable, these items can be eliminated and other items substituted in their place. Other methods rely on item analysis data. One technique is to rank items by their relative difficulty in the various groups. Items whose relative difficulty is much higher in one group than another (that is, items that are particularly difficult for a particular group) should be further investigated for possible bias. Another approach (Angoff & Ford, 1973; Lord, 1980; Scheuneman, 1979) is to compare the item difficulties using test takers of equal ability levels. That is, we could compare the responses of, say, black and white test takers who had equal ability (as measured by their total score or some external criteria). Items that varied in difficulty between groups would then be checked for possible bias. A third approach (e.g., Moss & Brown, 1979; Schmeiser & Ferguson, 1978) is to construct items that on a logical basis would seem to favor one group—for example, items on black and white literature. These items would then be administered to both black and white test takers and a significant item-by-test-taker interaction could indicate bias. Other techniques are described by Jensen (1980) and Rudner, Getson and Knight (1980).

Atmosphere Bias. The second type of possible bias refers to the effects of the testing conditions on test takers' performance. Examples include the type of motivation elicited, factors related to the examiner-examinee interaction, and factors in the evaluation and scoring of responses. (All three effects are likely to be more pronounced on individually administered tests.) The goal is to minimize any possible tester or test condition effects. This can usually best be accomplished by using standard testing conditions.

Here again, things are not as simple as they might seem at first glance. For example, directions on maximal performance tests stress doing the best one can and, often, responding rapidly. However, while this motivation may be common for middle-class test takers it may not be so universal for test takers from disadvantaged or lower-class backgrounds. Or, on individually administered tests, the nature of the examiner-examinee relationship may affect the level of performance exhibited. To counteract this possible bias, some people suggest that examiners should be members of the same group (e.g., race, sex, or ethnic group) as the test takers. Although the evidence on the magnitude of tester effects is by no means clear (Jensen, 1980), test users should be alert to this possibility and use testing conditions that minimize potentially biasing effects.

Bias in Use—Prediction. From one point of view, a test is biased if predictions or decisions based on test scores vary for different groups. However, since there are various ways of defining a biased prediction, a variety of statistical techniques for identifying prediction bias have been proposed.[11] Some of these were discussed in Chapter 6.

As a practical matter, whenever feasible, test users should investigate the validity of a test for various subgroups of the population studied; that is, for various racial, ethnic, or gender groups. Such studies can have various outcomes. If there are no significant differences between the prediction (regression) equations for the various groups, the same decision-making rules can be applied within each group. If the test is valid for each group but the prediction equations and/or cutting scores differ, separate prediction equations or cutting scores should be used in each group. If different predictors are valid in each group, separate prediction equations must be used. If the prediction procedure is not valid for one group, different assessment methods must be utilized for this group. The important point is that test users should be alert to differences in validity for various groups within a heterogeneous population and vary their prediction and decision-making procedures accordingly.

[11] See, for example, Cole, 1973, 1981; Einhorn & Bass, 1971; Hunter et al., 1979; Jensen, 1980; Linn, 1973, 1976; Linn & Werts, 1971; Novick & Ellis, 1977; O'Leary, 1973; Petersen & Novick, 1976; Sawyer, Cole, & Cole, 1976; Schmidt, Berner, & Hunter, 1973; Schmidt & Hunter, 1974; Shepard, 1981; Thorndike, 1971b; and *On bias in selection,* 1976.

Bias in Use—Social Consequences. Some critics of testing would say that the previous arguments miss the point. For example, a test may appear to be valid only because the criterion predicted is itself biased. Or a test might be a valid predictor of an outcome, but use of the test might lead to undesirable consequences (Messick, 1980b). More generally, the point is that we should always look beyond the predictive validity of a test; we must also look at the consequences of its use.

This means that we must always look at what happens as a consequence of test use. As Reschley states:

> Test use is unfair if opportunities are diminished or if individuals are exposed to ineffectual interventions as a result of tests. (Reschley, 1978, p. 33)

For example, even if a test clearly differentiated slow learners from other students, the use of the test would be unfair if the test scores were used to place students in special classes that allowed them less opportunity to learn. Note that this approach requires consideration of factors other than the quality of the test—in our example, the quality of the educational program provided. Thus fair use of tests involves more than psychometric validity; it encompasses the consequences of the decisions made on the basis of test scores as well. This point has also been clearly made by Messick (1980b).

A Caveat. In this section we have cautioned you to be constantly alert to the possibility of bias in tests and in test use. Such cautions must be taken seriously, both as a matter of good testing practice and on ethical and legal grounds. Yet it is equally important not to be so overwhelmed by the possibility of bias that you see bias when none is present. In an area so complex, confusing, and fast-changing as the study of test bias, this is no easy task. Only by being abreast of current developments and continually evaluating our testing procedures and uses of tests can we be assured we are using tests in a fair and unbiased manner.

summary

The purpose of maximal performance tests is to determine the test taker's best possible performance. There are three general classes of maximal performance tests: achievement tests, aptitude tests, and ability tests. Although these three types of tests vary in the nature of the domain measured, the specificity of the prior learning experiences, their time reference, and their uses, all measure developed abilities. That is, they all reflect the totality of an individual's learning experiences prior to testing.

Achievement tests measure command of the knowledge and skills in a well-defined domain and usually measure knowledge and skills that have been specifically taught. Their focus is on the past (what has been learned) or the present (what the person knows and/or what he can do). Two major distinctions within achievement tests are between teacher-built classroom tests and standardized achievement tests and between norm-referenced and content-referenced tests. Some achievement tests are survey tests, measuring command of a single subject or several subject matter areas. Others are diagnostic, readiness, or proficiency tests. For most uses, content validity is the primary concern when evaluating an achievement test.

Aptitude tests indicate the potential to learn, given appropriate training; thus their reference is to the future. Ability tests measure current status, and thus have a present reference. In contrast to achievement tests, aptitude and ability tests are not necessarily verbal; they may measure physical, perceptual, and psychomotor skills. Types of ability tests include general intelligence tests, academic ability tests, multiple aptitude tests, and tests of special abilities. When used in decision-making situations, criterion-related validity is most important; when used to define constructs and traits, construct validity is most important.

The quality of individual items can be determined by item analysis. Item analyses are concerned with three aspects of an item: difficulty (what percent of the test takers answer an item correctly?), discrimination (does the item differentiate between test takers with varying levels of ability?), and distracters (do they draw any responses?). Item analysis data can also be used to identify material students have or have not mastered and to study item bias.

When using maximal performance tests we must also be concerned with possible bias in items. Bias occurs whenever performance on an item (or a test) is influenced by factors irrelevant to the primary purpose of the testing. Content bias occurs when the content of the items, or the test takers' previous learning experiences, give an advantage to one group. Atmosphere bias occurs when the testing conditions favor one group. Prediction bias occurs when the form or level of predictive accuracy varies among groups. Bias in use involving social consequences occurs when treatments assigned on the basis of test results vary in quality. Although test users must be alert to possible test bias, they should understand that differences in average scores between groups are not sufficient, by themselves, to establish bias and that seeing bias when none is present is just as bad as overlooking bias when it is present.

Suggestions for Further Reading

Anastasi, A. Abilities and the measurement of achievement. *New Directions for Testing and Measurement,* 1980, *5*, 1–10. Discusses the connotations that have become attached to such terms as aptitude and intelligence and argues that maximal performance tests should be viewed as measures of developed abilities.

Cleary, T. A., Humphreys, L. G., Kendrick, S. A., & Wesman, A. Educational uses of tests with disadvantaged students. *American Psychologist,* 1975, *30*, 15–41. A review of the literature and a thoughtful discussion of the problems and issues in testing disadvantaged students.

Diamond, E. E. Minimizing sex bias in testing. *Measurement and Evaluation in Guidance,* 1976, *9*, 28–34. Identifies sources of sex bias in test items and describes procedures for detecting biased items.

Fincher, C. Using tests constructively in an era of controversy. *College Board Review,* 1979, *113*, 2–7. Suggests a number of ways tests can be used in education to assess competencies, evaluate programs, and facilitate learning.

Flaugher, R. L. The many definitions of test bias. *American Psychologist,* 1978, *33*, 671–679. As the title indicates, a review of the various proposed definitions of test bias.

Jensen, A. R. *Bias in mental testing.* New York: Free Press, 1980. A comprehensive, technical description and critical evaluation of the definitions, methods, and evidence on test and item bias.

McClelland, D. C. Testing for competence rather than for "intelligence." *American Psychologist,* 1973, *28*, 1–14. A critical evaluation of intelligence testing; suggests tests should focus on describing the range of an individual's competencies that are related to important life outcomes.

Nitko, A. J. Distinguishing the many varieties of criterion-referenced tests. *Review of Educational Research,* 1980, *50*, 461–485. Reviews the various definitions of criterion referencing and shows how the various concepts are alike and different.

On bias in selection. Journal of Educational Measurement, 1976, *13* (1). This entire issue of *JEM* is devoted to a discussion of various models for dealing with bias in selection situations.

Reschley, D. J. , & Sabers, D. L. Analysis of test bias in four groups with the regression definition. *Journal of Educational Measurement,* 1979, *16*, 1–9. A well-designed study which investigates the extent of bias in intelligence test scores in four ethnic groups.

Tyler, L. E. *Individuality.* San Francisco: Jossey-Bass, 1978. A very readable book arguing that tests should be used to describe the range of an individual's competencies.

Warrington, W. G. An item analysis service for teachers. *NCME Measurement in Education,* 1972, *3*(2). A description of the item analysis services at one university, including suggestions as to how the results can be used by classroom instructors.

Wesman, A. G. Intelligent testing. *American Psychologist,* 1968, *23,* 267–274. Description of the major issues in intelligence testing; argues that intelligence tests should measure past learnings that predict future outcomes and that there is no one definition of intelligence or one use of intelligence tests.

Chapter 11 • Classroom Achievement Tests

ALL students are familiar with the ubiquitous teacher-made classroom achievement test. In fact, you probably already have taken one or more tests covering the material in this book. The distinguishing features of these tests were that they were constructed by the course instructor, covered only material taught in a particular course, probably never have been (or ever will be) administered in exactly the same form to any other class, and were used to determine grades.

Similar tests are administered in thousands of classrooms every day; it is rare when examinations are not an integral part of a course. Because most classroom examinations are administered only once, to a particular class under a singular set of circumstances, the methods of constructing and evaluating classroom tests differ from those used to construct standardized achievement tests. Thus we shall discuss these two types of achievement tests separately.

Our discussion of classroom achievement tests will cover planning the test, the various types of test items, administering and scoring the test, analyzing the test, and using the test results. Our approach will be brief, illustrative, and evaluative. For more comprehensive discussions of classroom tests see, for example, Bloom et al. (1971, 1980), Brown (1981), Ebel (1972, 1979, 1980), or Gronlund (1977).

planning a classroom test

The first and most crucial decision in classroom testing is to determine *why* to administer a test. In the most general sense the answer is obvious: to measure students' achievement. But why? So grades can be assigned? So students will obtain feedback on the effectiveness of their learning? So the instructor can evaluate the effectiveness of his teaching? To encourage students to study harder? Or for some other purpose? Determining the purpose of testing usually answers many other questions, such as what material will be covered, when the test will be given, and what types of items will be used.

Viewed from a slightly different perspective, we can say that the nature of the test, and even the decision to test at all, should follow from the instructor's educational philosophy and his goals for the particular course. These basic views will determine not only the nature of the testing, but also the frequency and timing of exams. For example, if an instructor uses tests only to assign grades, he will probably give a final exam and several unit tests. If, however, the primary purpose of testing is to facilitate students' learning, he will use more frequent tests so as to maximize feedback.

One further possibility should always be considered: A test may not be the most appropriate method of assessing students' achievement. A teacher often has other methods of assessing students' achievement in addition to paper-and-pencil tests; for example, performance tests, observing students as they work, class recitation, homework, projects, and many other types of classroom activities. To cite but one obvious example, to determine whether students can tune an automobile engine we would be better advised to have them tune an engine than take a paper-and-pencil test covering the steps in tuning an engine.

Uses of Tests in the Classroom

By now it should be obvious that classroom tests can serve other purposes than just providing a basis for grading. Particularly we shall stress a point that too frequently is overlooked: Tests can be used to facilitate the learning process as well as to measure the outcomes of learning.

There are three points in the learning sequence where tests (or other assessment methods) may provide useful information. The first is at the beginning of a course or unit, prior to the start of instruction. Here we might administer a *pretest* to measure students' knowledge of prerequisite material and/or the material to be taught. If students have not mastered the prerequisite knowledge and skills, we will have to teach them; if they have already mastered some of the material to be taught, we can spend time on other topics. Pretests can also direct learning by pointing out important concepts and materials so that students can focus their attention on these areas. And, of course, pretests can provide baseline data to be used when evaluating the effectiveness of learning and instruction.

Tests can also be administered during the course of instruction. While these tests may be used for grading, a more important use is to facilitate learning. By providing students with feedback as to what material they have mastered and what material is still to be learned, tests can direct studying. Analysis of students' performance, particularly the errors they make, can be used by the teacher to diagnose problem areas and suggest remedial action. Tests given during instruction can also motivate students, either by showing them they need to work harder (if they do not do well) or by increasing their confidence (if they have been able to master difficult material). They can also be used to check whether students have understood the main points of a reading assignment or as a basis for discussion. The teacher can use the results to determine whether her instruction has been effective and to suggest what material should be reviewed or retaught using a different approach. Evaluations of learning made during the course of instruction are called *formative evaluations* (Bloom et al., 1971; Scriven, 1967).

The third point to measure achievement is at the end of a unit or course. These assessments are called *summative evaluations* and are designed to determine whether students have mastered the course objectives. Although summative evaluations are most frequently used as a basis for grading, they also indicate whether students have mastered the material and indicate whether the instruction has been effective. Since these assessments are collected at the end of instruction, and measure the results of learning, they are of less value for directing instruction and learning.[1]

The Test Plan

As indicated in Chapter 2, there are two general approaches to constructing achievement tests. One is to define the objectives for a particular course or unit, then write[2] items that measure attainment of these objectives. The other, which is probably more common, is to specify the content and cognitive skills covered in the course, then write items that sample these content and skill areas. We will call the first approach the objectives approach and the second the content/skills approach.

Objective-Based Tests.   In this approach to test planning, the first step is for the instructor to specify the objectives (goals and desired outcomes) for the course. This specification should, of course, occur when the instructor plans the course, not when he starts to build the exam. He will probably have several broad goals (for example, students should be able to interpret test scores) and many specific objectives (for example, students can interpret percentile ranks). These objectives define the domain to be covered by the exam.

To be useful in planning examinations (as well as for planning instruction), objectives must be expressed in behavioral terms. By behavioral objectives we mean statements that indicate what the student will be expected to know or do, as well as under what conditions and to what level of proficiency (Mager, 1962). It is not sufficient to state that students will "understand percentiles." Rather we must state objectives in the form: "Given a conversion table, the student can find the percentile rank for any raw score and give a verbal description of the person's performance."

Once objectives have been defined, the instructor can write the test items. Since all objectives are presumably important, he will, testing time permitting, write one or more items for each objective. Although some writers seem to imply that different types of items are needed on tests based on instructional objectives than on tests constructed using a content/skills test plan, the author has not found this argument convincing. What is crucial in this approach, however, is that the test items reflect the skills prescribed by the objectives. In other words, the difference is not in terms of the types of items but in why an item is included on the test.[3]

---

[1] Testing to measure retention and transfer may occur at some time after the completion of instruction. As such assessments are usually based on standardized tests, we shall discuss them in more detail in Chapter 12.

[2] Although some items are not, strictly speaking, written (for example, items on performance tests), we shall use the term "item writing" to refer to the process of constructing all types of test items.

[3] For a more detailed description of the objectives-based approach to test construction see, for example, Bloom et al. (1971, 1980), Popham (1973, 1981), and Popham & Lindheim (1980). For a description of the content/skills approach see Ebel (1972, 1979, 1980).

Content/Skills Test Plans.   The other approach to planning tests is to start by specifying what material is covered in the course or unit and then write items that sample this domain. On classroom tests the materials to be covered on any exam usually are clearly specified by the teacher—that is, the assignments for the unit. When using this approach, the test constructor must be concerned with two dimensions. First, he must sample the various content areas. For example, an exam on test scores should include items on several types of test scores, not just questions about, say, standard scores. The second dimension—skills—is often neglected. By skills we mean the cognitive process used to answer the item: processes such as knowledge, comprehension, application, analysis, synthesis, and evaluation (Bloom et al., 1956). That is, we generally do not want a test to measure only retention of facts; we also want to see whether students can apply their knowledge and draw appropriate conclusions.

As an example of this approach was given in Chapter 2, we will not repeat the discussion here. Rather we will only indicate that such test plans should specify the content and cognitive skills to be covered on the test and the relative emphasis to be given each content/skill category. Thus the test plan provides a basis for writing and selecting items as well as a means for determining the content validity of the completed test.

Other Considerations in Planning a Classroom Test

The test plan indicates what topics and skills will be covered on a test. This is a necessary first step. The test constructor, however, has to make several other decisions before writing the test items. These decisions have to do with the length of the test, the format of the items, and the difficulty of the items. Although the decisions made will vary with the purpose of the test, the subject matter, and the characteristics of the students tested, some general guidelines can be provided.

Probably the first factor the teacher will consider is the *length* of the test. This is not because length is the most important factor, but because of practical constraints, which are often hard to overcome. The obvious one is the length of class periods. Usually, except for final exams, teacher-built tests are designed so that they can be completed within one class period (45–50 minutes). Often a teacher will give short quizzes that take only a few minutes.

Regardless of the length of the test, a fundamental question is the number of items that can be completed within the time limits. Since the purpose of a classroom test usually is to determine the extent of students' knowledge rather than speed of response, time limits should be set so that all, or almost all, students can finish the test. The time needed will, of course, vary with the number of items, the difficulty of the items, the length of the items, the age of the students, and many other variables. The author's experience suggests that students can answer about one multiple-choice question per minute (except for math and problem items). The time to be devoted to essay questions will depend primarily on the question, the completeness of the response desired, and the ages of the students. Thus how much time to allow students to answer essay items can be determined only by experience in a particular course.

A second important consideration is the *item format.* Which format to use will be determined, at least partially, by the objectives or skills measured. For example, if a teacher is interested in students' ability to marshal arguments to support a point of view, he will probably use essay items. If a music teacher wants to see whether a trombone player can sight-read a new composition, he will use a performance test. If a math teacher wants to measure students' ability to apply an analytic technique to a new situation, he will use problems.

In many instances, however, the teacher will have a choice between several item formats. To consider a trivial example, a geography test on state capitals might use multiple-choice items:

The capital of New York State is:
   (a) Albany   (b) Buffalo   (c) New York City   (d) Rochester

or, alternatively, true-false items:

The capital of New York State is Albany. (TRUE   FALSE)

or completion items:

The capital of New York State is _____.

Since in many, if not most, circumstances alternative item formats may be appropriate, the choice between them will be made on the basis of other considerations—for example, the teacher's preference for, or skill in, writing different types of items.

In selecting an item format, the teacher should also consider several other factors. Does he want to include a large number of short items or a smaller number of broader items? Does he want students to rely on recall or recognition to answer the items? Does he want to use only one type of item or several different types? If he uses several types, what sort of mix of item types will be optimal? And so on.

Probably the major decision when choosing between item formats is whether to utilize a large number of specific items or a smaller number of fairly broad items—in other words, a choice between alternative-choice or short-answer items on one hand and essay questions on the other. The former procedure has the advantage of allowing for a more representative sampling of the material. Essay items concentrate coverage into certain areas rather than providing representative coverage of all content areas, but cover these areas in greater depth. Therefore, from a sampling point of view, more shorter items are preferred. However, since the two approaches also differ on a variety of other dimensions (such as skills tapped, ease of construction, testing time, and scoring ease), in choosing between the two formats the test constructor should realize that he will always be sacrificing one set of goals for another.

Another decision has to do with the *difficulty* of the items. Obviously, what is difficult varies with the type of course and characteristics of the students. What level is appropriate will depend on the purposes of the testing. If a teacher gives a quiz to check on whether students have read an assignment, he can use items that will be very easy for anyone who has read the material. Easy items are also appropriate to identify students who are lagging behind their classmates and as "warm-up" items (items used at the beginning of a test to get students into the swing of the test and to build confidence).

On content-referenced tests, items will be included if they measure an important instructional objective, regardless of their difficulty. Ideally, at the end of instruction every student should be able to pass every item. As this is an unrealistic goal, items are usually constructed so that most (usually at least 80 to 85 percent) of the students are expected to pass the item. If fewer students pass an item, it may be because the instruction was faulty, because the material was too difficult, or because the item was poorly written.

On norm-referenced tests, a different set of criteria apply. It can be shown that items of medium difficulty (that is, items answered correctly by 50 to 70 percent of the students) provide the widest distribution of scores. When the purpose of testing is to discriminate between students with varying degrees of knowledge of the material, items written at this level of difficulty are optimal. Items that are very easy or very difficult produce a narrower range of scores and therefore are less effective discriminaters.

Learning versus Learning Outcomes

In many discussions of the value of achievement tests, no clear distinction is made between the use of tests to facilitate learning and the use of tests to measure learning outcomes. Clarifying this distinction focuses the test construction process. That is, if the primary purpose of testing is to facilitate the learning process, items must be phrased so that incorrect responses suggest appropriate remedial action. To illustrate, consider a math item:

$$(2.5)^2 = \underline{\hspace{2cm}} \quad \text{(a) } 6.25 \quad \text{(b) } 5.25 \quad \text{(c) } 5.0 \quad \text{(d) } .625$$

In this item, selecting alternative (b) would result from a multiplication error, selecting (c) would result from misunderstanding what the exponent means, and selecting (d) would result from improper placement of the decimal point. By observing a student's incorrect answers, the teacher can identify learning problems and prescribe appropriate remedial action.

In contrast, when a test is used to measure the outcomes of learning, questions of why wrong answers were selected are of lesser importance. In these situations the critical consideration is whether the test validly measures the student's present level of achievement. For example, if a test requiring students to spot errors in sentences is highly correlated with the students' ability to construct good English sentences, then the recognition exam can be substituted for actually writing sentences. Note, we did *not* say that the ability to construct good sentences can be developed by identifying errors in other people's sentences; it may be that this ability can be developed only by having the student write sentences. What we did say was that the results of the learning process, however it occurred, can be measured by either technique.

varieties of test items

Given these basic decisions about the test format, the next step is to construct the test items. Writing good items is a skill that is developed only by practice. Even experienced item writers find it desirable to write many more items than will be included on the test. They then edit these items and select the best ones.

On paper-and-pencil classroom tests, both alternative choice and free response items may be used. On *alternative-choice items* students are given several possible answers and their task is to select the correct or best alternative. Examples of alternative-choice items are multiple-choice, true-false, and matching items. When using these items we assume that knowledge can be measured by the ability to discriminate between correct and incorrect alternatives—that is, by the ability to recognize the best answer presented. On *free response items* students must construct or supply the correct answer. Examples include short-answer and completion items, essay questions, and problems. Here the assumption is that achievement is better measured when the student must recall or construct an answer.

The relative merits of recall and recognition items have been widely debated. Advocates of recall items stress that they provide a more difficult, and thus better, test of a student's knowledge. They also point out that most "real-life" situations require the construction or production of a response, not a choice among a set of clearly labeled alternatives. Advocates of recognition items stress the technical superiority of recognition items (for example, their higher reliability) and the fact that it has not been clearly demonstrated that use of recall items results in superior learning or better retention. Advocates of both positions would probably admit that students will use differing study habits depending on the type of item expected on the test (Jacoby, 1973).

Sometimes a third type of item, performance items, is used. These items require some physical or psychomotor response. Examples include tasks such as tuning an automobile engine, sight reading a musical piece, throwing a pot, shooting free throws, giving a speech, and baking a cake. Although performance items may include verbal elements (for example, oral or written directions), the psychomotor component is usually the most important aspect of the response.

General Item Writing Guidelines

Before discussing specific types of items, we shall briefly discuss several general guidelines that apply to all types of achievement test items.

1. *Cover important material.* This is the prime requirement for any item. No item should be included on a test unless it covers an important fact, concept, principle, or skill. Furthermore, a test should not cover just one type of skill, say factual knowledge; some items should also measure higher-level skills such as comprehension, analysis, and evaluation.

2. *Items should be independent.* This does not mean you should ask only one question on any area. What it does mean is that the answer to one item should not be found in another item, and correctly answering one item should not be dependent on correctly answering a previous item.

3. *Write simply and clearly.* Use only terms and examples students will understand and eliminate all nonfunctional words. This will ensure that students will be able to answer on the basis of their knowledge of the material.

4. *Be sure students know how to respond.* This guideline applies particularly to free-response items but also applies to alternative-choice items. The point is that the item should define the task clearly enough that students who understand the material will know what type of answer is required and how to record their answers. For example, on essay questions the instructor may specify the length and scope of the answer required; on quantitative problems the amount of work to be shown and the required precision of the answer may be specified.

5. *Be flexible.* No one type of item is best for all situations or all types of material. In addition, some students can better display their knowledge on certain types of items. Thus, whenever feasible, any test should contain several types of items.

6. *Revise and edit.* Regardless of how skilled an item writer you are, not all of your first efforts will be perfect or even acceptable. Thus propective items should always be edited and revised before use. One technique I have found useful is to write a pool of items, then set them aside for a day or so. Then I come back and look at them again, revising, editing, and eliminating poorer items. It is surprising how many "good" items turn out to have obvious deficiencies when looked at a second time.

These guidelines are only suggestion, and all will be disregarded at one time or another. However, following these guidelines should result in simpler, clearer, and more valid items. Remember, too, that any guideline for writing items will be of less importance than the item content. Unless an item measures an important educational outcome it will be a poor item, regardless of how well it was written. Conversely, an item that tries to measure an important outcome will not succeed unless it is well written.

With these general guidelines in mind, we shall now discuss the various types of items commonly found on classroom tests. For each type we shall describe the basic characteristics, provide examples, give some variations on the item format, and discuss its advantages and limitations. Scoring problems will be discussed later in the chapter.

Multiple-Choice Items

A *multiple-choice item* consists of a stem and a set of alternatives (usually three to five). The student's task is to select the correct alternative from among the distracters (incorrect responses). For example:

If a test has set administrative procedures that are the same for all test takers, the test is said to be:
    (a) objective   (b) reliable   (c) standardized   (d) valid

The stem of a multiple-choice item may be either an incomplete statement (as in the above example) or a question.[4] In either case it should present the problem

---

[4] The stem may be more than one sentence long.

in enough detail that there is no ambiguity about what is being asked.

Distracters on multiple-choice items often are chosen to represent the most frequent incorrect responses. Thus, one empirical method of obtaining distracters would be to have a sample of students respond to a recall form of the item and determine which wrong answers are most prevalent; these responses would be incorporated as distracters. Other methods of selecting distracters include use of common misconceptions, logical alternatives, and distracters that maximize item validity. (See Cronbach & Merwin, 1955; Ebel, 1972; Wesman, 1971.)

Although multiple-choice items have been criticized for testing only factual material, if properly designed they can be used to test complex intellectual skills. For example, the ability to apply mathematical and statistical principles can be tested by a multiple-choice format:

> The mean on a test is 20 and the standard deviation is 5 points. Mike scores 13. Mike's T score would be:
> (a) 14   (b) 26   (c) 36   (d) 65

This item requires the student to go through the same sequence of steps that he would if the item were presented as a problem; the only difference is that he selects among alternatives rather than supplying an answer. Another example of an item requiring application of knowledge is:

> A scholastic aptitude test consists of mathematics and vocabulary items. There is only one form of the test, and less than 10 percent of the test takers complete all items within the time limits. To estimate the reliability of this test, you would use:
> (a) coefficient alpha
> (b) a coefficient of equivalence
> (c) a coefficient of stability
> (d) Kuder-Richardson formula 20

Many other examples could be given but the point is clear: Multiple-choice items can be used to measure complex reasoning skills.

Because a large number of multiple-choice items can be administered in a relatively short period, broad sampling of the domain is possible, and thus both reliability and validity are increased. Scoring of multiple-choice items is rapid and objective and items can be analyzed statistically, thereby providing data that can be used to improve item quality. A presumed disadvantage is their limited applicability (it is easier to write factual items than ones testing more complex skills); but, as indicated above, this is not an inherent limitation of the item format. Good multiple-choice items are, without doubt, difficult and time-consuming to construct.

There are several common variations of the multiple-choice format. One is to base a series of items on a reading passage, diagram, chart, or table. A similar format can be used with individual items—as, for example, when students are asked which of four cities is located at a particular place on a map. Another is to use an *analogies* format:

> Binet is to intelligence testing as Strong is to _____ testing.
> (a) achievement   (b) aptitude   (c) interest   (d) personality

Variations can also occur in the method of responding. For example, some instructors use multiple-choice items where more than one alternative (or no alternatives) can be correct. This procedure, in essence, changes the item into a series of true-false items, each having a common stem.

Guidelines for writing multiple-choice items are given in Table 11.1.

Table 11.1.
Guidelines for Writing Multiple-Choice Items

1. The stem should present the problem and include all qualifying phrases.
2. There should be only one correct alternative.
3. Distracters should be plausible but clearly incorrect.
4. Avoid negative wording.
5. Use "all of the above", "none of the above", and "some of the above" sparingly.
6. If an item contains controversial material, cite the authority whose opinion is being used.
7. Avoid irrelevant clues to the correct answer (e.g., grammar, length).
8. Each item should test one central idea or concept.
9. List alternatives in alphabetical or logical order; otherwise randomize so as to avoid patterns.

True-False Items

A *true-false item* is nothing more than a declarative sentence.[5] The test taker's task is to indicate whether the statement, as presented, is true or false.

The mean is a measure of the dispersion of a set of test scores. (T or F)
If a gas is heated within a container of constant volume, its pressure will increase. (T or F)

The test taker judges the correctness of the statement. If any part of the statement is incorrect the item is false.

Many people think that true-false items are restricted to factual content, but this format can be used to test applications and comprehension of principles (see the second example). As Ebel (1972) has convincingly argued, much knowledge is in the form of propositions (if-then statements), and propositional knowledge can readily be tested by true-false items.

True-false items are relatively easy to construct and can be scored rapidly and objectively. Because they tend to be rather short, many items can be administered in a given time period. Thus true-false tests can be quite reliable and the content domain can be sampled broadly. On the other hand, they should not be used in content areas where there are not specific correct and incorrect answers. They can be of value when we are less concerned with subtleties or exceptions, such as when testing younger children or checking to see whether students have understood the main points of a reading assignment.

There are other potential limitations of true-false items. Because there are only two possible responses, random guessing will produce a score of 50 percent correct and limit the range of scores. Then, too, some teachers write disproportionate numbers of true (or false) items. And it is only too easy to construct true-false items by lifting statements directly from the text or by only slightly altering a

[5] True-false items are sometimes more than one sentence in length.

text statement (for example, by inserting a "not" in a sentence. Slight changes in the wording of true-false items can change students' responses dramatically.

Probably the most common alternative format for true-false items is to require students to correct false statements. The major disadvantage of this procedure is that an item can be corrected in many ways, including a variety of trivial ways:

Item: Percentile ranks fall in a normal distribution. (T or F)
Correction: Percentile ranks do *not* fall in a normal distribution.
Intended correction: Percentile ranks fall in a rectangular distribution.

A simpler correction procedure would be to have the student only identify the false element in the statement, not correct the statement.

Guidelines for writing true-false items are presented in Table 11.2.

Tables 11.2
Guidelines for Writing True-False Items

1. Use words with definite and precise meanings.
2. The crucial element in the statement should be apparent.
3. The truth of the statement should not rest on trivia or trick phrases.
4. Avoid repetition or minor variations of textbook phrases.
5. Avoid specific determiners (words such as always, never).
6. When an item contains controversial material, cite the authority whose opinion is being used.
7. Include approximately equal numbers of true and false items.

Matching Items

Matching items consist of two parallel lists, one a series of stimulus words or phrases and the other a series of responses. The student's task is to match a response with each stimulus. A typical matching item might be:

DIRECTIONS: For each statement in the left column choose the method from the right column that is most appropriate. Each response alternative may be used once, more than once, or not at all.

1. Method used to determine the consistency of a classroom test	A. Stability
2. Method whose results are most affected by the speededness of the test	B. Equivalence
3. Method based on the intercorrelations among test items	C. Stability and equivalence
4. Method used to determine whether students' values change with college experience	D. Internal consistency

Note that this item could also be administered as four separate multiple-choice items; thus, in essence, a matching item is a series of multiple-choice items, with the same set of alternatives serving for all items.

Since matching items are essentially multiple-choice items, they have many of the same advantages, limitations, and uses as multiple-choice items. The major consideration in determining whether to use matching items is the amount of emphasis to be given the area covered by the matching item. Because the use of matching items will necessarily involve devoting four or five items to a topic, disproportionate weighting will occur unless this great an emphasis is desired.

Several other cautions must also be considered with matching items. Unless a matching item covers a single content area, the student can break the item into subsections, thus reducing the number of possible responses for any given stimulus. Frequently one sees matching items with a dozen or more stems and responses, covering several distinct areas. This approach puts a premium on reading and sorting skills at the expense of knowledge. This problem could be eliminated by using several matching items, each covering homogeneous material. Another problem concerns the number of response alternatives. If the number of responses equals the number of stimuli and each response can be used only once, the student can correctly answer the final item by a process of elimination and/or will get at least two items wrong if he does not know the answer to one. These possibilities can be eliminated by providing more responses than stimuli or by allowing each response to be used more than once.

Matching items do not need to use verbal stimuli. In fact, a common variation on the matching format is to have students match names or terms with locations on a map or diagram or with a series of specimens, such as types of rocks.

Guidelines for writing matching items are given in Table 11.3.

Table 11.3.
Guidelines for Writing Matching Items

1. All parts of the item should be homogeneous.
2. Limit the length of each list (use no more than about five stimuli and responses).
3. Each item (stem) should have only one correct response.
4. If the two lists have phrases of different lengths, use the longer ones as stimuli and the shorter ones as responses.
5. Arrange responses in alphabetical or logical order.

Short-Answer and Completion Items

Alternative-choice items require recognition of the correct response. In most situations, the same material could also be tested using a format that requires students to supply the correct response. For example, the multiple-choice item on page 239 could also be written as a completion item:

If a test has set administrative procedures that are the same for all test takers, the test is said to be (standardized).

or as a short-answer item:

A standardized test is one that has (set administrative procedures that are the same for all test takers).

The distinction between a short-answer and completion item is mainly the length and format of response. A *completion item* usually requires the student to provide a one- or two-word response, often within the body of the item; a *short-answer item* requires him to respond to a question in a sentence or two.

Short-answer and completion items generally cover the same type of material as alternative-choice items. Since there is no definitive evidence that either recognition or recall items are better, which format is used depends upon the preferences, item writing skills, and educational philosophy of the instructor. For example, if an instructor thinks that students should be able to recall material, rather than just recognize correct responses, she will use short-answer or completion items. This format is also appropriate for younger children, who are less likely to get confused with the mechanisms of responding than with a multiple-choice item. Also, it usually is easier and less time-consuming to compose a short-answer or completion item than to build a good multiple-choice item.

The major disadvantage of this format involves scoring. Not only does scoring take longer than for recognition items, it requires some decision making on the part of the scorer, and thus may decrease reliability. For example, in the item: "Reliability can be defined as _____," it is obvious that there are a large number of possible responses that will be wholly or partially correct. When scoring this item, the teacher would have to decide which responses were acceptable and how much credit would be allowed for each variation. Scoring can be made easier and more objective if the teacher prepares a scoring key prior to scoring the test. Even with a key, some students probably will give responses that are not on the key, and the teacher will have to use her best judgment in scoring these responses.

On completion items, teachers sometimes direct students' attention to the desired response by indicating the number of words in the correct answer or the first letter of the correct answer. There are also variations on the short-answer format. One is the *definition* item, where the students are asked to define terms or concepts. An analogous type of item in mathematics and science courses asks students to provide formulas. Or students may be asked to *identify* such things as organs of the body, parts of an automobile engine, or features on a topographical map. A variation on this approach is to ask students to describe the importance or function of the object identified. Other short-answer items require students to compare and/or contrast related terms, concepts, objects, or events.

Guidelines for writing short-answer and completion items are presented in Table 11.4.

Essay Questions

At some not clearly specifiable point, a short-answer item shades into an essay question. The distinction between the two types of items, however, is not solely in terms of their length; it also involves the function the item performs. Whereas short-answer items are best suited to measure factual knowledge, comprehension of principles, and the ability to identify and define concepts, essay questions provide a basis for evaluating the ability to organize, integrate, and evaluate knowledge. Responses to essay questions may also reflect students' attitudes, creativity, and verbal fluency—factors that may or may not be relevant to the purposes of the testing.

When constructing essay items, the teacher treads a thin line between making

Table 11.4.
Guidelines for Writing Short-Answer and Completion Items

1. Phrase items so that there is only one correct answer.
2. Be sure that students know what type of response is required.
3. Use new examples and situations.
4. Avoid overmutilated completion items; use no more than two blanks in an item.
5. On completion items, place the blank near the end of the sentence.
6. Make a key before administering the test.

the question too general and making the question excessively detailed. For example, the essay item, "Discuss the concept of reliability," is so general that a student could take any of a number of approaches when answering. On the other hand, an essay question phrased:

> Define reliability. Give the basic formula in terms of true and error variance. Define the coefficient of stability, the coefficient of equivalence, and coefficient alpha. List the sources of error that enter into each of these methods. Give an example of a situation in which each type might be used.

is little more than a series of short-answer items. This question might better be phrased:

> Define reliability verbally and by a formula. Identify and differentiate between three types of reliability by indicating their paradigm, the influencing error sources, and their appropriate uses.

This third version is not as specific as the second, and also places a greater premium on the student's ability to compare and evaluate the various methods of estimating reliability.

A primary advantage of essay questions is that they assess certain skills—particularly organization, integration, and evaluation—more effectively than do other item formats. Because of the semistructured nature, the student usually can approach an answer from several equally valid angles, thus yielding a flexibility not found in other formats. As with other recall items, faking and guessing are minimized.[6] The length of response allows the student to treat an area in depth. Although the ease of constructing essay items may be more apparent than real, essay tests are easier to write than multiple-choice tests, if for no other reason than that fewer items are required.

The major disadvantages of essay items become readily apparent when scoring begins. To read and grade essay items is a time-consuming task. Since each response will be different, comparing students who used different information and approached problems from different angles is an arduous task. Consequently, it is not surprising that the reliability of grades assigned responses to essay questions—from grader to grader, time to time, or question to question—is often unsatisfactory, even when scoring standards and procedures are clearly specified.

---

[6] Bluffing, or even guessing, is not completely eliminated. Students with well-developed writing skills can often write a response that reads well but, on closer examination, is superficial and does not show detailed knowledge of the material.

Graders may also be influenced by irrelevant factors such as length of responses, quality of prose, or neatness and handwriting (see, e.g., Coffman, 1966, 1971, 1972; Klein and Hart, 1968). Finally, as mentioned previously, essay exams do not provide as representative a sampling of the content domain as does the same amount of time devoted to multiple-choice or other "objective" items.

Variations on the essay question include take-home tests, using a composition (such as a poem, test manual, or journal article) as a stimulus for an evaluative essay, book reviews, and term papers.

Guidelines for writing essay questions are given in Table 11.5.

Table 11.5
Guidelines for Writing Essay Questions

1. The question should clearly define the task.
2. Indicate the scope and direction of the answer required.
3. Use questions that have correct answers.
4. Allow for "think time."
5. Use a large number of short essay items rather than a few longer ones.
6. Use optional questions sparingly, if at all.
7. Develop a scoring key before administering the test.

Problems

In certain subjects, particularly mathematics and the sciences, problems are often used as test items. Here the item describes a specific situation and gives some relevant data; the student's task is to solve the problem presented. Usually this solution involves identifying the question asked and the relevant conditions and data, setting up an equation or an analytic procedure, then applying the procedure to the data to obtain a solution. For example:

> An instructor administers a 50-item multiple-choice test to 200 students in an Introductory Psychology course. The mean is 37 and the standard deviation is 5 points. He grades on a curve and wants to give A grades to 16 percent of the students. What score will a student have to make to get an A?

To solve this problem the student must first recognize the general strategy, then apply the strategy to the specific data.

Problems are obviously well suited to testing computational skills, mathematical and scientific reasoning, and ability to apply knowledge to new situations. Although we generally think of problems presented on paper-and-pencil tests, the student may have to manipulate apparatus as, for example, in chemistry or physics experiments.

Construction of problem items is generally relatively simple and straightforward since the skills to be measured are well-specified and in most areas there will be a wide variety of possible problems. For example, to determine whether students can compute a mean, various data sets (which might vary widely in size and complexity) could be used. Scoring presents more of a problem, especially if one goes beyond an all-or-none, correct-or-incorrect approach. If you award partial credit, you will have to specify the conditions under which partial credit will be awarded. Often this is not very difficult. For example, when I ask students in my measurement class to compute the mean of a set of scores, I award one point for using the correct formula, another point for substituting the correct values into the formula, and a third point for correctly computing the answer.

Guidelines for writing problem items are listed in Table 11.6.

Table 11.6
Guidelines for Writing Problems

1: The problem statement should clearly set the task.
2. Indicate how the answer should be expressed.
3. Use new examples and situations.
4. Decide on scoring procedures before the test.

Performance Tests

In many situations we are more interested in students' ability to demonstrate their skill than in their ability to answer written questions. Many examples come readily to mind: tailoring a dress or making a soufflé (in home economics), assembling a carburetor (industrial arts), sight reading a musical composition (music), throwing a pot or painting a watercolor (art), being able to serve a tennis ball (physical education), or typing 40 words per minute. Other examples, which may not be so obvious, would include giving an extemporaneous speech, conducting an opinion poll, performing an engineering survey, conducting a counseling interview, or programming a computer. In each of these cases students must demonstrate their ability by an actual performance; hence the label "performance items."

When preparing performance items, there is one major guideline to follow: The task must be structured so that students know exactly what they are to do and under what conditions. The desired outcome usually serves to define the task. For example, asking the student to assemble a carburetor clearly defines the task. The other aspect, specifying the conditions, refers to such factors as the length of time the student is given to perform the task, what aids can be used (for example, whether a schematic diagram can be used to aid in the assembly of the carburetor), and any other variables that may affect performance.

Performance items are well suited to a criterion-referenced approach to evaluation. That is, in many cases it will be relatively easy to determine whether the student has met the minimally acceptable standards (Can she assemble the carburetor? Can he throw a pot?) but more difficult to make finer distinctions. Thus a content-referenced approach, with stress on completing the task to a minimally acceptable level rather than comparing students, is frequently more appropriate.

Guidelines for constructing performance test items are given in Table 11.7.

Table 11.7
Guidelines for Writing Performance Test Items

1. Clearly define the task.
2. Define any constraints or conditions.
3. Allow sufficient time for preparation and performance.
4. Develop evaluation criteria and methods before the test.

administering, scoring, and analyzing the test

Ideally, the teacher will write more items than are needed. She can then use those items that are best written, test more important concepts, and provide the emphases outlined in the test plan. More realistically, we might expect the teacher to write enough adequate items, reflecting the desired emphases, to obtain an acceptable measure of students' knowledge of the domain tested.

Since tests are evaluative situations, they often raise students' level of anxiety. For most students, much of this anxiety will be dissipated if they clearly understand what will be expected of them. Thus, several days prior to the test, the teacher should inform students when the test will be given, what topics and assignments will be covered, what types of items will be used, how long the test will be, and how the results will be used. Then students can plan their studying accordingly.

Another factor is often overlooked: Students need time not only to read and respond to items, but also to think about and plan their answers. This is particularly true on items that require organization and integration, such as essay items, and those requiring devising a strategy, such as problems. Many of us overlook this factor and thus make our tests too long. Since most classroom tests should be power tests, not speed tests, we generally would be better advised to administer shorter tests (containing only good items) rather than longer tests that require rapid, and perhaps careless, responding.

Administering the Test

Most commonly, test items are duplicated so that each student has a copy of the test. However, other procedures may be used. For example, a teacher may read the questions (such as on a spelling test or a foreign language dictation), the questions may be written on the board, or items may be projected on a screen. Although this latter procedure places definite time restrictions on responding, it is an excellent method of presenting certain types of identification items—for example, identifying sites on a map, the artist or characteristics of a painting, or the parts of the body. In a science class, the teacher might set up displays and ask students to identify designated characteristics. Or items might be presented by computers and the students would respond directly on the computer console.

There are several important considerations when administering a classroom test. The test proper should include explicit directions as to the time limits, how and where to respond, and scoring. If the item format changes within the test, a new set of directions may be needed. (Of course, with older students, or when a

test is similar to previous tests in the course, formal directions may be minimal.)
If special equipment is used (such as projectors or displays), each student should
be able to see, hear, or have access to the materials.

Another decision is where and how students should record their answers.
There are two possibilities: on the test or on a separate answer sheet. Responding
on the test is less confusing and thus is recommended for younger children. On
the other hand, scoring is more cumbersome, especially if the test is more than
one page long. If students answer on the test, make sure there is enough space
after each item for the response. Separate answer sheets are necessary when responses are scored by electronic machines. In this case, the answer sheets must
fit the specifications of the particular scoring machine used. Separate answer
sheets may also be used to facilitate hand scoring or when test booklets are to be
reused.

Unless the school operates on an honor system, the instructor will want to
proctor the test to prevent cheating. Even with an honor system it is a good idea
to remain in the room during testing to answer any questions that arise about the
test or to handle any emergencies, such as a student getting sick during the test.

Scoring the Test

Scoring procedures will depend on the types of items used. In all cases, however,
scoring involves comparing each student's responses to a key. A *scoring key* is
nothing more than a list of correct responses, acceptable variations, and the
weights assigned to each response. This key should be made up prior to scoring
any of the tests. In fact, constructing a key prior to administering the test often
identifies ambiguous or weak items, which can then be eliminated.

Alternative-Choice Items.   Scoring alternative-choice items is straightforward.
If hand-scoring procedures are used, each student's responses are visually compared to the key. If electronic scoring machines are available, the teacher will
have to construct an appropriate answer key.

The teacher must also assign weights to each item, a decision that should be
made when planning the exam. For alternative-choice items, and most completion and short-answer items, the simplest procedure will usually be to award one
point for each correct response (and 0 for incorrect answers). Problems, essays,
and some short-answer items may be worth several points. If the teacher wants to
award partial credit on items, he must clearly specify the bases on which partial
credit will be awarded. The sum of points assigned for correct responses will
generally be used as the (total) test score.

Correction for Guessing.   In some circumstances, when using alternative-
choice items, a teacher may want to apply a correction for guessing. This correction subtracts a portion of the wrong responses from the correct responses. The
general formula to correct for guessing is:

$$X_C = R - \frac{W}{A - 1}$$ (11.1)

where X_C is the score corrected for guessing, R is the number of correct responses, W the number of incorrect responses, and A the number of response alternatives per item. With true-false items the formula is:

$$X_C = R - W \tag{11.1a}$$

since there are only two possible alternatives: true and false. For multiple choice items with four alternatives, the formula is:

$$X_C = R - \frac{W}{3} \tag{11.1b}$$

These formulas assume that the student responds randomly when unsure of the correct response—a highly tenuous assumption in most cases.

To illustrate, consider a 50-item multiple-choice exam with four alternatives per item. Suppose that Mike answers 36 items correctly, 12 items incorrectly, and does not respond to 2 items. His score, corrected for guessing, would be:

$$X_C = 36 - \frac{12}{3} = 36 - 4 = 32$$

Note that omitted items are not considered in the correction; that is, omitted items are not considered as wrong answers.

Whether correcting for guessing is worthwhile is a debatable point (see, e.g., Davis, 1951, 1964; Ebel, 1965). Proponents argue that correcting for guessing produces scores that better reflect students' true achievement levels and discourages guessing. Opponents argue that the ranking of students will be approximately the same whether or not scores are corrected, that guessing patterns are not random (as assumed by the correction formulas), that the probability of obtaining a high score by guessing is exceedingly small, that applying the correction makes scoring more cumbersome, and that the making of rational guesses under conditions of uncertainty may be a habit worth cultivating. Also, if all students attempt all items—as is usually the case on classroom exams—correcting for guessing will not alter rankings, but only reduce scores. It would seem that the burden of proof would fall upon proponents of correcting for guessing; in this author's opinion they have not as yet made a compelling case.

Short-Answer and Completion Items.   Scoring short-answer and completion items, though not as simple as scoring alternative-choice items, is relatively easy and objective. Since responses are usually short (a word, phrase, or sentence or two) and the possible correct responses are limited (often only one possibility), few decisions need to be made. The only problems are deciding what variations on the correct response are acceptable and, on multipoint items, deciding when to give partial credit.

Essay, Problem, and Performance Items.   Some of the problems involved in scoring essay, problem, and performance items arise because of the length and/or complexity of the response. Others arise because there is usually more than one correct answer or solution and/or more than one way to arrive at a correct response. Thus there is more room for subjective judgment. The net effect is to reduce the reliability of the scores assigned.

The practical problem, therefore, is to devise methods for making scoring more objective and reliable, and hence more valid. One way to attain these goals lies within the task (items). When the task is clearly defined, the range of response options will be limited; thus scoring can be more standardized and consistent. The danger is that we will go overboard; for example, if we structure a problem in too much detail it may no longer present a problem, since we have, in essence, told the student how to go about solving it. Or if an essay question is too specific, it may become nothing more than a series of short-answer items. In both of these illustrations, a task requiring higher-order intellectual skills has been reduced to one requiring lower-level skills.

A second approach lies in clarifying the bases for assigning scores. If the instructor analyzes the task (both its overall nature and component parts) and considers the possible alternative responses at each point, he will have a guide to use when scoring any given response. This analysis should also indicate the relative weight assigned each part and each alternative response. In practice this would mean that on essay items the instructor would write several sample answers; on problems he would have to work through the solution using various possible methods. The point is that the instructor, insofar as possible, should anticipate the various responses students will make and determine how he will score them. In addition, he must decide what emphasis to place on factors other than content or method used; for example, on an essay exam will he consider factors such as organization and writing style when assigning scores?

A third area in which standardization can be achieved is through the mechanics of the scoring process. Some procedures that I have found useful are to scan several papers before starting scoring to get a baseline view of the type and level of responses; grading a sample of papers twice to see if I am, in fact, grading consistently; and scoring papers anonymously so as not to be influenced by students' performance in other aspects of the course. Another important mechanism is to grade items one at a time; that is, first grade all answers to item 1, then all responses to item 2, and so on. Of course, using a predetermined key helps; however, I always find some unanticipated responses.

Needless to say, not all of these approaches can be used on any test. The important point is to try to make your scoring as objective as possible by setting certain standards and prescribing certain rules, then following them consistently. My experience is that students recognize that some subjectivity is always involved in grading essay, problem, and performance items; all they ask is that the instructor consistently apply well-reasoned rules when scoring their papers. (For a more detailed discussion of essay scoring see Brown, 1981, or Coffman, 1971, 1972.)

Analyzing the Test

Although few teachers systematically analyze their tests, such analyses can improve test construction skills and provide useful information on the effectiveness of teaching and learning. Analyses may be of test scores (total scores), individual items, or groups of related items. Since item analysis was discussed in the previous chapter, we shall concentrate here on analyses of total scores.

Score Distributions.   What can score distributions tell the teacher? Consider first a norm-referenced test. The mean indicates the overall difficulty of the test. Like individual items, a mean score of between 50 and 75 percent generally is optimal if we wish to differentiate between students. In addition, a normal distribution provides good differentiation between students, particularly those whose scores fall at either end of the distribution. Thus, when tests are used for grading, a normal distribution with a mean score between 50 and 75 percent is optimal. If the distribution is negatively skewed, with many students obtaining high scores and few obtaining low scores, the test was quite easy. This distribution would discriminate only between students with lesser degrees of knowledge. If the purpose of the test was to check whether students had read an assignment or mastered basic material, such a distribution would be expected. If the distribution is positively skewed, with few persons obtaining high scores, the test would be difficult. However, such a distribution might be found for a pretest over unstudied material. Or, if a posttest, it could indicate poorly constructed items or incomplete learning.

On content-referenced and mastery tests a different distribution is desired. Since the goal is for the majority of students to master the material, a mean score of 85 to 90 percent is desired. If this occurs, the distribution will be negatively skewed. Thus, whereas there may be good discrimination between students with low scores, there will be little differentiation between students who attain the minimal level of mastery and those who know the material thoroughly. However, this will generally be of little concern.

On both norm-referenced and content-referenced tests, one other bit of information is valuable: How did the obtained distribution compare to the expected distribution? When there is a large discrepancy, the teacher should carefully consider why students did not perform as expected.

Setting Cutting Scores.   Many uses of classroom tests require the setting of cutting scores. When using a mastery approach to instruction, the teacher must determine what level of performance differentiates mastery from nonmastery. Or, when assigning grades, the teacher must decide which scores will differentiate the various grade levels. In both situations the question becomes: Where should the cutting line(s) be set?

Unfortunately, there is no completely objective method for setting cutting scores. In mastery learning approaches, the cutting line for mastery is generally set at 80 to 85 percent correct. Although this point has some empirical basis,[7] basically it is an arbitrary standard. Similarly, even teachers who grade on a percentage system (e.g., 90 percent for an A, 80 percent for a B) probably could not provide any empirical basis for these levels. Even systems using relative position

---

[7] Studies of programmed learning have shown that students who pass one unit with 80 to 85 percent mastery generally can succeed on the next unit in the instructional sequence.

(e.g., the top 20 percent of the students will get A's, the next highest 35%, B's, and so on) are based on logical, not empirical, bases.

On content-referenced tests, the problem is further complicated if we consider item difficulties (which, in turn, determine the difficulty of the test). Saying a score of 90 percent is needed for an A (or 85 percent for mastery) would make some sense if item difficulties were, in some sense, absolute. However, for any given topic, items of varying difficulty can be written. Thus a score of 90 percent might be a reasonable criterion for an A grade if a test contained items of easy or moderate difficulty, but would be almost impossible to attain if the instructor used only difficult items.

Although we seem to have an insoluble problem, in practice most instructors muddle through somehow. What appears to happen is that in most schools there is some consensus about the expected grade distribution. Most teachers, in turn, adjust their testing and grading practices to attain something approaching the desired distribution. Although this approach has obvious shortcomings in terms of scientific measurement, as a practical matter it appears to work quite well in most situations.

Consistency.   Since there usually is only one form of a classroom test and it will be administered only once, the methods of determining the reliability of a classroom test are limited to split-half and internal consistency measures. If the test consists of alternative-choice items, or items of (approximately) equal weights, the split-half method can be used. An odd-even split will generally suffice, assuming that items are positioned randomly. Of course, the Spearman-Brown correction formula must be used.

The other approach is to use a measure of internal consistency (for example, coefficient alpha or Kuder-Richardson 20). Although the knowledge and skills measured by the typical classroom exam are generally intercorrelated positively, whether they are so highly intercorrelated that they measure only one factor is problematical. Thus the assumptions of the internal consistency formula will be, at best, only approximated. (For an opposing view see Ebel, 1968).

In fact, computation of any reliability coefficient may seem unnecessary to the classroom teacher. After all, he has only one form of the test and will use the results regardless of the test's reliability. True; however, viewed from a longer-range perspective, computation of reliability estimates will indicate what types of tests and items produce the highest consistency and, therefore, enable the teacher to improve future tests by using similar test construction procedures.

Validity.   With achievement tests, including classroom tests, the prime concern is content validity; that is, do the test items representatively sample the domain of concern? The basic procedure is to compare the skills and content covered by the items with the test plan. If the items reflect the emphases in the plan, and cover important rather than trivial material, then the test has content validity. This process, of course, assumes that the test plan is a fair representation of the content domain and/or instructional goals.

Sometimes the validity of a classroom test can be supported by other evidence. For example, when courses are sequential, the relationship between scores on an exam in one course and success in the following course could be determined. Or scores on classroom exams could be correlated with standardized achievement tests covering the same general content area. If external measures are unavailable, data from within the class can be used. For example, if test scores do not parallel the teacher's judgment of students' knowledge and ability, the validity of the test might be called into question. (These results might, of course, also reflect upon the teacher's judgmental ability.) The scores on an exam could be correlated with scores on other exams or assignments—for example, term papers and reports. We might even be interested in comparing test scores and students' judgment of their learning. All of these data sources provide, albeit somewhat incomplete and biased, evidence of the validity of the test.

testing and instruction

For learning to occur, students must know whether their understanding of the material is correct or incorrect. This requires testing and other forms of assessment. Thus the question is not whether to assess students' achievement; rather, the important questions are: How often? In what manner? For what purpose?

Using Test Results

Earlier in the chapter we considered the places in the instructional sequence where testing could be used. We mentioned three points: prior to instruction (to assess students' entering knowledge), during instruction (to assess the progress of learning and the effectiveness of the instruction), and at the completion of instruction (to measure mastery of the material and the effectiveness of instruction). At each point we can consider performance on individual items, clusters of related items, or the test as a whole.

Alternatively, we can consider the functions achievement testing plays in instruction. The primary purpose of classroom testing is to increase and facilitate students' learning. This is accomplished in several ways: forcing students to study the material to be tested, by directing their attention to the more important material, and by providing rewards for good performance. Another way is by providing feedback regarding the effectiveness of learning—that is, by showing students what materials they have and have not mastered. Finding out what topics they have not mastered and where their weaknesses are enables students to direct further study to these areas; finding out they have mastered some material, especially if it is perceived as challenging or difficult, can be rewarding and motivating. Teachers can use the same information to diagnose students' learning problems and prescribe appropriate remedial or alternative instruction.

Teachers can also use the information provided by a test to improve their instruction. By finding out what topics are difficult for students, they can revise their instruction or use an alternative approach that may be more effective. If they teach the material using several different approaches, they can compare achievement under the different methods and see which is more effective, either for the class as a whole or for students having certain characteristics. And, of course, the teacher can use the information to improve their testing and assessment skills.

Another use of classroom testing is for grading. Although this is not the place for an extensive discussion of grading (see, e.g., Brown, 1981; Cureton, 1971; Ebel, 1972, 1979; Gronlund, 1974), we shall mention several important considerations briefly. First, grades should be based on sufficient evidence; that is, they should be based on a large number and variety of graded assignments. Second, any graded assignment should measure important instructional outcomes. Third, the procedures used to combine scores on various assignments should ensure that the desired outcomes are attained—for example, that each assignment is actually weighted as planned.

Finally, test results can be used for other types of educational decisions, such as placing students in reading groups or levels of a class. Here teacher-built tests have some advantages in that they can be adapted to the abilities and achievement of students in the particular class or school.

Issues in Classroom Testing

One issue that has caused a considerable amount of debate is the relative merits of alternative-choice and free response items—particularly multiple-choice and essay items. The resolution depends on the recognition that the two test formats are complementary, not opposed. Exams including essay and other free response items (such as problem and performance items) will be most appropriate with small classes, when time pressures are minimal, when the subject matter is to be covered in depth, and when the skills to be tested include application, organization, integration, evaluation, or creativity. Alternative-choice items will be used with large classes, for broad content sampling, with time pressures, and when testing of recognition skills is sufficient.

A second issue has to do with the amount of testing. Many critics of education suggest too much time is spent on testing, to the expense of learning. This view seems to imply that testing and learning are relatively independent. In reply, one could argue that a person cannot claim to have learned something unless they can demonstrate their learning by performance, either on a test or in some other manner. Furthermore, there is evidence from both laboratory studies and field studies suggesting that learning is increased more by time spent testing one's mastery rather than in further review of the material. These arguments suggest that there is probably too little testing rather than too much testing in education.

Third, many critics claim that testing dictates what is taught—that teachers spend too much time teaching students to do well on tests rather than teaching the course material. Although this argument is more frequently directed toward standardized tests, it also applies to classroom tests. This view has validity only if the test items do not cover important educational outcomes. If the test items measure the most important outcomes (as they should), preparing students to do well on tests will be the same as teaching them the important material from the course.

An Evaluation of Classroom Tests

Classroom tests do not meet all the psychometric requirements outlined in previous chapters. They are standardized to the extent that a common set of items is administered to all students under similar conditions. Scoring can be quite objective. Scores can be compared to a common norm group—the class—or to a predetermined standard of proficiency. Although the reliability of classroom tests is usually not determined, teachers can increase test reliability by writing clear and unambiguous items, using standardized testing conditions, and using a sufficient number of items. The content validity, which is the most important type of validity for classroom tests, can be ascertained by comparing the test items to the test plan or instructional objectives.

Compared to other types of assessment devices, such as standardized tests, classroom tests have several advantages. They can be adapted to the goals of a particular class. They have great flexibility in terms of length, types of items, time of administration, and coverage. Good items can measure all levels of cognitive skills. And the results can be used to improve learning and instruction in a variety of ways.

On the other hand, classroom tests also have certain limitations. Since they are usually constructed by only one teacher, that teacher's biases and preferences may be overemphasized. In addition, many instructors have difficulty writing good items and, regardless of the aims, write items measuring only knowledge. The reliability of classroom tests is often lower than desired. Moreover, some teachers rely solely on tests rather than using a broader range of assessment procedures.

In summary, the status of classroom tests is contradictory. Even people who vigorously attack other types of testing generally concede the need for classroom tests. Yet few teachers make the effort to increase their test construction skills or fully utilize tests as aids to learning. I would hope that those of you who become teachers will take the time and will make the necessary effort both to improve your tests and to use the results to increase your students' learning.

summary

Certainly the most widely used type of test is the teacher-built, classroom achievement test. These tests are usually constructed by one teacher, to measure the learning of material taught in a particular course or segment of a course. They can be used at the beginning of instruction (pretests) to determine what students already know so as to plan instruction, during instruction (formative evaluations) to check on the progress of instruction and the effectiveness of instruction, and at the end of instruction (summative evaluations) to determine whether students have learned the material taught and to evaluate the effectiveness of instruction.

After determining why tests are to be used, the next step is to write a test plan. This plan indicates what will be covered on the test and with what emphasis. It should both guide test construction and provide a basis for evaluating the completed test. Two common approaches are objectives-based tests and the content/skills blueprint. Other important considerations in planning a test include determining the length of the test, the type of items to be used, its difficulty, and whether the test will measure only the outcomes of learning or also give clues to the learning process.

Various types of items can be used on classroom tests. Alternative-choice items require the test taker to select the correct response from a given list of possible responses. Examples include multiple-choice, true-false, and matching items. Alternative-choice items allow for broad content sampling, can be used to measure most levels of cognitive skills, and can be rapidly and objectively scored. However, they are difficult to construct and are not the best type of item to measure skills such as analysis and integration.

Free response items require test takers to construct or supply the correct answer and thus measure recall rather than recognition. Examples include short-answer and completion items, essay questions, and problems. Essay questions are best used to measure integration and analysis skills, such as marshaling an argument to support a point of view. Problem items are most appropriate in math and science courses. Their major weakness is less than objective scoring. A third type of item, performance test items, require students to exhibit a physical or psychomotor skill as part of their response.

Guidelines were given for writing each type of item. Among the most important general guidelines are: cover important material, write simply and clearly, be flexible, and revise and edit. It was pointed out that item writing is not an easy task and requires much practice.

A teacher can obtain useful information from analyzing the results of a test, both for individual items and total test scores. The most essential step is to establish the content validity of the test.

The most frequent use of classroom tests is for grading. However, students can use the information provided by test results to determine what material they have and have not mastered and thus direct their further study. Teachers can use the results to get a better indication of their students' knowledge, to improve their assessment skills, and to plan and revise their instructional methods. These latter uses are more important than grading.

In short, in spite of some obvious psychometric limitations, classroom tests are an accepted and useful part of the educational process.

Suggestions for Further Reading

Anderson, R. How to construct achievement tests to measure comprehension. *Review of Educational Research,* 1972, *42*, 145–170. Argues that comprehension is more than recall and can best be measured by items requiring application of learned knowledge to new examples and situations.

Bloom, B. S., Hastings, J. T., & Madaus, G. F. *Handbook on formative and summative evaluation of student learning.* New York: McGraw-Hill, 1971. Describes the theory and practice of mastery learning, with emphasis on the measurement of mastery; includes large number of examples of items measuring various levels of cognitive skills in different subject matter areas; an excellent reference and guide.

Brown, F. G. *Measuring classroom achievement.* New York: Holt, Rinehart and Winston, 1981. An introduction to the construction and use of classroom achievement measures; includes many examples and practical applications.

Coffman, W. E. Essay examinations. In R. L. Thorndike (Ed.), *Educational measurement,* 2d ed. Washington, D.C.: American Council on Education, 1971. Discusses advantages, limitations, construction, and uses of essay questions; includes suggestions for writing good essay questions.

Coffman, W. E. On the reliability of ratings of essay examinations. *NCME Measurement in Education,* 1972, *3*(3). A shorter discussion focusing on the problems in grading essay questions.

Ebel, R. *Essentials of educational measurement,* 2d ed. Englewood Cliffs, N.J.: Prentice-Hall, 1972. An excellent defense of the use of norm-referenced measures of achievement, including examples of various types of test items and suggestions for improving classroom tests. (A briefer third edition was published in 1979.)

Ebel, R. Can teachers write good true-false items? *Journal of Educational Measurement,* 1975, *12*, 31–35. An empirical study comparing true-false and multiple-choice items; concludes true-false tests can be adequate measures of achievement.

Gronlund, N. E. *Constructing achievement tests,* 2d ed. Englewood Cliffs, N.J.: Prentice-Hall, 1977. Another good introduction to achievement testing.

Klein, S. P., & Hart, F. M. Chance and systematic factors affecting essay grades. *Journal of Educational Measurement,* 1968, *5*, 197–206. An empirical study illustrating how various factors influence the scores assigned to essay items.

McMorris, R. F., Brown, J. A., & Pruzek, R. M. Effects of violating item construction procedures. *Journal of Educational Measurement,* 1972, *9,* 287–295. An empirical study showing that faulty items are easier but as reliable and valid as well-written items.

Multiple-choice questions: A close look. Princeton, N.J.: Educational Testing Service, 1973. A brief description and evaluation of some complex multiple-choice items used on standardized achievement tests.

Popham, W. J., & Lindheim, E. The practical side of criterion-referenced test development. *NCME Measurement in Education,* 1980, *10*(4). An excellent, brief description of the amplified objectives approach to constructing criterion-referenced tests.

Chapter 12 • Standardized Achievement Tests

IN education, and in other instructional settings, there is often need for information based on broader, more standardized samples of performance than are provided by tests designed for use in one particular classroom. Common examples include measuring educational growth from year to year, comparing curricula or teaching methods, measuring integration of knowledge and transfer of skills, and placing students in appropriate courses or programs. In each of these situations classroom tests will generally not be adequate—thus the need for standardized achievement tests.

Although there are various types of standardized achievement tests, all share several important features:

- They are constructed (usually by a test publishing company) to meet detailed content specifications and involve extensive tryout, analysis, and revision of items.
- Standardized procedures for administering and scoring the test are developed and used.
- Methods for interpreting scores are clearly prescribed and normative data derived from carefully selected samples of test takers usually are available.

(These specifications also apply to other types of standardized maximal performance tests, such as intelligence, aptitude, and ability tests.)

This chapter discusses the construction and use of standardized achievement tests. We shall begin by outlining the steps in the construction of such tests, then discuss the various types of standardized achievement tests and their uses, and then evaluate these tests. Examples of specific tests will be used to illustrate principles and concepts.

constructing a standardized achievement test

In this section we shall give an overview of the steps in constructing a standardized achievement test. Although the exact steps will vary depending on the nature of the test, a typical sequence would be: planning the test, writing the items, pretesting and selecting items, establishing testing conditions, collecting reliability and validity data, obtaining normative data, and developing interpretive materials (ETS, 1965). As an illustration, we shall use a specific-subject survey test; variations required when constructing other types of tests will be discussed when considering specific types of tests.

The Test Construction Process

Standardized achievement tests are usually developed by subject matter specialists working in conjunction with test construction experts employed by a test publisher. Once the need for a test has been established, this group considers a number of questions: What content and skills will be covered? With what relative emphasis? What is the appropriate age range? What should the length of the test be? What is the relationship between this test and other tests in the battery and/or on the market? What item formats should be used? How many scores or subtests are needed? And so on, through many more questions. Their decisions regarding these questions form the general plans and guidelines for the test.

The Test Plan. As a standardized achievement test will be used in a variety of schools enrolling a wide diversity of students, the test must cover material that is commonly taught; for example, topics covered in the most frequently used textbooks in the subject. Consequently, the content domain sampled will be quite broad and no single topic will be covered in depth. If the test is part of a battery, the content will have to be articulated with that of other tests in the battery. And, of course, the reading level, difficulty, and content must be appropriate to the ages and educational level of the test takers.

Given these conditions, developing a test plan follows procedures similar to those used on classroom tests. The plan may be a content/skills grid or a listing of objectives. However, there will probably be many more dimensions and each dimension will be specified more completely and specifically (ETS, 1965; Popham & Lindheim, 1980; Tinkelman, 1971). In short, the process is the same as for classroom exams, the main difference being in the thoroughness of the test specifications.

Item Writing. Items may be written by subject matter specialists and/or professional item writers. They are then reviewed by other subject matter and testing specialists. This review covers content accuracy, grammatical construction, and possible bias in the items. Proposed items are edited, revised and rewritten, reviewed again, and so on until an acceptable item is attained. Note that items are written and independently reviewed by subject matter experts; the test specialists serve only as technical advisers. Thus the test includes items testing material that educators think important—not, as is sometimes charged, material that psychometricians feel is important.

It should also be noted that although the classroom teacher can use a variety of item formats, standardized tests will generally utilize alternative-choice items. The reasons are several: more adequate sampling of content, speed and accuracy of scoring, and higher reliability. Since multiple-choice items offer more advantages than other alternative-choice items, they are most widely used. The item writing task, thus, usually becomes one of writing multiple-choice items. Because of the importance of standardized tests, and the resources devoted to developing these tests, exceedingly sophisticated forms of multiple-choice items have been developed (see Figure 12.1 and *Multiple-choice questions: A close look,* 1973).

Many more items are written than will be needed. The best items are then selected to form preliminary versions of the test.

Item Pretesting and Selection. Although experienced item writers can construct items without obvious faults, there is no assurance that any given item will perform as expected when administered as part of a test. Thus the preliminary forms of the test are administered to samples of people who are similar to those who will take the final form of the test and relevant item statistics computed. On the bases of these analyses some items are eliminated, others revised, and others retained in their original form. If necessary, further tryouts and analyses are conducted.

The best items are then combined into one or more forms of the test. Several considerations must be balanced to produce a test with the desired characteristics. For example, the items should represent the various content/skill categories as outlined in the test plan; the number of items must be appropriate for the time limits; the test must be of the proper difficulty level; and a wide distribution of scores must be obtained. Moreover, these considerations apply to each form of the test and the various forms must be equated to each other. This balancing is an extremely delicate process, one that relies on both statistical data and rational judgment.

Specifying Testing Conditions. The test construction team must also develop procedures for administering and scoring the test. For example, if there will be time limits for the test, they must be specified. These limits will be determined both by practical considerations (how much time will be available for testing) and the data obtained from pretesting (how many items can be administered in a given time period; how many items will be needed for an adequate level of reliability). Directions will also need to be written, both for test takers and test administrators. Answer sheets must be developed, as well as scoring keys and procedures to ensure accurate and reliable scoring.

Psychometric Characteristics

To determine the psychometric qualities of the test, analyses of completed forms of the test are needed. We are interested in the average score (for various groups) and the distribution of scores. The consistency of the test scores must be determined, particularly equivalent forms reliability if there is more than one form of the test. The validity of the test—always content validity, but often also criterion-related—must be established. Normative data must be collected. Although the process of test development is designed to ensure that the test will be adequate in these respects, empirical studies are needed to confirm the effectiveness of the test construction process.

In the following paragraphs we shall briefly describe how the concepts of consistency, validity, and norms apply to standardized achievement tests. Our purpose here is to set some general guidelines that provide a framework for evaluating standardized achievement tests. When evaluating any particular test used for a specific purpose, the unique features of that particular test and testing situations must be taken into account.

Consistency. Some of the methods for estimating reliability are of only limited usefulness with standardized achievement tests. For example, although in education we are interested in retention of knowledge over relatively long time pe-

Figure 12.1. Examples of Multiple-choice Items Testing Higher-level Cognitive Skills

literature

Learning teacheth more in one year than experience in twenty; and learning teacheth safely when experience maketh more miserable than wise. He hazardeth sore that waxeth wise by experience. An unhappy master is he that is made cunning by many shipwrecks; a miserable merchant, that is neither rich nor wise but after some bankruptcies. It is costly wisdom that is bought by experience.

1. Which of the following best describes the style of the passage?
   (A) It uses a repeated balancing of parts rather than logical connectives.
   (B) It builds up to a climax by placing subordinate clauses first.
   (C) It is telegraphic in that subjects and occasionally predicates are omitted.
   (D) It uses a great number of long noun clauses to qualify the main statements.
   (E) It imitates conversation by using many parenthetical elements.

history

9. The following census data (in round numbers) are cited by a historian to demonstrate the "relatively restricted extent" of slavery in the South of 1860. All data are for the Southern states.
   - 12,250,000 total population of the South
   - 8,000,000 whites
   - 1,500,000 white families
   - 400,000 white slaveowning families
   - 4,000,000 slaves
   - 250,000 free Negroes

   Working with the same data, which of the following would be the most effective rebuttal to the historian's assertion?
   (A) The number of slaves was one-eighth the total United States population.
   (B) More than one out of every four white families owned slaves.
   (C) One out of every two people was either a slave or a member of a slaveowning family.
   (D) Less than 10% of the black population was free.
   (E) The black population was growing at a faster rate than the white.

4. "What is man born for but to be a reformer, a remaker of what man has made; a renouncer of lies; a restorer of truth and good, imitating that great Nature which embosoms us all, and which sleeps no moment on an old past, but every hour repairs herself, yielding every morning a new day, and with every pulsation a new life?"

   These sentiments are most characteristic of
   (A) fundamentalism   (B) Social Darwinism
   (C) pragmatism   (D) neoorthodoxy
   (E) transcendentalism

mathematics

10. If h, k, m, and n are positive numbers, k is greater than m, and n is greater than h, which of the following are true?

    I. $k + h$ is greater than $m + n$.
    II. $k + n$ is greater than $m + h$.
    III. $k + m$ is greater than $n + h$.

    (A) None   (B) I only   (C) II only   (D) I and II only   (E) I, II, and III

biology

10. An animal breeder crossed a black and a white guinea pig and a litter of three black offspring resulted. The breeder concluded that the black parent could not have been heterozygous (hybrid) for coat color because he thought that any cross between a black heterozygous guinea pig and a white guinea pig would yield a ratio of one black to one white offspring. His conclusion was unsound because he failed to realize that
   (A) the black parent may have been a male
   (B) mutations in coat color frequently occur
   (C) coat color in guinea pigs is not inherited
   (D) black coat color is dominant over white in guinea pigs
   (E) genetic ratios are reliable only for large numbers of offspring

physics

Questions 1-2

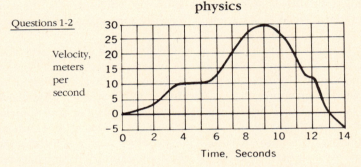

Velocity, meters per second

Time, Seconds

The graph above shows the velocity of a car as a function of time while the car moves along a straight track.

1. During the 7th second, the car is moving with constant
   (A) speed   (B) velocity   (C) acceleration   (D) momentum   (E) kinetic energy
2. During the first 3 seconds, the car has an average acceleration of about
   (A) $-\frac{8}{3}$ m/sec^2 (B) $-\frac{4}{3}$ m/sec^2 (C) 0 m/sec^2 (D) $\frac{4}{3}$ m/sec^2 (E) $\frac{8}{3}$ m/sec^2

Source: *About the Achievement Tests,* College Entrance Examination Board, 1975. Reproduced by permission.

riods, differential learning (and/or forgetting) will occur between testings. Thus a test that is sensitive to changes in knowledge will have a low coefficient of stability. But this instability would reflect true changes in ability, not error variance. Thus, stability estimates are inappropriate.

The typical standardized achievement test is broad and designed to measure a variety of abilities and skills. Thus measures of homogeneity generally will not be applicable. An obvious exception is subtests of diagnostic batteries. Here the goal is to measure component skills or abilities; hence, homogeneity will be a relevant consideration.

Thus we are left with two possibilities: measures of equivalence and split-half measures. The former is preferred. Needless to say, whenever an achievement test has more than one form, evidence of equivalent forms reliability is essential.

One factor that may influence the magnitude of a reliability coefficient deserves special mention. Standardized achievement tests generally are applicable at several grade levels. Inclusion of several grade levels in the sample used to determine reliability will increase the heterogeneity of the scores, and consequently increase reliability. But reliability estimates based on multigrade samples will be inflated compared with those based on single-grade samples. In most cases a more stringent, accurate, and useful estimate will be the reliability within a given grade level.

Validity. On achievement tests, the test items should sample the broader domain of knowledge and skills of interest. Thus the appropriate validity index is a measure of the adequacy of sampling—to wit, content validity. When establishing content validity the content domain must be clearly specified. An individual user may, however, define the relevant domain differently than the test developers. That is, the test will be more or less appropriate for his particular situation and purpose, depending on the congruence between the two definitions of the content domain, and the test user will have to judge the appropriateness of the test for his purposes.

In some circumstances, criterion-related validity evidence may be germane. When a standardized achievement test is used in making selection or placement decisions, the proportion of correct decisions or the increase in average criterion performance would be an appropriate validity index. Other types of validity evidence may also be of interest. If there are other tests measuring the same domain, the correlation between the two tests may provide validity evidence. And changes in scores between the beginning and completion of instruction establish that the test does measure the material covered in the instructional unit. We may also want to perform analyses to establish that performance on the test does not depend on irrelevant factors, such as reading ability and speed of responding.

Scores and Norms. Scores on standardized achievement tests may be either norm-referenced or content-referenced. In the norm-referenced approach, since score distributions will vary between groups, various norm groups may be needed. These groups will generally be defined by variables such as grade level, geographic area, type of school, socioeconomic level of the community, or type of school or curricula. Any of several types of scores may be used—for example, percentile ranks, standard scores, or grade-equivalent scores.

On content-referenced tests the test constructor has to set a proficiency standard. The usual procedure is to set a proficiency standard (say 80 percent correct), then select items so that the desired proportion of test takers will exceed this standard. However, this standard needs to be checked using data from administrations of the final form of the test. When using content-referenced scores, the test constructor may also provide some "pseudo-normative" data, such as the percentage of students in various grades, or types of schools, who attain the performance standard.

Test Manuals

The final step in the test development process is to write manuals and interpretive aids. One will be a technical manual containing information about the test construction process (including a definition of the domain, item specifications, bases for item selection, and item statistics) as well as normative, reliability, and validity data. Either in this manual, or in a separate manual, there should be detailed directions for administering and scoring the test.

The test developer should also supply materials to help test users interpret and use the test results. On norm-referenced tests these will include a variety of normative data, presented in a form that is technically correct yet readily understandable by test users. It may also include other materials such as interpretations of sample test profiles and suggestions for using scores. Although development of these aids may appear rather pedestrian in comparison with the sophisticated statistical analyses of the psychometrician, the quality and clarity of these interpretive aids probably contribute as much, if not more, than any other factor to proper use and interpretation of test scores.

types of standardized achievement tests

Having discussed the general principles for constructing and evaluating standardized achievement tests, we now turn to a more detailed consideration of the various types of standardized achievement tests. We shall discuss the salient features of each type of test and some of their possible uses. In the following section we shall look at standardized achievement tests again, this time organizing our discussion around the various uses for these tests.

Specific-Subject Tests

Survey achievement tests provide an index of a student's overall command of a particular content domain. One type of survey test, the *specific-subject test* covers only one particular course or an integrated series of courses; for example, first-year French, college algebra, American history, English literature, or introductory chemistry. Because these tests will be used in a variety of schools, they will include content that is commonly taught and will broadly sample the relevant content domain.

When constructing or evaluating a survey achievement test, several considerations are preeminent. First the content domain should be clearly specified.[1] Furthermore, the items should representatively sample the various subareas of the domain. Note, however, that when a test is used in a particular class, the test user's definition of the domain may not exactly parallel the domain as defined by the test constructor. Thus, when using a specific-subject test in a particular class, you should always compare the test constructor's definition of the domain and the item coverage to your objectives and emphases, to ensure that the test is a valid measure of what you are teaching in that particular class.

A second requirement is that the test measure achievement in the relevant domain, not other abilities. This requirement may be harder to attain than might be expected. Certain broad skills that influence performance on survey tests—for example, reading comprehension and test-taking skills—can and should be minimized. Also, unless there is some overwhelming argument otherwise, a survey test should be a power test, since our objective usually is to measure the breadth and depth of students' knowledge, not the speed with which they can respond.

A third requirement is that scores be expressed in meaningful units. Since survey tests measure overall command of an area, usually only one (total) score is reported. If the test is norm-referenced, the preferable scores are percentile ranks within grades or standard scores. Normative data on a variety of groups should be

[1] Specifying the content domain includes describing both the substantive aspects of the domain and the cognitive skills utilized when responding to items.

available, particularly data for each grade level in which the test may be used. If the test is content-referenced, the basis for developing the scoring scale should be clearly specified.

Finally, the test should be periodically revised and updated. Since knowledge is constantly increasing and curricula change, older tests may not reflect current curricular emphases.

Achievement Test Batteries

An alternative approach is to include tests of a number of different subject-matter areas in one integrated battery. For example, a survey battery might include tests of arithmetic (or mathematics), reading, language usage, social studies, and science. In addition, there may be subtests within an area. For example, within the arithmetic area there might be separate tests for computations, concepts, and problem solving, or the language usage test might be subdivided into subtests of spelling, grammar, punctuation, and effectiveness of expression. Some batteries also include tests measuring the ability to use reference materials, such as dictionaries and maps. Separate scores are obtained for each test (and subtest); a composite score (over all areas) may or may not be calculated.

Survey batteries vary in their relative emphasis on content and skills. Some batteries stress command of quite specific content and skills; others emphasize skills that can be applied in various situations and to a variety of problems. The former type would emphasize specific facts and principles; the latter, applications of general concepts, principles, and methods to new situations and examples. A common type of item on these tests is a reading paragraph followed by questions that require application of general concepts and principles to specific questions about the material read. The general principles are not included in the reading passages; however, the specific facts to which these principles are to be applied are contained therein.

Construction of Achievement Batteries.   When constructing (or evaluating) an achievement test battery, the requirements discussed under specific-subject tests should be met. That is, the content domain should be clearly defined, the items should representatively sample the various subareas of the domain, the tests should measure achievement rather than other factors, the content should be up to date, and scores should be expressed on meaningful scales.[2]

Certain problems arise on test batteries that do not occur on specific-subject tests. An achievement battery should cover all (or most) important curricular areas. For example, a battery designed for use in elementary grades that did not cover reading or arithmetic would obviously be incomplete. Furthermore, the various tests should be independent, each covering a distinct area, rather than similar content being covered on more than one test. In operational terms, the correlations between tests should be moderate; otherwise, all tests will be only different ways of measuring the same set of skills.

Scores on the various tests (and/or subtests) within the battery should all be

---

[2] These requirements apply to each separate subtest or test in the battery, not just to the battery as a whole.

expressed on the same scoring scale. That is, all scores should be transformed to percentile ranks or all to one type of standard scores. Furthermore, the same sample of test takers should be used to derive the normative data for every test. If different samples were used for each test, we could not directly compare a student's scores on the various tests comprising the battery since each score would be interpreted with reference to a different norm group. This does not mean that there can be only one norm group; indeed, normative data from various groups is desirable. The point is that, within any norm group, scores on all tests should be derived from the same sample.

If the battery is to be administered at more than one grade level, several forms of the test should be available so that the identical test will not be administered each year. And, since students' knowledge and skills change rapidly (especially at younger ages), there should be various levels of the test, each covering several grade levels. At younger ages, each level may be used in only one or two grades; at older ages, one level may be used in three or four grades. If the scores are used to measure growth from year to year, a common score scale or other basis for comparing performance across grade levels must be provided.[3] In short, there must be coordination between various levels of the test, both in terms of the content covered and the scoring scale used.

Examples. We shall neither attempt to survey all the published achievement test batteries nor evaluate any single test in depth. However, to give you the flavor of an achievement test battery, a description of one battery is given in Table 12.1, other batteries are listed in Table 12.2, and examples of types of items found on achievement test batteries are shown in Figure 12.2. For other descriptions and evaluations of common achievement test batteries see Buros (1978) or Mehrens and Lehmann (1980). Better yet, obtain copies of several achievement test batteries and their manuals and review the tests, keeping in mind the principles discussed in this and previous chapters.

Placement Tests

At the high school and college levels, students often must choose between several courses in a field; for example, between several possible biology, mathematics, physics, or chemistry courses. When these courses presume varying background in the subject or build on each other, it is important to place students in the course that best matches their preparation. One way to determine their level of knowledge, and hence the appropriate placement, is by placement examinations. These tests are similar to specific-subject tests in that they measure command of a specified course or domain; however, they are designed specifically for placement.

One example is the *CEEB Advanced Placement Program*. This program consists of both course work (typically taken in high school) and an examination program. Approximately 20 examinations are available in diverse subjects including Chemistry, European History, French, Physics, and Latin. Each examination predominantly consists of essay questions; some exams, however, are supplemented by objective questions, and the modern language tests include listening

---

[3] One approach to constructing such scales is use of latent trait models (see Chapter 9).

Table 12.1
Description of an Achievement Test Battery: The Stanford Achievement Tests

Test series: The Stanford Achievement Tests, 7th edition
Publisher: The Psychological Corporation (1981)

Standard Early School Achievement Test (K-grade 1.9)
The Environment (Social Studies, Science), Mathematics, Sounds and Letters, Word Reading, Sentence Reading, Listening to Words & Stories. Two levels.

Stanford Achievement Tests (grades 1.5–9.9)
Levels. Primary 1 (1.5–2.9), Primary II (2.5–3.9) Primary III (3.5–4.9), Intermediate I (4.5–5.9), Intermediate II (5.5–7.9), Advanced (7–9.9)
Tests. The following tests are included:

			Level			
Test	P1	P2	P3	I1	I2	Adv
Vocabulary	X	X	X	X	X	X
Word Reading	X	X				
Reading Comprehension	X	X	X	X	X	X
Word Study Skills	X	X	X	X	X	
Concepts of Number	X	X	X	X	X	X
Math Computations	X	X	X	X	X	X
Math Applications	X	X	X	X	X	X
Spelling	X	X	X	X	X	X
Language			X	X	X	X
Environment	X	X				
Social Science			X	X	X	X
Science			X	X	X	X
Listening Comprehension	X	X	X	X	X	X

Test of Academic Skills.
Levels: Level I (8.0–12.9), Level II (9–13)
Tests: Reading Comprehension, Reading Vocabulary, Math, Language (Spelling, English), Social Science, Science.

Items. See Figure 12.2.

Scoring. By hand or machine.

Scores. Percentile ranks, grade equivalents, stanines, scale scores. Profile provided for plotting scores. Also criterion-referenced scores.

Norms. On SAT, based on 275,000 students in 109 systems in 43 states. On TASK, based on 47,000 students from 29 states.

Validity. Basically content or curricular validity. Suggest compare content to local objectives.

Consistency. Report Kuder-Richardson 20, corrected split-half coefficients, and standard error of measurement. The reliability coefficients are generally .85 or higher.

Other services. Item analysis; diagnostic reading and arithmetic tests (two levels, 2.5–4.5 and 4.5–8.5), modern math concepts test (two levels, 5–6, 7–9).

Suggested uses. Measure achievement level; cumulative measurement of growth; diagnosis of strengths and weaknesses; selection and placement; curriculum planning and evaluation; guidance.

Table 12.2
Examples of Standardized Achievement Test Batteries

Adult Basic Learning Examination (Harcourt Brace Jovanovich). Measures basic learning of adults in four areas—Reading, Spelling, Arithmetic Computation, and Problem Solving; items focus on everyday situations; three levels (comparable to grades 1 to 12).

California Achievement Tests (California Test Bureau/McGraw-Hill). Tests of knowledge and understanding in Reading (Vocabulary, Comprehension), Arithmetic (Reasoning, Fundamentals), and Language (Mechanics, Spelling); five levels, grades 1 to 14.

Comprehensive Assessment Program, Achievement Series (Scott Foresman). Lower levels cover Reading and Vocabulary, Language, Math; Study Skills added in upper elementary grades; high school levels also test Writing, Science, and Social Studies; eleven levels, kindergarten to grade 12.

Comprehensive Tests of Basic Skills (California Test Bureau/McGraw-Hill). Covers Reading (Vocabulary, Comprehension), Language (Mechanics, Expression, Spelling), and Arithmetic Skills (Computation, Concepts, Applications); also has a Study Skills sections; four levels, grades 2 to 12.

Iowa Tests of Basic Skills (Houghton-Mifflin). Covers Vocabulary, Reading Comprehension, Language Skills, Arithmetic Skills, and Work-Study Skills; generally several subtests for each part; various forms, grades 1 to 9.

Iowa Tests of Educational Development (Science Research Associates). Emphasis on critical thinking, analysis, and applications; major sections are Reading (Comprehension, Vocabulary), Language Arts (Usage, Spelling), Mathematics, Social Science, Sciences, Use of Sources of Information; grades 9 to 12.

Metropolitan Achievement Tests (Harcourt Brace Jovanovich). All levels cover basic language (e.g., word knowledge, reading, spelling) and math skills (e.g., computations, concepts, problem solving); upper levels contain science and social studies tests; six levels, kindergarten to grade 10.

Sequential Tests of Educational Progress, Series II (Cooperative Tests, Educational Testing Service). Tests cover English Expression, Reading, Mechanics of Writing, Mathematics Computation, Math Basic Concepts, Science, and Social Studies; four levels, grades 4 to 14.

SRA Achievement Series (Science Research Associates). Battery for grades 1 to 4 covers Reading, Arithmetic, and Language Arts; for grades 4 to 9 includes Reading, Language Arts, Math, Social Studies, Sciences, and Uses of Sources; for Reading, Language Arts, and Math/Arithmetic there are several subtests.

Stanford Achievement Tests (Harcourt Brace Jovanovich). See text for description.

Tests of Academic Progress (Houghton Mifflin). Covers Social Studies, Composition, Science, Reading, Math, and Literature; three forms, grades 9 to 12.

---

comprehension sections. The exams are graded by special committees of secondary school and college teachers. The results are sent to the college the student enters and the individual college decides whether to grant credit and/or advanced placement.

By providing a student with a means for demonstrating competency in an area, advanced placement exams allow for flexibility in educational planning by allowing students to advance in accordance with their abilities rather than be required to take courses that repeat material already learned. By combining the test development skills of a test publisher with local standards for interpreting scores, the Advanced Placement Exams provide the test user with the best of both worlds. Many colleges use other standardized tests, or locally constructed achievement tests, to serve the same placement and credit-awarding functions.

Figure 12.2 Examples of Items on a Standardized Achievement Test: The Stanford Achievement Test, Intermediate II.

TEST 1: Vocabulary

STEPS TO FOLLOW

I. Listen to each sentence your teacher reads to you.
II. Choose the word from those below that *best* completes each sentence.
III. Look at the answer spaces at the right or on your answer sheet (if you have one).
IV. Fill in the space which has the same number as the word you have chosen.

SAMPLE

The name of a winter month is —

A 1 April   3 January
    2 October   4 June

TEST 2: Reading Comprehension

STEPS TO FOLLOW

I. Read each selection.
II. Read the questions that follow the selection.
III. Choose the *best* answer for each question.
IV. Look at the answer spaces at the right or on your answer sheet (if you have one).
V. Fill in the space which has the same number as the answer you have chosen.

SAMPLES

Joe is often quite tardy. This week, however, he has been on time every day.

A Joe is often —
   1 late   2 ill   3 tired   4 early

B This week he has been —
   5 worse   7 on time
   6 absent   8 late

TEST 4: Mathematics Concepts

STEPS TO FOLLOW

I. Read each statement or question.
II. Decide which answer is *best*.
III. Look at the answer spaces at the right or on your answer sheet (if you have one).
IV. Fill in the space which has the same letter as the letter beside your answer.

SAMPLE

A Which numeral has the greatest value?

  a seven   c eight
  b nine   d three

TEST 5: Mathematics Computation   Part A

STEPS TO FOLLOW

I. Read each mathematical sentence.
II. Decide which of these signs will make it true:
   > is greater than   < is less than   = is equal to
III. Look at the answer spaces at the right or on your answer sheet (if you have one).
IV. Fill in the space which has the same letter as the answer you have chosen.

SAMPLE

A $2 + 4 \bullet 4 + 2$

Part B

STEPS TO FOLLOW

I. Work each exercise.
II. Look at the possible answers beside each problem and see if your answer is here.
III. If it is, fill in the space at the right or on your answer sheet (if you have one) which has the same letter as your answer.
IV. If your answer is *Not Here*, fill in the space which has the same letter as the letter beside NH.

SAMPLE

B   25   a 97
    + 73   b 88
            c 98
            d 89
            e NH

TEST 6: Mathematics Applications

STEPS TO FOLLOW

I. Solve each problem. Unless you are told otherwise, there is no sales tax.
II. Look at the possible answers under the problem. Is your answer here?
III. If it is, fill in the space at the right or on your answer sheet (if you have one) which has the same letter as your answer.
IV. If your answer is *Not Here*, fill in the space which has the same letter as the letter beside NH.

SAMPLE

A Susan lost 2 beads. She now has 8 left. How many beads did Susan have at first?

  a 4   c 6
  b 12   d 10
         • NH

TEST 7: Spelling   Part A

STEPS TO FOLLOW (Questions 1-8)
I. Read each group of phrases. Look at the under-lined word in each phrase. One of the underlined words is misspelled for the way it is used in the phrase.
II. Find the word that is *not* spelled correctly.
III. Look at the answer spaces at the right or on your answer sheet (if you have one).
IV. Fill in the space which has the same number as the word you have chosen.

SAMPLE

A 1 <u>no</u> school today   3 a honey <u>be</u>
  2 <u>meet</u> at the bus   4 the two <u>dogs</u>

Part B

STEPS TO FOLLOW (Questions 9-60)
I. Read each group of words.
II. Find the misspelled word in each group.
III. Look at the answer spaccs at the right or on your answer sheet (if you have one).
IV. Fill in the space which has the same number as the word you have chosen.

SAMPLE

B 5 cow   7 sky
  6 bagg   8 tell

TEST 8: Language   Part A

STEPS TO FOLLOW (Questions 1-42)
I. Read each sentence.
II. Look at the four different ways in which you can fill in the blank.
III. Choose the best form to write in a school paper.
IV. Look at the answer spaces at the right or on your answer sheet (if you have one).
V. Fill in the space which has the same number as the answer you have chosen.

SAMPLES

A My teacher lives on ___
  1 Center street
  2 Center Stree.
  3 center street.
  4 center Street.

TEST 8: Language   Part C

STEPS TO FOLLOW (Questions 51-70)
I. Read each group of words.
II. Fill in, in the spaces at the right or on your answer sheet (if you have one), the space for:
  1 if the group of words makes *ONE* complete sentence with the addition of a period or question mark
  2 if the group of words makes *TWO OR MORE* sentences without changing or omitting any words
  N if the group of words is *NOT* a complete sentence.

SAMPLE

C It was raining
  a 1   b N   c 2

TEST 9: Social Science

STEPS TO FOLLOW
I. Read each question.
II. Choose the *best* answer.
III. Look at the answer spaces at the right or on your answer sheet (if you have one).
IV. Fill in the space which has the same number as the answer you have chosen.

SAMPLE

A Which one of the following is a continent?
  1 England   3 Mexico
  2 Africa   4 Canada

TEST 10: Science

STEPS TO FOLLOW
I. Read each question.
II. Choose the *best* answer.
III. Look at the answer spaces at the right or on your answer sheet (if you have one).
IV. Fill in the space which has the same number as the answer you have chosen.

SAMPLE

A The sun is a —
  1 planet   3 comet
  2 star   4 meteor

TEST 11: Listening Comprehension

Listen while I read the sample story. It says:

> After school, John went to the store. He took a loaf of bread home and then he went to Ken's home.

The question is: "After school, where did John go first? 1 home, 2 the library, 3 the store, 4 Ken's home." Which of the answers tells where John went first?

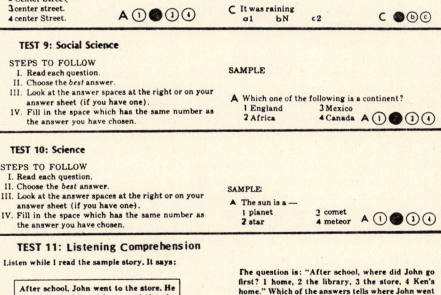

Diagnostic Tests

Survey tests, whether specific-subject tests or parts of batteries, give an overall indication of a student's command of a content area. For many purposes this is sufficient. For other purposes, such as when a student is having difficulty learning, we may want more detailed information that indicates what particular aspects of the subject are causing the student trouble. Although we could get some indication of these problem areas from a survey test by looking at the student's responses to individual items, or clusters of items measuring related skills, a better approach would be to construct tests specifically to provide information about the student's mastery of the component skills in an area. Diagnostic tests are designed to provide this type of information.

Diagnostic tests are most common in reading and arithmetic, primarily because both are fundamental educational skills that can be broken down into component skills. For example, one diagnostic reading test provides four major scores—word recognition, oral reading, silent reading, and auditory comprehension—plus supplementary measures of rate of silent reading and phonics. Another measures word recognition, comprehension, vocabulary, rate of reading, story comprehension, and both oral and silent word-attack skills. Use of subtests provides a more thorough understanding of a student's reading skills than a survey measure of reading speed and/or comprehension.

A diagnostic test must cover the component abilities and skills necessary for successful performance. The first step in constructing a diagnostic test, therefore, is to identify these component abilities. This will be based both on a logical understanding of the area tested and empirical evidence regarding the relationships between component skills. As the scores will be used to identify specific weaknesses and problem areas, items within each subtest should be constructed so students can make different types of errors. Thus each subtest will contain several items measuring each specific skill or operation. As we may also be interested in how complex an item a student can handle, items of varying difficulty are usually included on each subtest.

Several other requirements pertain to the construction of diagnostic tests. First, the skill must be such that dividing the overall performance into components does not destroy the nature of the total act; if it does, any partitioning of the skill will result in scores that will be of limited usefulness. Second, there will, necessarily, be several subtests or scales, each measuring a single component. Third, the various subtests should be homogeneous or, at least, measure combinations of skills that are, in some respects, inseparable. Fourth, the test battery should be inclusive; if certain fundamental skills are not measured, it will be impossible to ascertain the exact cause of a student's difficulty. Fifth, scores on each component test should be reliable, both because we want to make decisions about individuals and because we will be comparing scores on various subtests.

A final and extremely important requirement is that the scores should have implications for remedial work. Since the purpose of a diagnostic test is to identify an individual's strengths and weaknesses, the pattern of scores not only should identify these areas, but also should point to appropriate remedial action. Thus interpretation of diagnostic tests should be made by a person who has a thorough grounding in testing, the learning process, and the subject matter covered by the test, such as a school psychologist or a child clinical psychologist.

Brief descriptions of several diagnostic tests are given in Table 12.3.

Table 12.3
Examples of Diagnostic Tests

Diagnostic Reading Scales (California Test Bureau/McGraw-Hill). Covers word recognition, reading (oral reading, silent reading, and auditory comprehension,) and phonics and word analysis; (10 components, such as initial consonants and blends); grades 1 to 8; 1981 edition.

Gates-McGinitie Reading Tests (Riverside). Vocabulary (including decoding skills at lower ages) and comprehension; grades 1 to 12; 1978 edition.

Individual Pupil Monitoring System (Riverside). Criterion-referenced tests based on specified behavioral objectives; Reading test measures word attack, vocabulary and comprehension, and discrimination/study skills; also a Mathematics test; grades 1 to 8.

Key Math Diagnostic Arithmetic Test (American Guidance Service). Covers three major areas—Content (numeration, fractions, geometry and symbols), Operations (addition, subtraction, multiplication, division, mental computations, and numerical reasoning), and Applications (word problems, missing elements, money, measurements, and time); preschool through sixth grade.

Nelson-Denny Reading Test (Riverside). Covers vocabulary, reading comprehension, and reading rate; grades 9 to 12, college, and adult.

Prescriptive Mathematics Inventory (California Test Bureau/McGraw-Hill). Criterion-referenced, both traditional and modern math; three levels, grades 4 to 8; also a similar Reading Test.

Stanford Diagnostic Reading Test (Harcourt Brace Jovanovich). Measures reading comprehension, vocabulary, syllabication, auditory skills, phonetic analysis, and reading rate; grades 2 to 8.

Readiness Tests

Readiness tests, like diagnostic tests, are generally concerned with fundamental skills, particularly reading. The basic question to be answered by readiness tests is: "Does the student possess the necessary skills to succeed in a particular educational task?" In other words, is he or she ready to start to study a particular skill?

The first step in test construction, thus, is to identify the skills that are predictive of success. These skills may be of various sorts. In some instances they may be general intellectual or physical abilities; for example, before a child can learn to read, her visual discrimination must be developed to a level at which she can discriminate between printed letters. In other instances, the indication may be possession of an appropriate fund of knowledge; for example, a student must be able to count before he can learn to add, and know the names of objects and meanings of words before he can learn to read. One can also conceive of attitudes and predispositions toward learning and attacking problems as being essential aspects of readiness.

Readiness tests are usually encountered at the preschool and kindergarten age levels, where the interest is in determining readiness to begin formal educational programs, particularly instruction in reading. Since reading readiness tests are designed for use with children who have not yet learned to read, they usually consist of pictorial and symbolic materials administered with oral directions.

An example of a readiness test is the *Boehm Test of Basic Concepts.* The idea

Figure 12.3 Examples of Items on the Boehm Test of Basic Concepts

directions

1. Mark the pole with the flag at the *top*.
2. Mark the dog that is going *through* the hoop.

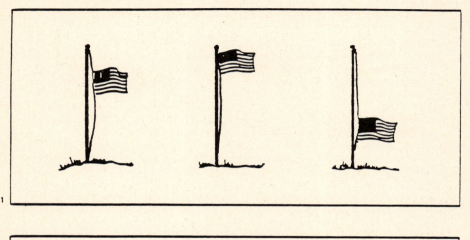

behind this test is that children have to understand certain basic concepts relating to space, quantity, and time in order to understand the directions and procedures used in schools. Examples include such concepts as top, below, larger, skip (a space), and next. Children who are unfamiliar with these concepts will have trouble following instructions and thus may not profit from instruction. The test consists of 50 sets of pictures (see Figure 12.3), each of which illustrates one concept. The teacher reads a description of the concept and students mark the picture that best illustrates this concept.

Other readiness tests are briefly described in Table 12.4.

Table 12.4
Examples of Readiness Tests

Analysis of Readiness Skills (Riverside). Separate tests for Reading and Mathematics; kindergarten and grade 1.

Boehm Test of Basic Concepts (Psychological Corporation). See text for description.

CIRCUS (Addison-Wesley). Includes 14 tests and three teacher-completed instruments; basic tests include How Much and How Many (counting, relations, numbers) and Listen to the Story (comprehension, interpretation and recall of oral language, vocabulary); other tests include receptive vocabulary, auditory discrimination, functional language, visual discrimination, letter-number recognition, perceptual-motor coordination; several levels, preschool through grade 3.

Metropolitan Readiness Test (Psychological Corporation). Measures beginning consonants, sound-letter correspondence, visual matching, finding patterns, school language, listening, quantitative concepts, quantitative operations; kindergarten and grade 1.

Tests of Basic Experiences (California Test Bureau/McGraw-Hill). Four areas—language, mathematics, science, social studies; preschool through grade 1.

One word of caution should be interjected regarding the use of readiness measures. Since these tests are typically administered to children whose test-taking skills are undeveloped, whose attention span is short, and whose emotional behavior is often erratic, the test results may well present a misleading picture of the child. Thus decisions about the child's readiness should never be based solely on tests; rather the test results should be supplemented by other information, such as observations by teachers and parents.

Proficiency Tests

Sometimes we want to determine whether a student has attained a particular level of competency[4] in an area. This may be proficiency in a complete course or on some specific skill, for example, the ability to make a particular type of weld, to use a microscope, or to type 30 words a minute. In these situations we need a proficiency test.

Developing a proficiency test involves two steps: defining the skill or domain and establishing the minimal level of competency. Often this is done by defining objectives then translating them into test items. Using this approach, the first step would be to define the skill, the conditions under which it is to be demonstrated, and the minimal level of acceptable performance. We would then construct a series of tasks measuring attainment of the objective. For example, if we were interested in typing skill, we might define the task as copying a 200-word passage within 6 minutes with less than four errors. If the student attains or surpasses this standard, he has demonstrated his proficiency; if he does not type enough words per minute, or makes more than the allotted number of errors, he has not demonstrated his proficiency.

Proficiency tests may also cover a particular subject matter area. One example is the *College Level Examination Program* (CLEP), sponsored by the College

---

[4] Although the terms "competency" and "proficiency" can have slightly different connotations, we shall use them interchangeably to refer to situations where the goal of testing is to ascertain whether a test taker has attained some minimum, predetermined standard of performance.

Board. These examinations were developed to serve the college student who is following a nontraditional pattern (that is, a pattern other than high school immediately followed by college). Thus, they are used for such purposes as establishing the level of educational attainment of adults returning to college, who, through independent study or vocational experiences, have developed knowledge and skills equivalent to those taught in college level courses. They can also be used to measure knowledge at a transition point—for example, at the end of the sophomore year of college or at the completion of junior college.

There are two types of exams: general and subject matter. The general exams measure achievement in broad areas of liberal arts (English Composition, Humanities, Mathematics, Natural Sciences, and Social Sciences–History) and are multiple-choice exams, 60 to 75 minutes in length. The subject examinations consist of a 90-minute multiple-choice section and an optional essay exam of the same length. The exams are designed to measure basic facts and concepts and the ability to apply these facts and concepts to the solution and interpretation of problems. Exams are available for approximately 30 undergraduate courses.

Minimum Competency Tests.   Minimum competency tests, as the name implies, are designed to establish whether students have attained a certain level of competency in an academic area. They generally are used either as a standard for graduation from high school or as a basis for promotion to the next grade level. The primary assumption underlying minimum competency tests is that each student should master certain knowledge and skills before being awarded a diploma or promoted to the next grade. Currently more than 30 states have some type of minimum competency testing program.

The two major problems involved in developing a minimum competency test are the same as those involved in developing any proficiency test: defining the domain and setting the competency level. However, because of the importance of the decisions made on the basis of minimum competency tests (Will a student receive a high school diploma? Will he be promoted to the next grade?), use of these tests has generated an intense amount of controversy over both political and psychometric issues. (For discussions of the issues and technical problems see, e.g., Bunda & Sanders, 1979; Ebel, 1978b; Glass, 1978; Jaeger & Tittle, 1980; Madaus & McDonagh, 1979; Pipho, 1978; Resnick, 1980; Shepard, 1980.)

In terms of content, the major problem is what should be covered on the test. For example, should the test measure only "basic" skills, such as reading, writing, and mathematics skills, or should they also cover other areas, such as science, government, and history? Even within a particular area there are disagreements as to what skills should be covered and how items should be framed. For example, in the mathematics area, should we only measure operations specifically taught in schools or should students be asked to apply these operations to practical problems, such as balancing a checkbook or filling out an income tax form? Proponents of the former view argue that it is unfair to test students on materials they have not been specifically taught; proponents of the latter view argue the true test of learning is whether students can apply what they have learned.

There are also arguments about where to set the minimum passing score. If it is set too high, many students will not pass the test and will be denied a diploma or forced to spend an additional year in the same grade. On the other hand, if the standard is set too low, students with weaker than desired achievement may pass. There are also a host of other, more political, problems involved in the use of minimum competency tests. For example, should the minimum proficiency level be the same for all schools in a state or should each school be allowed to set its own standards? What about students who repeatedly fail the test; should they receive a certificate of attendance rather than a diploma? Should students who pass the test early in their high school careers be allowed to leave school? Are the tests fair to members of minority groups? Thus, even though many people support the idea of minimum competency tests, a number of practical and political problems must be resolved before such a program can be implemented.

Vocational Proficiency Tests.   Although we generally think of achievement tests in connection with education, they are also used in industrial, military, and professional settings—for example, for selection and placement and as a basis for promotion.

Achievement tests are also used for licensing or certification in certain professions—such as medicine, law, accounting, and engineering. The basic assumption when achievement tests are used for certification is, of course, that there are certain skills or knowledge that an individual must possess if he or she is to engage successfully in a given occupation or practice a particular profession. The test serves as a mechanism for determining whether the individual possesses these competencies. Depending on the particular circumstances (for example, what occupation, whether the governing board is local or national) the examination may be informal and ad hoc, a standardized test, or, most commonly, something in between.

Content-Referenced Tests

In recent years content-referenced achievement testing has become quite popular. (This approach also goes by various other names, including criterion-referenced, objective-referenced, and domain-referenced.) Although the construction of content-referenced tests is similar in many ways to norm-referenced tests, there are several important differences. The first step is to clearly define the domain to be tested. In most cases this involves specification of behavioral objectives, that is, listing the knowledge and skills students should possess at the end of a unit or course of instruction. Test items are then generated to measure attainment of these objectives. Even though these items may not differ in format or content from items on norm-referenced tests, the sampling of items for inclusion on the test differs. On content-referenced tests we construct several items to measure each important objective, not just sample items to represent the content domain. In other words, items are selected to measure attainment of each objective.

Scores also differ on content-referenced tests. Generally we will examine performance on individual items, or clusters of items measuring the same objective. Scores are interpreted in terms of content mastery, not in relation to the performance of other students. How other students do is irrelevant; all students can demonstrate mastery or all can fail.

Some content-referenced tests cover a set content domain defined in terms of the skills and knowledge that are commonly taught. These tests are designed to apply in a wide variety of schools. However, the content-referenced approach also lends itself to tailoring tests for specific courses and schools. This can be done in the following way. For a given content area, a list of behavioral objectives is prepared. Then pools of items are written to measure attainment of each of these objectives. (The total collection of items is often referred to as an *item bank*.) An individual teacher, or teachers within a school, can look at the list of objectives and determine which ones are particularly appropriate for their situation. The required number and type of items are then selected from the item bank to form a test. This particular collection of items (the test) may never be used in other situations, since it is designed to fit the specifications of a particular situation. However, because the items from the bank are used in various classes (though not in the same combination), data on performance of other classes are available and can be used to provide some relevant normative information. The advantage of this approach is that a test can be developed to measure attainment of the objectives of a particular class or school, using items that have been carefully and systematically developed and validated.

uses of standardized achievement tests

A standardized achievement test (or any other assessment technique) should not be administered unless we plan to use the results. To administer a test, then file away the scores is a waste of time, time that better could be spent on other instructional activities. In this section we shall describe several possible uses of standardized achievement tests. The uses described are only suggestions and illustrations; other uses are possible.

When considering these examples, two complementary points should be kept in mind. First, the scores on a test may be used for various purposes. For example, scores on a test used to place students in sections of a course may also be used when planning or evaluating instruction. Second, scores on achievement tests should not be the only source of information used in making instructional decisions. To continue the same example, when making placement decisions you should consider such evidence as grades in prerequisite and related courses, ability test scores, and the student's educational goals, as well as the placement test scores.

Uses in the Instructional Process

The most important use of standardized achievement tests is to facilitate the instructional process—that is, to provide information that can be used to make instruction more effective, consequently increasing students' achievement. These uses include selection and placement, planning instruction, identifying students having special needs, and educational and vocational guidance.

Selection and Placement. Although placement decisions are more common at higher levels of education, they are made at all grade levels. For example, reading readiness tests are used at the kindergarten or first grade level to assign students various reading programs or groups. Throughout the elementary and high school years, standardized achievement tests are used to place students in various educational tracks or curricula, to determine when students should take a particular course (Should Kirk take algebra in eighth grade or wait until ninth grade?), and for assigning students to appropriate courses. And when students transfer to schools in another community, particularly ones having educational programs quite different from their previous school, test results may be helpful in placing them in the appropriate grade level or in specific courses.

At the college level, use of standardized achievement tests for placement is quite common. Because high school curricula vary widely and students have taken different courses, entering college freshmen differ in their level of achievement. Since most colleges offer a variety of courses in a given field, each presuming different backgrounds and knowledge, placement tests can be very useful when placing students in classes. Most commonly, placement tests are used in fields where courses build sequentially, such as mathematics and foreign languages, or in basic required courses where students exhibit various levels of skills, such as English composition. While many of these placement tests are constructed and administered locally, other colleges use scores on standardized achievement tests, such as the achievement test portions of the College Board (CEEB) Admissions Testing Program, or the CEEB Advanced Placement Examinations.

Achievement test scores can also be used when making selection decisions. Many selective colleges require applicants to submit scores on the CEEB achievement tests as part of their application and use these scores when making admissions decisions. Achievement tests are also used by graduate and professional schools. For example, achievement tests in various subject matter areas are included in the Graduate Record Examination, a test used by many graduate schools. These scores are used when selecting among applicants for admission to graduate programs. The Medical College Admission Test also has sections measuring the student's knowledge of basic science.

In all of these situations the ideal procedure is to use tests specifically designed for making placement and/or selection decisions. However, scores on survey tests are sometimes used. The crucial consideration is, of course, that the test used validly measures the prerequisite skills needed for the course, curriculum, or program.

Instructional Planning. Most instructional decisions, especially day-to-day and moment-to-moment decisions, are based on teacher-built tests and more informal methods, such as classroom observation. However, standardized achievement tests also can play a part in instructional planning, either for individual students or for the class as a whole.

At the beginning of instruction, instructors can use achievement test results to understand their students better—both their general level of achievement, as indicated by survey batteries, or their knowledge of a specific subject. Test scores can also be used to identify those students who already have mastered the material to be taught and thus can proceed to the next unit.[5] And, of course, readiness

---

[5] Teacher-built tests can also be used for this purpose (see Chapter 11).

tests are used to determine which students are prepared to begin a course of instruction.

During instruction, the progress of learning is usually assessed by teacher-built tests and informal methods. If standardized measures are used, they should be content-referenced since the primary goal is to determine what topics students have and have not mastered. However, diagnostic tests are frequently used when it becomes apparent that certain students are having trouble with the material.

Standardized achievement tests can be used at the end of instruction, to measure whether the instructional objectives have been attained. Here specific subject tests are most useful, as they focus on a particular subject matter domain. Depending on the nature of the course, either norm-referenced or content-referenced tests may be used.

Identifying Special Needs. In most courses there are some students who do not profit from the regular method of instruction and thus need a different type of instruction. Thus one function of testing should be to identify those students who have special needs. We have already mentioned one such example, the use of diagnostic tests with students having difficulty in a particular subject. Another example is students whose general mental abilities are either so high or so low as to require special classes. These latter two groups, however, will usually be identified by other methods, such as the teacher's observation and ability tests, rather than by achievement tests. There are, however, two groups of students whose special needs can be identified by achievement tests: those with learning disabilities and those having outstanding talent in a specific field.

The field of learning disabilities has received increasing attention in recent years, especially since passage of Public Law 94-142, the Education for all Handicapped Children Act of 1975. Although there is no universally agreed upon definition of what is meant by a learning disability, most definitions state that a learning disability is indicated by average or above average intellectual ability accompanied by significantly lower achievement in one or more areas. Thus, to identify a learning-disabled child requires measures of both ability and achievement. While below expected achievement may be indicated by classroom performance, it also may be indicated by scores on achievement tests, either specific-subject tests or survey batteries. If a discrepancy between ability and achievement is found, further evaluation and diagnostic procedures are used to establish the nature of the disability and the appropriate remedial action. For our discussion, however, the major point is that achievement tests may be used to identify children with learning disabilities and other types of learning problems.

There are also children whose achievement in a specific field is so far in advance of their classmates as to suggest that other than the traditional method of instruction would be more beneficial. An example of this situation is Stanley and his associates' work with mathematically precocious youth (Fox, Brody, & Tobin, 1980; George, Cohn, & Stanley, 1979; Keating, 1976; Stanley, 1980; Stanley, George, & Solano, 1978; Stanley, Keating, & Fox, 1974). Stanley thought many junior high students could learn mathematics much more rapidly than they would be taught in the regular school curriculum. He instituted a "talent search" to identify these talented students, using a variety of measures including the mathematics tests from the CEEB Admissions Program, a test usually administered only to high school juniors and seniors. He identified a number of junior high students who obtained very high scores on this test. He then provided a variety of special programs for these students, including accelerated mathematics courses taught on weekends and even early college admission for the most talented students. Using the test allowed these mathematically talented students to be placed in programs that enabled them to progress at a rate consistent with their superior skills and abilities.

Educational and Vocational Guidance and Planning. Taking an even broader view of the instructional process, we can consider the use of achievement tests in educational and vocational planning and guidance. Most people tend to select courses, college majors, and vocations in which they have high chances of success. One basis for making such choices is to consider those areas where one has previously achieved at a high level. Although most people make these judgments on bases such as course grades, they also consider performance on tests. These may be achievement test batteries; tests given for special purposes, such as college admission tests; or tests given during the counseling or guidance process.

To illustrate, consider a student who has received average grades in mathematics and science courses but above-average grades in English and history. Suppose also that his scores on an achievement battery show the same pattern of strengths and weaknesses, and that his overall achievement score is above average but not outstanding. When discussing his educational plans with the high school counselor, he could use this information to help choose a college and a major. For example, since his strengths are in verbal areas, he might decide to major in political science, business, or prelaw. And because his scores were good, though not outstanding, he might decide to apply to the state university and a good liberal arts college, but not to any highly selective colleges.

Measuring Outcomes

In many situations we want to know how well students have learned the course material and whether instruction has been effective. Consequently, we need to measure the outcomes of the learning process. As with the instructional use of tests, this evidence is often obtained from teacher-built tests and other locally constructed assessment procedures. However, standardized achievement tests also can be used.

In this section we shall discuss two situations where measures of educational outcomes are needed: grading and the establishment of proficiency.

Grading. The most common purpose of testing in education is as a basis for assigning grades. Although I would suggest that grades usually be based on teacher-built tests (and other locally devised assessment methods) since they can be tailored to fit the goals of a particular class, in two situations standardized tests may be used. One is when there are several sections of a course and the same examination is administered to students in all sections. The other is when we want to compare the performance of students in a particular class to a wider norm group. For example, I might want to know how the achievement of students in my general psychology class compares with that of students in similar classes throughout the country. This information could be obtained only by using a standardized test.

Another type of test is often used in classrooms, one that falls between standardized and teacher-built achievement tests. These are *text-based tests,* ones provided by the text publisher as part of an instructional package. Such tests are commonly provided with elementary and secondary level texts.[6] Although the same items can be administered in various classes, these tests lack many essential ingredients of good standardized tests. In particular, there generally is no description of the item construction process, there is no evidence of reliability and validity, and norms are not provided. Although these tests are convenient to use and cover the material in the text, the quality of items is frequently lower than would be desired. Teachers who use such tests should make sure the items are of good quality and reflect their instructional emphases.

Establishing Proficiency. The clearest example of educational use of proficiency tests is minimum competency tests. As mentioned previously, minimum competency tests are used to determine whether students should be promoted to the next grade or receive a high school diploma. Because there is a designated set of skills students are expected to master, and the goal of testing is to determine whether individual students have mastered this material to a prescribed level, content-referenced tests will be more useful than norm-referenced tests.

Establishment of proficiency also is important in other settings. A driver's license examination is an example. Various occupations and professions also have licensure or certification examinations. Examples include law, medicine, engineering, accounting, psychology, real estate sales, and various skilled trades, such as for plumbers and electricians. Although many of these licensing examinations are constructed by test publishing firms, administered nationwide, and include normative data, others are wholly, or in part, designed for use in a particular community or state. In all cases, however, the goal is to determine whether the test taker has the skills necessary to perform the job at an acceptable level of proficiency.

Evaluation of Instruction

Tests can also be used to evaluate the instructional process. Data from standardized tests can be used to evaluate teachers, curricula, instructional materials, educational programs, and instructional methods.[7] When used for these purposes, achievement test scores usually serve as the dependent variable or outcome measure. For example, when several different methods of instruction are compared,

[6] Tests are usually provided for each chapter or topic, with review tests for each unit. An alternative procedure, often used with college texts, is to provide a pool of items from which instructors select the items they wish to use.

[7] Although our examples will be concerned with classroom instruction, the same methods can also be applied to other instructional stituations, such as industrial training programs.

achievement test scores would be the criteria used to measure the effectiveness of the various approaches.

Standardized tests have certain advantages over teacher-built tests, and other ad hoc procedures, in evaluation studies. The content domain is clearly defined and items are carefully constructed. Testing conditions and procedures are standardized. Reliability generally is higher than on other types of measures. The test items cover those aspects of the material that are generally considered to be most important—that is, the material most commonly taught. (Of course, if there are important specific local goals, they should also be measured.) Normative data for various groups are available. Taken together, these characteristics ensure more accurate measurement and allow for comparisons with other groups of students and with similar studies.

When using standardized achievement tests to evaluate instruction or instructors, a point made earlier becomes especially crucial: A test should not be the only measure of effectiveness used. Various types of information should be collected so decisions are not made on the basis of only one type of evidence. Thus, for example, when comparing curricular materials, we would want to consider the content of the materials, students' and teachers' reactions, and the cost effectiveness, as well as effects on achievement. However, in our examples, we shall consider only the criterion of achievement.

As evaluation of instruction is a complex process, we shall consider only one example. Readers interested in more detailed discussions should see Anderson & Ball, 1978; Astin & Panos, 1971; Baker & Quellmalz, 1980; Berk, 1980b; Cronbach et al., 1980; Cronbach & Snow, 1977; Dressel, 1976; Madaus, Airasian, & Kellaghan, 1980; Popham, 1974; and Wittrock & Wiley, 1970.

Evaluating Educational Programs. Frequently one sees the average achievement test scores of students in a particular school or various schools in a community reported in newspapers. If the scores are higher than average, the implication is that the school is doing a good job educating children; if they are lower, the conclusion is often that the school needs improvement. Are such interpretations justified? Seldom. One reason is that such interpretations often fail to take into account the background and abilities of the students attending the schools. For example, average achievement (compared to national norms) by students in a school in a culturally deprived area may represent or reflect an excellent school system. Then, too, there is seldom any detailed investigation as to whether the test items measure the major educational goals of a particular school.

Even when we take the students' backgrounds and the educational goals into account, there may be subtle psychometric problems. For example, Madaus, Airasian, and Kellaghan (1980) have pointed out that the tests usually used as a basis for such comparisons contain items that were selected to discriminate between individual students. These may not be the same items that best differentiate between schools. Therefore, they suggest that program evaluations should use tests designed specifically to point out differences between schools. These would be content-referenced tests, which contain items measuring skills taught in some schools but not in others, rather than norm-referenced tests, which measure knowledge that is widely taught.

Research Uses

Standardized achievement tests also can be used to answer research questions. Some studies are purely descriptive; for example, we may want to describe the range of achievement in different subject areas of students in a particular school or community. Other studies test a particular hypothesis—for example, that mastery learning results in higher achievement than a traditional approach to instruction in biology. The goal of such research is to obtain information that can be used to improve instruction.

Rather than describing traditional research studies, we have chosen as examples two somewhat atypical uses of tests—atypical in the sense that the focus is not on the performance of individual students. The first is the National Assessment of Educational Progress, a program designed to determine what U.S. students of various ages know and can do. The other, the International Studies of Educational Achievement, explores the differential achievement in various countries and the factors relating to this differential achievement.

The National Assessment of Educational Progress. You have probably read articles that suggest that present-day students have learned much more than their parents did at the same age. About as frequently, you see articles that suggest that today's students are not as well prepared as those of previous generations, especially in basic subjects (see, e.g., Kline, 1974). Which view is correct? No one knows. One reason is that there is no baseline data to compare achievement at different times. The National Assessment of Educational Progress was designed to provide information on the knowledge, skills, and attitudes of American children and young adults (Committee on Assessing the Progress of Education, 1968; Martin, 1979; Tyler, Merwin, & Ebel, 1966; Womer, 1970). Because the focus is on providing baseline data, individual scores are not reported; in fact, each person takes only parts of the test battery.

The battery consists of ten tests (Literature, Science, Social Studies, Writing, Citizenship, Music, Mathematics, Reading, Art, and Vocational Education), representing areas taught in most schools. Within each area, objectives were developed and items written to measure these objectives. Although some questions measure knowledge (for example, name the U.S. Senators from your state), the emphasis is on understanding and applications (for example, being able to select a balanced diet or tell the consequences of disturbing a given ecological system). In addition to paper-and-pencil items, exercises involved observations, interviews, questionnaires, performance tests, and sample productions.

The exercises were administered to students at four age levels: 9, 13, 17, and young adults (26–35). As the primary goal of the Assessment is to measure change, each test will be repeated every several years. By not releasing all the items, some items can be used in following testing. The results of the two testings can be compared to see whether performance has increased or decreased.

To summarize, the National Assessment will provide two types of data: what students of various ages know and can do and how these knowledges and skills change over time.

The International Study of Educational Achievement.   The goals of these studies were to develop standard measures of educational achievement, describe the achievement level in various countries, and identify the factors that account for cross-national differences in achievement.

The first study (Husén, 1967) involved achievement in mathematics. In this study 133,000 students in 20 countries were tested; one group tested was 13-year-old students, the other students in the last preuniversity year. Besides achievement test scores, data were collected on student, teacher, and school characteristics.

The second phase of the study, the Six Subject Survey, covers Science (Comber & Keeves, 1973), Literature (Purves, 1973), Reading Comprehension (Thorndike, 1973), English and French as Foreign Languages, and Civic Education. Approximately 258,000 students in 20 countries (including several undeveloped nations) will be tested. The target populations include 10-year-olds, 14-year-olds, and students in the last year of precollege education (Härnquist, 1975).

When looking at the results of such studies, most people probably look first at the rank of their country. However, these rankings can be misleading. One problem, of course, is developing tests that are applicable in all nations. Although this is comparatively simple in mathematics, it is more difficult in areas like reading. Another problem is the different curricular emphases in the various countries. A third, and perhaps most difficult, problem is sampling students, particularly at older age levels. Consider the fact that U.S. high school seniors scored relatively low on the Mathematics, Science, and Reading Comprehension tests. What does this mean? On face value it might seem that the U.S. schools are not doing a good job. On the other hand, more than 70 percent of the children of this age are in school in the United States, whereas in other countries only one in 10 may be in school. Since students who are in school are likely to be the most able, the U.S. standing may reflect our policy of open access to education.

Both the National Assessment and the International Study show that important information can be obtained from testing programs, information that can be used to improve education without reporting scores for individual students.

some questions about standardized achievement tests

Having discussed the construction, types, and uses of standardized achievement tests, we now turn to several questions about these tests: Are they psychometrically sound measuring instruments? How do they differ from other types of maximal performance tests? What are the major issues in the use of these tests?

Psychometric Characteristics

Of all the varieties of psychological and educational tests, standardized achievement measures have, by and large, attained higher standards of consistency, validity, and normative data than any other type of test. This is not to say that all standardized achievement measures are satisfactory; far from it. Rather, there are a number of standardized achievement tests on the market, particularly survey tests, that are highly reliable, have content and predictive validity, and provide normative data from representative samples of the population. Thus a potential user has a high probability of finding a carefully constructed and technically satisfactory achievement test.

One area where psychometric requirements are not met as adequately as might be desired is the interpretation and use of scores. Many norm-referenced tests report scores on various subtests and content-referenced tests report scores on clusters of related items. Since these subtests and clusters frequently contain few items, scores may be unreliable and thus should be interpreted with caution. In addition, many standardized achievement tests report scores that are frequently misinterpreted. One example is the widespread use of grade-equivalent scores. Another is the use of educational and achievement quotients. As pointed out in Chapter 8, both of these types of scores have important limitations, which often result in the misinterpretation of scores.

Differences from Other Types of Maximal Performance Tests

After reading this chapter and the previous one, you should be aware of the differences between teacher-built and standardized achievement tests. As a review, the major differences are summarized in Table 12.5. When considering these types of tests, keep in mind that one type will not be better in all situations; each has its own advantages, limitations, and appropriate uses.

We could also ask how standardized achievement tests differ from other types of standardized maximal performance tests, such as aptitude, ability, and intelligence tests. They often use similar item formats, administrative procedures, and normative data. Furthermore, if you were to examine items from an ability test and an achievement test, particularly in areas such as vocabulary and arithmetic, you probably would not do much better than chance in assigning items to the appropriate test. Although this may seem surprising, it shouldn't, since both tests measure developed abilities.

How, then, do the tests differ? One dimension is content. For example, items measuring knowledge of specific areas, such as science and social studies, generally appear only on achievement tests. However, a more crucial distinction is in how items are selected and the tests are used. Achievement tests are designed to measure circumscribed content domains and to indicate what has been learned, whereas ability tests measure broader domains and indicate current status. In short, although their content may be similar, the method of selecting items and the uses of the tests are different.

Issues in Achievement Testing

Most people agree that measuring achievement is an essential part of the educational process: If we do not measure achievement, how can we know whether students have learned the material taught? However, there is disagreement about

Table 12.5
Comparison of Teacher-Built and Standardized Achievement Tests

Dimension	Teacher-Built Tests	Standardized Tests
Content coverage	Specific to class; narrow but in depth; class assignments	Common to many schools; broad, few items per topic; commonly taught material; covers several grade levels.
Items	Written by classroom teacher; various formats; seldom pretested; difficulty adaptable to class	Written by subject matter experts and professional item writers; usually alternative-choice; extensive pretesting; range of item difficulties
Forms	Usually only one	Usually equivalent forms
Administration	When needed	Generally once a year
Scores	Raw scores, grades	Percentile ranks, standard scores, grade-equivalent scores
Norms	Compare within class	National samples and subsamples (e.g., by type school, geographic region)
Reliability	Seldom estimated	Equivalent forms, internal consistency; generally quite high
Validity	Content validity, compared to goals for class	Content validity, compared to test plan
Uses	Grading; pretesting; formative evaluation; plan instruction	Growth from year to year; comparisons beyond class; diagnosis and identification of special needs; evaluating teachers and methods; research; placement and selection

how achievement should be measured. Standardized achievement tests have been the target of much criticism, even to the point where one national educational association has gone on record in favor of a moratorium on the use of standardized achievement tests in the schools.

In this section we shall consider some issues in the use of standardized achievement tests. Several other issues, such as the effects of coaching, that also apply to achievement testing will be discussed in Chapters 13 and 14.

Reliance on Alternative-Choice Items.   One set of criticisms revolves around the fact that standardized achievement tests rely, almost exclusively, on alternative-choice items. Critics (e.g., Hoffmann, 1961, 1962; Taylor, 1977; Wheeler, 1979) point out that not only do multiple-choice items fail to measure certain important skills (for example, integration, evaluation, and creativity), but that the item format also has certain imperfections (for example, items may be ambiguous or penalize students with a greater depth of knowledge). The conclusion of many of these critics seems to be that multiple-choice questions should be replaced by a better type of item. What this new type of item would be often is not clear; presumably it would be some form of a free response item.

There are several possible replies to this criticism. For one, it is not feasible to conduct a large-scale testing program using free response items because of the scoring problems (both time, and thus money, and scorer unreliability). Second, there is the learning-testing distinction mentioned earlier. It is clear that the results of learning can be assessed by methods different from the method used when learning. Therefore, if the goal of testing is to measure what a student knows or can do, there is no reason why the test must involve the same procedures as the learning process. Critics who point out that the multiple-choice approach cannot produce certain desired learnings may be correct; however, it does not follow that the results of some of these learning experiences cannot be assessed with objective tests. Third, in some cases, other types of items are used. For example, the CEEB Admission Testing Program has included a writing sample and the Advanced Placement Examinations utilize essay questions. These are exceptions because, as mentioned above, scoring problems are ubiquitous.

Norm-Referenced and Content-Referenced Tests.   Many proponents of a particular type of testing give the impression that test users must choose between norm-referenced and content-referenced tests—that there is no middle ground. Advocates of norm-referenced tests (e.g., Ebel, 1969, 1972, 1979, 1980) argue that what counts in most situations is relative achievement and thus tests should be designed to rank order students in terms of their relative achievement. Advocates of content-referenced tests (e.g., Bloom et al., 1971, 1980; Popham, 1973, 1981) argue that tests should indicate what students know or do not know and what they can or cannot do, and that this information can be obtained only from content-referenced tests.

I would hope by now that you realize that I think this is a false issue. Each type of test has its appropriate and inappropriate uses (Mehrens & Ebel, 1979). For competitive decisions, such as selection, and for comparing various groups or programs, norm-referenced tests are generally better. For making diagnoses and day-to-day instructional decisions, content-referenced tests are generally better. Needless to say, with either class of tests there are both good and bad tests. Test users must decide how they want to use a test and what type of tests will best suit their purposes, then select the best test from among the various possibilities.

Testing and the Curricula.   Another set of issues revolves around the questions of whether standardized tests determine the curricula and whether teachers teach to tests. This view presumes that teachers will be evaluated in terms of their students' performance. Thus, to make themselves look good, teachers will "teach to the test," stressing the materials that they know (or presume) will be covered on the test and neglecting other equally important materials. Although some teachers, no doubt, try to teach toward tests, the incidence of such behavior is unknown but probably overestimated. In addition, the evidence from coaching studies would indicate that such attempts to influence scores are likely to be unsuccessful.

Note also that this view assumes that the test measures outcomes other than the important outcomes of education. In fact, one sometimes hears that standardized tests are worthless because they measure what test publishers are interested in, not what educators say are the important outcomes. Such arguments only betray the ignorance of their proponents because, as was mentioned earlier, the content of achievement batteries is determined by subject matter experts, not psychologists and test specialists. And, although test publishers may claim that their tests reflect classroom practices, they may, in fact, lead classroom practices. If they lead, then, in effect, they do determine curricula. But the overriding issue is not whether tests lead or follow classroom practices but whether the test content reflects important educational outcomes.

Bias. Finally, we once again consider the question of bias. Are standardized achievement tests biased against certain groups or individuals? Here, as usual when discussing bias, the answer depends on how we define bias. If we think of bias as occurring whenever all students have not had equal opportunity to learn the material covered on the test, then there are situations in which tests will be biased. Since standardized achievement tests cover material that is commonly taught, some students will not have been exposed to the material covered. These include not only members of some minority groups but also students in schools where the material has not been taught or stressed.

If the material covered on the test has been taught, but members of several groups obtain different average scores, the implications are less clear-cut. Adopting our previous view that group differences are not sufficient to establish bias, we would have to look beyond differences in scores for two groups, and consider the item content and student abilities before concluding that the test was biased. In either instance the test scores still indicate the test taker's mastery or relative achievement as compared with that of other students. The implications drawn from the scores might differ, however, particularly if students in the various groups differed widely in their background or previous instruction.

summary

Standardized achievement tests differ from teacher-built tests in that they are constructed to meet more detailed content specifications, use standardized procedures for administration and scoring, and provide normative data and other methods for interpreting scores. The various types of standardized achievement tests can be classified in many ways—for example, by content area, grade level, or potential uses. They may be either norm-referenced or content-referenced.

They are usually constructed by test publishing firms, with items written by subject matter experts and professional item writers. The first step is to prepare a detailed list of test specifications, covering both the test content and the format of the items. A large pool of items is written and items are then subjected to extensive tryout and analysis. The best items are combined into one or more forms of the test. Care is taken to ensure that the tests meet acceptable standards of reliability and validity and a variety of normative data are collected. Test manuals and other interpretive materials are provided, both to describe the test construction process and to aid in the administration, interpretation, and use of the test.

There are various types of standardized achievement tests. Some are survey tests, which provide an overall index of a student's command of a content area. Some survey tests (specific-subject tests) cover one course or area; others are batteries covering a half-dozen or more content areas. Other types of standardized achievement tests include placement tests, diagnostic tests, readiness tests, and proficiency tests.

Standardized tests can be used for both formative and summative evaluations. Formative evaluations are made during the process of instruction and indicate how learning and instruction are progressing. Summative evaluations occur at the end of instruction and are used to evaluate learning or the quality of instruction.

Standardized achievement tests have several possible uses in the instructional process. They can be used to select students for courses or programs and to place students in appropriate courses or tracks. They can be used to describe what students know and thus plan instruction accordingly. They can be used to identify students with special needs, both those having learning problems and those with special talents. In a longer-range view, they provide information that can be used in educational and vocational planning and guidance.

They can also be used to measure the outcomes of learning: to see how much learning has occurred, for grading, and for establishing proficiency in a course or on a specific skill. When appropriate cautions are observed, they can be used to evaluate instructional methods or materials, curricula, instructors, and educational programs. Finally, they are often used in studies of the instructional process.

Although most people agree that measuring achievement is an essential part of the educational process, there is less agreement as to the proper role of standardized achievement tests. Common criticisms are that standardized achievement tests rely almost exclusively on alternative-choice items (thus do not measure some important skills), that they may determine what is taught, that items may be biased, and that norm-referenced achievement tests are sometimes used in situations where content-referenced tests would provide better information.

Suggestions for Further Reading

Airasian, P. W. A perspective on the uses and misuses of standardized achievement tests. *NCME Measurement in Education,* 1979, *10*(3). A brief description of the criticisms and misuses of standardized achievement tests with suggestions for proper uses in educational settings.

Breland, H. M. Can multiple-choice tests measure writing skills? *College Board Review,* 1977, *103,* 11–13, 32–33. Presents evidence to show that multiple-choice items can assess writing skills.

Breland, H. M., & Gaynor, J. L. A comparison of direct and indirect assessments of writing skill. *Journal of Educational Measurement,* 1979, *16,* 119–128. An empirical study comparing writing samples with multiple-choice items to assess writing ability; suggests both approaches should be used.

Bunda, M. A., & Sanders, J. R. (Eds.). *Practices and problems in competency-based measurement.* Washington, D.C.: National Council on Measurement in Education, 1979. A series of papers reviewing the current status of competency-based programs and the issues in measuring competency.

Green, B. F., Jr. In defense of measurement. *American Psychologist,* 1978, *33,* 664–670. A reply to critics and a defense of the use of multiple-choice items to measure achievement.

Harnischfeger, A., & Wiley, D. E. Achievement test scores drop. So what? *Educational Researcher,* 1976, *5*(3), 5–12. Review of the evidence on the decline in achievement test scores, discussion of suggested reasons for the drop, and discussion of some unanswered questions.

Jaeger, R. M., & Tittle, C. K. (Eds.). *Minimum competency achievement testing.* Berkeley, Calif.: McCutchan, 1980. A series of articles by both supporters and critics of the minimum competency movement, as well as reactions from people in various disciplines; a thorough, balanced presentation of the issues.

Madaus, G. F., Airasian, P. W., & Kellaghan, T. *School effectiveness: A reassessment of the evidence.* New York: McGraw-Hill, 1980. An excellent discussion of the data and problems in using tests to measure the effectiveness of schools, including suggestions for appropriate methods of assessment.

Martin, W. H. National Assessment of Educational Progress. *New Directions for Testing and Measurement,* 1979, *2,* 45–67. A good introduction to the National Assessment; describes the design of the project and discusses some illustrative results.

Mehrens, W. A., & Lehmann, I. J. *Standardized tests in education,* 3d ed. New York: Holt, Rinehart and Winston, 1980. A good introduction to the use of standardized tests in education; discusses problems and how to use achievement tests and describes many commonly used tests.

Schrader, W. B. (Ed.). *Measuring achievement: Progress over a decade. New Directions for Testing and Measurement,* 1980, *5*. A series of papers on current thinking about and approaches to the measurement of achievement.

Thorndike, R. L. (Ed.). *Educational measurement,* 2d ed. Washington, D.C.: American Council on Education, 1971. The most comprehensive discussion of measurement in education covering test design and construction, psychometric considerations, and uses of tests; individual chapters written by experts in specific areas.

Chapter 13 • Measures of General Mental Ability

HAVING described teacher-built and standardized achievement tests, we now turn to ability and aptitude tests. In this chapter we shall discuss measures of general mental ability, what most people refer to as intelligence tests. In the following chapter we shall discuss measures of more specific aptitudes and abilities. We shall not maintain any fine distinction between aptitude and ability, since the measurement procedures are quite similar. For example, at the operational level both types of tests often contain similar content and use similar item formats. They differ primarily in use: ability tests describe current status and aptitude tests predict future performance.

In this chapter we shall start by defining intelligence; we shall then describe various methods for measuring general intellectual ability—individual intelligence tests, group tests, tests for particular populations, and academic ability (scholastic aptitude) tests. The chapter will conclude with a discussion of some issues involved in the measurement of mental ability.

intelligence defined

A number of techniques have been proposed for measuring intelligence including individually administered tests, group tests, performance and nonverbal tests, and even neurophysiological measures. Because there is so much controversy over and misunderstanding of the term "intelligence," we shall present a definition of intelligence and describe some theories of intellectual structure before considering the variety of methods proposed for measuring general mental ability.

What Is Intelligence?

Intelligence is one of those terms that everyone thinks he understands yet few people can define precisely. My dictionary defines it as:

> a) the ability to learn or understand from experience; ability to acquire and maintain knowledge; mental ability. b) the ability to respond quickly and successfully to a new situation; use of the faculty of reasoning in solving problems, directing conduct, etc. effectively. (*Webster's New World Dictionary,* 1966, p. 760)

Note that this definition includes a variety of, albeit related, skills: the ability to learn or acquire knowledge, the ability to retain knowledge, reasoning ability, and the ability to respond to new situations. Note, also, that in each case intelligence is referred to as an ability, thus implying that it is a stable characteristic of the person (a trait).

Most people would probably say that this is a fairly accurate definition of intelligence. They might quibble about some aspects of the definition, or include other abilities, but, by and large, it would be satisfactory.

The same dictionary, however, includes a third definition of intelligence:

> c) in *psychology,* measured success in using these abilities to perform certain tasks. (*Webster's New World Dictionary,* 1966, p. 760)

This is a very important addition, and one that is often overlooked. Note what this part of the definition says. First, it says that intelligence is "measured success in using these abilities." What does this mean? It means that intelligence is an observable and measurable characteristic. Although we may postulate some underlying ability, we can only measure observable manifestations of the ability. That is, intelligence is indicated by the ability to perform. Perform what? Here the definition is not much help: It merely says "certain tasks." However, the implication is that only performance on certain types of tasks is considered to be a sign of intelligent behavior. The discussion in this chapter will further define the nature of these tasks. For the present we shall only say that the tasks are selected because they represent behaviors many people agree are signs of intelligence, because they predict criteria requiring use of intellectual abilities (e.g., academic success), and/or because they meet certain statistical and theoretical criteria (e.g., increase with age).

Why, then, is there so much controversy over intelligence tests? One reason is that people do not agree on what tasks should be considered as indications of intelligence. For example, intelligence tests have been criticized because they emphasize convergent rather than divergent thinking. This argument is true, but it misses the point. The fact that intelligence tests do not measure creative abilities does not imply that creative abilities are unimportant; it only indicates that they must be measured by other types of instruments.

Another reason for disagreement is the confusion between the measured performance and the (hypothetical) underlying ability. Most people think of intelligence as a basic characteristic of a person, one that is the cause of behavior. However, psychologists prefer not to think in this manner. They prefer to view intelligence as a description of the person's level of performance on certain types of tasks, not as a causal agent.

To summarize, intelligence is the ability to perform certain defined types of tasks. Or, as phrased in a frequently used definition: "Intelligence is what an intelligence test measures." Thus, scores on intelligence tests are nothing more than descriptions of a person's level of performance on the set of tasks measured by the test. To the psychologist, intelligence is a descriptive label, not an underlying characteristic or entity that causes other behavior.

Theories of Intellectual Structure

Given this definition, there is still the question of how intellectual abilities are structured and organized. For example, is intelligence a unitary ability reflected in performance on various types of intellectual tasks? Or can intelligence better be conceptualized as a small number of broad, but relatively independent abilities? Or is intelligence composed of a large number of quite specific and distinct abilities?

The development of a theory of intellectual structure has occupied the attention of a number of psychologists. Their attack has been both empirical and theoretical, but generally has been closely connected with intelligence testing and has utilized factor analysis as the primary research technique. To give a flavor of the various approaches, précis of several historically interesting and currently fashionable models are presented below.

General Intelligence Theories.   The simplest approach is to postulate that intelligence is a unitary ability, a single general capacity. This view holds that although intelligence may be expressed in diverse fashions or may be directed toward a variety of activities, basically it is a single ability. Any test that provides a single score (IQ) is, at least in a broad sense, representing a unifactor theory.

One type of general intelligence model is that of Spearman, who proposed a two-factor theory. The first factor was a general capacity or mental energy factor, which was basically a reasoning factor. In addition to this general factor (labeled *g*), each specific test was presumed to measure skills that were specific to that particular test. (see Figure 13.1a). Thus, although it assigns primary importance to the general factor, the theory does recognize that other specific factors (and even other general factors) must be considered. The implication for measuring intelligence, however, is that the best test would be one saturated with general intelligence.

Group Factors.   This approach assumes that intelligence can be represented by a relatively small number of fairly broad common factors (see Figure 13.1b). Although the exact abilities (group factors) found in any specific study depend upon several variables (such as the tests used, the nature of the sample tested, and the method of analysis), the following factors have appeared with some regularity and have been confirmed by several investigators:

Space. The ability to visualize geometric patterns in space
Perceptual speed. Quick and accurate noting of details
Number. Quickness and accuracy in simple arithmetic computations
Verbal comprehension. Knowing the meaning of, and relationships between, words
Word fluency. Ability to use many words
Memory. Immediate recall of rote materials
Induction. Ability to extract rules

To measure intellectual ability, therefore, one would administer a battery of tests, each of which measured one of the factors.

Guilford's Structure-of-Intellect Model.   A quite different model has been proposed by Guilford (1956, 1959, 1966, 1967, 1968) who conceived of intellectual functioning having three dimensions: operations, contents, and products (see

Figure 13.1 Models of Intellectual Structure. (a) General intelligence model. (b) Group factors model. (c) Structure-of-intellect model. (d) Hierarchical model.

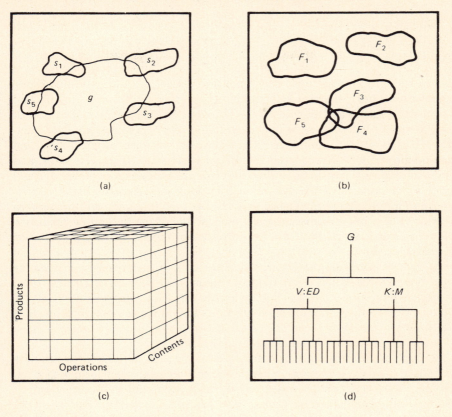

(a)

(b)

(c)

(d)

Sources: (c) Guilford, 1967; (d) Vernon, 1971.

Figure 13.1c). Operations are the processes involved in intellectual behavior: cognition, memory, divergent thinking, convergent thinking, and evaluation. The contents of these operations may be figural, symbolic, semantic, or behavioral, and the products may be units, classes, relations, systems, transformations, or implications. Thus the model contains 120 cells (5 operations × 4 contents × 6 products), each of which represents a distinct factor that is measured by a separate test. For example, in Guilford's scheme, the verbal comprehension factor (vocabulary) becomes the ability to cognize semantic units.

Vernon's Hierarchical Theory.   Both the group factors and Guilford's model conceive of intelligence as being composed of a number of relatively independent abilities. We could then ask whether these various abilities are all on the same level of generality or whether some are more comprehensive or include others. The latter approach would view intellectual structure as a hierarchy, extending from broad general factors (general intelligence), through group factors, to more and more specific factors. For example, Vernon (1971) has proposed a model (see Figure 13.1d) in which general ability (g) is at the apex of the hierarchy. This general factor is subdivided into two major group factors—a verbal-educational (V:ED) factor and a practical-mechanical (K:M) one. Each of these categories is further subdivided into group factors and then into more and more specific factors.

Other Approaches.   There are still other approaches to a theory of intellectual structure. For example, Cattell (1963, 1968) and Horn (1967) have suggested that intelligence can better be viewed as consisting of two general factors: fluid intelligence and crystallized intelligence. Crystallized intelligence has a heavy cultural component and is best measured by tests of vocabulary, numerical skills, and general and specific information. Fluid intelligence involves more perceptual and performance skills. Since the relative contributions of fluid and crystallized intelligence to intellectual performance vary from person to person and situation to situation, and by developmental level, the stability of intellectual performance will depend on the role fluid and crystallized components play in the behavior measured.

Other approaches are developmental. For example, there have been attempts to develop tests based on Piaget's theory of mental development (e.g., Hunt, 1976; Uzgiris & Hunt, 1975). Yet another approach is that of Sternberg (1977, 1979, 1980) who states that theories of intelligence should measure components. By a *component* he means the cognitive processes a test taker uses in answering questions, solving problems, or operating on information.

Although models are conceptual and heuristic devices, not all test constructors have based their work on a particular theory of intellectual structure. In fact, the dominant approach has been an empirical one of attempting to predict a specific criterion with maximal accuracy. Thus, tests of scholastic aptitude have been developed not in accord with a prevailing theory of intellectual structure, but by including skills that previous research has shown to be predictive of academic success.

individual intelligence tests

Throughout the twentieth century, attempts to measure intellectual ability (intelligence) have played a preeminent role in psychological testing (A. J. Edwards, 1971; Goslin, 1963). In earlier years the idea of general intelligence held forth; more recently attention has focused on the variety of intellectual abilities. However, measures of general intellectual ability are still widely used and, in spite of their theoretical deficiencies, have shown practical utility (A. J. Edwards, 1975; McNemar, 1964). Thus, we shall describe the most important individual intelligence tests, the *Stanford-Binet Intelligence Scale* and the various Wechsler intelligence scales.

The Stanford-Binet Intelligence Scale

The Stanford-Binet Intelligence Scale is the healthiest surviving direct descendent of Binet's original scale. Binet originally developed his test to identify slow learners in Paris schools. Using a definition of intelligent behavior that stressed the ability to take and maintain a definite direction or set, the capacity to adapt in order to obtain a given end, and the power of self-criticism, he developed a test that was first published in 1905. Three aspects were of greatest import: using complex tasks as test items, using age standards, and measuring general mental development rather than separate mental faculties.

Early Forms. As the test became popular, several attempts were made to translate the test and adapt it for American usage. Terman's version, first published in 1916, and known as the Stanford-Binet, was most successful. Terman's test was an extension and improvement on Binet's scale and, in many respects, uses Binet's scale only as a point of departure. The 1916 version was important for several reasons: It was the first test to provide detailed administrative and scoring instructions; the IQ was used; and representative normative data were provided.

In the 1937 revision, two forms of the test were constructed—L and M. Each form covered the age range from 2 years to adult and was standardized on more than 3000 children (ages 1½–18). Selection of items was based on three criteria: The item measured behavior considered intelligent; the percentage of children passing the item increased rapidly with age; and the mean mental age of children passing and failing the item differed significantly. The 1937 revision was undoubtedly the best measure of intellectual ability available, but it suffered several technical limitations in the composition of standardization sample and the IQ distribution. The test was also heavily loaded with verbal materials and the administrative procedure was time-consuming.

Another revision was made in 1960. Rather than constructing an entirely new test, the authors decided to update the items and restandardize the test (Terman & Merrill, 1960).

In 1972 the test was again restandardized (Terman & Merrill, 1973). In this revision the test content was not changed. The new normative sample consisted of approximately 2100 children tested in 1971–72; 100 in each half-year age range for ages 2.5–5 and 100 for each age from 6 to 18. One interesting finding was that scores tended to be higher than those obtained in previous standardizations.

Form L–M. Items[1] on Form L–M are grouped into 20 age levels. At the youngest age levels (ages 2 through 5) there is a separate set of items for each six months; from age 5 through 14, there is a set of items for each year. In addition, there is an Average Adult plus three Superior Adult levels. At each level, except Average Adult, there are six subtests plus an alternate subtest. A given subtest may appear at only one age level or occur at several age levels, with different levels of proficiency being required for passing at different age levels. For example, the Vocabulary subtest appears at age levels VI, VIII, X, XII, XIV plus the four adult levels. At age 6, successfully defining six words constitutes success; at the Superior Adult III level, 30 of the 45 items must be correctly defined in order to pass the subtest.

The composition of the test can best be appreciated by actual study of the test items. To give a flavor of the items, Table 13.1 briefly describes the items at four

---

[1] We shall use the term "item" to describe the tasks on the Stanford-Binet even though some tasks consist of more than one item.

Table 13.1
Examples of Items on the Stanford-Binet Intelligence Scale

AGE II
1. Three-Hole Form Board. Placing three geometric objects in form board.
2. Delayed Response. Identifying placement of hidden object after 10-second delay.
3. Identifying Parts of Body. Pointing out features on paper doll.
4. Block Building Tower. Building four-block tower by imitating examiner's procedure.
5. Picture Vocabulary. Naming common objects from pictures.
6. Word Combinations. Spontaneous combination on two words.

AGE VI
1. Vocabulary. Correctly defining six words on 45-word list.
2. Differences. Telling difference between two objects.
3. Mutilated Pictures. Pointing out missing part of pictured object.
4. Number Concepts. Counting number of blocks in a pile.
5. Opposite Analogies II. Items of form "Summer is hot; winter is_____."
6. Maze Tracing. Finding shortest path in simple maze.

AGE X
1. Vocabulary. Correctly defining 11 words on same list.
2. Block Counting. Counting number of cubes in three-dimensional picture, some cubes hidden.
3. Abstract Words I. Definition of abstract adverbs.
4. Finding Reasons I. Giving reasons for laws or preferences.
5. Word Naming. Naming as many words as possible in one minute.
6. Repeating Six Digits. Repeating six digits in order.

AVERAGE ADULT
1. Vocabulary. 20 words correct.
2. Ingenuity I. Algebraic word problems involving mental manipulation of volumes.
3. Differences between Abstract Words. Differentiating between two related abstract words.
4. Arithmetical Reasoning. Word problems involving simple computations.
5. Proverbs I. Giving meaning of proverbs.
6. Orientation: Direction II. Finding orientation after a verbal series of changes in directions.
7. Essential Differences. Giving principle difference between two related concepts.
8. Abstract Words III. Meanings of abstract adverbs.

age levels. Some of the distinct features of the test can be noted from this sample of items. Note that at Age II the test items involve sensorimotor skills, the ability to follow directions, and identification of objects and parts of the body; verbal and language skills play a minor role. By Age VI the tests are heavily weighted with verbal skills (Vocabulary, Analogies, Differences), and discriminations (Differences, Mutilated Pictures) and numerical concepts begin to appear. Age X again emphasizes verbal skills, but many of the items now involve abstract concepts rather than relying on concrete experience (as at Age VI). By the Average Adult level the test materials are almost entirely verbal, symbolic, and abstract.

The Stanford-Binet must be administered individually and, because of the complexity of the testing procedures, requires a trained examiner. Testing begins at the age level at which the child is likely to succeed, but not without some effort. Typically this will be the age level immediately lower than the child's chronological age. Explicit directions for administering the items (for example, the exact wording to be used) are provided in the manual. The testing proceeds until every set of items from the age level at which all items are completed successfully (the basal age) through the age at which all items are failed have been administered. Because testings continue until these limits are reached, the testing sessions are often quite long—frequently an hour and a half or longer.

Scores.   Each response is compared to a list of correct responses given in the test manual. Scoring is all-or-none for each item, with no partial credit. Each correct answer is given a certain number of months' credit. These credits, when added to the basal age, give the test taker's *mental age*.

There are two distinct, though related, ways of interpreting performance on the Stanford-Binet. The mental age gives an indication of the test taker's level of intellectual development. The mental age can be considered a type of content-referenced score since it indicates the type and complexity of tasks the child can perform. For example, a child with a mental age of 5 would be expected to be able to define simple words, identify parts of the body, fold a piece of paper into a triangle, draw an acceptable square, and note similarities and differences between common objects.

The *intelligence quotient* (IQ), in contrast, is a norm-referenced score. It indicates the child's relative rate of intellectual development compared to his or her agemates. On the Stanford-Binet, IQs are deviation IQs with a mean of 100 and a standard deviation of 16 IQ points at each age level. The higher the IQ (above 100), the more accelerated the intellectual development compared to children of the same age; the lower the IQ, the more delayed the development.

Consistency and Validity.   Data from extensive studies of Form L and M indicated that the coefficient of equivalence was generally .90 or higher with children aged 5 or older; other studies have shown test-retest reliabilities of similar magnitude (see A. J. Edwards, 1972). These levels of reliability can be translated in a standard error of measurement of approximately 5 IQ points. In general, reliability is higher for older than younger children and for children having lower rather than higher IQs. The method of item selection, requiring each item to correlate with the total score, assures that the test will be homogeneous. And, of course, the method of deriving IQs assures that the average level of performance will remain constant from year to year.

Since the Binet can most appropriately be viewed as a sign of intelligent behavior, construct validity becomes the central issue. Here several lines of evidence are relevant. The authors state that intelligent behavior is exhibited in the solution of problems such as analogies, opposites, vocabulary, comprehension, similarities and differences, absurdities, completion of verbal and pictorial materials, and memory for rote and meaningful materials. Thus, there is an implicit definition of the content universe sampled, one that is heavily weighted with verbal reasoning abilities. The item selection criteria (age differentiation, internal consistency) also serve to define the construct of intelligence. Second, factor analyses have shown that performance on the Stanford-Binet reflects a general factor, verbal reasoning, but that other abilities (for example, memory, perception) influence performance at certain age levels. Third, criterion-related validity studies have shown that Stanford-Binet IQs correlate with a variety of measures of academic accomplishment (for example, grades, years of education, teachers' ratings, achievement test scores) and that the correlations are usually slightly higher for verbal areas (for example, English, history, reading) than for mathematics and science areas.

In short, the Stanford-Binet is a good measure of the intellectual abilities, particularly verbal abilities, of school-age children. Because of its technical quality, plus its historical importance, it has come to serve as *the* standard for measuring intelligence, the standard against which all other purported measures of intelligence must be calibrated. Thus the strengths and limitations of the Stanford-Binet approach to measuring intelligence are, to a considerable extent, reflected in many other instruments.

The Wechsler Intelligence Scales

Although it can be used to measure adult intelligence, the item content and normative data on the Stanford-Binet are more appropriate for children. Thus, in 1939 David Wechsler published a test designed specifically to measure adult intelligence, the *Wechsler-Bellevue Intelligence Scale.* In 1955 this scale was modified and restandardized as the *Wechsler Adult Intelligence Scale* (WAIS). Recently, the WAIS was further modified and restandardized, with a revised edition (the WAIS-R) being published in 1981. Two other forms of the test, for younger age ranges, have also been published: the *Wechsler Intelligence Scale for Children,* revised edition (WISC-R) for ages 6 to 16, and the *Wechsler Preschool and Primary Scale of Intelligence* (WPPSI) for ages 4 to 6.5.

By defining intelligence as "the aggregate or global capacity of the individual to act purposefully, to think rationally, and to deal effectively with his environment" (Wechsler, 1958, p. 7), Wechsler adopts a general intelligence approach. This view is supported by the statement that the subtests are "different measures of intelligence, not measures of different kinds of intelligence" (1958, p. 64). Yet, paradoxically, Wechsler also stresses using the test as a diagnostic instrument by using patterns of subtest scores as a basis for making inferences about the individual's intellectual and emotional status. Although the IQ is viewed as "a comprehensive statement about the person's overall intellectual functioning ability" (1958, p. 156), an index of relative brightness compared to age peers, Wechsler also says that intelligence is not the mere sum of abilities tapped by the various subtests. Rather it is the configuration of abilities plus motivational and personality factors that produce intelligent behavior.

We shall first describe the various Wechsler scales, then contrast them with the Stanford-Binet.

The Wechsler Adult Intelligence Scale. The revised edition of the WAIS, the WAIS-R, consists of 11 subtests. Six tests (Information, Comprehension, Arithmetic, Similarities, Digit Span, and Vocabulary) form the *Verbal Scale;* the other five (Digit Symbol, Picture Completion, Block Design, Picture Arrangement, and Object Assembly) comprise the *Performance Scale.* All 11 tests make up the *Full Scale* (see Table 13.2).

TABLE 13.2
Description of WAIS-R Subtests

VERBAL SCALE

Information: 29 items that measure the range of the examinee's knowledge and retention of learned materials, and assess the examinee's cultural background. Items are of the form 'Where does wool come from?" and "Who wrote Paradise Lost?"

Comprehension: 16 items measuring judgment and "common sense." Includes translation of proverbs and items of form "Why should children be warned against playing with matches?"

Arithmetic: 14 items testing concentration, arithmetic ability, and problem-solving skill. All items have time limits and are simple word problems; for example, "If I have $15 and earn $8 more, how much money do I now have?"

Similarities: 14 items measuring logical thinking and conceptual ability; a good measure of general intelligence. Items are of the form "In what way are a car and a boat alike?"

Digit Span: Tests attention and immediate memory by items requiring examinee to repeat series of digits either forward or backwards.

Vocabulary: 35 words of varying difficulty. Is the best single index of Full-Scale IQ; indicates range of knowledge and cultural background.

PERFORMANCE SCALE.

Digit Symbol: Measures flexibility and ability for new learning through a task requiring the substitution of symbols for numbers. Speeded.

Picture Completion: 20 items that require examinee to tell what is missing in a picture of a common object. Measures perceptual ability, particularly ability to differentiate essential from unessential details.

Block Design: Examinee reproduces designs with colored blocks. Measures ability to analyze and organize. Good test for observing problem-solving strategy as well as distorted perception and visual-motor coordination. Generally considered best single performance test. Time limits. 9 items.

Picture Arrangement: Requires examinee to arrange a group of pictures (similar to comic strip panels) to tell a coherent story. Measures ability to comprehend a total situation. Bonus points for rapid solutions. 10 items.

Object Assembly: Task is to assemble pieces of a puzzle to form a common object. Speeded. Tests perceptual ability and persistence. 4 items.

Within each subtest, items are arranged and administered in order of difficulty, with testing being discontinued after a prescribed number of consecutive failures. Some items have time limits; others are untimed. As with the Stanford-Binet, the WAIS is individually administered and requires a trained examiner, and instructions for administration and scoring are spelled out in detail in the manual. The testing session is generally shorter than on the Binet, usually lasting 45 to 60 minutes.

Items are scored by comparing the response to a list of acceptable response variations given in the manual.[2] Points are assigned on the basis of correctness

[2] See Figure 2.3.

and, on several tests, speed of response. On some tests, differing number of points are awarded depending on the quality of the response. Thus, in contrast to the age scale approach of the Binet, the WAIS is a *point scale* (as are the other Wechsler scales).

Raw scores on each subtest are converted to standard scores ($\overline{X} = 10$ and $s = 3$ points). Subtest standard scores are then summed and converted into three IQ scores: a Verbal IQ, a Performance IQ, and a Full Scale IQ. Since test performance decreases with age, IQs are computed separately for several age groups;[3] hence, IQs indicate relative standing among age peers. The IQs are deviation IQs with $\overline{X} = 100$ and $s = 15$ (cf. the Stanford-Binet IQ), derived from a normative sample that, in essence, was a cross section of the U.S. adult population.

The Wechsler Intelligence Scale for Children. The *Wechsler Intelligence Scale for Children* (WISC) was an extension , to lower age levels, of the Wechsler-Bellevue. The format of the WISC is similar to the adult scales, and only one WISC subtest (Mazes) did not appear on the adult form. Many of the WISC scales were constructed by adding easier items to the adult scale and eliminating some of the more difficult items.

In 1974 a revised version of the WISC (the WISC-R) was published. As with the Stanford-Binet, this revision was more of a restandardization than a massive change. The same subtests were retained, but some items were revised and others were replaced with new items. A more representative normative sample was used for computing IQs. Perhaps the major change was shifting the age range; the WISC is now designed for children of ages 6 through 16.

As typically administered, the WISC-R consists of five Verbal tests (Information, Similarities, Arithmetic, Vocabulary, Comprehension) and five Performance tests (Picture Completion, Picture Arrangement, Block Design, Object Assembly, and Coding). Two additional tests, Digit Span and Mazes, can be used in certain situations.

The Wechsler Preshool and Primary Scale of Intelligence In 1967 another Wechsler scale, the *Preschool and Primary Scale of Intelligence* (WPPSI) was published. This test is designed for use at ages 4–6½, when the child is beginning formal schooling and accurate measures of intelligence may play an important part in many critical educational decisions. The format and subtests are quite similar to the WISC, but certain changes have been made (for example, including more nonverbal tasks) to make the test appropriate for preschoolers. In fact, about half of the WPPSI items also appear on the WISC. The goal of the WPPSI, however, is to include only items particularly appropriate to the 4–6½-year age range so that an accurate estimate of the child's intelligence can be made.

Consistency and Validity. When evaluating the psychometric properties of the Wechsler scales, one could ask a number of questions, among the most important

---

[3] On the WAIS-R, normative data are available for the following age ranges: 16–17, 18–19, 20–24, 25–34, 35–44, 45–54, 55–64, 65–69, and 70–74 (Wechsler, 1981).

of which are: How reliable are the various IQ scores? How reliable are the subtest scores? Is use of separate Verbal and Performance IQs justified? Can subtest scores be used for diagnoses? What evidence is there for the validity of the test? How adequate are the normative data?

Both the WISC-R and WAIS-R are highly reliable instruments. The average (over various age groups) split-half reliability coefficients for Verbal, Performance, and Full Scale IQs are over .90, with the full scale reliabilities being about .95; the Verbal IQs are slightly more reliable than the Performance IQs. Stability coefficients over short periods (two to seven weeks) are also .90 or above. Scores on the subtests, as might be expected, are less reliable, generally falling between .70 and .85 with WAIS-R coefficients generally being higher than WISC-R coefficients. The standard errors of measurement are about 3 points for the Verbal and Full Scale IQs and 4 points for the Performance IQ.

Various lines of evidence can be used to support the validity of the Wechsler IQs. Items were selected for inclusion by studying previous tests to determine what sorts of items best measured intelligent behavior, from clinical experience, and by trying out experimental items on groups having known characteristics. Wechsler has also presented a detailed justification of including each subtest as a measure of intelligence (Wechsler, 1955). Such procedures support the content and construct validity of the WAIS subtests. Factor analysis data are more complex. Sometimes a general factor is found; other analyses identify three factors: verbal comprehension, perceptual organization, and reasoning.

The manuals also provide data on the correlation between the Verbal, Performance, and Full Scale IQs and between scores on the individual subtests and Verbal, Performance, and Full Scale IQs. These data are reported for each age range and also as averages across age ranges. We shall consider only the latter. The average Verbal-Performance IQ correlation is .67 for the WISC-R and .74 for the WAIS-R, indicating that the Verbal and Performance tests do measure different sets of abilities (they share about half of their variance in common). The correlations between individual subtests and Verbal, Performance, and Full Scale IQs tend to be in the .50s and low .60s, although they range from as low as .33 (between Coding and the Performance IQ on the WISC-R) to as high as .85 (between Vocabulary and Verbal IQ on the WAIS-R). Several trends are apparent: Subtests correlate higher with their corresponding scale than with the other scale (i.e., verbal subtests correlate higher with Verbal than with Performance IQ); verbal subtests tend to have higher correlations with IQs than performance subtests; the Vocabulary subtest has a higher correlation with Verbal and Full Scale IQs than other verbal tests; and the Block Design subtest has higher correlations with Performance and Full Scale IQs than the other performance tests. Stated differently, Vocabulary and Block Design seem to be the most valid verbal and performance subtests, respectively. These data must be carefully considered when using the tests for diagnostic purposes since they provide the basis for determining whether observed performance differences are, in fact, significant or just reflect errors of measurement.

The standardization samples for each test seem to have been carefully chosen to represent a cross section of the American public (for the appropriate age range). The WISC-R standardization sample consisted of 2200 children stratified by age, sex, race, geographic region, parental occupation, and urban/rural residence. The standardization sample for the WAIS-R consisted of 1880 adults stratified by age, sex, race, geographic region, occupation, education, and urban/rural residence. Most samples contained at least 100 persons of each sex at each age level.

The Wechsler Scales and the Stanford-Binet. Although both the Wechsler and the Stanford-Binet are individually administered intelligence tests, there are a number of major differences between the two scales: (1) The Wechsler tests are arranged and administered by subtests; the Binet by age levels. (2) The Wechsler tests include both verbal and performance tasks; the Binet is heavily verbal in content. (3) The Wechsler scales provide three IQs—Verbal, Performance, and Full Scale—plus subtest scores; the Binet provides one overall IQ plus a mental age score. (4) The Binet is designed primarily for children of ages 2 to 18, but can be administered to adults; the WAIS was designed for adults (age 15 and over), but scales have been developed for children—the WISC-R for ages 6–16 and the WPPSI for ages 4 – 6½. (5) The Wechsler scales are point scales; the Stanford-Binet an age scale. (6) All subjects are administered identical subtests on the Wechsler scales; on the Stanford-Binet the content varies depending upon the age level. (7) The Wechsler scales are more adaptable to diagnostic uses.

The correlation between IQs on Wechsler and Stanford-Binet scales varies with the particular sample and age range used. The WISC-R manual (Wechsler, 1974) reports data showing the average correlation with Stanford-Binet IQs (over four age ranges) was .71 for Verbal IQs, .60 for Performance IQs , and .73 for the Full-Scale IQ; some studies have found slightly higher correlations. Thus, the relationship between scores on the two tests is relatively high but far from perfect.

Uses of Individual Intelligence Tests

Scores on individual intelligence tests provide an indication of a person's level of general intellectual functioning. Most frequently this information is useful when working with people at the ends of the intelligence distribution. For example, at the lower end, scores are often used as one basis for placement in special education classes or other programs for the mentally retarded. At the upper end of the distribution, scores are used to determine whether children should be accelerated educationally or be placed in programs for gifted children.

Scores can also be used for diagnostic purposes. Because the tests are administered individually, the examiner has ample opportunity to observe the test taker working on the tasks. Often these observations suggest hypotheses, such as brain damage, particular types of learning disabilities, or perceptual or memory problems. On the Wechsler scales, diagnoses are also made by comparing scores on the various subtests or the Verbal-Performance IQ discrepancies (Kaufman, 1979; Matarazzo, 1972). For example, a student who scores low on tests of immediate memory, such as the Digit Span or Coding, may have attention difficulties. Or a student who performs relatively poorly on Block Design may have a perceptual organization problem.

When making use of subtest score patterns in diagnosis, one has to be careful not to overinterpret small score differences. To prevent misinterpretations, the Wechsler manuals provide tables indicating how large a difference between subtest scores is needed for the difference to be statistically significant.[4] Although the exact number of points differs for various subtests, the median differences between subtests needed for significance at the 15 percent level is about 3 scale score points; for the Verbal-Performance IQ discrepancy, a significant difference is 6–7 points. Differences less than these amounts should not be considered to be significant.

As we have constantly emphasized, diagnoses or decisions should not be made from only one test or measure. Thus diagnostic information obtained from intelligence test scores should always be confirmed by other methods, either other types of tests or observations and interviews.

other approaches to the assessment of mental ability

Individual intelligence tests are the best single method of assessing intellectual functioning. However, because only one person can be tested at a time and a trained examiner is needed, they are quite costly and are inefficient when large numbers of people must be tested. Thus paper-and-pencil group intelligence tests have been developed for use when large numbers of persons must be tested. A different approach also may be needed when testing certain groups of people, such as very young children and persons having language or physical handicaps. Special types of tests have been developed for use with each of these groups.

There are also situations in which we want to measure general mental ability but have a somewhat more limited focus. The obvious example is in schools where we want to measure only those abilities needed for successful performance in academic situations, a somewhat different set of skills than measured by general intelligence tests. Such tests, called *academic ability* or *scholastic aptitude tests,* will be discussed in the next section.

Group Intelligence Tests

The original stimulus for the development of group intelligence tests was World War I, when the United States was faced with the task of mobilizing and organizing millions of men in a short time. Two tasks in particular, the screening out of men whose mental limitations made them unfit for military service and the identification of potential officer candidates, seemed to be appropriate areas for application of techniques of the then developing field of mental testing. However, use of the available methods for assessing intelligence, individually administered tests like Stanford-Binet, was obviously not feasible. Fortunately a psychologist, Arthur Otis, was developing a group intelligence test and turned his materials over to the armed services. This material was the basis of the *Army Alpha* test, which became the grandfather of group intelligence tests.

[4] Tables show the 15 percent confidence limits for differences between individual subtests and the 15 percent and 5 percent confidence levels for Verbal-Performance IQ differences.

In the years since World War I, many intelligence tests have been developed (see DuBois, 1970a, or Goslin, 1963). Group tests share certain common features. They can be administered to groups of people, and, because of less complex procedures, a highly trained administrator generally is not required. On the other hand, the test usually is administered with a time limit, direct observation of test-taking behavior is not feasible, and certain persons—for example, young children and other persons who cannot read—cannot be tested. Group tests are usually paper-and-pencil tests and use multiple-choice items.

This latter point, the restricted range of item types, is potentially the most serious limitation. Group intelligence tests typically are composed of several types of items: vocabulary, general information, arithmetic, and reasoning. In particular, they are often heavily weighted with vocabulary items, either in the traditional form or variations such as selecting the correct word to use in a sentence or analogies items. The emphasis on vocabulary items reflects the empirical finding that vocabulary is the best single index of intelligence. General information items ("The capital city of France is _____" and "The population of the United States is _____") are included to probe the individual's range of knowledge. Arithmetic items generally involve only simple computations, certainly no more complex than basic algebra. Reasoning items may be either verbal or nonverbal analogies, number series ("What is the next number in the sequence 1, 2, 4, 7, 11, . . . ?"), or other similar items.

Although group intelligence tests were originally designed to be economical substitutes for individual tests, and are still used in this manner, several varieties of group tests have assumed an existence of their own. For example, scholastic aptitude tests are designed to predict academic success. Other group intelligence measures are also used for industrial and business screening. These tests are generally short (often requiring only 15 to 30 minutes of working time), are constructed along traditional lines, and cover only the commonest components of intellectual ability. In both of these cases, the goal of testing is accurate prediction of the criterion of interest (academic or job success) rather than a representative sampling of intellectual abilities. Scores on these tests, however, generally correlate highly with scores on individual intelligence tests.

Infant and Preschool Tests

The testing of infants and preschool children presents enough special problems to merit separate consideration. One is that, typically, children do not learn to read nor write until they are in first grade (about 6 years old). Therefore, tests requiring reading skills are obviously inappropriate for preschool children (and even of questionable appropriateness in primary grades). Furthermore, even the relatively simple task of making a mark to indicate one of several objects, which is the response format used on many tests at the primary level, may be beyond their grasp. Thus, preschool tests are usually performance tests or require the child to respond orally to orally presented questions.

The age of the examinees also presents certain administrative problems. With infants it may be necessary to observe spontaneous behavior rather than relying on responses elicited by specific stimuli (items). Young children also have short attention spans, tire easily, may be shy or refuse to interact with the examiner, may prefer to play with the test materials rather than continue with the test, are easily upset, and may otherwise exhibit erratic behavior. Because they have limited conceptions of time, speeded items are generally inappropriate. In addition, scoring of infant and preschool tests often is not objective, frequently being based on ratings derived from behavioral observations. These factors serve to underscore the need for trained and perceptive examiners. They also often result in low reliability and may even call into question the validity of the scores obtained.

Content.   Infant tests typically assess gross and fine motor control, coordinated movements, ability to communicate by speech and other modalities (e.g., gestures, facial expressions), and social responsiveness. Preschool tests typically measure perceptual and motor skills (by tasks such as block designs, copying patterns, or form boards), simple discriminations (identifying which object in a set is different), recognition of incongruities (indicating what is missing or out of place in a picture), naming parts of the body or common objects and/or indicating their function, following simple directions, and immediate memory (repeating words or digits). Some tests include simple vocabulary items, often in pictorial form. Many batteries assess psychomotor and social development as well as mental abilities.

A good example is the *Bayley Scales of Infant Development,* which is designed for children 2 to 2½ years of age. The test provides three types of scores: mental development, motor development, and a behavior record. The Mental Scale measures perceptual, learning, memory, problem solving, and verbal communication skills. The Motor Scale measures both gross motor skills (e.g., standing, walking, climbing) and ability to manipulate hands and fingers. The Behavior Record, which is based on the examiners' observation and ratings, measures emotional and social development, attention span and persistence, goal directedness, and other personality characteristics.

Developmental Scales.   Most preschool and infant tests, either explicitly or implicitly, utilize a developmental approach. That is, they include only items and tasks that typify the behavior of children at various ages and that increase with age. This has several important implications for the test construction process. Items are selected because they are typical of a particular age level and/or increase with age. Consequently, an age differentiation criterion can be used to validate the test; a valid test will be one where scores increase with age. It also places tremendous importance on obtaining representative normative data; unless the norm groups are representative of the general population, interpretations of scores will be in error. Obtaining representative samples of infants and preschool children is no easy task; too often norm groups consist of volunteers or members of special groups (e.g., children from a particular clinic or preschool program), a practice that results in unrepresentative normative data.

The emphasis on a developmental approach has also led to construction of tests based on a particular developmental theory. For example, Hunt (Hunt, 1976; Uzgiris & Hunt, 1975) has developed scales to measure aspects of Piaget's sensorimotor stage of development: visual following and object permanence, means for obtaining desired environmental events, gestural imitation, vocal imitation, construction of operational causality, construction of object relations in space, and schemas for relating to objects. Each scale consists of a number of steps (7 to 14 on the various scales) representing the sequential steps in the development of the skill measured. Because these scales measure sequential steps in development, Hunt has called them ordinal scales of infant development.

Another example of a developmentally-based test is the *McCarthy Scales of Children's Abilities*. This battery, which is designed for children aged 2½ to 8½, consists of 18 subtests which are scored on six scales. Three scales—Verbal (5 subtests), Perceptual-Performance (7 subtests), and Quantitative (3 subtests)— measure various aspects of cognitive functioning. The scores on these 15 subtests are also summed to form the General Cognitive scale. The other two scales are the Memory scale (which includes 4 subtests also included in the General Cognitive Scale) and the Motor scale (5 subtests, 2 of which are scored on the General Cognitive scale and 3 of which are not).

Because the test includes many easy items (designed for testing very young children), it can be used for identifying the strengths and weaknesses of mentally retarded children. Conversely, it can be used to identify superior abilities of young children; however, it does not have a high enough ceiling to identify superior older children. And, as a variety of subtests are included, and the examiner can observe the child completing the tasks, various types of motor, sensory, speech, and perceptual difficulties can be identified.

Nonverbal and Performance Tests

All of the tests discussed thus far in this chapter are, to a greater or lesser degree, verbal tests. That is, they required use of oral or written language in the items, the responses, and/or the directions. When testing certain groups, however, use of verbal materials may present problems. Examples include people with speech or hearing problems, people who are illiterate, people being tested in other than their native language, the very young, and the mentally retarded. When testing these groups there is a need for items that measure memory, perceptual abilities, conceptualization, thinking, and problem solving skills without relying exclusively on verbal materials.

A variety of nonverbal and performance tests have been developed to meet this need. Most utilize nonverbal tasks and responses but rely on verbal (usually spoken) directions. However, some tests have been adapted so they can be administered using pantomime directions. Among the more commonly used tasks on these tests are:

Draw-a-person tests. The test taker is instructed to draw one or more persons; scores are based on the completeness and accuracy of the drawing.
Form boards. The task is to place cut-out geometric forms in the corresponding hole in a board; usually timed.
Block designs. The test taker uses multicolored cubes to reproduce a stimulus design.

Mazes. Examinee traces the shortest path through a printed maze.

Object assembly. Similar to a jigsaw puzzle, with the examinee fitting pieces together to form an object.

Note that similar tasks are included on individual intelligence tests; for example, the WISC-R Performance scale includes block design, object assembly, and maze tests.

Another use of nonverbal and performance testing is in cross-cultural testing. Nonverbal tests are used in this situation both to minimize language differences and to ensure that the tasks will not be highly culturally loaded. Two types of tests have been widely used in cross-cultural studies: draw-a-person tests and abstract reasoning tests, such as Raven's Progressive Matrices Test (see Chapter 10).

Although scores on nonverbal and performance tests generally have moderately high correlations with more verbal measures of intelligence, the correlations generally are not of such magnitude that one test can be substituted for the other. For example, on the WISC-R the average correlation between the Verbal and Performance scales is 0.67 and the average correlation between a particular Performance subtest and the Full Scale IQ is 0.66 (Wechsler, 1974).

Tests for the Physically Handicapped

Another situation in which a different type of test is needed is when testing physically handicapped individuals, such as the blind, the deaf, and persons with disabilities or illnesses that interfere with their responding. One approach is to develop special tests for each type of handicapped group. Another approach has been to adapt individual intelligence tests, such as the Stanford-Binet and Weschler scales, for use with these populations. Such adaptations have been made for deaf and blind persons. Note, however, that because these forms of the test use different administration conditions, scores should be compared with those of norm groups composed of people having the particular handicap rather than with the regular norms.

What sort of adaptations are needed? With visually handicapped persons, items presented orally (such as the Verbal sections of the WISC-R and WAIS-R) can be used in their usual fashion. However, performance items cannot be used unless they can be adapted so that stimuli can be identified using other modalities, such as touch. Written items can be administered orally, printed in large type (for persons with limited vision), or written in braille. Responses can be given orally and recorded by an examiner, typed, written in braille, or recorded on special answer sheets. Directions can usually be given verbally.[5]

Testing deaf individuals presents a different set of problems. Obviously verbal directions and items cannot be used unless the test taker is adept at lipreading. If the person can read, items can be presented in written form. In other situations directions may be presented in sign language or by pantomime. Because of the speech and language handicaps of deaf people, some tests emphasize nonverbal tasks. For example, a test designed for use with the deaf, the *Hiskey-Nebraska Test*

---

[5] Special forms of college and graduate school admission tests, including the SAT and GRE, are available for visually handicapped test takers.

of Learning Aptitude, contains subtests such as Picture Associations, Picture Identification, Block Patterns, Picture Analogies, and Spatial Reasoning.

Persons with certain types of physical disabilities, such as cerebral palsy, may have little trouble understanding written or verbal items and instructions, but may be limited in their ability to respond. If the test taker can respond orally, the examiner can record their responses. Others may be able to type their responses. Even test takers with more severe motor problems may be able to respond by pointing to, or otherwise indicating (e.g., by a nod) the correct response.

academic ability tests

Academic ability tests, or scholastic aptitude tests, as their name implies, are designed to predict performance in academic situations. They differ from general intelligence measures by having a more limited focus—predicting academic performance. However, since basic intellectual skills are important determiners of success in most educational settings, the content of scholastic aptitude tests does not differ markedly from that of general intelligence tests. Yet because of their distinctive features, and the fact that they are the most widely used type of general ability measure, we shall consider scholastic aptitude tests in detail.

Basic Features

It may be considered nitpicking to think of scholastic aptitude tests as distinct from group tests of intelligence. But since intelligence tests and scholastic aptitude tests are based on different philosophies (that is, the measurement of a general human trait versus prediction of academic success), rely on different types of validation (that is, construct versus criterion-related validity), and utilize different norm groups (that is, general population versus students), there are enough differences to warrant separate consideration.

Construction. Although the guiding principles used in constructing a scholastic aptitude test should now be obvious, it would be well to emphasize several points. First, the primary basis for item selection should be the validity of the item in predicting academic criteria. Second, the tests will, almost without exception, be paper-and-pencil tests. Furthermore, because they will be administered to large numbers of students, items will generally be cast in multiple-choice or other objective formats to facilitate scoring. Third, most scholastic aptitude tests are part of a series, with tests at various age levels. The pragmatic problem is deciding how many age levels to include, where to divide the levels, and articulation between age levels. The age level problem is also reflected in the norms; the test constructor must obtain representative samples of students at each grade level. Because each level of the test will be used in several adjacent grades, and periodic testing will probably occur, provision of equivalent forms at each level is highly desirable.

Finally, scholastic aptitude tests will be power tests. On a power test, you will recall, scores reflect the complexity or difficulty of the items the student can correctly answer. Since the important dimension of academic performance is the complexity of the material that can be mastered, not speed of responding, validity will be higher when a power test is used as a predictor.

Content.   Although various types of items could be included on scholastic aptitude tests, in practice the content is generally quite standardized. Among the most widely used item types are: *vocabulary,* or a variation such as analogies or sentence completion (selecting the proper word to complete a sentence); *reading comprehension,* where the student reads a paragraph and then answers questions based upon the information contained in the paragraph; *numerical ability,* tested through computation and/or word problems; measures of *abstract reasoning,* such as number series problems or nonverbal analogies; and *general information* items. The exact content will, of course, vary with the scope of the test and the age level of the students. For example, in the primary grades, before children have acquired any fluency in reading, vocabulary will be tested by picture vocabulary items, but at older ages more complex item forms, such as analogies, can be used.

Since the educational system is cumulative and past performance is usually the best predictor of future performance, it would be surprising if scholastic aptitude tests were not heavily loaded with skills developed by previous school learnings. And they are. However, to avoid being too closely tied to specific learnings and educational experiences, the tests concentrate on skills and materials that transfer to a wide variety of situations. Furthermore, whenever possible, items are constructed so that students must apply their repertoire of knowledge and skills to new situations; specific information, if needed, is provided in the item content. For example, a reading comprehension item, even though it covers a topic new to the student, can test his ability to extract salient features from what he has read. Or a graph interpretation item, though presenting a student with data he has never previously encountered, can test his ability to interpret graphs. Thus previous learning may play a role in test performance by influencing problem-solving strategies as well as being reflected in knowledge of specific factual material.

Validation.   As academic aptitude tests are designed to predict academic performance, the appropriate type of validity evidence is criterion-related validity. That is, these tests should be validated against a criterion that measures academic achievement. What criteria are used to validate scholastic aptitude tests? The most obvious and widely used are grades—in specific courses or overall grade point averages. But other criteria are also possible, such as scores on achievement tests, teachers' ratings, completion of an education program, prizes or awards won, or rate of learning. However, validation studies have generally utilized criteria such as grades. Consequently, the tests often predict a particular type of educational accomplishment, grade-getting ability.

The fact that academic ability tests contain only alternative-choice items has led to a common misunderstanding: that they are limited or invalid because they use only alternative-choice items. But this argument misses the point. Since the tests are designed to predict academic achievement, any type of item that predicts achievement can legitimately be included on the test. If alternative-choice items predict achievement, as indeed they do, they may be properly used on scholastic aptitude tests. This does not imply that they are the only type of item that can be used, or that they can test all important skills and abilities—only that they are reasonable predictors of achievement. Given their level of predictive accuracy, and their advantages when testing large numbers of students, they are used much more frequently than other types of items.

Examples of Academic Ability Tests

Academic ability tests are used at all levels of education, from the primary grades through graduate and professional school. In the public schools they are used primarily to describe the abilities of individual students; at the college, graduate, and professional school level they are used primarily as selection tools. Since the basic features of these tests should be quite obvious, each type of test will not be described in detail. However, we shall briefly describe some examples of tests at each level.

Elementary and High School Tests.   Although there are tests designed for a particular grade range, particularly at the primary grades, a more common approach is to develop a coordinated testing program that can be used in a wide range of grades. These *multilevel tests* have separate forms for different grade ranges, sometimes with more than one form being appropriate for a given grade level.[6] Although the content may differ slightly at various grade levels, the items generally cover vocabulary, verbal reasoning, general information, and quantitative thinking. Some tests include items measuring reading comprehension and nonverbal reasoning.

Examples of academic tests are described briefly in Table 13.3.

College Admission Tests.   There are two major national college admission testing programs: the College Entrance Examination Board's *Scholastic Aptitude Test* (SAT) and the *American College Testing Program Assessment* (ACT). Both are designed to aid college and university admission officers in evaluating the qualifications of applicants for admission. Prospective students take the ACT or SAT during their junior or senior year in high school, and scores are reported to colleges to which they have applied. Some colleges require (or recommend) the ACT, others the SAT, some accept both, and others do not require either test.

Although the ACT and SAT are both college admissions tests, they differ in both content and format. The ACT battery is composed of four tests: English, Mathematics, Social Studies, and Natural Science. A score is reported for each subtest and, in addition, the average of the four test scores is reported as a Composite score. The tests in the ACT battery are achievement-oriented, emphasizing the ability to apply developed skills. For example, the Social Studies and Natural Sciences tests place primary emphasis on the ability to interpret material presented in reading paragraphs.

The College Board program, in contrast, makes a clearer separation between

---

[6] The higher-level form might be used if students were above average in ability and the lower-level form if students were below average in ability.

Table 13.3
Examples of Academic Ability Tests

Cognitive Abilities Test (Riverside). Multilevel edition (grades 3–12) has three sections: Verbal (vocabulary, sentence completion, verbal classification, verbal analogies), Quantitative (quantitative relations, number series, equation building), and Nonverbal (figure classification, figure analogies, figure synthesis). Primary level (K–3) measures oral vocabulary, quantitative concepts, and relational concepts.

Developing Cognitive Abilities Test (Scott Foresman). Grades 2–12, five levels; measures verbal, quantitative, and spatial abilities.

Henmon-Nelson Tests of Mental Ability (Riverside). Grades K–12, four levels, also college edition; usual variety of items.

Lorge-Thorndike Intelligence Test (Riverside). Grades 3–13, eight levels, also separate college edition; verbal and nonverbal skills including pictorial and numerical items.

Miller Analogies Test (Psychological Corporation). For college and graduate level; very difficult test of verbal reasoning measured solely by analogies items; use restricted.

Otis-Lennon School Ability Test (Psychological Corporation). Grades 1–12, five levels; verbal comprehension and reasoning, numerical reasoning, abstract reasoning.

School and College Ability Test, Series III (Addison-Wesley). Grades 3–12, three levels; verbal and quantitative reasoning.

Test of Cognitive Skills (Publishers Test Service). Grades 2–12, five levels; sequences (finding rule or pattern in sequence of symbols, letters, or numbers), analogies, memory, and verbal reasoning.

---

its aptitude and achievement tests. The SAT is a measure of scholastic aptitude and provides two scores: a Verbal score and a Mathematics score. No composite score is obtained. As with the ACT, all items are in a multiple-choice format. The Verbal section consists of antonym, sentence completion, analogy, reading comprehension, and general understanding (information) items. The Mathematics section includes word and computational problems in algebra, geometry, and basic arithmetic processes, the interpretation of graphs and charts, and logical reasoning items. In addition to the SAT, a series of achievement tests covering various subjects, (and in some areas levels within subjects) and a Test of Standard Written English, are included in the program.

The scales for reporting scores on the two tests also are different, although both use standard score scales. Scores on the SAT range from 200 to 800 with the mean score for college-bound students being 500 and the standard deviation 100 points in the original norm sample. For the ACT, the range is 1–36 with the mean for college-bound students about 20 (again, in the original norm sample) and the standard deviation about 5 points. We have emphasized the phrase "original norm sample" because both tests have kept their original score scale, even though the average performance of college-bound students has changed over the years (see below). This means that a score of, say 600, on the SAT-Verbal represents the same absolute level of performance, regardless of the year the test was taken. However, since the distribution of scores changes from year to year, this score might result in different percentile ranks (compared to other test takers in a given year) if a student took the test in, say, 1978 or 1982.

Examples of items from a college admission test are shown in Figure 13.2.

Figure 13.2 Examples of Items from a College Admission Test: The College Board *Scholastic Aptitude Test* and *Test of Standard Written English*

SAT—Verbal

Antonyms. Select the word most nearly opposite in meaning.

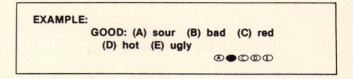

> **EXAMPLE:**
> GOOD: (A) sour (B) bad (C) red
> (D) hot (E) ugly

Analogies. Select the pair of words whose relation is most similar to that expressed in the original pair.

> **EXAMPLE:**
> YAWN : BOREDOM : : (A) dream : sleep
> (B) anger : madness (C) smile : amusement
> (D) face : expression
> (E) impatience : rebellion

Sentence Completion. Select the words that best fit the meaning of the sentence.

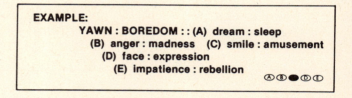

> **EXAMPLE:**
> Although its publicity has been ----, the film itself is intelligent, well-acted, handsomely produced, and altogether ----.
>
> (A) tasteless . . respectable (B) extensive . . moderate
> (C) sophisticated . . amateur (D) risqué . . crude
> (E) perfect . . spectacular

Reading Passages. Answer questions on the basis of what is stated or implied in the passage.

> That Plato's *Republic* should have been admired, on its political side by decent people, is perhaps the most astonishing example of literary snobbery in all history.
>
> Let us consider a few points in this totalitarian tract. The main purpose of education is to produce courage in battle. To this end, there is to be a rigid censorship of the stories told by

mothers and nurses to young children; there is to be no reading of Homer because that degraded versifier makes heroes lament and gods laugh; the drama is to be forbidden because it contains villains and women; music is to be only of certain kinds, which, in modern terms, would be military bands playing "My Country Tis of Thee" and "Stars and Stripes Forever."

1. The main point of the passage is to

   (A) cast contempt on the kind of music advocated in Plato's *Republic*
   (B) describe the content of Plato's *Republic*
   (C) discuss the positive and negative aspects of Plato's *Republic*
   (D) show how Plato's *Republic* influenced the lives of people at the time
   (E) criticize the political philosophy contained in Plato's *Republic*

4. The passage suggests that all of the following are forbidden in Plato's *Republic* EXCEPT

   (A) dance music
   (B) patriotic music
   (C) plays about villains
   (D) portrayals of the amusements of the gods
   (E) stories about poor people stealing to feed their families

5. The author's attitude toward Plato's *Republic* is one of

   (A) quiet concern   (B) cautious acceptance
      (C) reverent admiration   (D) outraged disapproval
         (E) total indifference

SAT—Mathematical

Standard Multiple-Choice Questions. Select the correct answer.

1. If $2a + b = 5$, then $4a + 2b =$

   (A) $\dfrac{5}{4}$ (B) $\dfrac{5}{2}$ (C) 10   (D) 20   (E) 25

6. If a car travels X kilometers of a trip in H hours, in how many hours can it travel the next Y kilometers at this rate?

   (A) $\dfrac{XY}{H}$ (B) $\dfrac{HY}{X}$ (C) $\dfrac{HX}{Y}$ (D) $\dfrac{H + Y}{X}$ (E) $\dfrac{X + Y}{H}$

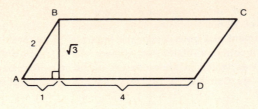

8. The figure above shows a piece of paper in the shape of a parallelogram with measurements as indicated. If the paper is tacked at its center to a flat surface and then rotated about its center, the points covered by the paper will be a circular region of diameter

(A) $\sqrt{3}$ (B) 2 (C) 5 (D) $\sqrt{28}$ (E) $\sqrt{39}$

Quantitative Comparison. See directions with item.

Directions: Each of the following questions consists of two quantities, one in Column A and one in Column B. You are to compare the two quantities and on the answer sheet blacken space

A if the quantity in Column A is greater;
B if the quantity in Column B is greater;
C if the two quantities are equal;
D if the relationship cannot be determined from the information given.

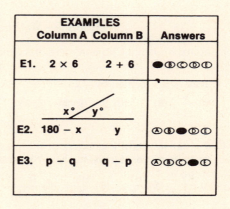

Test of Standard Written English

Usage. Indicate which underlined part contains an error in grammar, usage, diction, or idiom.

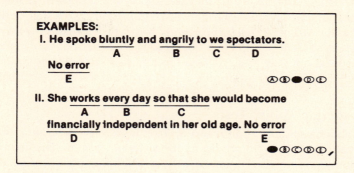

Sentence Correction. Select the answer that produces the most effective sentence.

2. Althea Gibson was the first black American to win major tennis championships and played in the 1950s.

- (A) Althea Gibson was the first black American to win major tennis championships and played in the 1950s.
- (B) Althea Gibson, being the first black American to win major tennis championships, and playing in the 1950s.
- (C) Althea Gibson, playing in the 1950s, being the first black American to win major tennis championships.
- (D) Althea Gibson, who played in the 1950s, was the first black American to win major tennis championships.
- (E) Althea Gibson played in the 1950s, she was the first black American to win major tennis championships.

Source: *Taking the SAT.* Educational Testing Service, 1978. Reproduced by permission.

Graduate and Professional School Admission Tests. Many graduate and professional schools, especially ones which have a selective admission policy, require applicants to submit scores on scholastic aptitude tests as part of their application for admission. These tests are quite similar in content to college admission tests, although they are more difficult. Some testing programs also contain achievement tests in content areas. As noted above, their primary purpose is to aid in the selection process.

An example is the *Graduate Record Examination* (GRE), a test used by many graduate schools. This battery consists of two parts—an aptitude test and an achievement test. The Aptitude portion provides three scores: Verbal, Quantitative, and Analytic Thinking. Students may also take an achievement test covering the material taught in undergraduate curricula. Achievement tests are available in over 20 fields, including Biology, Chemistry, French, History, Music, and Psychology. Some achievement tests also have subtest scores; for example, the History test has separate scores for European and American History.

There are also test batteries for various professional schools. Examples include the *Medical College Admission Test,* the *Law School Admission Test,* the *Veterinary Aptitude Test,* and the *Graduate Management Admission Test.* A slightly different type of test is the *National Teachers Examination,* which assesses the knowledge and abilities of students completing udergraduate teacher education programs. The NTE is used not only as a criterion for admission to graduate programs in education, but also as one basis for the certification and selection of teachers.

Using Academic Ability Tests

Academic ability tests are used for two major purposes: to describe individuals' general level of ability and to predict future academic success. The first purpose is more common in public schools, with the scores being used to place students in courses or academic tracks and to plan instruction, either for individuals or a class. The latter use is more common in higher education, especially in schools having selective admission policies. Here, too, results can be used in placement and academic advising.

In using academic ability tests for these purposes, several important considerations arise. Among the most important, or at least most debated, are: How accurately can academic performance be predicted from scores on academic ability tests? Are the tests biased against certain individuals or groups? Can scores be raised by coaching or special preparation? Are test scores declining? We shall consider each of these questions briefly.

Predictive Validity. There have been hundreds, if not thousands, of studies investigating the predictive accuracy of academic ability tests (see, e.g., ACT, 1972; Angoff, 1971b; Breland, 1979; Lavin, 1965). In most situations, correlations between test scores and measures of achievement (usually grades) are in the .50s or .60s. However, the correlations vary widely depending on the school and the course. For example, the validity of college admission tests varies from near zero to the .70s at various schools (Breland, 1979). And, as might be expected, scores predict performance more accurately in "academic" courses, such as English, history, and mathematics, than in more specialized subjects such as art or industrial education.

Although a high level of predictive accuracy might be considered to be desirable, some people have interpreted these results in a different manner. They suggest that the relatively high correlations imply that education has not been adapted to the needs and abilities of individual students. If education was directed to individual abilities, there would be a lower correlation between ability and achievement.

Bias. Some critics claim that academic ability tests are unfair to persons from atypical, disadvantaged, and culturally limited backgrounds. This criticism has been particularly directed to the use of academic ability tests as selection devices, particularly in college and professional school admissions. Although certain individuals from minority groups may be penalized, the available data indicate that the tests predict as well for disadvantaged minority group students as for white middle-class students (see, e.g., Bowers, 1970; Breland, 1979; Cleary, 1968; Cleary et al., 1975; Cole, 1973; Davis & Temp, 1971; Linn, 1973; Munday, 1965; Reschley & Sabers, 1979; Schmeiser & Ferguson, 1978; Stanley & Porter, 1967; Thomas & Stanley, 1969). In fact, the data suggest that any bias present is in the opposite direction from what is claimed; that is, tests overpredict the performance of minority students and underpredict for white students.

Here again, the data are open to various interpretations. That is, the data may reflect that fact that the same set of abilities are required both for success in academic situations and for effective performance on the tests. Thus minority group students would suffer the same handicaps in college as they do in testing situations. Whether this represents a criterion or prediction bias or reflects a fact of life depends on your point of view.

Two points that have been stressed throughout the book are also worth reemphasizing at this point: Test scores should not be the only basis for selection, and a test should be validated for every use.

Coaching. Another point that has been intensely debated, again particularly in connection with college admission tests, is the effects of coaching on test scores (see, e.g., Alderman & Powers, 1979; CEEB, 1968; Fremer & Chandler, 1971; Jackson, 1980; Messick, 1980a, 1981a; Messick & Jungeblut, 1981; Pike, 1978; Pike & Evans, 1972; Powers & Alderman, 1979; Slack & Porter, 1980). Although there is evidence that certain types of coaching can increase scores, particularly on mathematics items and when the test taker is not familiar with the testing procedures, these changes are generally slight, usually of the order of magnitude of the standard error of measurement of the test.

The debate over the implications of such changes is complicated by the failure of proponents to agree on two basic questions. One is what is meant by coaching. Do we mean short periods of preparation or more intensive, long-term review and preparation courses? As might be expected, greater improvement is found with more intensive training programs (Messick & Jungeblut, 1981). Critics argue that these findings suggest that coaching can increase scores; in response, other psychologists argue that since these programs increase performance by teaching the skills covered on the test, they are educational programs and thus are not properly considered as coaching. The other question revolves around how big a difference in scores is needed to have practical implications. Critics cite data showing that differences due to coaching are of the same magnitude as differences between accepted and unaccepted students, and thus coaching may make a difference in whether a student is accepted at a particular college. Their opponents argue that the improvements, if present, are not large enough to result in a student with a mediocre ability being accepted and that test scores are only one, often minor, consideration in deciding who will be accepted and who will be rejected.

The Decline (?) in Ability. A question that periodically arises is whether the average ability of the population is declining. In earlier years this problem was usually phrased in terms of the decline of intelligence in the general population. In more recent years the problem has again arisen because data have shown that the average scores on college admission tests have been declining over the past 15–20 years.

There is no doubt that scores on college admission tests have declined. For example, in the period between 1960 and 1977, the average score on the Verbal portion of the SAT has declined from 477 to 429 and the average score on the Mathematics test has declined from 498 to 471 (*On further examination,* 1977, p. 6).

The question is why this decline has occurred. Consider scores on the SAT. One possible explanation is that the test has become harder. However, analysis of the test items shows that the difficulty of the test has not increased; if anything, it has become easier. Another possible explanation is that the pool of people taking the test has changed. This factor does appear to account for much of the decline, especially in earlier years. As more and more students entered college, more students with poorer academic records took the SAT, thus lowering the average score. So, too, there were more test takers from groups who generally score below average on the test (e.g., students from lower socioeconomic levels and minority groups). But these factors alone do not account for the entire decline, especially in later years. Thus other causative factors have been postulated: the lesser emphasis on academic subjects in schools and greater emphasis on electives, national disruptions such as the Vietnam War and accompanying civil unrest, the increased use of drugs, increased television watching instead of reading, and even changes in family size and composition (Zajonc, 1976).

Another line of argument is that the decline is relatively unimportant because the test is outdated and no longer measures the abilities needed for college success. This argument has been refuted by studies showing that the test predicts college success as accurately now as in the past. Although it is true that schools teach things not measured by the test, these data suggest that the abilities measured by the tests are still required for college success.

Related data are provided by score patterns of younger children. We mentioned that scores on the restandardization sample of the Stanford-Binet were higher than those of the previous standardization sample. There is also evidence that scores of elementary school children on standardized achievement and ability tests have started to rise again, after a decline (Munday, 1979). The pattern of performance also varies between fields. For example, Jones (1981) has presented data showing that in contrast to the general trend, scores of students planning to study science and mathematics in college have not declined.

In short, the data clearly indicate that scores on college admission tests have been declining. What is not apparent is why they are declining, what can be done to halt the decline, and what implications the score decline has for the educational system and the careers of the students affected.[7]

[7] For further discussions of the score decline problem see, for example, Breland (1976), Flanagan (1976), Harnischfeger & Wiley (1976), Kendrick (1967), Munday (1979), *On further examination* (1977), Zajonc (1976), Zajonc & Bargh (1980).

issues in mental ability testing

There is no doubt that a number of carefully constructed, well-normed measures of general intellectual ability are available to the test user. This is true whether one considers individual intelligence measures, such as the Stanford-Binet and Wechsler scales, or paper-and-pencil measures, such as the SAT and ACT. The care devoted to the construction of these tests and the resultant technical sophistication provide models to be emulated. Procedures for administration and scoring are highly standardized. Available normative data are extensive and, generally, representative of the population the test is designed to serve. A possible exception is the representation of minority groups in normative samples. However, many tests currently include minority group members in normative samples and/or have developed normative data based on minority groups.

The points in the previous paragraph relate to the technology of measuring intelligence. But there are also other types of issues in intelligence testing. Some relate to the course of mental growth: Is intelligence stable over time? Does intelligence change with age? If so, in what ways? Is intelligence inherited? There also is a practical question: Do scores on intelligence tests predict success in "real-life" situations? There are also more theoretical questions, the most important of which is: Is intelligence a viable and useful construct? Before leaving our discussion of intelligence we shall consider these questions.

The Stability of Mental Abilities

The measured intelligence of most people (that is, their IQ) is relatively constant over long periods of time. One exception is the relation between mental ability measured in preschool years and as an adolescent or adult. Because infant and preschool tests are often unreliable and measure different skills than at older age levels and because intervening experiences vary widely, correlations between IQs obtained before age 5 or 6 and adult IQs are generally very low (Bayley, 1968; McCall, Hogarty, & Hurlburt, 1972). After this point, IQs remain more constant. The question is why.

Although earlier studies stressed the stability of the IQ, it is now recognized that the stability reflected the fact that most people experience relatively constant environmental conditions. As a consequence, environmental factors may not have a chance to demonstrate their effects fully. And since the greatest fluctuations in IQs occur with large changes in environmental conditions, environmental stability leads to stability in intelligence test scores. Moreover, the cumulative nature of intellectual development (and measurement) tends to produce artifacts that ensure a high correlation between successive IQ measures (J. Anderson, 1940). However, other data have shown that marked changes in IQ (20 IQ points or more) do occur under certain conditions.

What factors, then, produce greater than chance changes in the IQ? Some of the factors that may decrease intelligence are obvious: injury or illness, particularly if it effects the brain or central nervous system; and severe emotional trauma. Growing up in an extremely restricted or deprived environment may limit intellectual development. Conversely, the removal of an emotional block or provision of an especially stimulating environment or educational experiences may lead to increased intellectual growth (Bloom 1964; Brim & Kagan, 1980; Hunt, 1961; Rohwer, Ammon, & Cramer, 1974).

Changes with Age

It is obvious to even the most casual observer that abilities change with age. During childhood and adolescence almost all skills and abilities increase rapidly. (This fact is reflected in the use of age- and grade-equivalent scores on ability and achievement tests.) Not only do abilities increase during earlier years, they also decline in later life. Thus, if we were to plot intellectual development as a function of age, we would observe rapid growth during childhood, followed by a slower increase in adolescence and the early adult years. Mental ability then appears to reach a maximum in the early adult years, remains constant through middle age or later, and then declines.

Data on changes during the adult years are also available from standardization data on the WAIS-R. Table 13.4 shows how scores on the Verbal, Performance, and Full Scale IQs change with age for adult samples. The first three columns of the table show the sum of scores on the various subtests needed to obtain an IQ of 100 at various age levels. As can be seen, the score needed to obtain an IQ of 100 increases to age 25–34 (20–24 on the Performance scale), then decreases with increasing age. The fourth column shows the Full Scale IQ that the average person in each age range would obtain if IQs were based on the 25–34 norm group. These data again show that performance increases to age 25–34, then declines thereafter.

The previous discussion presented an oversimplified view. There are several reasons for this statement. One is that the shape of the curve will depend on the ability being tested. Some abilities, particularly speeded and perceptual tasks, peak and decline relatively early. Others, particularly more complex reasoning

Table 13.4
Changes in Intelligence Test Performance with Age

Age Range	Score Needed for IQ = 100			IQ Based on Age 25–34 Norms
	Verbal	Performance	Full Scales	
16–17	51	48	98	91
18–19	54	49	101	92
20–24	60	52	111	98
25–34	63	51	114	100
35–44	61	47	107	96
45–54	59	43	102	93
55–64	57	39	96	89
65–69	54	34	89	85
70–74	51	31	81	81

Source: Wechsler (1981).

skills, develop more slowly and decline less readily. Thus, rather than making general statements about the growth and decline of abilities, we must always refer to the growth curve for a specific ability. The growth curve is also affected by the experiences of the particular person. This is particularly apparent with the decline of abilities. If an ability is constantly used, its decline will be less rapid. For example, the decline in the ability to do arithmetic computations will be pronounced if a person does not use this skill, whereas it will remain high, or even increase, in people who practice the skill.

Not only is the rate of growth different at various ages, the organization of abilities changes with age (see, e.g., Horn, 1970; Reinert, 1970). We have already referred to this phenomenon when we noted that intelligence tests measured different skills at various age levels. During the preschool years the tests measured perceptual skills; in later years the emphasis was on verbal reasoning abilities. These changes in emphasis reflect differences in experiences at various ages as well as changes associated with physiological and neurological development.

Although abilities can change as a result of maturation and specific training, the empirical evidence shows that most abilities are relatively stable, even over long periods of time. Why is this so? When considering this question, keep in mind that most evidence of stability refers to the relative position of individuals. That is, although intellectual abilities increase with age, a person's position relative to that of his agemates remains relatively constant. Why? One reason is that similar skills are tested at each age. Thus, persons who have high ability can build on this foundation and remain ahead while people whose ability is weak continue to lag behind. Another reason is the consistency of the environment. Large changes in ability tend to occur as a consequence of large changes in one's environment. Since, for most people, the environment remains relatively stable, at least when considered in the context of the wide variety range of possible environments in a society, we would expect their abilities to remain relatively unchanged. Then, too, as Ferguson (1954) has pointed out, ability tests tend to measure overlearned skills. That is, we measure skills that are so well established that little change can be expected.

Heredity and Environment

Underlying both of the previous questions is an even broader question: Are abilities such as intelligence inherited? This is, needless to say, a highly debated question, one that constantly reappears in the psychological literature (see, e.g., Anastasi, 1973; Block & Dworkin, 1976; Bodmer & Cavalli-Sforza, 1970; Bouchard & McGue, 1981; Eysenck & Kamin, 1981; Herrnstein, 1971; Jencks et al., 1972; Jensen, 1969, 1973, 1980; Kamin, 1974; Loehlin, Lindzey, & Spuhler, 1975; Loehlin & Nichols, 1976; Nichols, 1978; Scarr, 1981).

Most people would probably agree that intelligence depends on hereditary characteristics, environmental learning experiences, and the interaction of these two sources of influence. Thus the question is usually phrased in terms of the relative influences of these various influences. A variety of sources of data have been used in an attempt to answer this question: studies of the correlations between intelligence test scores of people having various degrees of relationship;

studies of twins, particularly identical twins reared apart; selective breeding studies; studies of environmental manipulations; and so on. The most common statistical procedure is to estimate the *heritability* of intelligence; that is, the percent of variation in intelligence within a population that is due to inherited differences.

Investigators have reached widely divergent conclusions as a result of these studies. Some have concluded that hereditary differences account for as much as 80 percent of the observed differences in intelligence; others have concluded that hereditary effects are lower, in the range of 40 to 60 percent; others have concluded that hereditary differences have only a minor effect and that most differences in observed intelligence are due to environmental differences. Some have concluded that the methodological problems make the question essentially unanswerable. Still others have suggested that the question is so fraught with social and political ramifications that the question should not even be investigated.

Intelligence and Life Success

Another area that has been the subject of a large amount of research is the relationship between intelligence and socially relevant criteria, such as educational and vocational success. Binet's test, you will recall, was originally developed to identify slow learners. Since Binet's time, innumerable studies have been conducted relating intelligence measures to a wide variety of educational outcomes. Considering the diversity of tests, samples, and criteria used, the results of these studies have been amazingly consistent; the correlations between scores on general intelligence tests and measures of academic success generally fall in the .40–.70 range. Correlations are generally higher when the criterion is a standardized measure of achievement, in more academic and verbal areas, and with younger children. Intelligence scores are also related to the level of education completed. In short, measures of general intellectual ability predict a variety of academic criteria (McNemar, 1964).

The relationship of intelligence test scores to occupational success is also a controversial area. On the one hand there are studies (Harrell & Harrell, 1945) that have shown that occupations can be ranked in terms of the intellectual ability of persons working within these occupations. Then, too, it is well documented that occupational membership is closely related to educational attainment and that educational attainment can be predicted from intelligence test scores (see, e.g., Herrnstein, 1971). On the other hand, there are studies (e.g., Thorndike & Hagen, 1959) that show little relationship between ability and occupational success when predicting relative success within an occupational group. Perhaps the best reconciliation of the present knowledge is that many occupations may have minimal intellectual requirements, but given the minimal level of intellectual ability, an individual's performance in an occupation will be determined by factors and abilities other than general intellectual ability.

Intelligence as a Construct

Any evaluation of general intelligence tests is, in many ways, an evaluation of the construct of general intelligence. There is no doubt that general intelligence tests reliably sample a certain constellation of abilities (vocabulary, fund of general information, numerical ability). However, the question remains as to whether the concept of general intelligence is a viable one.

There would, at first blush, appear to be many reasons for rejecting the notion of general intelligence. The tests themselves are composed of several different types of items, and factor analyses have confirmed the existence of a number of distinct intellectual abilities. Other studies have shown that performance on general intelligence tests is a function of different sets of abilities at different age levels; again, an argument against the general intelligence view. Why, then, do psychologists persist in building general intelligence tests and use a single score, usually the IQ, to summarize an individual's intellectual abilities? One reason no doubt is historical tradition; the early tests used this approach, and their descendants have followed in their footsteps. But this is hardly a sufficient reason. More important is the fact that scores on general intelligence tests predict a variety of educational and vocational criteria. Furthermore, as we shall see later in the discussion of multiaptitude batteries, in the majority of situations prediction using multiple abilities has proved to be no more effective than predicting from a single index of general intelligence (cf. McNemar, 1964).

The debate over the concept of general intelligence also illustrates the distinction between basic research on the structure of abilities and application of knowledge gained to the technology of test construction. It would be hard to argue against the view that intellectual ability is best conceived of as a number of intelligences or, if you will, a number of quite distinct intellectual abilities. However, although test constructors have been able to develop tests measuring these abilities, the tests do not have greater predictive efficiency than do general intelligence measures. Thus many persons prefer to use general intelligence tests, even though they realize the theoretical limitations of such measures.

Another approach to evaluating the usefulness of the construct of intelligence has been suggested by Resnick, who suggested, " . . . a more basic question [should be] asked concerning intelligence—what *is* it, rather than who *has* it." (Resnick, 1976a, p. 4). She is pointing out that most studies of intelligence have been directed toward measuring individual differences in intelligence and establishing empirical correlates of intelligence. She feels that more progress would be made by concentrating efforts on understanding the nature of intelligence, particularly what cognitive processes are involved in intelligent behavior. Some attempts have been made in this area (Carroll, 1976; Estes, 1974; Sternberg, 1977, 1979). The common thread in all these approaches is an attempt to reconcile our knowledge of intelligence, as studied by the individual differences approach, with knowledge obtained from studying learning and cognitive processes.

summary

This chapter focused on measures of general mental ability. These tests are designed to provide an overall index of general mental functioning; consequently they are survey tests and usually report only one score—or, at most, several scores covering broad areas of intellectual functioning. Various types of tests fall within this category: individually administered intelligence tests, group intelligence tests, tests for special populations (e.g., the very young, the retarded and verbally handicapped, the physically disabled), and academic ability tests.

Intelligence, to the psychologist, is a descriptive label applied to the test taker's level of performance on certain classes of tasks. Most intelligence tests are primarily tests of verbal reasoning ability (as measured by items such as vocabulary, same-opposites, and analogies) but may also include items measuring general information, numerical reasoning, memory, and perceptual and organizational skills. Psychologists disagree on how the various components of mental ability are organized; some think that intelligence is a general ability that pervades all types of cognitive tasks, others think of it as a small number of relatively broad abilities, and still others prefer to think in terms of a large number of discrete abilities. An emerging trend in the measurement of intelligence is to attempt to better integrate the measurement of mental abilities with knowledge of basic cognitive process.

Individually administered tests were the first type of intelligence test to be developed and still provide the best single approach to the assessment of intellectual functioning. We described the two major individual intelligence tests: the Stanford-Binet Intelligence Scale and the various Wechsler scales (the Wechsler Adult Intelligence Scale, the Wechsler Intelligence Scale for Children, and the Wechsler Preschool and Primary Scale of Intelligence). Although they differ on various dimensions (e.g., appropriate age range, content, administration, scoring), all are carefully constructed, valid measures of intelligence. The Wechsler scales, however, appear to be more useful for diagnosing specific areas of intellectual dysfunctioning.

Because individual intelligence tests are inefficient when testing large numbers of persons, a number of group intelligence tests have been developed. These are paper-and-pencil tests that use alternative-choice items. Typical content includes verbal reasoning, numerical, general information, and nonverbal reasoning items. They are used in education and business and industry to obtain a relatively quick, objective index of the test taker's level of intellectual functioning. Scores on group tests generally correlate quite highly with scores on individually administered intelligence tests.

Other tests have been developed for use with specific populations. For example, infant and preschool tests take a developmental approach and tend to emphasize perceptual abilities. As might be expected, they generally have low correlations with measures of adult intelligence. Other tests have been developed for testing mentally retarded and illiterate persons. These tests often contain nonverbal items such as draw-a-person tasks, form boards, block designs, and puzzles. Special tests and testing procedures have also been developed for persons with sensory or physical problems that interfere with their perception of items or their responding.

Academic ability, or scholastic aptitude, tests have a more limited focus than general intelligence tests, being designed to measure only those abilities essential for academic success. Like group intelligence tests, they tend to be paper-and-pencil tests and use alternative-choice items. Their content is similar to that of group intelligence tests (e.g., vocabulary, numerical, nonverbal reasoning, general information), but they include reading comprehension items as well. As the lower grade levels, academic ability tests are used primarily to describe students' abilities and plan instruction; in higher education they are used for selection, placement, and counseling and guidance. These latter tests may be designed for general use or for a specific purpose, such as selecting students for a particular type of graduate or professional education.

The chapter concluded with a discussion of some recurrent issues in the measurement of intelligence and mental ability. We pointed out that most people's mental ability, compared to their age-mates, remains relatively stable over time, primarily because their environments do not change drastically. While the peak on mental ability appears to be in the early twenties, whether a given individual's abilities will decline thereafter depends on the particular function tested and the use the person makes of this ability. We also noted that although the effects of heredity and environment on mental ability have been extensively studied, there is little agreement as to their relative contributions. Finally, we concluded that although the concept of general mental ability (that is, intelligence) has certain theoretical and empirical weaknesses, by and large it has proved to be a useful concept for guiding test construction.

Suggestions for Further Reading

Estes, W. K. Learning theory and intelligence. *American Psychologist,* 1974, *29,* 740–749. Argues that the construction of intelligence tests should be based on our knowledge of the learning process.

Herrnstein, R. IQ. *Atlantic,* September 1971, 43–64. A review of intelligence testing and the hereditary bases of intelligence and a discussion of the implications for the stratification of society.

Kamin, L. J. *The science and politics of IQ.* New York: Wiley, 1974. A harsh criticism of the notion of intelligence and intelligence testing.

Lennon, R. T. The anatomy of a scholastic aptitude test. *NCME Measurement In Education,* 1980, *11*(2). A consideration of the problems in measuring ability illustrated by a description of the process used to construct a commercially published scholastic aptitude test.

Loehlin, J. C., Lindzey, G., & Spuhler, J. N. *Race differences in intelligence.* San Francisco: Freeman, 1975. A comprehensive review of the evidence and issues regarding racial differences in measured intelligence.

McNemar, Q. Lost: Our intelligence. Why? *American Psychologist,* 1964, *19,* 871–882. A defense of the usefulness of the concept of general intelligence.

On further examination: Report of the advisory panel on the Scholastic Aptitude Test score decline. New York: College Entrance Examination Board, 1977. The summary report of the commission investigating the SAT score decline; gives empirical data and suggests reasons for the decline.

Resnick, L. B. (Ed.). *The nature of intelligence.* Hillsdale, N.J.: Erlbaum, 1976. A series of papers examining the cognitive and adaptive processes involved in intelligence and how these processes can be better reflected in measures of intelligence.

Sattler, J. M. *Assessment of children's intelligence and special abilities,* 2d ed. Boston: Allyn and Bacon, 1982. A comprehensive description of various methods for measuring children's abilities and intelligence; a basic reference on the psychoeducational assessment of children.

Sternberg, R. J. The nature of mental abilities. *American Psychologist,* 1979, *34,* 214–230. A good introduction to Sternberg's approach to the measurement of cognitive and intellectual functions.

Test use and validity. Princeton, N.J.: Educational Testing Service, 1980. A reply by ETS to Ralph Nader's criticisms of the SAT.

Thorndike, R. L. Mr. Binet's test 70 years later. *Educational Researcher,* 1975, *4*(5), 3–7. A brief review of the changes in the Binet intelligence test over a 70-year period.

Wechsler, D. Intelligence defined and undefined: A relativistic appraisal. *American Psycholgist,* 1975, *30,* 135–139. A leader in the measurement of intelligence discusses his thinking on the nature of intelligence and its measurement.

Chapter 14 • Aptitude and Ability Tests

THE tests discussed in Chapter 13 were designed to measure general mental ability. Consequently, they described performance by a single score, such as an IQ, or by several scores covering quite broad domains. Many psychologists, however, think this conception is too simplistic, preferring to think in terms of cognitive abilities (in the plural), rather than just a single unitary ability. They point out that studies have shown that even individual intelligence tests measure more than one ability. On a practical level, the need to consider diverse abilities is also apparent. Educational psychologists are concerned with matching students' abilities with schools or courses; industrial psychologists are interested in placing workers in jobs that match their skills and abilities; counselors consider abilities when helping their clients to make educational and vocational plans. In all of these situations, reliance on a single score would be unnecessarily restrictive; what is needed are measures of various abilities.

Test constructors have typically taken one of two approaches to measuring these diverse characteristics. Some have attempted to develop integrated test batteries that measure a small number of quite broad abilities. The other approach has been to develop separate tests for each specific ability. Sometimes this approach is used because the test constructor's interests are confined to a specific area; for example, he may only be interested in studying, say, creativity or musical ability. In other cases a test may be developed in response to a particular demand; for example, an industrial psychologist may develop a test of a particular ability needed on a specific job.

In this chapter we shall discuss a wide variety of aptitude and ability tests, including tests of cognitive and perceptual-motor abilities. We shall first discuss multiaptitude test batteries and then tests designed to measure specific abilities. The chapter will conclude with a review of maximal performance tests.

multiaptitude test batteries

In the multiaptitude approach a person's abilities are described using a relatively small number of tests, each of which measures a relatively independent ability. The assessment of these abilities requires an integrated battery of tests, each of which measures only one ability and is relatively independent (that is, uncorrelated) with other tests in the battery.

This philosophy has important implications for test construction and use. For example, how many abilities (tests) should be included in the battery? Should the battery be comprehensive or measure only the more important abilities? Most test constructors take a pragmatic view and measure only a small number, usually 6 to 12, major abilities. There is also the question of whether the individual tests will measure "factorially pure" abilities or whether they will be comprised of items measuring closely related abilities. The former is called a multifactor approach, the latter a multiaptitude approach. And, since the importance and structure of abilities changes with age, different sets of tests may be included in batteries at various age levels.

Other considerations relate to the interpretation and use of scores. To permit intraindividual comparisons (that is, determination of an individual's relative strengths and weaknesses in various ability areas), scores on all tests in the battery must be compared with a common norm group or groups. If intraindividual comparisons are to be made, each test must measure a distinct ability and have high reliability and a low standard error of measurement.

When using multiaptitude batteries, the same set of scores can be used to predict various academic and/or vocational criteria, even criteria requiring use of quite different skills. The empirical question is which scores to use and what weight each score will receive in predicting a particular criterion. This is a simple multiple regression problem; if scores on each test in the battery are correlated with each of the various criteria, the multiple regression equations will indicate the optimal weight to assign each test for predicting each criterion. The efficiency obtained by using the same set of scores for predicting various outcomes is an advantage of the multiaptitude approach.

With these general considerations in mind, we shall now briefly describe several multiaptitude batteries.

The Differential Aptitude Tests

As our primary example of a multiaptitude battery we have chosen the *Differential Aptitude Tests* (DAT) published by the Psychological Corporation. This battery of eight tests was designed to serve as an aid in the educational and vocational guidance of students in grades 8 through 12. First published in 1947, with the latest revision in 1982 (Forms V and W), the DAT is probably the most widely used multiaptitude battery on the secondary school level.

The development of the DAT was guided by certain general principles. The two most important were that the test battery measure multiple abilities and that the test should be useful in educational and vocational guidance. In addition, the tests in the battery were designed to measure abilities considered to be independent by counselors and other users, rather than factorially defined constructs, and be power tests (an exception is the Clerical Speed and Accuracy Test). The test authors also wanted the test to contain practical materials, to be easy to administer, and to have alternative forms. To aid in interpretation, great care was taken to obtain good normative data.

In reviewing the guiding philosophy of the DAT, one can see the interplay of theoretical and practical demands and the necessity for tempering a purely psychometric approach with the requirements of developing an instrument that provides meaningful scores to students and counselors. In constructing the DAT the authors satisfied the essential psychometric requirements but never lost sight of the needs of the test user.

Content.   The DAT consists of eight separately administered tests. Three tests—Verbal Reasoning (VR), Numerical Ability (NA), and Abstract Reasoning (AR)—measure broad intellectual abilities. The items on VR and NA, in particular, are similar to items on many general intelligence and scholastic aptitude tests, whereas the AR items measure nonlanguage reasoning ability. To ensure that a common core of experience was tapped, items on VR and NA use materials commonly taught in U.S. schools. VR utilizes a special form of analogies item that requires students to use reasoning rather than mere associations (see Figure 14.1 for illustrations of DAT items). The authors propose using the combined VR and NA scores as an index of scholastic aptitude.

The other five tests are more specific in content and function. Three of the tests—Clerical Speed and Accuracy (CSA), Mechanical Reasoning (MR), and Space Relations (SR)—would seem to be most valuable in vocational counseling. CSA is the only test in the battery placing primary emphasis on speed, measuring speed of performing a simple perceptual task. MR measures comprehension of mechanical and physical principles as expressed in familiar situations. SR measures the ability to visualize and mentally manipulate concrete materials. The other two tests—Language Usage (LU) and Spelling (Sp)—are both achievement tests. The authors justify their inclusion in the battery because "they represent basic skills that are necessary in so many academic and vocational pursuits" (Bennett, Seashore, and Wesman, 1966, pp. 1–9).

The authors recommend administering the entire battery of eight tests so that the pattern of scores can be considered when counseling the student. Total testing time is slightly over 3 hours, with time limits varying from 6 to 30 minutes per test.[1] The tests can be administered by the classroom teacher, are printed in a reusable booklet, and utilize separate answer sheets, permitting hand or machine scoring.

Consistency and Validity.   The DAT manual reports a large amount of reliability and validity data.[2] For example, data from various sex and grade level groups show that the large majority of corrected split-half reliability coefficients are .90 or higher on all tests and that scores are relatively stable (r's of .58–.87) from over the three-year period from grades 9 to 12.

Because the pattern of test scores is considered important when counseling students, the intercorrelations between tests become of paramount importance. The intercorrelations between tests vary widely, with the largest number falling in the .51–.69 range. Thus, although the separate tests are by no means independent (nor do the authors claim them to be), neither are they so highly related as to be considered all measures of the same ability.

[1] The DAT also contains a Career Planning Questionnaire. The times given are for the ability tests.
[2] Most of the validity data reported are for previous forms of the test. However, since the test content has not changed radically, similar results would be expected for the newer forms.

Figure 14.1 Examples of Items on the Differential Aptitude Tests.

Verbal Reasoning
Pick out words that will fill the blanks so that the sentence will be true and sensible.
Example X. . . . . is to water as eat is to . . . .

A	continue—drive	D	girl—industry
B	foot—enemy	E	drink—enemy
C	drink—food		

Example Z. . . . . is to one as second is to . . . .

A	two—middle	D	first—two
B	first—fire	E	rain—fire
C	queen—hill		

Numerical Ability
Select the correct answer.

Example X			*Example Y*		
Add 13	A	14	Subtract 30	A	15
12	B	25	20	B	26
	C	16		C	16
	D	59		D	8
	E	none of these		E	none of these

Abstract Reasoning
Select the answer figure that completes the series begun in the Problem Figures.

PROBLEM FIGURES   **ANSWER FIGURES**

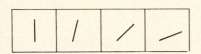 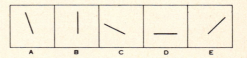

Clerical Speed and Accuracy
Mark the blank on the answer sheet corresponding to the underlined combination on the Test-Items.

TEST ITEMS

V.	**AB**	AC	AD	AE	AF
W.	aA	aB	BA	Ba	**Bb**
X.	A7	7A	B7	**7B**	AB
Y.	Aa	Ba	**bA**	BA	bB
Z.	3A	3B	**33**	B3	BB

SAMPLE OF ANSWER SHEET

	AC	AE	AF	AB	AD
V	::::	::::	▬	::::	::::
	BA	Ba	Bb	aA	aB
W	::::	::::	::::	::::	::::
X	7B ▬	B7 ::::	AB ::::	7A ::::	A7 ::::
Y	Aa ::::	bA ::::	bB ::::	Ba ::::	BA ::::
Z	BB ::::	3B ::::	B3 ::::	3A ::::	33 ::::

Mechanical Reasoning

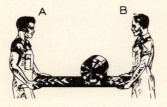

X

Which man has the heavier load?
(If equal, mark C.)

Figure 14.1 (continued)

Space Relations
Decide which figure can be made from the pattern at the left.

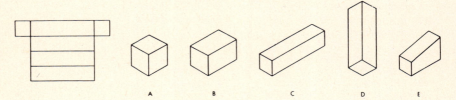

A B C D E

Spelling
Indicate whether the word is spelled correctly or incorrectly.

EXAMPLES

W. man

X. gurl

Y. catt

Z. dog

SAMPLE OF
ANSWER SHEET

	RIGHT	WRONG
W	▮	⫶
X	⫶	▮
Y	⫶	▮
Z	▮	⫶

Language Usage
Indicate which part of the sentence contains an error.

EXAMPLE   SAMPLE OF ANSWER SHEET

Ain't we / going to the / office / next week / at all.

A   B   C   D   E

A	B	C	D	E
▮	⫶	⫶	⫶	▮

Over the years, an abundance of validity data has been collected for the DAT. The bulk of the data presented involves prediction of grades in specific high school courses. Although any attempt to summarize these data necessarily involves oversimplification, several trends are apparent:

- Grades in the common high school courses are best predicted by VR, NA, and LU, and by the VR + NA composite.
- By and large, course grades are best predicted by the corresponding test; for example, VR and LU are the best predictors of English grades, NA of math grades, and LU in language courses.
- In courses such as art and industrial arts, there is some, but far from overwhelming, support for the validity of the DAT tests.
- When results are considered on a school-by-school basis, there is a wide range of validity coefficients.

Other validity data show that the predictive accuracy of the DAT decreases only slightly over a period of several years. Evidence is also presented showing that DAT scores are often highly correlated (for example, .70–.80) with scores on achievement test batteries administered either concurrently with or after the DAT. Finally, several large-scale follow-up studies indicate that students who obtain different amounts of post-high school education and/or enter different occupations can be differentiated on the basis of their (high school) DAT scores; however, the difference appears to be as much a function of the level of DAT scores as the pattern of scores.

Score Interpretation. In many ways the DAT procedures are a model for the interpretation of test scores. Normative data are presented for large representative samples of high school students with separate norm tables available for each grade (8–12) and sex grouping and for fall and spring testings. On CSA, a highly speeded test, there are even separate norms depending on what type of answer sheets were used. Percentile rank and stanine conversion tables are available. Percentile ranges are reported to emphasize the fact that each score contains some measurement error and to caution the user against overinterpretation. Normal percentile charts are used to present the test scores graphically (see Figure 8.4). Note that the profile is constructed so that significant differences on two tests are indicated by nonoverlapping bars. Finally, the test authors stress the value of collecting local validity data and suggest use of expectancy tables to interpret scores.

Other Multiaptitude Test Batteries

The DAT illustrates the approach and many of the considerations involved in the construction and use of multiaptitude batteries. However, several other batteries have features that are worth noting. The SRA[3] *Primary Mental Abilities* test is important historically and is an example of an educationally oriented battery. The *Flanagan Aptitude Classification* and *Flanagan Industrial Tests* and the *General Aptitude Test Battery* are examples of tests designed for use in occupational and industrial settings. Guilford's tests are an illustration of tests developed from a comprehensive research program on the structure of abilities, the University of Southern California Aptitudes Research Project.

The Primary Mental Abilities. The PMA is important historically because it was developed from Thurstone's pioneering research on the structure of abilities and was the first multifactor battery. The current revision has five levels, covering the K–12 grade range, with four or five test at each grade level. The factors measured include: Verbal Meaning—the ability to deal with words and verbal concepts; Number Facility—facility in doing simple numerical tasks; Spatial Relations—ability to visualize and conceptualize; Reasoning—the ability to think logically; and Perceptual Speed—ability to distinguish sizes and shapes. The Verbal Meaning, Number Facility, and Spatial Relations Tests occur at each level; Perceptual Speed is tested only at younger ages (grades K–6), and Reasoning at older age levels

---

[3] SRA refers to Science Research Associates, the publisher of the test.

(grades 4–12). Two other of Thurstone's original factors, Word Fluency and Memory, are not represented in the battery.

The Flanagan Aptitude Classification and Industrial Tests. These are two separate, though overlapping, test batteries. The *Flanagan Aptitude Classification Tests* (FACT) consists of 16 tests; the *Flanagan Industrial Tests* is a battery composed of 18 tests. In contrast to the DAT and PMA, these batteries were explicitly designed to tap abilities that are important in successful occupational performance. Systematic job analyses were conducted to identify elements that are common to a number of jobs and related to successful job performance. Tests were then constructed to measure these job elements, using content that was directly relevant to the occupational world. For example, the Inspection test requires the subject to compare pictures of small parts and identify ones having imperfections (see Figure 14.2). Or, to use another example, the Assembly test consists of a picture of a number of disassembled parts followed by a series of pictures of completed parts; the subject's task is to choose the completed object that can be made from the disassembled parts. On other tests in the battery (for example, Arithmetic and Vocabulary) the content is not as specifically vocational.

The General Aptitude Test Battery. In contrast to the multiaptitude batteries discussed previously, the GATB, which was developed by the U.S. Employment Service, includes several performance measures. Two of the nine factors measured—Finger Dexterity and Manual Dexterity—utilize performance tests; the other seven factors (Intelligence, Verbal Aptitude, Numerical Aptitude, Spatial Aptitude, Form Perception, Clerical Perception, and Motor Coordination are measured by conventional paper-and-pencil tests. In all, the GATB includes 12 tests requiring approximately 2½ hours of testing time.

The GATB was designed for use in preemployment counseling of high school students and adults seeking employment. Its major purpose is to provide a basis for job placement and referral. Also, an extensive program of research, including longitudinal studies, is being carried out to increase the pool of validity and interpretive data. The paradigm used in the majority of these studies involves identifying the aptitudes needed in a given occupation and then establishing the minimum test scores needed for successful job performance.

The USES program also includes two other tests that are used for job applicants having limited reading ability. The *Nonreading Aptitude Test Battery* is an adaptation of the GATB that provides nine scores: intelligence, verbal, numerical, spatial, form perception, clerical perception, motor coordination, finger dexterity, and manual dexterity. The latter three tests are the same as those on the GATB; the others are adaptations that require no reading and include tasks and material familiar to disadvantaged high school students and adults. Typical test items measure matching and use of coins, tools, and familiar objects. The *Basic Occupational Literacy Test* includes tests of reading vocabulary, reading comprehension, arithmetic computation, and arithmetic reasoning. Each test has three or four levels, each at a different level of competency. Items contain practical content and are designed to measure the literacy level of disadvantaged students and adults.

Figure 14.2 Examples of Items on the FACT Assembly and Inspection tests.

A. Inspection

Task is to identify parts having flaws—that is, ones that do not match first part in row.

SAMPLE PROBLEMS

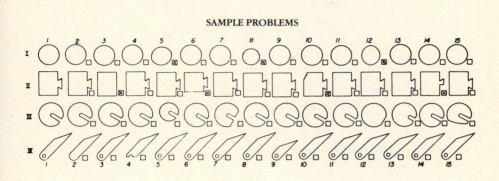

B. Assembly

Task is to indicate which completed part can be made by assembling component parts.

PRACTICE PROBLEMS

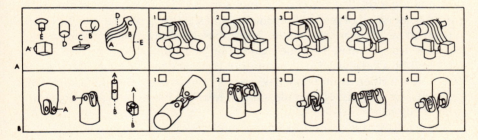

Guilford's Tests. When discussing theories of intellectual structure in Chapter 13, we mentioned Guilford's structure-of-intellect model. This model, as you will recall, suggested that there are 120 intellectual abilities which can be classified along three dimensions: operations, contents, and products. In the course of his research, Guilford has developed tests for many of these abilities. While not a formal test battery, in the sense of the DAT or GATB, these tests are similar to those included on multiaptitude batteries, and normative and reliability data are available for many of the tests.

Each component can be measured by one or more types of test items. For example, the ability to cognize[4] symbolic units can be measured by a Disemvoweled Words Test:

Put vowels in the blanks to make real words: P_W_R   C_RT_N

or a Scrambled Words test:

Rearrange the letters to make real words: RACIH   TVOES

The ability to cognize semantic units can be measured by a Vocabulary test:

GRAVITY means _____   VIRTUE means _____

Other tests measure divergent production. For example, divergent production of symbolic units can be measured by a Word Fluency test:

Write words containing the letter P.

and the divergent production of semantic classes can be measured by an Alternative Uses test:

List possible uses for a newspaper other than its common use.

Although these examples all use verbal material, other tests use nonverbal tasks. For example, the divergent production of figural systems is measured by a Making Objects test, which requires test takers to draw a specified object that incorporates a given geometric figure.

Evaluation of Multiaptitude Batteries

Multiaptitude tests, like any class of tests, vary widely among themselves. However, consideration of several fundamental questions will serve to put these tests in perspective. First, are multiaptitude tests based on any explicit rationale? Multiaptitude tests are based on the assumption that human performance can be described by a relatively small number of basic abilities. Many of the tests are based on a further assumption: The appropriate strategy for identifying these traits is factor analysis. Thus multiaptitude tests are based on a specific, clearly defined rationale.

Second, have the desired technical standards of test construction been attained? Although there are wide differences among the tests, it is clear that highly adequate levels of consistency and sufficient normative data can be obtained (for example, the DAT).

Third, do the multiaptitude tests cover a wide range of abilities? The batteries discussed covered from four to twenty-odd abilities. In some cases (such as the DAT and PMA), coverage was limited to academically related abilities that can be measured by paper-and-pencil tests; others (such as FACT) have a broader coverage of skills and use more ingenious formats. Especially for vocationally oriented batteries, more performance and motor tests would be desirable.

Finally, do the tests demonstrate differential validity? This is the central issue; yet, here, support for the multiaptitude approach is the weakest. Although the

---

[4] Cognize means to discover or recognize.

empirical evidence shows that single tests within multiaptitude batteries, or combinations of tests, can predict specific educational outcomes, there is little strong evidence that the tests are differentially predictive—either in terms of different tests predicting different outcomes or by increasing predictive accuracy by using patterns of scores. The validity of multiaptitude tests in predicting vocational criteria is even less well established. Multiaptitude tests, even when well constructed and technically sound, have not clearly demonstrated the ability to accomplish their stated goal—the differential prediction of various criteria from a common set of test scores.

measures of specific aptitudes and abilities

Multiaptitude batteries attempt to measure a wide range of abilities within the context of a single, integrated test battery. As indicated earlier, there is another approach to measuring abilities: building separate tests to measure each specific aptitude or ability. In this section we shall discuss examples of this approach. Some of the tests we shall consider focus on abilities germane to an academic setting; others tap occupational and vocational skills; still others are used in various clinical settings.[5] All focus on a specific ability, or small group of related abilities, rather than attempting to provide a comprehensive picture of an individual's abilities and skills.

Using this approach has both advantages and limitations. The major advantage of constructing specific aptitude tests is that the ability of concern can be measured in more depth. That is, by concentrating on a single ability, one can probe its various facets in more detail. And since the test is usually developed for a specific purpose or situation, it should be a more valid indicator for that particular situation. On the other hand, such an approach can lead to overspecificity and lack of generality. Then, too, if a test user wishes to measure several abilities, he will have to develop his own test battery by combining several existing tests. In some ways this is good, in that he can pick the most relevant tests for his purposes rather than accepting an existing battery. But this may require developing a new battery for each person or situation. Furthermore, since the various tests will have been developed on different populations, normative data will not be comparable, and thus there will be interpretation problems, especially when scores on various measures are compared.

Tests of Specific Academic Abilities

In previous chapters we described a variety of achievement and mental ability tests used to predict performance in specific courses or course areas. In most cases, the test items sampled the types of tasks to be encountered in the course, the assumption being that if a student can perform well on these sample tasks, they can master the subject matter.[6]

---

[5] In this section, as elsewhere in the book, we shall only illustrate some of the variety of tests available; we shall not attempt to comprehensively survey all possible types of tests.

[6] In content and format these tests are similar to achievement tests, particularly readiness tests. However, their use is more similar to aptitude tests.

At the elementary and secondary levels there are tests designed to predict performance in various subject matter areas; for example in mathematics courses such as algebra and geometry. There are also tests measuring skills, such as listening comprehension and critical thinking, which can be applied in various content areas. For example, the *Watson-Glaser Critical Thinking Appraisal* measures the ability to draw sound inferences, recognize assumptions, reason by deduction, draw conclusions, and evaluate arguments.

Another area where several tests are available is the learning of foreign languages. These tests often include both paper-and-pencil and audio-visual items. For example, the *Modern Language Aptitude Test* consists of five tests. Two tests, Number Learning and Phonetic Script, utilize an artificial language; the former is presented aurally and the latter audiovisually. The other three tests—Spelling Clues, Words in Sentences, Paired Associates—measure students' sensitivity to subtler aspects of the English language. All measure skills that have been shown to be essential for learning a foreign language. Another well-known test, the *Test of English as a Foreign Language* (TOEFL), is administered to foreign applicants to American universities and covers four areas: listening comprehension, English structure and written expression, reading comprehension, and vocabulary. Although the TOEFL is an achievement test, it is used by colleges and graduate schools to determine whether foreign students have enough proficiency in the English language to succeed academically in American universities. When used in this manner it functions as an aptitude test.

Creativity

Creativity has been an area of interest to many psychologists and educators (see, e.g., Arieti, 1976; Barron, 1963, 1968, 1969, 1972; Getzels & Jackson, 1962; Guilford, 1968; MacKinnon, 1962; Nicholls, 1972; Stanley, 1977; Taylor & Getzels, 1975; Torrance & Myers, 1970; Wallach, 1971; Wallach & Wing, 1969; Welsh, 1975). Some of the interest has been generated because creativity is a requisite skill in certain occupations—for example, art, architecture, creative writing, and scientific research. Other people have been interested in creativity as a cognitive ability, focusing on individual differences in creativity. Still other investigators have been interested in creativity as a problem-solving method. As a consequence, some investigators have concentrated on the skills and personal and background characteristics of creative persons and others have studied the creative process. Since this book is concerned with testing, we shall focus on the measurement of creative ability.

Defining creativity is an exercise in convergent and discriminant validity. The various skills and functions proposed as manifestations of creativity not only must be intercorrelated (convergent validity), they also must be distinct from other abilities, particularly intelligence (discriminant validity). There is general agreement that in order for a behavior to be indicative of creativity, or a test classed as a measure of creativity, responses must be produced rather than just selected from among available alternatives. A second essential element of creative behavior is that the responses be, in some sense, original. Although some writers appear to accept all original responses as being of equal value, most writers insist that the response be useful or relevant so as to eliminate obviously absurd responses.

Tests of Creativity. The search for characteristics that identify creative persons and pleas for identification and training of creative talent have far outstripped the development of tests for measuring creativity. However, several tests have been developed. Some of the tests developed from Guilford's structure of the intellect model, particularly those that measure aspects of divergent thinking, can be classed as tests of creativity. Examples would include Guilford's tests of Word Fluency (rapid listing of words containing a given letter), Ideational Fluency (naming things or objects that belong in the same class), Associational Fluency (producing synonyms), Alternative Uses (listing possible uses for an object, other than its normal uses), and Consequences (listing the various possible consequences of a given act). All these tests require verbal responses. Other tests in the model require figural responses, for example, the Making Objects test, which involves drawing specified objects utilizing a specified set of stimulus designs.

The *Torrance Tests of Creative Thinking* are divided into two major sections: Thinking Creatively with Words and Thinking Creatively with Pictures. The tests are structured as games or activities and are presumed to be applicable from kindergarten through graduate school, although certain modifications are made for younger children. Thinking Creatively with Words consists of a variety of activities. Three are based on a single sketch, with the subject's task being to list the questions he would ask to find out what is happening in the picture, guess the possible causes of the action in the sketch, and guess the possible consequences of the action pictured. Other activities require suggesting improvements for a toy, suggesting unusual uses for a common object, asking questions about the same common object, and guessing the consequences of an improbable action. Scoring is on three dimensions: fluency (number of relevant responses), flexibility (variety of response classes), and originality. Thinking Creatively with Pictures consists of three tasks: utilizing a colored shape to construct an original picture, sketching objects using pairs of specified irregular lines (see Figure 14.3), and constructing designs either from pairs of parallel lines or circles. These tests are scored on the basis of fluency, flexibility, originality, and elaboration.

Figure 14.3. An Item Similar to Those on Torrance's Test of Thinking Creatively with Pictures.

Evaluation. Certain problems are apparent on creativity tests. For example, both the Torrance and Guilford tests have time limits. Scoring, of course, cannot be completely objective. However, data show that trained scorers using a scoring manual can attain acceptable levels of scorer reliability. Still, the reliability of creativity tests are lower than desirable. Normative data are limited. Guilford's test construction procedures ensure that his tests will have both factorial and discriminant validity; however, correlations with other tests and socially relevant criteria are generally lacking. Torrance's tests, in contrast, have been related to a variety of criteria, but his research has lacked the systematic nature of Guilford's. Consequently, no clear pattern of validity results has emerged. Thus, although several creativity tests are available for research use, the tests have not yet reached the stage of development that allows for meaningful interpretations of individual scores.

Musical and Artistic Abilities

Tests of musical and artistic ability can be considered together because many of the same problems are encountered in both areas. For example, in both music and art one can clearly distinguish between appreciation and performance. It is one thing to be able to paint a picture, throw a pot, or cast a statue; it is another to be able to understand and appreciate a work of art. The two skills are not necessarily highly intercorrelated: Many persons can evaluate the merit of a work of art but are themselves able to produce only stereotyped works. Consequently, tests of the two types of skills must be quite different. Similarly, music appreciation and the ability to play an instrument (or sing) are distinct abilities.

The format of most art appreciation tests is quite similar: The test taker is presented with representations of two works of art—one a work of proven and judged merit, the other the same or similar object in slightly modified form—and is asked to indicate which work is aesthetically superior. Data suggest that scores do discriminate between relevant groups; for example, artists and art teachers obtain higher scores than do other persons.

Standardized tests of musical and artistic abilities generally assess only component skills rather than attempt to measure complex performance skills. For example, the *Seashore Measures of Musical Talents* measures skills such as pitch, rhythm, timbre, loudness discrimination, and tonal memory. In the pitch test the subject indicates which of two tones is higher (or lower) in pitch; the rhythm test requires the subject to compare two rhythm patterns and judge whether they are similar or different. Performance tests in art typically require the examinee to produce drawings under restricted conditions (for example, using a set of irregular lines as part of a picture). Scoring, requiring quality ratings, is subjective and often unreliable.

Tests of artistic and musical skill would seem to be prime candidates for a minimum proficiency approach to interpretation. That is, low scores indicate lack of necessary skills, thus indicating that chances for attaining success are virtually nonexistent. (A person who has trouble discriminating between tones will never learn to play the violin well.) However, because of the myriad of factors that determine artistic or musical success, performance above the threshold level would indicate only that the person has the minimal level of necessary ability.

Physical and Psychomotor Abilities

Although there are wide and obvious differences in physical abilities between people, they have been of little concern to psychologists. One reason, perhaps, is that the methods of measuring these abilities are more straightforward than measuring psychological characteristics. However, the measurement of these abilities is very important in other professions. For example, physicians measure visual and auditory acuity and a variety of physiological functions, such as blood pressure, respiration, and brain functioning. Physiologists are interested in various types of measures, such as cardiovascular functions and muscular activity. Measurement plays a large part in physical education and athletics as witnessed by the emphasis on speed, coordination, and muscular strength in the recruitment and training of athletes and the variety of statistics kept in all sports.

Psychologists interested in psychomotor abilities usually have taken one of two approaches. Some have been interested in identifying the basic dimensions of psychomotor performance: the skills and abilities individuals bring to learning new tasks, which are related to performance on a variety of tasks. For example, spatial visualization ability has been found to be related to performance on such diverse tasks as aerial navigation, blueprint reading, and dentistry (Fleishman, 1972). The other approach is to develop tests for specific abilities, such as finger dexterity and hand-eye coordination. Generally these tests have been developed for use in vocational selection and placement.

A Taxonomy of Perceptual-Motor Abilities.   As an example of the first approach, consider the work of Fleishman (1964, 1972, 1975). Through an extensive series of experimental and factor analytic studies using several hundred tasks, Fleishman identified 11 perceptual-motor and 9 physical proficiency factors. The perceptual-motor factors are:

Multilimb coordination: coordinated movement involving more than one limb, as when operating controls
Control precision: precise adjustment of controls using larger muscles
Response orientation: rapid selection or movement of controls
Reaction time: speed in response to an auditory or visual stimuli
Speed of arm movement: speed in making gross, discrete arm movements when accuracy is not required
Rate control: precise timing of continuous responses in reaction to changes in speed or direction of moving target
Manual dexterity: manipulating large objects under speeded conditions
Finger dexterity: manipulation of small objects using fingers
Arm-hand steadiness: precise arm-hand positioning where strength and speed requirements are minimal
Wrist-finger speed: rapid tapping within relatively large areas
Aiming: rapid dotting within a small area

The last two factors are more limited in scope and can be measured by paper-and-pencil tests; the others are more general and require apparatus for testing.

Fleishman also identified nine physical proficiency factors, which are abilities relevant to athletic and gross physical performance. These are as follows:

Static strength: maximum force exerted against external objects, such as in lifting weights

Dynamic strength: muscular endurance in exerting force continuously or repeatedly; ability to propel, support, or move one's body, such as pull-ups

Explosive strength: ability to mobilize energy for bursts of muscular effort, such as in sprints or jumping

Trunk strength: dynamic strength specific to trunk muscles, such as leg lifts or sit-ups

Extent flexibility: flexing or stretching trunk and back muscles

Dynamic flexibility: repeated, rapid, flexing trunk movements and resistance of muscles in recovery from strain, such as bending to touch floor

Gross body coordination: ability to coordinate action of several parts of the body while it is in motion

Gross body equilibrium: ability to maintain balance without visual cues

Stamina: capacity to sustain maximum effort requiring cardiovascular exertion

Fleishman suggests that these factors measure basic physical fitness.

When measuring psychomotor performance, the stage of practice must be taken into account. Most motor tasks require a warm-up period but, as practice continues, performance increases as muscles get in tone and the person learns how to perform the task. After a point, however, fatigue sets in and performance declines. In addition, as we practice a new skill, the intellectual component (thinking about how to do the task) decreases and performance becomes more automatic. Thus, in evaluating performance on psychomotor tasks one must consider both the individual's learning curve in mastering the task and the stage of the particular practice session, taking into account the effects of such factors as fatigue.

Fleishman also distinguished between ability and skill. By ability he means the more general traits of an individual. By skill he means the level of proficiency in performing a specific task, such as flying an airplane, serving a tennis ball, or operating a machine. The assumption is that the skills involved in performing a complex activity are determined by the more basic abilities (such as the factors he has identified). Whether abilities do, in fact, determine skill in any task can only be determined by validity studies in each particular situation. However, as noted, Fleishman has studied several hundred tasks and found that the abilities he identified account for the majority of variance in task performance.

Tests of Specific Skills.   The other approach is to construct tests to measure specific abilities. As these tests measure such factors as coordination, strength, or manipulative and dexterity skills, they will generally be performance rather than paper-and-pencil tests.

As an example, consider the *Purdue Pegboard* test. This test measures two types of dexterity: arm-and-hand and finger dexterity. The test apparatus consists of a board with two parallel rows of holes drilled down the center and a set of shallow trays at one end; the trays contain metal pins, collars, and washers. The test consists of four separately timed portions: (1) placing pins in the holes, one at a time, with the right hand; (2) the same task using the left hand; (3) the same task using both hands simultaneously; and (4) assembling pin-washer-collar-washer combinations using both hands. The test would seem to be a promising selection aid for assembly, packing, and other precise manipulative jobs; however, few validity data are available.

Other tests of manipulative abilities involve tasks such as placing cutouts into a form board and manipulating objects with a tweezers or other tools.

Vocational Aptitude Tests

Certain intellectual aptitudes, such as verbal and numerical reasoning, are important determiners of vocational success, especially in occupations requiring extensive academic preparation. Other aptitude measures focus on vocationally related skills, measuring both cognitive skills and motor and manipulative abilities. Although many vocational aptitude tests use a paper-and-pencil format (for administrative and scoring ease), they are not restricted to this format. Furthermore, many tests have restrictive time limits, either because speed is an essential element in successful job performance or because the basic task is so simple that the only meaningful way to discriminate between individuals is in terms of their speed of response.

Since the primary goal is to predict job performance, the first step in validating vocational aptitude tests is to conduct a *job analysis* to determine what skills and abilities are needed to perform the job successfully. The next step is to identify or construct tests that measure these abilities. We then do a validity study to determine the relationship between scores on the various tests and the criteria of job success. As a result of these studies, decision rules are developed to indicate how applicants will be selected or placed on jobs.

Another approach (Dunnette, 1966) focuses on job elements or skills. This approach recognizes that different persons may perform the same job in different ways (by using different skills or job elements). It also recognizes the interaction of situational factors with job skills.

Examples of Vocational Aptitude Tests.   In the previous section we described several performance tests that can be used for vocational selection and placement. Other vocational abilities can be measured by paper-and-pencil tests. An example is the *Bennett Mechanical Comprehension Test,* the test from which the DAT Mechanical Comprehension section was derived. This test measures the ability to understand physical principles expressed through practical situations. Because the test measures understanding of principles, it is most appropriate for predicting success on skilled technical jobs and semiskilled jobs involving the use of complex machinery.

Another vocationally relevant ability that can be assessed by paper-and-pencil tests in spatial visualization—the ability to visualize two- and three-dimensional objects as they are rotated, manipulated, or changed in some manner. For example, on the *Minnesota Paper Form Board* the stimuli consist of several geometric pieces; the test taker is asked to select, from among several alternatives, the geometric design that can be made by assembling the pieces. The DAT Spatial Relations test uses a slightly different task. Note that these tests require mental, rather than physical, manipulation of the object.

A quite different ability that also can be assessed by paper-and-pencil tests is clerical aptitude. Tests of this ability (for example, The *Minnesota Clerical Test* and the Clerical Speed and Accuracy section of the DAT) might equally well be called tests of perceptual speed and accuracy, since they assess the ability to note details quickly and accurately. The typical format requires comparing pairs of names or numbers; the task is to indicate whether the two elements are identical or different (in any respect). Clerical tests are probably the best example of a pure speed test. The tests are speeded because the skill tested is so simple that almost anyone could attain 100 percent accuracy given sufficient time; however, people differ widely in the speed with which they can perform the task.

The tests discussed are all standardized measures published by testing companies and designed for use in both counseling and selection. The armed services and many individual companies have developed their own tests to aid in selecting among applicants and placing workers in positions. Being designed for a particular job, these tests are often better job samples than standardized tests, which necessarily are more general.

Proficiency Tests. The tests discussed in the previous paragraphs measured broad skills and are used to predict occupational success. An alternative approach in testing vocational skills can also be used; we could measure whether an individual has developed the knowledge and skills necessary to perform an occupation. Such tests would be proficiency or competency tests.

An example of competency testing is the National Occupational Competency Testing Program (ETS, 1973). This program was instituted because it was recognized that many skilled craftsmen had developed high levels of skill through experience on their jobs. Certification of these skills would be valuable for several purposes, including awarding college credit and as a basis for certifying the occupational proficiency of prospective teachers of vocational subjects in community and junior colleges. Tests have been developed for 24 specialities in 13 industrial areas (including auto mechanics, plumbing, architectural drafting, printing, quantity food cooking, cabinet making, and millwork). Each test consists of a 3-hour written test plus a 4- to 6-hour performance section.

Other Methods. Vocational skills and abilities often are measured by procedures other than tests. A common procedure is to rely on biographic data, the assumption being that a person's skills can be assessed by information regarding his or her past education, training, and job experience (Owens, 1971). At other times, data are obtained by performance ratings, either obtained on the job, on simulated job samples, or in specific evaluation settings. Another approach, used for both training and placement, is the assessment center. This method utilizes a variety of evaluative procedures, including tests, observations and ratings, interviews, and simulated tasks. The goal is to obtain a comprehensive picture of an individual's strengths and limitations, information that can then be used to place individuals on appropriate jobs or to provide suggestions for training that will increase the skills needed to perform a job effectively.

Evaluation.   Any general statements about the validity of vocational aptitude tests must be qualified since, as might be expected, validity coefficients are highly situation-specific. It is clear, however, that vocational aptitude tests do not predict vocational criteria as well as intelligence and scholastic aptitude tests predict academic criteria. It is also clear that prediction generally is better when the criterion is performance in a training program rather than on-the-job performance.

Clinical Testing

School psychologists, clinical psychologists, and counselors often work with children and adults who are having difficulty functioning in school, on the job, or in everyday life. Sometimes the client's difficulties arise from problems in cognitive functioning, or clients may have difficulty mastering the tasks of everyday living; at other times the problem is in the area of personal or social adjustment. If the person is to function more effectively, the source of the problem must be identified and appropriate remedial treatment provided. Although identification of such problems are often made by interviews, observations, and other less formal assessment methods, there are tests designed for use in these situations. In this section we shall discuss two types of tests: measures of cognitive dysfunction and adaptive behavior measures.[7]

Cognitive Dysfunction.   Since cognitive abilities play an important role in all areas of life–in school, on the job, and in everyday living–any dysfunction of cognitive processes can seriously affect an individual's ability to function effectively in society. An obvious example is mental retardation. However, in this section we shall not be concerned with general retardation but instead will focus on more specific problems, such as the diagnosis of brain damage and learning disabilities.

A variety of methods have been proposed for diagnosing various types of cognitive dysfunctioning. One common technique is to utilize scores on individual intelligence tests. Although observation of performance on any individual intelligence tests may provide clues to the possible brain damage or other areas of cognitive dysfunctioning, the Wechsler scales are particularly appropriate for use in these situations because separate scores are obtained on a number of subtests. The usual procedure is to look at the pattern of scores on the various subtests. One clue is provided by low scores on certain subtests. For example, a low WISC-R Block Design score may indicate problems in integrating and reproducing perceptual material. This may be either a reception problem (the child cannot accurately perceive the elements of the task), a conceptual problem (the child does not understand the nature of the task),or a reproduction problem (the child perceives and understands the task but cannot reproduce the pattern). Other evidence may be obtained by looking at the scatter and pattern of scores on the

[7] Diagnosis of personal, emotional, and social problems will be considered in Chapters 15–17.

various subtests or looking at scores on subtests presumed to measure certain critical functions. Although there are diverse opinions on the validity of such pattern analyses (see, e.g., Kaufman, 1979; Matarazzo, 1972), this method of diagnosis is widely used.

There are also tests designed to measure brain damage and cognitive dysfunction. Block Design tests (similar to those on the WAIS-R and WISC-R) are frequently used for this purpose. Another widely used test is the *Bender-Gestalt (The Bender Visual Motor Gestalt Test)*. This test consists of nine cards, each containing a simple design (Figure 14.4). The subject copies the design with the card present. Although many clinicians use the test informally, normative data are available. There is also evidence that scores on the test predict school achievement and can be used to diagnose brain damage (Koppitz, 1975).

Another example is the *Goldstein-Scheerer Tests of Abstract Thinking* which include such tasks as block designs, color-form sorting, object sorting, and reproducing figures. There have also been attempts to use electrophysiological measures, such as the EEG, to diagnose learning problems (see Gresham & Evans, 1979, for a review).

In education, the focus has been on learning disabilities. As mentioned previously, a learning disability is a specific area of weakness in a child of average or above-average intelligence. Diagnosis is usually made from a variety of evidence, with one essential element being a significant difference between performance on an achievement measure and on a measure of intelligence. Thus diagnoses are made from scores on standardized tests, taken in conjunction with classroom observations and other sources of information.

To get more detailed information about the specific nature of the disability, tests of more specific functions are often administered. These may be diagnostic reading or mathematics tests, tests of the ability to understand verbal and written communication, perceptual tests, or short-term memory tests. One test that is frequently used is the *Illinois Test of Psycholinguistic Abilities*. This test is based on Osgood's model of the communication process, which contains three elements: channels (auditory-vocal, visual-motor), processes (receptive, organizing, or expressive), and levels (representational or automatic). The battery consists of ten tests that measure various combinations of dimensions—for example, items requiring the use of the visual-motor channel and expressive process at the representational level. The purpose is to locate the specific source of the disability.

Some Problems.   Making clinical assessments and diagnoses from patterns of test scores, either on a single instrument such as the WISC-R or a battery of tests, presents certain difficulties that are worth reviewing because they point out ubiquitous problems in psychological and educational assessment. Some of these problems are psychometric. For example, the difference between the scores being compared must be large enough to be statistically significant. Too often small, unreliable differences are interpreted as if they reflected true differences. As the size of the difference needed for significance depends on the reliability of the measures and the correlation between the measures, significant differences

Figure 14.4 Items Similar to Those on the Bender-Gestalt.

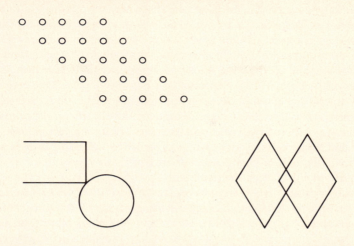

are most likely to be found when the individual tests are highly reliable and the tests measure distinctly different characteristics (that is, have low intercorrelations). Then, too, as atypical cases are a small minority of the total population, we must be concerned with the base rates. Particularly, there will be a tendency to identify too many false positives.[8] Because we are often dealing with many bits of data (e.g., many test scores), a particular diagnostic sign may be significant but only represent a chance finding.[9] Thus all indices should be cross-validated. And, of course, when diagnostic signs derived from one sample are used in other populations, they should be validated in the population in which they are used.

Other problems exist at a more conceptual level. Since behavior is multiply determined, a particular diagnostic sign may hold for some, but not all, persons having the specific disability. Conversely, different patterns of characteristics may result in the same diagnosis. Thus relying on the same pattern of scores for all persons may result in inaccurate classifications, both of false positives and false negatives. Finally, many of the diagnostic categories are not clearly defined. The widely used terms "minimal brain dysfunction" and "learning disability" are good examples. Obviously it will be difficult to measure a construct that is not clearly defined.

Adaptive Behavior. Adaptive behavior skills are those skills needed for effective everyday living. Measures of adaptive behavior are often used in conjunction with more traditional measures of mental ability to assess a child's ability to function in society.

---

    [8] False positives are persons erroneously identified (here, by the test) as having a characteristic or syndrome when in fact they do not; false negatives are persons who have the characteristic or syndrome but are not identified by the test.
    [9] When a large number of comparisons are made, some differences will be significant by chance. For example, since the WISC-R contains 10 subtests, there are 45 possible comparisons between subtests. If we use the 5 percent level of confidence, two comparisons will be significant by chance.

One well-known example is the *Vineland Social Maturity Scale* (Doll, 1965), which measures the child's ability to take responsibility and look after his or her personal needs. Responses are obtained from an interview with the child or an observer (e.g., a parent). Items cover eight categories including self-direction, self-help in eating and dressing, locomotion, communication, and socialization. A similar approach is used on the *Adaptive Behavior Scale* (American Association on Mental Deficiency, 1974). This form consists of two parts. One covers ten behavioral domains, including independent functioning (eating, care of clothing, use of toilet), physical development, language development, economic activity, self-direction, responsibility, and socialization. The other part consists of 14 aspects of maladaptive behavior, such as destructive behavior, hyperactivity, and withdrawal. The goal of both these instruments is to assess children's ability to function adequately in their environment.

A recent approach is the *Adaptive Behavior Inventory for Children* (ABIC), a part of the *System of Multicultural Pluralistic Assessment* (Mercer, 1979). This scale is designed to assess a child's performance in roles other than as a school learner. Again, responses are obtained from a knowledgeable observer, usually a parent. The instrument consists of 242 items of the form:

> How often does *(name)* pay part or all of the costs of his/her entertainment with money he/she has earned?
> Most of the time——Some of the time——Never——

Items are grouped into six scales: Family, Community, Peer Relations, Nonacademic School Roles, Earner/Consumer, and Self-Maintenance. As with the other instruments, the major function of the ABIC is to assess children's ability to function independently in their environment.

Cognitive Styles

Besides differences in abilities, people differ widely in how they attack problems. Some people are reflective, pondering various possibilities before deciding how to proceed; others are impulsive, offering the first answer that occurs to them. Some people tend to group objects, events, or data into broad classes; others use highly specific classes. Some people can tolerate uncertainty and incongruity; others are unwilling to tolerate experiences that go against their conventional experience.

Dimensions such as these are called *cognitive styles* because they reflect different habitual approaches (styles) of dealing with problems and cognitive material. Because they reflect habitual ways of dealing with material, they could be considered to be measures of typical performance. On the other hand, because they influence how a person deals with cognitive problems and the effectiveness of problem solving, they are similar to measures of maximal performance. Although they probably fall between the cracks of maximal and typical performance tests, we shall consider cognitive styles as abilities.

A variety of cognitive styles have been identified (Kogan, 1971; Messick, 1970; Witkin & Goodenough, 1977; Witkin, Moore, Goodenough & Cox, 1977). However, to illustrate the nature and measurement of cognitive styles we shall consider only one: field independence/field dependence (FI/FD). Field independence can be defined as:

an analytic, in contrast to a global, way of perceiving (which) entails a tendency to experience items as discrete from their backgrounds and reflects ability to overcome the influence of an embedding context. (Kogan, 1971, p. 246)

In other words, field independent people are analytic, can separate details from their context, and rely on internal frames of reference. Field dependent people, in contrast, think more globally and are influenced, even distracted, by the context of a problem or situation. The FI/FD dimension is related to a number of other criteria including attentiveness to social cues, social relationships, problem solving, preferences for courses and instructors, and choice of an occupation (Witkin & Goodenough, 1977).

How is FI/FD measured? The original studies used the Body Adjustment Test and the Rod and Frame Test. The Body Adjustment Test places the subject in a tilted chair within a tilted room; the task is to adjust the chair to a true vertical position. In the Rod and Frame Test the subject is put in a darkened room and presented with a luminous rod within a luminous frame. Both the rod and frame can be tilted in various directions; the subject's task is to align the rod in a true vertical direction. FI/FD can also be measured by a paper-and-pencil test, the *Embedded Figures Test*. This test consists of a series of complex geometric figures in which simpler figures are embedded (see Figure 14.5). The subject's task is to locate rapidly the simpler figures within the complex figures. All three tests are reliable and valid measures of FI/FD. Of interest is the fact that the same construct, field independence/field dependence, can be measured by several distinctly different types of tests—a clear illustration of convergent validity.

a review of maximal performance tests

In the past five chapters we have considered various types of maximal performance tests: teacher-built and standardized achievement tests, measures of general ability (intelligence), and a variety of tests designed to measure specific abilities. Before leaving our discussion of maximal performance tests, we shall briefly review some important points and look at the emerging trends in the measurement of abilities and achievement.

Achievement tests are certainly the most widely used type of test, and there is little disagreement that achievement testing is a necessary part of the educational process, particularly teacher-built classroom tests. Standardized achievement tests have not received such uncritical acceptance. Critics have argued that they measure only a limited range of skills, that they are biased against members of certain minority groups, and that they are improperly used to evaluate teachers and curricula. All of these arguments have some merit, inasmuch as tests have

Figure 14.5 Type of Item Used on the Embedded Figures Test.

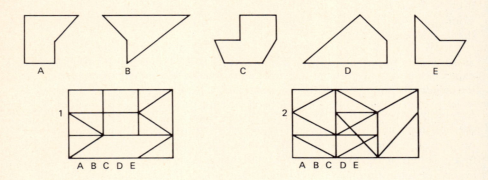

been misused. On the other hand, one could equally well argue that education can only be improved if changes are based on solid empirical data, such as provided by good tests (Ebel, 1964, 1981). I believe that tests should be used more in education, especially to provide information that will aid in improving instruction and facilitate learning.

The major trend in achievement testing has been the increased emphasis on content-referenced (criterion-referenced) testing. The argument here is that by showing what students do and do not know, what they can and cannot do, content-referenced tests provide more useful information for planning instruction for classes or individual students. This point of view cannot be denied. It should also be realized, however, that many decisions in education are comparative; thus, norm-referenced achievement tests continue to have a place. Since the two types of tests have varying purposes, they should be viewed as providing complementary types of information, not as examples of proper and improper testing (which is the way many people view them).

Tests of general and specific abilities can also be used for a variety of purposes, in education, in business and industry, and in counseling and guidance. Of all the types of ability tests, intelligence tests have come under the most fire. Some criticism results from how they are used, for example, as one basis for placing individuals in special education courses or for selecting students for college, graduate, and professional schools. Even though some critics claim that the tests do not predict performance adequately, there is ample data to support their use in a variety of situations. Of course, any test should be validated for each use. Other criticisms reflect a lack of understanding of what the tests are designed to measure. This is particularly true of intelligence tests. Since the everyday use of the term "intelligence" suggests a much broader constellation of abilities than the psychologists use, to many people the tests appear to fall short of their goals. However, one must realize that intelligence and academic ability tests are designed to measure a limited subset of skills, not all types of mental abilities.

Other Factors Determining Performance

One of the truisms of psychology is that behavior is determined by multiple causes. In terms of ability testing, this means that abilities are only one factor in determining performance; interests, values, personality characteristics, motivation, and a myriad of other factors also are important. Moreover, few jobs or academic courses are so simple or specific that only one ability is required. Furthermore, situational factors are important; that is, demands and requirements vary widely, even on presumably similar jobs or courses. The moral is obvious: When trying to predict performance, one must consider more information than just abilities. In addition, we must recognize that there are various ways to attain the same performance level—that is, that people will use different abilities to attain the same level of performance. Or, as Gough has phrased it, psychologists must recognize that there is "no one true path to grace."

For the researcher, the problem is to determine what variables determine success, and their relative contribution (importance). Since situations (for example, jobs, schools, courses) vary widely, this must be determined in each particular setting. The usual research strategy is multiple regression. Typical test users probably will not have the time or the resources to conduct such studies; however, they should familiarize themselves with the relevant research literature so they will understand what factors are likely to determine success in settings similar to the one in which they are working.

Some New Approaches

What are the emerging trends in ability measurement? One is the increased flexibility in testing procedures allowed by use of computers. Not only can computers present items in verbal or numeric language, they can also present graphs and pictorial material. Moreover, test takers can also indicate their answers on the computer, which in turn can score the responses and derive various types of scores. Item banks can be stored in computers and tests constructed by sampling from a pool of potential items, thus allowing different tests to be used for different classes or even each individual.

In terms of psychometric advances, an area of intense work is the application of item characteristic curve (latent trait) theory to test construction. This approach, as you will recall, scales items in terms of difficulty and people in terms of ability. Here again, different tests can be built for different persons; thus, even though each person may take different samples of items, their scores can be reported on a common scale of ability.

The combination of computer technology and the latent trait theory has led to yet another development, *tailored* or *sequential testing* (Betz & Weiss, 1975; Lord, 1977, 1980; Urry, 1977; Weiss, 1974; Wright & Stone, 1979). A computer can be programmed both to administer and score items and to make decisions as to which item should be administered. Sequential testing makes use of this capability. To illustrate, suppose that all students were first administered an item of mod-

Figure 14.6 Paradigm for Sequential Testing

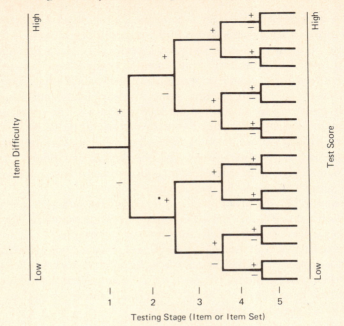

Testing Stage (Item or Item Set)

erate difficulty.[10] Some will pass the item and others will not. If a student passes the first item, a more difficult item is administered next; if the student fails the first item, an easier item is administered. This procedure is then repeated through a series of items (see Figure 14.6 for a schematic diagram of the process). If the items are accurately scaled by difficulty, a person's position on an ability continuum can be ascertained using fewer items than on a conventional test. On a conventional test, examinees answer some items that are easy for them and encounter some that are beyond the limits of their ability. On a sequential test, in contrast, test takers answer only items near the threshold of their ability, not ones that are very easy or too hard. Consequently, fewer items are needed to obtain an ability estimate.

Another trend is the development of tests for different types of abilities, ones that previously have not been measured. Tests of cognitive styles and for identifying learning disabilities are good examples. So, too, are tests devised for special populations, such as entering schoolchildren, children with various handicaps, and tests for minority students. In addition, materials have been developed to help people learn test-taking skills. Content-referenced tests also represent an expanded approach to measurement.

Other developments concern the basic nature of ability measurement. We have noted that several people have suggested that there should be a closer tie between the measurement of abilities and learning theory. For example, Estes (1974) at-

[10] Some approaches use a small set of items (5–10) rather than a single item at each stage of the process.

tempted to integrate learning theory with ability measurement. His major point was that knowing a person's score on an ability test tells us little about the learning processes that led to the score. Thus he suggests the development of measures that more directly indicate the nature of the learning process used. Glaser (1972, 1981), in contrast, looked more to the use of ability tests. His concern was that aptitudes should be defined in terms of the type of performances or learning they predict. That is, we should first determine the nature of learning tasks, and then develop tests that predict success in these types of learning. Both are suggesting a more developmental view of abilities.

Finally, McClelland (1973) and Tyler (1978) both have suggested that the goal of measurement should be to assess each individual's range of competencies rather than to compare all individuals on the same set of abilities, thus presuming that the same abilities are equally important to all people. Although this approach does not necessarily imply that different sorts of tests should be developed, it does have implications for how tests are interpreted and used.

summary

This chapter described a wide variety of tests designed to measure specific aptitudes and abilities. These tests were developed using one of two approaches. Some are multiaptitude test batteries, which are an integrated series of tests designed to measure a number of abilities. The other approach is to construct separate tests for each ability. The former approach is more efficient, provides a common set of normative data, and allows for identification of patterns of relative strengths and weaknesses within an individual. The latter approach often results in more valid measurement, since each test is constructed for a specific purpose, but lacks cross-situational generality and presents problems when making intraindividual comparisons.

A multiaptitude test battery consists of a small number of tests (usually 6–20), each of which measures a relatively broad ability. The abilities may be defined logically or empirically, such as by factor analysis. A good example is the Differential Aptitude Tests, a battery of eight paper-and-pencil tests measuring both academic and vocational abilities and designed for use in counseling high school students. Other batteries measure academic abilities (e.g., the Primary Mental Abilities) or vocational abilities (the General Aptitude Test Battery, the Flanagan Industrial Tests). Batteries which emphasize vocational abilities usually include performance tests and frequently use vocationally related content.

Individual tests are available in many areas. Some are tests of specific academic abilities. These are generally paper-and-pencil tests and may cover a particular course or area (e.g., algebra, foreign language) or measure skills utilized in various course areas (e.g., critical thinking, listening comprehension). Creativity tests measure divergent and original thinking and use both verbal and nonverbal stimuli. Musical and artistic aptitude tests either measure appreciation or the component skills needed for satisfactory performance in an area.

The study of vocational skills has also taken two approaches. One is to develop tests for specific abilities, such as finger and hand dexterity, spatial visualization, and clerical and mechanical aptitude. The other approach, exemplified by Fleishman's work, attempts to identify basic perceptual and psychomotor abilities. Fleishman, as the result of an extensive series of statistical and experimental studies, identified 11 perceptual-motor and 9 physical proficiency factors. These abilities have been shown to predict skill on a large number of tasks. When developing a test battery to predict vocational behaviors, the first step is to do a job analysis, then identify the abilities and skills needed on the job, then try out the tests, then develop decision rules. It is important to validate the tests and decision rules for each job and to consider any situational constraints.

When testing for cognitive dysfunctions and learning disabilities, diagnoses are often made from analyses of patterns of scores on tests such as the WISC-R, or by using tests specifically designed to diagnose particular types of disabilities. Pattern analysis (and diagnosis in general) presents a number of psychometric and definition problems; thus these problems were considered in some detail. We also described measures of adaptive behavior and cognitive styles. These latter tests are somewhat atypical since cognitive styles include elements of both maximal performance and typical performance.

The chapter concluded by reviewing some of the major points made in the discussion of maximal performance testing. We emphasized that test scores are only one source of information used when making decisions. Because behavior in any situation is multiply determined, various sources of information should be used when making decisions or diagnoses, when drawing conclusions, or when making hypotheses.

We also discussed some emerging trends in ability measurement including the development of new types of tests and approaches to measurement (such as content-referenced tests), the increasing use of computers in testing, and tailored testing. We also mentioned the view that tests should provide a better integration between the traditional approach to measurement, the individual differences approach, with knowledge of cognitive processes and the view that the goal of testing should be to determine each individual's range of competencies rather than measuring the same characteristics for all persons. In short, the major emerging trends are attempts to integrate testing with cognitive psychology and to individualize testing, so as to provide information that will be more useful to individuals in developing their skills.

Suggestions for Further Reading

Bersoff, D. N. Silk purses into sow's ears: The decline of psychological testing and a suggestion for its redemption. *American Psychologist,* 1973, *28,* 892–899. Suggests alternatives to traditional assessment procedures and advocates assessing specific behaviors and their consequenses.

Dick, W., Watson, K., & Kaufman, R. Deriving competencies: Consensus versus model building. *Educational Researcher,* 1981, *10*(8), 5–10,13. A description and comparison of two methods for identifying basic skills and competencies.

Ebel, R. L. The future of the measurement of abilities II. *Educational Researcher,* 1973, *2*(3), 5–12. A discussion of the trends and problems in measuring abilities, with particular emphasis on assessment in education.

Fincher, C. Standardized tests, group differences, and public policy. *College Board Review,* 1977, *103,* 19–31. A summary of the controversies and their implications for policy regarding the use of standardized tests in educational settings.

Fleishman, E. A. On the relation between abilities, learning, and human performance. *American Psychologist,* 1972, *27,* 1017–1032. A good introduction to Fleishman's work on physical and psychomotor abilities, which describes both his taxonomy and some representative studies.

Frederiksen, N., & Ward, W. C. Measures for the study of creativity in scientific problem-solving. *Applied Psychological Measurement,* 1978, *2,* 1–24. Describes the development and validation of several measures of scientific and creative thinking ability.

Glaser, R. Individuals and learning: The new aptitudes. *Education Researcher,* 1972, *1* (6), 5–13; The future of testing: A research agenda for cognitive psychology and psychometrics. *American Psychologist,* 1981, *36,* 923–936. In these two articles Glaser argues for a closer integration between ability testing and knowledge derived from studies of learning and cognitive processes.

Rudman, H. C. The standardized test flap. *Phi Delta Kappan,* 1977, *59*(3), 179–185. An evaluation of the arguments presented by critics of standardized testing, distinguishing between valid and invalid criticisms.

Taylor, I. A., & Getzels, J. W. (Eds.). *Perspectives in creativity.* Chicago: Aldine, 1975. A series of papers on the measurement and training of creative abilities.

Witkin, H. A., Moore, C. A., Goodenough, D. R., & Cox, P. W. Field-dependent and field-independent cognitive styles and their educational implications. *Review of Educational Research,* 1977, *47,* 1–64. A review of the research on this cognitive style with emphasis on its educational implications; a good introduction to this area of research.

Zigler, E., & Trickett, P. K. IQ, social competence, and evaluation of early childhood intervention programs. *American Psychologist,* 1978, *33,* 789–798. Authors argue that increased social competence is a more appropriate criterion for intervention programs than IQ increases and discuss problems in measuring social competence.

• part five •
typical
performance
tests

IF you were asked why you like certain people, you would probably mention their personality characteristics and the fact that their attitudes, values, and interests are similar to yours. If you were asked why you selected a particular career or college major, you would probably reply that you like the types of activities involved in the area and find the people in the field to be compatible. If asked to describe your philosophy of life, you would probably describe your values and your attitudes about certain questions and issues.

In each of these examples—whether talking about personality characteristics, interests, opinions, values, or attitudes—you were describing how you typically act or feel. Because of their importance in our lives, psychologists are also interested in these typical behaviors and reactions. Their interest may be more theoretical, as when developing a personality theory or theory of career development, or more practical, as when working with clients in counseling or therapy. To measure these characteristics we use typical performance tests.

As might be expected, the measurement of typical performance presents a different set of problems and concerns than measuring maximal performance. In this unit we shall consider a variety of approaches to typical performance measurement. Chapter 15 is an overview, describing the various methods and some problems in constructing, interpreting, evaluating, and using typical performance tests. Chapter 16 discusses self-report inventories, techniques which have test takers describe their own behavior by responding to self-descriptive statements. Chapter 17 describes other methods of personality assessment, including projective techniques, situational tests, observations, and ratings. When reading these chapters keep in mind two questions: How are the basic principles of psychological measurement used in typical performance measurement? And, how do typical performance tests differ from maximal performance tests?

Chapter 15 • Measures of Typical Performance

THE primary distinction between measures of maximal and typical performance is in the purpose of the measurement. On maximal performance tests the goal is to obtain an indication of the test taker's best possible performance; on typical performance measures, in contrast, we are interested in the test taker's habitual or usual performance or reactions. Although the set for maximal or typical performance is usually apparent from the nature and purpose of the test, it is specifically engendered by the test directions. On maximal performance tests, test takers are instructed to do their best, to obtain the highest possible score; on typical performance tests they are instructed to report their usual reactions or behaviors.

The two classes of tests also differ in other ways. One is the types of behavior measured. Maximal performance tests measure achievement, abilities, and aptitudes; typical performance tests measure interests, personality characteristics (both normal and abnormal), attitudes, values, and opinions. On maximal performance tests there usually is some logical basis or external criterion for differentiating between correct and incorrect responses. In contrast, on typical performance measures responses are usually keyed to represent the predominant response tendency of some designated group. This does not necessarily mean that scoring will be less objective, only that the basis for keying responses is different.

This and the following two chapters discuss measures of typical performance. This chapter will be an overview, briefly discussing various approaches to and problems in typical performance measurement, emphasizing the ways in which the measurement of typical performance differs from the measurement of maximal performance.

types of typical performance measures

More than other areas of psychological and educational testing, personality[1] measurement is characterized by a variety of approaches. The reasons for this diversity are several. Personality, as usually defined, encompasses a broad and heterogeneous area and includes a plethora of concepts and constructs (see, e.g., Hall and

---

[1] Although typical performance measures cover diverse types of behaviors and reactions (e.g., interests, attitudes, preferences, values), we will use the generic term "personality" to refer to all domains measured by typical performance tests.

Lindzey, 1978). And, historically, the personality area has been the subject of much theorizing, with different theories leading to different approaches to both the definition and measurement of central concepts. Consequently, a number of different methods of measuring personality have been developed. In this section we shall briefly discuss several of the more widely used techniques; each will then be considered in more detail later.

Self-Report Measures

One method of measuring personality characteristics is to have an individual describe or characterize himself. He may be presented with a list of adjectives and asked to check the ones that describe his personality; he may be asked whether a series of statements describe him; he may be asked to report his attitudes, interests, or values. The common element in these situations, and in all self-report techniques, is that the individual provides a description or report of his own behavior and/or reactions.

The basic assumption behind this approach is quite simple: The individual is in the best position to observe, describe, and report upon his or her own behavior. After all, you are the only person that is within your skin 24 hours of a day, 365 days of the year; you are always present to observe your own behavior. Any observer would not be privy to all aspects of your life. She could not know your attitudes or reactions to certain events, your thoughts, and your reasons for taking certain actions, although she could ask you about them or infer them from your overt behavior. In short, only you can observe yourself in all situations; thus you can base your report on the widest possible range of observations.

A corollary of the assumption, that people will report their behavior in an unbiased manner, rests on less solid ground. Many personality theories, in fact, imply that most people will present a somewhat biased picture of themselves. Thus, when constructing and scoring self-report techniques, it becomes necessary either to eliminate the opportunity to present a biased report or to identify the degree to which such tendencies operate. In fact, much effort in developing personality tests and much of the controversy over the value of personality measures is directly related to this issue.

Of the many possible methods that could be used to elicit self-descriptions, the most widely used is the *personality inventory*. An inventory consists of a relatively large number of statements, such as:

I frequently get headaches.
I enjoy competitive games.
New and different experiences excite me.
People often expect too much of me.

Test takers respond true (or agree, or some other variation) if the item describes or characterizes them, and false (or disagree) if the statement does not describe them. Because all persons respond to the same set of questions, an inventory can be likened to a standardized interview.

Self-report techniques are often referred to as objective personality tests. If we follow our previous usage of objectivity as referring to recording and scoring procedures, self-report techniques are objective measures. However, if, in addition, we consider that responses to the items reflect personal needs and characteristics, a subjective or projective element clearly enters into the measurement (Meehl, 1945).

Projective Methods

Projective techniques present the test taker with ambiguous stimuli and ask him to interpret or impose some structure upon them. This methodology follows from the projective hypothesis that states that an individual, when confronted with an ambiguous stimulus situation, will impose a structure on the stimulus that reflects his or her particular personality organization. Thus by knowing how a person interprets and structures ambiguous stimuli we can infer something about that person's personality.

An example of a projective technique, which is familiar to most persons, is the *Rorschach Method* (inkblot test). The Rorschach consists of a series of designs that resemble inkblots; the test taker's task is to tell what he sees in the blots. Here, obviously, the stimuli have no inherent meaning; therefore, any meaning must be supplied by the subject, the meaning he projects into the blots. Another widely used variety of projective method is the *Thematic Apperception Test* (TAT). The TAT consists of a series of semiambiguous pictures showing persons engaged in various activities; the test taker's task is to construct a story describing the characters and action. Another approach is the *sentence completion test.* Here, sentence stems such as "My greatest failure was . . ." serve as stimuli, and the task is to complete the sentence.

The validity and usefulness of projective methods have often been questioned. Some people question the basic assumptions underlying these methods; others react negatively to the artificiality of the stimulus material; still others point out the myriad of psychometric problems involved in their use. Even so, they continue to be used extensively in clinical practice (Wade & Baker, 1977).

Situational Methods

In the third general class of personality assessment methods, the common requirement is that individuals are placed in a situation that calls for some action or reaction, their behavior is observed and/or recorded, and a rating is made of the personality characteristics displayed. For example, several people might be brought together and instructed to devise a plan for an advertising campaign. By observing how they interact with each other, how they present their ideas, how their ideas are accepted by other members of the group, who emerges as a leader, how they handle assignments, and other relevant behaviors, an observer could rate these individuals along several personality dimensions (for example, leadership, sociability, effectiveness of expression, dominance, cooperativeness).

A widely used, perhaps overused, situational method is the interview. Although we usually think of one person interviewing another, it is possible to have several interviewers (as in a press conference or selection boards) and/or several candidates being interviewed simultaneously by one interviewer. The interview procedure itself can vary from a highly structured sequence of questions to an open-ended encounter that follows the interests of the participants.

Two characteristics of situational methods deserve special mention. First, the scores derived can either be objective indices of performance or, more commonly, ratings. To use our previous example (designing an advertising campaign) as an illustration, scores could either be the number of suggestions made or ratings of the quality of the suggestions made. Second, situational tests can serve as maximal performance tests as well as typical performance measures. Again, using the same example, if the focus was on the quantity or quality of suggestions made, it would be a maximal performance measure; if the focus was on interpersonal relations, it would be a typical performance measure. Of course, it could serve both functions simultaneously.

Observations and Ratings

In personality assessment, as well as in everyday life, knowledge of an individual's personality can be based on observation of his or her interactions with other people or problem-solving attempts. Thus another approach to personality assessment is direct observation. Frequently these observations are based on naturally occurring situations—as, for example, when students and teachers observe each other in classroom settings. At other times, observations are based on specifically designed evaluation procedures, as in the case of situational tests.

Assessments based on observations can be summarized and reported in various ways. One is by a narrative description, such as in a letter of recommendation. At other times, observations are summarized in a more formal manner. Perhaps the most common way is to use rating scales. *Rating scales* indicate where on the dimension being rated the rater thinks the person's behavior falls. Responses may be points on a quantitative scale or descriptive categories. If the latter approach is used, quantitative values are usually assigned the various categories for data analysis.

Behavioral Assessment

To a psychologist with behavioristic leanings, the approaches to measurement we have been discussing seem inappropriate (cf. Mischel, 1968). Behaviorists would argue that the concepts of traits as characteristics that guide and direct an individual's reactions have no meaning unless we can specify the behavioral referents. This suggests to the behaviorist that the focus of measurement is wrong. Rather than focusing on characteristics of the individual, behaviorists argue that we should look to the environmental conditions and the individual's behavior, not at traits.

Perhaps an illustration will clarify the difference between the trait and behavioristic approaches. Suppose a student tells a counselor that he gets tense, nervous, and uptight on exams and consequently obtains low grades. A counselor using the trait approach would concentrate on assessing characteristics of the student that might relate to his problem—for example, his degree of anxiety, attitude toward school, personality characteristics. The behavioral assessment approach, in contrast, would focus on specifying the conditions under which the student became anxious. In other words, we would look for the situational conditions that are present whenever the student became anxious. Assessment would also focus on specifying, in behavioral terms, the student's behaviors or reactions to these conditions. In short, the goal is to specify the stimulus and response contingencies in the anxiety-provoking situations.

The behavioral assessment approach also emphasizes use of direct measures of behavior rather than reports of behaviors. An example is provided by the study of phobias. Suppose that an individual is afraid of high places. To measure the degree of fear, the behaviorist might actually measure how high off the ground an individual will venture. Or, if a person is afraid of snakes, the behaviorist would measure how closely the individual will approach a snake.

In summary, the behaviorist position emphasizes that behavior is a function of stimulus conditions. To change behavior, you must change the stimulus situation. Measurement enters into the process only to provide a precise description of the stimulus conditions and client behaviors.

Unobtrusive Measures

One of the major problems in personality measurement is that the measurement process may affect the test taker's behavior and, in turn, the results obtained from the measurement. In other words, measurement is *reactive* (Webb et al., 1966). Reactive effects can be manifested in various ways. For example, awareness of being tested may cause the subject to view himself in a different manner or to select a particular role or set in an attempt to meet what he views to be the experimenter's demand.

Because these reactive tendencies alter the individual's behavior or responses, they may result in invalid or distorted responses. The question then becomes: Can we measure behavior by methods that are not reactive? In their book, Webb et al. (1966) describe a number of ingenious ways of obtaining information nonreactively. They call these measures *unobtrusive* because they do not in any way intrude upon the performance.

One obvious method is to use archival records. For example, to study a sales ability, we could look at production records; to study "accident proneness," we could look at accident records.

Another approach is simply to observe people's behavior. For example, if we wanted to study people's reactions to minority groups, we could observe social contacts. We might, for example, have a black worker sit at a table in a company cafeteria and observe whether other employees will sit with him and/or engage him in conversation. Such approaches have been widely used in studying race relations (Crosby, Bromley, & Saxe, 1980).

One problem in observational studies is that many crucial phenomena often do not occur on any predictable schedule. Thus we have to take them as they occur. Even systematic observation, unless involving continuous monitoring, may miss the phenomena. Analysis of retrospective records allows for the identification of patterns and frequency of these critical and important behaviors. However, since these records are retrospective, we cannot study the behavior as it occurs.

Other Approaches

A variety of other approaches are also used to study personality. Certainly one of the most commonly used methods is the clinical (diagnostic) interview. In diagnostic interviews, the therapist asks directive, leading, and open-ended questions and uses the responses as a basis for making judgments about the client's personality structure or degree of pathology. Descriptive information can also be obtained from biographical inventories and life histories. We can also use anecdotal records, which are brief summary reports of behaviors that are either very typical or atypical of a person.

Other methods focus on describing the characteristics of a group of people or of a culture, rather than individuals. An approach that is receiving increasing attention is the use of ethnographic techniques (Rist, 1980; Smith, 1978). Examples of techniques used include the ethnographic interview, where the investigator obtains information from a knowledgeable informant (Spradley, 1979), and the participant observer technique, where the investigator becomes an active member of the group being studied (Spradley, 1980). Paper-and-pencil inventories and ratings have also been used to describe groups of individuals.

Because behavior varies with the situation, methods have also been developed to describe situations and environments (Barker, 1968; Frederiksen, 1972; Moos, 1973, 1974). A related example is scales that describe college and university environments (Pace, 1963, 1979; Stern, 1970).

problems in typical performance measurement: conceptual

In most respects the measurement of maximal performance is quite straightforward. Content domains usually can be defined unambiguously, there are definite correct and incorrect answers, testing procedures can be standardized, statistical methods are available for evaluating consistency and validity, and standards and procedures for interpreting scores have been developed. The measurement of typical performance is more difficult. The constructs and domains measured often are not completely or clearly defined, testing procedures are not always standardized, validation is more indirect, and different interpreters may reach different conclusions from the same set of responses or scores.

In the remainder of this chapter we shall discuss some of the persistent problems in measuring typical performance, both conceptual and psychometric. Many of these problems will be discussed further when describing specific types of instruments. Thus, this chapter will provide an overview for Chapters 16 and 17 and alert you to considerations to take into account when reading about or using specific tests and approaches to personality measurement.

What Is Measured?

In Chapter 2 we stated that the first steps in developing any test are to define the characteristic(s) being measured and to specify the domain of items subsumed under this definition. The reason was obvious: Unless the characteristic being measured has been defined, we do not know what items to include on the test or how to evaluate validity. In the measurement of maximal performance, this generally presented few problems. However, when measuring typical performance the situation is much more complex. Let us consider some of the reasons.

The Variety of Personality Theories.   The content areas covered by typical performance measures are extremely diverse, including interests, personality characteristics, attitudes, and values. Moreover, within each of these areas there are a variety of theoretical approaches, each of which emphasizes a somewhat different set of salient characteristics. For example, in the personality area, there are a dozen or more major theoretical approaches (see, e.g., Corsini, 1977; Hall & Lindzey, 1978). Consequently, with the variety of different theoretical approaches, there are a large number of characteristics that could be measured.

Not only do the theoretical approaches differ in the characteristics (personality dimensions) they consider most important, they also differ in their analytic approach. Endler and Magnusson (1976) have identified four major models. Trait and psychodynamic models focus on personal factors as the main determinants of behavior. Situational models consider environmental factors and stimuli to be the major determinants of behavior. Interactional approaches consider both personal and situational variables and emphasize the importance of person-situation interactions. Each approach not only requires consideration of a different set of variables but also suggests different methods and techniques for measuring personality characteristics.

The Variety of Descriptors.   One reason for the variety of theoretical approaches is the large number of terms that can be used to describe personality—that is, the large number of potential stimuli or items. For example, Edwards and Walsh (1963) constructed a pool of 3000 personality items; there are 18,000 adjectives in the English language used to describe personality (Allport & Odbert, 1936); and as many as 40,000 different terms or phrases have been used to describe personality (Norman, 1963, 1967). Furthermore, because people seem to respond to the nuances of personality items, minor differences in content and wording often produce large differences in response rates. And, since behavior is determined by many factors, to sort out the effects of any given variable requires a large number of items. The designation "typical performance" also implies that the behavior measured occurs in a wide variety of situations. Thus, the number of items on personality tests usually is much larger than on maximal performance tests; in fact, most personality inventories consist of several hundred items.

The situation is further complicated by the fact that many of the concepts used in the various personality theories are vaguely or incompletely defined. Thus what characteristic is being measured, or what items should be used to measure a postulated characteristic, is often unclear.

Behavior and Reported Behavior.   One further question can be raised, particularly when using self-report measures. If a person responds "yes" to the item "I frequently have headaches," how shall we interpret this response? We can, of course, accept the statement at face value as an accurate report. Or should we accept the response only as the second best source of information about the individual, the best source being direct observation? Or, should we view the response as an interesting bit of verbal behavior and determine the meaning of the response by empirical studies? (Dahlstrom, 1969; Meehl, 1945). In this view, what is important are the behavioral correlates of making the particular response. This third viewpoint is espoused by persons supporting the empirical keying of personality inventories. In this approach the meaning of response is determined by what the response signifies—that is, by its empirical correlates.

In more general terms, the question concerns the relation between a person's description or presentation of her personality and her actual behavior. It is not hard to think of situations where people's reports of their behavior may not be reflected in their actual behavior. For example, an employer may say that he believes in equal rights but not hire members of minority groups, a student may say she is honest yet cheat on a test if given the opportunity, a person may be unwilling to admit to being afraid of flying. Thus, there is always a question of whether persons' reported behaviors or reactions reflect their actual behaviors.

How Are Behaviors Organized?   A final question concerns how individual behaviors and reactions are organized in personality structure. Aptitude and ability tests assume a trait model, and the purpose of the measurement is to establish an individual's scale position for each trait measured. An analogous approach can be used in personality measurement. Since each individual's pattern of trait scores will differ from every other individual's, each individual will have a unique personality structure (cf. Allport, 1955). If, however, we cluster individuals on the basis of the similarity of their trait patterns we have a *typology,* with "types" being defined by the similarity of their scores on various traits. Note that this typology does not involve mutually exclusive types; rather, it is a typology formed by using a multidimensional trait model.

Recently several investigators have proposed modified versions of a trait approach to studying personality. Epstein (1979, 1980) has shown that although individual measures of personality can be quite unstable, aggregating data over a number of situations and/or occasions can yield highly reliable measures that have greater generality. He used a methodology that utilized repeated measures daily over a period of a month. A somewhat different approach was taken by Harris (1980), who aggregated data derived from different methods: inventories, self-ratings, and ratings by others. He found that descriptions derived by aggregating over various methods were more reliable and useful than individual measures.

Both Epstein and Harris used methods that focused more intensively on particular individuals than the traditional individual differences approach, which emphasizes interindividual trait differences. This emphasis on studying the personality patterns of individuals has also been emphasized by Lamiell (1981), who suggested that the proper focus of studies of personality is on what a person tends to do (in contrast to what he chooses not to do) rather than on what a person can do or how he differs from other people. Like Epstein, Atkinson (1981) emphasized repeated measurements of the same individual. In contrast, however, he rejected the trait approach, and focused on the varying strength of different motives over a period of time. His approach, like Lamiell's, looks at the strength of, or tendency to perform, certain activities.

Person-Situation Interactions

Although the trait approach to studying personality has been, and continues to be, widely used, there is considerable dissatisfaction with this approach. One reason is the limited predictive validity of scores on personality measures; validity coefficients frequently do not exceed .30 (Mischel, 1979). These low correlations have led investigators to question the utility of the trait approach:

> Although behavior patterns often may be stable, they usually are not highly generalizable across situations. (Mischel, 1968, p. 282)

> People who are supposed to differ in some personality disposition or trait have never expressed that difference very consistently in different behaviors, in different situations, or at different times. (Atkinson, 1981, p. 117).

In short, these authors suggest that personality traits have limited generalizability or predictive power.

What is the reason for this limited predictive power? The view adopted by many people is that the trait approach does not adequately take into account situational variables and influences:

> . . . complex human behavior tends to be influenced by many determinants and reflects the almost inseparable and continuous interaction of a host of variables both in the person and in the situation. . . . if human behavior is determined by many interacting variables—both in the person and in the environment—then a focus on any one of them is likely to lead to limited predictions and generalizations. (Mischel, 1977, p. 246)

In other words, the study of personality must consider personal variables (traits), environmental variables, and the interaction of the two sources of influence.

The focus on person-situation interactions started with a book by Mischel (1968). Since that time, numerous articles have been written on this issue (see, e.g., Bem & Allen, 1974; Bem & Funder, 1978; Block, 1968; Bowers, 1973; Endler & Magnusson, 1976; Hogan, DeSoto, & Solano, 1977; Mischel, 1969, 1976, 1977, 1979). With the exception of the article by Hogan and his colleagues, all these authors believe that the usefulness of personality measures will be improved by a better understanding of the effects of situational variables.

To illustrate, consider dominance. If dominance were truly a trait, there would be individual differences in dominance; that is, a person who scored high on a measure of dominance would be expected to take a domineering role in various types of interpersonal interactions. But our experience tells us that this is not always the case. For example, a student who is consistently dominant in his relations with his peers may become quite submissive when interacting with parents or instructors. If this were the case, to predict when a person would and would not be dominant, we would have to know the nature of the situation; in this example, whom the person was interacting with in the situation. Such examples lead people to adopt an interactionist view.

An interactional view is not the only alternative to a trait approach. Some psychologists adopt a psychodynamic view. Whereas this view is similar to a trait view in its stress on personal characteristics, it differs widely in the types of personal variables considered, focusing on core psychological structures such as the id, ego, and superego. One could also adopt a purely situational approach, considering situational variables as the crucial determinants of behavior and putting little, if any, emphasis on personal characteristics. This is the approach taken by learning theorists (e.g., Skinner, 1953, 1969, 1974) and, in the personality area, by social learning theorists (e.g., Bandura, 1971; Mischel, 1973; Rotter, 1954).

To summarize, although trait approaches have proved useful when measuring maximal performance, many psychologists feel they have limited applicability to typical performance measurement, particularly the measurement of personality characteristics. They argue that to predict how a person will react in a given situation, one must also consider the characteristics of the situation and the nature of the person-situation interaction. We shall see, however, that many personality measures have been developed using a trait approach and that these instruments often have proved to be valid predictors of behavior.

Personality Assessment and the Individual

Most test takers view testing as an evaluative situation, thus have some anxiety when being tested. This feeling is often exacerbated when taking personality tests, because what is being measured and how the results will be used is not as clear as with maximal performance measures and also because many people believe that the tests will reveal facets of their personality they do not want uncovered. Thus, in personality assessment, the testing situation presents certain problems not found in maximal performance measurement. We shall discuss two of these factors: how testing may affect the individual and the question of invasion of privacy. We shall conclude by discussing some proper, and improper, uses of personality tests.

Effects on Test Takers. One feature that distinguishes psychological measurement from physical measurement is the degree to which the measurement process may affect the object (person) being measured. In the measurement of maximal performance it is recognized that the test may affect the test taker's behavior, but this effect frequently occurs only after the testing is completed. For example, students who are unable to answer many of the questions on an exam may vow to study harder in the future. There are exceptions, however, as when a student experiences failure in the early part of a test and, consequently, gives up and does not try on the remaining items. (It is precisely for this reason that it was suggested that tests begin with several easy items.)

Tests of typical performance appear to be more susceptible to changes produced by the testing situation. It is not uncommon for a counselee who has just taken a test to tell the counselor "You know, when I started to think about my interests when taking that interest inventory, I decided that I really don't like engineering after all." But there are also effects that influence responses to the test items. For example, when confronted with items that force them to think about themselves, some people become defensive; others are unwilling to say other than pleasant and socially desirable things about themselves.

If these reactions carry over outside the testing situation, the person has literally been changed by the testing. If they are manifested only on the test and do not carry over outside the test, the validity of the test becomes questionable.

Invasion of Privacy.   Although there has been some reaction against ability and aptitude tests, most people consider these tests, when used properly, to be impartial methods of assessing competence. The major complaints in these domains are often not with tests per se (except, possibly, intelligence tests), but with the consequences of test use. In the realm of personality testing, however, there has been a reaction against the idea of testing itself. One view is that personality tests invade an individual's privacy. In particular, items about certain subjects—usually politics, religion, and sex—have come under fire (Berdie, 1971; Dahlstrom & Dahlstrom, 1980, part IV).

But assuming that the test is valid and is used for a legitimate purpose, we can still ask whether personality measurement does invade privacy. Here the issue becomes a legal as well as a psychological one, for in our society the question of what constitutes the limits of privacy will ultimately be determined by legal and legislative action. Legal rulings are necessary because, although we all supply personal information in many situations, individuals differ in what they consider a reasonable request. Where one person may feel that a request for certain personal information may be unreasonable and invade his privacy, to another person the same request may seem reasonable, or even innocuous. The disagreement is in where to draw the line.

Perhaps the key to the issue is found in the fact that people often react negatively to personality assessment because they either do not understand how the test will be used or do not feel that they have any role in deciding how the results will be used. In short, the test is threatening because the situation is ambiguous. If the purposes and uses of the test are known, the objections often vanish. For example, most counselors have encountered students who adamantly refuse to take an interest or personality inventory but who, after having the purposes of the testing explained to them, have no further objections. The moral for the test user is obvious.

The issues discussed in the preceding paragraph have direct relevance for the invasion-of-privacy issue. For only if the test taker understands the nature of the test and how the results will be used can he make an informed decision as to the value of the test for himself. If he understands the purpose of the test, he can decide whether the test will invade his privacy, and then give (or withhold) his *informed consent* to the testing. If he gives his informed consent he is, in essence, saying that he does not believe that the testing will invade his privacy.[2]

---

[2] For further discussions of the issue of invasion of privacy see, for example, *Privacy and Behavioral Research* (1967), Ruebhausen & Brim (1966), and Smith (1981).

Uses of Personality Tests

Misuse of personality measures is relatively common, in spite of formal codes of ethics developed by professional organizations (e.g., Ethical principles of psychologists, 1981), and standards for test construction and use (*Standards,* 1974). One type of misuse occurs when persons untrained in the use of a particular technique nevertheless use it in applied psychological work. Another type of misuse involves applying a test in situations in which its validity has not been demonstrated. For example, the author once encountered a situation in which cutting scores on a personality inventory were used as a basis for admitting students into a teacher training program. The cutting scores used represented one psychologist's judgment of the acceptable score range; no objective evidence of the relationship between test scores and success, either in the program or as a teacher, was ever collected.

Another misuse of typical performance measures occurs when scores are misinterpreted or misunderstood. For example, scores on interest inventories measure the similarity of a person's interests to people working in the various occupations. Yet it is a common occurrence to hear test takers report that a high score on the, say, Psychologist scale of an inventory means that they would be a good psychologist or should go into psychology. Misinterpretations also occur because of the labels attached to scales on personality measures. For example, the original diagnostic scales on the Minnesota Multiphasic Personality Inventory represented clinical diagnostic categories. Thus persons scoring high on the Schizophrenia scale may (falsely) conclude that they are schizophrenic or have schizoid tendencies. Another common error is to imply that deviant scores on masculinity-femininity indices imply homosexual tendencies when, in fact, these scales measure masculinity or femininity of interests rather than heterosexual behavior. The moral is clear: Test interpreters should clearly explain what each scale measures, and test developers should avoid possibly misleading scale labels.

In a broader sense, many misinterpretations occur because test users fail to remember that the tests are measuring typical performance, not maximal performance. Thus a leadership inventory would measure a person's typical leadership style, not whether she knows how to be a good leader; an introversion/extroversion scale measures a person's habitual interpersonal behaviors, not whether that person can be extroverted if the situation demands such behavior. If we want to measure whether a person can react or perform in a particular manner, we should clearly structure the testing situation as a measure of maximal performance. This is particularly crucial if we are using the test to make a selection or placement decision, where we are more interested in what a person can do than how he or she typically reacts.

What, then, are appropriate uses of personality measures? They are most often used in clinical and counseling situations, to help the therapist understand a client's personality structure or estimate the severity of personal problems and to help clients understand their personality. They are also used in counseling and guidance situations to measure personal characteristics that might influence the choice of an occupation or career. Typical performance measures are also used in a variety of research studies—for example, studies of normal and abnormal personality, studies to find what factors influence performance or behavior in various situations, and studies of opinions of or attitudes toward various institutions or events. In all of these uses we are interested in typical or usual behaviors or reactions.

problems in typical performance measurement: psychometric

When considering the psychometric properties of typical performance measures, we will be concerned with the same dimensions as when measuring maximal performance: standardization of procedures, consistency, validity, and score interpretation. However, because of the differences in content and purposes of the measurement, certain procedures will be more appropriate and different problems will be encountered. In addition, some problems arise in typical performance measurement that do not occur, or at least are less crucial, in the measurement of maximal performance. The concern with dissimulation (faking) is an obvious example.

In this section we shall introduce some psychometric problems occurring in the measurement of typical performance. These problems will be discussed in more detail when considering specific tests and types of typical performance measures. At this point, however, we shall note that many typical performance instruments use less formal procedures for administration and scoring, and thus lack some of the desired psychometric properties. To hardheaded psychometricians, this is a disadvantage. To many clinicians, however, the flexible procedures are seen as an advantage, one that allows instruments to be adapted to particular individuals, situations, and uses and, consequently, provides more useful information.

Standardization

Standardization, you will recall, refers to three aspects of testing: content, administration, and scoring. In terms of content, most typical performance measures can be considered standardized because the same items, or set of stimulus materials, are presented to all test takers. However, because of the nature of the items, differences in how individual test takers interpret an item may introduce some uncontrolled variance. For example, a typical item on a self-report personality inventory might be: "I frequently get headaches." In this item, the word "frequently" could have various interpretations; some test takers may interpret it to mean every couple of days, whereas others may think once a month is frequent. Thus, even though the item is the same for all test takers, their interpretations of the item may vary. Whether this constitutes a problem depends on your point of view about personality measurement. As noted above, one view is that the differences in interpretation by various test takers are what make the item useful. Similar reasoning applies to projective test items; although the stimulus is the same for all test takers, differences in how the stimulus is interpreted provide diagnostic information.

Typical performance measures also vary widely in the standardization of administrative and scoring procedures. Self-report inventories, and other paper-and-pencil techniques such as ratings, generally have standardized administrative and scoring procedures. However, many individually administered personality measures, such as many projective techniques, allow greater variations in administrative and scoring conditions. Sometimes different items are administered to different people; at other times, the same items are administered but there are various possible scoring systems. For example, there are several different scoring systems for the Rorschach, the Thematic Apperception Test, and sentence completion tests. On other measures, general descriptions rather than specific, objective scores are reported. Thus, to the extent that administrative and/or scoring conditions can vary, the instruments are not completely standardized.

Consistency

Most typical performance measures provide more than one score. Self-report inventories usually provide scores for a dozen or more separate scales, projective methods are scored on a number of dimensions, and ratings usually involve a number of different characteristics. Thus, when considering the consistency of typical performance measures, we can be concerned with either individual scales (scores) or with profiles.

Consider first individual scales[3] or dimensions. Few typical performance measures have equivalent forms since it is difficult to develop equivalent forms or even comparable items.[4] Thus equivalent forms reliability usually is not computed. If the characteristic being measured is presumed to be stable over time, the coefficient of stability should be computed. If the scale is designed to measure a single characteristic, as most personality scales are, a measure of internal consistency such as coefficient alpha or Kuder-Richardson formula 20 should be computed. If the scale is more heterogeneous, such as the occupational scales on interest inventories, the corrected split-half reliability coefficient can be used.

When dealing with profiles of scores, the problem is how to determine the consistency of the pattern of scores. One approach is to consider all scores on the profile. For example, we could compute the correlation[5] between each person's profiles on the two occasions, then obtain the average correlation over all individuals. Another approach is to consider only certain salient scores, usually the highest scores. In this situation we would determine what percent (or proportion) of the highest scores remained consistent over the two administrations. When a profile of scores is summarized by a narrative description, or when various scores

---

[3] A scale, you will recall, is a group of items that are scored together but are not necessarily administered as a separate unit within a test. On most typical performance measures the items comprising any scale are scattered throughout the test and are treated as a unit only when scoring the test.

[4] This is because minor changes in the wording of an item often change its meaning drastically. Even putting "not" in an item does not necessarily produce the opposite response from test takers.

[5] This could be either Pearson's r or a rank-order correlation coefficient. Of course, to compute a correlation between profiles, scores on all scales must be expressed on the same scoring scale (e.g., all should be T scores) and based on the same norm group.

are reported on different scales, the problem is much more complex. If specific statements or predictions are made (e.g., a person is schizophrenic), the consistency of such predictions can be computed over testings. These same approaches can be used to determine consistency over different interpreters or different scoring systems.

On some personality dimensions a distinction can be made between long-term patterns of reacting and momentary dispositions. Anxiety is one example. On the one hand, we can look at stable differences between people in level of anxiety, differences that occur in various situations and persist over time. In this case we would be measuring *trait anxiety*. On the other hand, people also vary in their level of anxiety at a particular point in time, say just before taking a final examination in a course. These more momentary differences in anxiety may be situation-specific and not highly related to trait anxiety. In this case we are measuring *state anxiety*. While we may be able to measure a person's momentary level of anxiety at a particular point in time (their state anxiety) with some accuracy, this measurement may not be an accurate predictor of the person's anxiety level in another situation or at another time. However, if there are consistent cross-situational differences in anxiety level (and there are), we can also measure trait anxiety.

Validity

Determining the validity of typical performance measures may involve three different types of data: scores on individual scales, score profiles, and interpretations drawn from individual scores or score profiles. Each type uses different data and, as a consequence, may suggest a different validation method or result in different implications. For example, when we validate a description or prediction made by a test interpreter, we will be studying the effectiveness of the interpreter as well as the test scores. That is, since different interpreters may draw different conclusions from the same set of test scores, the validation study may have more to say about the test interpreters than the test per se.

The question of the relationship between reported and actual behaviors is also important in the validation of typical performance measures, particularly self-report techniques. Remember we said that a person's report of his behavior may not parallel his actual behavior; a person who claims to be open-minded and tolerant may not actually behave that way or be perceived as acting that way by other people. How can this be handled? One approach is, of course, to determine the correspondence between reported behavior and actual behavior whenever possible. That is, determine whether reports of behavior are valid indicators of actual behavior. But we can also accept the reported behaviors or reactions at face value. When using this approach, we would study the empirical correlates of the reported behaviors; in other words, consider the reported behaviors (the test responses) as data that have meaning in and of themselves (Dahlstrom, 1969; Meehl, 1945).

With these considerations in mind, let us look briefly at the content, criterion-related, and construct validation of typical performance measures.

Content Validity. In typical performance measurement, content validation is most appropriate at the individual scale level. Each scale (or score) should represent a particular trait, characteristic, or personality dimension. Thus there should be an underlying domain of items associated with this particular trait or characteristic and the items on the scale should be a representative sample of this domain. This requirement is basic but not always easy to obtain. As noted above, the constructs measured by typical performance tests are not always clearly defined and the potential domain may include various and diverse items. For these reasons, content validation of typical performance measures is more difficult than for maximal performance measures.

If the construct and domain of potential items are adequately defined, the process of content validation is similar to that used with maximal performance tests. That is, we compare the items on the scale to the specified domain and make a subjective judgment of the adequacy of the content sampling. To illustrate, if we were interested in test-taking anxiety, the domain would consist of items reflecting the variety of situations in which a person might display test-taking anxiety and the various reactions a person might have to anxiety-producing evaluative procedures. For a test of test-taking anxiety to have content validity, it would have to sample these various situations and reactions adequately.

Since personality measures usually cover more than one dimension, we must also be concerned with the adequacy of the coverage of the entire test. This is particularly true when the test is designed to give a comprehensive picture of personality or of a particular subset of personality dimensions. For example, although an interest inventory cannot be expected to cover all possible occupations (after all, there are over 20,000 occupations), to be useful the inventory should include scales representing various types of occupations. Of course, not only should the test as a whole represent the various possible occupations, each individual scale should be a valid measure of the domain associated with that particular occupation.

Criterion-Related Validity. When scores on typical performance measures are used to make specific predictions, criterion-related validity is the appropriate methodology. For example, scores on interest inventories can be validated against occupational choice, scores on personality inventories can be validated against a criterion of therapeutic success or by their ability to differentiate between people falling into various diagnostic categories, and ratings of job performance can be validated against measures of output. The procedures used would be those described in Chapter 6. In each of these situations we may validate scores on individual scales, a score profile, or a description or prediction made by a test interpreter.

Two aspects of the validation process merit special consideration. One is the importance of base rates. Many behaviors predicted from typical performance measures occur with relatively low frequency; that is, they have a low base rate. For example, only a small proportion of people enter any particular occupation and only a small proportion of people develop any psychiatric syndrome. Thus predictions from test scores will probably identify a large number of false positives. Consider, as an example, predicting occupational choice from scores on an interest inventory. Many more people will have high scores on a particular scale, say for psychology, than will enter that occupation. Thus, if a validation study looks at the proportion of people who score high on the psychology scale who become psychologists, the hit rate will probably be quite low, because most of the people with high scores on the psychologist scale will not enter psychology. However, if we look at the data from a different point of view, and contrast scores on the psychology scale of people who do and do not enter psychology, the results may be more promising.

The other consideration is differential validity. In typical performance testing, the ability of test scores to distinguish between various possible outcomes is often more important than predicting a single outcome. For example, it may be more important to distinguish between schizophrenics, depressives, hypochondriacs, and psychopaths than to predict whether a person will develop a psychiatric syndrome or personality disorder. Thus many criterion-related studies focus on differential diagnosis or prediction rather than on the prediction of a single outcome.

Construct Validity. Because most scales on personality measures are designed to measure "basic" dimensions of personality, construct validation is generally the most important type of validation for personality tests. This is particularly true because the constructs measured are often incompletely defined or are presumed to be at a more basic, or at least a different level of generality, than indicated by their observed features or correlates. In other words, the test scores serve as signs, pointing out the nature of the construct being measured. Thus the purpose of a validation study is to define more clearly the nature and scope of the construct being measured.

All of the methods described in Chapter 7 can be used to establish the construct validity of personality measures. Studies of internal structure indicate whether the characteristic is unidimensional and stable over time. Correlations with other measures indicate what other traits and characteristics are related to the score being investigated. Criterion-related studies show what outcomes or behaviors can be predicted from the test scores. Experimental manipulations show the range of situations over which the empirical relations hold and the effects of varying conditions on test scores. Perhaps, most crucial, however, are studies of convergent and discriminant validity, including use of the multitrait-multimethod matrix. Since each scale should measure a separate dimension and the various scales should measure different traits, evidence of convergent and discriminant validity is particularly important in establishing what each scale measures, that the same trait can be measured by different tests or methods, and that different scales do measure distinctly different traits.

Score Interpretation

The interpretation of scores also presents a distinct set of problems. As might be expected, one concerns the level of analysis. That is, when more than one score is obtained (the usual case), should each dimension be considered individually or should some more holistic method analysis be used? Advocates of holistic analyses claim that analyzing personality in a piece-by-piece fashion necessarily fragments and destroys the phenomena being studied. In reply, proponents of the trait approach insist that scientific measurement occurs only when dimensions are treated individually. Although there is no reason why both approaches cannot be used (after all, gross and microscopic anatomy are both respectable subjects), psychologists usually defend one or the other. Perhaps, the question should be rephrased: What is the appropriate way to combine scores? In answer to this question, the trait camp would say collect scores on individual traits, then synthesize them into an overall view; the holistic camp would emphasize synthesis, with specific reactions being deduced from the general personality picture.

Scores on various scales may be combined actuarially or by clinical judgment. The interpretation may be a general personality description or a more specific statement or prediction. That is, it may be a narrative summary of the salient features of the test taker's personality or it may be a statement such as: "John has interests similar to electrical engineers," "Client-centered counseling is likely to be an effective technique with Jane," or "Karen is likely to become hostile when she does not get her own way."

Since there are no clear dividing lines between acceptable and unacceptable or normal and abnormal behavior, most interpretations will be norm-referenced. For most typical performance measures, the appropriate norm group will be a cross section of the population. However, more limited norm groups can be developed based on dimensions such as sex, socioeconomic level, education, or some combination of these dimensions (e.g., adult males). Needless to say, obtaining representative samples of adults is no easy task.

One further point should be mentioned. When describing personality, we usually emphasize a person's most salient characteristics. These may be characteristics that a person possesses to a greater degree than most other people or ones that are stronger than their other characteristics. In other words, we can either compare a person's personality characteristics to those of other people or compare the relative strength of characteristics within an individual. The former approach is called *normative,* the latter *ipsative.* [6]

To illustrate the difference between normative (interindividual) and ipsative (intraindividual) comparisons, consider a vocational interest inventory that provides scores on broad interest areas such as science, business, social sciences, and art. The normative approach to interpretation would compare a person's interest in each area to those of other people. Thus, we might say that Janet had stronger interest in science than 90 percent of college students or that her interest in art was higher than 20 percent of the students. The ipsative approach, in contrast, would compare the relative strengths of various interests within an individual. Thus, even if Jason's interest in all areas was moderate, we would determine

---

[6] The term "ipsative" also has other, more specific definitions. For example, it is applied to tests where the sum of scores over all scales must add up to a certain value. On these tests, increases in the score on one scale will necessarily result in lower scores on another scale or scales. This procedure also forces some correlations between scales to be negative, even ones that would be positively correlated if other scoring procedures were used.

whether his interest in, say, business was higher than his interest in social sciences. As might be expected, items on instruments using an ipsative approach often require a choice between two or more possibly competing interests or behaviors.

Dissimulation

A problem encountered on typical performance measures, which is of lesser concern on maximal performance measures, is the possibility that test takers may systematically distort their responses. On maximal performance measures the only ways test takers can distort their scores are by consciously selecting wrong answers or by certain guessing habits (e.g., refusing to guess, always selecting true on true-false items when unsure of the correct answer). However, on typical performance tests the problem is so crucial that test constructors use a variety of strategies to identify and control these response biases. These methods will be described in detail in the next chapter. At this point we shall just indicate the nature of the problem.

One possibility is that a person will answer items so as to present a particular picture of himself rather than responding honestly. For example, a test taker may alter her responses on a personality inventory in an attempt to picture herself in a more (or less) desirable light. Or a test taker may attempt to present a particular picture of himself—for example, as being aggressive, sociable, religious, or as having the interests of physicians. To bias responses in this manner, the test taker responds as he thinks a person with the characteristics he is trying to emulate would respond. He can do this only if the test items are such that he has some basis for knowing what response is expected. Thus this bias is content-dependent. Responding so as to present a particular picture of oneself is called a *response set*.

There is also another type of bias, one that is relatively independent of the item content. These are called *response styles* and are systematic methods of responding when an item is ambiguous and/or the test taker is uncertain how to respond. Examples include agreeing with statements regardless of their content (acquiescence), avoiding the use of extreme categories on ratings (the error of central tendency), and selecting a particular alternative (say, C) on multiple-choice items.

The investigation of response sets and styles has been an active area of research since Cronbach (1946, 1950) first raised concern about them. Most psychologists view response biases as a source of error. Thus much of the research has been directed to attempts to identify response biases and to develop methods for controlling their effects. However, some investigators consider response biases to be stable personality dimensions, worthy of study in their own right.

summary

In typical performance measurement we are concerned with a person's usual or habitual behaviors, reactions, and feeling. Thus typical performance measures focus on interests, normal and abnormal personality characteristics, attitudes, values, and opinions. Although the set for typical performance may be apparent from the nature and purposes of the testing, it is specifically engendered by the test directions.

A wide variety of approaches to the measurement of typical performance have been used. On self-report techniques individuals describe their own behavior, usually by agreeing or disagreeing with a large number of self-descriptive statements. Projective methods involve presenting an ambiguous stimulus and having the test taker interpret the stimulus, the assumption being that how a person structures the situation will reveal facets of his personality. Situational methods involve observing and rating a person's behavior in either a natural or a contrived situation. In contrast to the previous approaches, which stress measurement of personality traits and components, behavioral assessment focuses on the measurement of overt behaviors.

A major problem in the measurement of typical performance is determining exactly what to measure. This is a problem because there are a wide variety of personality theories and methodological approaches to studying personality, because a plethora of constructs and behaviors can be measured, because personality dimensions are often not clearly defined, and because a person's reported behavior may not parallel his or her actual behavior. In addition, many theorists question the utility of studying personality traits. They suggest that to understand how a person will behave in a particular situation one must consider the situational variables and constraints and the nature of the person-situation interaction. That is, the appropriate level of analysis is the reciprocal interaction between personal and environmental factors.

Typical performance measures also present a number of psychometric problems. These occur because administrative and scoring conditions often are not standardized and because different levels of analysis can be used. Thus many personality measures do not have the desired psychometric properties described earlier in this book. However, determining how well they meet these criteria is important because they will be good measuring instruments only to the extent that they meet these requirements.

Two types of reliability data are important on typical performance measures. Stability indices are needed if the characteristic measured is presumed to be stable over time. However, it is possible to measure states (momentary dispositions) as well as traits (longer-term reaction patterns). Indices of internal consistency are appropriate when a scale is designed to measure only a single trait. All types of validity indices can be used, but in most cases evidence of construct validity is most important since the tests are designed to measure "basic" components of personality. However, any personality scale should have content validity and, if used in decision-making situations, criterion-related validity.

Interpretation of scores can be based on individual scales or score profiles, or consist of a descriptive summary or specific statements made by an interpreter. This latter approach, being based on the clinical judgment of the test interpreter, confounds the data obtained from the test scores with the test interpreter's analysis of the test scores. Interpretations can be normative, comparing a person's scores to those of other individuals, or ipsative, comparing the relative strengths of various personality components within an individual. When interpreting personality measures, particularly self-report measures, one must also be aware of the possibility of dissimulation or faking.

Suggestions for Further Reading

Atkinson, J. W. Studying personality in the context of an advanced motivational psychology. *American Psychologist,* 1981, *36,* 117–128. Describes the weaknesses of traditional psychometric approaches to the measurement of motivation and suggests an alternative approach.

Endler, N. S., & Magnusson, D. Toward an interactional psychology of personality. *Psychological Bulletin,* 1976, *83,* 956–974. Describes the basic features and assumptions of various approaches to personality measurement and argues for more stress on person-situation interactions.

Fiske, D. W. *Measuring the concepts of personality.* Chicago: Aldine, 1971. A thoughtful discussion of the nature of personality measurement and its role in assessment and research.

Goldberg, L. R. Some recent trends in personality assessment. *Journal of Personality Assessment,* 1972, *36,* 547–560. An overview and provocative discussion of the status of personality assessment; describes the major approaches to measuring personality.

Gough, H. Some reflections on the meaning of psychodiagnosis. *American Psychologist,* 1971, *26,* 160–167. Describes the functions of diagnosis and differentiates between different types of diagnoses—clustering symptoms, identifying the illness, and determining etiological factors.

Holt, R. R. *Assessing personality*. New York: Harcourt Brace Jovanovich, 1971. A brief overview of personality assessment, illustrated with an extensive case study.

Jackson, D. N. The dynamics of structured personality tests: 1971. *Psychological Review,* 1971, *78,* 229–248. Gives principles for developing personality scales that utilize both psychological and psychometric knowledge; stresses need for broad item pools, control of bias, and separating trait and method variance.

Korchin, S. J., & Schuldberg, D. The future of clinical assessment. *American Psychologist,* 1981, *36,* 1147–1158. A review of the current status of and emerging trends in clinical assessment; argues that although assessment is needed, its methods can be improved.

Mischel, W. *Personality and assessment*. New York: Wiley, 1968. The book that activated the person versus situation debate; argues for measuring situations rather than traits.

Mischel, W. On the future of personality measurement. *American Psychologist,* 1977, *32,* 246–254. An updated version of Mischel's thinking, again arguing for the consideration of situational variables and person-situation interactions.

Wiggins, J. S. *Personality and prediction: Principles of personality assessment*. Reading, Mass.: Addison-Wesley, 1973. As the author states, "a relatively sophisticated introduction to the art and science of personality assessment"; stresses an empirical, scientific approach.

Chapter 16 • Self-Report Inventories

THE common element in all self-report techniques is that test takers serve as observers and reporters of their own behaviors, reactions, attitudes, and feelings. As mentioned previously, the basic assumption underlying this approach is that people are in the best position to observe and describe their own behaviors, attitudes, interests, values, and personality characteristics. This is particularly true of those feelings and reactions that may not be apparent from overt behavior.

A variety of self-report methods are used in personality assessment: inventories, checklists, attitude scales, and self-ratings. This chapter will focus on inventories, particularly interest and personality inventories. An *inventory* consists of a large number of self-descriptive statements; test takers respond by indicating whether each statement does or does not describe them. Other common characteristics of inventories are that they are paper-and-pencil instruments; scores are reported on a number of scales, each of which measures a separate trait, characteristic, or dimension; interpretation of scores is norm-referenced; and procedures are built into the test to identify and control response biases.

Because the meaning of any score depends on the manner in which the scale was constructed and because there are several distinct approaches to constructing scales on inventories, we shall begin with a description of several scale construction strategies. We shall than describe examples of instruments for measuring vocational interests and personality characteristics. Finally we shall consider the problem of response biases in some detail.

scale construction methods

The typical interest or personality inventory is composed of a number of different scales, each of which measures a separate dimension or characteristic. A scale, you will recall, is a group of items that is scored as a unit, though not necessarily administered as a unit. In some cases a given item may be scored on only one scale, in other cases it may be scored on more than one scale. In the latter situation the same response (e.g., "true") may be scored on more than one scale or one response may be scored on one scale and an alternative response on another scale (e.g., "true" responses scored on one scale, "false" responses on another scale).

Scales are usually constructed using one of three strategies (Goldberg, 1972). These methods of scale development differ in how items are selected for inclusion on a scale. In *logical keying*, items are included because there is some rational basis for presuming they measure the characteristic of interest. This approach is also referred to as a priori or intuitive keying. In *empirical keying,* items are selected because of their observed relationship with some external criterion, usually membership in a group exhibiting the characteristic of interest. This approach is also called criterion or external keying. In *homogeneous keying,* item selection is based on the intercorrelations between the items comprising the scale. That is, only items that intercorrelate positively are included on a particular scale. This approach is also called internal keying.

Logical Keying

One approach to scale construction, which was used on most earlier instruments, is to assign items to scales on theoretical or rational bases. In practice, this means once the test constructor has decided on the trait to be measured, he writes items that *appear* to measure that trait. For example, a scale measuring "introversion" would probably be composed of items such as the following:

> I blush easily.
> At a party, I introduce myself to people I do not know.
> I prefer small parties with friends to large gatherings.
> Reading is one of my favorite activities.

Keying of the items would be on rational bases only. Although there might not be universal agreement regarding the keying of any single item, the scale construction procedure favors items whose keying is obvious. (Note that you probably could easily tell what response to each of the sample items would be scored for introversion.)

The construction of a personality inventory often begins in this manner, by writing items that appear to bear a relationship to the trait being measured. But this approach must be treated as only a beginning, since items that appear to measure a given trait may not, in fact, measure that trait. Also, a test composed only of obvious items would be exceedingly prone to distortion and dissimulation. In short, logically keyed inventories are of limited value.

Empirical Keying

In this approach, items are selected on the basis of their observed relationship with an external criterion measure. Suppose, for example, we wanted to measure the vocational interests of psychologists. As a criterion group of psychologists we might select a sample of members of the American Psychological Association (APA). We would also have to develop a pool of items which measure vocational interests. Usually these would be statements that describe vocational and avocational activities, such as: Listening to classical music, Doing scientific research, Attending sports events, Gourmet dining. Test takers would respond by indicating whether they like or dislike the activity described in the statement. Originally we would need a large pool of items.

Next we might administer these items to our sample of psychologists and compute the proportion of the sample responding "like" to each item. This approach would indicate what activities the average psychologist does and does not like. However, it would not answer another, more important question: How do the interests of psychologists differ from people in other occupations? To answer this question we would have to administer the same items to a group of people who are not psychologists. For this group, we might use a cross section of people in other occupations and professions. Note that our main concern is how the interests of psychologists differ from people in other occupations, not just what the interests of psychologists are.

Suppose that we follow the procedure described and obtain the following (hypothetical) results:

| | Proportion Responding "Like" | | |
Item	Psychologists	Others	Difference
Listening to classical music	.35	.15	.20
Doing scientific research	.60	.20	.40
Attending sports events	.75	.80	-.05
Gourmet dining	.30	.25	.05

Which items distinguish psychologists from other people? To answer this question, we look for items which show large differences between psychologists and other people. If we consider a difference of .20 to be significant,[1] the first two items would be included on the psychologist scale and the last two eliminated. By repeating this procedure with all the items in the pool we could develop a scale consisting of items that differentiated psychologists from people in other occupations.

Several points about the item selection procedure should be noted. First, an item that typifies a criterion group will not be included on the scale unless it differentiates between the criterion and the comparison group. The third item illustrates this point. Conversely, an item that is not typical of the majority of the criterion group may be included if it discriminates. The first item illustrates this point. Second, items included on the scale may or may not be logically related to the criterion. Consider the first two items. While we might have predicted that psychologists would be more interested in scientific research than people in other occupations, there is no basis for predicting that they would be more likely to enjoy listening to classical music. Yet because this latter item discriminated, it would be included on the scale. Third, although we could include all discriminating items on the final scale, as a practical matter we will include only as many as are needed to obtain the desired content balance, a reliable and valid scale, and the desired score distribution.

The empirical method of item selection guarantees that the scale developed will have concurrent validity. Since each item included on the scale differentiates between psychologists and other people, a combination of the most discriminating items (the scale) will also differentiate between the two groups. And by re-

[1] In test construction the minimum difference would be determined by statistical criterion; for example, we might consider only items where the difference was significant at the .05 level.

peating the procedure, using the same items but different criterion groups, we could develop scales for various occupations. Each occupational scale would include those items that best discriminated members of the occupation from people in other occupations.

Inasmuch as items on each scale are keyed to a particular criterion group, the nature of the criterion group will be reflected in the scale. In our example we defined psychologists as members of the APA. If we had used a different sample of psychologists, we might have selected a different set of items. The major point is: When using empirically keyed scales, score interpretations will always be relative to the original criterion group.

A related concern is the generalizability of the scale. The test construction procedure has guaranteed that the scale will have concurrent validity. But will it predict criteria other than membership in the original criterion group? Does the test make any theoretical sense? Such questions can be answered only by further study of the test. Whereas the first question is a straightforward empirical question, the second is more complicated. Because the items were chosen on empirical bases, their theoretical importance was irrelevant. Yet if we wish to use tests to measure constructs in a theory, we have to be able to make theoretical sense out of empirical results. An important consideration then becomes how to integrate seemingly meaningless empirical results (for example, the fact that psychologists like to listen to classical music) into the theoretical network. We have, in short, an exercise in construct validation.

Homogeneous Keying

A third strategy for scale development is based on the view that only homogeneous scales can be used to measure psychologically meaningful variables. That is, the *sine qua non* in scale construction is that the scale must be homogeneous. Thus, when scales are being developed, items not correlating with the other scale items are eliminated because they are considered to be measuring a different trait or construct. Only those items that correlate with other items in the scale are retained.

The scale development process proceeds as follows. First, a large number of items are administered to an appropriate standardization group—usually a representative sample of the population in which the test will be used. The intercorrelations among items are then subjected to some analytic procedure that clusters items into homogeneous groups (for example, factor analysis). These homogeneous item groupings form the basis of a scale. The content of the items comprising the scale give meaning (and a name or label) to the scale.

To illustrate, suppose that the items described in our example of empirical keying were administered to a group of people. Suppose also that some additional items were: Repairing your own car, Doing home repairs, Reading automotive and mechanical magazines, Operating machinery. If we intercorrelated all these items, we would probably find that these last four items would be positively intercorrelated but that they would have low correlations with the previous items (Listening to classical music, etc.). These latter four items, then, could form the basis of an homogeneous scale. (In practice, we would, of course, use many more items.) To determine what the scale measures, we would look at the content of the items. Since the common thread appears to be interest in mechanical activities, we might call this a Mechanical Interest Scale.

The process of homogeneous keying results in unidimensional scales that have some construct validity. Whether the scales have criterion-related validity is another question, one that can be answered only by empirical data. Although psychologists who advocate homogeneous keying feel that the scale construction procedure ensures that scales will measure important dimensions, more empirically oriented persons will demand proof of the scale's validity. So, too, psychologists who prefer homogeneous keying demand that the empiricist explain the meaning of their scales. In short, the difference between empirical and homogeneous keying is in the methods, data preferences, and research styles.

Other Considerations

Logical, empirical, and homogeneous keying represent three major approaches to the construction of scales for self-report personality inventories. Although the rational approach is no doubt the weakest, all approaches use rational methods when selecting items in the earliest stages of test construction. That is, items are included in the pool of potential items only if there is some rationale for doing so. The other two approaches, though often not differing significantly in validity (Hase & Goldberg, 1967), do represent distinctly different philosphies of test construction.

Perhaps the optimal test construction strategy is a combination of empirical and homogeneous keying. In this approach, homogeneous scales would first be constructed. These homogeneous keys would then be validated against empirical criteria, and those items that did not demonstrate empirical validity would be eliminated. The final scale would be both homogeneous and empirically valid—and thus both practically and theoretically useful.

Regardless of which scale construction strategy is adopted, the final version of the scale must be subjected to further analysis. For example, the score distribution must have an appropriate mean and sufficient variability. To aid in interpretation of scores, normative data must be collected. The reliability of the scale should also be determined and validity studies conducted.

We shall now turn to a consideration of some specific tests and inventories that exemplify the various approaches to scale construction. We will show how the approach was used in the development of the test, describe the test that resulted, and briefly discuss the validity, usefulness, and limitations of the test. Because of the obvious deficiencies of scales developed on purely a priori bases, we will not discuss tests developed by purely logical methods. The reader should be aware, however, that many of the earliest personality inventories (some of which, unfortunately, are still available on the market) utilized this mode of test construction.

vocational interest inventories

That people who work in different occupations have different abilities, interests, attitudes, values, and personality characteristics is a well-established fact. In this section we shall discuss the measurement of one of these areas, vocational interests. Our discussion will focus on the instruments developed by two pioneers in interest measurement, E. K. Strong, Jr., and G. F. Kuder, because the tests they developed are widely used and also illustrate the various problems and considerations involved in the construction, evaluation, interpretation, and use of interest inventories.

Before discussing specific tests, however, we first need to consider several basic issues in the measurement of vocational interests.

Approaches to Interest Measurement

Vocational interests refer to the likes and dislikes, and patterns of preferences, that characterize people in various occupations and differentiate between occupations. These preferences may involve occupations and occupational activities, hobbies and amusements, leisure time activities, school subjects, or types of people. Most interest measures use an inventory approach. Test takers respond either by indicating their liking or disliking for each activity or by ranking them in order of preference. Although the stimuli (items) do not have to be specifically vocationally related, they should be familiar to people who take the test.

When constructing an instrument for measuring vocational interests, the test constructor must make two fundamental decisions, ones that will determine the nature of the instrument developed. These decisions are whether to measure interest in specific occupations or in broader vocational areas, and how to key responses. Let us consider each decision briefly.

The first decision is whether to measure interests in specific occupations or in broad vocational areas. If one opts for the former approach, the inventory would have scales measuring interest in, say, medicine, law, real estate sales, psychology, elementary school teaching, and other occupations. Using the latter approach would result in scales covering broad vocational areas—for example, scientific, mechanical, artistic, sales, or linguistic interests. In other words, we can adopt a rather broad-gauged or narrow-gauged approach.

The second decision concerns the method of scale construction and item keying. The approach may be logical, with items assigned to scales on a rational, a priori basis; empirical, with items assigned to scales on the basis of their observed relationship to some criterion; or homogeneous, with items assigned to scales on the basis of their intercorrelations. Each of these approaches has been applied to the development of interest inventories, with the empirical method appearing to predominate at this time.

With these considerations in mind, we shall now describe some of the more widely used interest inventories.

The Strong-Campbell Interest Inventory

The *Strong-Campbell Interest Inventory* (SCII)[2] was originally published as the *Strong Vocational Interest Blank* (SVIB) in 1927. The SVIB had separate forms for

---

[2] The complete name of the test is the *Strong-Campbell Interest Inventory: Form T325 of the Strong Vocational Interest Blank*. For brevity we shall refer to it as the Strong-Campbell Interest Inventory or the SCII.

men and women and measured only interests in specific occupations. Over the years, the test has been revised several times. In the 1969 revision the Basic Interest Scales, which measure interest in broad vocational areas, were added. In a more comprehensive revision in 1974, the separate men's and women's forms were merged into one form and the General Occupational Themes were introduced. These latter scales provide a unifying theoretical framework for the SCII.

A further revision was published in 1981. This revision added new occupational scales and matched all male-normed occupational scales with corresponding female-normed scales, and vice versa. In addition, more recent criterion groups were used to norm the various occupational scales and a number of psychometric analyses were made.

The Inventory.   The SCII consists of 325 items divided into seven sections (see Table 16.1 for a description of the types of items included). On most items, test takers respond by indicating whether they like, are indifferent to, or dislike the activity mentioned; however, items on Part VI require a choice between two activities and those on Part VII require test takers to indicate whether or not a characteristic describes them. Items are written at a sixth grade reading level. The test is untimed and the median time for completion is 25 to 35 minutes. Because of the number of scales (see below), special machine scoring is needed; several agencies are licensed to score the test.

Since the interests of most people do not stabilize until age 17 or 18, or even later for some people, the SCII typically is administered to high school juniors and seniors, college students, and adults. Although the test is sometimes used with mature younger students, routine use at younger ages is not recommended.

The most common use of the SCII is for counseling high school and college students regarding their vocational plans. It may seem absurd that a person would have to take an interest test to find out his or her interests; however, because of limited work experiences, misperceptions of jobs, and a common inability to view oneself objectively, an inventory can often clarify interests. Although the SCII can be utilized for selection and placement, both in academic and business settings, the fact that it can be faked would dictate caution when using the inventory in this manner. Other uses include as an aid counseling workers regarding job dissatisfaction or changing occupations and as a research tool when studying differences between occupational groups. Needless to say, for all these purposes an interest inventory should be only one of several sources of information. For example, when counseling with students regarding educational or vocational plans, one also should consider factors such as abilities, past achievement and academic performance, values, and economic considerations.

Types of Scales.   The SCII reports scores on 6 General Occupational Theme scales, 23 Basic Interest Scales, and 162 Occupational Scales. There are also two special scales and a number of administrative indices. A copy of the score profile is shown in Figure 16.1.

The *General Occupational Themes* represent the broadest classification of interests reported on the test and were derived from Holland's (1973) theory of

TABLE 16.1
Types of Items on the Strong-Campbell Interest Inventory

Part I. *Occupations* (131 items; respond L (Like), I (Indifferent to), or D (Dislike)) Sample items: Actor/Actress, Advertising Executive, Architect

Part II. *School Subjects* (36 items; L-I-D) Sample items: Algebra, Art, Philosophy

Part III. *Activities* (51 items; L-I-D) Sample items: Adjusting a carburetor, Making a speech

Part IV. *Amusements* (39 items; L-I-D) Sample items: Golf, Playing chess, Jazz or rock concerts

Part V. *Types of People* (24 items; L-I-D) Sample items: Emotional people, Babies, Nonconformists

Part VI. *Preferences between Two Activities* (30 pairs) Sample items: Airline pilot—Airline ticket agent, Dealing with things—Dealing with people, Having a few close friends—Having many acquaintances

Part VII. *Your Characteristics* (14 items; yes-no) Sample items: Win friends easily, Have patience when teaching others

---

vocational interests. In essence, Holland suggests that there are six idealized occupational types, each based on a constellation of interest-personality types (see Figure 16.1). Holland believes that each type of person seeks out a different type of occupational environment. Thus, the tenor of any occupation is determined by the personality characteristics of the workers as well as its skill requirements. Scores on the General Occupational Themes can be used to direct students' attention to more specific interest areas or occupations.

Each scale consists of 20 items with "Like" responses scored positively and "Dislike" responses scored negatively. Norms are based on a general sample of 600 persons (300 males and 300 females), with scores reported as standard scores with a mean of 50 and a standard deviation of 10 points. In addition to standard scores, interpretive comments (e.g., very high, average) are printed on the profile. Because the distributions of scores for men and women differ, the interpretive comment for a given standard score may vary depending on the sex of the test taker. The profile also shows the distribution of scores for each sex (by a bar showing the 25th–75th percentile range and a line showing the 10th–90th percentile range).

The *Basic Interest Scales* were formed by clustering items that are highly intercorrelated; that is, they are homogeneously keyed scales. Scales are arranged in clusters corresponding to their predominant General Occupational Theme and reflect interest in broad vocational areas such as Agriculture, Science, Teaching, and Sales. As with the General Occupational Themes, "Like" responses were weighted positively and "Dislike" responses negatively. Thus test takers who give many "Like" responses are likely to obtain higher scores on the Basic Interest Scales than people who give more "Dislike" responses.

Scores were normed using the general norm group, again using standard scores with a mean of 50 and a standard deviation of 10 points. Thus, like the General Occupational Themes, a score of 50 is average for people in general and higher scores indicate more intense interest. Interpretive comments are included as are the distributions for each sex. People in occupations falling within a Basic Interest area generally score about 8–10 points above the average; for example,

Figure 16.1 The Strong-Campbell Interest Inventory Profile

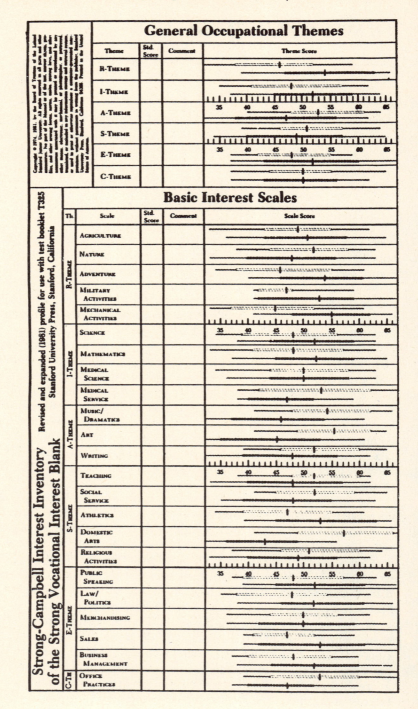

SVIB-SCII Profile for

Code	Scale	Sex Norm	Std Score	Very Dis.	Dissim.	Mod Dis.	Mid Range	Mod Sim.	Similar	Very Sim.
RC	Air Force Off's	f								
RC	Air Force Off's	m								
RC	Army Officer	f								
RC	Army Officer	m								
RC	Navy Officer	m								
R	Navy Officer	f								
RE	Police Officer	f								
RE	Police Officer	m								
RCE	Voc. Agric. Tchr.	m								
RC	Farmer	f		12	21	27	39	45	54	60
R	Farmer	m								
R	Forester	m								
R	Skilled Crafts	m								
R	Rad. Tech. (x-ray)	f								
RI	Rad. Tech. (x-ray)	m								
RI	Forester	f								
RI	Engineer	f								
RI	Engineer	m								
RI	Veterinarian	m		12	21	27	39	45	54	60
RIC	Lic. Pract. Nurse	f								
RAS	Occup. Therapist	f								
RAS	Occup. Therapist	m								
IR	Veterinarian	f								
IR	Chemist	f								
IR	Chemist	m								
IR	Physicist	f								
IR	Physicist	m								
IR	Geologist	f		12	21	27	39	45	54	60
IR	Geologist	m								
IR	Med. Technol.	f								
IR	Med. Technol.	m								
IR	Dental Hygienist	f								
IR	Dentist	f								
IR	Dentist	m								
IR	Optometrist	f								
IR	Optometrist	m								
IR	Phys. Therapist	f		12	21	27	39	45	54	60
IR	Phys. Therapist	m								
IR	Physician	f								
IR	Physician	m								
IRS	Regist. Nurse	m								
IRS	Math-Sci. Tchr.	m								
IRC	Math-Sci. Tchr.	f								
IRC	Systems Analyst	f								
IRC	Systems Analyst	m								
IRC	Computer Progr.	f		12	21	27	39	45	54	60
IRC	Computer Progr.	m								
IRE	Chiropractor	f								
IRE	Chiropractor	m								
IE	Pharmacist	m								
I	Pharmacist	f								
I	Biologist	f								
I	Biologist	m								
I	Geographer	f								

Administrative Indexes

TOTAL RESPONSE	Response %				
	LP	IP	DP		
INFREQUENT RESPONSE				Occupations	
				School Subjects	

continued

Occupational Scales

Code	Scale	Sex Norm	Std Score	Very Dis.	Dissim.	Mod. Dis.	Mid-Range	Mod. Sim.	Similar	Very Sim.	Code	Scale	Sex Norm	Std Score	Very Dis.	Dissim.	Mod. Dis.	Mid-Range	Mod. Sim.	Similar
I	Geographer	m									SE	YMCA Director	m							
I	Mathematician	f									SE	School Adminst.	f							
I	Mathematician	m									SE	School Adminst.	m							
IA	College Prof.	f									SCE	Guid. Counselor	m							
IA	College Prof.	m									SEC	Guid. Counselor	f							
IA	Sociologist	f									SEC	Social Sci. Tchr.	f							
IA	Sociologist	m									SEC	Social Sci. Tchr.	m							
IAS	Psychologist	f									EA	Flight Attend't.	f							
IAS	Psychologist	m									EA	Flight Attend't.	m							
AIR	Architect	f		12	21	27	39	45	54	60	EA	Beautician	m		12	21	27	39	45	54
AIR	Architect	m									E	Beautician	f							
AI	Lawyer	f									E	Dept. Store Mgr.	f							
AI	Lawyer	m									E	Dept. Store Mgr.	m							
AE	Public Rel. Dir.	f									E	Realtor	f							
AE	Public Rel. Dir.	m									E	Realtor	m							
AE	Advertising Exec.	f									E	Life Ins. Agent	f							
AE	Advertising Exec.	m									E	Life Ins. Agent	m							
AE	Int. Decorator	f									E	Elect. Publ. Off.	f							
AE	Int. Decorator	m		12	21	27	39	45	54	60	E	Elect. Publ. Off.	m		12	21	27	39	45	54
A	Musician	f									E	Public Administ.								
A	Musician	m									EI	Invest. Fund Mgr.	m							
A	Comm'l. Artist	f									EI	Marketing Exec.	f							
A	Comm'l. Artist	m									EI	Marketing Exec.	m							
A	Fine Artist	f									E	Personnel Dir.	f							
A	Fine Artist	m									E	Personnel Dir.	m							
A	Art Teacher	f									E	Ch. of Comm. Ex.	m							
A	Art Teacher	m									E	Restaurant Mgr.	f							
A	Photographer	f		12	21	27	39	45	54	60	EC	Restaurant Mgr.	m		12	21	27	39	45	54
A	Photographer	m									EC	Ch. of Comm. Ex.	f							
A	Librarian	f									EC	Buyer	f							
A	Librarian	m									EC	Buyer	m							
A	For. Lang. Tchr.	f									EC	Purchas'g Agent	f							
A	For. Lang. Tchr.	m									EC	Purchas'g Agent	m							
A	Reporter	f									ERC	Agribus. Mgr.	m							
A	Reporter	m									ES	Home Econ. Tchr.	f							
A	English Teacher	f									ECS	Nurs. Home Adm.	m							
AS	English Teacher	m		12	21	27	39	45	54	60	EC	Nurs. Home Adm.	f		12	21	27	39	45	54
SA	Speech Pathol.	f									EC	Dietitian	f							
SA	Speech Pathol.	m									ECR	Dietitian	m							
SA	Social Worker	f									CER	Exec. Housek'r	f							
SA	Social Worker	m									CER	Exec. Housek'r	m							
SA	Minister	f									CES	Bus. Ed. Teacher	f							
SIE	Minister	m									CES	Bus. Ed. Teacher	m							
SI	Regist. Nurse	f									CE	Banker	f							
S	Lic. Pract. Nurse	m									CE	Banker	m							
S	Special Ed. Tchr.	f		12	21	27	39	45	54	60	CE	Credit Manager	f		12	21	27	39	45	54
S	Special Ed. Tchr.	m									CE	Credit Manager	m							
S	Elem. Teacher	f									CE	IRS Agent	m							
S	Elem. Teacher	m									CE	IRS Agent	f							
SR	Phys. Ed. Tchr.	f									CA	Public Administ.	m							
SR	Phys. Ed. Tchr.	m									C	Accountant	f							
SRE	Recreat. Leader	f									C	Accountant	f							
SRE	Recreat. Leader	m									C	Secretary	f							
SE	YWCA Director	f									C	Dental Assistant	f							

Administrative Indexes | | Special Scales

Response %			Response %			Response %			
LP	IP	DP	LP	IP	DP	LP	IP	DP	**Academic Comfort**
	Activities			Types of People			Characteristics		
	Amusements			Preferences			All Parts		**Introversion-Extroversion**

lawyers would score about 60 on the Law/Politics Basic Interest Scales. Scores are relatively stable across age ranges with the exception of the Adventure Scales. On this scale teenage boys score 8–10 points higher than do adults.

The *Occupational Scales* were developed by contrasting the responses of men and women working in an occupation with a general sample. Thus they are empirically keyed scales. The criterion groups consisted of 200–300 persons in an occupation who were between the ages of 25 and 55; had been in the occupation for at least three years; reported they enjoyed their work; meet minimal standards of occupational performance; and pursued their occupation in a fashion typical for that occupation. All but eight of the 162 Occupational Scales have both male and female criterion groups. Data for more than half the criterion groups were collected in 1978–1979, another quarter between 1972 and 1978, and none before 1966.[3]

In contrast to the other types of scales, standard scores on the Occupational Scales are normed on the criterion groups. Thus a score of 50 on any Occupational Scale is the average score for people in that occupation. For example, a score of 50 on the Biologist scale is the average score obtained by biologists in the criterion group, *not* the average score of people in general on the Biologist scale. Besides the standard scores, each score is described on a seven-step descriptive scale which ranges from "very dissimilar" through "midrange" to "very similar".

Scores are also reported on two special scales. Items on the Academic Comfort (AC) scale are ones that differentiate between students who do well in educational settings and those who do not. The Introversion-Extraversion (IE) scale measures liking for working with other people or working alone. The Administrative Indexes include the percent of "Like," "Indifferent," and "Dislike" responses made to each content category and an index of infrequent responses. This latter index can be used to determine the validity of the profile by identifying persons who responded randomly or skipped many items.

Interpretation.   Scores on the SCII are presented on a profile (see Figure 16.1). Although an excellent description of how to interpret scores is given on the back of the test taker's copy of the score profile,[4] interpretation is quite complex and is best done by a counselor or other person familiar with the SCII and vocational interests. However, some of the important points to consider when interpreting scores are discussed below.

Scores on the General Occupational Themes, which represent the broadest classification of interests, should be looked at first. High scores indicate areas of interest; low scores represent areas where the test taker's interests are dissimilar to persons in these vocational areas. The General Occupational Themes also pro-

---

[3] The restandardization sample consisted of 40,197 test profiles drawn from the 162 occupational groups. Each person in the sample was selected as a typical representative of that occupation, using the criteria described in the text. The revision resulted in 99 new Occupational Scales, some replacing old scales and others entirely new.

[4] A similar, more technical description is printed on the back of the counselor's copy of the profile. For further information see the *SVIB-SCII* (1981) or Campbell (1971).

vide an integrated theoretical and interpretive framework for the rest of the test. This is illustrated by the fact that scores on the Basic Interest and Occupational Scales are clustered according to their General Occupational Themes. On the Occupational Scales the predominant theme for each scale is indicated by letters next to the scale title. For example the "RC" by Air Force Officer indicates that people in this occupation score highest on the Realistic theme and second highest on the Conventional theme.

Next look at the Basic Interest Scales, particularly those scales falling under Themes where the test taker obtained high scores. Since the Basic Interest Scales measure interest in relatively broad occupational areas, they are most useful when counseling persons whose interests have not fully crystallized and for giving an indication of interest in occupations not covered by an Occupational Scale.

Next look at specific Occupational Scales. Although we would look particularly at occupations in the areas where the test taker scored highest on the General Occupational Themes and Basic Interest Scales, we would look at all high scores. And, of course, we would look closely at scores on any occupations the test taker has considered entering.

When looking at the profile, but particularly Occupational Scales, we should consider patterns of scores as well as individual scores. Some of the reasons for considering patterns are illustrated by the following points: (1) Not all occupations are represented by scales. To obtain an indication of a person's interest in a nonrepresented occupation we could consider his scores in related occupations (the group the occupation would fall in) and on the relevant Basic Interest Scales. (2) Since there are various ways of performing any occupation and various jobs within an occupation, the pattern of scores may give a clue to the specialty or type of position to be considered. For example, a combination of high interests in Psychology and social service occupations (S-coded occupations) might indicate clinical or counseling psychology, whereas Psychology interests combined with high interests in physical sciences would be more compatible with experimental psychology. (3) A preponderance of high scores in several related occupations reinforces that the person's interests are in that area. (4) Low scores indicate areas in which the individual's interests are definitely dissimilar to persons currently employed in the field. (5) The relative scatter of scores—whether there are pronounced likes and dislikes or whether most scores are near the average—gives an indication of the relative strengths of various interests.

Psychometric Properties.   The SVIB-SCII has been one of the most extensively studied typical performance measures. Rather than reviewing all the data, we shall concentrate on three areas: the stability of the scores, the validity of the scores, and sex differences. (For a description of the research results see Campbell, 1971, or the *Manual for the SVIB-SCII,* 3d ed., 1981).

The most important type of reliability data for an interest inventory concerns stability. This is particularly true when the inventory is used as an aid in making an occupational choice. For example, when college students are selecting a vocation, they are interested not only in their current interests but, more important, whether their interests will remain the same over the 30 or more years they may be in an occupation. If interests change, the test score will be of little value since their interests at, say, age 40 will not be the same as their current interests.

Scores on the Occupational Scales are remarkably consistent. The median test-retest correlations over short periods (a month or less) are about .90 and are only slightly lower (.87) over a three-year period. Median test-retest correlations for the General Occupational Themes, Basic Interest Scales, and Special Scales are only slightly lower (median r's .81–.91) over similar periods. Scores are also quite consistent over longer time periods. In what must surely be one of the longest term test-retest studies, Strong (1955) found a median r of .67 for the Occupational Scales over a 22-year period!

Other types of consistency data are also of interest. We noted that the interests of most people stabilize in their late teens or earlier twenties, with few major changes thereafter. And, in a series of ingenious studies, Campbell (1965, 1966a, 1966b) found that the interests of individuals holding the same position have not changed greatly over time. For example, he tested persons holding the same position in particular banks in 1934 and 1964, thirty years apart, and found their interests to be remarkably similar. These data seem to fly in the face of the view that occupational requirements are rapidly changing.

The empirical keying of the Occupational Scales guarantees their concurrent validity. The median overlap of the criterion and reference samples is 34 percent, which is a difference of about two standard deviations in average scores. Determination of the predictive validity of the Occupational Scales is more difficult because of the base-rate problem (Brown, 1961). That is, since there are numerous occupations and people have interests similar to people in more than one occupation (i.e., obtain several high scores), many people who obtain high scores on a particular Occupational Scale will not enter an occupation. A reasonable summary of the data is that about half of the people obtaining a high score on an Occupational Scale go into that or a closely related occupation (Dolliver, 1969; Spokane, 1979).

Another concern is sex differences in responding. Although some people argue that interest inventories should not use separate sex norms, the empirical data argue otherwise. For example, approximately half of the SCII items show a 15 percent or greater difference in responses between men and women. Thus the SCII reports separate sex norms for all types of scales.

The Kuder Interest Inventories

The other major pioneer in interest measurement is G. F. Kuder. Over the years, Kuder has developed several interest inventories, some of which utilize empirical keying and others of which use homogeneous keying. We shall discuss three of these inventories: the *Kuder Vocational Preference Record,* the *Kuder General Interest Survey,* and the *Kuder Occupational Interest Survey.*

One of the distinguishing features of Kuder's approach is the item format. On the Kuder inventories, each item consists of three statements. A typical triad is shown on page 394.

a. write a story about a sports event
b. play in a baseball game
c. teach children to play a game

The test taker responds by indicating which activity he most prefers and which he least prefers. This enables all possible pairs of items to be compared.

The Kuder Vocational Preference Record.   This test is the prototype of a homogeneously keyed interest inventory. Like the other Kuder inventories, the items are presented in triads. Unlike the SVIB and Kuder OIS, which assess interest in specific occupations, the Kuder Vocational measures interest in broad vocational areas. Thus, it is appropriately used in situations in which the concern is with identifying broad areas of interest, rather than choosing a specific occupation; for example, with junior high and high school students.

The process of scale construction proceeded as follows. After an item pool had been developed, a priori item keys were constructed. Thus, for example, all items that appeared to measure literary interests were included on one scale, all items denoting scientific interests on another, and so on. The items were then administered to an experimental sample, and items that did not correlate with the total score on the a priori key were eliminated. By this procedure the scoring keys were made more homogeneous. These analyses resulted in the scrapping of some a priori scales and the restructuring of others. Analogous procedures were used to add scales. The present form of the test consists of ten scales—Outdoor, Mechanical, Computational, Scientific, Persuasive, Artistic, Literary, Musical, Social Service, and Clerical.

Although the scale construction procedure guarantees that the scales will be homogeneous, it raises some problems when interpreting scores. Because responding to the inventory items requires a choice between alternatives that are scored on different scales, any response will increase the score on one scale but consequently limit the maximal possible score on another scale. Thus the sum of the raw scale scores, over all scales, will be the same for all persons; that is, scores are ipsative. As a consequence, a person who has strong interests in several areas may find that these preferences cancel each other out and he or she does not obtain high scores on any scale. Conversely, a person who has no strong interests except in one area will obtain a very high score on that scale. Furthermore, we must consider the average level of interest in each area. For example, the average male probably is more interested in mechanical than clerical activities. Thus, even though scores at the 70th percentile on both scales indicate the same relative position compared to other males, they may not represent equal degrees of interest. Considerations such as these make interpretation of scores more difficult than might appear on first glance.

The Kuder General Interest Survey.   This test is an extension of the Kuder Vocational Preference Record designed for use in grades 6 through 12. It reports the same scores as the Kuder Vocational Preference Record, but scores are compared to a different norm group, one composed of students in grades 7–12. Many schools now use the General Interest Survey instead of the Vocational Preference Record.

The Kuder Occupational Interest Survey.   The Kuder Vocational Preference Record and General Interest Survey contain homogeneously keyed scales which report interest in broad vocational fields. The Kuder Occupational Interest Survey (KOIS, Form DD), in contrast, uses empirically keyed scales and reports interests in specific occupations and college majors. Like the SCII, the KOIS is designed primarily for use in the educational and vocational counseling of high school and college students and adults. The basic philosophy underlying the KOIS is that people in different occupations have different patterns of preferences, and a match between the preferences of an individual and people in an occupation is likely to lead to greater job satisfaction.

The KOIS consists of 100 triads whose content was sampled from 17 vocational and personal preference areas related to occupational choice and job satisfaction (Kuder, 1977). Items were written at the sixth grade level and most people can complete the test in 30 minutes. In contrast to the SCII, specific job titles and activities are not used in the items.

As on the SCII, the KOIS reports scores for specific occupations. The current form of the test reports scores for 126 occupational scales, 52 with male norms only, 20 with female norms only, and 54 (27 occupations) with both male and female norm groups. Unlike the SCII, the KOIS also reports scores for 48 college majors. Of the college major scales, 23 have male norms, 13 female norms, and 12 (6 majors) have both male and female norm groups. The defining characteristics of the occupational criterion groups were similar to those used on the SCII but, of course, they do not include the same people. Thus, scores on SCII and KOIS scales having the same occupational title may not be highly correlated (Zytowski, 1968).

Scores on the KOIS are based on a different scoring system than the one used on the SCII. On the KOIS, scores are reported as lambda coefficients, which are an index of the similarity of the person's pattern of preferences to the average person in an occupation or college major.[5] The higher the lambda, the more similar the individual's interests to people in the criterion group. Rather than grouping occupations by their similarity (as on the SCII), the KOIS profile lists the test taker's scores in order of the decreasing magnitude of the lambda coefficients (see Figure 16.2). Test takers are advised to consider any occupation (or major) whose scores fall within .06 of their highest scores.

Most reliability studies have investigated the stability of KOIS profiles rather than of individual scales. Median profile stability coefficients are about .90 over short periods and Zytowski (1976) has found that profiles are relatively stable over periods as long as 12 years.

The test manual reports data from several studies which show that about 60 percent of the people in an occupation obtained their highest score on the cor-

---

[5] The lambda coefficient is essentially a form of correlation between the individual's profile and the average profile of members of the criterion group.

Figure 16.2 The Kuder Occupational Interest Survey Profile (Form DD)

Report of Scores   Kuder Occupational Interest Survey   Form DD

NAME ALONZO RAMON L   MALE   00001   DATE 06/18/79

OCCUPATIONAL SCALES	NORMS M	NORMS F
STATISTICIAN	.50*	
CHEMIST	.49*	
OPTOMETRIST	.48*	
>COMPUTR PROGRAMR		.47*
>SCIENCE TCHR, HS		.47*
>COMPUTR PROGRAMR	.47*	
PODIATRIST	.47*	
PSYCHOLOGY PROF	.47*	
ENG, MINING/METAL	.46*	
MATHEMATICIAN	.46*	
PSYCHIATRIST	.46*	
PSYCH, COUNSELING	.46*	
>SCIENCE TCHR, HS	.46*	
DIETITIAN, ADMIN		.45*
OSTEOPATH	.45*	
>PSYCH, CLINICAL	.45*	
PSYCH, INDUSTRIAL	.45*	
HOME EC TCHR COL		.44*
>AUDIOL/SP PATHOL	.44*	
ENGINEER, MECH	.44*	
PEDIATRICIAN	.44*	
>X-RAY TECHNICIAN	.44*	
>DENTIST	.43	
ENGINEER, CIVIL	.43	
METEOROLOGIST	.43	
>PHYS THERAPIST	.43	
>DENTIST		.42*
NUTRITIONIST		.42*
ENGINEER, ELEC	.42	
>MATH TCHR,HI SCH	.42	
>ACCOUNTANT		.41*

OCCUPATIONAL SCALES	NORMS M	NORMS F
>COUNSELOR,HI SCH		.35
PRINTER	.35	
SCHOOL SUPT	.35	
TV REPAIRER	.35	
>BOOKSTOR MANAGER		.34
SECRETARY		.34
>SCC WORKER,GROUP		.34
BUYER	.34	
SALES ENG,HT/AIR	.34	
TRAVEL AGENT	.34	
>LIBRARIAN		.33
>SOCIAL CASEWORKR		.33
SCC WORKER,MEDIC		.33
FORESTER	.33	
RADIO STATON MGR	.33	
>SOC WORKER,PSYCH		.32
ELEM SCHL TCHR	.32	
PHOTOGRAPHER	.32	
NURSE	.31	
SOC WORKR,SCHOOL		.31
BANKER	.31	
>BOOKKEEPER	.31	
CLOTHIER, RETAIL	.31	
SUPERVSR,INDUSTR	.31	
>BOOKKEEPER		.30
HOME DEMONST AGT		.30
POSTAL CLERK	.30	
REAL ESTATE AGT	.30	
RELIGIOUS ED DIR		.29
COUNTY AGRI AGT	.29	
INSURANCE AGENT	.29	

COLLEGE MAJOR SCALES	NORMS M	NORMS F
>MATHEMATICS	.50*	
PHYSICAL SCIENCE	.48*	
PREMED/PHAR/DENT	.48*	
>PSYCHOLOGY	.46*	
>BIOLOGICAL SCI	.45*	
ENGINEERING,CHEM	.44*	
ENGINEERING,ELEC	.44*	
>BIOLOGICAL SCI		.42*
>ELEMENTARY EDUC	.42	
>MATHEMATICS		.41*
>FOREIGN LANGUAGE	.41	
HEALTH PROFES		.40*
>SOCIOLOGY	.40	
ECONOMICS	.39	
>HISTORY	.39	
>MUSIC & MUSIC ED	.39	
>PSYCHOLOGY		.38*
>ENGLISH	.38	
>POLITICAL SCI	.38	
ENGINEERING,MECH	.37	
ENGINEERNG,CIVIL	.36	
>ENGLISH		.35
>PHYSICAL EDUC		.35
>PHYSICAL EDUC	.35	
>FOREIGN LANGUAGE	.34	
LAW-GRAD SCHOOL	.34	
AIR FORCE CADET	.34	
HOME ECON EDUC	.33	

>PHYS THERAPIST .41*
>PHYSICIAN .41*
>PSYCHOLOGIST .41*
>X-RAY TECHNICIAN .41*
>COUNSELOR,HI SCH .41

ENG.HEAT/AIR CON .41
ENGINEER, INDUS .41
>LIBRARIAN .41
>PHYSICIAN .41
>ACCT,CERT PUBLIC .40
>BOOKSTOR MANAGER .40
JOURNALIST .40
>PSYCH, CLINICAL .39
PHARMACIST .39

DEAN OF WOMEN .38
DIETITIAN,SCHOOL .38
>MATH TCHR,HI SCH .38
>LAWYER .38
PERSONNEL MANAGR .38
>SOC CASEWORKR .38
SOC WORKER,GROUP .38
VETERINARIAN .38
>AUDIOL/SP PATHOL .37

>LAWYER .37
OCCUPA THERAPIST .37
ARCHITECT .37
MINISTER .37
UNIV PASTOR .37
DENTAL ASSISTANT .36
PHARMACEUT SALES .36
>SOC WORKER,PSYCH .36
YMCA SECRETARY .36

PLANT NURSRY WKR .29
STENOGRAPHER .27
>BLDG CONTRACTOR .27
>INTERIOR DECRAT .27
BANK CLERK .26

>INTERIOR DECORAT .26
>FLORIST .26
PLUMBING CONTRAC .26
>FLORIST .25
PRIMARY SCH TCHR .25
FARMER .24
OFFICE CLERK .24
POLICE OFFICER .24
ELECTRICIAN .23

MACHINIST .23
BEAUTICIAN .22
BRICKLAYER .22
AUTO SALESPERSON .21
WELDER .21
PLUMBER .20
PAINTER, HOUSE .19
AUTO MECHANIC .18
DEPT STORE SALES .18

TRUCK DRIVER .16
CARPENTER .14

NURSING .33
>POLITICAL SCI .33
BUS ACCT AND FIN .33
FORESTRY .33

>ELEMENTARY EDUC .32
>HISTORY .32
ARCHITECTURE .32
BUS MANAGEMENT .32

MILITARY CADET .32
SOCIAL SCI, GENL .31
>MUSIC & MUSIC ED .31
BUS ED & COMMERC .30

BUS & MARKETING .29
DRAMA .28
TCHG CATH SISTER .27
AGRICULTURE .27

>ART AND ART EDUC .27
>ART AND ART EDUC .26
>SOCIOLOGY .26
ANIMAL HUSBANDRY .24

	V 46		
M	.36	S	.33
MBI	.41	F	.38
W	.34	D	.27
WBI	.41	MQ	.28

Your scores are reported to you in rank order, on all scales. They show to what extent the choices you marked were like those typical of satisfied people in the occupations and college majors listed. Your top scores are followed by an asterisk (*). (For additional information and for an alphabetical list of scales, see the other side of this report.) > INDICATES TWIN SCALES, WITH SCORES IN M AND F COLUMNS.

responding occupational scale and 90 percent of their scores on the most similar scale are within .06–.07 of their highest score. These results confirm the suggestion that test takers consider occupations falling within .06 of their highest score. A study of the predictive validity of the KOIS over a 12- to 19-year period was done by Zytowski (1976). He found that about half the students were in occupations that were within .06 of their highest KOIS score and another quarter were in occupations that were within .07–12 of their highest score. The best predictions occurred when the test was taken at an older age, by a college student, and when the student selected a higher-level occupation in a scientific or technical field.

Other Vocational Interest Inventories   The inventories developed by Strong and Kuder illustrate many of the approaches to and problems in the measurement of vocational interests. But a number of other instruments are also available. Rather than describe them, we have listed some of them in Table 16.2.

Table 16.2
Examples of Vocational Interest Inventories

Kuder General Interest Survey (Science Research Associates). See text for description.

Kuder Occupational Interest Survey (Science Research Associates). See text for description.

Kuder Vocational Preference Record (Science Research Associates). See text for description.

Ohio Vocational Interest Survey (Psychological Corporation). Grades 8–13; items measure interest in work activities; 24 scales (e.g., machine work, crafts, management, teacher-counselor, clerical, medical).

Self-Directed Search (Consulting Psychologists Press). A self-assessment package based on Holland's theory; items involve self-ratings of interests, abilities, competencies, and occupational choices.

Strong-Campbell Interest Inventory (Stanford University Press). See text for description.

Vocational Preference Inventory (Consulting Psychologists Press). Measures the six occupational/personality types in Holland's theory.

Work Values Inventory (Riverside). Covers 15 value areas related to work (e.g., intellectual stimulation, relations with associates, job security, variety); grades 7 to adult.

Using Vocational Interest Inventories

The primary use of vocational interest measures is as an aid in vocational and educational counseling, particularly to help high school and college students and adults select occupations and careers. As mentioned above, the basic assumption is that people are likely to be more satisfied and remain in an occupation when their preferences and interests match those of other people working in the occupation. This does not mean that persons whose interests are quite dissimilar to most people in an occupation will be dissatisfied; if their job is atypical, or they perform it in a different manner, they may be very satisfied. However, the weight of the evidence suggests otherwise; for example, people who change jobs tend to move to ones more consistent with their interests.

Interest inventories can also be used to place people on jobs. For example, a company may hire various types of engineers: some to work on production, some for sales, and others for research positions. It is quite possible that scores on interest inventories can help match the engineers with the most appropriate job. Except in rare cases, they should not be used for selection, both because there is little empirical support for such use and because there is a greater probability of biased responding when a test is used to select applicants for a job or a professional school.

Although interests play an important role in occupational choice, they are not the only consideration. Certainly one must consider abilities and past achievement. There is a moderate positive relationship between abilities and interest, but the magnitude of this relationship (r's seldom higher than .30) is not sufficient to conclude that strong interest indicates high ability. There are also personal and social factors to consider when selecting an occupation. That these are important is illustrated by a study by McArthur (1954). He found that the SVIB was a better predictor of occupational choice for middle-class than upper-class students. One could speculate that upper-class students are more likely to be influenced by family traditions and pressures to enter certain businesses or professions (e.g., a family-owned business), whereas middle-class students try to maximize their opportunities for success by entering occupations that are consistent with their interests (and abilities).

Two problems in interest measurement are yet to be completely resolved. Although it has been relatively easy to construct inventories measuring interests in professional and higher-level occupations, it has been more difficult to measure interests in technical and nonprofessional fields. This is because people in professions have more distinct patterns of preferences, whereas people in technical areas have less differentiated interests; that is, their interests are more similar to people in general. The other question is what to do about sex differences. Even though access to any occupations should not be restricted on the basis of sex, the empirical fact remains that men and women in the same occupation have different patterns of preferences. Part of this difference may be due to different roles within an occupation; for example, male and female psychologists may tend to be in different specialty areas. The typical solution (used on the SCII and KOIS) is to use separate male and female norm groups but to report each person's scores on both norm groups. To many, this may not be an ideal solution, but it reflects the current empirical reality.

personality inventories

Just as work on group intelligence tests and interest inventories began around the time of World War I, so did the development of personality inventories. During the period between World War I and World War II a number of personality inventories were developed, some of which are still used. The inventories of this era were, by and large, keyed by a priori methods, measured only one or a few dimensions, and lacked empirical validity evidence. Then a major landmark in the development of self-report personality inventories occurred with the publication of the *Minnesota Multiphasic Personality Inventory* (MMPI) in 1942. The MMPI has so influenced the course of personality measurement and research since its publication that we shall first look at the MMPI in detail, then consider several other instruments which illustrate particular approaches to personality measurement.

The Minnesota Multiphasic Personality Inventory

The 550 MMPI items are self-descriptive statements taken from other inventories, textbook descriptions, psychiatric case write-ups, medical records, and self-descriptions. The content of these items was related to areas such as general health; neurologic, physical, and physiological symptoms; family and marital relations; religious, sexual, and social attitudes; morale and affect; obsessions, compulsions, delusions, hallucinations, and phobias. Typical items are of the form:

> I frequently find myself worrying about something.
> At times I feel like smashing something.
> I am happy most of the time.
> I cry easily.
> I am afraid when I look down from a high place.

Subjects respond yes, no, or cannot say (?), depending on whether or not the statement described them.

Although other methods of administration can be used,[6] items usually are presented in a test booklet with responses made on a separate answer sheet. The test is untimed and the reading level is very low; thus most people complete the test in 45 minutes to an hour.

Scores are typically obtained for ten clinical (diagnostic) scales and four validity scales (see Figure 16.3). The clinical scales, while having labels which correspond to the original criterion groups, generally are referred to by either their abbreviation or scale number. These scales are:

1	Hs	Hypochondriasis	6	Pa	Paranoia
2	D	Depression	7	Pt	Psychasthenia
3	Hy	Hysteria	8	Sc	Schizophrenia
4	Pd	Psychopathic deviate	9	Ma	Hypomania
5	Mf	Masculinity-feminity	0	Si	Social introversion-extraversion

Scores are expressed as T scores (standard scores with a mean of 50 and a standard deviation of 10 points) based on a general population norm group. Higher scores represent the "abnormal" end of each scale.

Development of the MMPI. The test authors hoped to develop a new kind of personality inventory—"an objective instrument for the 'multiphasic' assessment of personality by means of a profile of scales" (Hathaway, 1960, p. vii). By multiphasic they meant an instrument that would measure many facets of personality simultaneously (in contrast to the limited number of traits measured by tests available at that time). Furthermore, they hoped to include only empirically developed scales that could be used for diagnostic purposes.

---

[6] For example, each individual item can be printed on a separate card with the test taker sorting the cards into three piles: true, ?, and false.

Figure 16.3 The Minnesota Multiphasic Personality Inventory Profile

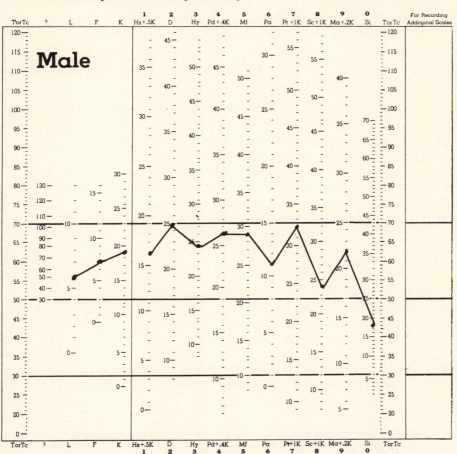

The basic procedure used was empirical keying. Criterion groups were composed of persons classified into one of the then prevalent psychiatric diagnostic categories—for example, hysterics, hypochondriacs, psychopaths, schizophrenics. Members of each criterion group were carefully selected to represent unambiguous manifestations of the syndrome being studied. Responses of the criterion group members were compared to the responses of a normal sample to select those items that differentiated between normals and members of the diagnostic group. Both validation and cross-validation samples were used. Responses of criterion group members were also contrasted with responses of patients hospitalized for physical complaints. This procedure was used because an item might differentiate between normals and a criterion (psychiatric) group but really be discriminating only between hospitalized and nonhospitalized persons. However, if the item also discriminated between persons hospitalized for mental and for physical complaints, it could be assumed to be tapping an essential aspect of the psychiatric disorder.

Although the process of developing and purifying the scales varied between scales, in general the responses of each criterion group were compared to those of various normal groups.[7] Originally scales were developed for eight diagnostic groups (scales 1–4 and 6–9). However, the profile usually includes two other scales (5 and 0), which do not represent clinically defined syndromes.

Reliability estimates for the MMPI scales, as is true of most personality measures, are lower than reliabilities on measures of maximal performance. For example, retest reliabilities range from .60 to .90 over short periods (a month or less) with normal subjects. The reliabilities decrease over long time periods, but do not seem to be noticeably lower for deviant groups. Although the MMPI scales were not designed to be homogeneous, internal consistency estimates of .90 and higher have been obtained for several of the scales.

The MMPI has proved to be a fertile item pool for persons wishing to construct special scales. More than 200 scales have been developed from the item pool, bearing such diverse labels as anxiety (several scales), ego strength, academic achievement, impulsivity, originality, pharisaic virtue, and ulcer personality. There is nothing to prevent an investigator from choosing a criterion group having certain characteristics, having them take the MMPI, and comparing their responses to the norm group, thus developing a new scale. There are also a number of short forms of the test that reduce the number of items and/or scales (Dahlstrom, 1980; Faschingbauer & Newmark, 1978).

Validity Scales.   One major innovation of the MMPI was the incorporation of scales to identify various test-taking attitudes. These are called *validity scales* since deviant scores on these scales invalidate the rest of the scores or, at least, call their validity into question. One of the indices is simply a count of the number of omitted items. If a large number of items are omitted, the test may be discarded or the test taker may be asked to complete the test; a small number of omissions are generally neglected and the test scored as usual.

On personality inventories, some persons will try to present themselves in the best possible light. To identify these people, a *Lie (L) scale* was constructed. The items on the L scale are virtues that few mortals possess, at least in the degree indicated by the items (such as: I do not always tell the truth; Once in a while I put off until tomorrow what I ought to do today; At times I feel like swearing). Persons who answer many of the items in the keyed direction either are trying to present a good impression or are very moral persons (in the conventional and straightlaced sense). The items are quite obvious to any one with much sophistication.

---

[7] Various "normal" groups were used. The basic one was hospital visitors, which turned out to be a good cross section of the adult population. Other groups (e.g., college students) were also used in some analyses.

Just as there are situations in which a person might want to present a good impression, there also are situations in which a person might want to appear more disturbed or give a poorer impression—for example, to increase the probability of being accepted into therapy or to avoid an onerous assignment. These persons can be detected by their scores on the *F scale,* a scale consisting of items that are infrequently answered in one direction (for example, I have nightmares every few nights; My soul sometimes leaves my body; Someone has been trying to poison me). However, high scores can also be obtained by people who do not understand the testing process, by answering randomly, and by people who are truly disturbed.

The fourth validity index, the *K scale,* consists of items that are susceptible to distortion or faking. The scale was developed in an attempt to reconcile MMPI scores with psychiatric diagnoses for several subsets of individuals whose MMPI scores did not typify their behavior (Meehl & Hathaway, 1946). Persons scoring high on the K scale tend to be defensive and deny personal inadequacies and problems of self-control; low scores indicate a willingness to say socially undesirable things about oneself. Correcting certain of the diagnostic scales with the K score increases the validity of the diagnostic scales; thus corrected K scores are used on certain of the clinical scales.

One further method of identifying possible invalid scores should be mentioned. Because the items comprising each scale were selected empirically, some items do not bear any logical relationship to the label of the scale. For example, the item "I often feel as if things were not real" could probably be identified as being on the Sc scale, whereas the item "I enjoy children" would not seem to bear any obvious relation to any diagnostic category. The former item is obvious, the latter one subtle. For a diagnostic scale, two subscales thus can be constructed: one of obvious items and the other of subtle items. If a scale is scored on both subsets of items, differences in scores would provide another method of detecting dissimulation.

Interpretation. Although the diagnostic scales were constructed empirically, it soon became apparent that using the MMPI solely as a diagnostic sorting device was a tremendous waste of information. The item pool of the MMPI was too rich to be used for so limited a purpose. Furthermore, it also became apparent that to make maximum use of the information provided, scores would have to be interpreted, not by treating each scale individually, but in terms of patterns of scores.

To interpret scores configurally requires specifying rules and procedures for arranging and summarizing the pattern of scores. To facilitate the interpretation, each scale was given a number and profiles were coded as a sequence of numerals corresponding to the rank ordering of scale scores. This procedure (of referring to scales by number rather than name) also focuses attention on the broader meaning of the scale, not just the label derived from the original criterion group.

Several alternative coding systems are available—the distinction between them being primarily in the complexity of the symbolization used. One simple system uses only the two highest scale scores to form the code. Thus, a profile with the highest score on scale 4 (Pd) and the second highest score on scale 9 (Ma) would be classified "49." Slightly more complex systems use a combination of the three highest scales and the lowest scale; for example, a code might be 498-2. Highly complex systems use various symbols to indicate the absolute level of scores and which scores differ by only one point. Coding permits objective classification of MMPI profiles—by similarity of profile codes—and thereby enables one to search for behavior patterns that typify a particular profile code, thus providing a basis for interpreting scores on the test.

It would not be unfair to say that many of the major advances in the objective interpretation of personality test scores have resulted directly from attempts to interpret the MMPI. One of the first approaches was the Atlas approach (Hathaway & Meehl, 1951). The *MMPI Atlas* consists of a collection of MMPI profiles, arranged by profile codes, with each profile being followed by a brief narrative description of the characteristics of the person whose profile was presented. The test user could look in the Atlas for examples of profiles with similar coding, read the personality descriptions, and get a flavor of the behavior characterizing persons having that particular profile pattern.

As use of the MMPI expanded, a folklore of interpretation clues developed based on patterns of profile scores. Thus, a profile with scales 1 and 2 coded highest was said to indicate a neurotic pattern with depression and probably pain and/or somatic complaints; if scale 8 was significantly higher than scale 7, the indication was that the person was psychotic rather than neurotic; the relation of scores on scales 3 and 4 was said to indicate the amount of libidinal energy; and so on. Some of these folklore interpretations were supported by hard data, others were the distillation of clinical experience, and others probably represented severe cases of selective retention. Because of their unsystematic nature, these proposed interpretations lacked many of the requisites for being acceptable scientific knowledge.

What was needed were more systematic data regarding the characteristics of persons obtaining certain patterns of MMPI scores; or, as Meehl phrased it, what was needed was a good cookbook (Meehl, 1956). Good cookbooks (or codebooks, as they came to be known) would be empirically derived; would be based on a representative, or at least specifiable, population; and would summarize the characteristics of persons having a given MMPI profile that differentiated them from other persons (Table 16.3). Because there are many possible MMPI patterns, and data must be available for a number of people having the same profile in

Table 16.3
Example of Codebook Entries

MMPI Code	Actuarial Description
27	Anxious; socially insecure; depressed; shy; lacks self-confidence; study problems.
28	Lacks skills with opposite sex; anxious; depressed; indecisive; shy; socially insecure; nervous; exam jitters.

order to ensure stable results, the development of a cookbook requires tremendously large samples. However, several cookbooks have been developed (e.g., Drake & Oetting, 1959; Marks & Seeman, 1963; Marks, Seeman, & Haller, 1974).

With the advent of computers, the test interpretation process has been further mechanized. Scoring rules and interpretive comments can be stored in a computer. If item responses are entered, the computer can score the test and print a copy of the test profile. It can also look up the appropriate descriptive comments and print a verbal interpretation of the scores (see Table 16.4). Computers can also be programmed to make diagnostic decisions, such as whether the score profile is normal or abnormal or what diagnostic category the test taker's scores most closely resemble. This process involves storing the diagnostic rules in the computer, then applying these rules to the test scores (Butcher, 1971; Fowler, 1979; Kleinmutz, 1972, 1975).[8]

Table 16.4
Example of a Computerized Interpretation of an MMPI Profile

The test results appear to be valid. He has followed the instructions and seems to have answered truthfully. There is no sign of undue defensiveness.

The client tends to be tense, overanxious, and impulsive. He has a high energy level and is aroused quite easily. He may find it difficult to stick to tasks, especially those assigned by others. Although he will probably be outgoing and sociable, he may lack consideration and judgment. He is quite concerned about what others think of him. His performance on a job or task may be erratic. He will frequently ask for reassurance that he is proceeding correctly. However, because he is impulsive, he may continue to make mistakes, particularly foolish ones. He will be more concerned with finishing a job, and others' evaluation of his performance, than with his own standards of success. He may be easily swayed by other people's opinions.

Contributions of the MMPI. The MMPI as probably the most widely used self-report personality inventory. It is used as a diagnostic aid, as a screening device, as a counseling and psychotherapeutic tool, and as a research instrument. It is used for both decision-making and descriptive purposes. Its wide usage attests to the fact that many psychologists consider it to be both valid and useful in both clinical and research settings. But the MMPI is also important for its influence on the development of personality assessment. No other test has influenced objective personality assessment procedures as much as the MMPI.

What then are its major contributions? For one, the MMPI demonstrated that personality measurement could be an objective, empirically based procedure. Previously, personality measures had used a priori scoring keys or, at best, had used statistical criteria based on item distribution properties. The MMPI, in contrast, incorporated scales derived by empirical methods. Second, the MMPI included validity scales to control distortion. Although several previous tests had made passes at validity keys, the MMPI was the first to incorporate validity scales

---

° For further discussions of the interpretation of the MMPI see, for example, Dahlstrom, Welsh. & Dahlstrom (1972), Good & Branter (1974), Graham (1977), and Greene (1980).

as an integral part of the testing (and interpretation) procedure. Third, research on the MMPI demonstrated that not only could the process of test construction be empirical and objective, so also could the test interpretation process. The development of coding systems, atlases, configural scoring rules, and cookbooks all represented attempts to objectify the interpretation process. Fourth, and by no means least, the MMPI has provided a large item pool that has been used for development of further scales and in research projects of various sorts. Particularly important is the fact that new scales could be developed without changing the stimulus situation for the test taker, thus increasing the comparability of results obtained in different settings.

The interest in the MMPI has also spawned a wide variety of research studies. This research is so voluminous that it would be impossible to summarize in a few pages; interested readers should see, e.g., Butcher, 1969, 1979; Butcher & Pancheri, 1976; Dahlstrom & Dahlstrom, 1980; Dahlstrom, Welsh, & Dahlstrom, 1972, 1975; or Newmark, 1979.

Other Personality Inventories

The MMPI illustrates many of the considerations and problems involved in constructing and interpreting self-report personality inventories. But the MMPI is only one of a large number of self-report inventories (Buros, 1978). In this section we shall briefly describe three instruments that illustrate particular approaches to personality measurement. The *California Psychological Inventory* is an example of an inventory that focuses on normal personality traits. The *Edwards Personal Preference Schedule* illustrates how a particular problem, the control of the social desirability response set, can influence test development. The *Bem Androgyny Scale* is a test developed to measure one characteristic rather than a number of dimensions. Descriptions of some other tests are given in Table 16.5.

The California Psychological Inventory.   One frequently heard complaint about the MMPI concerns its "pathological" nature. In many ways the *California Psychological Inventory* (CPI) can be considered an MMPI for normal personality. The CPI consists of 480 statements, including some MMPI items, that are presented in a format similar to the MMPI. In contrast to the MMPI, however, the CPI scales are designed to measure dimensions of normal personality—for example, dominance, sociability, tolerance, achievement via independence, flexibility. The 18 scales are grouped into four categories: measures of poise, ascendancy, and self-assurance; measures of socialization, maturity, and responsibility; measures of achievement potential and intellectual efficiency; and measures of intellectual and interest modes.

The majority, though not all, of the scales were developed by empirical methods. For example, the Dominance scale was validated (1) by its ability to differentiate between groups of students rated as "most" and "least" dominant by teachers and/or principals, and (2) by correlating dominance scores with the ratings of dominance by peers or psychologists. In short, scales were validated against "real-life" social criteria. The goal was to develop scales that would measure important and socially relevant personality dimensions. This, then, is the

Table 16.5
Examples of Self-report Personality Inventories

Adjective Check List (Consulting Psychologists Press). Standard list of 300 adjectives; can be scored on 24 scales.

California Psychological Inventory (Consulting Psychologists Press). See text for description.

Edwards Personal Preference Schedule (Psychological Corporation). See text for description.

Eysenck Personality Questionnaire (Educational and Industrial Testing Service). Three basic dimensions of personality—Psychoticism (tough-mindedness), Extraversion, and Neuroticism (emotionality).

IPAT Anxiety Scale (Institute for Personality and Ability Testing). Brief measures of five dimensions of anxiety; adolescents and adults.

Minnesota Counseling Inventory (Psychological Corporation). For use in counseling high school students; three areas of adjustment and four modes of adjusting.

Minnesota Multiphasic Personality Inventory (Psychological Corporation). See text for description.

Omnibus Personality Inventory (Psychological Corporation). Fourteen scales covering intellectual values, attitudes, social-emotional adjustment, and modes of responding (e.g., Thinking Introversion, Autonomy, Practical Outlook, Social Extraversion); college.

Sixteen Personality Factors Questionnaire (Institute for Personality and Ability Testing). Based on Cattell's research; 16 scales (e.g., Assertiveness, Emotional Maturity, Impulsiveness, Self-Sufficiency, Tension); adults; also editions for high school and elementary levels.

State-Trait Anxiety Inventory (Consulting Psychologists Press). For research studies on anxiety; measures Anxiety Proneness (trait) and Current Level of Tension (state).

Study of Values (Houghton Mifflin). Often referred to as Allport-Vernon-Lindzey Study of Values; measures six basic motives—Theoretical, Economic, Aesthetic, Social, Political, and Religious; high school, college, and adult.

---

important aspect of the CPI; it illustrates that empirical keying procedures can be applied to measuring "normal" personality.

The Edwards Personal Preference Schedule.   The EPPS is a self-report personality inventory, consisting of 225 items in forced-choice format. It is scored on 15 scales corresponding to Murray's need categories (see Figure 8.4). Whether the EPPS, in fact, adequately measures the dimensions that it supposedly taps is of secondary importance for our purposes. Of primary importance is the fact that the EPPS was designed to control the effects of one of the major response sets, social desirability.

Edwards showed that there was a high correlation between the rated social desirability of an item and the probability of endorsement of that item. This finding cast doubt on the validity of all self-report inventories by opening the possibility that the test takers were responding not solely to the content of a test item but also to its social desirability. Thus scores on, say, the MMPI might as readily be interpreted as measures of the test taker's willingness to say socially undesirable things about himself. The test constructor, consequently, must decide how to control for this possibility and ensure that the scale scores reflect trait differences rather than differences attributable to the social desirability variable.

Edwards reasoned that the best way to control social desirability was to force the test taker to choose between two equally desirable (or undesirable) alternatives, each of which measured different traits. By pairing alternatives having the same rated social desirability but measuring different traits, the test taker must respond on the basis of item content (as both statements in the pair are equally desirable or undesirable). Thus, confronted with the choice between two equally desirable alternatives, for example:

> I like to help my friends when they are in trouble.
> I like to do my very best in whatever I undertake.

or two equally undesirable alternatives, for example:

> I feel depressed when I fail at something.
> I feel nervous when giving a talk before a group.

the test taker will respond primarily on the basis of content. Of course, on any particular item, one statement may be more socially desirable for a given individual than the other but—averaging over all items on the test—the effects of social desirability should cancel out.

By this procedure of constructing items by systematically pairing alternatives with similar social desirability ratings but representing different traits (needs), Edwards constructed an inventory that presumably eliminated the influence of social desirability. How well did he succeed in attaining his goal? The preponderance of evidence seems to indicate that although the influence of social desirability is much less on the EPPS than on the typical personality inventory, its influence has by no means been completely eliminated.

Two other important consequences of Edwards' attempt to control social desirability by use of a forced-choice format should be mentioned. First, utilization of the forced-choice format necessarily resulted in ipsative scores, thereby introducing complications into both the interpretation and statistical analyses of the scores. And, second, concentration on controlling the effects of the social desirability variable evidently resulted in less care being devoted to item selection, with the only apparent criterion for inclusion being the logical relation of the item content to one of Murray's need categories. Thus it appears that in test construction, as in other endeavors, an attempt to maximize one value frequently results in the sacrifice of another.

The Bem Androgyny Scale. A particularly messy area in personality research has been the measurement of psychological masculinity-femininity (MF). MF scales typically measure the interests, preferences, and values of males and females. That is, scales are developed by selecting items that differentiate between the "average" man and "average" woman. For example, if more women than men express interest in classical music, preferences for classical music would be scored "feminine." The result is a scale with feminine interests at one end and masculine at the other.

Bem (1974) suggested that this approach is inappropriate because it forces persons to one or the other end of the scale, whereas many people may have both masculine and feminine characteristics. Thus she developed a test with separate scales for masculinity and femininity. The items on the scale are adjectives that were placed on either the masculine or feminine scale on the basis of the ratings of judges. That is, adjectives that were seen as more typically masculine were placed on the masculine scale. The test taker indicates, on a 7-point scale, whether an item describes him. Thus, he receives two scores: one on masculinity and one on femininity. Thus, it is possible for a person to score high on both scales—that is, have the characteristics of both sexes.

In addition, an *androgyny* score can be obtained by comparing scores on the M and F scales. People whose scores are similar are androgynous and have the characteristics of both sexes. Persons whose scores differ widely are sex-typed. The test promises to be useful in studies of sex differences and sex role development.

Alternative Approaches

All the examples described in this chapter were inventories. Several other self-report techniques are described below. As with inventories, the common feature of all these methods is that test takers provide a description of their own behaviors, reactions, or feelings.

Scales on inventories typically measure personality traits and dimensions. An alternative approach is to identify problems or areas of concern. Once salient problems are identified, remedial treatment can be started. In these situations one can use a *problem checklist,* which is nothing more than a list of potential problems. The respondent checks the ones of greatest concern. Checklists can be used to identify personal, interpersonal, or social problems (e.g., I have trouble making friends, I do not get along with my parents) or for areas such as study habits (I have trouble getting to work, I lose my concentration easily). In some instances, checklists are filled out by an observer, such as a teacher, rather than by the individual. Checklists can also be used to assess skills, such as those needed to do research.[9]

Closely related are *self-ratings.* Although most ratings are of other people, individuals can also rate their own behaviors. We shall discuss rating scales in the next chapter.

Another approach is the *Q-sort.* In a Q-sort the individual is presented with a series of self-descriptive statements, usually printed on individual cards, and asked to sort these cards into categories from the most to least descriptive (Stephenson, 1953, 1980). The number of categories used, and the number of statements placed in each category, are specified in advance. For example, the individual might be presented with 100 statements and asked to select the one that is most descriptive, the three next most descriptive, the next six, and so on. Usually the number of cards to be placed in each category is chosen so that the final sorting will approximate a normal distribution. Since the procedure requires making intraindividual comparisons, it is ipsative—and the relative salience of different statements for the individual can be determined.

Q-sorts have several other uses. If Q-sorts are obtained from a number of people, we can intercorrelate their responses and cluster people in terms of the similarity of their sortings. This procedure identifies classes of people who have

---

[9] For further discussion of checklists see Brown, (1981) or Mehrens & Lehmann (1978).

similar personalities. Another variation is to ask the person to complete several different sorts; for example, one's actual self and one's ideal self. This approach has often been used in studies of self-concepts and to provide information for use in therapy and counseling.

dissimulation

At various places in our discussion of typical performance measurement we have mentioned the possibility of biased responding and faking. While certain types of response biases can occur on projective and situational methods, and even on maximal performance tests, the problem is most apparent on self-report measures because individuals, for various reasons, may not be objective and unbiased observers of their own behavior and reactions. This distorted pattern of responding has been called response bias, faking, and dissimulation.

Because biased responding is possible, test contructors and users must be concerned with the possible effects. The first step is to identify the possible response biases. Then we must attempt to control, eliminate, or correct for their effects. In this section we shall describe various types of response biases that may occur on typical performance measures and some methods that have been used to measure them.

Response Sets and Styles

Previously we distinguished between two classes of response biases: response sets and response styles (Rorer, 1965). A *response set,* you will recall, is content-dependent and occurs when test takers attempt to present a particular picture of themselves. Examples include trying to appear psychologically sick or healthy (faking bad and faking good), attempting to exhibit a particular trait or characteristic (e.g., attempting to look like a physician on the SCII), or making only socially desirable responses.

To illustrate a response set, consider social desirability. A. L. Edwards (1957b, 1967) has shown that personality items can be ranked, with high reliability, along a dimension that indicates whether the statement is considered socially desirable or undesirable. For example, the statement "I am an intelligent and creative person" would almost certainly be judged as highly desirable, whereas the statement "I often have temper tantrums when something doesn't go my way" would almost certainly be rated as socially undesirable. By having judges rate items on social desirability, we could obtain a social desirability scale value for each item and/or develop a social desirability scale. As would be expected, items that are rated as being socially desirable are endorsed with greater frequency than items rated as being socially undesirable; in fact, there is a very high positive correlation between the social desirability rating of an item and the probability of its being endorsed.

Response sets, such as social desirability, are dependent upon the content of the item. That is, a test taker cannot alter his responses to produce the desired picture unless he can see the relationship between the item content and the probable keying of the item. In addition to content-dependent response sets, various content-independent response tendencies, or *response styles,* have been identified. Examples include the tendency to select some response when unsure of the correct response (guessing), the tendency to agree with a statement when having no informed basis for agreeing or disagreeing (acquiescence), and the tendency to avoid extreme responses (central tendency). Note than an essential condition for manifestation of a response style is that the test taker has no rational way of choosing between responses, usually because the item is ambiguous, meaningless, or difficult. In these situations it is postulated that the test taker will respond, not at random, but in accord with a particular response style. Note, also, that response styles may operate on tests of maximal performance as well as tests of typical performance; for example, when unsure of the correct response to true-false items, most people respond true.

Methods for Identifying and Controlling Response Biases

Given that response biases can occur, and there is ample evidence that they do occur on all types of typical performance measures, the problem becomes how to identify and control these tendencies. Four types of methods have been used: eliciting the test taker's cooperation, structuring the task to minimize bias, use of special scales, and looking at inconsistencies in data obtained from various sources.

Cooperation.   Perhaps the ideal way to control response biases is to make sure that test takers have no reason for biasing their responses—that is, by structuring the testing situation so that test takers feel it is to their advantage to respond honestly. Often this can be accomplished by simply explaining the nature and purpose of the test to the test taker. If test takers know what the test measures and how the results will be used, they will have little reason to distort their responses. This approach is most appropriate in counseling and therapeutic interactions, where the counselor and client are working together to solve a problem. It is obviously less useful in situations, such as selection, where the test taker may have something to gain by biasing his responses. However, even in therapeutic situations, there may be reasons to dissemble. For example, if a clinic cannot serve all prospective clients and screening is done on the basis of severity of symptoms as shown by a personality inventory, a prospective client may "fake bad" in order to increase his chances of being accepted for therapy. Or a client who wants to terminate therapy may deny some problems (i.e., fake good) so as to appear to show improvement.

Task Structure.   Another approach is to structure the task so that biased responding is difficult. Here, interestingly, two opposite approaches have been used. One is to make the testing situation or stimuli so ambiguous that test takers do not know how to bias their responses. This approach is illustrated by projective methods. Or the true purpose or nature of the testing may be concealed from the test taker.[10] At the other extreme, the situation or items can be so highly structured

[10] Since disguising the purpose of the testing raises ethical questions, it generally is not an acceptable way to control response biases.

and clear that biases have little room to creep in. An example is rating observable behaviors using a highly specific rating category. This approach leaves less room for bias than rating broad, general personality traits.

Another possibility is to use a response format that decreases the possibility of bias. The forced-choice method is a good example. For example, we saw how Edwards used a forced-choice format to eliminate the effects of social desirability. That is, he required test takers to make a choice between two equally desirable or equally undesirable statements. If each statement were rated individually, a person could bias their responses (i.e., give the socially desirable response); however, by pairing the stimuli on social desirability the person has to respond on the basis of content, not social desirability. Similar procedures can be used on ratings; for example, we can ask the rater to indicate which of two equally desirable or undesirable terms or statements better describes an individual. We can also use person-to-person rating scales, where raters have to select which of two people they would, for example, rather have as a working partner. This procedure avoids the possibility of a person saying that all partners would be desirable. If the procedure is repeated over all possible pairs of potential co-workers, we can obtain a rank ordering of prefered co-workers.

Special Scales. A third approach is to use special scales to identify response biases. At the simplest level we could count the number of items that the test taker did not answer. This might indicate his degree of defensiveness. Or we could, as is done on some inventories, repeat some items. We could then check to see how often the person responded in the same mannner. If many responses were different, the validity of the test would be called into question.[11]

Other types of special scales have already been described—for example, the validity scales on the MMPI. These scales are used in two ways. On one hand, they are reported separately and interpreted in their own light. On the other hand, scores on the K scale are also used as a correction factor to increase the validity of the clinical scales. Other examples of special scales include the atypical response scale on the SCII, the social desirability scales used on many instruments, and the subtle-obvious keys on the MMPI.

Inconsistent Data. A final method looks at inconsistencies in data, either between scales within a test or between the test and other sources of information. The MMPI subtle-obvious keys could be an index of the former type. Another example would be obtaining a normal MMPI profile from a person hospitalized for a psychiatric disorder. In this case we might well question the validity of the test profile, even though the validity indices were in the normal range.

An example from the author's experience illustrates the use of various sorts of data. My adviser once found an SVIB-SCII profile that had a pattern of scores widely divergent with what he, and I, expected. Since the handwriting was mine,

---

[11] Note that these approaches may identify people who misunderstood the test procedures or responded haphazardly, as well as people who are deliberately faking. The Atypical Response scale on the SCII also does this.

there was no question that I had taken the test. On checking, we determined that it was the profile for a SVIB-SCII I had taken in a class when challenged by an instructor to prove that I could fake my responses to the test. Only the fact that my scores were so different from what was known about me suggested that the test responses may have been biased.

Using Information on Response Biases.   Although we have been discussing response biases as if they always reflected deliberate attempts to distort responses, extreme scores on validity keys may also result from the test taker misunderstanding how to respond to the test. Examples include the MMPI "?" and F scales and the SCII Atypical Response Scale. Thus we must always determine whether atypical scores result from deliberate attempts to bias responses (response sets), systematic response tendencies (response styles), or misunderstanding of testing procedures.

If there is evidence that responses may have been biased, what can be done? Obviously, if the bias is extreme, the test results should not be interpreted or used. If possible, the person should be retested. If the degree of bias is less and the bias can be taken into account when interpreting scores, we can interpret scores, but with caution.

an evaluation of self-report inventories

Having looked at a number of examples of personality inventories, albeit in a cursory fashion, we might ask: What does it all mean? Can personality be measured by self-report inventories? To be consistent with our view that validity is the most important characteristic of any test and that validity is situation-specific would dictate a response that such questions are essentially unanswerable. And in one important sense they are: The test user must always evaluate any test in light of the particular requirements of the particular situation (see, especially, Mischel, 1968). Nevertheless, certain recurring themes appeared throughout our discussion. We shall review these by asking several questions.

Does the self-report approach to the construction of personality measures work? If by this question is meant, "Can inventories based on self-reports be constructed?", the answer is obviously yes, for many have been constructed. If the question means, "Can the self-report format be adapted to the measurement of a wide variety of traits or aspects of personality?", the answer is again yes, since self-report inventories have been developed to measure vocational interests, psychiatric syndromes, normal personality, cognitive styles, and values—everything from schizophrenic tendencies to interest in baking, from religious values to psychopathic tendencies, from aggression to nurturance. If the question is rephrased to mean, "Do the inventories measure the basic components of an individual's personality?", no answer can be given. Instead, one must ask, what is meant by "basic components"? If, like some factor analysts, one means well-documented factors, then the answer is yes; if, like some personality theorists, you mean some intangible underlying motivating agent, then the answer is "probably not."

Do self-report personality inventories attain the desired standards of consistency and validity? The evidence shows that the consistency of personality measures—be it stability or internal consistency—is generally lower than on other types of measures. But is this a function of the phenomenon we are dealing with or the mode of measurement? There is evidence that well-constructed inventories can meet rigorous standards of internal consistency and stability (for example, Strong's 18-year follow-up). Validity is another question. In most cases the appropriate method of establishing validity is construct validity, and construct validity can neither be established overnight nor be summarized by a single index. Certainly, there is evidence showing that scores on personality inventory do relate to a variety of other variables. However, in the large majority of instances the relationships are disappointingly low.

What is the relationship between personality measurement and personality theory? With several exceptions, tests developed to reflect a particular theory have not been epitomes of good test construction methodology and, conversely, the most rigorous test construction methods have been adopted by persons whose philosophic viewpoint approaches dust-bowl empiricism. Personality inventories have, of course, been used to test concepts in, and deductions from, personality theory, but too often the tests used have been accepted uncritically, been developed on an ad hoc basis, or have been used for purposes for which they were not designed. In short, the relation between personality theory and personality measurement is far from the desired level.

Have empirical correlates of personality inventory scores been established? If anything is certain in personality measurement it is that scores on the widely used personality inventories have been, or will be, correlated with practically any variable imaginable. For example, the Eighth Mental Measurements Yearbook lists 5000 references for the MMPI, 1500 for the SVIB, and 1600 for the Edwards PPS. So there is no doubt that there is a plethora of data: the problem is making any sense out of the data. Since much of the data are situation-specific, collected on particular samples in a particular place at a particular time for a particular purpose, rather than as part of systematic attempts to understand the meaning of a particular test or test score, the data are almost impossible to comprehend. One can only admire the attempts made to summarize the data on particular tests—attempts like those of Dahlstrom et al. (1972, 1975) for the MMPI, Campbell (1971) for the SVIB, Super and Crites (1962) for a variety of tests, and some of Buros' reviewers.

What impact do response sets, response styles, and faking have on inventory scores? In spite of concentrated research and attempts at control, it is clear that the effects of these variables have not been completely eliminated from any of the extant inventories. Although the identification of the direction and amount of possible dissimulation (as in the MMPI validity scales) and incorporation of these data into the test interpretation process is a desirable step, adoption of a test format that would eliminate their effects would be an even more desirable solution. The most systematic attempt to accomplish this end (Edwards' work) has been only partially successful. Furthermore, since much of the research on these variables has involved only intratest measures and not extratest variables, it is impossible to ascertain definitely whether their effects are test-specific or represent broader personality traits. But, without doubt, response sets and styles do influence test scores and faking of personality inventories is possible.

Is empirical or homogeneous keying a more effective approach to construction of self-report inventories? To answer this question, of course, requires another question: more effective for what purpose? There is no question but that empirically keyed tests (such as the MMPI and SCII) are more widely used, receive stronger support from the research literature, and have had a greater impact on personality assessment. These conclusions hold in spite of the fact that the homogeneously keyed instruments, theoretically, should possess the advantages of an empirically keyed instrument plus have the advantage of providing homogeneous, and hence hopefully more readily interpretable, scores. The reasons for the failure of the homogeneously keyed instruments is unclear; one possible reason is that the existing inventories do not tap all the relevant factors. Ideally, of course, the instrument should include items that are *both* empirically and homogeneously keyed, not in the sense of the scales on the SCII or MVII, but in the sense that the items included on a scale have surmounted both empirical and homogeneous selection hurdles.

Are different item formats differentially effective? For the most part, constructors of items for self-report personality inventories have not been noticeably creative, relying primarily on two basic item formats: statements requiring an agree-disagree response, and/or a forced choice between two or more alternatives. Although the latter approach has certain benefits in controlling irrelevant variables, it also leads to ipsative scores and, consequently, problems in analyzing and interpreting scores. Thus lacking any persuasive argument based on differential reliability and/or validity, there may be some slight advantage for the simpler yes-no approach. One would hope, however, that the test constructors might show more ingenuity in attempting to develop new item formats. To cite only one example of what might be done, Goldberg has experimented with an item format that requires the respondent to indicate whether he has engaged in an activity in the past (say, climbing a mountain or telling off a teacher), what his subjective reaction to the experience was (did he like it or dislike it?), and what the probability is that he will engage in the activity in the future. This format not only provides a large amount of response data from a single stimulus item, it also allows for the analysis of response patterns.

Finally, for what practical purposes can self-report inventories be used? Because of the openness of self-report inventories to faking and other varieties of dissimulation, they should be used only in circumstances in which the test taker will treat the test as a measure of typical performance. The empirical data certainly support the use of interest inventories in vocational counseling and planning, and, if used with caution, in educational and vocational placement. The more traditional personality inventories exhibit such low relationships with real-life criteria that their use for purposes other than hypothesis building and to make statements about the general characteristics of individuals or groups seems quite tenuous.

summary

On self-report methods, test takers observe and report their own behaviors, reactions, attitudes, and feelings. The basic assumption is that the test taker is in the best position to observe these characteristics, and thus can respond using the widest possible range of experience. Their main limitation is that since test takers may not be objective judges of their own behavior, they may consciously or unconsciously distort their responses.

A variety of self-report methods are used, including inventories, checklists, and attitude scales. Inventories are the most common. An inventory is a collection of self-descriptive statements, often several hundred items. Test takers respond by indicating whether or not the statements describe them. Typically scores are obtained on a number of independent scales or dimensions.

Scales on inventories can be constructed by three methods. With logical keying, the items selected are ones that appear to measure the characteristic of concern. Empirical keying involves selecting items that have an observable relation with some external criterion, such as membership in an occupational or diagnostic group. Homogeneous keying selects items that are highly intercorrelated, thus producing homogeneous scales.

The inventory approach is widely used to measure vocational interests. As illustrations we focused on the inventories developed by Strong and Kuder. The Strong-Campbell Interest Inventory measures both interests in broad vocational areas (the General Occupation Themes and Basic Interest Scales) and in specific occupations (the Occupational Scales). Both homogeneous and empirical keying is used; homogeneous for the Basic Interest Scales and empirical for the Occupational Scales. The Kuder Vocational Preference Record and General Interest Survey use homogeneous keying and report interests in broad vocational areas. In contrast, the Kuder Occupational Interest Survey uses empirical keying and reports interest in occupations and college majors. The Kuder and Strong inventories are carefully constructed, reliable, valid, and are used primarily in the educational and vocational counseling of high school and college students and adults.

Inventories also are extensively used in personality measurement. Here the Minnesota Multiphasic Personality Inventory was used as the prime example. The MMPI contains empirically keyed clinical scales, which originally were developed to aid in psychiatric diagnosis. However, the test is now used as a more general personality assessment technique. It also contains a number of validity scales designed to identify various types of response biases. We used the MMPI to illustrate various approaches to interpreting personality test profiles: clinical lore, profile analysis, atlases, codebooks, and computer-based interpretations.

As responses to self-report inventories can be faked, the problem of response biases (dissimulation) was considered in detail. We distinguished between response sets (content-dependent response patterns designed to present a particular picture) and response styles (systematic patterns of responding that are content-independent). We also described various methods used to identify and control response biases: eliciting cooperation, structuring the task to minimize bias, use of special scales, and considering incongruities among various sources of data.

Self-report inventories are standardized, objective tools for personality assessment. The better ones have good normative data, have adequate reliability, and have been subjected to extensive research. The major problem is in combining data from the various scales into an integrated picture of the test taker's personality structure.

Suggestions for Further Reading

Butcher, J. N. (Ed.). *New developments in the use of the MMPI.* Minneapolis: University of Minnesota Press, 1979. Chapters cover the use of the MMPI in a variety of applied problems—such as studies of aging, cross-cultural differences, criminals, and medical patients—and in personnel selection.

Dahlstrom, W. G., & Dahlstrom, L. (Eds.). *Basic readings on the MMPI.* Minneapolis: University of Minnesota Press, 1980. Covers scale development, response sets and styles, special scales, uses of the test, and objections to the test.

Dawis, R. V. Measuring interests. *New Directions for Testing and Measurement,* 1980, *7,* 77–92. A good, brief introduction to interest measurement, covering both the theory and methods of measuring interests.

Edwards, A. L. *The measurement of personality traits by scales and inventories.* New York: Holt, Rinehart and Winston, 1970. A quantitative introduction to the methodology of constructing personality scales; the emphasis is on statistical methods and the control of response sets.

Goldberg, L. R. Objective diagnostic tests and measures. *Annual Review of Psychology,* 1974, *25,* 343–366. A review of the status of objective personality measurement.

Hase, H. D., & Goldberg, L. R. Comparative validity for different strategies for constructing personality inventory scales. *Psychological Bulletin,* 1967, *67,* 231–248. An empirical study contrasting the validity of six methods of constructing personality inventory scales.

Kleinmutz, B. *Computers in personality assessment.* Morristown, N.J.: General Learning Press, 1972. A description of how computers can be used in personality assessment, with particular reference to the MMPI.

Kuder, G. F. Some principles of interest measurement. *Educational and Psychological Measurement,* 1970, *30,* 205–226. Kuder's philosophy of interest measurement summarized in 12 principles.

Prediger, D. J. Alternatives for validating interest inventories against group membership criteria. *Applied Psychological Measurement,* 1977, *1,* 275–280. Points out the difference between using interest inventories to suggest what occupation an individual should enter and to suggest what occupations an individual should consider.

SVIB-SCII: The 1981 Revision. Stanford, Calif.: Stanford University Press, 1981. An introduction to the SCII, including a copy of the test profile, the interpretive material, summaries of the test development and salient research, and suggestions for using the test.

Zytowski, D. G. (Ed.) *Contemporary approaches to interest measurement.* Minneapolis: University of Minnesota Press, 1973. Descriptions of a number of widely used interest inventories, including their construction, interpretation, and use.

Chapter 17 • Other Methods for Personality Assessment

IN most respects, self-report inventories follow the same psychometric tradition as do achievement and ability tests. This is seen clearly in the emphasis on objectivity and standardized testing conditions, the use of empirical data to select items and validate scores, and the focus on measurement of separate traits and dimensions. They differ from maximal performance measures in the goals of the measurement, content, and the uses of scores, rather than in the basic measurement methodology.

Although many psychologists consider such "objective" measures to be the best method for assessing personality characteristics, others would disagree. One objection is that the emphasis on methodology, particularly as illustrated by empirical keying, has relegated personality theory to a subsidiary role. That is, what is measured on inventories often seems to be less important than how it is measured. A related criticism is that self-report techniques are too atomistic, that they focus on the independent dimensions of personality rather than attempting to present an integrated, dynamic picture.

Finally, personality inventories have been criticized because they represent measurement in an artificial situation. What is needed, critics suggest, are assessments obtained in more real-life, naturalistic settings. Rather than ask how a person would react, critics argue, we should observe how a person actually does react. This, of course, implies that the assessment situation should be as similar to a real-life setting as possible.

In this chapter we shall discuss a variety of alternative approaches to personality measurement that are designed to overcome some of these objections. We shall first discuss projective methods, an approach that, by and large, has been more theory-based and holistic than other approaches to personality measurement. We shall then discuss two methods, situational tests and observations, that focus on assessment in more naturalistic settings. We shall also describe a number of other approaches, such as attitude scales and questionnaires, which are used in particular situations. The chapter will conclude with a review and evaluation of typical performance measurement.

projective techniques

Projection refers to the process by which individuals' personality structure influences the ways in which they perceive, organize, and interpret their environment and experiences. When tasks or situations are highly structured their meaning usually is clear, as is the appropriate way to respond to the situation. Thus, operation of the mechanism of projection can best be seen (and measured) when an individual encounters new and/or ambiguous stimuli, tasks, or situations.

The implication for test construction is obvious: To study personality, one should present an individual with new and/or ambiguous stimuli and observe how he reacts and structures the situation. From his responses we can then make inferences concerning his personality structure. The crucial requirements are that the stimulus situation lack definitive structure and that the test taker be given wide latitude in his mode of response; unduly restricting response options would, in effect, be structuring the task.

Not all authors agree that these are the essential features of projective methods. Lindzey (1961), for example, after surveying the various definitions of projective techniques, concluded that the hallmarks of projective techniques were their sensitivity to unconscious or latent aspects of personality, the multiplicity of responses permitted the subject, the fact that several personality dimensions are measured simultaneously, the subject's unawareness of the purpose of the testing,[1] and the richness of the response data elicited. In addition, certain other characteristics frequently are noted, but are not of prime importance: the ambiguity of the stimulus, the use of holistic analyses, the evocation of fantasy responses, and the fact that there are no correct or incorrect responses.

Rather than haggling further over a definition, we shall describe several widely used projective methods. After reading these descriptions, you can decide which dimensions are fundamental and which are incidental.

The Rorschach Method

Perhaps no other psychological test is as well known, has intrigued the layman as much, or caused as much division of opinion among psychologists as the *Rorschach Method*. The test consists of ten cards, each of which contains an amorphous design resembling an inkblot (see Figure 17.1). All of the designs are symmetrical and printed on a white background; half are in shades of gray and black, others are gray plus color, and others are completely chromatic.

Since the stimuli are ambiguous, how the test taker structures and responds to the cards—that is, what he "sees" in the blots—represents his projection of meaning into the stimuli. These projected meanings, in turn, are used as the basis for making inferences about his personality structure and dynamics.

The use of "inkblots" as stimuli illustrates an important aspect of projective testing: the unimportance of item content. The only requirement is that the stimulus be unstructured but capable of having a structure imposed upon it. The inkblots are, of course, essentially meaningless; yet because they resemble and suggest real objects, they are capable of being structured, allowing the subject to

---

[1] Awareness is a relative concept; for example, a person may be aware that he is being tested but not know what characteristics are being measured and/or how the scores will be used. As Kelly (1958) has stated: An objective test is one where the test taker tries to guess what the examiner is thinking; a projective test is one where the examiner tries to guess what the test taker is thinking.

Figure 17.1 An Inkblot Similar to Those Used in the Rorschach Method

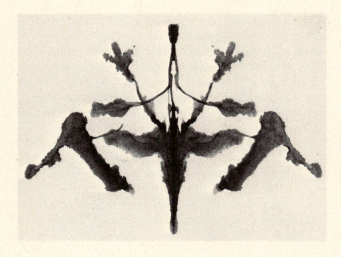

project meaning onto them. Thus they are ideally suited to serve as stimuli, even though they have no inherent meaning.

Administration and Scoring.   Administration of the Rorschach typically occurs in two stages. During the first stage the test administrator presents the cards, one at a time, in a set order. The subject is instructed to report what the blots resemble or suggest to him. The examiner records the subject's responses and keeps a record of several other aspects of performance—for example, the latency of the first response to each card, the total time spent on a card, how the card is turned. The second stage of the administration is an inquiry. In this stage the subject goes through the cards a second time, commenting upon the features of the blots that caused him to make a particular response. The administrator may actively question the test taker during the inquiry, seeking to clarify the responses or their basis. The test is administered to only one individual at a time and requires a highly trained administrator.

There are several approaches to scoring the Rorschach (see, e.g., Aronow & Reznikoff, 1976; Beck et al., 1961; Exner, 1974; Klopfer & Davidson, 1962). Although certain dimensions (location, determinants, and content) are scored in all systems, there is disagreement on exact scoring techniques, the relative emphasis to be given each score, and the other dimensions scored. *Location* refers to the portion of the blot used as the basis of the response. It can vary from use of the whole blot, through use of a major detail, to use of minor details of the blot, or even use of white background space. *Determinants* refer to which aspects of the blot determined the response: the shape or form, shading or texture, coloring, and whether movement was perceived. *Content,* of course, refers to the category the percept falls into—for example, a human, details of humans, an animal, a plant. Every response is scored on all three dimensions: location, determinant, and content.

These scores, plus other data (for example, total number of responses, reaction times, various ratios between scores, whether the responses were popular or original) are combined into a *psychogram*. From this point, interpretation becomes a highly individualized matter. Some clinicians rely on actuarial patterns and signs; others proceed on a completely intuitive basis. Some emphasize the pattern of scores; others emphasize individual responses. Some pay particular attention to content; others pay little attention to the content. It is at this point, consequently, that the Rorschach loses its objectivity. Although actuarial validity data could be developed, these have not become popular because of certain statistical problems (Cronbach, 1949)—for example, different numbers of responses are given by different subjects—and because many Rorschach users feel that statistical treatment destroys the dynamic and holistic nature of the interpretation.

Interpretation and Validity.   Although the literature is replete with studies of the Rorschach (Buros, 1978, lists almost 5000 studies using the test), the validity of the method is often questioned. Opinions range from the view that the Rorschach's validity is beyond question to the view that it is a worthless instrument (Karon, 1978; Peterson, 1978, Wade & Baker, 1977). The reasons for these differences of opinion are numerous. The statistical problems with scores, for one, render much of the validity data meaningless or at least inconclusive. Then, too, since control of relevant variables is difficult, the results of any study are open to various interpretations. Third, because the test presumably measures unconscious motivating factors, and criterion measures reflecting these factors are not available, direct validity evidence is lacking. Conversely, some Rorschach advocates consider studies of the relationship between Rorschach scores and objective criterion measures to be trivial. And forth, although the test is supposed to reflect basic personality structures, changes in the testing situation can alter the test taker's responses (Klopfer & Taulbee, 1976; Masling, 1960).

Because interpretations of Rorschach scores are highly individualized, studies are actually validating a particular examiner's interpretation of the Rorschach.[2] That is, the test and examiner are confounded. For example, suppose that Dr. Chiaroscuro looks at Rorschach psychograms of students at Waterman College and identifies the students needing counseling. Any study relating his diagnoses to an independent criterion will, in essence, be validating Dr. Chiaroscuro's interpretation of the Rorschach, not the test. What validity should be attributed to the good doctor and what to the test is an unanswerable question. To validate Rorschach scores one would, of course, have to relate psychogram scores to the criterion directly, without the examiner's interpretation.

---

[2] The confounding of test scores with the interpreter's analysis of the scores occurs whenever subjective judgment enters into the score interpretation process. The problem is more obvious on projectives, however, because scoring and interpretation rules are less standardized.

To counter the problems with holistic, interpreter-confounded interpretations, some investigators have focused on validating individual scores or scores on prognostic rating scales (see Klopfer & Taulbee, 1976, for a review). Others (Ames et al., 1971, 1973, 1974) have provided normative data for the Rorschach. Both of these approaches make interpretations more objective and empirically based.

The Holtzman Inkblot Test. A test which could be considered as a modification of the Rorschach is the *Holtzman Inkblot Test* (Hill, 1972; Holtzman, 1981; Holtzman et al., 1961). This test can be administered to groups and has more objective scoring procedures. It differs from the Rorschach in several ways: There are many more cards; the subject is allowed only one response per card; scoring is restricted to a small number of important dimensions; quantitative scoring weights are used; and several forms of the test have been developed. These changes result in reliable scores, avoid many of the statistical problems inherent in the Rorschach, and simplify administration while retaining many of the desirable projective features of the original test.

The Thematic Apperception Test

On a continuum measuring the degree of structure, self-report inventories would fall at the high-structure end and projective methods at the unstructured end. But projectives vary among themselves in degree of structure. Whereas the Rorschach presented the test taker with a highly ambiguous stimulus situation and permitted wide latitude in response, the *Thematic Apperception Test* (TAT) presents the subject with a more structured stimulus and response situation.

The TAT consists of a set of 20 cards, 19 of which picture scenes varying in content and ambiguity—typically of people engaged in some activity—and one blank card (see Figure 17.2). The cards are presented, one at time, to the subject, who is requested to make up a story about the card. This story should include details such as what is happening, who the people involved are, what actions have preceded the scenes, what will happen, and what the actors are thinking and feeling.

The basic rationale of the test depends heavily on the mechanism of identification. The major assumption is that the test taker will identify with one of the characters in the scene, particularly the central character. Since the stimuli on the TAT generally involve people pursuing various activities, the test has more face validity than does the Rorschach.

As with the Rorschach, there are several scoring systems. The original scoring system emphasized analysis of the needs of the main actor and the environmental presses that impinge upon him; an emphasis that followed directly from Murray's (1938) theory of personality. In general, the various scoring and interpretation systems rely heavily on an analysis of the thematic content of the stories, with structural properties playing a relatively minor role.

The exact content (that is, cards used) varies with the age and sex of the subject. Thus, some flexibility in adapting the test to the subject is possible. Special sets of cards have also been developed for use with various groups—for example, blacks

Figure 17.2 A Stimulus Card Similar to Those on the TAT

and children. Other sets have been developed to measure particular personality variables, such as McClelland's use of a modified set of TAT cards to study achievement motivation (McClelland, 1961, 1965, 1978; McClelland et al., 1953).

Determining the validity of the TAT is a difficult task. The first question one has to answer is whether the stories actually reflect the test taker's personality or are only stereotypic reactions to the situations pictured. Even assuming the former, can we assume that the test taker identifies with the "hero"; that the hero's problems, reactions, and pressures acting upon him reflect aspects of the test taker's life? Lack of agreement on a single scoring and interpretation system complicates the task. Thus acceptable validity data are hard to find. These problems have led reviewers to comment, "We seem to be approaching the conclusion that the TAT is not a psychometric instrument at all, but rather a multidimensional method for studying complex personality and for evaluating needs, values, motivations, and attitudes." (Klopfer & Taulbee, 1976, p. 554).

Other Projective Methods

Although the Rorschach and TAT, and their modifications, are the most common projective techniques, a number of other approaches can also be used. One is the *word association technique*. On word association tests, the examiner reads a list of words and the subject responds with the first word that comes to mind. As might be expected, the ideal stimulus words are ones that permit a wide variety of associations, some of which have diagnostic significance. By analyzing the pattern of responses, recurrent themes, hesitations in responding, and other signs, inferences about personality dynamics are made. Although most interpretations are based on content analysis, empirically keying methods can be applied to word association tests. For example, a scale to identify depressed individuals could be developed by identifying responses that occur more frequently in protocols of depressed persons than in normals.

Another well-known method is the *sentence completion test*. These tests typically consist of sentence stems, with the subject's task being to complete the sentence in his or her own words. As on word association tests, ideal stems are ones that can be completed in several ways and deal with diagnostically relevant topics. Scoring usually is subjective, stressing content analysis, but can be objective.

A third type of projective method, *figure drawings,* have been used for the assessment of both cognitive and personality characteristics. The simplest form of this technique requires the test taker to draw a person; more complex versions require the subject to draw several persons or draw a person in relation to other objects. Scoring and interpretation, though more objective than with most projective techniques, are far from standardized. However, most systems rely on characteristics of the drawing, the method of attack, and comments made by the individual, either spontaneously or in response to the examiner's inquiry. Since the test content is universal, the technique can be applied in almost any group. Thus it is often used in cross-cultural studies, with retarded children, and with children having language handicaps.

Finally, several projective methods can be subsumed under the label *expressive methods.* These include role-playing techniques and psychodrama , where subjects act out a particular role or part, and play techniques, where a child is presented with a variety of objects and asked to play with them in a particular manner. There are also reproduction techniques, such as the *Bender-Gestalt,* that require the subject to remember and reproduce designs. In short, almost any unstructured situation can be used as stimulus material.

An Evaluation of Projective Techniques

Although the use of projective techniques is decreasing, several projective methods are still among the most frequently used instruments in clinical psychology (Klopfer & Taulbee, 1976; Wade & Baker, 1977; Weiner, 1972). But is the use of projective methods justified by the validity evidence? Is any information provided by projectives that is not obtainable by other methods? Are there particular situations in which projective methods are most useful?

Before considering these validity questions, one might ask a prior question: Are projective methods tests? A test, you will recall, was defined as a systematic procedure for measuring a sample of behavior. For the current purposes the crucial phrase is "systematic procedure"; in other words, standardization.

By and large, the content of projective techniques is as standardized as that of other tests. The administrative procedures, though more flexible than those on standardized aptitude and achievement tests and self-report personality inventories, are comparable to the procedures used on individual intelligence tests. However, with a couple of notable exceptions (e.g., Holtzman's Inkblot Test), scoring procedures are unstandardized and/or there is disagreement between several alternative scoring systems. Hence, if we adhere to a literal interpretation of the definition, projective methods are not tests.

The lack of standardized scoring procedures has other important consequences. Without quantifiable scores, consistency estimates cannot be made. Without objective scoring, adequate normative data cannot be developed. (A weakness of almost all projective methods is the lack of adequate normative data.) And, without adequate normative data, interpretation of scores must be idiographic, rather than normative or nomothetic.

In personality measurement the basic concern is construct validity. Here we encounter an impenetrable barrier. If projective techniques measure basic components of personality, and if these facets are, by definition, unconscious (thus inaccessible to observation and measurement), then one can never directly validate a projective method. Several indirect lines of evidence, however, can be brought to bear. For example, if a projective method (or any other personality test) measures "basic" traits, scores should be relatively unaffected by ephemeral conditions associated with the particular test administrator, the conditions of test administration, slight changes in the stimulus materials or responding mode, or transient states of the test taker. Yet all of these factors influence responding on projective techniques. Also, dissimulation is possible on projective methods. Thus, whatever projectives measure, they are not pervasive, immutable aspects of personality structure.

What sort of evidence do projective techniques provide that is not available from other methods of measuring personality? One presumed advantage of projective measures was the richness of responses generated, and, consequently, the variety of dimensions tapped. However, one would be hard put to find a variable measured by a projective technique that has not also been measured by more objective methods.

What can we conclude about projective methods? By the standards of traditional psychometric theory, most would be rated as unacceptable. Yet many clinicians find them useful. Can they be wrong? Possibly. But one could also defend the view that instruments that better attain the desired psychometric properties, such as inventories, are limited and represent only one approach to assessing personality. In addition, projectives serve as a type of semistandardized diagnostic interview that requires a close interaction between the tester and the test taker. The nature of this interaction may enable the tester to pick up clues that would not be obtained using other assessment methods. But these clues may result largely, if not entirely, from the tester's acumen rather than from the test itself.

situational methods

Self-report and projective methods measure reactions in a somewhat artificial testing situation. Although a testing situation possesses certain definite advantages (for example, control of irrelevant variables by standardized conditions), it is still one step removed from "real life." Thus interpretations of behaviors and responses exhibited on tests are open to the criticism that the subject's behavior might have been different in a more natural situation. We can partially vitiate this argument by establishing the relationship between test performance and external criteria. However, failure to find a significant relationship between a test-defined variable and an external criterion measure always has at least two explanations:

There is, in fact, no relationship between the two variables or the test does not measure the variable it is designed to measure.

The need for the testing situation to be as natural as possible is particularly critical when measuring typical performance. Ideally, we would study the behavior a person exhibits, not her reports of how she does or would behave. To illustrate, suppose we were interested in "sociability." If we administered a self-report inventory, test takers could present deliberately biased reports or, for other reasons, not give an accurate indication of their sociability. An alternative approach would be to observe a person interacting with other people and, on the basis of her behavior in these interactions, rate her sociability. This interaction might be in naturally occurring situations or in situations especially designed to permit observation of the subject's sociability—for example, placing the person in a situation where she had to meet and interact with persons she had not previously met. This latter approach would be an example of a *situational test*.

Although we shall discuss situational tests in the context of typical performance measurement, they can also be used as maximal performance measures. Earlier we used an example of a leaderless group discussion where the participants were asked to design plans for an advertising campaign. If we measured the quantity or quality of suggestions made, we would be using the test as a measure of maximal performance. Situational tests are also used to measure behaviors requiring use of both skills and personality characteristics. Assessing leadership behaviors would be one such example.

Examples of Situational Methods

Situational tests are time-consuming and expensive to administer and score. One obvious exception is the interview, which is probably the most widely used assessment procedure. Although the other examples of situational methods we shall discuss have not been used as extensively, they illustrate approaches that have proved useful in certain situations.

The Interview. You have probably been interviewed many times—for example, when applying for college or a job. This was an example of a selection interview. But there are also other types of interviews: diagnostic interviews, medical history interviews, counseling interviews, and public opinion interviews, to name but a few. We shall focus on interviews designed to assess personality characteristics.

Although an interview usually is a one-to-one situation, there are a number of possible variations on this traditional procedure. A *panel interview* involves one person being confronted by a panel of interviewers. This procedure has the obvious advantage of decreasing repetition that would occur if each member of the panel interviewed the candidate individually. Another variation is the *stress interview,* where the interviewer attempts to subject the interviewee to stress by constant probing, asking personal and embarrassing questions, trying to confuse the interviewee, and other similar techniques. The purpose of this type of interview is to see how the subject reacts under anxiety-producing conditions, the presumption being that this will give a more valid assessment than a nonstressful situation.

In evaluating interviews, several questions are of prime importance: Can reliable ratings be obtained from an interview? Is any information obtained from interviews that cannot be obtained by other methods? What is the validity of the interview as an assessment tool?

It is well known that different interviewers often arrive at widely divergent conclusions after interviewing the same candidate. One reason is lack of standardization: Not only do different interviewers cover different topics, they also look for different qualities in an individual. So, too, the interviewee may react differently to various interviewers. The reliability of interview judgments can be increased by structuring interviews so that the same topics are covered by all interviewers, and the traits to be rated and the rating procedure are clearly specified. Given reliable ratings, we encounter a second question: Does the interview provide information that cannot be obtained by other methods? Factual information and estimates of personality traits can be collected more economically in other ways (for example, by application blanks and self-report inventories, respectively). Thus, the maximal payoff will be attained by concentrating on social behavior and information that would particularly qualify or disqualify the person (for example, speech problems, unique abilities or accomplishments). Finally, evidence shows that interview ratings decrease validity as often as they increase it. The main reason for this finding is that interviewers overemphasize the particular traits they think are important. Still interviews continue to play a major role in many assessment procedures, apparently because everyone feels that he or she is an excellent judge of other people.

Indirect Tests.   Some methods might best be described as indirect tests. By indirect we mean that the test serves primarily as a vehicle for observing the subject's behavior, not as end in itself. An example is the *leaderless group discussion*. In this technique a group of persons are brought together and asked to discuss some (usually controversial) topic. In other situations, they may be asked to devise a plan of operations (for example, a sales campaign), to construct some object or device, or to solve a problem (for example, how to cross a natural barrier, such as a stream or canyon, using only selected materials). Although success in completing the task may be scored, the focus is usually on characteristics displayed in attacking the problem—ones such as perseverance and leadership.

The OSS Assessment.   One of the most intensive assessments ever conducted was that done by the Office of Strategic Services during World War II (OSS Assessment Staff, 1948). In order to select personnel for intelligence-related assignments, a three-day assessment procedure was developed. Groups of candidates were brought to an assessment center and subjected to a wide variety of assessment techniques, including paper-and-pencil tests, stress interviews, problem-solving exercises, and numerous ingenious situational tests. Performance on these tasks was rated by the Assessment Staff (which included psychologists, physicians, and military officers), and ratings were also obtained from peers. On the basis of these ratings, a formulation of the personality structure of each individual was developed and a prognosis of his success on OSS assignments made. Because of the nature of the criterion, a systematic validity study was largely precluded. Because of the time and expense of such an approach, and its doubtful validity (Vernon, 1964), similar procedures are used only with highly sensitive positions and for research purposes (Barron, 1963; MacKinnon, 1962).

The In-Basket Test.   An interesting example of an attempt to assess candidates' job performance is the *In-Basket Test* (Frederiksen et al., 1957). Variations of the test have been constructed for several occupations, including school administrators and military officers. In each case the person is provided with a variety of materials (organizational charts, technical reports, surveys, and memoranda) that provide background knowledge of the situation. He is then presented with materials that might be found in the "in-basket" on his desk and is asked to take action on these matters. For example, a school administrator might have to decide whether to hire (or fire) a particular teacher, how to handle children who damaged some school property, plan a campaign for a school bond issue, decide on the adoption of new texts, plan how to handle teachers' demands for higher salaries, and so on. The candidate can handle each problem by making a decision, requesting further information, deferring action until a later date, assigning the job to a subordinate, or in any other manner he could use on the job. Decisions will be made on the basis of his repertoire of job skills, taking into consideration the characteristics of the particular situation (as described in the background materials). Scoring is on a variety of dimensions, involving both process and outcome, but stresses general styles or patterns of handling administrative tasks. The nature of the In-Basket Test makes it suitable as a training device as well as a selection test.

Evaluation of Situational Methods

One obvious disadvantage of situational tests is their cost. They involve large amounts of both the candidates' and raters' time, can be applied to only one or a few candidates simultaneously, require trained judges to observe and rate performance, and often require expensive materials. The fundamental question is, however, not their absolute cost but whether their advantages justify the additional costs. We would probably have to conclude that any increase in validity does not overbalance the additional costs. This conclusion would hold even considering that the technique is generally employed only when selecting personnel for jobs in which a mistake in judgment can involve great costs (for example, military officers, school superintendents, CIA agents). In these cases a costly selection device might well repay its costs. On the other hand, these techniques may be used for training as well as assessment.

Scoring and interpretations of scores also present problems. Frequently scores are ratings, which can have undesirable properties (see below). And, even though we may be attempting to assess typical performance, test takers—because they know they are being evaluated—may adopt a maximal performance set and attempt to show their best behavior rather than their typical behavior. There also may be problems in synthesizing and expressing the results of the assessment.

For example, situational tests generally involve measurement along more than one dimension, with scores combined to produce an integrated picture of the individual. If the end product of this combination is a global personality description, direct predictions of specific behaviors may not be possible. If, on the other hand, the data are expressed as a series of specific predictions, an integrated picture will not be obtained. In either case, the problem is to find an appropriate method of combining the various scores. This problem is further complicated by the fact that the data (that is, scores and ratings) often have undesirable statistical properties (for example, they are unreliable, have a limited range of values, are expressed on an ordinal scale). In short, many of the most difficult problems in psychological measurement are encountered when synthesizing data from situational tests.

observations and ratings

The methods we have been discussing involve obtaining responses in a testing situation. However, personality assessments also can be based on observations of a person's behavior. These observations may be obtained in naturally occurring situations, such as in a classroom or on a job, or in situations especially designed for the purpose of observation. While such observations can be used to measure achievement, abilities, and skills (Brown, 1981), we shall focus on their use in measuring personality characteristics.

An observation is a vehicle for obtaining information about an individual. But this information must be summarized in some manner. The most common method is to use rating scales. Thus we shall also describe rating scales and other methods for summarizing data obtained from observations.

Observations

Self-report methods are based on the assumption that people are the best observers of their own behaviors, reactions, feelings, and attitudes. But much information about these attributes can be obtained by observing a person. While it is true that an observer cannot know an individual's feelings and attitudes, if we observe a person over a relatively long period of time and in a variety of situations, we can both obtain a good sampling of her behavior and have a strong basis for inferring her feelings and attitudes. For example, teachers and employers often can give accurate descriptions of their students' or employees' personality characteristics.

As mentioned above, observations may be made in naturally occurring situations or in specially designed evaluative situations. In many ways, the former are preferable because they are more realistic and because the people being observed are less likely to alter their behavior to make a favorable impression. This latter point suggests that observations should be as unobtrusive as possible, regardless of the setting.

Observations also vary widely in length and scope. Some observations are based on long-term contacts with the person observed; sometimes in only one situation, such as a particular class, other times in a variety of situations, such as when you rate a friend. At other times observations are based on a short time period and a limited sample of behavior, as when a school psychologist observes a student in a single class or a therapist forms an impression of a client from a brief, initial interview.

Observations have two characteristics that make them particularly valuable. One is that they allow you to observe a person working on a problem, or interacting with others, not just observe the outcome of the interaction or the person's report of the outcome. The other is somewhat paradoxical: Although we are interested in typical behavior, observations can be a good method of noting atypical behaviors or behaviors in rare or unusual situations. These reactions often tell more about a person's personality than typical behavior or behavior in more ordinary situations. For example, observing a lifeguard's reaction to a near drowning may tell more about her ability to cope with stress than observing her performing the more routine functions of the job.

Making Observations. Most of us think we are perceptive observers and interpreters of other people's behavior. We readily can recall instances when we observed something about a person, perhaps some seemingly trivial behavior, that told us something important about the person. On the other hand, we usually forget the times we missed what, in retrospect, were obvious clues and the times when our inferences were in error. Thus making good observations may not be as easy as it might seem. However, the accuracy and usefulness of the information obtained from observations can generally be improved by following certain guidelines. Although these guidelines apply particularly to planned, evaluative observations, most have relevance for more informal, everyday observations of behavior.

1. *Specify the characteristic(s) to be observed.* Although you may find out something of interest fortuitously, you are more likely to obtain useful information when you determine in advance what you are looking for and focus your attention in that direction. For example, in a leaderless group discussion we might focus on the participants' dominance and reactions to criticism.

2. *Observe specific behaviors.* Not only must the general traits or characteristics of interest be specified, but the specific behaviors that are signs of these characteristics must be identified as well. Thus, if we were interested in dominance, we might look at such variables as the amount of time a person spent speaking, whether the person tried to steer or direct the discussion, whether he or she argued strongly against opposing views, and so on. Concentrating on specific behaviors makes observations more objective and provides a better basis for any later attempts to change the behavior.

3. *Focus on a small number of characteristics and behaviors.* One common problem is that we try to observe too many characteristics at one time. Consequently we lack focus and miss many important clues. Generally we should focus on only two or three characteristics; other characteristics can be assessed at other times.

4. *Make observations as unobtrusive as possible.* There are two reasons for this suggestion. One is that people often change their behaviors when they know they

are being observed and evaluated. The other is that when an observer intrudes in a situation, the nature of the situation will be changed; consequently, you may not be able to observe the behaviors you want to observe. To illustrate, in a course I teach (The Teaching of Psychology), I observe graduate students teaching classes. The first time I observe (even if I just sit in the back of the room), both the teacher and students are aware of my presence and react differently than they normally do. However, after I have come to class several times, both the teacher and the students relax and ignore me. Then I get a better indication of the teacher's typical behaviors and style of interaction with the class.

5. *Obtain as many observations as possible.* The goal in making observations is to obtain a representative sample of a person's behavior. This can best be done by observing the person several times and in various situations; a single observation may give a misleading picture. For example, when observing graduate students teaching, I attempt to visit their classes several times (sometimes announced, sometimes unannounced) and to observe them teaching different topics and using different methods (e.g., lecture, discussion).

6. *Use several observers.* One reason for the use of more than one observer is that some people are better observers of certain types of characteristics; for example, some are better at observing cognitive skills and others are better at observing social interactions. Another reason is to prevent biases, either because of the observer's previous knowledge about the person being observed or because of ideas about the behaviors being rated. And, of course, if the observation is being done in the context of another relationship (e.g., a therapist observing a client, a teacher observing a student), the primary activity may demand so much attention and effort that accurate observation is not possible.

7. *Defer inferences and conclusions.* When observing, the focus should be on identifying and recording behaviors and reactions, not on what they mean. After we have completed the observation, we can look for patterns and draw inferences. Focusing on behaviors and reactions prevents too rapid jumping to conclusions, particularly ones which may bias future observations.

Summarizing Observations. The results of an observation must be summarized in some manner. Here there are several possibilities. One is to use a *checklist,* which is nothing more than a list of behaviors and/or reactions of interest. To continue our example of assessing dominance by observing a leaderless group discussion, the checklist might contain statements such as:

___ Structured the task.
___ Gave suggestions about how to proceed.
___ Interrupted another person to state his/her opinion.

The observer checks those behaviors that were exhibited by the person being observed.[3]

[3] Checklists may be filled in during or after the observation. In this case, the observer would check each behavior as it occurred.

Sometimes the observer indicates the frequency of occurrence of a particular behavior, either by counting the number of times it occurs or by a summary judgment. For example, the last item might be phrased:

Interrupts another

__ Frequently   __ Sometimes   __Seldom   __ Never

This procedure is a type of *rating scale.* (Rating scales will be discussed in detail below.)

Observations also can be summarized in a narrative report. Common examples are *letters of recommendation* and a counselor or therapist's *case notes,* which summarize an interview. At other times, *anecdotal reports* may be used. These are brief summaries of specific events that illustrate either particularly typical or atypical behaviors. An anecdotal record should include a description of the situation, a description of the behaviors observed, and may include the observer's interpretation of the behavior (Brown, 1981; Thorndike & Hagen, 1977).

The purpose of all summaries is to condense the major points of the observation into usable form, either for statistical analyses or for use in making diagnoses or changing behavior. If these summaries and the observations are to be of value, they must be used. Too often we make observations, and even summarize them, and then file them away and make no use of them.

Rating Scales

Results of observations are often summarized on rating scales. (So, too, is information obtained from situational and performance tests.) In ratings, a trained judge observes an individual and assigns a score on a preestablished scale. Although rating scales have many different formats, all have the same goal: assigning a value to the individual's performance on some dimension. This score may be a point on a continuum or one of a set of ordered categories.

On *comparative rating scales,* persons are compared with each other. At the simplest level people can be ranked in order along the continuum of interest. More commonly, several categories (levels) are given and the rater assigns the person to the category he thinks best describes the person's performance (see Figure 17.3a). When using comparative rating scales, the composition of the comparison group must be specified so that it can serve as a frame of reference for the rater. For example, when rating applicants for graduate school it would be necessary to specify whether the applicant is being compared to undergraduates or graduate students.

In contrast to comparative rating scales, *standard rating scales* use response categories that describe various levels of performance. Thus raters are making an absolute rather than a comparative judgment. Ideally, the categories should be defined behaviorally (see Figure 17.3b).

A variation used with both comparative and standard rating scales is the *graphic rating scale.* Here the rating task is the same but the response format differs. On graphic rating scales the various categories are arranged along a continuum (graph) and the rater checks a category on the continuum (see Figure 17.3c and d). Instead of discrete categories, some graphic rating scales allow raters to check any point along the continuum (Figure 17.3e).

Figure 17.3 Examples of Rating Scales.

a. *Comparative*
Ability to select and apply appropriate statistical analyses.*
— Upper 10%
— Upper 25% but not top 10%
— Middle 50%
— Lowest 25%

b. *Standard*
Which of the following statements best describes the student's ability to select and apply appropriate statistical analyses?
— Can select methods independently and apply correctly
— Can select and correctly apply methods with some guidance
— Can select and apply methods only with extensive guidance
— Can apply methods in cookbook fashion if told what to do
— Is unable to use common statistical techniques

c. *Graphic (comparative)*
Ability to select and apply appropriate statistical analyses.
Top 20%   Next 20%   Middle 20%   Next 20%   Lowest 20%
L_____|_____|_____|_____|_____⌐

d. *Graphic (standard)*
Ability to select and apply appropriate statistical analyses.

Undergraduate   Beginning   M.S. candidate   Ph.D. candidate   Post Ph.D. level
    level   graduate level
L_____|_____|_____|_____|____⌐

e. *Graphic (continuum)*
Check the place on the continuum that best describes the student's ability to select and apply appropriate statistical analyses.

Weak   Average   Excellent
L_____|_____|_____|_____⌐

f. *Numerical*
Rate the student's ability in the following areas on a 7-point scale with 7 being the highest rating, 4 average, and 1 the lowest rating.
— Ability to select and apply appropriate statistical analyses
— Ability to draw valid conclusions from data and analyses
— Ability to design a well-controlled study
— Ability to generate testable research hypotheses

g. *Forced choice*
Which of the following statements is a better description of the student?
— Can select and apply appropriate statistical analyses
— Can generate testable research hypotheses

h. *Forced choice (man to man)*
Which student is better able to select and apply appropriate statistical analyses?
— Dan Rudolph
— Scott Sellers

*An appropriate frame of reference would be other graduate students in items where comparisons to a norm group were made.

Numerical rating scales require the rater to assign one of a set of arbitrary numerical values to the person being rated (Figure 17.3f). Although these numerical values have no intrinsic meaning except in relation to the anchor points on the scale, relative strengths and weaknesses can be identified by comparing ratings on various dimensions. For example, an instructor might obtain high ratings on "States goals and objectives" but lower rankings on "Answers students questions clearly."

Another variation is a *forced-choice rating scale*. Two types are used. In one, the rater is presented with two characteristics and must select the one that best describes the person (Figure 17.3g). In the other, a dimension is specified and the rater must choose which of two persons best fits the description (Figure 17.3h). This latter type is called a *man-to-man rating scale*.

Rating Errors. Because ratings depend on subjective judgment, they are open to various types of errors and biases. Although training raters to be alert to the various types of errors can reduce bias, errors also can be controlled by the construction of the scales and by the directions for their use.

One type of error, the *error of central tendency,* refers to the rater's avoidance of extreme categories and the overreliance on middle (average) categories. Sometimes this error results from the lack of sufficient opportunity to observe the behavior being rated; in the absence of evidence to the contrary, the person is given an average rating. The solution to this problem is to allow more opportunity for observation. At other times, this error results from raters not wanting to go out on a limb and use extreme categories. This can be controlled by using procedures that require the rater to rank-order subjects or place a certain number of people in each rating category.

The *error of leniency* is a tendency to be overly generous in ratings. This error is very frequent, perhaps because we tend to see the best in people. These errors can be controlled by statistical transformations of scores (i.e., transforming ratings to standard scores), by making rating categories more precise and realistic, and by using forced-choice methods or procedures that require placing a certain number of people in each category. The opposite type of error, the *severity error,* occurs when raters are too stringent. The same sorts of corrections can be used as for the error of leniency.

Another common error is called the *halo effect.* Here raters allow their general opinion of a person to influence their ratings of specific characteristics. For example, if a student likes an instructor, he may rate her high on all dimensions on an instructor evaluation form, regardless of her actual behavior. For example, he may rate the instructor as organized regardless of her actual degree of organization. Again, the best protection is to use clearly defined categories or procedures that require rank-ordering the various characteristics of the person being rated.

A *logical error* occurs when the rater assumes that two characteristics are related when, in fact, they are not necessarily related. For example, a rater may assume that creativity and intelligence are related abilities, thus give a person similar ratings on both characteristics. This error can be prevented by using specific, behavioral descriptions of the characteristics rated.

Obtaining Accurate Ratings. Obtaining accurate ratings is more difficult than might be expected on first glance. The first essential requirement is that raters have the opportunity to observe the behavior to be rated. This means the persons being rated must be observed in situations in which they can exhibit the behaviors being rated and that raters will expend the time and effort needed to make accurate ratings.

Incorporating certain characteristics into the rating procedure can also improve ratings. The behaviors to be rated should be clearly and unambiguously defined. Rating specific behaviors is preferable to rating broad personality traits. Scales should use clearly defined response categories. And, whenever possible, more than one rater should be used. For example, in diving and gymnastics competitions, scoring is based on the average rating of several judges, not the opinion of one judge.

In all cases, raters should be trained in the use of the rating scales and procedures. A good procedure is, first, to explain the rating procedure to the judges, and then try a few practice ratings. The judges can then compare their ratings and modify their procedures to obtain more standardized, and hence more accurate, ratings.

One final question might be mentioned: What characteristics should be rated? Ideally, ratings should be made only on characteristics that, through validity studies, have been shown to be important. And, because ratings are subject to numerous errors, they should be used only when more objective data is not available. Still, how do we know what behaviors to study originally? Flanagan (1954) has suggested one method. He pointed out that what distinguishes between good and poor workers is how they handle certain critical situations. Thus he suggested that we start by collecting incidents that represent particularly good or poor performance (for example, how a physician handled a particular emergency or what a worker did when his machine failed). These *critical incidents,* then, would be the behaviors to be given most importance in ratings.

a miscellany of other methods

The methods of personality assessment we have described, though representing the major approaches to personality assessment, do not exhaust all the possibilities. In this section we shall discuss three other types of typical performance measures: attitude scales, questionnaires and surveys, and measures for determining the meaning of constructs. Several other methods that are sometimes used will not be discussed—for example, sociometric techniques, ethnographic methods, measures of values, and behavioral assessment.[4]

Attitude Scales

An *attitude* refers to an organized predisposition to think, feel, perceive, and behave in a certain manner toward some referent or cognitive object (Dawes, 1972; Kerlinger, 1973). The referent of an attitude may be an object or event, an institution, a type of behavior, a person or group of people, or even an idea. Thus

---

[4] For an introduction to sociometric methods see Kerlinger (1973, Chapter 32). For discussions of ethnographic measures see Spradley (1979, 1980). For discussions of behavioral assessment see Haynes (1978), Haynes & Wilson (1979), or Hersen & Bellack (1976).

we can measure attitudes toward the Catholic Church, civil rights, or working women, to cite but a few examples.

Types of Attitude Scales. There are various approaches to constructing attitude scales (see, e.g., Dawes, 1972; Edwards, 1957a; Guilford, 1954; or Summers, 1970). We shall briefly describe two common types: Likert scales and Thurstone scales.

In the behavioral sciences *Likert scales* are used most frequently because they are easier to construct and generally are as reliable and valid as the more complex types of attitude scales. On a Likert scale test takers are presented with a series of statements and indicate their degree of agreement (or disagreement) with each item (see Figure 17.4a). Responses are usually made on a 5- or 7-point scale, with response categories ranging from "strongly agree" to "strongly disagree." All items are considered to be of equal value, and responses are weighted to reflect the degree of agreement. The score may be either the total number of points (over all items) or the average score per item.

The construction of a *Thurstone scale* is more complex. A pool of potential items is given to a group of expert judges who rate each item in terms of how strong an attitude is reflected by agreement with the item. The mean and variance of each item, and the intercorrelations among the items, are then computed. Based on these analyses, items are selected for the final scale. These are items that represent different positions on the attitude continuum (have different scale values), whose placement is consistent across judges (have low variances), and that measure the attitude (correlate positively with other items selected). These items are then administered to test takers, who indicate whether they agree or disagree with the item (see Figure 17.4b). The individual's score is the average scale value of the items endorsed.

Figure 17.4 Examples of Attitude Scale Items.

a. *Likert Scale item*
　　Capital punishment should be used for crimes such as armed robbery.
　　　　Strongly agree
　　　　Agree
　　　　Undecided
　　　　Disagree
　　　　Strongly disagree

b. *Thurstone scale items*
　　Capital punishment should be used for all crimes where a person is killed or threatened to be killed. (6.3)
　　Capital punishment should be used only for treason or killing a police officer. (4.1)
　　Capital punishment should never be used. (0.3)
　　(Note: Scale values, in parentheses, would not appear on the test; they are included here for illustration only.)

Uses of Attitude Scales. Attitude scales are frequently used to obtain normative data on the attitudes of various groups. Thus, for example, politicians are interested in the attitudes of various subgroups of the U.S. population on controversial issues such as abortion, increases in military spending, and gun control. But they are also a valuable tool in many other types of studies. They can be used as independent variables in studies where attitudes may influence outcomes—for example, the effect of attitudes toward education on enrollment in higher education or performance in different types of curricula. They can also be used as dependent variables—for example, when evaluating the reactions to different types of therapy or teaching methods. And, of course, they are used to measure the effectiveness of various means of changing attitudes, such as exposure to different types of persuasive messages. (For a summary of recent research on attitudes see Cialdini, Petty, & Cacioppo, 1981.)

When attitude scales are used, two questions must be faced. First, how accurate are subjects' reports of their attitudes? As with self-report techniques, attitude scales are open to various types of biases, such as social desirability, and rating errors, such as central tendency and leniency. The second question concerns the relationship between attitudes and behavior. Just because people hold a particular attitude does not guarantee that they will behave in a manner consistent with their attitude. For example, a person's reported attitudes toward members of minority groups may not accurately reflect how he or she will actually behave when interacting with members of a minority group.

Questionnaires and Surveys

Questionnaires and surveys are very flexible assessment methods. They can be used to ascertain factual information, opinions, reactions, or attitudes. They can be administered in written form or orally. They can use questions that require a choice between given responses or open-ended questions. If a fixed-response format is used, the respondent may only have to answer yes or no, or may respond by selecting one of a small number of predetermined categories (e.g., Is your annual income: less than $10,000; $10–20,000; $20–30,000; or over $30,000), or by completing a rating or attitude scale. They may be very brief, consisting of only a few questions, or quite long, often requiring several hours for completion.[5]

Usually questionnaires and surveys are used to obtain the reactions of a particular population. When used in this manner, obtaining a representative sample of the target population becomes of paramount importance. Sometimes, as when students complete an instructor evaluation questionnaire, the entire population can be sampled. Usually, however, we only obtain responses from a sample of the population. To ensure representative sampling, highly sophisticated sampling techniques have been developed. Perhaps the best example is polling of preferences for candidates in presidential elections. Here techniques have been developed that allow accurate predictions of voter preferences to be determined by sampling about 1500 voters. Other examples include Gallup's annual survey of attitudes toward education and Astin's annual survey of the characteristics and attitudes of entering college freshmen.

Examples. The public opinion poll, such as illustrated by the election poll, is but one type of questionnaire survey. Several other types are also familiar to you. For example, an interview can be considered as a type of questionnaire. This is particularly true of *structured interviews,* where the interviewer asks a predetermined set of questions. Although a structured interview can be used to obtain factual information or use fixed-response questions, these are inefficient uses of

---

[5] See Kerlinger (1973) for an excellent discussion of writing questionnaire items.

the method since this type of information can be obtained more efficiently by a written questionnaire. A better use is to concentrate on reactions, opinions, attitudes, and explanations and clarifications of previously obtained information. (For example: Why did you leave your last job?) This approach would use more open-ended questions.

Another widely used method is the *biographical information form*. This approach is illustrated by application blanks for colleges, professional schools, and jobs. Applications and other types of biographical information forms may be very brief—or they may be quite extensive, as are some applications for colleges and professional schools and forms used in research (Owens, 1971). The shorter ones usually focus on factual information; longer ones may probe reactions, opinions, and attitudes.

You are also probably familiar with *course and instructor evaluation forms*. These usually focus on students' opinions and ratings rather than on more factual information. Some forms ask you to describe the instructor's behaviors (Did the instructor summarize each lecture?), others ask for evaluations of these behaviors (How effective were the lecture summaries?). On some, items are quite specific (Knows students' names; Willing to answer questions); others use broader categories (Interaction with class members). Some ask for opinions on a variety of instructor characteristics and behaviors; others may ask only one question (What grade would you assign the instructor?).

A slightly different type of approach is illustrated by the *College and University Environment Scales* (CUES), developed by Pace (1963, 1967). The purpose of the CUES is to provide a description of the college environment as perceived by students. The test consists of 150 statements that describe college environments; for example:

T F   Students are generally quite friendly on this campus.
T F   There is a lot of pressure to obtain high grades.

Students or other observers indicate whether each statement describes the college. Items are grouped into five scales called Practicality, Community, Awareness, Propriety, and Scholarship. By summing across raters, a description of the college is obtained. By comparing CUES profiles of various colleges, prospective students can obtain a picture of the differing atmospheres of various colleges and select the one that best fits their preferences.

The Meaning of Constructs

As final examples we shall consider two methods that focus on how individuals organize, structure, and give meaning to constructs they use. One, the *Semantic Differential,* was originally developed as a method for measuring the psychological meaning of constructs (Osgood, Suci, & Tannenbaum, 1957). For example, what are the connotations of terms such as "school," "teacher," and "principal"? The other, the *Role Construct Repertory Test* (Rep Test) was designed to identify the constructs people use when they perceive objects, events or people, those constructs which structure and direct their behavior (Kelly, 1963).

The Semantic Differential.   The scales on the *Semantic Differential* are bipolar pairs of adjectives, such as good-bad, clean-dirty, strong-weak, fast-slow, active-passive. The concept to be rated is listed at the top of a page with the pairs of adjectives listed below. Varying numbers of adjective pairs can be used; usually about 15 pairs are used for each concept. Subjects respond by checking the place on a seven-point scale that corresponds with their evaluation:

School

Good	__:__:__:__:__:__	Bad
Slow	__:__:__:__:__:__	Fast
Strong	__:__:__:__:__:__	Weak

If more than one concept is rated, the scales are repeated for each concept.

Scores on several scales (item pairs) are generally combined into clusters or factors. Usually three factors[6] are used: Evaluation (e.g., good-bad, beautiful-ugly, clean-dirty), Potency (e.g., large-small, heavy-light, strong-weak), and Activity (e.g., active-passive, sharp-dull, fast-slow). Depending on the research problem, an investigator may use adjectives representing all three factors or only one or two of them.

Although our illustrations concerned an institution (school) and occupational roles (teacher, principal), the same procedure can be used to evaluate other types of concepts such as occupations, particular people (my father, a specific teacher, the governor of your state), or even oneself.

The Rep Test. The *Rep Test* is based on the assumption that each person uses certain concepts to organize his perceptions of objects, events, and people, and to differentiate between them. Since different people may use different constructs, the constructs they use are important clues to their personality structure. Although the test can be administered in several ways, its basic principles can be illustrated quite simply. The examiner first gives the person a list of role titles (e.g., father, close friend, teacher, someone you dislike) and asks the person to name a specific person fitting each role. The examiner then selects three people from the list and asks the subject to indicate an important way that two of the three people are alike and differ from the third. This indicates a construct the person uses to differentiate between people. The procedure is repeated with various triads, thus eliciting other important organizing constructs.

Although the test can be interpreted qualitatively, quantitative methods or interpretation are possible. For our purposes, the Rep Test is notable because the objects being sorted are people and, more important, because test takers generate the dimensions used to describe their own personalities. That is, the constructs identified are ones the test taker uses to differentiate between people, not dimensions previously defined by the test constructor.

a review and evaluation of typical performance measures

Having described a variety of approaches to measuring typical performance, we shall now review some of the major points and evaluate the various methods and

---

[6] These three factors are ones typically found in the factor analyses of *Semantic Differential* scales.

techniques. To put the discussion in context, consider the relationship between personality measurement and personality theory. Although there is a clear relationship between personality measurement and psychometric theory, there is not as close a relationship between personality measurement and personality theory. Some of the tests described have had their roots in a particular theory—for example, the Edwards PPS and TAT in Murray's need-press theory and the Rorschach in psychoanalytic theory. Otherwise, personality measures have only fleeting connections with personality theory. Systematic attempts to build tests measuring the basic constructs of a given theory, or attempts to build a theory of personality around a particular test, are few and far between.

This lack of relationship between personality theory and measurement implies that we should evaluate the instruments more in terms of their methodology than their relationship to personality theory. Not everyone would agree with this view. For example, we have mentioned that Atkinson (1981) has questioned the applicability of traditional psychometric methods to the measurement of motivation, and other writers (e.g., Epstein, 1980; Harris, 1980; Lamiell, 1981) have suggested that traditional methods cannot be applied without modification.

Psychometric Properties

When discussing particular tests and approaches we have mentioned instances where instruments or procedures did not meet the psychometric standards outlined earlier in the book and in the *Standards*. Thus it would be well to review the psychometric properties of typical performance measures.

Standardization. One requirement of a psychological test is standardization of content, administrative procedures, and scoring. Although the content of some personality measures may be varied to suit the needs of a particular individual or situation, by and large the content is quite well standardized. Similarly, administrative procedures are generally relatively standardized. It is in scoring procedures that many personality measures fall short. Projective methods, in particular, seem prone to use of unstandardized and subjective scoring methods.

Even among measures having standardized scoring procedures, a common weakness of personality measures is the lack of representative normative data. On most personality measures, general population norms are desirable. Readily available populations, such as students, are not representative of the general population, but are too often used.

Dissimulation. Responses on personality measures may reflect both item content and response biases. What, then, can be done to minimize the effects of response biases? At least three approaches are possible. First, structure the testing situation so that the test taker is not motivated to dissemble. The most effective method is also the simplest: Enlist cooperation by explaining the purpose of the testing and how scores will be used. Second, include dissimulation indices on the test so that you can assess the degree of bias. And, third, establish empirical relations between test scores and extratest criteria. This will allow the meaning of the score to be determined independently of any biases.

Consistency. Consistency can be established by three methods: equivalence, stability, and internal consistency. Since there seldom are alternative forms of typical performance measures, estimates of equivalent forms reliability usually are not available. Scores on personality measures usually are responsive to situational differences and to change over time, thus yielding less stable measurements than scores on maximal performance measures. However, some characteristics, such as vocational interests, can be quite stable over time.

A personality scale used to define a personality trait or dimension should be internally consistent. Thus measures of homogeneity (internal consistency) should be obtained for most personality scales. Many scales have acceptable internal consistency, even ones developed by empirical keying (e.g., the MMPI clinical scales). Of course, many scales are developed using procedures that guarantee high internal consistency; for example, the homogeneously keyed scales on the KOIS and SCII and Thurstone attitude scales.

Other types of consistency data are also important. On inventories such as the SCII, KOIS, and MMPI, indices of profile stability are important and should be reported. As noted, the stability of profiles on interest inventories is quite high, at least over short periods. Whenever scores on various scales within a test are compared, as when making diagnoses, the correlations between scales and, more particularly, the reliability of difference scores should be ascertained. Although the former data are usually available, at least in the case of self-report inventories, the latter frequently are not reported.

Validity. On typical performance measures the construct measured and the limits of the domain sampled often are not clearly and specifically defined. Furthermore, appropriate external criteria for validating scales may not be readily apparent. What, for example, would be an appropriate criterion for validation of a test of flexibility or dominance? In some cases, particularly with projective techniques, the variables measured are defined so as to preclude use of external criteria. All these considerations suggest that personality measures are best conceived as signs (rather than samples or predictors) and, consequently, the appropriate method of validation is construct validation.[7]

Although all types of evidence on construct validity can be used, and have been used, two types are particularly important: convergent and discriminant validity. That is, different measures of the same construct should have high intercorrelations (convergent validity), and measures of presumably different constructs should have low intercorrelations (discriminant validity).

Three other questions regarding the validity of typical performance measures are also of interest. First, how does the validity of personality measures compare with that of achievement and aptitude tests? Second, which of the general approaches to personality measurement is most valid? And, third, within a given approach, which specific technique is most valid? Of course, since validity is situ-

---

[7] This is not to imply that content- and criterion-related validity are not important for typical performance measures. When items on scales are usually selected to represent a particular content domain, content validity should be established. And whenever scores are related to an external criterion, criterion-related validity should be determined.

ation-specific, any answer to these questions will reflect the trends of the evidence rather than give a definitive answer applicable to all situations.

The first question has several answers. Looking at the absolute magnitude of validity coefficients, one would conclude that validity generally is lower for personality tests than for other types of measurement. Yet, because different situations and criteria are involved, one cannot conclusively state that personality measurement is inherently less valid than the measurement of aptitudes and achievement. If we look at incremental validity, we find that there are few situations in which the addition of personality variables significantly increases predictive accuracy over measures of maximal performance. However, the situations in which tests are typically used as predictors (such as academic success or job performance) are ones in which the criteria are heavily weighted in favor of intellectual skills.

The author's conclusion in regards to the second question should be obvious from the amount of space devoted to the three major approaches. However, one could argue that this only reflects the author's bias toward the traditional psychometric approach to validity. Granted; but until alternative methods of assessing the effectiveness of measurement procedure are developed, these are the only acceptable standards available. Finally, in spite of the theoretical advantages of homogeneous keying, the hard evidence supports empirical keying as the better method of keying self-report inventories.

Psychometric Properties: A Summary.   As has been suggested, both in this review and throughout the last three chapters, measures of typical performance often lack some or many of the desired pyschometric properties of good measuring instruments. Certainly they do not meet these standards as well as measures of maximal performance do. Thus some people have questioned whether they should even be classified as tests and/or be evaluated using the same standards and guidelines. For example, it is suggested in the *Standards* (1974, Principle B1.1.1, p. 13) that even self-report measures be referred to as inventories rather than as tests.

Does this mean that the methods currently available for measuring typical performance should not be used? Some people, undoubtedly, would say yes; that unless better methods are developed we should not attempt to measure typical performance. But this is avoiding the issue, for there are times when information about personality characteristics is neccessary or useful. How, then, should one proceed? One common approach is to view personality measures as a type of semistandardized interview, as an opportunity to observe an individual in a relatively standardized, controlled situation. The information obtained can be used to suggest hypotheses about the individual's behavior, feelings, and reactions. These hypotheses can then be confirmed by information from other sources, such as interviews, further testing, or observation. It should be noted, however, that this approach, while providing information that may be quite useful in practical situations, leaves much to be desired in terms of the scientific validation of personality measures.

Interpretation and Use

Assuming that we have used an instrument that meets at least the minimal psychometric requirements, the next questions are how scores can be interpreted and what the possible and appropriate uses of the scores are.

Interpretation.   Since different measures utilize different types of scores, there are various methods of interpreting scores. For example, if only qualitative information is obtained or if no satisfactory normative data are available, only narrative descriptions can be used. On the other hand, if scores are expressed quantitatively and normative data are available, scores can be interpreted in the usual normative fashion (see Chapter 8). Of course, adjustments must be made if the scoring procedures result in ipsative scores.

Perhaps the major question, however, concerns the appropriate level of analysis; that is, whether scores and scales should be interpreted individually or whether we should use more holistic methods of analysis.

When making holistic analyses, such as on projectives, we encounter an interesting phenomenon, called *the Barnum effect,* which must be taken into account when determining the validity of personality descriptions. The Barnum effect suggests that by relying on vague statements and going with the base rates, one can produce a personality description having superficial validity. For example, consider the following personality description:

> Although not brilliant, the subject is well above average in intelligence with a streak of creativity. Many of his talents go unnoticed by other people, but when he sets his mind on a task, he does an excellent job. Although his moods are generally fairly even, he has periods of the blues and, at other times, has boundless energy and accomplishes a great deal in a short period. He is fair in his dealings with other persons. He is quite sociable, generally liking the company of other people, but there are times when he would rather be alone.

Most people would probably accept this statement as being a reasonably good description of their personality. The main point is not that such descriptions can be prepared without the aid of test scores, which is true. The point is that in situations in which scoring and interpretive processes are ill-defined, and holistic descriptions are used (as is typically the case with projectives), such statements frequently are presented as interpretations of test scores. Because of the vagueness of the interpretive procedures and the generality of the description, it is impossible to establish direct links between specific test scores or signs and specific descriptive statements. Yet, the apparent validity of the description suggests that the test is valid.

To summarize, I would suggest using normative interpretations whenever possible. Although you can focus on particular scales, more useful information usually will be obtained from analyzing the pattern of scores—that is, from profile analyses. When normative information is not available, more subjective analyses must be made. The conclusions and implications drawn from these interpretations should be viewed as hypotheses, not facts, and confirmed by other sources of information.

Uses of Typical Performance Measures. Because of their psychometric limitations, especially the fact that responses can be distorted, most typical performance measures generally should not be used in making selection and placement decisions. (A possible exception is placing workers on jobs that fit their interests.) Like maximal performance measures, if typical performance measures are used in selection and placement, there should be validity evidence to support their use.

What, then, are appropriate uses for typical performance measures? The most frequent use is as aids in counseling and therapy. Here they can serve various purposes. They can be used for diagnosis, to ascertain the nature and severity of a client's psychological problems. They can be used to help the counselor better understand the client's personality structure or to help clients better understand themselves. They can be used as one basis for decision making, as when clients use scores on interest inventories to help select a vocation. They can also be used to evaluate the effectiveness of counseling and therapy. For example, changes in personality characteristics or attitudes are used as criteria for assessing the effectiveness of counseling and therapy.

They can also be used for program planning. For example, if a teacher knows her students' personality characteristics, attitudes, and interests, she can better plan instruction that will fit their needs and interests. Or if certain attitudes are interfering with effective performance by workers, training programs can be developed to explore the bases for these attitudes and to change them.

Another use is in research. Here typical performance measures can serve as either independent or dependent variables.[8] As an example, consider two scales on the CPI, Achievement via Conformity and Achievement via Independence, which represent different methods of attaining desired ends. If we identified two groups of students, one who scored high on one scale and the other who scored high on the other scale, and compared their classroom achievement, we would be using the test scores as independent variables. Conversely, the scales could be used as dependent measures, say in a study to determine whether a particular approach to a course results in changes in students' method of studying. Or, as another example, consider need achievement (N:Ach). Here we might see whether salesmen with high N:Ach scores make more customer calls than ones with lower N:Ach scores (using N:Ach as an independent variable) or whether a particular type of family environment increases achievement needs (using N:Ach as a dependent variable). Other examples of research uses include studies of attitude changes, evaluations of counseling and therapy outcomes, reactions to particular courses or instructional methods, and attempts to identify the basic dimensions of personality.

---

[8] In yet other studies, personality variables that may influence results are controlled either by the experimental design (e.g., by random selection of subjects or by matching) or by statistical procedures.

Some Opposing Views

Our evaluation of typical performance measures has followed a traditional view; thus we evaluated these measures using the same criteria as used for maximal performance measures. But, as we have mentioned, not everyone would agree with this view. Some people (e.g., Atkinson, 1981; Harris, 1980; Lamiell, 1981) question whether traditional psychometric criteria can be applied to typical performance measures. Two other camps also would question this approach, but on more conceptual or theoretical bases. One is the behaviorists, who would argue that we should measure overt behaviors, not personality traits. The other is those people who believe that differences in behavior result primarily from situational variables or from person-situation interactions. Both these groups would question the emphasis on the measurement of personality traits. Which approach is most valid and useful is still an open question, one that will be decided only when more evidence is collected.

summary

Objective personality measures, such as self-report inventories, have been criticized for taking a piecemeal approach, focusing on individual traits and characteristics, and for stressing psychometric considerations more than personality theory. In this chapter we discussed other approaches to personality assessment that are more holistic (projectives), assess behavior in more naturalistic situations (situational tests and observations), or focus on specific types of reactions (attitude scales).

Projective techniques are based on the assumption that when confronted with an ambiguous or unstructured situation, a person will organize the situation in a manner that reveals his or her personality characteristics. The best known, and most widely used, projective technique is the Rorschach Inkblot Method. Other projectives include the Thematic Apperception Test (TAT), sentence completion tests, word association techniques, and figure drawings. Because scoring procedures on many projective methods are not standardized, interpretations often confound the examiners' observations with information derived from the test. Thus they are best viewed as a type of structured interview.

Situational measures use naturalistic settings or structured simulations as a basis for observing an individual's personality characteristics. They use complex, realistic tasks and provide an opportunity to observe performance, but generally they are time-consuming and expensive. Although objective indices of performance can be collected, reports are usually narrative descriptions or ratings.

Observations are closely related to situational tests. Since good observations are hard to obtain, a set of guidelines were provided. As with situational measures, observations are usually summarized by narrative reports, checklists, or rating scales, with rating scales being most common. On a rating scale, an observer indicates a person's position on a continuum describing a behavior or characteristic. Several common types of rating scales were described, including comparative, standard, graphic, and forced-choice rating scales. Because ratings are open to several types of errors, the common rating errors and procedures for obtaining accurate ratings were described.

Several other assessment methods were also discussed. Attitude scales measure a person's predisposition to think, perceive, behave, feel, or react to specified objects or persons. Two types were discussed: Thurstone and Likert scales. Questionnaires and surveys can be used to obtain factual information or to measure opinions, reactions, and attitudes. The Semantic Differential and the Rep Test measure constructs individuals use to describe people or objects.

The chapter concluded with a review of typical performance measures. Although many typical performance measures have standardized content and administrative procedures and acceptable reliability, scoring and interpretation is often quite subjective. In addition, since the tests are designed to measure personality dimensions, construct validity is the most important type of validity evidence. Because many typical performance measures lack certain essential psychometric properties, it was suggested that they be used primarily for descriptive rather than decision-making purposes and, when used to assess individuals, as a source of hypotheses rather than as conclusive evidence.

Suggestions for Further Reading

Aiken, L. R. Attitude measurement and research. *New Directions for Testing and Measurement,* 1980, *7,* 1–24. Reviews the construction, evaluation, and use of attitude scales; a good, brief introduction to this area.

Costin, F., Greenough, W. T., & Menges, R. J. Student ratings of college teaching: Reliability, validity, and usefulness. *Review of Educational Research,* 1971, *41,* 511–535. A comprehensive review of the literature on the usefulness of student ratings of college instructors.

Dawes, R. M. *Fundamentals of attitude measurement.* New York: Wiley, 1972. A somewhat technical and theoretical discussion of methods for measuring attitudes; a good overview of attitude measurement.

Ferber, R., Sheatsley, P., Turner, A., & Waksberg, J. *What is a survey?* Washington, D.C.: American Statistical Association, 1980. A brief, nontechnical introduction to the design and use of sample surveys.

Hogan, R., DeSoto, C. B., & Solano, C. Traits, tests, and personality research. *American Psychologist,* 1977, *32,* 255–264. A response to five common criticisms of personality assessment, defending personality measurement and differentiating it from other areas of the study of personality.

Kerlinger, F. N. *Foundations of behavioral research,* 2d ed. New York: Holt, Rinehart and Winston, 1973. Part 9 (Chapters 28–34) covers interviews, objective tests, projectives, observations, sociometry, the semantic differential, and Q methodology; includes many examples.

McClelland, D. C. Managing motivation to expand human freedom. *American Psychologist,* 1978, *33,* 201–210. An illustration of how research on one personality characteristic, achievement motivation, has been applied to a variety of socially important problems.

Rabin, A. I. (Ed.). *Assessment with projective techniques: A concise introduction.* New York: Springer, 1981. Contains chapters describing the common projective techniques, including research and clinical uses.

Saal, F. E., Downey, R. G., & Lahey, M. A. Rating the ratings: Assessing the psychometric quality of rating data. *Psychological Bulletin,* 1980, *88,* 413–428. A review of the definitions and measurement of common rating errors with suggested procedures for identifying rating errors; some parts are technical but the major points are clearly presented.

Schrauger, J. S., & Osberg, T. M. The relative accuracy of self-predictions and judgments by others in psychological assessment. *Psychological Bulletin,* 1981, *90,* 322–351. A review of the literature comparing self-assessments to other methods in a variety of areas, such as intellectual achievement, vocational interests, job performance, and personal adjustment.

Semeonoff, B. *Projective techniques.* New York: Wiley, 1976. An introduction to a variety of projectives, their interpretation and use.

Wade, T. C., & Baker, T. B. Opinions and use of psychological tests: A survey of clinical psychologists. *American Psychologist,* 1977, *32,* 874–882. A survey of 500 clinical psychologists, focusing on their use and opinions about psychological tests in clinical practice.

• part six •
evaluating educational and psychological tests

"**N**OBODY's perfect!" How often have you heard that comment? But even though we live in an imperfect world, we cannot become paralyzed into inaction by that realization. Nor should we adopt a Pollyanna attitude. Rather we must be aware of our limitations and the limitations of the tools that we use, and attempt to improve conditions.

Testing is no exception to this view. No test is perfect and no use of tests, however well intentioned, is without limitations and possible undesirable effects. But by carefully selecting tests and thoughtfully considering the consequences of testing, we can use tests in a manner that is beneficial to both test takers and test users.

In Chapter 18 we shall discuss the considerations in selecting and evaluating tests, suggesting how to identify the best test(s) for your purpose. Chapter 19 will review the current status of testing, consider some pervasive and current problems and issues in testing, and suggest some future developments. Together these chapters should provide a review and integration of the material presented in previous chapters and leave you with some questions to consider in your future use of tests.

Chapter 18 • Selecting and Evaluating Tests

THROUGHOUT this book we have discussed a number of requirements for and characteristics of "good" tests. For the most part, these characteristics have been treated separately and often quite abstractly. Since most readers will apply the knowledge gained from this book as test users, rather than as test developers or researchers, questions regarding test interpretation and use will be of most immediate interest and concern. But before a test can be interpreted or used, someone has had to decide to use the particular test.

Two separate but related problems will be considered in this chapter. The first is identifying and selecting, from among the myriad of published tests, those tests that seem most appropriate for one's needs and purposes. The second is evaluating those tests chosen for further consideration and possible use.

At this point let me remind you of an important point made in the first chapter: A test is only one of various possible methods for measuring the characteristics of individuals. In some situations a test may not be the best or most efficient method of obtaining the desired information. Thus, in a broader sense, your problem is to identify and select the most appropriate assessment method(s). However, since this book focuses on tests, we will assume that tests can provide the desired information and concentrate on the problems in selecting and evaluating tests.

selecting tests

Imagine that you are in charge of setting up a testing program for use in your school district. The program is to cover all testing for grades kindergarten through 12. How would you begin? Where would you look for information about tests? What sort of questions would you ask about the tests you consider? How would you decide which ones to use? These are the sorts of questions addressed in this chapter. We shall discuss them in two stages. In this section we shall consider how to identify tests that appear to meet your requirements; in the next section we shall consider the evaluation of the tests selected for further consideration.

Factors in Test Selection

When identifying a pool of possible tests, the test user must consider various factors: the purpose of the testing, what characteristics are to be measured, how the test results will be used, who will take the test, the qualifications of the people who will interpret the scores and use the results, and any practical constraints. Consideration of these factors will reduce the pool of possible tests to a manageable number, thereby allowing for detailed review of the best prospects.

The Two Basics: Purpose and Population. When selecting tests, the first question always should be: Why do we want to test? For example, is the purpose to place students in course sections, to diagnose learning deficiencies or psychological problems, or to evaluate the effectiveness of a training program? Specifying why we are testing also indicates what characteristics need to be measured. Thus, for example, if we are interested in measuring knowledge of general chemistry, we need look only at chemistry achievement tests; if we are interested in vocational interests, we can limit our search to vocational interest inventories; and so on.

Not only does specification of the test purpose indicate which characteristics will be measured, it also often suggests appropriate item formats and types of scores. If, for example, an English grammar test is needed to place students in various sections of an English course, a test with comprehensive content coverage would be required, but one summary score would be sufficient. However, if the grammar test were to be used for diagnostic purposes, we would need a test that covered the various areas of grammar and provided separate scores for each subarea.

A second consideration is the nature of the group tested. Are we testing adults or children? Groups with particular educational or cultural backgrounds? People with particular handicaps or special abilities? Since tests are developed for certain age, educational, and cultural groups, the characteristics of the group to be tested will further limit the number of possible tests. Thus, knowing that we need a grammar test limits our search; moreover, the additional requirement that the test be appropriate for junior high students further limits the field of potential tests.

The particular characteristics to be considered will, of course, depend on the nature of the situation and the purpose of the testing. These characteristics, in general, are the same as those considered in forming norm groups—for example, age, education, socioeconomic status, and level of particular skills (such as reading ability). Whenever test performance varies as a function of some characteristic, that characteristic should be considered when selecting the test.

User Qualifications. Perhaps the most overlooked consideration in the test selection process is the qualifications of the people who will use the test. The term "test user," you will recall, refers to anyone "who chooses tests, interprets scores, or makes decisions based on test scores" (*Standards,* 1974, p. 1). If test users are not qualified, a test may be improperly administered, misinterpreted, or used in an inappropriate manner.

What are the necessary qualifications of test users? One approach is to consider the problem in terms of types of tests. The 1966 revision of the *Standards* listed three levels of tests:

Level A. Tests or aids that can adequately be administered, scored and interpreted with the aid of the manual and a general orientation to the kind of institution or organization in which one is working (e.g., achievement or proficiency tests).

Level B. Tests or aids that require some technical knowledge of test construction and use, and of supporting psychological and educational fields such as statistics, individual differences, psychology of adjustment, personnel psychology, and guidance (e.g., aptitude tests, adjustment inventories applicable to normal populations).

Level C. Tests and aids that require substantial understanding of testing and supporting psychological fields, together with supervised experience in the use of these devices (e.g., projective tests, individual mental tests). (*Standards*, 1966, p. 10)

You can see that different qualifications are needed to use different types of tests.

The 1974 edition of the *Standards* contains several principles relating to qualifications of test users. While stating that test publishers have the responsibility to inform potential users of the qualifications necessary for the proper use of a test, the *Standards* also states that all test users must ultimately decide whether they have the necessary qualifications. That is, test users should be aware of their own qualifications and how well they match the qualifications required for use of a specific test (Principle C1.1, p. 58). These qualifications include basic knowledge of the principles of psychological measurement and the limitations of test interpretation, and the technical knowledge necessary to evaluate the claims made in the test manual. For all but the least complex tests, this would generally require knowledge equivalent to that gained in an introductory course in educational or psychological measurement (such as the one you are now taking).

But test users must have more than general knowledge of testing procedures and practices. They must know the literature relevant to the specific tests they are using and the testing problems they may encounter. This is particularly important when tests are used to make decisions about individuals. In short, anyone who interprets and uses tests should thoroughly understand the general principles of psychological measurement and know the relevant information about the particular tests they are using.

Practical Considerations.   Test selection is also governed by a number of practical constraints, such as the time available for testing and the cost of the testing program.

Consider, first, *testing time*. Usually we are not able or willing to devote unlimited time to testing. For example, an employer may use a test only if it can be administered in a half hour; an instructor may require a test that can be administered within one class period; a college admission test may have to fit into a half-day testing session. Probably the most common limitation is the need for tests given in public schools to conform to class schedules. In this situation, the test must be able to be administered within one class period, or a multiple of a class period, or must have subtests that can be administered within a single class period.

A second practical consideration is *cost*. Users must choose tests that fit their budgets. These costs include not only test booklets and answer sheets but also scoring and reporting expenses. Costs can be minimized in many ways; for example, using separate answer sheets and staggered testing sessions can reduce the number of test booklets required. We must also take into account indirect costs, including staff time to prepare, administer, and interpret the test, and any special equipment or facilities needed.

These practical constraints must be placed in perspective. Rather than being hard-and-fast determinants, they are better viewed as flexible guidelines. Certainly, practical considerations are much less important than the technical quality of the test. Also, practical limitations sometimes are more apparent than real. Of all the considerations involved in selecting tests, practical ones are the least important.

Sources of Information

Once the type of test needed has been identified, the next step is to locate tests that appear to fit the desired specifications. These may be either commercially published tests and/or unpublished tests. Although the former are easier to identify, some sources include unpublished instruments (see below). In this section we shall consider the various sources test users can consult to locate tests.

Compilations of Tests. By a compilation we mean a sourcebook that lists, and usually briefly describes, the various tests available in a given field. Although these sources list the available tests (often including unpublished instruments), they may not be exhaustive in coverage, become out of date, and generally provide only minimal information about the instruments listed. However, they do identify available tests and indicate how copies of the test and further information can be obtained.

The most well-known compilation is *Tests in Print II* (Buros, 1974). This is a comprehensive bibliography of tests used in psychology, education, and business. Although some confidential and restricted tests (for example, the SAT and GRE) are included, most of the almost 2500 tests listed are available to qualified users. The tests are listed by type, thus allowing the test user to focus his search. Each entry includes the title of the test, the examinees and level for which the test was designed (for example, grades 4–6), the author, publisher, publication date, parts or subtests, scores, and comments (for example, "new form available annually," "for research use only"). In addition, each entry is cross-referenced to other categories of test within *Tests in Print* and to the *Mental Measurements Yearbooks*.

The main use of *Tests in Print* is to determine whether any published tests are available in a given category. Thus it is a good place to start a search. Since it provides only minimal information about each test, you will have to consult other sources for more detailed information.

Other compilations describe the instruments available in a designated area. These may be quite comprehensive; for example, one (Chun, Cobb, & French, 1975) describes 3000 sources. Some examples include compilations of self-concept measures (Wylie, 1974), mental health measures (Comrey, Backer, & Glaser, 1973), measures used in child development (Johnson, 1976; Johnson & Bommarito, 1971), measures for early childhood education (Goodwin & Driscoll, 1980), measures of social psychology attitudes (Robinson & Shaver, 1973), and measures for the assessment of children's intelligence and special abilities (Sattler, 1982). It should also be noted that there are numerous books available describing specific tests (e.g., the MMPI and Rorschach) or particular classes of tests (e.g., intelligence tests, projective methods).

A third source is the ERIC Clearinghouse on Tests and Measurements, which is located at the Educational Testing Service. This organization abstracts and indexes information on tests used in education and psychology and periodically publishes reviews of the literature on selected measurement topics (e.g., Backer, 1977). Several professional journals also publish lists of newly developed or revised tests.

The Mental Measurement Yearbooks. The single most important source of information about published tests is the *Mental Measurements Yearbook* series instituted by Oscar Buros and now located at the University of Nebraska. In spite of the name, the *MMY* is not an annual publication. Rather, volumes are published every several years; the sixth edition was published in 1965, the seventh in 1972, and the eighth in 1978. The *Yearbooks* have three major objectives: (1) to provide a readily available, comprehensive, up-to-date bibliography of tests and sources of information about test construction, validation, and use; (2) to encourage more sophisticated and higher-quality critical evaluations and appraisals of tests and testing practices; and (3) to encourage publication of fewer, but better, tests. The first purpose has been accomplished by the *Yearbooks* themselves and the second encouraged by the high critical standards of the *Yearbook* reviews. Unfortunately, the third goal has not yet been attained.

The *Yearbooks* are the test users' bible. The entry for each test includes the test title; author, publisher and publication date; groups for which the test is intended; part scores, levels, forms; method of scoring; cost; time, both working time and total administration time; pages; and an indication of whether reliability and validity data are available (see Figure 18.1). There is also a bibliography for the test, and cross-references to other editions of the *Yearbook*.

Although this descriptive material is of great value, the heart of the *Yearbook* is the critical reviews of tests. Not every test is reviewed, but reviews are given of widely used, new, and revised tests. These reviews vary in length from a few paragraphs to several pages. They are frankly critical and evaluative. About half the tests are reviewed by more than one person, with reviews written from different perspectives. For example, a French test might be reviewed by a psychologist, who would focus on the technical quality of the test, and by a French teacher, who would evaluate the content and coverage of the test.

The *MMY* also includes reviews of books about testing, a directory of periodicals that publish articles on testing and measurement, a directory and index of test publishers, and several indices (by test name, title, classification).

The publisher of the *Yearbooks,* the Institute of Mental Measurements, also

Figure 18.1   A Sample Page From a *Mental Measurements Yearbook*

origin and not of a kind likely to be useful to an American user. A reference is made to the use of the test in the measurement of mental deterioration. Two references in French are given to deterioration studies.

Until the publishers produce evidence that this test is equal or superior to the many non-verbal tests published in the United States, it has little to commend it for use in guidance situations. The fact that it is a test of a single item type may make it useful for certain factor analytic studies.

[455]

★Deeside Non-Verbal Reasoning Test: English-Welsh Bilingual Version. Ages 10–12; 1961–63; 2 forms: test 1 ('61), test 2 ('63), (16 pages); separate mimeographed manuals for test 1 ['61, 17 pages], test 2 ['63, 19 pages]; distribution restricted to directors of education; 25s. per 25 tests; 7s. 6d. per manual; postage and purchase tax extra; 37–38(60) minutes; W. G. Emmett; George G. Harrap & Co. Ltd. *

[456]

★Doppelt Mathematical Reasoning Test. Grades 16–17 and employees; 1954–63; IBM; Form A ('54, 4 pages); manual ('58, 10 pages); bulletin of information ('63, 36 pages); revised procedures for testing center operation ('63, 8 pages); distribution restricted and test administered at specified licensed university centers; scoring and reporting handled by the local center; examination fee to centers: $1 per examinee; fees to examinees are determined locally and include reporting of scores to the examinee and to 3 institutions or companies designated at the time of testing; additional score reports may be secured from the publisher at a fee of $1 each; 50(60). minutes; Jerome E. Doppelt; Psychological Corporation. *

REFERENCES

1. SCHWARTZ, MILTON M., AND CLARK, F. EUGENE. "Prediction of Success in Graduate School at Rutgers University." *J Ed Res* 53:109–11 N '59. * (*PA* 35:1223)
2. ROEMMICH, HERMAN. "The Doppelt Mathematical Reasoning Test as a Selection Device for Graduate Engineering Students." *Ed & Psychol Meas* 21:1009–10 W '61. *

W. V. CLEMANS, *Director, Test Department, Science Research Associates, Inc., Chicago, Illinois.*

The *Doppelt Mathematical Reasoning Test* contains 50 problems that differ from the usual pattern for multiple choice questions in that there are no stems. The task facing the examinee is defined once for the entire set in the directions which state:

Each problem in this test consists of five mathematical figures or expressions. Four of these have something in common which is not shared by the remaining one. You are to choose the *one* figure or expression which does *not* belong with the other four and mark the letter corresponding to your choice in the proper place on the answer sheet.

None of the problems involves mathematics beyond the usual secondary school level. The test can be easily administered to large groups or to individuals.

The manual states that the test "was designed primarily as an aid in the selection of students for graduate work" and that it "may also be useful in the classification and assignment of college graduates applying for positions in industry which require mathematical reasoning."

Correlations of the DMRT with faculty ratings or grades for three groups of 41, 57, and 109 graduate students taking mathematics suggest that the test may have some value for selecting graduate students. The coefficients obtained were .52, .71, and .43, respectively. Similar coefficients are reported for 28 graduate students in chemistry and 26 undergraduates in a psychometrics course, but a coefficient of only .32 was found for 29 medical students. This latter finding is hardly significant, but is the only coefficient reported for a criterion group whose course work is not primarily quantitative. The Psychological Corporation supplies summaries of five studies reported by independent investigators that tend to corroborate the claim that the test relates to measures of success in graduate study in mathematics or statistics. Apparently no systematic approach has been made to determining how valuable the test is for graduate students in other areas. Validity data for industrial criteria have not yet been supplied.

In the norms section of the manual percentile equivalents are given for five small student samples ranging in size from 102 to 145 students selected from 15 colleges and universities. The groups consisted of senior psychology students, medical students, psychology majors, education majors, and graduate students taking courses in statistics. Percentile equivalents are also given for a group of 388 engineers from one industrial organization.

Reliability coefficients were computed for each of the six groups using the odd-even approach and the Spearman-Brown formula. The coefficients range from .78 to .85. The author points out that the lowest values were found for the most homogeneous groups. He fails to point out, however, that the three groups yielding the highest reliability coefficients (all .85) not only had the largest standard deviations but also the lowest means. This phenomenon suggests to this reviewer that the higher values may have been due to speeded-

Source: Buros (1965).

publishes a series of monographs describing particular categories of tests. These monographs incorporate relevant information from the *Yearbooks* and *Tests in Print* and are designed for test users whose interests are limited to one or a few types of tests. Four of the monographs cover relatively broad areas of testing: personality tests, intelligence tests, reading tests, and vocational tests. For example, *Intelligence Tests and Reviews* (Buros, 1975a) consists of the intelligence test sections of the first seven *Yearbooks* and *Tests in Print II* and covers 394 intelligence tests. The other five monographs focus on specific subject matter areas: English, foreign languages, mathematics, science, and social studies. For example, *English Tests and Reviews* (Buros, 1975b) covers 292 English tests.

When selecting tests, no other single source can match the *Yearbooks* (and the associated monographs). The descriptive information provides a basis for determining whether a test will meet your needs, the bibliography helps locate further information about the test, and the critical reviews provide opinions on the merits and limitations of the test. All test users should become familiar with, and use, this reference.

Other Sources. Textbooks on educational and psychological testing also provide descriptions and evaluations on various tests. General texts, such as the one you are reading, do not provide exhaustive coverage or extensive descriptions of particular tests, but do discuss the more widely used tests and methods. Others, with more specific focuses, cover individual tests in more depth—for example, standardized tests used in education (Mehrens & Lehmann, 1980), vocational interest tests (Zytowski, 1973), projective methods (Rabin, 1981), and tests used by vocational guidance counselors (Kapes & Mastie, 1982). Books devoted to individual tests are too numerous to be listed here.

Educational and psychological journals and periodicals are another source of information. Some journals periodically review tests (e.g., *Journal of Educational Measurement, Measurement and Evaluation in Guidance*). Others include reviews of the literature on specific tests, types of tests, or testing problems (e.g., the *Annual Review of Psychology, Psychological Bulletin,* and *Review of Educational Research*). A wide variety of journals include articles on various aspects of testing.[1] The best use of journals is not to identify tests but to obtain more detailed information on the usefulness and validity of the tests selected and to identify possible problems. The search for relevant articles can be facilitated by using the reference lists in the *MMY* or consulting indices to published literature, such as the *Psychological Abstracts* or the *Education Index*.

The Center for the Study of Evaluation at the University of California at Los Angeles also publishes monographs containing critical reviews of tests in several

[1] Among the journals and periodicals containing articles relating to tests and testing problems are the *American Psychologist, Journal of Applied Psychology, Journal of Counseling Psychology, Journal of Consulting and Clinical Psychology, American Educational Research Journal, Journal of Educational Measurement,* NCME *Measurement News,* NCME *Measurement in Education, Measurement and Evaluation in Guidance, Applied Psychological Measurement, Educational and Psychological Measurement, Harvard Educational Review, College Board Review, Personnel Psychology, Journal of Vocational Behavior,* and *Journal of Personality Assessment.*

areas—for example, elementary school tests; tests for cognitive, affective, and interpersonal skills; preschool/kindergarten tests; and criterion-referenced tests.

Most colleges and universities, and many public school systems, have persons on their staffs who are knowledgeable about testing. In addition, there are psychologists who work for public or private agencies or in business and industry, or who are in private practice. These persons generally can suggest appropriate tests, direct the test user to information sources, or suggest persons or agencies that can help with a testing problem.

For the most detailed information about a particular test, one should contact the test publisher. Each publisher prints a catalog, which can be used to locate possible tests. Of more interest, however, is the fact that publishers also provide *specimen sets* of most tests. A specimen set (which usually can be obtained for a minimal fee) consists of a copy of the test, the answer sheet, scoring key, and technical and interpretive manuals. The potential test user can study these materials and evaluate the content, administration, and technical quality of the test.

The Order of Search. You may want to use any or all of these sources when searching for a test that fits your purposes. The most efficient way is to start with the *MMY, Tests in Print,* or a compilation (if there is one in your area of interest), then look to other sources such as journals and textbooks. Once the field of potential tests has been narrowed to a small number, the test user should obtain specimen sets and use them as a basis for a detailed study of the tests.

Sometimes no test will be found that meets your requirements. In this situation you have several alternatives. One is to look for another (nontest) method of obtaining the relevant data. Or certain of your original requirements might be changed, or relaxed. A third possibility is to construct a new test to meet your requirements. Since test construction is both time-consuming and expensive, this is usually the least feasible alternative.

The Need for Multiple Assessment

Our discussion may have given the impression that you are searching for one test that will meet your purposes. In some situations this may be true. If it is, your task is to select the best test from among various possibilities. However, generally this will be an oversimplified view. In most circumstances, your decision (and hence test use) will involve several characteristics, and since most tests measure only a limited set of characteristics, you will be searching for the best test of each characteristic. In other situations you may want to measure a given characteristic by more than one method. Here you would be looking for several good measures of the characteristic.

Another situation in which you will be looking for more than one test is when you are trying to develop a testing program that can be used with a variety of persons to make a number of different decisions. Here you would be looking for the optimal blend of instruments to accomplish your various goals.

An Example: School Testing Programs. To illustrate, consider the situation used to introduce this topic, developing a testing program for use in grades K–12 of a public school system.

Your first task would be to identify the various potential uses of tests in the school system. Consulting with teachers, administrators, students, counselors, school psychologists, and parents, you might come up with a list like the following:

- Identification of readiness for school
- Identification of readiness for instruction in a particular subject (e.g., reading, algebra),
- Measurement of what students have learned, both general skills (e.g., reading) and in specific subjects
- Identification of students' academic abilities
- Placement in courses or academic tracks
- Identification of students with special needs
- Establishment of competency in basic skills (reading, mathematics)
- Aids for vocational and educational guidance

All of these decisions would require information provided by tests.[2]

Your next task would be to identify tests to meet these various needs. Without going into detail here (see, e.g., Ahmann & Glock, 1975; Mehrens & Lehmann, 1978; or Thorndike & Hagen, 1977) we shall just give some examples of the types of tests you would need. To identify students' academic abilities you would want a scholastic aptitude test; to measure general learning outcomes you would want a survey achievement battery. For both of these purposes you would prefer tests that have different levels for various grades so that same test could be administered in each grade. To measure competency, you would need content-referenced achievement tests. As aids in vocational guidance, you would need an interest inventory and perhaps a multiaptitude battery such as the DAT. And so on. The point is that you would have to consider a variety of types of tests.

After you have identified potential tests in each category, you would critically evaluate these tests and select the ones that best fit the requirements of your particular school system. (Here, again, consultation with the affected parties would be advisable.) Furthermore, you would want to coordinate your selection so as to minimize the number of tests and amount of testing needed. One way would be to select tests that could serve several purposes. For example, perhaps the achievement battery used to measure overall learning could also be used as a basis for placing students in course sections or academic tracks.

evaluating tests

Let us assume that you have identified several tests that appear to meet your general requirements. Your task then becomes to evaluate these tests and select the best one(s) for your particular situation and purposes. These evaluations will be made using the materials in the specimen set. For example, the content and coverage of the test can be ascertained by studying the individual test items; the test

---

[2] Information needed to make these decisions also can come from other sources, such as evaluations by teachers. And the program might also include tests administered by external agencies, such as college admission tests.

takers' task from the test, answer sheet, and directions; and the technical adequacy of the test from the reliability, validity, and normative data presented in the manual.

The Test Manual

The *test manual* is the basic source of information about the constructions, standardization, psychometric properties, and interpretation of the test.[3] It should provide all the information necessary to evaluate the test. Thus, obtaining and studying the test manual (and the accompanying material in the specimen set, such as a copy of the test) is the most important step in evaluating a test.

What sort of information should be contained in the test manual? The manual should "provide enough information for a qualified user to make sound judgments regarding the usefulness and interpretation of test scores" (*Standards,* 1974, p. 5). More specifically, any test manual should include certain types of information.[4] It should describe the basic rationale of the test, what characteristics it is designed to measure, and suggest appropriate uses for the test; describe, in detail, the rationale and procedures for selecting items and developing scales; clearly describe all administrative and scoring procedures and point out potential problems in administration and scoring; describe the procedures used to establish the reliability and validity of all scores and scales, presenting not only conclusions but also relevant data; and present sufficient data, including norm tables, to allow for correct interpretation of scores. Ideally, the manual should also contain a bibliography of any other sources that more clearly describe the rationale of the test or the test construction processes, and of studies using the test. In short, it should contain all the information potential users need to answer their questions about the development, interpretation, and use of the test.

When evaluating tests one must take a skeptical and critical attitude. Although most test developers and publishers are honest and ethical, a test is a commercial product and hence the manual will attempt to picture the test in the best light. Thus, the *Standards* cautions, "A manual is to be judged not merely by its literal truthfulness, but by the impression it leaves with the reader" (*Standards,* 1974, p. 5). Thus not only should you adopt a critical attitude toward the information contained in a test manual, you should also pay particular attention to questions that are not answered in the manual.

The Standards for Educational and Psychological Tests

At several points we have mentioned the *Standards for Educational and Psychological Tests.* This pamphlet was prepared by three professional organizations concerned with testing: the American Educational Research Association (AERA), the American Psychological Association (APA), and the National Council on Measurement in Education (NCME). The current (1974) edition is the third; previous

---

[3] Some tests have several manuals, most commonly one dealing with administration and scoring and another dealing with technical aspects (test construction, reliability, validity, and norming).

[4] The types of information are spelled out in the *Standards.*

C1. The manual should report the validity of the test for each type of inference for which it is recommended. If its validity for some suggested interpretation has not been investigated, that fact should be made clear. ESSENTIAL

C1.1. Statements in the manual about validity should refer to the validity of particular interpretations or of particular types of decision. ESSENTIAL

[Comment: It is incorrect to use the unqualified phrase "the validity of the test." No test is valid for all purposes or in all situations or for all groups of individuals. Any study of test validity is pertinent to only a few of the possible uses of or inferences from the test scores.

If the test is likely to be used incorrectly for certain areas of decision, the manual should include specific warnings. For example, the manual for a writing skills test states that the test apparently is not sufficiently difficult to discriminate among students "at colleges that have selective admissions."]

C1.2. Wherever interpretation of sub-scores, score differences, or profiles is suggested, the evidence in the manual justifiying such interpretation should be made explicit. ESSENTIAL (Also see B4.4.)

[Comment: One aptitude test manual indicates the difficulties involved in computing the statistical significance of differences between scores in a profile. In an effort to cope with this problem a convenient method of approximating the significance of plotted differences is provided. Cautions and limitations of this type of profile interpretation are suggested.]

C1.21. If the manual for an inventory suggests that the user consider responses to separate items as a basis for personality assessment, it should either present evidence supporting this use or call attention to the absence of such data. The manual should warn the reader that inferences based on responses to single items are subject to extreme error, hence should be used only to direct further inquiry, as, perhaps, in a counseling interview. ESSENTIAL

C2. Item-test correlations should not be presented in the manual as evidence of criterion-related validity, and they should be referred to as item-discrimination indices, not as item-validity coefficients. ESSENTIAL

[Comment: It is, of course, possible to make good use of item-test correlations in reasoning about construct validity. However, such correlations are not, in themselves, indicators of test validity; they are measures of internal consistency.]

Content Validity

C3. If a test performance is to be interpreted as a sample of performance or a definition of performance in some universe of situations, the manual should indicate clearly what universe is represented and how adequate is the sampling. ESSENTIAL

[Comment: Some consideration should be given to the adequacy of sampling from both the appropriate universe of content and the universe of behaviors that the items are intended to represent. For example, the manual of a test of achievement in American history might not only describe the item types used and the coverage of the subject matter, but also should describe to what extent responding to the test items serves as an adequate sample of the examinee's attainment of such skills as critical reading of historical material, including evaluation of evidence, analysis of cause and effect relationships, and whatever other behaviors are considered to be "achievement in American history."]

C3.1. When experts have been asked to judge whether items are an appropriate

Source: *Standards*, 1974, p. 18.

editions were published in 1954 and 1966, and a fourth edition is being prepared. It is directed to two audiences: test users (who must evaluate the information presented in test manuals) and test publishers (who prepare manuals and other information about tests).

Three major areas are covered. The first involves standards for tests, manuals, and reports. Subareas are concerned with the dissemination of information, aids to interpretation, directions for administration and scoring, and scores and norms. This section is primarily concerned with ways of communicating information about the test to the test user. The second major section covers standards for reliability and validity. The third section focuses on the use of tests, considering such factors as qualifications of test users, choosing tests, administration and scoring, and the interpretation of scores.

A page from the 1974 edition of the *Standards* is shown in Figure 18.2. This particular page contains principles related to the manual's presentation of information regarding test administration and scoring. Note that there are general principles (C1, C2, C3), subprinciples (C1.1, C1.1.1, and so on), and explanatory comments. Note also that some principles are considered essential[5] requirements (e.g., C1, C1.1, C1.1.1), others very desirable (e.g., C1.1.2), and others desirable (e.g., C2). These principles should be referred to when evaluating a test. In fact, I would suggest that every test user own, study, and constantly use the *Standards*.

The *Standards* may appear quite technical to some test users, especially those with minimal training in educational and psychological measurement. For these people, a related publication, *Guidelines for Test Use: A Commentary on the Standards for Educational and Psychological Tests* (Brown, 1980) will provide a useful summary and companion to the *Standards*. Other related publications deal with evaluation studies and with the validity of selection tests (*Principles for the Validation and Use of Personnel Selection Procedures,* 1975).

The Evaluation Process

As with techniques of studying, singing styles, and golf putting stances, there is no one format or procedure for evaluating a test. Any individual who consistently evaluates tests will, in time, develop his own format and procedures, emphasizing the characteristics of tests that he thinks most important. There are, however, common elements that must be included in any test evaluation.

Figure 18.3 shows, in outline form, the information I consider when evaluating a test. This guide, as any other,[6] should be treated as a series of basic questions. In any particular evaluation, other questions may also be asked. For example, if a test is too long or comprehensive, the prospective user might want to know the answers to such questions as: Can certain sections be eliminated? What effect will

---

[5] The principles labeled "essential" represent the minimal amount of information that should be presented in the manual.

[6] Other evaluation forms can be found in Anastasi (1982, Appendix C), Payne (1974, pp. 344–346), and Thorndike & Hagen (1977, pp. 107–110). One can, of course, use the *Standards* as an evaluation guide.

Figure 18.3 A Format for Evaluating Tests

1. General Information
   Title:
   Author:
   Publisher:
   Publication date:
   Forms and levels:
   Manual and other technical aids:

2. Purposes and Uses
   Purpose as stated by author:
   Other purposes/uses implied by author:
   Other purposes/uses reported in literature:

3. Practical Considerations
   Direct costs: (booklets, answer sheets, scoring, etc.)
   Indirect costs:
   Time: (working time, total administration time)

4. Format and Layout
   Editorial quality:
   Arrangement of items and subsection/parts:
   Appeal/face validity:
   Test takers' ease of comprehension and response:

5. Items and Their Coverage
   Basis of item selection:
   Coverage: (especially, over- and underrepresented areas)
   General quality of items:
   Variety of item formats:
   Item difficulty:

6. Consistency
   Evidence (amount and quality) of:
      equivalence:
      stability:
      internal consistency:
   Factors possibly influencing reliability:
   Reliability of subtest scores (if applicable):
   Reliability of difference scores (if applicable):
   Standard error of measurement (total, subtest/scales):
   Consistency for different groups of subjects:

7. Validity
   Evidence (amount and quality) of:
      content validity:
      construct validity:
      criterion-related validity:
   Validity of subtest/part scores:
   Generalizability of validity data:

8. Scores and Norms
    Norm groups: (variety and quality):
    Scales used to report scores:
    Interpretative aids available:
    Information on subtest scores:

9. Administration and Scoring
    Administration problems:
    Qualifications for test administrator:
    Apparatus, equipment needed for administration:
    Instructions (for administrator, for test taker):
    Scoring (how done; who can do; problems; what aids provided?):

10. Other Information
    Comments by reviewers/users:
    Test part of series or battery:
    Auxiliary services available/provided:

this have on validity? Will the scores obtained from the revised test be comparable to those obtained using the entire battery?

The evaluations utilize information obtained from various sources. General information (time, scores, age level, forms, and so on) can be obtained from reference sources (e.g., Buros). This information can be confirmed, and missing data supplied, from the test manual. Next we study the test itself, focusing on the format and layout and on the content and coverage of the individual items. Here some reference will have to be made to the manual, to determine the rationale and method of selecting items. After study of the test itself, we turn to the psychometric characteristics of the test—its reliability, validity, scores, and norms. Data for these sections will come primarily from the test manual. The manual will also provide the information regarding administration and scoring. Finally, we take into account any other information, from the test publisher's material or outside sources (e.g., Buros, test reviews) that may be relevant to our evaluation.

Once the evaluation has been completed, the test user must make a decision. If he has been evaluating only one test, he must decide whether it looks promising enough to use. If he has been evaluating several tests, he must choose between them (or possibly reject them all). Reaching this decision is a rational, judgmental process. The test user must weigh the advantages and limitations of the various tests in question, make a decision, and then proceed on the basis of that decision.

The evaluative procedure does not end at this point. Because each testing situation is unique, it is impossible to predict with absolute certainty that the test(s) chosen will, in fact, work. Thus, if possible, a preliminary tryout should be conducted before the test is put into widespread or routine use. (Ideally, a tryout would involve the use of several tests with the final selection of a test being based on the results of the tryout.) If a tryout is not feasible, a test should be adopted tentatively and its usefulness constantly reviewed and evaluated. In all circumstances, the value of a test will not be determined until validity data, based on studies of the test in the actual situation, are available.

summary

The material in this chapter can best be summarized by reviewing the steps in selecting and evaluating tests. I have suggested the following sequence of steps:

1. Outline your general requirements: the purpose of testing, the characteristics to be measured, and the nature of the group to be tested. Consider also the qualifications of test users and practical constraints.
2. Identify what tests are available which appear to meet your needs. Here sources like *Tests in Print,* the *Mental Measurements Yearbooks,* test publishers catalogs, and test compilations will be most helpful.
3. Obtain further information about these tests from texts, journals, reference books, and consultation with people who have used this type of test.
4. Select the most promising tests. Obtain samples (specimen sets) of these tests.
5. Make a detailed evaluation of these tests, keeping in mind the unique requirements of your situation. On the basis of these evaluations, select the test(s) to be used.
6. If at all possible, conduct an experimental tryout of the test before putting it to use.
7. Use the test. Constantly monitor and evaluate its usefulness and effectiveness.

The process of selecting and evaluating tests is a systematic, though judgmental, process. If a test is to be effective, rigorous critical standards must be followed when evaluating potential tests, and the use of the test must be constantly monitored. If at any point in the process the test fails to meet your requirements, its use should be discontinued and other tests or procedures substituted.

Suggestions for Further Reading

Brown, F. G. *Guidelines for test use: A commentary on the Standards for Educational and Psychological Tests.* Washington, D.C.: National Council on Measurement in Education, 1980. An explanation and discussion of the implications of the *Standards;* written for nontechnically trained test users.

Buros, O. K. The story behind the Mental Measurements Yearbooks. *Measurement and Evaluation in Guidance,* 1968, *1,* 86–95. The history of the *MMY* as described by their developer.

Buros, O. K. Fifty years in testing: Some reminiscences, criticisms, and suggestions. *Educational Researcher,* 1977, 6(7), 9–15. Buros' personal reflections on important historical developments in testing, the quality of tests, and needed improvements in testing.

Buros, O. K. (Ed.). *The eighth mental measurements yearbook.* Highland Park, N.J.: Gryphon Press, 1978. The consumer's guide to published tests; all test users should be familiar with this reference.

Katz, M. *Selecting an achievement test: Principles and procedures.* Princeton, N.J.: Educational Testing Service, 1973. A pamphlet describing the important questions to ask when selecting an achievement test.

Lerner, B. The Supreme Court and the APA, AERA, NCME Test Standards: Past references and future possibilities. *American Psychologist,* 1978, *33,* 915–919. Describes how the Supreme Court has used the *Standards* and federal agency guidelines in deciding cases involving testing.

Novick, M. R. Federal guidelines and professional standards. *American Psychologist,* 1981, *36,* 1035–1046. Examination of the role of various types of guidelines in determining issues of test quality, of test fairness, and in balancing the interests of the various parties involved in testing.

Principles for the validation and use of personnel selection procedures. Washington, D.C.: American Psychological Association, Division of Industrial/Organizational Psychology, 1975. A pamphlet outlining procedures for validation research, personnel selection, and promotion; an application of the relevant sections of the *Standards.*

Standards for educational and psychological tests. Washington, D.C.: American Psychological Association, 1974. The basic statement of three professional organizations concerned with testing; gives guidelines for providing information on test construction, evaluation, interpretation, and use; "must" reading.

Thorndike, R. L., & Hagen, E. P. *Measurement and evaluation in psychology and education,* 4th ed. New York: Wiley, 1977. Chapter 12 discusses the problems and concerns in developing a school testing program.

Chapter 19 • Problems, Issues, and Trends

IN the previous chapters we discussed the basic concepts and principles of educational and psychological testing and illustrated how they apply to the construction, interpretation, evaluation, and use of various types of tests. In this chapter we shall discuss some current problems and issues and identify some emerging trends in testing.

To provide a framework for the discussion we shall first review some of the major concepts and principles of educational and psychological testing. When reading this chapter keep in mind a point emphasized in the first chapter: While we have focused on tests, the problems and issues we have discussed, and will discuss in this chapter, apply to all methods used to assess human characteristics; they are not particular to tests.

a recapitulation

A test was defined as a systematic procedure for measuring a sample of behavior. The phrase "systematic procedure" implies that the same (or comparable) items are administered to all test takers, under similar conditions, and that all responses are scored using the same procedures. Because a test is a measuring instrument, procedures must be developed to express performance on a quantitative scale. The term "sample" refers to the fact that the items on any particular test usually are only a subset of all possible items in the domain of interest. And, because only overt behaviors can be measured, conclusions regarding hypothetical underlying abilities and traits are inferences based on the test taker's responses.

Most tests utilize a trait or individual differences model. That is, they are designed to measure certain constellations of characteristics or abilities (traits), with the assumption being that all test takers possess the trait in some degree but that individuals differ in the amount of the trait they possess. Furthermore, tests measure developed abilities and characteristics. That is, whereas a test score describes the person's present status on the characteristic measured, present performance reflects the individual's experiences prior to testing and, perhaps, even genetic predispositions.

Good tests have certain properties. The domain to be sampled and the purpose of the testing must be specified in advance, both to guide the test construction process and to provide a basis for evaluating the completed test. The test should have standardized administrative conditions in order to reduce measurement errors (thus increasing reliability) and to allow for comparisons between the scores of different individuals. A test should be reliable and valid. There should be normative data, standards, or other procedures that provide a basis for interpretation of scores. Finally, a good test is practical and efficient.

Of these characteristics, the most important is validity. Validity, you will recall, refers to how well a test measures a trait or characteristic or predicts some external behavior. Validity is the most important property of a test because unless we know what a test measures or predicts, we have no firm basis for interpreting scores. In turn, unless the purpose of the test has been defined, we have no basis for establishing validity and, if testing conditions are not standardized or the test is not reliable, its potential validity will be limited.

The three major types of validity—content, criterion-related, and construct—parallel the three major functions of tests: as samples, as predictors, and as signs, respectively. A test serves as a sample when the items represent (i.e., sample) a clearly defined content or behavorial domain. Classroom exams illustrate this function. A test serves as a predictor when scores are used to forecast some qualitatively different behavior, as when a college admission test is used to predict college grades. A test serves as a sign when it helps clarify the nature of a (still incompletely defined) construct; for example, determining what variables or outcomes are related to scores on an intelligence test may help clarify what is meant by intelligence.

When tests are used as decision-making aids, two aspects of validation are of primary importance. First, validity data will be situation-specific. That is, a test that is valid for one use may not be valid when used for similar purposes, in different populations, and/or in apparently similar situations. Thus a test must be validated for each particular use and in each specific situation. Second, the usefulness of a test depends on the amount of additional or unique information it provides; information that adds to what we already know. In other words, incremental validity, broadly defined, is the most important index of the effectiveness of a test in decision-making situations.

When tests are used to measure a particular characteristic or to describe an individual's level of performance, we can talk of the test's validity in a more general sense. Here our primary concern is with how well the test measures the characteristic of interest. In these descriptive uses, validation involves establishing that the test does, in fact, measure the characteristic of interest. This requires various types of evidence and is a continual process in that each additional piece of evidence further clarifies the nature of the characteristic being measured and its relation with other variables. In other words, construct validation is essential.

There are three types of score interpretation: norm-referenced, content-referenced, and outcome-referenced. Accurate interpretation of each type of score requires, either directly or indirectly, validity evidence. Norm-referenced interpretations report a person's performance as a relative rank within a specified comparison group. Here validity evidence is needed, for without it we have only a relative ranking, and nothing more. Content-referenced scores indicate whether the test taker has attained some minimal level of mastery or competence in a defined content or skills domain. Again, unless the test is a valid measure of the domain, statements about mastery will have no meaning. Outcome-referenced scores interpret performance as a predicted performance level on some other measure. The accuracy of such predictions will, of course, vary with the degree of relationship between test scores and the external measure—that is, with the test's validity. Although the three types of scores provide different types of information, and often require different test construction strategies, they are best viewed as complementary ways of viewing performance, not as independent categories.

The basic rationale underlying testing is quite simple. There are numerous situations in which information about characteristics of individuals is needed, either to describe individuals or to make decisions about the individuals or about methods or treatments. These decisions should be based on the best available information. Tests are often a valid, efficient, and objective method of obtaining such information. If they are, they should be used. However, if other methods are more objective, valid, or efficient, they should be used instead.

problems and issues in testing

In previous chapters a number of problems and limitations of current testing procedures and practices were mentioned. In this section we shall review and discuss some of the major concerns, focusing on three areas: the range and availability of tests, psychometric problems, and the social consequences of testing. For other discussions of these issues consult the suggested readings at the end of this chapter.

The Range and Availability of Tests

By now it should be obvious that tests have been developed to measure a wide variety of abilities and personality characteristics. It also should be obvious that available tests vary widely in coverage and quality. In general, the measurement of maximal performance (achievement, abilities, and aptitudes) is more highly developed, both in the range of characteristics measured and in technical sophistication, than is the measurement of typical performance (personality). Although there are exceptions, such as the measurement of interests and attitudes, the measurement of personality characteristics is, by and large, at a more primitive state.

Content and Formats. Development of measures in previously neglected areas is continually proceeding; the measurement of cognitive styles and use of content-referenced tests are good examples. Yet there are also areas where measurement has been less than successful, motivation being a prime example. The problems involved in measuring motivation include the inability to agree on a definition of motivation, the situational-specific nature of motives, and the possibility that the traditional measurement models may be inappropriate for measuring motivation (Atkinson, 1981). Other areas lacking good tests include many complex skills such as writing, creativity, and problem solving.

Existing tests, particularly standardized tests developed by test publishers, have used a limited range of item formats. Almost without exception, these tests have used only multiple-choice items. In spite of the objectivity, reliability, validity, and efficiency of multiple-choice items, there are objections to the reliance on one type of item, and, more generally, to the seeming overemphasis on paper-and-pencil tests. Although performance measures are increasingly being used (for example, on vocational proficiency tests), exploration of alternative test item formats should be encouraged.

The methods of reporting and interpreting test scores have also been somewhat limited. Traditionally, most tests have been norm-referenced and designed to maximize individual differences. However, in the past decade, the pendulum has started to swing in the other direction. Developments such as mastery testing and competency-based measurement have shown the need for, and value of, content-referenced approaches.

At a more general level, the emphasis on tests designed to compare individuals, and determine who is "best," has been questioned. For example, McClelland (1973) and Tyler (1978) have suggested that the focus of measurement should be on determining each individual's range of competencies rather than comparing all individuals on a common set of measures. It should also be noted that measuring the magnitude of individuals' performance on some dimension is not the only possible approach; for example, measurement models that determine the similarity of individuals to specified groups can also be used (Dawes, 1972).

Availability of Tests.   Another set of problems relate to the availability of tests. Although professional organizations concerned with testing have developed standards for test use (*Standards,* 1974) and codes of ethics (e.g., Ethical Principles of Psychologists, 1981), and although test publishers attempt to control the distribution of their tests, there is no foolproof method for preventing unqualified persons from gaining access to tests. More important, there is no guarantee that unqualified persons will not use tests to make decisions about individuals or evaluate the effectiveness of a program. Control of access to test materials rests primarily with test publishers, however, for the current standards are without legal force or other sanctions. Most publishers do take steps to ensure that only qualified persons can purchase tests; however, a completely effective control mechanism, which does not unduly restrict qualified users, has not yet been developed.

On the other hand, there is no effective way to remove out-of-date and invalid (or unvalidated) tests from the market.[1] Oscar Buros, when instituting the *Mental Measurements Yearbooks,* hoped that publication of critical reviews of tests would expedite the removal of poor tests from the market; this effort, he feels, has not succeeded (Buros, 1968). Ideally, test users would identify the deficiencies of these poor tests and not purchase them, thus making their publication unprofitable and forcing the publisher to revise the test or withdraw it from circulation. Unfortunately, such an ideal has not been realized.

Psychometric Problems

The current status of the science and technology of maximal performance testing has been summarized by Carroll and Horn, who stated, "There is much that is not

---

[1] This problem is not unique to testing. For example, Thurow (1980) states that one of the major problems of American society is terminating unproductive companies and outdated agencies.

known about human abilities, but there is much that is known, and what is known provides a reasonable basis for building a technology of ability assessments" (Carroll & Horn, 1981, p. 1013). Less is known about typical performance measurement, but, as we have seen, even here a technology of testing has been developed. In this section we shall discuss some of the unresolved problems and limitations of psychometric theory and technology.

Factors Influencing Test Performance. An increasingly active area of research is concerned with the effects of environmental, situational, and personal variables on test performance. Must of the interest in this area has developed out of practical concerns such as declining scores on college admissions tests, the effects of coaching, and the effects of test anxiety (particularly on mathematics tests). Other stimuli include the study of person-situation interactions and generalizability theory. Research in these areas has shown that test scores can be influenced by a wide variety of personal and stituational variables. Thus test scores cannot be naively interpreted as precise indices of relatively immutable psychological traits. Rather, when interpreting test scores, either to make practical decisions or as measures of psychological constructs, test users must always consider the possible effects of a variety of factors.

Validity. Since validity is the central concept in testing, any problems in the conceptualization of validity and the design of validation studies will have a significant impact on the value of the information provided by a test. In the discussion of criterion-related validity we mentioned a number of common shortcomings of validity studies: the use of unrepresentative or restricted validation samples, problems in identifying and operationalizing appropriate criterion measures, failure to consider base rates when determining validity, using an inappropriate index of validity, and the failure to consider incremental validity and utility. In addition, test users often fail to consider the situation-specific nature of validity data, and thus employ tests without obtaining validity evidence for their particular situation.

A second type of validity problem is the level of predictive accuracy obtained by present tests. Validity coefficients for predicting academic performance from academic ability tests generally do not exceed .60 (Breland, 1979; Hills, 1971; Lavin, 1965). That is, present methods account for less than half of the criterion variability, certainly far from an optimal level. Predictions of nonacademic outcomes, such as job performance, are no more accurate. Furthermore, this level of predictive accuracy has been essentially constant over the past several decades, even when new measures and analytic techniques have been used.

It might seem that using additional predictors (e.g., personality measures in addition to ability measures) would increase predictive accuracy. However, the results of numerous studies show that although predictions made from a combination of variables are generally more accurate than predictions from single variables, the increase in predictive accuracy is slight, even when using the optimal combination of predictors. Attempts to increase predictive accuracy by using multiple aptitudes batteries, differential prediction strategies, moderator variables, configural scoring, and other more complex methods also have not substantially increased the level of predictive accuracy obtained. Although a high level of predictive accuracy may not always be desirable (see, e.g., Goslin, 1963; Young, 1961; and below), one would hope for a higher level of predictability, especially when tests are used to make decisions about individuals.

A related problem has to do with the application of validity data. Validity data is always based on data from groups. But even when a test is quite valid for a group, many incorrect decisions will be made at the individual level. The implications of this fact vary with one's perspective; certainly they are of greater import when viewed from the perspective of the individual affected. Although the use of decision-making accuracy indices gives accurate data on the number of incorrect decisions made within a group, no method identifies which individuals will be incorrectly classified. This question of fairness to individuals or to groups is also an unresolved issue in the area of test bias.

At a more general level, the concept of validity presents some problems. The concept of validity involves an amalgam of practical and theoretical considerations. Furthermore, since there are various types of validity, some or all of which may be relevant in a particular situation, there can be disagreement as to what type of validity evidence is relevant in a given situation. To illustrate, some authors claim that content validity is essential for measures used to select among job applicants; that is, any test used to select applicants should measure the skills needed on the job. Other authors make a distinction between the content validity of a test and its job relatedness. Still others claim that if a test predicts job or training outcomes, content validity is unnecessary.

There also are people who claim all other types of validity are but subcategories of construct validity. In a sense this is true since the fundamental question about any test is what skill or characteristic it measures; however, this viewpoint skirts the issue of determining the effectiveness of a test for making specific types of decisions.

Setting Standards. The developing emphasis on content-referenced tests and their use to establish mastery, competency, and proficiency has spawned another issue—setting passing scores. All of these tests require establishment of a minimum passing score; the question is how and where to set this score. Glass (1978) has argued that any such standards are, of necessity, arbitrary. If one uses the term "arbitrary" in a very broad sense, this is undoubtedly true. But this does not mean that the standards are pulled out of thin air; rather it should mean that they are based on the best available evidence. Yet there is no completely objective way to set standards; all, to a greater or lesser degree, involve some degree of subjective judgment.

The use of content-referenced scores also raises psychometric issues. For example, how does one determine the reliability of content-referenced scores? What item analysis procedures should be used to select items? How can the validity of these tests be established? For many of these questions, procedures derived from classical test theory are of limited applicability due to the limited variability of scores. Thus alternative statistical methods need to be developed, ones that are more appropriate for content-referenced tests. As yet, there is no universal agreement on acceptable statistical procedures, although many methods have been proposed.

The Model.   The discussion of setting standards pointed out another issue: The usual test theory model may not be appropriate for all types of tests. The classical model is an individual differences model. When the purpose of testing is to differentiate between individuals, the model works well; for other problems, such as determining mastery or competency, the model is of less value. Thus other models and statistical methods are being developed.

Two models seem to hold promise for resolving some unsettled problems. One is the item characteristics curve, or latent trait, approach. This model, you will recall, allows for independent determination of item parameters and ability levels. Thus it overcomes many of the problems of both norm-referenced and content-referenced testing; however, one has to make certain assumptions that some people find too restrictive or unrealistic. The other approach is generalizability theory. This model is particularly useful in alerting test developers and users to the variety of dimensions over which test scores vary and provides methods for evaluating the extent of variability.

A common element in many of the newer approaches is their higher level of statistical complexity. Although the use of these approaches in test development and analysis may produce more accurate test scores, it widens the gap between test developers and psychometricians on the one hand and test users on the other. What is crucially needed are ways of translating the meaning and implications of these newer approaches into language that is understandable to the typical test user.

Social Consequences of Testing.

Whereas psychologists and test developers are concerned with improving the technical quality of tests, test users and test takers are more concerned with the practical and social consequences of using tests as decision-making aids. This is not to imply that the test developers are unconcerned with the consequences of testing; on the contrary, in recent years a significant portion of the professional literature and convention time has been devoted to these issues. The concern is also shown by the number of articles in the popular press, actions by the legislative and executive branches of government, and the number of court cases involving testing.

To illustrate, consider the use of tests in selecting students for college, graduate schools, or professional schools, or in hiring workers. Although tests are fairer and more accurate indices of ability than other methods often used as selection devices (e.g., skin color, wealth, social or political influence), they can perpetuate certain undesirable practices and attitudes. For example, a biased test may limit opportunities or result in the disqualification of a disproportionate number of members of certain minority groups. Moreover, the use of tests as selection devices may promote the belief that only qualities that can be tested are important or may appear to limit applicants' ability to present a case for themselves. Thus, as

Messick (1980b) and others have pointed out, test users must always be concerned with two questions: How accurately the test measures (its validity) and how the test will be used. Failure to consider both of these questions can result in improper test use.

In this section we shall consider some of the pervasive issues arising out of the use of tests. Although issues discussed do not exhaust the social concerns about testing, they will give a flavor of the types of social and political issues surrounding the use of tests.

Testing in Education.   Testing plays a central role in education. Tests are used to assign grades, to determine eligibility for promotion or graduation, to plan instruction, to evaluate instructors and curricula, to select students for higher education, to place students in courses, to determine eligibility for special programs, and for a variety of other purposes. Although there has been little debate over the role of teacher-built tests, there have been numerous criticisms of the use of standardized ability and achievement tests, particularly when they are used to establish minimum competency, to select students for higher education, and to place students in special education classes. This criticism has become so intense that several professional education associations have advocated a moratorium on the use of standardized tests in the schools.

One way to clarify the role of testing in education is to consider the consequences of using and not using tests in education. For example, Ebel (1964) has identified four consequences that critics of testing have implied might result from educational testing programs. First, testing may place on the child a stamp of intellectual status—whether superior, mediocre, or inferior—and influence self-esteem, decrease motivation (if scores are low), and consequently help determine adult social status. Second, testing may lead to a narrow conception of ability or to the pursuit of a single goal, thus reducing the diversity of talent in society. Third, testing may place test publishers in the position of determining educational content. And, fourth, testing may encourage inflexible, impersonal, and mechanical methods of appraisal, thereby reducing human freedom.

In his article, Ebel pointed out that these arguments are often based more on opinion than facts and that they are criticisms of how tests are used rather than of the tests themselves. In this and a later article (Ebel, 1981) he also listed some of the harmful consequences of *not* testing. Not testing would handicap communities seeking excellence in their schools by eliminating a source of data that could be used to determine what students had learned and whether schools were attaining their goals. It would handicap minorities and other students by not giving them an opportunity to demonstrate their achievements and abilities. It would limit teachers' ability to reward and motivate their students and would limit students' opportunities to obtain feedback on the progress of their learning. It would limit the information available to researchers and administrators who want to study conditions promoting learning, the effectiveness of instructional methods and curricula, and instructional innovations. It would also provide less evidence to rebut critics who complain about the quality of schools and education.

Ebel suggests several ways that the use of tests could be improved. One is to use tests to identify strengths and weaknesses and thereby help students improve their performance, rather than using tests primarily to identify and label present status. Second, by developing tests in many different areas we would foster the idea that a wide variety of talents are important in our society. Third, we should communicate the results of the tests to the individuals concerned so they can make plans on the basis of solid evidence. And, fourth, we should decrease the emphasis on using tests to make decisions about other people and encourage their use as a basis for helping individuals make their own decisions about their life plans and goals.

These suggestions of Ebel, in many ways, are similar to those people who advocate that test development should be more closely related to cognitive abilities (Estes, 1974; Glaser, 1972, 1981; Resnick, 1976a; Sternberg, 1979) and those (McClelland, 1973; Tyler, 1978) who suggest assessing each individual's range of competencies. They also have much in common with Gordon and Terrell (1981) who argue:

> The proper course of assessment in the present age is not merely to categorize an individual in terms of current functioning, but also to describe the process by which learning facility and disability proceed in a given individual so that it is possible to prescribe developmental treatment if necessary. (p. 1170)

In short, testing, if properly used, provides information that can be used to improve learning and instruction. If we do not test students, we will be deprived of a useful source of information and may have to rely on less adequate assessment methods.

This is not to imply that all testing in education is useful, or even appropriate. There are serious questions involved in using tests to evaluate instructors and curricula. We have also pointed out that the instruments typically used as a basis for evaluating educational programs, standardized norm-referenced tests, may not be the most appropriate method of evaluation (Madaus et al., 1980). However, good tests, properly used, can be a valuable aid. In many cases, good tests are available or can be developed. A more crucial problem is to see that they are used properly.

Test Fairness.   Another area of concern is the fairness of tests to members of certain populations, particularly ethnic minorities and women. Interestingly, the question of fairness has arisen in different contexts for these two groups. With blacks and other ethnic minority groups (such as Spanish-speaking and native Americans) the concern has usually been with the use of ability tests to establish minimum competency, to select students for higher education or workers for jobs, and to place students in special education classes. With women the focus has been on typical performance measurement, particularly vocational interests; however, some attention has been devoted to abilities, especially in mathematics.

As should be obvious from the discussion of bias in previous chapters, fairness (or, conversely, bias) is a complex and confusing issue. One problem is the variety of definitions of bias (see, e.g., Bond, 1981; Cole, 1981; Flaugher, 1978; Jensen, 1980; Shepard, 1981). For example, some definitions of bias result in practices that are fair to individuals but not to groups, whereas others produce the opposite effect. There is also disagreement as to what types of evidence are sufficient to establish bias. For some people differences in average scores between groups are sufficient to establish bias; others would say that different average scores warrant further investigation into possible bias but are not sufficient by themselves to establish bias. Then, too, various types of bias are possible; bias may reside in the test content, in the test administration, in prediction, or in how the test results are interpreted and used.

What, then, can be done to minimize bias? There are various ways to minimize content bias. Representatives of the potentially affected groups can screen and eliminate potentially biased items during the test construction. Although this procedure can eliminate objectionable items, an item that appears to be biased may not actually be. Various empirical methods can be used to detect biased items; examples include different relative difficulty and content-by-race interactions. Alternatively, tests could include only items measuring skills that are so basic that there is agreement that all persons, regardless of sex or gender, should master them. In some situations, different sets of predictors, or different prediction equations, can be used for the various subgroups.

On norm-referenced tests, the nature of the normative data must be considered. Members of minority groups should be proportionately represented in the norm groups. But what if different average scores and distributions are obtained for various groups? Some people advocate interpreting each person's score in comparison with subgroup norms based on people sharing certain salient characteristics; for example, blacks would be compared with blacks and women with women. Although this procedure will indicate how a person compares to others having similar backgrounds, it does not provide comparisons with a wider norm group, comparisons that are often necessary or useful.

The concerns over test bias undoubtedly will be with us for a long time, given the various points of view as to what constitutes a fair test. Even if we could agree on ways to identify and control bias in test content, administration, and prediction, social and political factors may influence how the test results are used. Suppose, for example, that measures deemed unbiased by psychometric criteria were used to select students for law school, but that these measures resulted in a disproportionately low number of members of a particular minority group meeting the criteria for admission. In this case, some minority group applicants not meeting the psychometric criteria would probably be admitted. Thus, psychometric fairness is essential to fair use of tests; it will not resolve all the problems involved in providing equal opportunities to all persons.

Prediction as a Goal. When tests are used as decision-making aids, the goal is the accurate prediction of some socially important external behavior. This is clearly shown by the emphasis on criterion-related validity in the evaluation of tests. Although the goal of obtaining accurate predictions is usually accepted without question, two questions need to be considered. What is being predicted? And, would more accurate predictions be an unmixed blessing?

The first question is the criterion question. Various possible criteria could be used in most situations, but tests are validated against only one, or a few, of the possible criteria. As a consequence, the test will identify those people who have the types of skills needed to perform well on that criterion. If the various possible criteria measures are highly intercorrelated, there is no problem. However, if the various criterion measures are relatively independent, reliance on the test will result in selecting people with certain characteristics (i.e., those measured by the test) and rejecting others with equally desirable, though different, characteristics.

Consider two examples. Admission tests for graduate and professional schools predict academic success better than applied performance. But, the ability to apply what one knows is not necessarily highly correlated with measures of academic achievement, such as grades (Taylor & Barron, 1963). Thus academic ability tests used to select medical students may identify students who do well in medical school courses but not necessarily in medical practice. Or the GRE may select graduate students who will get high grades in graduate courses in psychology but not those who will make the greatest research contributions or become the best clinical or counseling psychologists. The obvious solution is to use multiple predictor tests, which indicate potential success in various areas rather than relying on only certain types of evidence.

A second example has been provided by Astin (1975), who pointed out that college admission tests serve a sorting function; that is, they differentiate between students having different potentials for success under current conditions. The students who score highest on these tests, and perform best in college, are those who already have highly developed academic skills. As an alternative, he suggests that we could (even should) select students who are likely to gain the most from college experience. These will not necessarily be the same persons who score highest on admission tests.

At a broader level, one can also question the practice of using tests (and other measures) to predict future performance. Here our concern is not with the accuracy of prediction but with the idea of prediction. The reason for predicting is, of course, to maximize the fit between the individual and the treatment applied— for example, to ensure that those persons chosen to enter a training program are the ones who are most likely to profit from that program. But if, as some people have argued, the very act of predicting may influence the outcome—that the test scores might be part of a self-fulfilling prophecy—then persons predicted to succeed, by virtue of the prediction, have a higher probability of success. Superficially such predictions would be valid, but in actuality their validity would be spurious and illusory. At a different level, one must be concerned with the possible side effects of excessive reliance on prediction and preselection. Some gross manifestations include possible creation of an elite group based on test-taking ability, loss of motivation and hope, and reward for potential rather than performance.

Access to Information.   We have argued that test takers should always know why they are being tested, what skills and abilities will be tested, and how the scores will be used, as well as being informed of their scores. Yet this is often not the case. Test takers sometimes are asked (or required) to take tests without a clear idea of why they are being tested, what will be covered, or how the results will be used. Sometimes test takers are not even informed of their scores; for example, before 1958 SAT scores were only reported to colleges, not to individual test takers. Even when test takers receive their scores, they often do not have a chance to review their performance on individual items. Although restricting access to individual items is sometimes necessary to preserve test security (e.g., on selection tests), many classroom instructors do not return tests to students for review. No wonder students do not look upon tests as facilitating their learning.

In recent years, more information regarding testing practices has been provided to test takers. For example, publishers of college, graduate, and professional school admission tests have provided test takers with booklets describing the nature of the test, including sample tests and items, and giving suggestions for preparing for the test.[2] Colleges have also released more information, such as the weight tests are given in the admission process and the range of scores of successful and unsuccessful applicants. Several test publishers have also developed materials that familiarize potential test takers with testing procedures. All of these clarify how the tests will be used and enable test takers to improve their preparation for the test.

Another development has been the "truth in testing" movement. Here the concern is with giving test takers an opportunity to check the scoring of their test and review their answers. For example, a law has been passed in New York State requiring college and professional school admission testing programs to provide the test items and scoring key to test takers who request them. Although only relatively few test takers have requested this information, its availability has led to the discovery of several errors in the tests. On the other hand, the legislation has also resulted in fewer testing dates and higher testing fees. It has also raised serious concerns about maintaining the quality of the tests, since items that are released to the public cannot be used on further administrations of the test. This legislation has not been in effect long enough to provide the opportunity for an adequate assessment of its impact on testing practices.

Legal Issues. In a society where tests are used to make many important decisions about individuals and where legislation and litigation are a way of life, it is not surprising that all branches of the government have become more involved in testing controversies. Legislative involvement is illustrated by truth-in-testing laws. The involvement of the executive branch is shown by guidelines set by federal agencies (e.g., Equal Employment Opportunity Commission, 1970; EEOC et al., 1978, 1979; U.S. Government Accounting Office, 1978) regarding the use of tests in employment.

Testing issues have also been the basis of litigation in the state and federal courts.[3] Litigation has occurred in various areas including the use of intelligence

---

[2] An excellent example is the *GRE Information Bulletin* (1981). Similar publications are available for most college, graduate, and professional school admission tests.
[3] For reviews see, for example, Bersoff (1981), Lerner (1978, 1981) and *Educational Measurement and the Law* (1978).

tests for placement in special education classes, minimum competency testing, use of tests to select and promote workers, selection of applicants for medical schools, and access to test results and testing materials.

Bersoff (1981) reviewed the relationship between testing and the law and identified three areas of current concern. One is cultural bias, which is best illustrated by challenges to the use of tests for placement in special education programs. An example of a case in this area is *Larry P.* v. *Riles,* which was a challenge to the procedures used to assign students to classes for educationally mentally retarded (EMR) children in California schools. In this case, the California court ruled that intelligence tests unfairly discriminated against minority children and thus should not be used in classifying EMR children. The judge reasoned that unless a test yielded equal means and distributions for all groups and predicted relevant criteria, such as classroom grades, it was discriminatory. Needless to say, some psychologists, including Bersoff, feel that these requirements are psychometrically unsound and prejudge the issue of possible group differences in performance. Interestingly enough, a judge in another case in a different state (*PASE* v. *Hannon*) reached the opposite conclusion, deeming intelligence tests not to be culturally biased.

A second area of litigation involves the content validity of employment tests. Here the first major case was *Griggs* v. *Duke Power Co.* In this case the U.S. Supreme Court ruled that a test could be discriminatory in practice if it had an adverse effect on a minority group (even if the test was not designed to discriminate unfairly) and that all selection devices must measure the knowledge and skills required on the job; that is, tests must be job-related. In effect, the Court was saying that tests of broad skills could not be used unless the skills measured could be shown to be job-related. In another case *(Albermarle Paper Co.* v. *Moody)* the court took a similar stand. However, in *Washington* v. *Davis* the court expanded the decision to include skills necessary for successful completion of a training program, not just skills used on the job. This court also ruled that plaintiffs would have to prove that the intent of testing was to discriminate, not just that discriminatory effects had occurred. Other cases adjudicated by federal and state courts now suggest that other types of validation, such as criterion-related and construct validity, can be used where direct evidence of content validity is not appropriate.

The third area concerns making information about tests more available to test takers. The truth-in-testing legislation is one such example. Other examples include rulings that allow parents to see clinical records used as a basis for placement in educational programs and a decision *(Detroit Edison* v. *NLRB)* that denied the request of a union to obtain copies of a test used for promotion, except under certain restricted conditions.

Bersoff concluded his discussion by stating that although legal scrutiny of psychological testing will continue and although "the legal system has often been misguided and naive in its judgments about testing" (Bersoff, 1981, p. 1055), there are beneficial effects of the involvement of legislatures and courts in testing. This involvement has alerted psychologists, and society in general, to the fact that apparently benign practices may perpetuate discrimination; it has made psychologists aware that they are responsible for their practices and thus must more carefully scrutinize their procedures and recommendations. Moreover, it has shown the need for improved and alternative methods of assessments—ones that more validly describe individual's skills and abilities.

In this section we have attempted to give a flavor of some of the social issues involved in testing. As Novick (1981) has pointed out, there are three groups of participants in the testing process: test producers, test users, and test takers. Each has its own priorities, concerns, and objectives, which are not always congruent. Thus problems can arise out of the conflicts of interest between the groups. These problems can be resolved by placing the interests of one group over the others or, preferably, by developing approaches to assessment that balance the interests of all three groups.

some emerging trends

In each of the previous editions of this book I predicted some emerging trends in psychological and educational testing. To continue this tradition, I shall suggest several trends I see for the 1980s.

One trend will be an increasing tendency to view tests as measures of developed abilities rather than as indicators of relatively unchanging characteristics. Consequently, there will be less emphasis on "aptitudes" and more emphasis on measuring achievement and competencies. Furthermore, since maximal performance tests will be more closely linked with learning and cognitive theories, they will provide more useful diagnostic information rather than just measuring current status. Stated differently, the emphasis will be on the identification of each individual's range of competencies and the use of test information to develop programs to strengthen and broaden these competencies.

A closely related trend will be to integrate testing practices into the instructional process more effectively. Educational tests will be used increasingly for diagnostic purposes, to identify learning difficulties and prescribe appropriate instruction, rather than for selection and sorting. Test scores will be reported more often in ways that have more direct educational usefulness, such as content-referenced interpretations and the use of latent trait scores. Measurement of skills and characteristics related to learning, such as cognitive styles, will be increasingly used. And tests will continue to be used, probably increasingly so, to measure the various outcomes of education and to evaluate curricula and teaching methods.

There will be increasing concern with the effects of variables that influence test performance. Studies will focus on racial and gender bias, as well as factors such as test-taking skills, coaching, and test anxiety. Test developers will try to design tests to minimize these influences and programs to counteract these effects (e.g., test anxiety clinics, test-taking schools) will proliferate.

More information about the nature and uses of tests will be made public. Test publishers will provide more information to test takers on how to prepare to take tests, opportunities to review scores and items will be more common, and test users will more clearly explain their practices to test takers.

More generally, there will be greater concern over the social consequences of testing. Some of this concern may restrict test development and use, as is already exemplified by the increasing legislative and judicial control of testing practices.

Conversely, because test developers and test users will become more aware of the possible (and often unintended) outcomes of testing, testing practices will be more carefully scrutinized and better and fairer techniques developed.

There will be increasing flexibility in testing formats. Although computers have long been used to score and analyze tests, they will increasingly be used as a method of presenting test items. This will allow for new testing formats (such as sequential testing), individualized testing, and use of complex and different forms of items (e.g., ones using computer graphics or computer-stored data bases).

New psychometric models will be developed. The emergence of generalizability theory and latent trait models is already apparent in the literature. For example, at present the use of latent trait models is restricted to a few tests and to research; they will increasingly find their way into day-to-day test use.

Finally, since current procedures are found to be limited, traditional models have proved to be inadequate, and testing practices are being restricted by judicial and legislative actions, alternative methods of assessment will be developed. However, these new methods must be subjected to the same careful evaluation as are current methods and models. Unless they are more valid, fair, and/or efficient, they will not be an improvement over current methods.

a concluding comment

In this book we have tried to accomplish several goals: to present the basic concepts of psychological measurement, to indicate how tests are developed and used, to identify factors that influence test performance and show how these factors operate, and to illustrate the variety of psychological and educational tests. But, more important, we have attempted to develop a critical attitude, so that when you are confronted with the need to select or interpret a test you will approach the task with deliberate caution, carefully weighing the multitude of factors that must be considered. No book can completely prepare you for this task; it can only be developed by continual study of and experience in the development, validation, and use of educational and psychological tests. Thus, this book is but a beginning.

I believe that in many situations tests provide useful information, information that could not be obtained from other sources. I am also not unaware of the consequences that result from the use, both proper and improper, of tests. However, the fact remains that decisions frequently have to be made about individuals. In these circumstances, we should use the best information available. If it can be obtained from test scores, then tests should be used; if some other method provides better information, then tests should not be used. What is important is that we evaluate the effectiveness of the various methods (i.e., sources of information) and look at the consequences of adopting each approach. To proceed in ignorance or to throw out less-than-perfect methods (as tests are) and substitute even less perfect methods is not the answer. The only rational approach is to make informed decisions based on critical evelutions of all options, then apply the selected procedure fairly, objectively, and as humanely as possible.

This view has also been stated by Carroll and Horn (1981), who, when reviewing the current status of ability testing, stated:

We conclude that despite aberrations, false starts, misapplications, and unfortunate crystallizations of methods and interpretations, the differential psychology of cognitive abilities is a precious part of psychological knowledge about human beings. Properly used, this knowledge can do much to improve the human condition. (p. 1019)

In short, although tests are imperfect, and often have been misued, they have important contributions to make.

Finaly, in a discussion that has focused on the methods of educational and psychological testing, it is easy to overlook the most important point: It is not the test that is of prime importance; it is the individual who takes the test. Test scores may influence decisions that will alter the course of the individual's life. Therefore, when using tests, our foremost concern must always be with the effects of the testing on the person. Keeping this fact in mind will be the greatest single deterrent to the misuse of tests.

Suggestions for Further Reading

Allen, M. J., & Yen, W. M. *Introduction to measurement theory*. Monterey, Calif.: Brooks/Cole, 1979. Chapter 10 describes some current issues in measurement theory and newer psychometric models.

Cronbach, L. J. Five decades of public controversy over mental testing. *American Psychologist,* 1975, *30,* 1–14. Reviews the controversies over testing, particularly intelligence testing, between World War I and the 1970s.

Ebel, R. L. The social consequences of educational testing. *College Board Review,* 1964, *52,* 10–15; The social consequences of *not* testing. *New Directions for Testing and Measurement,* 1981, *9,* 31–37. In these two articles Ebel rebuts common criticisms of testing and describes some of the undesirable consequences of not testing.

Educational measurement and the law. Proceedings of the 1977 ETS Invitational Conference. Princeton, N.J.: Educational Testing Service, 1978. A series of articles on the relationship of testing and the law; considers such issues as admission testing, measurement standards, validity, and the difference between psychometric and legal evidence.

Holtzman, W. H. The changing world of mental measurement and its social significance. *American Psychologist,* 1971, *26,* 546–553. Describes a number of innovations in testing that provide more useful information to educational decision makers.

Lerner, B. Tests and standards today: Attacks, counterattacks, and responses. *New Directions for Testing and Mesaurement,* 1979, *3,* 15–31. Reviews and evaluates criticisms and legal rulings on minimal competency testing.

Lerner, B. Representative democracy, "men of zeal," and testing legislation. *American Psychologist,* 1981, *36,* 270–275. Reviews ten opinion surveys and concludes that critics' attitudes toward testing do not reflect the attitudes of the general public and, often, not even the groups they claim to represent.

Novick, M. R., & Ellis, D. D., Jr. Equal opportunity in educational and employment selection. *American Psychologist,* 1977, *32,* 306–320. Reviews major definitions of fairness and concludes that the concept of test fairness should be applied to individuals, not to groups.

Testings: Concepts, policy, practice and research. American Psychologist, 1981, *36*(10). A special issue of *AP* devoted to testing with articles covering the scientific foundations of testing, issues in testing, the practical uses of tests, and the social and scientific context of testing; an excellent introduction to the current status of testing.

Testing and the public interest. Proceedings of the 1976 ETS Invitational Conference. Princeton, N.J.: Educational Testing Service, 1977. A series of articles on the implications of testing practices for public policy decisions.

Tyler, R. W., & Wolf, R. M. (Eds.). *Critical issues in testing*. Berkeley, Calif., McCutchan, 1974. An examination of some major issues in testing, such as testing minority groups, using tests to group students, criterion-referenced tests, evaluating instruction, and testing and privacy.

Appendix A • Areas of the Normal Curve

THE normal curve is frequently used as a model for interpreting test scores. The normal curve model is useful because in a normal distribution there are specifiable relationships between standard (z) scores and the proportion of scores falling in various areas of the distribution. These relationships are shown in the table below, which can be read as follows:

Column A shows z scores in .05 intervals. (Tables with intervals of .01 can be found in many statistics books.) A z score indicates how far a raw score is from the mean in standard deviation units (see equation 3.7). The tabled values are all positive and thus can be used directly for scores above the mean; corresponding scores below the mean can be obtained by using negative z values.

Column B shows the proportion of the scores in the distribution which falls between the mean and the corresponding z score. To illustrate, when $z = 0.50$, approximately 19 percent (.1915) of the scores will fall between the mean and the score $z = 0.50$ and 38 percent (.3830) will fall within ± 0.50 of the mean (.1915 between the mean and $z = +0.50$ and another .1915 between the mean and $z = -0.50$).

Column C shows the proportion of scores falling in the larger portion of the distribution. For scores above the mean (positive z's) this will be the proportion of scores below the tabled z value; for scores below the mean, this will be the proportion above the tabled value. To continue the same example, 69 percent (.6915) of the scores will fall below $z = +0.50$ and, conversely, 69 percent will fall above $z = -0.50$.

Column D shows the proportion of scores between the tabled z score and the nearer end of the distribution. To illustrate, when $z = +0.50$, approximately 31% (.3085 = 1.000 − .6915) of the scores will be higher than $z = +0.50$ and the same proportion will be lower than $z = -0.50$.

The table can also be used to obtain *percentile rank* equivalents for any tabled z score. For scores above the mean, multiply the value in Column C by 100; for scores below the mean multiply Column D by 100. Thus for $z = +0.50$ the percentile rank equivalent is 69 (.6915 × 100) and for $z = -0.50$ the percentile rank equivalent is 31 (.3085 × 100). Percentile rank equivalents are shown in Columns E and F.

Finally, the table can be used to obtain T score equivalents by multiplying the z score by 10 and adding 50 ($T = 50 + 10z$). Thus for $z = +0.50$, the corresponding T score will be 55 and for $z = -0.50$ the corresponding T score will be 45. T score equivalents are shown in Columns G and H.

Areas, percentile ranks, and T scores for values falling between the tabled z scores can be found by interpolation (or by consulting a more detailed table).

The proportion of scores, represented in columns B–D of the table are shown in the accompanying figure. This figure depicts the relationships for z scores falling above the mean; z scores falling below the mean would be shown by the mirror image of this figure.

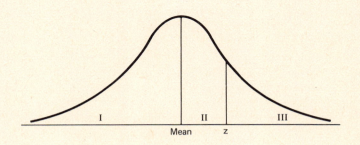

Column B, the proportion of scores between the mean and z, is represented by area II.

Column C, the proportion of scores in the larger portion, is represented by areas I & II.

Column D, the proportion of scores in the smaller portion, is represented by area III.

(A)	(B)	(C)	(D)	(E)	(F)	(G)	(H)
				Percentile Rank		T	
	Area mean to	Area larger	Area smaller				
z	z	portion	portion	$+z$	$-z$	$+z$	$-z$
0.00	.0000	.5000	.5000	50	50	50	50
0.05	.0199	.5199	.4801	52	48		
0.10	.0398	.5398	.4602	54	46	51	49
0.15	.0596	.5596	.4404	56	44		
0.20	.0793	.5793	.4207	58	42	52	48
0.25	.0987	.5987	.4013	60	40		
0.30	.1179	.6179	.3821	62	38	53	47
0.35	.1368	.6368	.3632	64	36		
0.40	.1554	.6554	.3446	66	34	54	46
0.45	.1736	.6736	.3264	67	33		
0.50	.1915	.6915	.3085	69	31	55	45

(A)	(B)	(C)	(D)	(E)	(F)	(G)	(H)
	Area mean to	Area larger	Area smaller	Percentile Rank		T	
z	z	portion	portion	$+z$	$-z$	$+z$	$-z$
0.55	.2088	.7088	.2912	71	29		
0.60	.2257	.7257	.2743	73	27	56	44
0.65	.2422	.7422	.2578	74	26		
0.70	.2580	.7580	.2420	76	24	57	43
0.75	.2734	.7734	.2266	77	23		
0.80	.2881	.7881	.2119	79	21	58	42
0.85	.3023	.8023	.1977	80	20		
0.90	.3159	.8159	.1841	82	18	59	41
0.95	.3289	.8289	.1711	83	17		
1.00	.3413	.8413	.1587	84	16	60	40
1.05	.3531	.8531	.1469	85	15		
1.10	.3643	.8643	.1357	86	14	61	39
1.15	.3749	.8749	.1251	87	13		
1.20	.3849	.8849	.1151	88	12	62	38
1.25	.3944	.8944	.1056	89	11		
1.30	.4032	.9032	.0968	90	10	63	37
1.35	.4115	.9115	.0885	91	9		
1.40	.4192	.9192	.0808	92	8	64	36
1.45	.4265	.9265	.0735	93	7		
1.50	.4332	.9332	.0668	93	7	65	35
1.55	.4394	.9394	.0606	94	6		
1.60	.4452	.9452	.0548	95	5	66	34
1.65	.4505	.9505	.0495	95	5		
1.70	.4554	.9554	.0446	96	4	67	33
1.75	.4599	.9599	.0401	96	4		
1.80	.4641	.9641	.0359	96	4	68	32
1.85	.4678	.9678	.0322	97	3		
1.90	.4713	.9713	.0287	97	3	69	31
1.95	.4744	.9744	.0256	97	3		
2.00	.4772	.9772	.0228	98	2	70	30
2.05	.4798	.9798	.0202	98	2		
2.10	.4821	.9821	.0179	98	2	71	29
2.15	.4842	.9842	.0158	98	2		
2.20	.4861	.9861	.0139	99	1	72	28
2.25	.4878	.9878	.0122	99	1		
2.30	.4893	.9893	.0107	99	1	73	27
2.35	.4906	.9906	.0094	99	1		
2.40	.4918	.9918	.0082	99	1	74	26
2.45	.4929	.9929	.0071	99	1		
2.50	.4938	.9938	.0062	99	1	75	25
2.55	.4946	.9946	.0054	99.5	0.5		
2.60	.4953	.9953	.0047	99.5	0.5	76	24
2.65	.4960	.9960	.0040	99.6	0.4		
2.70	.4965	.9965	.0035	99.6	0.4	77	23
2.75	.4970	.9970	.0030	99.7	0.3		
2.80	.4974	.9974	.0026	99.7	0.3	78	22
2.85	.4978	.9978	.0022	99.8	0.2		

| (A) | (B) | (C) | (D) | (E) | (F) | (G) | (H) |
| | Area mean to | Area larger | Area smaller | Percentile Rank | | T | |
z	z	portion	portion	$+z$	$-z$	$+z$	$-z$
2.90	.4981	.9981	.0019	99.8	0.2	79	21
2.95	.4984	.9984	.0016	99.8	0.2		
3.00	.4987	.9987	.0013	99.9	0.1	80	20

Appendix B • Statistical Symbols

E Error score

f Frequency of a particular score or within a score interval

n Number of observations or scores

r_{xy} (a) Pearson product moment correlation; (b) validity coefficient

p Proportion of responses, scores, or people in a given category

r_{xx} Reliability coefficient

$R_{y.123}$ Multiple correlation coefficient

Σ Sigma (the sum of)

s_{est} Standard error of estimate

s_{meas} Standard error of measurement (also s_m)

s_x Standard deviation

s_x^2 Variance

T (a) T score; (b) True score

X Observed score on variable X

x Deviation score $(X - \overline{X})$

$\overline{X}$ Mean

Y Score on the criterion variable

z Standard score (x/s)

Notes:

1. Scores on variables are in capital letters if expressed in raw score units (e.g., X) and in lower case letters if expressed as deviation scores (e.g., x).
2. Subscripts refer to the variable used to compute the statistic; e.g., s_x is the standard deviation for variable x.
3. When more than one variable is used, variables can be denoted by different letters (x, y) or numbers (1, 2, 3), or by subscripts (x_1, x_2, x_3).

Glossary

ability test   A test that measures current level of knowledge or skill in a particular area.

academic ability test   A test measuring skills (e.g., vocabulary, reading, mathematics) necessary for successful performance in academic settings. See also *scholastic aptitude test.*

achievement test   A test that measures the extent to which a person has acquired certain information or mastered certain skills, usually as the result of specific instruction.

age score   Score expressing performance in terms of the average performance of children of various ages. For example, an age score of 10.6 means that the child obtained the same score as the average child who is 10 years and 6 months old.

alternate forms   See *parallel forms.*

alternate forms reliability   See *coefficient of equivalence.*

alternative-choice item   Any item requiring test takers to select the correct response from a set of given alternatives; for example, multiple-choice, true-false, and matching items. Sometimes called recognition items.

aptitude test   A test designed to predict future learning, or performance on some task. *Aptitude* refers to those characteristics that indicate the ability to learn or develop proficiency, given appropriate training or conditions.

assessment   Any systematic basis for making inferences about characteristics of people, usually based on various sources of evidence; the global process of synthesizing information about individuals in order to understand and describe them better.

attitude scale   A test measuring the predisposition to think, feel, perceive, or believe in a certain manner toward some referent or cognitive object.

base rate   The rate of occurrence of a phenomenon in an unselected population. In selection, the proportion of people in an unselected group, or a group selected using current procedures, who are judged satisfactory.

battery   An integrated set of tests, standardized and normed on the same sample of people, but each measuring a different ability. More loosely, any group of tests administered together.

behavioral assessment   Assessment based on observations of overt behaviors (in contrast to tests or ratings).

behavioral objective   See *objective, instructional*.

bias   Refers to situations where the testing procedures result in a systematic advantage (or disadvantage) to members of some subgroup in comparision to other test takers, with the source of the advantage being irrelevant to the purposes of testing. Bias can be present in the test content, in the administrative procedures, in prediction, and/or in how the test is interpreted and used.

central tendency   The average or typical score in a distribution. Measures include the mean, median, and mode.

checklist   A list of behaviors or reactions used to indicate whether behaviors occurred, how frequently, and/or in what order.

clinical judgment   Combining scores to obtain a description or make a prediction using subjective, intuitive methods.

cluster analysis   Any method for grouping objects, events, or people into categories on the basis of similarity of salient characteristics.

coefficient alpha   A measure of internal consistency; interpreted as the expected correlation between tests of the same length randomly drawn from the same domain.

coefficient of equivalence   A measure of reliability obtained by correlating scores on two parallel forms of a test. Also called *alternate forms reliability, equivalent forms reliability,* and *parallel forms reliability*.

coefficient of stability   A measure of reliability obtained by correlating scores on two administrations of the same measure that are separated in time. Also called *test-retest reliability*.

coefficient of stability and equivalence   A measure of reliability obtained by correlating scores on two forms of a test administered at different times. Also called *coefficient of equivalence and stability*.

cognitive style   A characteristic way of approaching problems or other situations involving cognitive material—for example, reflection-impulsivity or field independence-field dependence.

comparable scores   Scores on two tests that represent the same relative position in a common norm group. Scores are considered to be *equivalent* if, in addition to being comparable, the test items sample the same domain(s).

completion item   An item consisting of a statement with one or more words or phrases omitted; the test taker supplies the missing words or phrases.

composite score   A score obtained by combining two or more other scores (i.e., scores on several items, subtests, scales, tests, or measures). The individual scores making up the composite may or may not be differentially weighted.

concurrent validity   The degree of relationship (usually the correlation) between test scores and a criterion measure when both measures are collected at the same point in time; a type of criterion-related validity.

confidence interval   The range within which scores (or statistics) will fall, at a given probability level, taking into account the error involved in the measurement. The two extreme values of the confidence interval are called the *confidence limits*.

congruent validity   The correlation between scores on a test and scores on another test that is an established measure of the same construct.

consistency   A general term used synonymously with reliability.

construct   A label used to describe a related set of characteristics of an individual; a label applied to a dimension along which individuals vary.

construct validity   The degree to which a test measures the psychological trait or characteristic it is designed to measure.

content validity   The degree to which items on a test representatively sample the underlying content/skills domain or instructional objectives.

content-referenced scores   Scores that are interpreted in comparison with a predetermined performance standard or as degree of mastery of a defined domain (e.g., percent correct and mastery scores). Also called *criterion-referenced scores*.

content-referenced test   A test that measures the degree of command of a specified content/skills domain or a list of instructional objectives, with scores interpreted by comparison to a performance standard. Also called a *criterion-referenced test*.

convergent validity   The degree to which two measures of the same construct, or two methods of measuring the same construct, produce similar results (i.e., are positively intercorrelated).

conversion table   An ordered table showing equivalent derived scores for each raw score in a distribution. A conversion table may include more than one type of derived score or derived scores for more than one norm group.

correction for attenuation   A statistical correction for the correlation between two measures taking into account the unreliability of measures, thus giving the hypothetical correlation between error-free measures of the two variables.

correction for guessing   A deduction from the number correct score that is equivalent to the number of points presumably gained by guessing.

correlation coefficient   An index of the degree of relationship between two sets of measures obtained from the same sample of individuals. The value can range from $+1.00$ to -1.00, with the absolute value indicating the degree of relationship (the higher the correlation, the closer the relationship) and the sign indicating the direction the variables are scored. Unless otherwise indicated, refers to the Pearson product-moment correlation coefficient (r).

criterion   The measure or standard against which a test is evaluated; the external variable a test is designed to predict. A *criterion measure* is a variable used to measure the (conceptual) criterion.

criterion contamination   Refers to the situation where assignment of criterion scores is influenced by knowledge of predictor scores.

criterion-referenced scores   See *content-referenced scores*.

criterion-referenced test   See *content-referenced test*.

criterion-related validity   The degree to which test scores are related to, or predict, scores on an external measure (the criterion).

cross-validation   Checking the validity of a predictor-criterion relationship by repeating the validation process on another sample similar to the original validation sample, preferably another sample randomly drawn from the same population.

culture-fair test   A test containing only items that do not produce a systematic advantage for one or more cultural groups, excluding items particular to a given culture, or otherwise controlling critical, culturally related variables.

cutting score   The test score that divides a group into two or more categories. In selection, the score that differentiates those predicted to succeed from those predicted to fail; in placement, scores that differentiate between treatment groups; on mastery tests, the minimum passing score.

decile   Any of the nine score points that divide a distribution into ten equal parts, each containing 10 percent of the scores. The first decile is the tenth percentile rank, the lowest 10 percent of scores is called the first *decile rank,* and so on.

decision-making accuracy   An index of criterion-related validity that indicates the proportion of correct decisions that would be made using the test scores as predictors. Indices are the *total hit rate* and the *positive hit rate* (see *hit rate*).

derived scores   See *transformed scores.*

developmental scales   Scales or tests that compare a test taker to the average or typical child at various ages.

deviation IQ   See *intelligence quotient.*

deviation score   A score expressed in terms of the number of raw score points from the mean; deviation score (x) = raw score $-$ mean.

diagnostic test   A test designed to identify a test taker's strengths and weaknesses, or level of proficiency in component areas of a skill, and used as a basis for prescribing appropriate remedial treatment.

difference score   A score derived by computing the difference between scores on two tests. When the scores are from two administrations of the same test, such as pretests and posttests, it is called a *change score.*

differential prediction   Using different combinations of variables to predict different outcomes (criteria) or to predict in different populations.

differential weighting   Assigning different weights to each element in a composite, either on the basis of their perceived importance or by their contribution to predictive accuracy.

difficulty   See *item difficulty.*

discriminant validity   Lack of relationship between measures of different traits or characteristics.

discrimination   See *item discrimination.*

dissimulation   Faking or other deliberate attempts to respond to items so as to present a biased or distorted picture.

distracter   An incorrect response on an alternative-choice item.

distribution   See *frequency distribution.*

domain   The hypothetical pool of all possible items measuring the characteristic of interest; the area of knowledge, skill, or behavior measured by a test.

empirical keying   A method of keying scales on self-report inventories where items are selected on the basis of their observed relationship with some external criterion. Also called criterion or external keying.

equivalent forms   See *parallel forms*.

equivalent forms reliability   See *coefficient of equivalence*.

equivalent scores   See *comparable scores*.

error   Any factor or variable that reduces the accuracy or validity of measurement. *Systematic errors* are produced by variables that have constant effects but are irrelevant to the purpose of the measurement; *random errors* are influences of variables that produce differences in scores on various measurements of the same trait.

error of measurement   See *measurement error*.

essay item   An item requiring test takers to write a narrative response to a question or problem situation.

evaluation   Judgment of the quality, value, or worth of some performance or program. Evaluations are usually based on various sources of evidence, including test scores.

expectancy table   A table showing the proportion (or percentage) of people at each predictor score level who obtain each outcome or criterion score; a type of outcome-referenced score.

face validity   Whether the test, on casual inspection, appears to measure the trait or characteristic it is said to measure.

factor analysis   A statistical method for determining how many factors are needed to account for the intercorrelations between a set of variables. A *factor* is a combination of variables that are intercorrelated and thus measure the same characteristic.

forced-choice item   An item, on a self-report inventory or rating scale, requiring a choice between two or more descriptors or persons.

formative evaluation   Evaluations obtained during the process of instruction (or other treatment) and used to assess learning progress or the effectiveness of instructional methods and materials.

free response item   Any item requiring test takers to construct or supply a response, such as short-answer, completion, definition, and essay items. Also called recall or supply items.

frequency distribution   An ordered table showing the number of people who obtain each score or range of scores.

generalizability   The degree to which scores are consistent or have the same meaning when administered under different conditions, in different populations, or in different situations.

grade-equivalent scores   Scores that report performance by comparing an individual to the typical or average child at various grade levels. Also called *grade-placement scores*.

group test   A test that can be administered to more than one person at a time (usually, but not necessarily, a paper-and-pencil test).

hit rate An index of decision-making accuracy. The *total hit rate* is the ratio of correct decisions to total decisions; the *positive hit rate* is the proportion of selected applicants deemed successful.

homogeneity The degree to which all items on a test measure the same trait or characteristic; operationally, a test whose items are all positively intercorrelated.

homogeneous keying A method of keying scales on self-report inventories in which items are selected on the basis of their intercorrelations. Also called internal keying.

incremental validity The increase in validity obtained by the addition of another predictor to a set of predictors.

intelligence quotient (IQ) An index of an individual's performance on an intelligence test relative to others of the same age. *Deviation IQs* are standard scores with a mean of 100 and a standard deviation of 15 or 16 points at each age level. *Ratio IQs,* now obsolete, are ratios of mental age to chronological age times 100.

intelligence test A test measuring those developed abilities considered to be a sign of intelligence. *Intelligence* is the ability to perform certain types of tasks considered to reflect intellectual ability in a given culture.

interest inventory A self-report inventory used to measure interests in specific occupations and/or broad vocational areas.

internal consistency A type of reliability that indicates whether the items comprising a test (or subtest or scale) are positively intercorrelated and thus all measure the same trait or characteristic; the degree to which a test measures only one characteristic. Usual indices are coefficient alpha and Kuder-Richardson formula 20.

interval scale A measurement scale having equal-size units.

inventory A collection of a large number of self-descriptive statements, or other stimuli, to which test takers respond by indicating whether the statement describes them or by otherwise endorsing items. Usually scores are obtained for several scales, each measuring a different characteristic.

ipsative measurement Broadly, any method based on intraindividual comparisons of the strengths of various traits; more specifically, measurement procedures in which the sum of scores over all scales is constant for all test takers.

item A single question or exercise on a test.

item analysis A statistical procedure used to determine the quality of individual test items. Usually includes analyses of difficulty, discrimination, and distracters.

item bank A collection of test items measuring a specified domain of knowledge, skills, of instructional objectives. Items can be sampled from the bank to construct tests to meet the specifications of individual test users.

item difficulty The percent or proportion of test takers in a specified group who answer an item correctly.

item discrimination The degree to which a test item differentiates between people having various levels of ability or knowledge of the material tested. When an external criterion is used as a basis for differentiating ability levels it is called *item validity.*

key, scoring   A list of correct responses, acceptable variations, and scoring weights for individual items. Test takers' responses are compared to the key, using specified procedures, to determine their raw scores.

Kuder-Richardson formula 20 (K-R 20)   A measure of internal consistency reliability applicable to dichotomously scored items.

latent trait   The hypothetical trait or dimension underlying test performance. By using specified statistical models, one can derive *latent trait scores,* which indicate the test taker's position on this continuum.

Likert scale   A type of attitude scale in which test takers indicate their degree of agreement with a set of statements measuring the attitude.

linear transformation   Any transformation of scores from one scale to another such that the plot of the relationship between the two sets of scores will be a straight line.

local norms   Norms that show the distribution of performance within a particular, specified local population such as a particular class, school, or city.

logical keying   A method of keying scales on self-report inventories by means of which items are selected on the basis of their rational relationship to the characteristic measured. Also called a priori and intuitive keying.

manual, test   A booklet providing information about the development, administration, scoring, reliability, validity, interpretation, and use of a test.

mastery score   The minimum passing score on a mastery test; the lowest score a person can obtain and still be classified as having mastered the material tested.

mastery test   A test that determines the extent to which a test taker has command of certain material or can perform a particular skill, with scores interpreted with reference to a predetermined standard of proficiency. Usually designed to measure attainment of specified instructional objectives.

matching item   An item requiring the test taker to associate elements on one list with the corresponding elements on a second list.

maximal performance test   A test measuring a test taker's best possible level of performance—for example, achievement, ability, and aptitude tests.

mean   The arithmetic average of a set of scores.

measurement   (a) The assignment of numbers to objects or events according to specified rules and operations. (b) The result (i.e., quantitative value assigned) of the measurement process.

measurement errors   Inconsistencies in scores from occasion to occasion attributable to the effects of variables operating in a nonsystematic (i.e., random) manner; broadly, both random and systematic errors.

median   The score that divides an ordered distribution into upper and lower halves; the 50th percentile rank.

mental age   A score on a mental ability test obtained by comparing an individual's performance with that of average children at various ages.

Mental Measurements Yearbook A periodically published compilation of published tests that includes basic information about each test, a bibliography of references to the test, critical reviews of tests, and other test-related information.

method variance Positive intercorrelations between measures of different characteristics obtained when different traits are measured by similar methods.

minimum competency test A test measuring whether test takers have attained a minimal level of proficiency in a given academic area. Used to establish eligibility for high school graduation or promotion to the next higher grade level.

modal-age grade norms Norms based on the performance of students who are of the typical age for their grade level.

mode The score that occurs most frequently in a distribution. If the two highest scores have approximately equal frequencies and are separated by one or more scores of lower frequency, the distribution is *bimodal*.

moderator variable A variable that identifies subgroups of people who are differentially predictable.

multilevel test An achievement or ability test having separate forms for various age or grade levels.

multiple aptitude test battery An integrated series of aptitude tests, each of which measures a different ability, but normed on the same population; also called *multiaptitude test*. If the aptitudes have been defined by factor analysis, it is called a *multifactor test battery*.

multiple correlation The correlation between a set of predictors, considered jointly (i.e., as a composite), and a single variable. The degree of relationship is indicated by the *multiple correlation coefficient (R)*.

multiple cutoff A noncompensatory method of combining scores where persons scoring above the cutting score on all variables are accepted and all others are rejected. When the predictor variables are administered sequentially, the method is called *successive hurdles*.

multiple regression A compensatory model for combining scores to predict scores on another variable where in each predictor variable is weighted in proportion to its contribution to prediction accuracy. The equation showing the weights assigned to each predictor variable is the *multiple regression equation*.

multiple-choice item An item where test takers select, from a list of given alternatives, the response that best completes a statement or answers a question.

norm group A representative sample of a specified population used as the basis for interpretation of individual test scores.

normal distribution The (hypothetical) symmetric, bell-shaped distribution of scores used as a model for many scoring systems and test statistics.

normal percentile chart A score profile in which scores are reported as percentile ranks, but the score dimension is scaled to correspond to a standard score scale.

normalized standard scores Standard scores that are derived so as to fall into a normal distribution.

normative data (norms) A set of scores that represent the distribution of test performance in a particular norm group and used as a basis for the interpretation of individual scores.

norm-referenced scores Scores that report performance in terms of the test taker's relative position in a specified norm group; for example, percentile ranks, standard scores, deviation IQs.

norm-referenced test A test designed to differentiate between persons having varying degrees of the ability or characteristic measured and interpreted by comparing the test taker's performance with that of others in a norm group.

objective, instructional A statement of an intended outcome of instruction. If an objective specifies the knowledge or skill to be demonstrated, the conditions under which the performance will be demonstrated, and the minimal level of proficiency, it is called a *behavioral objective*.

objective scoring Scoring using procedures that ensure high agreement between trained scorers. Objective scoring requires unambiguous recording of responses, a scoring key, and specification of procedures for comparing responses to the key to obtain scores.

outcome-referenced scores Scores interpreted in terms of the expected level of performance on some other variable or measure, for example, an expectancy table.

parallel forms Two or more forms of a test that cover the same domain, use the same item format(s), and are of equal difficulty. If the forms also have similar means, variability, and distributions they are called *equivalent forms*.

parallel forms reliability See *coefficient of equivalence*.

passing score See *cutting score*.

percent correct score A score expressing performance in terms of the percent of the maximal number of points attained.

percentile The 99 points on the score scale that divide the distribution into 100 segments, each containing the same number of scores. The point on the score scale corresponding to a given percentile rank is called the *percentile point*.

percentile rank The test taker's relative standing, in percentage terms, within a norm group; the percent of scores in a norm group that are equal to or lower than a given score.

performance test A test requiring some physical or psychomotor response—for example, manual dexterity tests and physical skills tests.

personality inventory An inventory measuring personality characteristics.

placement The process of assigning individuals to one of several alternative treatments (e.g., courses, jobs) with each person being assigned to one treatment. Tests used to aid in placement decisions are called *placement tests*.

point scale Any test or scale where the score is derived by summing the points obtained on various items.

power test A test designed to determine the test taker's maximum level of performance in some area. Power tests have items of varying levels of difficulty and are administered with no time limit, or a very liberal one.

practice effect   The influence of previous experience with the same or similar tests on scores on a later test administration; the increase in scores resulting from such practice.

predictive validity   The relationship, usually expressed as a correlation, between scores on a predictor test and a criterion measure collected at a later time; a type of criterion-related validity.

pretest   (a) A test given prior to instruction to assess students' mastery of prerequisite material and/or knowledge of the material to be taught. (b) An experimental form of a test used to collect item analysis data.

proficiency test   A test that measures whether test takers have attained a specified minimal level of competency in a given area or on a specified skill.

profile   A graphic presentation of scores on several tests, subtests, or scales, with all scores reported on the same scoring scale and compared to the same norm group.

projective methods   A class of tests in which test takers are presented with ambiguous stimuli or tasks and are asked to interpret or structure the stimuli.

random error   See *error* or *measurement error*.

random sample   See *sample*.

range, score   The difference between the highest and lowest score in a distribution.

rating scale   A series of descriptive statements, behavioral categories, or other sitmuli that an observer uses to indicate the degree of a characteristic a person possesses.

ratio IQ   See *intelligence quotient*.

raw score   The score derived directly from scoring the test responses—for example, number correct, number of errors, or time to completion.

readiness test   A test that measures whether an individual has the prerequisite skills necessary to learn or profit from instruction in an area.

regression equation   An equation showing the relative weights assigned to each independent variable when predicting some criterion. Weights are assigned so as to minimize the squared errors of prediction.

reliability   How consistently a test measures over time, occasions, or samples of items; the degree to which test scores are influenced by measurement errors. Indices include reliability coefficients and the standard error of measurement.

reliability coefficient   A quantitative index of the degree of reliability derived by correlating scores on various forms of a test, correlating scores on repeated administrations of a test, or from the intercorrelations of the items comprising a test.

representative sample   See *sample*.

response set   A content-dependent response bias that occurs when test takers respond to items so as to present a particular, distorted picture of themselves; examples include social desirability, faking good, and faking bad.

response style   A content-independent but systematic response tendency used when a test taker is unsure of the appropriate response—for example, always selecting alternative *c* on a multiple-choice test when uncertain, or the error of central tendency in ratings.

restriction of range The situation where, because of the nature of the sample studied, the variability of scores on one or both variables is lowered. Has the effect of reducing the magnitude of the correlation between the variables.

sample A subset of observations (e.g., of items, people, or scores) drawn from a larger population. If each observation has an equal opportunity chance of being selected, the sampling is *random;* if observations are selected so as to obtain proportional representation in terms of certain salient dimensions, the sampling is stratified or *representative.*

scale (a) A set of items, not necessarily administered as a separate subsection of a test, measuring a particular trait or characteristic. (b) A continuum, having quantitative units, that reflects varying levels of a trait or characteristic.

scholastic aptitude test A test that measures those abilities that are predictive of success in academic settings.

score The quantitative value assigned to an individual's performance on a test.

score band The range of scores within which an individual's score falls, taking into account the error of measurement. Usually the observed score plus or minus some multiple of the standard error of measurement.

scoring key See *key, scoring.*

selection The process of choosing the most-qualified persons from a pool of applicants where not all applicants can be chosen.

selection efficiency The degree to which a predictor correctly identifies those people who will be successful on some criterion task.

selection ratio The proportion of people selected using a particular method and cutting score; the number selected divided by the number of applicants.

self-report method In general, any method in which an individual provides a report of his or her own behavior or reactions; more specifically, paper-and-pencil typical performance measures, such as inventories, where the test takers are presented with a series of self-descriptive statements and endorse those that they think describe them.

sequential test A test that presents individual items, or subsets of items, in such a manner that responses to previous items determine which of several possible items are administered next. Also called a *tailored test.*

short-answer item An item requiring test takers to respond in a word, phrase, or sentence or two; examples include definition, identification, translation, and completion items.

situational method A testing procedure that provides an opportunity for the test taker's behavior to be observed or measured in a simulated or real-life situation.

skewed distribution A unimodal distribution that is asymmetric about the mean. If scores cluster at the high end and tail off toward the low end, the distribution is *negatively skewed;* if scores cluster at the low end and tail off toward the high end, the distribution is *positively skewed.*

social desirability   A response set in which test takers respond to items on the basis of what is considered desirable behavior by most other people.

Spearman-Brown formula   A formula for estimating the effects on reliability when the number of items is increased or decreased.

speed test   A test measuring differences in test takers' rate of responding. Usually consists of very simple items administered with a highly restrictive time limit.

split-half reliability coefficient   A measure of reliability obtained by correlating scores on two randomly selected or otherwise equivalent sections of a single test, then correcting the correlation between halves by the Spearman-Brown formula.

standard deviation   A measure of variability, expressed in raw score terms, of the dispersion of test scores around the mean.

standardization   The development of a standard set of procedures for selecting items for a test, administering the test, and scoring the test. Some definitions also require provision of normative data.

standardized test   A test having specified content, prescribed procedures for administration and scoring, and normative data or other procedures for interpreting scores.

standard error of estimate   In regression analysis, an index of the magnitude of prediction errors; the standard deviation of the distribution of prediction errors (prediction error is the difference between actual and predicted criterion scores).

standard error of measurement   An index of the amount of measurement error in test scores; theoretically, the standard deviation of the distribution of observed scores around an individual's true score. Used to estimate the range in which the true score will fall or the amount of change expected on retesting.

standard score   A type of transformed score that reports performance in terms of the number of standard deviation units the raw score is from the mean—for example, z scores and T scores.

Standards for Educational and Psychological Testing   A publication of three national professional organizations concerned with testing (the American Psychological Association, the American Educational Research Association, and the National Council on Measurement in Education) which gives standards and guidelines for the development, evaluation, interpretation, communication of information, and uses of tests and other assessment instruments.

stanine   A nine-step standard score system with mean of 5 points and standard deviation of 2 points, with all steps (except the extremes) being 0.5 standard deviation wide.

subtest   A set of items administered and scored as a distinct portion of a test.

summative evaluation   Evaluations obtained at the end of instruction to determine whether students have mastered the objectives and whether instruction has been effective.

survey test   A test providing an overall measure of achievement in an area, usually reporting only one total score.

systematic error   See *error*.

T *score*   A standard score scale with a mean of 50 and a standard deviation of 10.

test   A systematic procedure for measuring a sample of behavior.

test bias   See *bias*.

test plan   A specification of the proposed coverage of a test indicating content and cognitive skills to be included, and the relative emphasis on each subcategory. May also include specification of item formats and sample items.

test user   Anyone who chooses tests, interprets scores, or makes decisions based on test scores.

test-retest reliability   See *coefficient of stability*.

trait   A hypothetical characteristic (e.g., intelligence, dominance) on which people vary and that is relatively stable over time and situations; operationally, a cluster of intercorrelated behaviors or reactions; a category for the orderly description of behavior.

transformed scores   Scores expressed on scales other than raw scores and derived by some specified statistical operation—for example, percentile ranks, standard scores. Also called *derived scores*.

true score   The score an individual would obtain if a test were perfectly reliable; the score that would be obtained if the individual took all possible items in a domain; a person's average score over a large number of equivalent forms of a test.

true-false item   A statement that the test takers judge as being either correct or incorrect.

typical performance measure   Any method of measuring a test taker's usual or habitual behaviors, reactions, feelings, or attitudes; examples include personality inventories, interest inventories, and attitude scales.

typology   A system for describing personality that categorizes individuals into mutually exclusive, qualitatively different categories.

unidimensional test   A test that measures one, and only one, characteristic; operationally, a test in which all items are drawn from the same domain and are positively intercorrelated.

unobtrusive measure   Any measure that can be obtained nonreactively—that is, in a manner that does not intrude upon or affect performance.

utility   The usefulness of a test as determined from a costs/benefits analysis.

validity   The degree to which a test measures the characteristic it is designed to measure or predicts some outside variable; the proportion of observed score variance that is relevant to the purpose of the testing. See also *content validity, construct validity, criterion-related validity*.

validity coefficient   The correlation between scores on a predictor variable and a criterion measure.

validity generalization   The extent to which scores can be interpreted similarly, or inferences made from test scores apply, to other situations, populations, or methods of determining validity.

validity scales Special scales on self-report inventories designed to detect response sets and styles.

variability How widely scores in a distribution are scattered or dispersed. Usually measured by the standard deviation or variance.

variance An index of the total amount of variability in a set of test scores; the square of the standard deviation.

z score A type of standard score that expresses performance in terms of the number of standard deviations from the mean; computationally, the raw score minus the mean divided by the standard deviation.

Bibliography

Ahmann, J. S., & Glock, M. D. *Evaluating pupil growth* (5th ed.). Boston: Allyn and Bacon, 1975.

Aiken, L. R. Attitude measurement and research. *New Directions for Testing and Measurement,* 1980, *7,* 1–24.

Airasian, P. W. A perspective on the uses and misuses of standardized achievement tests. *NCME Measurement in Education,* 1979, *10*(3).

Alderman, D., & Powers, D. E. *The effects of special preparation on SAT-Verbal scores.* Princeton, N.J.: Educational Testing Service, 1979.

Allen, M. J., & Yen, W. M. *Introduction to measurement theory.* Monterey, Calif.: Brooks/Cole, 1979.

Allport, G. W. *Becoming.* New Haven: Yale University Press, 1955.

Allport, G. W. Traits revisited. *American Psychologist,* 1966, *21,* 1–10.

Allport, G. W., & Odbert, H. S. Trait-names: A psycholexical study. *Psychological Monographs,* 1936, *47*(1).

American Association on Mental Deficiency. *Adaptive behavior scale: Manual.* Washington, D.C.: American Association on Mental Deficiency, 1974.

American College Testing Program. *Assessing students on the way to college* (2 vols.). Iowa City: American College Testing Program, 1972.

Ames, L. B., Metraux, R. W., Rodell, J. L., & Walker, R. N. *Rorschach responses in old age.* New York: Brunner/Mazel, 1973.

Ames, L. B., Metraux, R. W., Rodell, J. L., & Walker, R. N. *Child Rorschach responses.* New York: Brunner/Mazel, 1974.

Ames, L. B., Metraux, R. W., & Walker, R. N. *Adolescent Rorschach responses.* New York: Brunner/Mazel, 1971.

Anastasi, A. Heredity, environment and the question "How?" *Psychological Review,* 1958, *65,* 197–208.

Anastasi, A. On the formation of psychological traits. *American Psychologist,* 1970, *25,* 899–910.

Anastasi, A. *Common fallacies about heredity, environment, and human behavior.* Research Report No. 58. Iowa City: American College Testing Program, 1973.

Anastasi, A. *Psychological testing* (4th ed.). New York: Macmillan, 1976.

Anastasi, A. Abilities and the measurement of achievement. *New Directions for Testing and Measurement,* 1980, *5,* 1–10.

Anastasi, A. *Psychological testing* (5th ed.). New York: Macmillan, 1982.

Anderson, J. E. The prediction of terminal intelligence from infant and preschool tests. *Thirty-ninth Yearbook, National Society for the Study of Education,* 1940, Part I, 385–403.

Anderson, N. H. Scales and statistics: Parametric and nonparametric. *Psychological Bulletin,* 1961, *58,* 305–316.

Anderson, R. C. How to construct achievement tests to assess comprehension. *Review of Educational Research,* 1972, *42,* 145–170.

Anderson, S. B., & Ball, S. *The profession and practice of program evaluation.* San Francisco: Jossey-Bass, 1978.

Angoff, W. H. How we calibrate College Board scores. *College Board Review,* 1968, *68,* 11–14.

Angoff, W. H. Scales, norms, and equivalent scores. In R. L. Thorndike (Ed.), *Educational measurement* (2d ed.). Washington, D.C.: American Council on Education, 1971. (a)

Angoff, W. H. (Ed.) *The College Board Admissions Testing Program.* New York: College Entrance Examination Board, 1971. (b)

Angoff, W. H. Criterion-referencing, norm-referencing, and the SAT. *College Board Review,* 1974, *92,* 2–5, 21.

Angoff, W. H., & Ford, S. F. Item-race interaction on a test of scholastic aptitude. *Journal of Educational Measurement,* 1973, *10,* 95–106.

Arieti, S. *Creativity: The magic synthesis.* New York: Basic Books, 1976.

Aronow, E., & Reznikoff, M. *Rorschach content interpretation.* New York: Grune & Stratton, 1976.

Arvey, R. D. Unfair discrimination in the employment interview: Legal and psychological aspects. *Psychological Bulletin,* 1979, *86,* 736–765.

Astin, A. V. Standards of measurement. *Scientific American,* June 1968, 50–52.

Astin, A. W. Criterion-centered research. *Educational and Psychological Measurement,* 1964, *24,* 807–822.

Astin, A. W. The myth of equal access. *The Chronicle of Higher Education,* September 29, 1975.

Astin, A. W., & Panos, R. J. The evaluation of educational programs. In R. L. Thorndike (Ed.), *Educational measurement* (2d ed.). Washington, D.C.: American Council on Education, 1971.

Atkinson, J. W. Studying personality in the context of an advanced motivational psychology. *American Psychologist,* 1981, *36,* 117–128.

Backer, T. E. *A directory of information on tests.* ERIC Tests and Measurements Report No. 62, 1977.

Baglin, R. F. Does "nationally" normed really mean nationally? *Journal of Educational Measurement,* 1981, *18,* 97–107.

Baker, E. L., & Quellmalz, E. (Eds.) *Educational testing and evaluation.* Beverly Hills, Calif.: Sage, 1980.

Bandura, A. *Social learning theory.* Morristown, N.J.: General Learning Press, 1971.

Barker, R. G. *Ecological psychology.* Palo Alto, Calif.: Stanford University Press, 1968.

Barron, F. *Creativity and psychological health.* New York: Van Nostrand, 1963.

Barron, F. *Creativity and personal freedom.* New York: Van Nostrand, 1968.

Barron, F. *Creative person and creative process.* New York: Holt, Rinehart and Winston, 1969.

Barron, F. *Artists in the making.* New York: Seminar Press, 1972.

Bayley, N. Behavioral correlates of mental growth: Birth to thirty-six years. *American Psychologist,* 1968, *23,* 1–17.

Bechtoldt, H. Construct validity: A critique. *American Psychologist,* 1959, *14,* 619–629.

Beck, S. J., Beck, A. G., Levitt, E. E., & Molish, H. B. *Rorschach's test. I. Basic processes* (3d ed.). New York: Grune & Stratton, 1961.

Bejar, I. I. A procedure for investigating the unidimensionality of achievement tests based on item parameter estimates. *Journal of Educational Measurement,* 1980, *17,* 283–296.

Bem, D. J., & Allen, A. On predicting some of the people some of the time: The search for cross-situational consistencies in behavior. *Psychological Review,* 1974, *81,* 506–520.

Bem, D. J., & Funder, D. C. Predicting more of the people more of the time: Assessing the personality of situations. *Psychological Review,* 1978, *85,* 485–501.

Bem, S. L. The measurement of psychological androgyny. *Journal of Consulting and Clinical Psychology,* 1974, *42,* 155–162.

Bennett, G. K., & Doppelt, J. E. *Test Orientation Procedure.* New York: Psychological Corporation, 1967.

Bennett, G. K., Seashore, H. G., & Wesman, A. G. *Manual for the Differential Aptitude Tests* (4th ed.). New York: Psychological Corporation, 1966.

Berdie, F. S. What test questions are likely to offend the general public? *Journal of Educational Measurement,* 1971, *8,* 87–93.

Berk, R. A. A consumer's guide to criterion-referenced test reliability. *Journal of Educational Measurement,* 1980, *17,* 323–349. (a)

Berk, R. A. (Ed.) *Educational evaluation methodology: The state of the art.* Baltimore: Johns Hopkins University Press, 1980. (b)

Bersoff, D. N. Silk purses into sow's ears: The decline of psychological testing and a suggestion for its redemption. *American Psychologist,* 1973, *28,* 892–899.

Bersoff, D. N. Testing and the law. *American Psychologist,* 1981, *36,* 1047–1056.

Betz, N. E., & Weiss, D. J. *Empirical and simulation studies of flexilevel ability testing.* Psychometric Methods Program Report 75-3. Minneapolis: University of Minnesota, Department of Psychology, 1975.

Birnbaum, M. H. Reply to the Devil's Advocate: Don't confound model testing and measurement. *Psychological Bulletin,* 1974, *81,* 854–859.

Block, J. Some reasons for the apparent inconsistency of personality. *Psychological Bulletin,* 1968, *70,* 210–212.

Block, J. H. (Ed.) *Mastery learning: Theory and practice.* New York: Holt, Rinehart and Winston, 1971.

Block, J. H. (Ed.) *Schools, society, and mastery learning.* New York: Holt, Rinehart and Winston, 1974.

Block, N. J., & Dworkin, G. (Eds.) *The I.Q. controversy.* New York: Pantheon, 1976.

Blommers, P. J., & Forsyth, R. A. *Elementary statistical methods in psychology and education* (2d ed.). Boston: Houghton Mifflin, 1977.

Bloom, B. S. *Stability and change in human characteristics.* New York: Wiley, 1964.

Bloom, B. S. Mastery learning. In J. H. Block (Ed.), *Mastery learning.* New York: Holt, Rinehart and Winston, 1971.

Bloom, B. S. Time and learning. *American Psychologist,* 1974, *29,* 682–688.

Bloom, B. S. *Human characteristics and school learning.* New York: McGraw-Hill, 1976.

Bloom, B. S. The new direction in educational research: Alterable variables. *New Directions for Testing and Measurement,* 1980, *5,* 17–30.

Bloom, B. S., et al. *Taxonomy of educational objectives. Handbook I: Cognitive domain.* New York: McKay, 1956.

Bloom, B. S., Hastings, J. T., & Madaus, G. F. *Handbook on formative and summative evaluation of student learning.* New York: McGraw-Hill, 1971.

Bloom, B. S., Madaus, G. F., & Hastings, J. T. *Evaluation of student learning.* New York: McGraw-Hill, 1980.

Bodmer, W. F., & Cavalli-Sforza, L. L. Intelligence and race. *Scientific American,* 1970, *223*(4), 19–29.

Bond, L. Bias in mental tests. *New Directions for Testing and Measurement,* 1981, *11,* 55–77.

Bornmuth, J. R. *On the theory of achievement test items.* Chicago: University of Chicago Press, 1970.

Bouchard, T. J., Jr., & McGue, M. Familial studies of intelligence: A review. *Science,* 1981, *212,* 1055–1059.

Bowers, J. The comparison of GPA regression equations for regularly admitted and disadvantaged freshmen at the University of Illinois. *Journal of Educational Measurement,* 1970, *7,* 219–225.

Bowers, K. S. Situationism in psychology: An analysis and critique. *Psychological Review,* 1973, *80,* 307–336.

Breland, H. M. *The SAT score decline: A summary of related research.* Princeton, N.J.: Educational Testing Service, 1976.

Breland, H. M. Can multiple-choice tests measure writing skills? *College Board Review,* 1977, *103,* 11–13, 32–33.

Breland, H. M. *Population validity and college entrance measures.* Research Monograph No. 8, New York: The College Board, 1979.

Breland, H. M., & Gaynor, J. L. A comparison of direct and indirect assessments of writing skill. *Journal of Educational Measurement,* 1979, *16,* 119–128.

Brennan, R. L. Applications of generalizability theory. In R. A. Berk (Ed.), *Criterion-referenced measurement: The state of the art.* Baltimore: Johns Hopkins University Press, 1980.

Brennan, R. L., & Kane, M. T. Generalizability theory: A review. *New Directions for Testing and Measurement,* 1979, *4,* 33–51.

Brim, O. G., Jr., Glass, D. C., Neulinger, J., & Firestone, I. J. *American beliefs and attitudes about intelligence.* New York: Russell Sage, 1969.

Brim, O. G., Jr., & Kagan, J. (Eds.) *Constancy and change in human development.* Cambridge, Mass.: Harvard University Press, 1980.

Brogden, H. E. On the interpretation of the correlation coefficient as a measure of predictive efficiency. *Journal of Educational Psychology,* 1946, *37,* 65–76.

Brogden, H. E. A new coefficient: Application to biserial correlation and to estimation of selective efficiency. *Psychometrika,* 1949, *14,* 169–182.

Brown, F. G. A note on expectancy ratios, base rates, and the Strong Vocational Interest Blank. *Journal of Counseling Psychology,* 1961, *8,* 368–369.

Brown, F. G. *Guidelines for test use: A commentary on the Standards for Educational and Psychological Tests.* Washington, D.C.: National Council on Measurement in Education, 1980.

Brown, F. G. *Measuring classroom achievement.* New York: Holt, Rinehart and Winston, 1981.

Bunda, M. A., & Sanders, J. R. (Eds.) *Practices and problems in competency-based measurement.* Washington, D.C.: National Council on Measurement in Education, 1979.

Buros, O. K. (Ed.) *The sixth mental measurements yearbook.* Highland Park, N.J.: Gryphon Press, 1965.

Buros, O. K. The story behind the Mental Measurements Yearbooks. *Measurement and Evaluation in Guidance,* 1968, *1,* 86–95.

Buros, O. K. (Ed.) *The seventh mental measurements yearbook.* (2 vols.). Highland Park, N.J.: Gryphon Press, 1972.

Buros, O. K. (Ed.) *Tests in print II.* Highland Park, N.J.: Gryphon Press, 1974.

Buros, O. K. (Ed.) *Intelligence tests and reviews.* Highland Park, N.J.: Gryphon Press, 1975. (a)

Buros, O. K. (Ed.) *English tests and reviews.* Highland Park, N.J.: Gryphon Press, 1975. (b)

Buros, O. K. Fifty years in testing: Some reminiscences, criticisms, and suggestions. *Educational Researcher,* 1977, *6*(7), 9–15.

Buros, O. K. (Ed.) *The eighth mental measurements yearbook* (2 vols.). Highland Park, N.J.: Gryphon Press, 1978.

Butcher, J. N. (Ed.) *MMPI: Research developments and clinical applications.* New York: McGraw-Hill, 1969.

Butcher, J. N. *Objective personality assessment.* New York: General Learning Press, 1971.

Butcher, J. N. (Ed.) *New developments in the use of the MMPI.* Minneapolis: University of Minnesota Press, 1979.

Butcher, J. N., & Pancheri, P. *A handbook of cross-national MMPI research.* Minneapolis: University of Minnesota Press, 1976.

Campbell, D. P. The vocational interests of American Psychological Association presidents. *American Psychologist,* 1965, *20,* 636–644.

Campbell, D. P. Stability of interests within an occupation over 30 years. *Journal of Applied Psychology,* 1966, *50,* 51–56. (a)

Campbell, D. P. The stability of vocational interests within occupations over long time spans. *Personnel and Guidance Journal,* 1966, *44,* 1012–1019. (b)

Campbell, D. P. *Handbook for the Strong Vocational Interest Blank.* Stanford, Calif.: Stanford University Press, 1971.

Campbell, D. T. Recommendations for APA test standards regarding construct, trait, or discriminant validity. *American Psychologist,* 1960, *15,* 546–553.

Campbell, D. T., & Fiske, D. W. Convergent and discriminant validation by the multitrait-multimethod matrix. *Psychological Bulletin,* 1959, *56,* 81–105.

Carroll, J. B. A model of school learning. *Teachers College Record,* 1963, *64,* 723–733.

Carroll, J. B. Problems of measurement related to the concept of learning for mastery. In J. H. Block (Ed.), *Mastery learning.* New York: Holt, Rinehart and Winston, 1971.

Carroll, J. B. Psychometric tests as cognitive tasks: A new "Structure of Intellect." In L. B. Resnick (Ed.), *The nature of intelligence.* Hillsdale, N.J.: Erlbaum, 1976.

Carroll, J. B., & Horn, J. L. On the scientific basis of ability testing. *American Psychologist,* 1981, *36,* 1012–1020.

Carver, R. P. Two dimensions of tests: Psychometric and edumetric. *American Psychologist,* 1974, *29,* 512–518.

Cattell, R. B. Theory of fluid and crystallized intelligence: A critical experiment. *Journal of Educational Psychology,* 1963, *54,* 1–22.

Cattell, R. B. Are I.Q. tests intelligent? *Psychology Today,* March 1968, 56–62.

Chun, K-T., Cobb, S., & French, J. R. P., Jr. *Measures for psychological assessment: A guide to 3,000 original sources and their applications.* Ann Arbor: Institute for Social Research, University of Michigan, 1975.

Cialdini, R. B., Petty, R. E., & Cacioppo, J. T. Attitude and attitude change. *Annual Review of Psychology,* 1981, *32,* 357–404.

Cleary, T. A. Test bias: Prediction of grades of negro and white students in integrated colleges. *Journal of Educational Measurement,* 1968, *5,* 115–124.

Cleary, T. A., Humphreys, L. G., Kendrick, S. A., & Wesman, A. Educational uses of tests with disadvantaged students. *American Psychologist,* 1975, *30,* 15–41.

Clemans, W. V. Test administration. In R. L. Thorndike (Ed.), *Educational measurement* (2nd ed.). Washington, D.C.: American Council on Education, 1971.

Coffman, W. E. On the validity of essay tests of achievement. *Journal of Educational Measurement,* 1966, *3,* 151–156.

Coffman, W. E. Essay examinations. In R. L. Thorndike (Ed.), *Educational measurement* (2d ed.). Washington, D.C.: American Council on Education, 1971.

Coffman, W. E. On the reliability of ratings of essay exams. *NCME Measurement in Education,* 1972, *3*(3).

Cole, N. S. Bias in selection. *Journal of Educational Measurement,* 1973, *10,* 237–255.

Cole, N. S. Bias in testing. *American Psychologist,* 1981, *36,* 1067–1077.

College Entrance Examination Board. *Effects of coaching on Scholastic Aptitude Test scores.* New York: College Entrance Examination Board, 1968.

College Entrance Examination Board. *Taking the SAT.* New York: College Entrance Examination Board, Admissions Testing Program, 1978.

Comber, L. C., & Keeves, J. P. *Science education in nineteen countries: An empirical study.* New York: Wiley, 1973.

Committee on Assessing the Progress of Education. *How much are students learning? Plans for a National Assessment of Education.* New York: Committee on Assessing the Progress of Education, 1968.

Comrey, A. L., Backer, T. E., & Glaser, E. M. *A sourcebook for mental health measures.* Los Angeles: Human Interaction Research Institute, 1973.

Corsini, R. (Ed.) *Current personality theories.* Itasca, Ill.: Peacock, 1977.

Costin, F., Greenough, W. T., & Menges, R. J. Student ratings of college teaching: Reliability, validity, and usefulness. *Review of Educational Research,* 1971, *41,* 511–535.

Cronbach, L. J. Response sets and test validity. *Educational and Psychological Measurement,* 1946, *6,* 475–494.

Cronbach, L. J. Statistical methods applied to Rorschach scores: A review. *Psychological Bulletin,* 1949, *46,* 393–429.

Cronbach, L. J. Further evidence on response sets and test design. *Educational and Psychological Measurement,* 1950, *10,* 3–31.

Cronbach, L. J. Coefficient alpha and the internal structure of tests. *Psychometrika,* 1951, *16,* 297–334.

Cronbach, L. J. *Essentials of psychological testing* (3d ed.). New York: Harper & Row, 1970.

Cronbach, L. J. Test validation. In R. L. Thorndike (Ed.), *Educational measurement* (2d ed.). Washington, D.C.: American Council on Education, *1971.*

Cronbach, L. J. Five decades of public controversy over mental testing. *American Psychologist,* 1975, *30,* 1–14.

Cronbach, L. J. Equity in selection—where psychometrics and political philosophy meet. *Journal of Educational Measurement,* 1976, *13,* 31–41.

Cronbach, L. J., et al. *Toward reform of program evaluation: Aims, methods, and institutional arrangements.* San Francisco: Jossey-Bass, 1980.

Cronbach, L. J., & Furby, L. How should we measure "change"—Or should we? *Psychological Bulletin,* 1970, *74,* 68–80.

Cronbach, L. J., & Gleser, G. C. *Psychological tests and personnel decisions.* Urbana: University of Illinois Press, 1957.

Cronbach, L. J., & Gleser, G. C. *Psychological tests and personnel decisions* (2d ed.). Urbana: University of Illinois Press, 1965.

Cronbach, L. J., Gleser, G. C., Nanda, H., & Rajaratnam, N. *The dependability of behavioral measurements.* New York: Wiley, 1972.

Cronbach, L. J., & Meehl, P. E. Construct validity and psychological tests. *Psychological Bulletin,* 1955, *52,* 281–302.

Cronbach, L. J., & Merwin, J. C. A model for studying the validity of multiple-choice items. *Educational and Psychological Measurement,* 1955, *15,* 337–352.

Cronbach, L. J., Rajaratnam, N., & Gleser, G. C. Theory of generalizability: A liberalization of reliability theory. *British Journal of Statistical Psychology,* 1963, *16*(2), 137–163.

Cronbach, L. J., & Snow, R. E. *Aptitudes and instructional methods: A handbook for research on interactions.* New York: Irvington, 1977.

Crosby, F., Bromley, S., & Saxe, L. Recent unobtrusive studies of black and white discrimination and prejudice: A literature review. *Psychological Bulletin,* 1980, *87,* 546–563.

Cureton, E. E., et al. *The multi-aptitude test.* New York: Psychological Corporation, 1955.

Cureton, L. W. The history of grading practices. *NCME Measurement in Education,* 1971, *2*(4).

Dahlstrom, W. G. Recurrent issues in the development of MMPI. In J. N. Butcher (Ed.), *MMPI: Research developments and clinical applications.* New York: McGraw-Hill, 1969.

Dahlstrom, W. G. Altered versions of the MMPI. In W. G. Dahlstrom & L. Dahlstrom (Eds.), *Basic readings on the MMPI.* Minneapolis: University of Minnesota Press, 1980.

Dahlstrom, W. G., & Dahlstrom, L. (Eds.) *Basic readings on the MMPI: A new selection on personality measurement.* Minneapolis: University of Minnesota Press, 1980.

Dahlstrom, W. G., Welsh, G. S., & Dahlstrom, L. E. *An MMPI handbook. Vol. 1: Clinical interpretation.* Minneapolis: University of Minnesota Press, 1972.

Dahlstrom, W. G., Welsh, G. S., & Dahlstrom, L. E. *An MMPI handbook. Vol. 2: Research applications.* Minneapolis: University of Minnesota Press, 1975.

Darlington, R. B. Another look at "culture-fairness." *Journal of Educational Measurement,* 1971, *8,* 71–82.

Davis, F. B. Item selection techniques. In E. F. Lindquist (Ed.), *Educational measurement.* Washington, D.C.: American Council on Education, 1951.

Davis, F. B. *Educational measurements and their interpretation.* Belmont, Calif.: Wadsworth, 1964.

Davis, J. A., & Temp., G. Is the SAT biased against black students? *College Board Review,* 1971, No. 81, 4–9.

Dawes, R. M. *Fundamentals of attitude measurement.* New York: Wiley, 1972.

Dawes, R. M. Graduate admissions variables and future success. *Science,* 1975, *187,* 721–723.

Dawes, R. M. Suppose we measured height with rating scales instead of rulers? *Applied Psychological Measurement,* 1977, *1,* 267–273.

Dawis, R. V. Measuring interests. *New Directions for Testing and Measurement,* 1980, *7,* 77–92.

Diamond, E. E. Minimizing sex bias in testing. *Measurement and Evaluation in Guidance,* 1976, *9,* 28–34.

Dick, W., Watson, K., & Kaufman, R. Deriving competencies: Consensus versus model building. *Educational Researcher,* 1981, *10*(8), 5–10, 13.

Doll, E. A. *Vineland social maturity scale: Manual of directions* (rev. ed.). Minneapolis: American Guidance Service, 1965.

Dolliver, R. H. "3.5 to 1" on the Strong Vocational Interest Blank as a pseudo-event. *Journal of Counseling Psychology,* 1969, *16,* 172–174.

Drake, L. E., & Oetting, E. R. *An MMPI code book for counselors.* Minneapolis: University of Minnesota Press, 1959.

Dressel, P. L. *Handbook of academic evaluation.* San Francisco: Jossey-Bass, 1976.

DuBois, P. H. *A history of psychological testing.* Boston: Allyn and Bacon, 1970. (a)

DuBois, P. H. Varieties of psychological test homogeneity. *American Psychologist,* 1970, *25,* 532–536. (b)

Dudek, F. J. The continuing misinterpretation of the standard error of measurement. *Psychological Bulletin,* 1979, *86,* 335–337.

Dunnette, M. D. A note on *the* criterion. *Journal of Applied Psychology,* 1963, *47,* 251–254.

Dunnette, M. D. *Personnel selection and placement.* Belmont, Calif.: Wadsworth, 1966.

Dunstan, M. R. Using educational measurement for educational change. In W. E. Coffman (Ed.), *Frontiers of educational measurement and information systems.* Boston: Houghton Mifflin, 1973.

Ebel, R. L. Must all tests be valid? *American Psychologist*, 1961, *16*, 640–647.

Ebel, R. L. Content standard test scores. *Educational and Psychological Measurement*, 1962, *22*, 15–25.

Ebel, R. L. The social consequences of educational testing. *College Board Review*, 1964, *52*, 10–15.

Ebel, R. L. *Measuring educational achievement*. Englewood Cliffs, N.J.: Prentice-Hall, 1965.

Ebel, R. L. The value of internal consistency in classroom examinations. *Journal of Educational Measurement*, 1968, *5*, 71–73.

Ebel, R. L. Knowledge vs. ability in achievement testing. In *Toward a theory of achievement measurement*. Proceedings of the 1969 Invitational Conference on Testing Problems. Princeton, N.J.: Educational Testing Service, 1969.

Ebel, R. L. *Essentials of educational measurement* (2d ed.). Englewood Cliffs, N.J.: Prentice-Hall, 1972.

Ebel, R. L. The future of the measurement of abilities II. *Educational Researcher*, 1973, *2*(3), 5–12.

Ebel, R. L. And still the dryads linger. *American Psychologist*, 1974, *29*, 485–492.

Ebel, R. L. Can teachers write good true-false items? *Journal of Educational Measurement*, 1975, *12*, 31–35.

Ebel, R. L. The case for norm-referenced measurements. *Educational Researcher*, 1978, *7*(11), 3–5. (a)

Ebel, R. L. The case for minimum competency testing. *Phi Delta Kappan*, 1978, *59*(8), 546–549. (b)

Ebel, R. L. *Essentials of educational measurement* (3d. ed.). Englewood Cliffs, N.J.: Prentice-Hall, 1979.

Ebel, R. L. *Practical problems in educational measurement*. Lexington, Mass.: Heath, 1980.

Ebel, R. L. The social consequences of *not* testing. *New Directions for Testing and Measurement*, 1981, *9*, 31–37.

Echternacht, G., & Plas, J. M. Grade equivalent scores: If not grade equivalent scores—then what? *NCME Measurement in Education*, 1977, *8*(2).

Educational Measurement and the Law. Proceedings of the 1977 ETS Invitational Conference. Princeton, N.J.: Educational Testing Service, 1978.

Educational Testing Service. *ETS builds a test*. Princeton, N.J.: Educational Testing Service, 1965.

Educational Testing Service. Competency tests help tradesmen earn academic credit. *ETS Developments*, Fall 1973, 1, 5.

Edwards, A. J. *Individual mental testing: I. Mental tests*. New York: Intext, 1971.

Edwards, A. J. *Individual mental testing: II. Measurement*. New York: Intext, 1972.

Edwards, A. J. *Individual mental testing: III. Research and interpretation*. New York: Intext, 1975.

Edwards, A. L. *Techniques of attitude scale construction*. New York: Appleton, 1957. (a)

Edwards, A. L. *The social desirability variable in personality assessment*. New York: Holt, Rinehart and Winston, 1957. (b)

Edwards, A. L. The social desirability variable: A review of the evidence. In I. A. Berg (Ed.), *Response set in personality assessment*. Chicago: Aldine, 1967.

Edwards, A. L. *The measurement of personality traits by scales and inventories*. New York: Holt, Rinehart and Winston, 1970.

Edwards, A. L. *An introduction to linear regression and correlation*. San Francisco: Freeman, 1976.

Edwards, A. L. *Multiple regression and the analysis of variance and covariance*. San Francisco: Freeman, 1979.

Edwards, A. L., & Walsh, J. A. Relationships between various psychometric properties of personality items. *Educational and Psychological Measurement*, 1963, *23*, 227–238.

Einhorn, H. J., & Bass, A. R. Methodological considerations relevant to discrimination in employment testing. *Psychological Bulletin*, 1971, *75*, 261–269.

Endler, N. S., & Magnusson, D. Toward an interactional psychology of personality. *Psychological Bulletin*, 1976, *83*, 956–974.

Engelhart, M. D. A comparison of several item discrimination indices. *Journal of Educational Measurement*, 1965, *2*, 69–76.

Epstein, S. Explorations in personality today and tomorrow: A tribute to Henry A. Murray. *American Psychologist*, 1979, *34*, 649–653.

Epstein, S. The stability of behavior. II. Implications for psychological research. *American Psychologist*, 1980, *35*, 790–806.

Equal Employment Opportunity Commission. Guidelines on Employee Selection Procedures. *Federal Register*, 1970, *35*, 12333–12336.

Equal Employment Opportunity Commission, Civil Service Commission, Department of Labor, & Department of Justice. Adoption by four agencies of Uniform Guidelines on Employee Selection Procedures. *Federal Register,* 1978, *43,* 38290–38315.

Equal Employment Opportunity Commission, Office of Personnel Management, Department of Justice, Department of Labor, & Department of the Treasury. Adoption of questions and answers to clarify and provide a common interpretation of the Uniform Guidelines on Employee Selection Procedures. *Federal Register,* 1979, *44,* 11996–12009.

Estes, W. K. Learning theory and intelligence. *American Psychologist,* 1974, *29,* 740–749.

Ethical principles of psychologists. *American Psychologist,* 1981, *36,* 633–638.

Exner, J. E., Jr. *The Rorschach: A comprehensive system.* New York: Wiley, 1974.

Eysenck, H. J., & Kamin, L. *The intelligence controversy.* New York: Wiley, 1981.

Faller, J. E. Precision measurement of the acceleration of gravity. *Science,* 1967, *158,* 60–67.

Faschingbauer, T. R., & Newmark, C. S. *Short forms of the MMPI.* Lexington, Mass.: Lexington Books, 1978.

Feldt, L. S., & Hall, A. E. Stability of four item discrimination indices over groups of different average ability. *American Educational Research Journal,* 1964, *1,* 35–46.

Ferber, R., Sheatsley, P., Turner, A., & Waksberg, J. *What is a survey?* Washington, D.C.: American Statistical Association, 1980.

Ferguson, G. A. On learning and human ability. *Canadian Journal of Psychology,* 1954, 8, 95–112

Fincher, C. Personnel testing and public policy. *American Psychologist,* 1973, *28,* 489–497.

Fincher, C. Is the SAT worth its salt? An evaluation of the use of the Scholastic Aptitude Test in the University System of Georgia over a thirteen-year period. *Review of Educational Research,* 1974, *44,* 293–305.

Fincher, C. Standardized tests, group differences, and public policy. *College Board Review,* 1977, *103,* 19–31.

Fincher, C. Using tests constructively in an era of controversy. *College Board Review,* 1979, *113,* 2–7.

Fiske, D. W. *Measuring the concepts of personality.* Chicago: Aldine, 1971.

Flanagan, J. C. The critical incident technique. *Psychological Bulletin,* 1954, *51,* 327–358.

Flanagan, J. C. Changes in school levels of achievement: Project TALENT ten and fifteen year retests. *Educational Researcher,* 1976, *5*(8), 9–14.

Flaugher, R. L. The new definitions of test fairness in selection: Developments and implications. *Educational Researcher,* 1974, *3*(9), 13–16.

Flaugher, R. L. The many definitions of test bias. *American Psychologist,* 1978, *33,* 671–679.

Fleishman, E. A. *The structure and measurement of physical fitness.* Englewood Cliffs, N.J.: Prentice-Hall, 1964.

Fleishman, E. A. On the relation between abilities, learning, and human performance. *American Psychologist,* 1972, *27,* 1017–1032.

Fleishman, E. A. Toward a taxonomy of human performance. *American Psychologist,* 1975, *30,* 1127–1149.

Fowler, R. D. Use of computerized MMPI in correctional decisions. In J. N. Butcher (Ed.), *New developments in the use of the MMPI.* Minneapolis: University of Minnesota Press, 1979.

Fox, L. N., Brody, L., & Tobin, D. (Eds.) *Women and the mathematical mystique.* Baltimore: Johns Hopkins University Press, 1980.

Frederiksen, N. Towards a taxonomy of situations. *American Psychologist,* 1972, *27,* 114–123.

Frederiksen, N., Saunders, D. R., & Wand, B. The In-Basket Test. *Psychological Monographs,* 1957, *71*(9).

Frederiksen, N., & Ward, W. C. Measures for the study of creativity in scientific problem-solving. *Applied Psychological Measurement,* 1978, *2,* 1–24.

Fremer, J., & Chandler, M. O. Special studies. In W. H. Angoff (Ed.), *The College Board Admissions Testing Program.* New York: College Entrance Examination Board, 1971.

Gaito, J. Measurement scales and statistics: Resurgence of an old misconception. *Psychological Bulletin,* 1980, *87,* 564–567.

Gardner, E. F. Bias. *NCME Measurement in Education,* 1978, *9*(3).

Gardner, P. L. Scales and statistics. *Review of Educational Research,* 1975, *45,* 43–57.

George, W. C., Cohn, S. J., & Stanley, J. C. (Eds.) *Educating the gifted: Acceleration and enrichment.* Baltimore: Johns Hopkins University Press, 1979.

Getzels, J. W., & Jackson, P. W. *Creativity and intelligence.* New York: Wiley, 1962.

Ghiselli, E. E. Dimensional problems of criteria. *Journal of Applied Psychology,* 1956, *40,* 1–4.

Ghiselli, E. E. *Theory of psychological measurement.* New York: McGraw-Hill, 1964.

Ghiselli, E. E., Campbell, J. P., & Zedeck, S. *Measurement theory for the behavioral sciences.* San Francisco: Freeman, 1981.

Glaser, R. Instructional technology and the measurement of learning outcomes. *American Psychologist,* 1963, *18,* 519–521.

Glaser, R. Individuals and learning: The new aptitudes. *Educational Researcher,* 1972, *1*(6), 5–13.

Glaser, R. The future of testing: A research agenda for cognitive psychology and psychometrics. *American Psychologist,* 1981, *36,* 923–936.

Glaser, R., & Nitko, A. J. Measurement in learning and instruction. In R. L. Thorndike (Ed.), *Educational measurement* (2d ed.). Washington, D.C.: American Council on Education, 1971.

Glass, G. V. Primary, secondary, and meta-analysis of research. *Educational Researcher,* 1976, *5*(10), 3–8.

Glass, G. V. Integrating findings: The meta-analysis of research. *Review of Research in Education,* 1977, *5,* 351–379.

Glass, G. V. Standards and criteria. *Journal of Educational Measurement,* 1978, *15,* 237–261.

Gleser, G. C. Cronbach, L. J., & Rajaratnam, N. Generalizability of scores influenced by multiple sources of variance. *Psychometrika,* 1965, *30,* 395–418.

Gold, A. M. The use of separate-sex norms on aptitude tests: Friend or foe? *Measurement and Evaluation in Guidance,* 1977, *10,* 162–171.

Goldberg, L. R. Some recent trends in personality assessment. *Journal of Personality Assessment,* 1972, *36,* 547–560.

Goldberg, L. R. Objective diagnostic tests and measures. *Annual Review of Psychology,* 1974, *25,* 343–366.

Goldberg, L. R. The reliability of reliability: The generality and correlates of intra-individual consistency in responses to structured personality inventories. *Applied Psychology Measurement,* 1978, *2,* 269–291.

Goldman, L. *Using tests in counseling* (2d ed.). New York: Appleton, 1971.

Good, P. K.-E., & Branter, J. P. *A practical guide to the MMPI.* Minneapolis: University of Minnesota Press, 1974.

Goodenough, F. L. *Mental testing.* New York: Holt, Rinehart and Winston, 1949.

Goodwin, W. L., & Driscoll, L. A. *Handbook for measurement and evaluation in early childhood education.* San Francisco: Jossey-Bass, 1980.

Gordon, E. W., & Terrell, M. D. The changed social context of testing. *American Psychologist,* 1981, *36,* 1167–1171.

Goslin, D. A. *The search for ability.* New York: Russell Sage, 1963.

Goslin, D. A. *Teachers and testing.* New York: Russell Sage, 1967.

Gough, H. Some reflections on the meaning of psychodiagnosis. *American Psychologist,* 1971, *26,* 160–167.

Graham, J. R. *The MMPI: A practical guide.* New York: Oxford University Press, 1977.

GRE 1981–82 Information Bulletin. Princeton, N.J.: Educational Testing Service, 1981.

Green, B. F., In defense of measurement. *American Psychologist,* 1978, *33,* 664–670.

Green, B. F. A primer of testing. *American Psychologist,* 1981, *36,* 1001–1011.

Greene, R. L. *The MMPI: An interpretive manual.* New York: Grune & Stratton, 1980.

Gresham, F., & Evans, J. R. Recent developments in electrophysiological measurement: Implications for school psychology. *Psychology in the Schools,* 1979, *16,* 314–321.

Gronlund, N. E. *Improving marking and reporting in classroom instruction.* New York: Macmillan, 1974.

Gronlund, N. E. *Constructing achievement tests* (2d ed.). Englewood Cliffs, N.J.: Prentice-Hall, 1977.

Guilford, J. P. *Psychometric methods* (2d ed.). New York: McGraw-Hill, 1954.

Guilford, J. P. The structure of the intellect. *Psychological Bulletin,* 1956, *53,* 267–293.

Guilford, J. P. Three faces of intellect. *American Psychologist, 1959, 14,* 469–479.

Guilford, J. P. Intelligence: 1965 model. *American Psychologist, 1966, 21,* 20–26.

Guilford, J. P. *The nature of human intelligence.* New York: McGraw-Hill, 1967.

Guilford, J. P. *Intelligence, creativity, and their educational implications.* San Diego: Robert Knapp, 1968.

Guion, R. M. Open a new window: Validities and values in psychological measurement. *American Psychologist, 1974, 29,* 287–296.

Guion, R. Content validity—the source of my discontent. *Applied Psychological Measurement, 1977, 1,* 1–10.

Guttman, L. A basis for analysing test-retest reliability. *Psychometrika, 1945, 10,* 255–282.

Hall, C. S., & Lindzey, G. *Theories of personality* (3d. ed.). New York: Wiley, 1978.

Hall, J. L. Stabilized lasers and precision measurement. *Science, 1978, 202,* 147–156.

Hambleton, R. K. On the use of cut-off scores with criterion-referenced tests in instructional settings. *Journal of Educational Measurement, 1978, 15,* 277–290.

Hambleton, R. K. Latent ability scales: Interpretations and uses. *New Directions for Testing and Measurement, 1980, 6,* 73–97.

Hambleton, R. K., & Cook, L. L. Latent trait models and their use in the analysis of educational test data. *Journal of Educational Measurement, 1977, 14,* 75–96.

Hambleton, R. K., & Novick, M. R. Toward an integration of theory and method for criterion-referenced tests. *Journal of Educational Measurement, 1973, 10,* 159–170.

Hambleton, R. K., Swaminathan, H., Cook, L. L., Eignor, D. R., & Gifford, J. A. Developments in latent trait theory: Models, technical issues, and applications. *Review of Educational Research, 1978, 48,* 467–510.

Harnischfeger, A., & Wiley, D. Achievement test scores drop. So what? *Educational Researcher, 1976, 5*(3), 5–12.

Härnquist, K. The International Study of Educational Achievement. *Review of Research in Education, 1975, 3,* 85–109.

Harrell, T. W., & Harrell, M. S. Army General Classification Test scores for civilian occupations. *Educational and Psychological Measurement, 1945, 5,* 229–239.

Harris, C. W. (Ed.). *Problems in measuring change.* Madison: University of Wisconsin Press, 1963.

Harris, C. W., Alkin, M. C., & Popham, W. J. *Problems in criterion-referenced measurement.* CSE Monograph Series in Evaluation, No. 3. Los Angeles: Center for the Study of Evaluation, University of California at Los Angeles, 1974.

Harris, J. G., Jr. Nomovalidation and idiovalidation: A quest for the true personality profile. *American Psychologist, 1980, 35,* 729–744.

Hartnett, R. T., & Willingham, W. W. The criterion problem: What measure of success in graduate education? *Applied Psychological Measurement, 1980, 4,* 281–291.

Hase, H. D., & Goldberg, L. R. Comparative validity of different strategies for constructing personality inventory scales. *Psychological Bulletin, 1967, 67,* 231–248.

Hathaway, S. R. Foreword to W. G. Dahlstrom & G. S. Welsh (Eds.), *An MMPI handbook.* Minneapolis: University of Minnesota Press, 1960.

Hathaway, S. R., & Meehl, P. E. *An atlas for the clinical use of the MMPI.* Minneapolis: University of Minnesota Press, 1951.

Hattie, J. A., Conditions for administering creativity tests. *Psychological Bulletin, 1977, 84,* 1249–1260.

Haynes, S. N. *Principles of behavioral assessment.* New York: Gardner Press, 1978.

Haynes, S. N., & Wilson, C. C. *Behavioral assessment.* San Francisco: Jossey-Bass, 1979.

Hays, W. L. *Statistics* (3d ed.). New York: Holt, Rinehart and Winston, 1981.

Henryssen, S. Gathering, analyzing, and using data on test items. In R. L. Thorndike (Ed.), *Educational measurement* (2d ed.). Washington, D.C.: American Council on Education, 1971.

Herrnstein, R. I.Q. *Atlantic,* September 1971, 43–64.

Hersen, M., & Bellack, A. S. *Behavioral assessment.* Elmsford, N.Y.: Pergamon, 1976.

Hill, E. F. *The Holtzman Inkblot Technique: A handbook for clinical applications.* San Francisco: Jossey-Bass, 1972.

Hills, J. R. Use of measurement in selection and placement. In R. L. Thorndike (Ed.), *Educational measurement* (2d ed.). Washington, D.C.: American Council on Education, 1971.

Hively, W., Maxwell, G., Rabehl, G., Sension, D., & Lundin, S. *Domain-referenced curriculum evaluation: A technical handbook and a case study from the MINNEMAST Project.* AERA Monograph Series on Curriculum Evaluation, No. 1. Los Angeles: Center for the Study of Evaluation, University of California at Los Angeles, 1973.

Hively, W., Patterson, H. L., & Page, S. H. A "universe-defined" system of arithmetic achievement tests. *Journal of Educational Measurement,* 1968, *5,* 275–290.

Hoffmann, B. The tyranny of multiple-choice tests. *Harpers,* March 1961, 37–44.

Hoffmann, B. *The tyranny of testing.* New York: Macmillan, 1962.

Hogan, R., DeSoto, C. B., & Solano, C. Traits, tests, and personality research. *American Psychologist,* 1977, *32,* 255–264.

Holland, J. L. *Making vocational choices: A theory of careers.* Englewood Cliffs, N.J.: Prentice-Hall, 1973.

Holt, R. R. *Assessing personality.* New York: Harcourt Brace Jovanovich, 1971.

Holtzman, W. H. The changing world of mental measurement and its social significance. *American Psychologist,* 1971, *26,* 546–553.

Holtzman, W. H. Holtzman Inkblot Technique (HIT). In A. I. Rabin (Ed.), *Assessment with projective techniques: A concise introduction.* New York: Springer, 1981.

Holtzman, W. H., Thorpe, J. S., Swartz, J. D., & Herron, E. W. *Inkblot perception and personality: Holtzman Inkblot Technique.* Austin: University of Texas Press, 1961.

Hopkins, K. D., & Glass, G. V. *Basic statistics for the behavioral sciences.* Englewood Cliffs, N.J.: Prentice-Hall, 1978.

Horn, J. L. Some characteristics of classroom examinations. *Journal of Educational Measurement,* 1966, *3,* 293–295.

Horn, J. L. Intelligence: Why it grows, why it declines. *Trans-Action,* November 1967, 23–31.

Horn, J. L. Organization of data on life-span development of human abilities. In L. R. Goulet & P. B. Baltes (Eds.), *Life-span developmental psychology.* New York: Academic Press, 1970.

Horst, P. A technique for the development of a differential prediction battery. *Psychological Monographs,* 1954, *68*(9).

Horst, P. A technique for the development of a multiple absolute prediction battery. *Psychological Monographs,* 1955, *69*(5).

Hoyt, C. Test reliability obtained by analysis of variance. *Psychometrika,* 1941, *6,* 153–160.

Hunt, J. McV. *Intelligence and experience,* New York: Ronald, 1961.

Hunt, J. McV. Ordinal scales of infant development and the nature of intelligence. In L. B. Resnick (Ed.), *The nature of intelligence.* Hillsdale, N.J.: Erlbaum, 1976.

Hunter, J. E., & Schmidt, F. L. Critical analysis of the statistical and ethical implications of various definitions of *test bias. Psychological Bulletin,* 1976, *83,* 1053–1071.

Hunter, J. E., Schmidt, F. L., & Hunter, R. Differential validity of employment tests by race: A comprehensive review and analysis. *Psychological Bulletin,* 1979, *86,* 721–735.

Hunter, J. S. The national system of scientific measurement. *Science,* 1980, *210,* 869–874.

Husén, T. (Ed.) *International study of achievement in mathematics* (2 vols.). New York: Wiley, 1967.

Huynh, H. On consistency of decisions in criterion-referenced testing. *Journal of Educational Measurement,* 1976, *13,* 253–264.

Jackson, D. N. The dynamics of structured personality tests: 1971. *Psychological Review,* 1971, *78,* 229–248.

Jackson, R. The Scholastic Aptitude Test: A response to Slack and Porter's "Critical appraisal." *Harvard Educational Review,* 1980, *50,* 382–391.

Jacoby, L. L. Test-appropriate strategies in retention of categorized lists. *Journal of Verbal Learning and Verbal Behavior,* 1973, *12,* 675–682.

Jaeger, R. M. The national test-equating study in reading. *NCME Measurement in Education,* 1973, *4*(4).

Jaeger, R. M. Some exploratory indices for selection of a test equating method. *Journal of Educational Measurement,* 1981, *18,* 23–38.

Jaeger, R., & Tittle, C. (Eds.) *Minimum competency achievement testing.* Berkeley, Calif.: McCutchan, 1980.

Jencks, C., et al. *Inequality: A reassessment of the effect of family and schooling in America.* New York: Basic Books, 1972.

Jensen, A. R. How much can we boost IQ and scholastic achievement? *Harvard Educational Review,* 1969, *39,* 1–123.

Jensen, A. R. *Educational differences.* London: Methuen, 1973.

Jensen, A. R. The effect of race of examiner on mental test scores of white and black pupils. *Journal of Educational Measurement,* 1974, *11,* 1–14.

Jensen, A. R. *Bias in mental testing.* New York: Free Press, 1980.

Johnson, O. G. *Tests and measurements in child development—Handbook II.* San Francisco: Jossey-Bass, 1976.

Johnson, O. G., & Bommarito, J. W. *Tests and measurements in child development—Handbook I.* San Francisco: Jossey-Bass, 1971.

Jones, L. V. The nature of measurement. In R. L. Thorndike (Ed.), *Educational measurement* (2d ed.). Washington, D.C.: American Council on Education, 1971.

Jones, L. V. Achievement test scores in mathematics and science. *Science,* 1981, *213,* 412–416.

Kamin, L. J. *The science and politics of IQ.* New York: Wiley, 1974.

Kapes, J. T., & Mastie, M. M. (Eds.) *A counselor's guide to vocational guidance instruments.* Falls Church, Va.: National Vocational Guidance Association, 1982.

Karon, B. P. Comment: Projective tests are valid. *American Psychologist,* 1978, *33,* 764–765.

Katz, M. *Selecting an achievement test: Principles and procedures.* Princeton, N.J.: Educational Testing Service, 1973.

Kaufman, A. S. *Intelligent testing with the WISC-R.* New York: Wiley, 1979.

Keating, D. P. (Ed.) *Intellectual talent: Research and development.* Baltimore: Johns Hopkins University Press, 1976.

Kelly, E. L. *Assessment of human characteristics.* Belmont, Calif.: Brooks/Cole, 1967.

Kelly, G. A. The theory and technique of assessment. *Annual Review of Psychology,* 1958, *9,* 323–352.

Kelly, G. A. *A theory of personality.* New York: Norton, 1963.

Kendrick, S. A. When SAT scores go down. *College Board Review,* 1967, *64,* 5–11.

Kerlinger, F. N. *Foundations of behavioral research* (2d ed.). New York: Holt, Rinehart and Winston, 1973.

Kerlinger, F. N., & Pedhazur, E. J. *Multiple regression in behavioral research.* New York: Holt, Rinehart and Winston, 1973.

Klein, S. P., & Hart, F. M. Chance and systematic factors affecting essay grades. *Journal of Educational Measurement,* 1968, *5,* 197–206.

Kleinmutz, B. *Computers in personality assessment.* Morristown, N.J.: General Learning Press, 1972.

Kleinmutz, B. The computer as clinician. *American Psychologist,* 1975, *30,* 379–387.

Kline, M. *Why Johnny can't add.* New York: Vintage, 1974.

Klopfer, B., & Davidson, H. H. *The Rorschach Technique: An introductory manual.* New York: Harcourt Brace Jovanovich, 1962.

Klopfer, W. G., & Taulbee, E. S. Projective tests. *Annual Review of Psychology,* 1976, *27,* 543–567.

Koffler, S. L. A comparison of approaches for setting proficiency standards. *Journal of Educational Measurement,* 1980, *17,* 167–178.

Kogan, N. Educational implications of cognitive styles. In G. S. Lesser (Ed.), *Psychology and educational practice.* Glenview, Ill.: Scott Foresman, 1971.

Kolen, M. J. Comparison of traditional and item response theory methods for equating tests. *Journal of Educational Measurement,* 1981, *18,* 1–11.

Kolen, M. J., & Whitney, D. R. Methods of smoothing double-entry expectancy tables applied to the prediction of success in college. *Journal of Educational Measurement,* 1978, *15,* 201–211.

Koppitz, E. M. *The Bender Gestalt Test for Young Children. Vol. 2: Research and application, 1963–73.* New York: Grune & Stratton 1975.

Korchin, S. J., & Schuldberg, D. The future of clinical assessment. *American Psychologist,* 1981, *36,* 1147–1158.

Krathwohl, D. R., & Payne, D. A. Defining and assessing educational objectives. In R. L. Thorndike (Ed.), *Educational measurement* (2d ed.). Washington, D.C.: American Council on Education, 1971.

Kuder, G. F. Some principles of interest measurement. *Educational and Psychological Measurement,* 1970, *30,* 205–226.

Kuder, G. F. *Acitivity interests and occupational choice.* Chicago: Science Research Associates, 1977.

Kuder, G. F., & Richardson, M. W. The theory of estimation of test reliability. *Psychometrika,* 1937, *2,* 151–160.

Lamiell, J. T. Toward an idiothetic psychology of personality. *American Psychologist,* 1981, *36,* 276–289.

Lavin, D. E. *The prediction of academic performance.* New York: Russell Sage, 1965.

Lennon, R. T. The anatomy of a scholastic aptitude test. *NCME Measurement in Education,* 1980, *11*(2).

Lerner, B. The Supreme Court and the APA, AERA, NCME Test Standards: Past references and future possibilities. *American Psychologist,* 1978, *33,* 915–919.

Lerner, B. Tests and standards today: Attacks, counterattacks, and responses. *New Directions for Testing and Measurement,* 1979, *3,* 15–31.

Lerner, B. Representative democracy, "men of zeal," and testing legislation. *American Psychologist,* 1981, *36,* 270–275.

Light, R. J., & Smith, P. V. Accumulating evidence: Procedures for resolving contradictions among different studies. *Harvard Educational Review,* 1971, *41,* 429–471.

Lindzey, G. *Projective techniques and cross-cultural research.* New York: Appleton, 1961.

Linn, R. L. Fair test use in selection. *Review of Educational Research,* 1973, *43,* 139–161.

Linn, R. L. In search of fair selection procedures. *Journal of Educational Measurement,* 1976, *13,* 53–58.

Linn, R. L. Demands, cautions, and suggestions for setting standards. *Journal of Educational Measurement,* 1978, *15,* 301–308.

Linn, R. L., & Werts, C. E. Considerations for studies of test bias. *Journal of Educational Measurement,* 1971, *8,* 1–4.

Livingston, S. A. Criterion-referenced applications of classical test theory. *Journal of Educational Measurement,* 1972, *9,* 13–26.

Loehlin, J. C., Lindzey, G., & Spuhler, J. N. *Race differences in intelligence.* San Francisco: Freeman, 1975.

Loehlin, J. C., & Nichols, R. C. *Heredity, environment, and personality.* Austin: University of Texas Press. 1976.

Loevinger, J. A systematic approach to the construction and evaluation of tests of ability. *Psychological Monographs,* 1947, *61*(4).

Loevinger, J. Objective tests as instruments of psychological theory. *Psychological Reports,* Monograph Supplement 9, 1957, 635–694.

Lonner, W. J. The SVIB visits German, Austrian and Swiss psychologists. *American Psychologist,* 1968, *23,* 164–179.

Lord, F. M. Do tests of the same length have the same standard error of measurement? *Educational and Psychological Measurement,* 1957, *17,* 510–521.

Lord, F. M. Practical applications of item characteristic curve theory. *Journal of Educational Measurement,* 1977, *14,* 117–138.

Lord, F. M. *Applications of item response theory to practical testing problems.* Hillsdale, N.J.: Erlbaum, 1980.

Lyman, H. B. *Test scores and what they mean* (3d ed.). Englewood Cliffs, N.J.: Prentice-Hall, 1978.

Lyman, H. B. Metrics used in reporting test results. *New Directions for Testing and Measurement,* 1980, *6,* 17–34.

Macdonald-Ross, M. Graphics in texts. *Review of Research in Education,* 1977, *5,* 49–85.

MacKinnon, D. W. The nature and nurture of creative talent. *American Psychologist,* 1962, *17,* 484–495.

Madaus, G. F., Airasian, P. W., & Kellaghan, T. *School effectiveness: A reassessement of the evidence.* New York: McGraw-Hill, 1980.

Madaus, G. F., & McDonagh, J. T. Minimum competency testing: Unexamined assumptions and unexplored negative outcomes. *New Directions for Testing and Measurement.* 1979, *3,* 1–14.

Mager, R. F. *Preparing instructional objectives.* Palo Alto, Calif.: Fearon, 1962.

Magnusson, D. *Test theory.* Reading, Mass.: Addison-Wesley, 1967.

Manual for the SVIB-SCII (Form T325) (3d ed.). Stanford, Calif.: Stanford University Press, 1981.

Marks, P. A., & Seeman, W. *The actuarial description of abnormal personality: An atlas for use with the MMPI.* Baltimore: Williams & Wilkins, 1963.

Marks, P. A., Seeman, W., & Haller, D. L. *The actuarial use of the MMPI with adolescents and adults.* Baltimore: Williams & Wilkins, 1974.

Marso, R. N. Test item arrangement, testing time, and performance. *Journal of Educational Measurement,* 1970, *7,* 113–118.

Martin, W. H. National Assessment of Educational Progress. *New Directions for Testing and Measurement,* 1979, *2,* 45–67.

Masling, J. The influence of situational and interpersonal variables in projective testing. *Psychological Bulletin,* 1960, *57,* 65–85.

Matarazzo, J. D. *Wechsler's measurement and appraisal of adult intelligence* (5th and enlarged ed.). New York: Oxford University Press, 1972.

Mayo, S. T. Mastery learning and mastery testing. *NCME Measurement in Education,* 1970, *1*(3).

Mayo, S. T. (Ed.) Interpreting test performance. *New Directions for Testing and Measurement,* 1980, *6.*

McArthur, C. Long-term validity of the Strong Interest Test in two subcultures. *Journal of Applied Psychology,* 1954, *38,* 346–353.

McCall, R. B., Hogarty, P. S., & Hurlburt, N. Transitions in infant sensorimotor development and the prediction of childhood IQ. *American Psychologist,* 1972, *27,* 728–749.

McCall, W. A. *How to measure in education.* New York: Macmillan, 1922.

McClelland, D. C. *The achieving society.* New York: Van Nostrand, 1961.

McClelland, D. C. Toward a theory of motive acquisition. *American Psychologist,* 1965, *20,* 321–333.

McClelland, D. C. Testing for competence rather than for "intelligence." *American Psychologist,* 1973, *28,* 1–14.

McClelland, D. C. Managing motivation to expand human freedom. *American Psychologist,* 1978, *33,* 201–210.

McClelland, D. C., Atkinson, J. W., Clark, R. A., Lowell, E. L. *The achievement motive.* New York: Appleton, 1953.

McHugh, R. B. The interval estimation of a true score. *Psychological Bulletin,* 1957, *54,* 73–74.

McMorris, R. F., Brown, J. A., & Pruzek, R. M. Effects of violating item construction principles. *Journal of Educational Measurement,* 1972, *9,* 287–295.

McNemar, Q. Lost: Our intelligence? Why? *American Psychologist,* 1964, *19,* 871–882.

McNemar, Q. On so-called test bias. *American Psychologist,* 1975, *30,* 848–851.

Meehl, P. E. The dynamics of "structured" personality tests. *Journal of Clinical Psychology,* 1945, *1,* 296–303.

Meehl, P. E. *Clinical versus statistical prediction.* Minneapolis: University of Minnesota Press, 1954.

Meehl, P. E. Wanted—A good cookbook. *American Psychologist,* 1956, *11,* 263–272.

Meehl, P. E., & Hathaway, S. R. The K factor as a suppressor variable in the MMPI. *Journal of Applied Psychology,* 1946, *30,* 525–564.

Meehl, P. E., & Rosen, A. Antecedent probability and the efficiency of psychometric signs, patterns, or cutting scores. *Psychological Bulletin,* 1955, *52,* 194–216.

Mehrens, W. A., & Ebel, R. L. Some comments on criterion-referenced and norm-referenced achievement tests. *NCME Measurement in Education,* 1979, *10*(1).

Mehrens, W. A., & Lehmann, I. J. *Measurement and evaluation in education and psychology* (2d ed.). New York: Holt, Rinehart and Winston, 1978.

Mehrens, W. A., & Lehmann, I. J. *Standardized tests in education* (3d ed.). New York: Holt, Rinehart and Winston, 1980.

Mercer, J. R. *SOMPA: System of Multicultural Pluralistic Assessment Technical Manual.* New York: Psychological Corporation, 1979.

Meskauskas, J. A. Evaluation models for criterion-referenced testing: Views regarding mastery and standard-setting. *Review of Educational Research,* 1976, *4,* 133–158.

Messick, S. The criterion problem in the evaluation of instruction: Assessing possible, not just probable, intended outcomes. In M. C. Wittrock & D. E. Wiley (Eds.), *The evaluation of instruction.* New York: Holt, Rinehart and Winston 1970.

Messick, S. The standard problem: Meaning and values in measurement and evaluation. *American Psychologist*, 1975, *30*, 955–966.

Messick, S. *The effectiveness of coaching for the SAT: Review and reanalysis of research from the fifties to the FTC.* Princeton, N.J.: Educational Testing Service, 1980. (a)

Messick, S. Test validity and the ethics of assessment. *American Psychologist*, 1980, *35*, 1012–1027. (b)

Messick, S. The effectiveness of coaching for the SAT. *New Directions for Testing and Measurement*, 1981, *11*, 21–53. (a)

Messick, S. Evidence and ethics in the evaluation of tests. *Educational Researcher*, 1981, *10*(9), 9–20. (b)

Messick, S., & Jungeblut, A. Time and method in coaching for the SAT. *Psychological Bulletin*, 1981, *89*, 191–216.

Millman, J. Passing scores and test lengths for domain-referenced measures. *Review of Educational Research*, 1973, *43*, 205–216.

Millman, J. Criterion-referenced measurement. In W. J. Popham (Ed.), *Evaluation in education.* Berkeley, Calif.: McCutchan, 1974.

Millman, J., Bishop, H., & Ebel, R. An analysis of test-wiseness. *Educational and Psychological Measurement*, 1965, *25*, 707–726.

Mischel, W. *Personality and assessment.* New York: Wiley, 1968.

Mischel, W. Continuity and change in personality. *American Psychologist*, 1969, *24*, 1012–1018.

Mischel, W. Toward a cognitive social learning reconceptualization of personality. *Psychological Review*, 1973, *80*, 252–283.

Mischel, W. *Introduction to personality* (2d ed.). New York: Holt, Rinehart and Winston, 1976.

Mischel, W. On the future of personality measurement. *American Psychologist*, 1977, *32*, 246–254.

Mischel, W. On the interface of cognition and personality: Beyond the person-situation debate. *American Psychologist*, 1979, *34*, 740–754.

Mitchell, S. K. Interobserver agreement, reliability, and generalizability of data collected in observational studies. *Psychological Bulletin*, 1979, *86*, 376–390.

Moos, R. H. Conceptualizations of human environments. *American Psychologist*, 1973, *28*, 652–655.

Moos, R. H. Systems for the assessment and classification of human environments. In R. H. Moos & P. M Insel (Eds.), *Issues in social ecology.* Palo Alto, Calif.: National Press Books, 1974.

Moss, J. D., & Brown, F. G. Sex bias and academic performance: An empirical study. *Journal of Educational Measurement*, 1979, *16*, 197–201.

Multiple choice questions: A close look. Princeton, N.J.: Educational Testing Service, 1973.

Munday, L. A. Predicting grades in predominantly Negro colleges. *Journal of Education Measurement*, 1965, *2*, 157–160.

Munday, L. A. Changing test scores: Basic skills development in 1977 compared with 1970. *Phi Delta Kappan*, 1979, *60*, 670–671.

Murray, H. A. *Explorations in personality.* New York: Oxford University Press, 1938.

Newmark, C. S. (Ed.) *MMPI: Clinical and research trends.* New York: Praeger, 1979.

Nicholls, J. G. Creativity in the person who will never produce anything original and useful. The concept of creativity as a normally distributed trait. *American Psychologist*, 1972, *27*, 717–729.

Nichols, R. C. Policy implications of the IQ controversy. *Review of Research in Education*, 1978, *6*, 3–46.

Nitko, A. J. Distinguishing the many varieties of criterion-referenced tests. *Review of Educational Research*, 1980, *50*, 461–485. (a)

Nitko, A. J. Criterion-referencing schemes. *New Directions for Testing and Measurement*, 1980, *6*, 35–71. (b)

Norman, W. T. Toward an adequate taxonomy of personality attributes: Replicated factor structure in peer nomination personality ratings. *Journal of Abnormal and Social Psychology*, 1963, *66*, 574–583.

Norman, W. T. *2800 personality trait descriptors: Normative operating characteristics for a university population.* Ann Arbor: University of Michigan, Department of Psychology, 1967.

Novick, M. R. Federal guidelines and professional standards. *American Psychologist*, 1981, *36*, 1035–1046.

Novick, M. R., & Ellis, D. D., Jr. Equal opportunity in educational and employment selection. *American Psychologist*, 1977, *32*, 306–320.

Nunnally, J. *Psychometric theory* (2d ed.). New York: McGraw-Hill, 1978.

O'Leary, L. R. Fair employment, sound psychometric practice, and reality: A dilemma and a partial solution. *American Psychologist*, 1973, *28*, 147–150.

On bias in selection. *Journal of Educational Measurement*, 1976, *13*(1), entire issue.

On further examination: Report of the Advisory Panel on the Scholastic Aptitude Test score decline. New York: College Entrance Examination Board, 1977.

Oosterhof, A. C. Similarity of various item discrimination indices. *Journal of Educational Measurement*, 1976, *13*, 145–150.

Osgood, C. E., Suci, G. J., & Tannenbaum, P. H. *The measurement of meaning.* Urbana: University of Illinois Press, 1957.

OSS Assessment Staff. *Assessment of men.* New York: Holt, Rinehart and Winston, 1948.

Owens, W. A. A quasi-actuarial basis for individual assessment. *American Psychologist*, 1971, *26*, 992–999.

Pace, C. R. *College and University Environment Scales: Technical Manual.* Princeton, N.J.: Educational Testing Service, 1963.

Pace, C. R. *Analyses of a national sample of college environments.* Los Angeles: University of California at Los Angeles, 1967.

Pace, C. R. *Measuring outcomes of college.* San Francisco: Jossey-Bass, 1979.

Page, E. B. Seeking a measure of general educational advancement: The Bentee. *Journal of Educational Measurement*, 1972, *9*, 33–43.

Payne, D. A. *The assessment of learning: Cognitive and affective.* Lexington Mass.: Heath, 1974.

Perrin, D. W., & Whitney, D. R. Methods for smoothing expectancy tables applied to the prediction of success in college. *Journal of Educational Measurement*, 1976, *13*, 223–231.

Petersen, N. S., & Novick, M. R. An evaluation of some models for culture-fair selection. *Journal of Educational Measurement*, 1976, *13*, 3–29.

Peterson, R. A. Review of the Rorschach. In O. K. Buros (Ed.), *The eighth mental measurements yearbook.* Highland Park, N.J.: Gryphon Press, 1978.

Pike, L. W. *Short-term instruction, testwiseness, and the Scholastic Aptitude Test: A literature review with research recommendations.* Princeton, N.J.: Educational Testing Service. 1978.

Pike, L. W., & Evans, F. R. *Effects of special instruction for three kinds of mathematics aptitude items.* New York: College Entrance Examination Board, 1972.

Pillemer, D. B., & Light, R. J. Synthesizing outcomes: How to use research evidence from many studies. *Harvard Educational Review*, 1980, *50*, 176–195.

Pipho, C. The minimum competency testing movement. *Phi Delta Kappan*, 1978, *5*(9), entire issue.

Popham, W. J. *Criterion-referenced measurement: An introduction.* Englewood Cliffs, N.J.: Education Technology Publishers. 1973.

Popham, W. J. (Ed.) *Evaluation in education.* Washington, D.C.: American Educational Research Association, 1974.

Popham, W. J. The case for criterion-referenced measurements. *Educational Researcher*, 1978, 7(11), 6–10.

Popham, W. J. *Modern educational measurement.* Englewood Cliffs, N.J.: Prentice-Hall, 1981.

Popham, W. J., & Husek, T. R. Implications of criterion-referenced measurement. *Journal of Educational Measurement*, 1969, *6*, 1–9.

Popham, W. J., & Lindheim, E. The practical side of criterion-referenced test development. *NCME Measurement in Education*, 1980, *10*(4).

Powers, D. E., & Alderman, D. L. *The use, acceptance, and impact of Taking the SAT.* Princeton, N.J.: Educational Testing Service, 1979.

Prediger, D. J. Alternatives for validating interest inventories against group membership criteria. *Applied Psychological Measurement*, 1977, *1* 275–280.

Principles for the validation and use of personnel selection procedures. Washington, D.C.: American Psychological Association, Division of Industrial-Organizational Psychology, 1975.

Privacy and behavioral research. Washington, D.C.: Government Printing Office, 1967.

Purves, A. C. *Literature education in ten countries.* New York: Wiley, 1973.

Rabin, A. I. (Ed.) *Assessment with projective techniques: A concise introduction.* New York: Springer, 1981.

Reinert, G. Comparative factor analytic studies of intelligence throughout the human life-span. In L. R. Goulet & P. B. Baltes (Eds.), *Life-span developmental psychology.* New York: Academic Press, 1970.

Reschley, D. J. *Non-biased assessment.* Des Moines: State of Iowa, Department of Public Instruction, 1978.

Reschley, D. J. Nonbiased assessment. In G. Phye & D. J. Reschley (Eds.), *School psychology: Perspectives and issues.* New York: Academic Press, 1979.

Reschley, D. J., & Sabers, D. L. Analysis of test bias in four groups with the regression definition. *Journal of Educational Measurement, 1979, 16,* 1–9.

Resnick, D. Minimum competency testing historically considered. *Review of Research in Education, 1980, 8,* 3–29.

Resnick, L. B. Introduction: Changing conceptions of intelligence. In L. B. Resnick (Ed.), *The nature of intelligence.* Hillsdale, N.J.: Erlbaum, 1976. (a)

Resnick, L. B. (Ed.) *The nature of intelligence.* Hillsdale, N.J.: Erlbaum, 1976. (b)

Richardson, M. W., & Kuder, G. F. The calculation of test reliability coefficients based on the method of rational equivalence. *Journal of Educational Psychology, 1939, 30,* 681–687.

Ricks, J. H., Jr. *Local norms: When and why.* Test Service Bulletin No. 58. New York: Psychological Corporation, 1971.

Rist, R. C. Blitzkrieg ethnography: On the transformation of a method into a movement. *Educational Researcher, 1980, 9(2),* 8–10.

Robinson, J. P., & Shaver, P. R. *Measures of social psychological attitudes* (rev. ed.). Ann Arbor: Institute for Social Research, University of Michigan, 1973.

Rohwer, W. D., Jr., Ammon, P. R., & Cramer, P. *Understanding intellectual development.* Hinsdale, Ill.: Dryden, 1974.

Rorer, L. G. The great response-style myth. *Psychological Bulletin, 1965, 63,* 129–156.

Rosenthal, R. Combining results of independent studies. *Psychological Bulletin, 1978, 85,* 185–193.

Rotter, J. B. *Social learning and clinical psychology.* Englewood Cliffs, N.J.: Prentice-Hall, 1954.

Rowley, G. L. Which examinees are most favored by the use of multiple choice tests? *Journal of Educational Measurement, 1974, 11,* 15–23.

Rudman, H. C. The standardized test flap. *Phi Delta Kappan, 1977, 59(3),* 179–185.

Rudner, L. M., Getson, P. R., & Knight, D. L. A Monte Carlo comparison of seven biased item detection techniques. *Journal of Educational Measurement, 1980, 17,* 1–10.

Ruebhausen, D. M., & Brim, O. G., Jr. Privacy and behavioral research. *American Psychologist, 1966, 21,* 423–437.

Rumenik, D. K., Capasso, D. R., & Hendrick, C. Experimenter sex effects in behavioral research. *Psychological Bulletin, 1977, 84,* 852–877.

Saal, F. E., Downey, R. G., & Lahey, M. A. Rating the ratings: Assessing the psychometric quality of rating data. *Psychological Bulletin, 1980, 88,* 413–428.

Sarason, I. G. (Ed.) *Test anxiety: Theory, research, and applications.* Hillsdale, N.J.: Erlbaum, 1980.

Sarnacki, R. E. An examination of test-wiseness in the cognitive test domain. *Review of Educational Research, 1979, 49,* 252–279.

Sattler, J. Racial "experimenter effects" in experimentation, testing, interviewing, and psychotherapy. *Psychological Bulletin, 1970, 73,* 137–160.

Sattler, J. M. *Assessment of children's intelligence and special abilities* (2d ed.). Boston: Allyn and Bacon, 1982.

Sawyer, R. L., Cole, N. S., & Cole, J. W. L. Utilities and the issue of fairness in a decision theoretic model for selection. *Journal of Educational Measurement, 1976, 13,* 59–76.

Scarr, S. *Race, social class, and individual differences in IQ.* Hillsdale, N.J.: Erlbaum, 1981.

Scheuneman, J. A method of assessing bias in test items. *Journal of Educational Measurement, 1979, 16,* 143–152.

Schmeiser, C. B., & Ferguson, R. L. Performance of black and white students on test materials containing content based on black and white cultures. *Journal of Educational Measurement,* 1978, *15,* 193–200.

Schmidt, F. L., Berner, J. G., & Hunter, J. E. Racial differences in validity of employment tests: Reality or illusion? *Journal of Applied Psychology,* 1973, *58,* 5–9.

Schmidt, F. L., & Hunter, J. E. Racial and ethnic bias in psychological tests: Divergent implications of two definitions of test bias. *American Psychologist,* 1974, *29,* 1–8.

Schrader, W. B. (Ed.) Measuring achievement: Progress over a decade. Proceedings of the 1979 ETS Invitational Conference. *New Directions for Testing and Measurement,* 1980, *5.*

Schrauger, J. S., & Osberg, T. M. The relative accuracy of self-predictions and judgments by others in psychological assessment. *Psychological Bulletin,* 1981, *90,* 322–351.

Scriven, M. The methodology of evaluation. In R. Tyler et al., *Perspectives on curriculum evaluation.* AERA Monograph Series on Curriculum Evaluation, No. 1. Chicago: Rand McNally, 1967.

Seashore, H. G., & Ricks, J. H., Jr. *Norms must be relevant.* Test Service Bulletin No. 39. New York: Psychological Corporation, 1950.

Sechrest, L. Incremental validity. *Educational and Psychological Measurement,* 1963, *23,* 153–158.

Semeonoff, B. *Projective techniques.* New York: Wiley, 1976.

Serling, A. M. The measurement of public literacy. *College Board Review,* Winter 1979–80, *114,* 26–29.

Shepard, L. A. Technical issues in minimum competency testing. *Review of Research in Education,* 1980, *8,* 30–82.

Shepard, L. A. Identifying bias in test items. *New Directions for Testing and Measurement,* 1981, *11,* 79–104.

Shoemaker, D. M. Toward a framework for achievement testing. *Review of Educational Research,* 1975, *45,* 127–147.

Skinner, B. F. *Science and human behavior.* New York: Macmillan, 1953.

Skinner, B. F. *Contingencies of reinforcement: A theoretical analysis.* New York: Appleton, 1969.

Skinner, B. F. *About behaviorism.* New York: Knopf, 1974.

Slack, W. V., & Porter, D. The Scholastic Aptitude Test: A critical appraisal. *Harvard Educational Review,* 1980, *50,* 154–175.

Smith, D. Unfinished business with informed consent procedures. *American Psychologist,* 1981, *36,* 22–26.

Smith, L. M. An evolving logic of participant observation, educational ethnography and other case studies. *Review of Research in Education,* 1978, *6,* 316–377.

Smith, M. L., & Glass, G. V. Meta-analysis of psychotherapy outcome studies. *American Psychologist,* 1977, *32,* 752–760.

Spokane, A. R. Occupational preferences and the validity of the Strong-Campbell Interest Inventory for college women and men. *Journal of Counseling Psychology,* 1979, *26,* 312–318.

Spradley, J. P. *The ethnographic interview.* New York: Holt, Rinehart and Winston, 1979.

Spradley, J. P. *Participant observation.* New York: Holt, Rinehart and Winston, 1980.

Standards for educational and psychological tests. Washington, D.C.: American Psychological Association, 1974.

Standards for educational and psychological tests and manuals. Washington, D.C.: American Psychological Association, 1966.

Stanley, J. C. Reliability. In R. L. Thorndike (Ed.), *Educational measurement* (2d ed.). Washington, D.C.: American Council on Education, 1971.

Stanley, J. C. On educating the gifted. *Educational Researcher,* 1980, *9*(3), 8–12.

Stanley, J. C., George, W. C., & Solano, C. H. (Eds.) *The gifted and the creative: A fifty-year perspective.* Baltimore.: Johns Hopkins University Press, 1978.

Stanley, J. C., Keating, D. P., & Fox, L. H. *Mathematical talent: Discovery, description, and development.* Baltimore: Johns Hopkins University Press, 1974.

Stanley, J. C., & Porter, A. C. Correlation of Scholastic Aptitude Test scores with college grades for Negroes versus whites. *Journal of Educational Measurement,* 1967, *4,* 199–218.

Stephenson, W. *The study of behavior: Q-technique and its methodology.* Chicago: University of Chicago Press, 1953.

Stephenson, W. Newton's fifth rule and Q methodology: Application to educational psychology. *American Psychologist,* 1980, *35,* 882–889.

Stern, G. G. *People in context: Measuring person-environment congruence in education and industry.* New York: Wiley, 1970.

Sternberg, R. J. *Intelligence, information processing, and analogical reasoning: The componental analysis of human abilities.* Hillsdale, N.J.: Erlbaum, 1977.

Sternberg, R. J. The nature of mental abilities. *American Psychologist* 1979, *34,* 214–230.

Sternberg, R. J. Factor theories of intelligence are all right almost. *Educational Researcher,* 1980, *9*(8), 6–13, 18.

Stevens, S. S. Mathematics, measurement, and psychophysics. In S. S. Stevens (Ed.), *Handbook of experimental psychology.* New York: Wiley, 1951.

Strahan, R. F., Todd, J. B., & Inglis, G. B. A palmar sweat measure particularly suited for naturalistic research. *Psychophysiology,* 1974, *11,* 715–720.

Strong, E. K. *Vocational interests 18 years after college.* Minneapolis: University of Minnesota Press, 1955.

Summers, G. F. (Ed.) *Attitude measurement.* Chicago: Rand McNally, 1970.

Super, D. E., & Crites, J. O. *Appraising vocational fitness.* New York: Harper & Row, 1962.

SVIB-SCII: The 1981 Revision. Palo Alto, Calif.: Stanford University Press, 1981.

Taylor, C. W., & Barron, F. *Scientific creativity: Its recognition and development.* New York: Wiley, 1963.

Taylor, E. F. Tests that send kids "Through the looking glass." *Des Moines Register,* November 20, 1977.

Taylor, H. C., & Russell, J. T. The relationship of validity coefficients to the practical effectiveness of tests in selection: Discussion and tables. *Journal of Applied Psychology,* 1939, *23,* 565–578.

Taylor, I. A., & Getzels, J. W. (Eds.) *Perspectives in creativity.* Chicago: Aldine, 1975.

Terman, L. M., & Merrill, M. A. *Measuring intelligence,* Boston: Houghton Mifflin, 1937.

Terman, L. M., & Merrill, M. A. *Stanford-Binet Intelligence Scale: Manual for the third revision, Form L-M.* Boston: Houghton Mifflin, 1960.

Terman, L. M., & Merrill, M. A. *Stanford-Binet Intelligence Scale: Manual for the third revision, Form L-M* (1973 Norms Edition). Boston: Houghton Mifflin, 1973.

Terwilliger, J. S., & Lele, K. Some relationships among internal consistency, reproducability, and homogeneity. *Journal of Educational Measurement,* 1979, *16,* 101–108.

Test use and validity. Princeton, N.J.: Educational Testing Service, 1980.

Testing and the public interest. Proceedings of the 1976 ETS Invitational Conference. Princeton, N.J.: Educational Testing Service, 1977.

Testing: Concepts, policy, practice and research. *American Psychologist,* 1981, *36*(10), entire issue.

Thomas, C. L., & Stanley, J. C. Effectiveness of high school grades for predicting college grades of black students: A review and discussion. *Journal of Educational Measurement,* 1969, *6,* 203–215.

Thorndike, R. L. Reliability. In E. F. Lindquist (Ed.), *Educational measurement.* Washington, D.C.: American Council on Education, 1951.

Thorndike, R. L. (Ed.) *Educational measurement* (2d ed.). Washington, D.C.: American Council on Education, 1971. (a)

Thorndike, R. L. Concepts of culture-fairness. *Journal of Educational Measurement,* 1971, *8,* 63–70. (b)

Thorndike, R. L. *Reading comprehension education in fifteen countries.* New York: Wiley, 1973.

Thorndike, R. L. Mr. Binet's test 70 years later. *Educational Researcher,* 1975, *4*(5), 3–7.

Thorndike, R. L., & Hagen, E. P. *Ten thousand careeers.* New York: Wiley, 1959.

Thorndike, R. L., & Hagen, E. P. *Measurement and evaluation in psychology and education* (4th ed.). New York: Wiley, 1977.

Thurow, L. C. *The zero-sum society.* New York: Basic Books, 1980.

Tilton, J. W. The measurement of overlapping. *Journal of Educational Psychology,* 1937, *28,* 656–662.

Tinkelman, S. N. Planning the objective test. In R. L. Thorndike (Ed.), *Educational measurement* (2d ed.). Washington, D.C.: American Council on Education, 1971.

Torrance, E. P., & Myers, R. E. *Creative learning and teaching.* New York: Dodd, Mead, 1970.

Traub, R. E., & Fisher, C. S. On the equivalence of constructed-response and multiple-choice tests. *Applied Psychological Measurement,* 1977, *1,* 355–369.

Tryon, G. S. The measurement and treatment of test anxiety. *Review of Educational Research,* 1980, *50,* 343–372.

Tufte, E. R. (Ed.) *The quantitative analysis of social problems.* Reading, Mass.: Addison-Wesley, 1970.

Tufte, E. R. *Data analysis for politics and policy.* Englewood Cliffs, N.J.: Prentice-Hall, 1974.

Tukey, J. W. *Exploratory data analysis.* Reading, Mass.: Addison-Wesley, 1977.

Tyler, L. E. *Individuality.* San Francisco: Jossey-Bass, 1978.

Tyler, L. E., & Walsh, W. B. *Tests and measurements* (3d ed.). Englewood Cliffs, N.J.: Prentice-Hall, 1979.

Tyler, R. W., Merwin, J. C., & Ebel, R. L. Symposium: A National Assessment of Educational Progress. *Journal of Educational Measurement, 1966, 3,* 1–17.

Tyler, R. W., & Wolf, R. M. (Eds.) *Critical issues in testing.* Berkeley, Calif.: McCutchan, 1974.

U.S. Government Accounting Office. Report to the Congress by the comptroller general of the U.S.: Problems with the federal Equal Employment Opportunity Guidelines on Employee Selection Procedures need to be resolved. Washington, D.C.: U.S. Government Accounting Office, 1978.

Urry, V. W. Tailored Testing: A successful application of latent trait theory. *Journal of Educational Measurement, 1977, 14,* 181–196.

Uzgiris, I. S., & Hunt, J. McV. *Assessment in infancy: Ordinal scales of psychological development.* Urbana: University of Illinois Press, 1975.

Vernon, P. E. *Personality assessment: A critical survey.* London: Methuen, 1964.

Vernon, P. E. *Structure of human abilities.* New York: Barnes & Noble, 1971.

Vernon, P. E. *Intelligence and cultural environment.* London: Methuen, 1972.

Vernon, P. E. *Intelligence: Heredity and environment.* San Francisco: Freeman, 1979.

Wade, T. C., & Baker, T. B. Opinions and use of psychological tests: A survey of clinical psychologists. *American Psychologist, 1977, 32,* 874–882.

Wainer, H. Estimating coefficients in linear models: It don't make no nevermind. *Psychological Bulletin, 1976, 83,* 213–217.

Wainer, H., & Thissen, D. Graphical data analysis. *Annual Review of Psychology, 1981, 32,* 191–241.

Wallach, M. A. *The intelligence/creativity distinction.* New York: General Learning Press, 1971.

Wallach, M. A., & Wing, C. W. *The talented student: A validation of the creativity-intelligence distinction.* New York: Holt, Rinehart and Winston, 1969.

Ward, W. C., Frederiksen, N., and Carlson, S. B. Construct validity of free-response and machine-scorable forms of a test. *Journal of Educational Measurement, 1980, 17,* 11–29.

Warrington, W. G. An item analysis service for teachers. *NCME Measurement in Education, 1972, 3*(2).

Webb, E. J., Campbell, D. T., Schwartz, R. D., & Sechrest, L. *Unobtrusive measures: Nonreactive research in the social sciences.* Chicago: Rand McNally, 1966.

Webster's New World Dictionary (College Ed.). Cleveland: World, 1966.

Wechsler, D. *Manual for the Wechsler Adult Intelligence Scale.* New York: Psychological Corporation, 1955.

Wechsler, D. *The measurement and appraisal of adult intelligence.* Baltimore: Williams & Wilkins, 1958.

Wechsler, D. *Manual for the Wechsler Intelligence Scale for Children-Revised.* New York: Psychological Corporation, 1974.

Wechsler, D. Intelligence defined and undefined: A relativistic appraisal. *American Psychologist, 1975, 30,* 135–139.

Wechsler, D. *WAIS-R Manual* (Wechsler Adult Intelligence Scale—Revised). New York: Psychological Corporation, 1981.

Weiner, I. E. Does psychodiagnosis have a future? *Journal of Personality Assessment, 1972, 36,* 534–546.

Weiss, D. J. *Strategies of adaptive ability measurement.* Psychometric Methods Program Report 74–5. Minneapolis: University of Minnesota, Department of Psychology, 1974.

Weitz, J. Criteria for criteria. *American Psychologist, 1961, 16,* 228–231.

Welsh, G. S. *Creativity and intelligence: A personality approach.* Chapel Hill: Institute for Research in Social Science, University of North Carolina, 1975.

Wesman, A. G. *Comparability vs. equivalence of test scores.* Test Service Bulletin No. 53. New York: Psychological Corporation, 1958.

Wesman, A. G. Intelligent testing. *American Psychologist, 1968, 23,* 267–274.

Wesman, A. G. Writing the test item. In R. L. Thorndike (Ed.), *Educational measurement* (2d ed.). Washington, D.C.: American Council on Education, 1971.

Wheeler, T. C. The American way of testing. *New York Times Magazine,* September 2, 1979, 40–42.

Wiggins, J. S. *Personality and prediction.* Reading, Mass.: Addison-Wesley, 1973.

Wine, J. Test anxiety and direction of attention. *Psychological Bulletin,* 1971, *76,* 92–104.

Wing, H. Practice effects with traditional mental test items. *Applied Psychological Measurement,* 1980, *4,* 141–155.

Witkin, H. A., & Goodenough, D. R. Field dependence and interpersonal behavior. *Psychological Bulletin,* 1977, *84,* 661–689.

Witkin, H. A., Moore, C. A., Goodenough, D. R., & Cox, P. W. Field-dependent and field-independent cognitive styles and their educational implications. *Review of Educational Research,* 1977, *47,* 1–64.

Wittrock, M. C., & Wiley, D. E., (Eds.). *The evaluation of instruction.* New York: Holt, Rinehart and Winston, 1970.

Wolins, L. Interval measurement: Physics, psychophysics, and metaphysics. *Educational and Psychological Measurement,* 1978, *38,* 1–9.

Womer, F. B. National Assessment says. *NCME Measurement in Education,* 1970, *2*(1).

Wright, B. D. Solving measurement problems with the Rasch Model. *Journal of Educational Measurement,* 1977, *14,* 97–116.

Wright, B. D., & Stone, M. H. *Best test design.* Chicago: MESA Press, 1979.

Wylie, R. C. *The self-concept: A review of methodological considerations and measuring instruments* (Vol. 1). Lincoln: University of Nebraska Press, 1974.

Young, M. *The rise of the meritocracy.* Baltimore: Penguin Books, 1961.

Young, R. K., & Veldman, D. J. *Introductory statistics for the behavioral sciences* (4th ed.). New York: Holt, Rinehart and Winston, 1981.

Zajonc, R. B. Family configuration and intelligence. *Science,* 1976, *192,* 227–236.

Zajonc, R. B., & Bargh, J. Birth order, family size, and decline of SAT scores. *American Psychologist,* 1980, *35,* 662–668.

Zigler, E., & Trickett, P. K. IQ, social competence, and evaluation of early childhood intervention programs. *American Psychologist,* 1978, *33,* 789–798.

Zytowski, D. G. Relationships of equivalent scales on three interest inventories. *Personnel and Guidance Journal,* 1968, *47,* 44Z49.

Zytowski, D. G. (Ed.) *Contemporary approaches to interest measurement.* Minneapolis: University of Minnesota Press, 1973.

Zytowski, D. G. Long-term stability of the Kuder Occupational Interest Survey. *Educational and Psychological Measurement,* 1976, *36,* 689Z692.

Name Index

Subject Index

Ability, defined, 209
  developed, 210
Ability tests, 209–210, 214–217,
    328–354, 485
  college admission, 312–317
  creativity, 338–340
  intelligence, 296–310
  psychomotor, 341–343
  types of, 215–216
  validation of, 216–217
Academic ability tests, 216, 305,
    310–320, 337–338, 485
  bias in, 318–319
  college admission, 312–317
  construction of, 310–311
  graduate and professional
    school admission, 317–318
  score decline, 320
  validation of, 311–312, 318
Achievement quotient, 171
Achievement tests, 208, 209,
    210–214, 485
  batteries, 266–267, 268–269
  classroom, 232–257
  content-referenced, 277–278
  diagnostic, 272–273
  issues in use of, 286–289
  minimum competency,
    276–277
  norm-referenced vs. content-
    referenced, 212–213,
    288–289
  proficiency, 275–277
  readiness, 273–275
  specific subject, 265–266
  standardized, 259–290
  survey, 212
  types of, 211–213
  validation of, 213–214
Adaptive Behavior Inventory for
    Children (ABIC), 348
Adaptive Behavior Scale, 348
Adaptive behavior scales, 348
Admission tests, college,
    312–317
  graduate and professional
    school, 317–318

Advanced Placement Program,
    267, 269
Age scales and scores, 168–169,
    485
Alternate forms reliablility, see
    coefficient of equivalence
Alternative-choice items, 26,
    238, 485
  scoring of, 249
  use on standardized tests, 288
  see also matching items,
    multiple-choice items,
    true-false items
American College Testing
    Program (ACT), 312–313
Anecdotal reports, 432
Aptitude, 209, 214–215, 485
Aptitude tests, 208–209,
    214–217, 328–345, 485
  multiple aptitude test
    batteries, 328–337
  musical and artistic, 339–340
  vocational, 343–345
  see also ability tests
Army Alpha test, 305
Artistic ability, tests of, 339–340
Assessment, 14–15, 485
  behavioral, 362–363
Atmosphere bias, 228
Attitude scales, 435–436, 485

Barnum effect, 443
Base rates, 111, 123–124, 485
Basic Occupational Literacy
    Test, 334
Bayley Scales of Infant
    Development, 307
Behavioral assessment,
    362–363, 485
Bem Androgyny Scale, 406,
    408–409
Bender-Gestalt (Bender Visual
    Motor Gestalt Test), 346
Bennett Mechanical
    Comprehension Test, 343
Bias, defined, 224, 472–473, 486
  in maximal performance

Bias, (cont.)
  tests, 224–229, 289
  in prediction, 127–128,
    228–229
  types of, 227–229
Biographical information forms,
    438
Boehm Test of Basic Concepts,
    274–275

California Psychological
    Inventory, 406–407
Central tendency, measures of,
    40, 41–43, 486
Change scores, interpretation
    of, 199–200
  reliability of, 93
Checklists, 409, 431
Classroom achievement tests,
    232–257
  administration, 248–249
  analysis of scores, 251–254
  instructional uses, 233–234,
    237, 254–255
  item types, 238–248
  planning of, 232–237
  reliability of, 252
  scoring of, 249–251
  validation of, 253–254
Clinical testing, 345–348
Coaching, effects on test scores,
    63, 319
Codebooks, 404
Coefficient alpha, 83, 486
Coefficient of determination, 51,
    105
Coefficient of equivalence, 67,
    77–79, 486
Coefficient of stability, 67,
    76–78, 486
Coefficient of stability and
    equivalence, 67, 78–79, 486
Cognitive dysfunction tests,
    345–346
Cognitive styles, 349–353
College admission tests,
    312–317